PEOPLES *and* CULTURES *of* ASIA

PEOPLES *and* CULTURES *of* ASIA

Edited by
Raymond Scupin
Lindenwood University

Upper Saddle River, New Jersey 07458

Library of Congress Cataloging-in-Publication Data

People and cultures of Asia / edited by Raymond Scupin.
p. cm.
Includes bibliographical references and index.
ISBN 0-13-118110-6
1. Asia—Civilization—Textbooks. I. Scupin, Raymond.

DS12.P48 2006
950—dc22 2005050967

Publisher: Nancy Roberts
Editorial Assistant: Lee Peterson
Full Service Production Liaison: Joanne Hakim
Senior Marketing Manager: Marissa Feliberty
Marketing Assistant: Anthony DeCosta
Manufacturing Buyer: Benjamin Smith
Cover Art Director: Jayne Conte
Manager, Cover Visual Research & Permissions: Karen Sanatar
Cover Art: Alan Evrard/Robert Harding World Imagery
Director, Image Resource Center: Melinda Reo
Manager, Rights and Permissions: Zina Arabia
Manager, Visual Research: Beth Brenzel
Photo Researcher: Melinda Alexander
Photo Coordinator: Carolyn Gauntt
Composition/Full-Service Project Management: GGS Book Services, Atlantic Highlands
Printer/Binder: R. R. Donnelley and Sons

Pearson Education LTD., London
Pearson Education Singapore, Pte. Ltd
Pearson Education, Canada, Ltd
Pearson Education—Japan
Pearson Education Australia PTY, Limited
Pearson Education North Asia Ltd
Pearson Educación de Mexico, S.A. de C.V.
Pearson Education Malaysia, Pte. Ltd
Pearson Education, Upper Saddle River, New Jersey

10 9 8 7 6 5 4 3 2 1
ISBN 0-13-118110-6

This book is dedicated to Donald E. Brown,
who taught so many about the anthropology of Asia

CONTENTS

PART III East Asia

PREFACE

Anthropologists have been doing ethnographic research in Asia for more than a hundred years. Based on this empirical research, they have developed a profound understanding of the diverse cultures of this region. Surprisingly, these anthropological insights on Asian cultures have not been communicated as widely as they should be among the undergraduate audience in the United States. One major reason for this is the lack of a comprehensive, incisive, and substantive text that focuses upon this region. In light of the increasing geopolitical developments in Asia, undergraduate students need to be better informed and have a developed perspective about this region of the world. They read about Afghanistan, China, and Korea in the news but they lack a historical, political, and cultural context for thinking about these countries.

Recent Asian developments and issues have had immense effects on both U.S. and global political trends, and have resulted in misconceptions and simplistic stereotypes illustrated in the well-known phrase "the clash of civilizations." In particular, this clash of civilization thesis was widely reinforced by the Western media following the tragedy of 9/11/01 in the United States. This thesis tended to perpetuate the stereotypical notion that Muslims and Asians had radically different cultural and political traditions from that of Western culture and civilization. Theses cultural differences would result in an inevitable clash between the East and the West. In contrast to this simplification of Asian and Muslim societies, anthropologists have found that there are no monolithic forms of Asian or Muslim culture or tradition. Asia is a culturally diverse region with a wide variety of languages, ethnic groups, and religions.

This region contains a majority of the world's population—over three billion people. Different forms of societies have developed in Asia, ranging from the hunter-gatherer and horticultural societies of the tropical rainforests, to the pastoral nomads of northern China, to the complex agricultural societies, to the advanced industrial societies such as those in Japan and Korea. Local-level ethnographic fieldwork that anthropologists have done within these societies has been extremely helpful in elucidating the political and cultural complexities and trends within Asia. An anthropological understanding of Asian societies and cultures has been helpful to officials in government, the diplomatic corps, and international agencies in overcoming simplistic and rigid formulations of the so-called Orient. These findings need to be communicated to the undergraduate audience.

Based on our teaching experiences, we find that undergraduates are more eager than ever to understand this area of the world. For example, in Chapter 2 on Afghanistan we provide a section with a comprehensive overview of the religious and political history of the Islamic tradition. This will provide a context for understanding later chapters dealing with the Islamic countries of Pakistan and Indonesia. We believe that a textbook such as this gives undergraduate students some foundation and background to understand the global developments that have arisen within the Islamic world and the rest of Asia today.

One of the major objectives of anthropology is to comprehend both the differences and similarities of different groups of humans throughout the world. A major lesson derived from anthropological research is that as different groups learn about each other's cultural values, norms, behaviors, goals, and aspirations, the less likely they are to maintain rigid stereotypes and misconceptions about one another. Thus, one of the practical results of this anthropological research on Asia is a reduction of rigid racist stereotypes, ethnocentrism based on simplistic static images, and animosities and tensions among different groups. As students learn to discern what anthropologists have learned about the peoples and cultures of Asia they are more likely to be able to adjust and become productive citizens in an increasingly multicultural and globally integrated world. A sound comprehensive understanding of the cultures of Asia and the global impact that Asia has had on the world is a fundamental aspect of a well-rounded liberal arts education.

DESCRIPTION OF THE TEXTBOOK

This textbook is a collection of comprehensive but highly readable chapters on Asia. Part I discusses prevalent stereotypes and cultures of the countries in Asia and introduces students to anthropological vocabulary. Part II focuses on Southwest and South Asia, including chapters on Afghanistan, India, and Pakistan. Part III covers East Asia and includes chapters on China, Japan, and Korea. Part IV focuses on mainland and island Southeast Asia. Each chapter is written by an anthropologist who has done ethnographic research in the respective area. The chapters address the geography, prehistory, languages, demography, and history of each country and discuss contemporary developments in the economy, family, gender issues, ethnicity, politics, and religion in these various countries. The textbook is written for the undergraduate student with no background in anthropology or Asian studies. As mentioned, the opening chapter introduces some of the fundamental concepts of anthropology such as culture, ethnicity, globalization, and other basic terminology.

FEATURES OF THIS BOOK

The unique aspect of this textbook on the peoples and cultures of Asia is that it is the only single textbook available at this time that highlights the importance of this region of the world. Although the textbook is written by anthropologists, it is not aimed at an anthropological audience. Written for the general undergraduate from the sophomore to senior level, this textbook is aimed at undergraduate students ranging from community college level to four-year liberal arts, and research universities. It is written for nonmajors or students who may be taking an Asian culture course as their only course about this region during their entire undergraduate experience. At the same time, the book includes recent references to current anthropological research for those students who want to pursue studies in the area of Asian studies. The textbook does not emphasize minor theoretical debates within the discipline of anthropology among specialists, which may deflect attention away from the major insights that have been gained within anthropology about the region of Asia. Therefore, the text could be used in a variety of Asian studies courses for the undergraduate student. The text is written to challenge naive concepts of the Asian mind and culture and to stimulate critical thinking among undergraduate students.

The chapters of this textbook are written by ethnographers who have done local-level fieldwork and in-depth research in these various areas of the world, and have acquired a first-hand understanding of these regions. These chapters will provide students with a basic holistic understanding of these communities, and will assist students in building a global perspective and in doing so will help reduce some of the superficial, media-based characterizations and representations of Asian cultural traditions and contemporary developments.

We believe that our textbook—with chapters focusing on particular countries emphasizing the interrelationships among the demography, economy, social life, gender, ethnic relations, politics, and religions with a solid historic and prehistoric background—is more useful for the student who is taking a course on modern Asia or the ethnography of Asia. Our chapter-by-chapter account of the various countries of Asia enables the student to grasp a holistic understanding of these countries of Asia and the region as a whole.

ACKNOWLEDGMENTS

A comprehensive textbook on the anthropology of Asia requires a team approach. We would like to thank all of the authors for their important contributions to this project. We would like to thank the reviewers of various chapters for the text including Donald E. Brown, University of California Santa Barbara; Richard O'Connor, University of the South; Karel (Carool) Kersten, Payap University (Thailand); Nancy Abelmann, University of Illinois—Urbana-Champaign; Michael S. Billig, Franklin & Marshall College; James F. Eder, Arizona State University; David B. Edwards, Williams College; H. Leedom Lefferts, Drew University; Carole McGranahan, University of Colorado, Boulder; Kathryn Howard, University of Pennsylvania; Harumi Befu, Stanford University; Kathleen Nadeau, California State University, San Bernardino; and Cabeiri deBergh Robinson, University of Washington. We would also like to express our thanks to Nancy Roberts, anthropology editor for Prentice Hall, for her support for this project, managing editor Joanne Hakim, photo editor Melinda Alexander, cartographer Steve Hyde, and Scott Garrison, for his technical assistance.

PEOPLES *and* CULTURES *of* ASIA

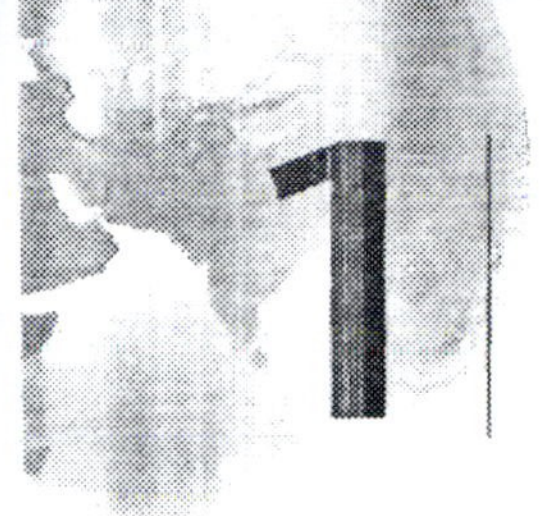

INTRODUCTION TO ASIA

Raymond Scupin

Asia is a geographically and culturally diverse region with a wide variety of languages, ethnic groups, political systems, and religions. This textbook focuses on Southwest and South Asia (Afghanistan, India, and Pakistan), East Asia (China, Japan, and North and South Korea), mainland Southeast Asia (Myanmar [Burma], Thailand, Kampuchea [Cambodia], Laos, and Vietnam), and island Southeast Asia (Malaysia, Singapore, Brunei, Indonesia, and the Philippines). These countries contain most of the world's population—over three billion people. The variant ecological and historical circumstances in Asia have resulted in a wide range of societies and cultures. As you will see, the populations and cultures of the various countries of Asia have been shaped by traditional cultural beliefs and practices, as well as by cultural traditions and practices that developed as a result of contacts with other countries of Asia and the West. The countries of Asia had many economic, political, and religious connections with one another for centuries resulting in the diffusion or spread of cultural traditions and practices within the Asian region. Yet, these diffused cultural traditions and practices have always been selectively integrated and modified in the context of prior traditions and practices.

This same process of diffusion, selective integration, and modification of cultural traditions and practices occurred through the contacts developing between the West and the region of Asia. These contacts began with the exploration and colonization of some areas of Asia sponsored by Western countries such as Spain, Portugal, England, France, Holland, and the United States. Although these colonized regions of Asia ultimately became independent of the Western colonial regimes, the process of what has been called "globalization" continued with the spread of capital, labor, technology, and culture across many national borders in Asia. Today, globalization continues to occur through the increasing spread of industrial technology, including electronic and satellite communications such as the telephone, television, the Internet, email, and fax, into the countries of Asia. Yet, again, the cultural traditions and practices rooted in globalization have been selectively transformed, modified, and integrated by the peoples of Asia. This textbook will provide a broad understanding of both the local sources of cultural traditions and practices and how these traditions and practices are being influenced by globalization processes throughout Asia.

PREVALENT STEREOTYPES OF ASIA

From the Western media we gain conflicting images and stereotypes of Asian cultures and peoples. In some of these stereotypes Asian peoples are portrayed as excessively mystical, otherworldly, passive, and fatalistic, whereas in

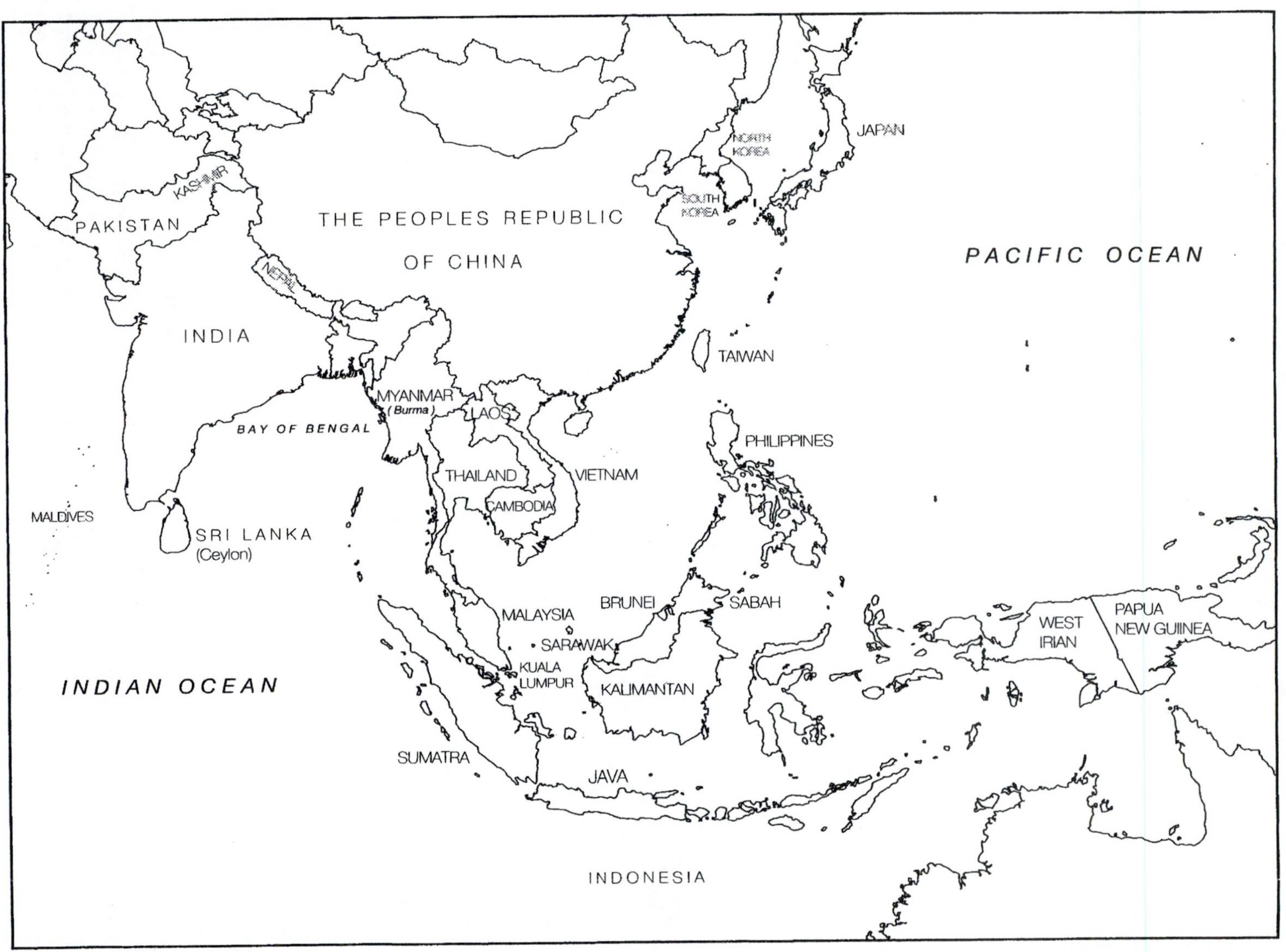
JAPAN
NORTH KOREA
SOUTH KOREA
KASHMIR
PAKISTAN
THE PEOPLES REPUBLIC
OF CHINA
PACIFIC OCEAN
NEPAL
INDIA
TAIWAN
MYANMAR
(Burma)
LAOS
BAY OF BENGAL
PHILIPPINES
THAILAND
VIETNAM
CAMBODIA
MALDIVES
SRI LANKA
(Ceylon)
BRUNEI
SABAH
MALAYSIA
SARAWAK
WEST
IRIAN
PAPUA
NEW GUIINEA
KUALA
LUMPUR
KALIMANTAN
INDIAN OCEAN
SUMATRA
JAVA
INDONESIA

another contrasting image they are portrayed as fanatical religious adherents who are willing to promote violence and terrorism to obtain their political and religious ends. These images and stereotypes have a long history in the West stemming from the time of the earliest European contacts with Asia. Early contacts and colonization frequently led to violent resistance and conflict, which influenced stereotypes of Asians versus Westerners. Later, as Western scholars began to translate the religious and philosophical texts of Asia, they produced generalizations and conclusions about the inherent characteristics of Asian peoples, and their societies. This type of scholarship is known as Orientalist scholarship or Orientalist interpretations. These Orientalist interpretations and images have had the effect of perpetuating distorted stereotypes of the peoples and cultures of Asia.[1] The early contacts with the West and Orientalist scholarship led to generalizations expressed in the nineteenth-century phrase of Rudyard Kipling's "East is East, and West is West, and never the twain shall meet." Following numerous contemporary anthropological and critical historical studies these stereotyped descriptions of Asian peoples and cultures have been found to be wholly inadequate and superficial. Anthropologists and other scholars have penetrated beyond the surface appearances represented in the Western media and Orientalist textual scholarship to understand and explain the actual complexities and tremendous variations of the cultural traditions and practices of these various countries of Asia. The chapters of this textbook written by anthropologists will provide a basis for undermining the superficial stereotypes and images of Asian peoples and cultures.

ANTHROPOLOGY: AN INTERDISCIPLINARY PERSPECTIVE

All of the contributing authors of this textbook are anthropologists who have conducted research in various countries of Asia. However, this textbook is not written only for anthropology students. It is a textbook written for the student who wants to gain a comprehensive understanding of the peoples and cultures of Asia. Thus, regardless of whether you are a student of the sciences, humanities, the arts, or any other discipline, this textbook will provide you with a broad context for assessing and evaluating information about Asia from the media and other sources.

The word *anthropology* stems from the Greek words *anthropo,* meaning "human beings" or "humankind," and *logia,* translated as "knowledge of or the study of." Thus, we can define anthropology as *the systematic study of humankind.* This definition in itself, however, does not distinguish anthropology from other disciplines. After all, historians, psychologists, economists, sociologists, and scholars in many other fields systematically study humankind in one way or another. Historically, anthropology developed within the context of four subdisciplines, or subfields, that bridge the natural sciences, the social sciences, and the humanities. These four subdisciplines—physical anthropology, archaeology, linguistic anthropology, and cultural anthropology—gave anthropologists a broad approach to the study of humanity the world over, both past and present.

These subfields of anthropology emerged in Western society in an attempt to understand non-Western peoples including those of Asia. Europeans had been exploring and colonizing areas of Asia since the fifteenth century. Various European travelers, missionaries, and government officials had begun to describe Asian peoples and cultures. By the nineteenth century, anthropology had developed into one of the primary disciplines for understanding these Asian societies and cultures. The major questions that these nineteenth-century anthropologists grappled with had to do with the basic differences and similarities of human societies and cultures, and the physical variations of people in Asia and other areas of the world.

Presently, however, anthropology does not limit itself to its own four subfields to realize its research agenda. Cultural anthropology, for instance, is closely related to sociology. Anthropology also overlaps the fields of psychology, economics, and political science. Finally, anthropology dovetails considerably with the field of history, which, like anthropology, encompasses a broad range of events. Every human event that has ever taken place in the world is a potential research topic for both historians and anthropologists. Historians describe and explain human events that have occurred throughout the world; anthropologists place their biological, archaeological, linguistic, and ethnographic data in the context of these historical developments. In addition to its interconnections with the natural and social sciences, the discipline of anthropology is also aligned with the humanistic fields of inquiry. This is particularly true with respect to the field of cultural anthropology because these researchers are involved in the study of different contemporary cultures. Many anthropologists explore the creative cultural dimensions of humanity, such as myth, folklore, poetry, art, music, and mythology. Thus, contemporary anthropologists have continued the use of a strong interdisciplinary tradition through systematic research efforts within the four fields as well as many other fields of scholarship. The chapters that follow in this textbook on Asian cultures are based on a fully developed interdisciplinary approach.

An archaeological site in Vietnam.

Physical anthropology, the branch of anthropology concerned with humans as a biological species, is the subdiscipline most closely related to the natural sciences. Physical anthropologists conduct research in two major areas: human evolution and modern human variation. The investigation of human evolution presents one of the most tantalizing areas of anthropological study. Much of the evidence for human origins consists of fossils, the fragmentary remains of bones and living materials preserved from earlier periods. These scientists are sometimes called paleoanthropologists. Another group of physical anthropologists focuses their research on the range of physical variation within and among different "modern" human populations. These anthropologists study human variation by measuring physical characteristics, such as body size, variation in blood types, differences in skin color, or various genetic traits. An increasingly important area of research for these physical anthropologists is genetics, the study of the biological "blueprints" that dictate the inheritance of physical characteristics.

Through archaeology, the branch of anthropology that seeks out and examines the artifacts of past societies, we learn about the culture of those societies—the shared way of life of a group of people that includes their values, beliefs, and norms. Artifacts, the material products of former societies, provide clues to the past. We will provide the most recent discoveries and findings of archaeologists in each of the chapters to illustrate the development and emergence of the ancient civilizations of Asian societies. Linguistics, the study of language, has a long history that dovetails with the discipline of philosophy but is also one of the integral subfields of anthropology. Some linguistic anthropologists concentrate on the comparison and classification of different languages to discern the historical links among languages. By examining and analyzing grammatical structures and sounds of languages, researchers are able to discover rules for how languages change over time, as well as which languages are related to one another historically. As will be seen, each chapter will introduce some of the conclusions regarding the linguistic history and how language influences the culture and the politics in these different Asian countries.

Cultural anthropology is the subfield of anthropology that examines various contemporary societies and cultures throughout the world. Cultural anthropologists do research in all parts of Asia, from the tropical rainforests of Southeast Asia, to the deserts of inner China, to the mountains of Afghanistan, to the urban areas of India. In the past, anthropologists used to study small-scale communities, but presently cultural anthropologists study many complex societies in a wide range of settings. Cultural anthropologists use a unique research strategy in conducting their fieldwork in different settings. This research strategy is referred to as *participant observation*, which involves learning the language and culture of the group being studied by participating in the group's daily activities. Through this intensive participation, the cultural anthropologist becomes deeply familiar with the group and can understand and explain the society and culture of the group as an insider. Presently, many anthropologists use the term *etic* to refer to the description of a culture by the anthropologist, and *emic* to refer to the natives' point of view of their own culture.

The results of the fieldwork of the cultural anthropologist are written up as an ethnography, a description of a society. A typical ethnography reports on the environmental setting, economic patterns, social organization, political system, and religious rituals and beliefs of the society under study. This description of a society is based on what anthropologists call ethnographic data. The gathering of ethnographic data in a systematic manner is the specific research goal of the cultural anthropologist. A typical ethnography includes a description of the physical environment (geography), demography (population), technology (tools and knowledge), the economy (the organization of production, distribution, and consumption of goods and services), social structure (including family and marriage, and gender), relations among ethnic groups, political organization and processes, and religion. Although this is not a complete list of the different variables studied by cultural anthropologists, it provides the general framework for understanding a society. All of these variables are discussed in relationship with one another to produce what is known as a "holistic understanding" of a society. The various chapters on countries and regions will provide a holistic understanding through a discussion of these different aspects of the relevant societies in the Asian area.

THE CONCEPT OF CULTURE

Culture is a fundamental concept within the discipline of anthropology. Anthropologists were the first scholars to utilize this term with a general purpose meaning to include everything that is constructed by humans. This general view suggests that culture includes tools, weapons, fire, agriculture, animal domestication, metallurgy, writing, the steam engine, glasses, airplanes, computers, penicillin, nuclear power, rock-and-roll, video games, designer jeans, religion, political systems, subsistence patterns, science, philosophy, sports, and social organizations. Culture contains all the plans, rules, techniques, designs, and policies for living. All culture is transmitted to individuals through learning or what anthropologists refer to as *enculturation*, in contrast to biological traits which are passed to us through genetics. Most anthropologists today would accept a broad conception of culture as a shared way of life that includes values, beliefs, and norms transmitted within a particular society from generation to generation.

The human capacity for culture and enculturation is based on our linguistic and cognitive ability to symbolize. Symbols are abstract ideas that are embodied within language. Language is the standardized system of symbols that allows people to communicate with one another. Language ensures the continuity of a cultural heritage. As human children learn their language, symbols and culture are transmitted from generation to generation. One aspect of language that is recognized is that humans can speak using complicated phonological, syntactical, and grammatical rules, while not being conscious of those rules. Speakers and listeners of language cannot consciously express those complicated rules. Presumably, some aspects of human culture are unconscious also. As humans learn language, both consciously and unconsciously, they learn how to subsist, how to socialize, how to govern their society, and what gods to worship. Culture is the historical accumulation of symbolic knowledge that is shared by a society. This symbolic knowledge is transmitted through learning, and it can change rapidly from parents to children and from one generation to the next. Generally, however, people in societies go to great lengths to preserve their culture and symbolic traditions. As we will see in later chapters, the persistence of cultural and symbolic traditions, the basis of one's ethnic and national identity, is as widespread as cultural and ethnic change.

It is apparent that cultural understandings are not shared equally by all members of a society. Even in small-scale societies, culture is shared differently by males and females or by young and old. Some individuals in these societies have a great deal of knowledge regarding agriculture, medical practices, or religious beliefs, whereas others have less. In the complex multicultural and multiethnic Asian societies considered in this textbook culture consists of a tremendous amount of information and knowledge regarding technology, social and political life, and other aspects of society. Different people learn different aspects of culture, such as maintaining rice fields, elaborating religious rituals, using childcare techniques, or making decisions in the stock market. Hence, to some extent, culture varies from person to person, from region to region, from age to age grouping, from gender to gender, and from ethnic group to ethnic group. An *ethnic group* is a collectivity of people who believe they share a common history, culture, or ancestry. There may be some overlap in shared practices and culture among different individuals or ethnic groups but there are various degrees of commitment to particular aspects of a common culture. In many cases, the so-called common culture may be contested and struggled against. Thus, anthropologists do not believe that "cultures" are discrete units with homogeneous values, beliefs, and norms that are shared by everyone within the society. The extent to which an individual or a particular ethnic group in a society shares a particular culture is an empirical question that the anthropologist has to investigate.

The concept of culture has two dimensions that are sometimes distinguished by anthropologists: material and nonmaterial culture. Material culture consists of the physical products of human society (ranging from clothing styles to housing and building types, to technologies of transportation). Material culture can become important ethnic boundary markers, which are used to differentiate one group from another. Clothing styles are often used to distinguish one ethnic group from another. Nonmaterial culture refers to the intangible products of human society (symbols and language, values, beliefs, and norms). Values are the standards by which members of an ethnic group define what is good or bad, holy or unholy, beautiful or ugly. They are assumptions that are shared within the ethnic group. *Values* are the abstract generalizations that underlie beliefs. All ethnic groups have *beliefs*, which are cultural conventions that concern true or false assumptions, including specific descriptions of the nature of the universe and one's place in it. Some beliefs may be combined into an ideology. An *ideology* consists of cultural symbols and beliefs that reflect and support the interests of specific ethnic groups or within a particular ethnic group. Particular ethnic groups promote ideologies for their own ends as a means of maintaining and justifying economic and political authority.

Norms, the rules of right and wrong behavior manifested within a society, are another aspect of nonmaterial culture. Norms are shared rules or guidelines that define how a group "ought" to behave under certain circumstances. Norms are generally connected to the values, beliefs, worldviews, and ideologies of an ethnic group. Some anthropologists use the term *ethos* to refer to the socially acceptable norms within an ethnic group. Norms guiding ordinary usages and conventions of everyday life are known as folkways or etiquette. Thus, among different ethnic groups there are a variety of rules for greeting people, exchanging gifts, exhibiting table manners, and behaving on innumerable social occasions. *Mores* or morality norms have much stronger sanctions than folkway or etiquette norms. Members of ethnic groups believe that their mores are crucial for the maintenance of a decent and orderly way of life. People who violate mores are usually severely punished, though punishment for the violation of mores varies from one ethnic group to another. It may take the form of ostracism, vicious gossip, public ridicule, exile, losing one's job, physical beating, imprisonment, commitment to a mental hospital, or even execution.

The terms for nonmaterial culture including values, beliefs, norms, ideologies, ethos, and worldviews are used by many anthropologists in their fieldwork research. However, not all anthropologists agree with concise, clear-cut distinctions among these terms. Instead these terms are based on the models that anthropologists build on when studying and interpreting other cultures. Terms such as *values*, *beliefs*, *norms*, or *worldviews*, and *culture* itself are used as heuristic devices and research aids to help explain behavior and understand the complex symbols shared by different groups within a society. Contemporary anthropologists recognize that these models are only partial solutions to explaining and understanding the empirical and existential realities of people within a particular country or region.

A reaction that many students have when first confronting cultures and religions other than their own is known as ethnocentrism. *Ethnocentrism* is the practice of judging another society by the values and standards of one's own society. Ethnocentrism usually involves the belief that one's own culture is superior to that of other cultures. To some degree, ethnocentrism is a universal phenomenon. As humans learn the basic values, beliefs, and norms of their society, they tend to think of their own culture as the most preferable, ranking other cultures as less desirable. In fact, members of a society become so committed to particular cultural traditions that they cannot conceive of any other way of life. They often view other cultural traditions as strange, alien, inferior, crazy, or immoral. Anthropologists recognize that ethnocentrism inhibits an understanding of other cultures. To combat the problem of ethnocentrism, twentieth-century anthropologists developed the concept of cultural relativism. *Cultural relativism* is the view that any cultural tradition must be understood within the context of a particular society's solutions to problems and opportunities. All societies must provide solutions to getting enough to eat, curing illnesses, raising children, and satisfying both material and spiritual needs. Every culture has its own particular history that led to specific practices and beliefs. Because cultural traditions represent somewhat unique adaptations and symbolic systems for different societies, these traditions must be understood as objectively as possible. Cultural relativism offers anthropologists a means of investigating other societies without imposing ethnocentric assumptions. At the same time, anthropologists, as other humans, are sometimes confronted with values and practices that may lead to harm to individuals or society as a whole. Therefore, anthropologists do not suggest that any set of values, norms, and practices are equally permissible. Extreme forms of relativism are not acceptable within the field of anthropology.

ANTHROPOLOGICAL VOCABULARY AND KINSHIP

Anthropologists have conducted research on family and kinship throughout the world. Though family and kinship are universal features, ethnographic research has demonstrated that the forms of family, kinship relations, and social organization are manifested differently in various societies. In attempting to understand and explain the different forms of family, kinship, and social structures anthropologists have developed a specialized vocabulary. As will be seen in the following chapters on Asian societies, the anthropologists will use terms such as *patrilineal descent, bilateral descent, clans, extended or joint families, polygynous marriages,* and *matrilocal residence.* To provide a context for understanding the family, kinship, and social organization in Asia, it is necessary to introduce some of this anthropological vocabulary and terminology.

The term *family* is used by anthropologists to refer to the individuals residing in a household related by blood, marriage, or adoption. The two major types of families found throughout the world are the nuclear and extended families. A typical nuclear family is composed of two parents and their immediate biological offspring or adopted children. Some anthropologists believe that the nuclear family is a universal feature of all societies.[2] What is meant by this is that all societies have a male and female who reproduce children and are the core of the kinship unit. However, as will be seen in later chapters, the nuclear family is not the principal kinship unit in most Asian societies. In most rural and some urban areas of Asia the predominant form is the extended family, which is composed of parents, children, and other kin relations bound together as a social unit. The extended family takes different forms dependent on the particular circumstances within the society. One type of extended family is known as the *stem family* that consists of two or more married couples of different generations. Thus, a stem family might have a married couple with children that are married residing in the same household. Another form of extended family is the *joint family* consisting of married couples of the same generation. A joint family may have several brothers, their wives, and their children living within the household. The joint family may also have several generations within the household: the grandparents, parents, and children. It must be emphasized that all of the individuals within a family, whether nuclear or extended, do not reside together throughout the life of the family cycle. In other words, the family cycle changes; older children may marry and leave the family, children may be adopted out, and ultimately some family members die.

A Chinese family.

In most Asian societies the family is a product of marriage, a social bond sanctioned by society between two or more people that involves economic cooperation and culturally approved sexual activity. Two general patterns of marriage exist: *endogamy*, which is marriage between people of the same social group or category; and *exogamy*, marriage between people of different social groups and categories. Endogamous marriages may be preferred by a specific ethnic group within a society. Exogamy may involve individuals who marry outside their own particular village into another village. In some cases, a marriage may include two or more partners. Monogamy involves two individuals in the marriage. Though this is the most familiar form of marriage in Western industrial societies, it is not the only type of marriage practiced in Asia. Some Asian societies practice some form of polygamy, marriage involving a spouse of one sex and two or more spouses of the opposite sex. There are two forms of polygamy: *polygyny*, marriage between one husband and two or more wives, and *polyandry*, marriage between one wife and two or more husbands. Cousin marriage is also found in some Asian societies, as in other areas of the world. Anthropologists note two preferred forms of cousin marriage in Asia: *cross-cousin marriage*, whereby a male marries his mother's brother's daughter, or father's sister's daughter, or *parallel-cousin marriage*, typically when a male marries his father's brother's daughter.

Descent and residence rules are frequently important within the family and kinship relations in Asian societies. As we will see in some Asian societies the most significant group for tracing one's descent is the *lineage*, a group composed of relatives, all of whom trace their relationship through consanguineal (blood) or affinal (marriage) relations to an actual, commonly known ancestor. Everyone in the lineage knows exactly how she or he is related to this ancestor. Unilineal descent groups are lineage groups that trace their descent through only one side of the lineage or through only one sex. The most common type of unilineal descent group found in Asian societies is a *patrilineal descent group*, or patrilineage, composed of people who trace their descent through males from a common, known male ancestor. Another form of unilineal descent group that exists in some areas of Asia is the *matrilineal descent group*, or matrilineage, whose members calculate descent through the female line from a commonly known female ancestor. In some areas of Asia, especially Southeast Asia, a number of groups practice *bilateral descent*, in which relatives are traced through both maternal and paternal sides of the family simultaneously. This type of descent system does not result in any particular lineal descent grouping. In those cases in which bilateral descent is found, a loosely structured group known as a kindred is used to mobilize relatives for economic, social, or political purposes. *Kindreds* are overlapping relatives from both the mother's and father's side of a family that an individual recognizes as important kin relations.

Another form of descent group found in Asia is known as a clan. A *clan* is a form of descent group whose members trace their descent to an unknown ancestor in the past. Members of clans usually share a common name but are not able to specify definitive links to an actual genealogical figure. Some clans are patriclans, a group distinguished by a male through whom descent is traced. Other clan groupings are matriclans, whose descent is traced through a female. Some Asian societies have both clans and lineages. In such a system, clans are larger groupings, consisting of several different lineages. In most of these Asian societies, marriages are usually exogamous in respect to lineage and clan; that is, individuals are supposed to marry outside their own clan and lineage. However, as we will see in some areas of Asia, individuals are encouraged to marry within their own lineage or clan grouping for economic or political purposes.

In addition to descent rules that govern marriage, postmarital residence rules following marriage are often preferred in many Asian societies. Anthropologists indicate that the rules for residence after marriage in Asian societies are related to the forms of descent groups. For example, the vast majority of Asian societies have patrilineal descent groups and *patrilocal rules* of residence. In other words, the wife of the male resides with the male's father's family after marriage. Another, less frequent, pattern of postmarital residence in Asia is *matrilocal residence,* in which the newly wedded couple lives with or near the wife's parents. The other predominant form of postmarital rule is *neolocal residence* whereby the married couple sets up a new residence outside their paternal or maternal family household.

Descent groups and marriage rules provide distinctive organizational features for many Asian societies. Descent groupings such as clans, lineages, or kindreds may become corporate social units, meaning that they endure beyond any particular individual's lifetime. Thus, they can play a key role in regulating the production, exchange, and distribution of goods and services over a long period of time. Family rights to land, livestock, and other resources are usually defined in relation to these corporate descent groups. Sometimes in societies with bilateral descent, noncorporate kindreds are the basic labor-cooperative groups for production and exchange. People living in bilateral societies can turn to both the mother's and father's side of the family for economic assistance. In Southeast Asia, the kindred is a much more loosely structured group. The kindred is highly flexible and allows for better adaptation in certain environmental circumstances.

Descent groups and marriage rules in Asian societies provide a means to manage their economic rights and obligations. Within the descent groups, individual nuclear families may have rights to particular land and animals. For example, among patrilineally organized peoples, land

Bilateral descent The tracing of descent through both paternal and maternal lines.

Clan A form of descent group whose members trace their descent to an unknown ancestor in the past.

Cross-cousin marriage When a male marries his mother's brother's daughter or father's sister's daughter.

Endogamy Marriage between people of the same social group or category.

Exogamy Marriage between people of different social groups and categories.

Extended family Comprised of parents, offspring, and additional relatives within a household.

Joint family Married couples of the same generation within a household.

Kindred The loosely structured group of relatives that results from calculating bilateral descent.

Lineage A group composed of relatives, all of whom trace their relationship through consanguineal (blood) or affinal (marriage) relations to an actual, commonly known ancestor.

Matrilineal descent group A group that traces their descent through the maternal line.

Matrilocal residence The postmarital residence rule in which a newly married couple must reside with the wife's parents' household.

Neolocal residence The postmarital residence rule in which the newly married couple establishes a new household.

Nuclear family Composed of two parents and their immediate biological offspring or adopted children within a household.

Parallel-cousin marriage Typically when a male marries his father's brother's daughter.

Patrilineal descent group A group that traces their descent through the paternal line.

Patrilocal residence The postmarital residence rule in which a newly married couple must reside with the husband's father's household.

Polyandry Marriage between one wife and two or more husbands.

Polygamy Marriage with multiple spouses.

Polygyny Marriage between one husband and two or more wives.

Primogeniture The form of inheritance in which property and land are transmitted from generation to generation through an eldest male.

Stem family Two or more married couples of different generations within a household.

Ultimogeniture The inheritance rule in which property and land are passed to the youngest son.

is sometimes transmitted from generation to generation through an eldest male, an inheritance pattern known as *primogeniture.* Another, less common, pattern is *ultimogeniture,* in which property and land are passed to the youngest son. We realize that the introduction of this family, marriage, kinship, and social organization terminology may be confusing outside a particular context of a society's practices. Therefore, we provide the above box with the definitions of the terms used in the chapters that follow.

It must be emphasized that descent, marriage, and residence rules are not static in Asian societies. Rather, they are flexible and change as ecological, demographic, economic, and political circumstances change. For example, ethnic groups with rules of preference for marriage partners make exceptions to those rules when the situation calls for it. If an Asian society has norms that prescribe cross-cousin or parallel-cousin marriage, and an individual does not have a cousin in the particular category, various options will be available for the individual. There are usually many other candidates available for an arranged marriage. Anthropologists have demonstrated over and over again that much strategizing goes on in Asian societies in determining marital choice, residence locales, and descent. Factors such as property and the availability of land, animals, or other resources often influence decisions about marital arrangements. Often, parents will be involved in lengthy negotiations or even advertising regarding marital choices for their offspring. These people, like others throughout the world, are not automatons responding automatically to cultural norms. Kinship and marital rules are ideal norms, and these norms are often violated through strategic decision making by individuals in various circumstances.

WHY STUDY ASIA?

Many students today may have questions about the practical benefits of their educational experience. Hence, you might ask "Why study Asia?" First, studying another region of the world contributes to a general liberal arts education, which helps students develop intellectually and personally, as well as professionally. Numerous studies indicate that a well-rounded education contributes to a person's success in any chosen career, and because of its broad interdisciplinary and multicultural dimensions, the study of Asia is especially well suited to this purpose. In the context of a liberal arts education, the study of a cultural region of the world will help cultivate critical thinking skills. The chapters on the different countries and regions of Asia rely on constant evaluation of, and critical thinking about, ethnographic data collected in the field. By being exposed to the cultures and lifestyles of unfamiliar societies, students may adopt a more critical and analytical stance toward conditions in their own society. Critical thinking skills enhance the reasoning abilities of students wherever life takes them.

The study of Asia also creates an expanding global awareness and an appreciation for cultures other than our own. In this age of rapid communication, worldwide travel, and increasing economic interconnections, young people preparing for careers in the twenty-first century must recognize and show sensitivity toward the cultural differences that exist among peoples, while understanding the fundamental similarities that make us all distinctly human. In this age of cultural diversity and increasing internationalization, sustaining this dual perception of underlying similar human characteristics and outward cultural differences has both practical and moral benefits. Nationalistic, ethnic, and racial bigotry are rife today in many parts of the world, yet our continuing survival and happiness depend on greater mutual understanding. Asia and the West, including the United States, are bound together inextricably through global political and economic connections. The study of Asia promotes a cross-cultural perspective that allows us to see ourselves as part of one human family in the midst of tremendous cultural diversity. This global perspective developed through the study of Asia can be parlayed into an enhanced understanding of other regions of the world.

In addition, following September 11, 2001, many Americans and Westerners were dismayed at why such a tragedy could occur within their own society. Westerners and Americans found that they did not have an understanding of why other people throughout the world had grievances that could sustain such an act of violence. As a result of 9/11 some Americans and Westerners began to discern that earlier geopolitical strategies in areas such as Afghanistan, an unknown region, were directly related to what had occurred. After 9/11 a political and military relationship with Pakistan created more awareness of the turbulent relations between Pakistan and India. Terrorist activities in such areas as Indonesia and the rise of Islamic movements in South and Southeast Asia have become staples of the Western media since 9/11. The recent discoveries of nuclear weapons capabilities in North Korea and the widespread global instability that could arise from such developments have also arisen within the Western media. Concerns about the status of China as it develops more economic and political interconnections with the United States and the West have become explicit topics of discussion on the daily pages and televisions of the American audience. Japan's continuing struggle to arise from its economic difficulties and the impact that this will have on America and the West is another subject matter addressed by many. All of these concerns have created ambiguities, anxieties, and apprehension by many Westerners and Americans about the region of Asia. A better comprehension and a richer understanding of the peoples and cultures of Asia will help provide a more comprehensive and accurate intellectual framework for resolving these ambiguities and concerns. One of the major goals of this textbook is to provide such a comprehensive and accurate understanding of the countries and regions of Asia.

Results of the 9/11/01 tragedy.

It is also the hope of the authors of this textbook that the study of Asia offers some practical and more pragmatic agendas. Given the increasingly multicultural and international focus of today's world, students who go on to careers in business, management, marketing, health care, or public service may find it advantageous to have an understanding of this important area of the world. The concepts and knowledge gleaned from the study of Asia may enable students to find practical applications in dealing with issues of cultural and ethnic diversity and multiculturalism on a daily basis.

Education majors preparing for the classroom can draw on their background in the study of Asia to provide a more insightful context for some of these issues that they will face with their future students. A better knowledge of the countries and cultures of Asia will hopefully produce more productive citizens that can enhance improved relationships between the West and the East. Our increasingly global environment needs citizens not just of some local region or group but also, and more importantly, we need world citizens who can work cooperatively in an inescapably multicultural and multinational world to solve our most pressing problems of bigotry, poverty, and violence.

NOTES

1. Edward W. Said wrote the first sustained critique of Western scholarship and its production of distorted stereotypes within the Middle East in his book *Orientalism* (New York: Vintage Press, 1979). Anthropologist Stephen Inden has written about Orientalism with respect to India in *Imagining India* (Oxford England: Blackwell, 1990). A number of scholars have critiqued the history of China such as Arif Dirlik's essay "Chinese History and the Question of Orientalism," *History and Theory* 35, 70.4 (1996): 96–119. All of the recent scholarship on Asia has been written with an awareness of the critique of Orientalism and its problems of perpetuating distorted, essentialized conceptions of Asian peoples and cultures.

2. Anthropologist George Murdock proposed that the nuclear family was the basis of all social organization throughout the world in his classic *Social Structure* (New York: Macmillan, 1949).

2 AFGHANISTAN

H. Sidky
Deborah S. Akers

INTRODUCTION

During the 1980s Afghanistan attracted considerable international interest as a result of the Soviet invasion in 1979 and the armed resistance by the Afghan people. In Western perceptions and political discourse Afghanistan was portrayed as the land of a proud freedom-loving and courageous people fighting for their country against a ruthless foreign aggressor possessing superior firepower. The American media and leaders like President Jimmy Carter and his successor Ronald Reagan hailed the Afghan resistance groups, called *mujahideen* (singular *mujahid*—those who undertake *jihad* or religious struggle in defense of the faith), as heroic "freedom fighters" and "holy warriors."

In addition to high praise and sympathy, the United States and its allies showered the mujahideen with vast sums of money and a massive array of armaments. The Soviets poured in an equal amount of cash and weaponry to the Kabul regime, which they were supporting. Ten years of brutal fighting ensued until the Soviets withdrew in 1989. With the subsequent breakup of the Soviet Union, ending the Cold War, international attention shifted elsewhere and Afghanistan more or less dropped out of the limelight of global politics and Western media attention. The one exception was an incident in 1998, when the United States on President Bill Clinton's orders fired 74 Tomahawk cruise missiles at terrorist training camps near Khost and Jalalabad in Afghanistan in retaliation for the bombings of the American embassies in Kenya and Tanzania. It seems that things had changed inside Afghanistan from what they were before.

By the start of the twenty-first century, there was an entirely different American perception of Afghanistan. It was now viewed as a grim "Kalashnikov culture," located near some other "stan," the home of heavily armed militant Muslims, warlords, opium czars, and terrorists, a place where women were oppressed and beaten in public, and where Islam "had gone crazy."[1] Many in the West did not understand what was transpiring in Afghanistan and many more simply did not care. The September 11, 2001, attacks on New York City and Washington, DC changed all of that. *Afghanistan* became a

We wish to sincerely thank the following scholars who reviewed this work in manuscript form for their thoughtful comments and suggestions: Dr. David Edwards, Associate Professor of Anthropology at Williams College and Director of the Williams Afghan Media Project, Professor Karel (Carool) Kersten, a noted Islamic scholar now teaching in Thailand, and Dr. Thomas Barfield, Professor of Anthropology and chairman of the Department of Anthropology at Boston University.

UZBEKISTAN
TAJIKISTAN
TURKMENISTAN
HINDU KUSH MOUNTAINS
AFGHANISTAN
PAKISTAN
IRAN
Kabul
Kandahar
Hazara
Tajik
Uzbek
Pashtun
other

household word. It was also in the days immediately after the collapse of the Twin Towers that some Americans to their horror first heard of *al Qaeda,* Osama bin Laden, and the "atavistic" bearded radicals, called the *Taliban,* and their global jihad or holy war against the United States.

The September 11 tragedy not only brought Afghanistan back into the center stage of global politics, but it also brought to the fore the fundamentally problematic nature of the relationship between the United States and the Islamic world. This is well illustrated in the proclivity of American political leaders to construe the terrorist attacks in simplistic terms as a war between the forces of good versus evil, declarations by political scientists about "a clash of civilizations," or "the West versus the Rest," and ill-informed Western stereotypes that overlook the historical complexity and ethnographic richness and diversity of the Islamic world, all of which serve to perpetuate significant misunderstandings and misperceptions. As a consequence, Afghanistan, terrorism, anti-Americanism, and Islam have become inextricably linked. Unfortunately, misperceptions such as these, which continue to guide how many Americans construe Islamic and Muslim peoples, serve as barriers for cross-cultural understanding at a time when what is most needed is for us to comprehend and constructively engage the Islamic world.

The case of Afghanistan epitomizes all of the misperceptions noted above. The majority of Afghans, and Muslims in general, do not subscribe to the radical political vision of Osama bin Laden and his followers or the policies and agendas of the Taliban. The Afghan people suffered horrific atrocities at the hands of al Qaeda fighters, who turned their country into a base of operations, and the Taliban, whose draconian interpretation of Islamic law was unprecedented and objectionable not only to most Afghans, but also to most Muslims around the world. Moreover, none of the individuals who orchestrated and carried out the 9/11 attacks were Afghans. Yet it was the Afghans who paid a heavy price when the United States sent its military to exact retribution.

A mere 35 years ago, Afghanistan was one of the most moderate, peaceful, and safest societies in the Islamic world, if not the whole of Asia. Enforced compliance of religious duties was unheard of. There was a great deal of tolerance for members of other sects and other faiths. Women enjoyed considerable freedoms and access to education and were engaged in a wide range of professions, including ministerial posts in the government. Americans and Westerners were welcomed graciously as honored guests. Afghans were proud of their artistic traditions and their long and rich historical and cultural heritage, both pre-Islamic and Islamic.

The unfortunate circumstances linking Afghanistan to the tragic events of September 11 are recent developments. Why Afghanistan became the nexus of the global jihad against the United States, why radical groups like the Taliban emerged, why Osama bin Laden found refuge in Afghanistan, and why al Qaeda targeted the United States are questions to which the answers lie well beyond Afghanistan and extend into broader geopolitical circumstances, twentieth-century superpower rivalries, Soviet and U.S. foreign policies, the manner in which Afghanistan has been integrated into the global system, and the broader regional political forces at work during the closing decades of the twentieth century.

Every aspect of Afghan society was affected in some way by the war that began with the communist takeover in 1978, followed by the Soviet invasion in 1979, and which continues in its latest permutation as the United States' "War on Terror," which started in October 2001. The war in its international, regional, and local dimensions looms central in the anthropological narrative presented here. Unfortunately, as a result of the disruption of scholarship and cessation of anthropological research due to the war we have insufficient knowledge about the nature of the massive sociopolitical transformations that took place in Afghanistan over the last 24 years. A general picture, however, is slowly emerging. The information presented here is in part based upon the ethnographic literature produced prior to the war and in part on a range of other sources, such as historical accounts, analyses by political scientists, information provided by international humanitarian agencies working inside the country, and archival materials that became available during the period after the Soviet withdrawal.[2]

In this chapter we attempt to address the questions raised above within the framework of a general discussion of Islam and an overview of Afghanistan, its geography, prehistory, history, languages, religious composition, and contemporary culture. Hopefully this will provide the reader with a better understanding of Afghanistan and its people and an appreciation of the complex nature of the circumstance that launched the War on Terror, and a broader perspective with which to think about the related issues in a more informed and responsible fashion.

GEOGRAPHIC SETTING

Afghanistan is a landlocked mountainous country lying in the heart of the Eurasian continent. Encompassing roughly 401,450 square miles (647,500 square kilometers) making it slightly smaller than the state of Texas, it borders Pakistan to the south and east 1506 miles (2,430 km), Iran to the west 580 miles (936 km), Turkmenistan 461 miles (744 km) to the northwest, Tajikistan 748 miles (1,206 km) and Uzbekistan 85 miles (137 km) to the north, and China 47 miles (76 km) to the northeast.[3]

Before its emergence as a recognized nation state in the nineteenth century the name *Afghanistan* applied solely to the territory inhabited by one of the country's dominant ethnic group, a people known as "Afghans," or the Pashtuns (Pushtuns). However, construing Afghanistan as the "homeland of the Pashtuns" is misleading and obscures the complex sociocultural diversity of the people who are citizens of Afghanistan. In the context of the state, *Afghanistan* refers to the homeland of all individuals who are legal citizens of the country.

Lying at the intersection between the Middle East, Iran, Central Asia, and the Indian subcontinent, and more broadly between China and the Persian Gulf, northern Europe, and the Mediterranean world, Afghanistan has been described as "a land bridge between the world's major civilizations." Afghanistan's cultural, political, and economic development and demographic structure have been powerfully shaped by its position at the "cross-roads" of civilizations. Waves of migrating peoples, traders, invading armies, and colonizers who brought with them diverse cultural traditions through the centuries are evident in the country's rich and diverse archaeological remains and in its present-day demographic, cultural, and ethnolinguistic mosaic.

Afghanistan has an extremely complex topography with considerable vertical relief over most of its terrain. For this reason it is difficult to divide the country into clearly defined geographic and climatic zones. In general, the geophysical and topographic features of the country—which consist of a central mountainous highland area, surrounding foothills, and plains and deserts to the north, west, and southwest—make for ecologically diverse landscapes ranging from snowcapped peaks to dusty steppes, oases, fertile valleys, and burning deserts, with different potential for human subsistence and economic productivity. Demographic, settlement, and subsistence patterns to a large extent are linked to local ecological conditions that are strongly affected by topography, altitude, and aspect.

The massive Hindu Kush Mountains and sub-branches dominate the country's geography and overall ecology. *Hindu Kush* means literally "killer of Hindus" and, according to the renowned Moroccan traveler Ibn Battuta who passed through this area in the fourteenth century, the mountains were so named on account of the many slaves brought from India to be sold in the slave markets of Muslim Central Asia who perished as a result of heavy snows and cold temperatures. The Hindu Kush bisects Afghanistan into two uneven halves and forms a natural boundary between Central and South Asia. Afghanistan's extreme rugged terrain and vertical relief have posed severe logistical challenges for overland travel, the development of highway systems, and military operations. This has contributed both to the country's physical isolation from the outside world and to internal regional isolation. Different parts of the country are accessible through a network of difficult-to-negotiate roads and strategic high mountain passes that since ancient times have functioned to channel the flow of people, material goods, and ideas along certain routes.

Until the middle part of the twentieth century travel in Afghanistan was mainly by caravans of pack animals (camels, horses, and donkeys) that traversed tortuous, slender trails and unpaved roads. All-weather highway construction began only during the 1950s, with massive foreign aid from the United States and the Soviet Union. Internal communication was thus considerably impeded and as a result political, social, and economic integration was very slow. More than two decades of warfare beginning with the communist coup in 1978 and Soviet invasion the following year has resulted in severe damage to the meager transportation infrastructure that was in place before the war. Efforts are now under way to repair the major highways.

There are 16 mountain passes, but only three have been historically significant. The Salang Pass 9,449 feet (2,880 m), about 112 miles (180 km) north of Kabul, with its 1.68 miles (2.7 km)-long tunnel throught the heart of the mountain built by the Soviets in 1964, provides the fastest all-season route between northern and southern Afghanistan. The Salang road was the principal highway used by the invading Soviet army in 1979 on its way from Termiz, in Uzbekistan. Until the construction of the Salang tunnel the main transit to the north was by way of the Shibar Pass 10,696 feet (3,260 m) and the Bamiyan valley, overlooked by the colossal Buddhas carved into the cliffs that were destroyed by the Taliban. Marco Polo traveled along this route, as did Chinese pilgrims who were carrying sacred Buddhist texts from India to China. Access to the north is also possible through the Khawak 11,824 feet (3,550 m) and Anjuman 12,657 feet (3,858 m) passes in the Panjsher valley. In 330 BC Alexander the Great led his army through the Panjsher valley and over the Khawak Pass to conquer Bactria (Balkh) in northern Afghanistan. Other conquerors, such as Tamerlane and Genghis Khan, used this pass on their march to India.

Passage from the Kabul valley to eastern Afghanistan is possible through the Lataband Pass 8,199 feet (2,499 m) over the mountains that lie between Kabul and the plains of Jalalabad. A road clinging to the side of the Tang-i-Gharu gorge of the Kabul River, completed in 1960, forms the main road from Kabul to Jalalabad and Pakistan. Access to Peshawar, Pakistan, is through the famous Khyber Pass 3,369 feet (1,027 m), a 28 mile (45-km)-long passage through the Safed Koh Mountains. Alexander the Great marched through here on his way to India. During the nineteenth century British armies marched to Afghanistan through the Khyber Pass. During the twentieth century the Khyber Pass and Tang-i-Gharu became the main artery for the flow of military supplies and humanitarian conveys, refugees, and smuggled trade goods.

No mountain barriers exist between Afghanistan and its neighbors to the north, west, and southwest. The mountains and foothills to the north gradually merge into the Central Asian steppes. The plateaus and deserts to the west and southwest merge with the desert terrain in Iran.

The climate of Afghanistan is arid to semiarid. Much of the precipitation falls in winter and in the form of snow at high altitudes. Precipitation ranges from 28 to 32 inches (700 to 800 mm) in the east to 12 inches (300 mm) or less in the plains and lowlands. Temperature regimes vary considerably with altitude. Lower elevations are nearly frost-free with hot summers, whereas higher elevations have arctic conditions in winter and mild summers. Desert or semidesert conditions characterize most of the country. Water therefore constitutes one of the critical limiting factors for human subsistence, whether farming, herding, or hunting and gathering.

Terrain above 2604 feet (4,200 m) is generally barren and permanent snow covers elevations above 2160 feet (5,000 m). At lower altitudes grasslands and scrub vegetation is present. At one time the eastern ranges of the Hindu Kush were covered with dense forest. However, the years of conflict and uncontrolled exploitation and illegal timber operations have contributed to a massive reduction of the forest cover. Further to the west, the forest cover changes into grasslands creating pastures in the higher valleys, drawing nomads from the plains to the south, who come here in the summers to graze their livestock herds.

The Hindu Kush Mountains contain the high watershed that is the source of Afghanistan's principle river systems: the Amu Darya, Hari Rud, Hilmand-Arghandab, and Kabul systems. For centuries Afghan farmers have relied upon these rivers for irrigation.

Of the total surface area of the country approximately 5 percent is under intense irrigation agriculture, 7 percent is under rainfed agriculture, 47 percent is rangeland, and the remaining 41 percent of the country includes urban settlements and barren rocky outcrops. The inhabitants of Afghanistan have attempted to exploit the wide range of environments and overcome environmental constraints by adopting a variety of subsistence strategies, including intensive irrigation farming, dry farming, arboriculture (grapevine and fruit tree cultivation), and transhumant and nomadic pastoralism based upon sheep and goat herding.

PREHISTORY

Prehistoric archaeology in Afghanistan did not begin in earnest until the 1950s and was still in its initial stages of development when the outbreak of the war in 1979 interrupted all such research.[4] Despite the limited number of sites excavated and the resultant gaps in the archaeological record of the country, some preliminary observations are possible.

The human occupation of Afghanistan has substantial antiquity, although precise dates are difficult to establish. The earliest evidence comes from Dasht-i-Nawar, on the shores of a large brackish lake in Ghazni province, where archaeologists discovered a concentration of quartzite tools, including cleavers, large scrapers, choppers, and pebble tools thought to represent a Lower Paleolithic tool industry. Although subsequent surveys failed to yield additional traces of Lower Paleolithic tools, sites dating to this period have been discovered in southern Tajikistan about 62 miles (100 km) from the Afghan border, yielding pebble tools and a flake industry along with chopping tools and retouched flakes. This supports the possibility of the existence of potential Lower Paleolithic sites in northern Afghanistan, which appears to have been part of a broader and well-documented worldwide adaptive pattern resulting in the expansion of humans into the continental interiors of Asia.

There is better documentation for the human occupation of Afghanistan during the Middle Paleolithic period. Dara-i-Kur, a rock shelter site near the village of Chanar-i-Gunjus Khan in Badakshan province has yielded a tool industry consisting of flaked tools with a high occurrence of blades and a few side scrapers, but no hand-axes. Charcoal samples from a hearth have yielded a date of 29,000 to 30,000 years or older. In addition the site has yielded a hominid right temporal bone, which is so far the only known hominid material to be found in context for this period in Afghanistan. Comparisons of this material with Neanderthal and modern *Homo sapiens sapiens* indicates morphological similarities to modern humans, although it is within the range of the more anatomically modern Neanderthal populations such as the Es-Skhul skull found in Mount Carmel, Israel.

In addition, Dara-i-Kur has yielded faunal (animal) remains of wild sheep, goats, and possibly cattle, suggesting the establishment of a basic hunting adaptation during this time that continued until the end of the Paleolithic period. Moreover, the identification of these potentially domesticable species at such an early period indicates that the region was within the natural range of these species before the Neolithic (agricultural) Revolution in Southwest Asia. The appearance of these animals later on as domesticated species cannot be explained in terms of diffusion from some other location. Although the evidence is scanty, the implication here is that the Neolithic in Afghanistan may have occurred independently.

The Late Paleolithic is known from sites north of the Hindu Kush. Kara Kamar in the Haibak area has yielded an early Upper Paleolithic stone tool industry based on blade technology. Carbon dating has yielded an age of between 25,000 to 32,000 BP (before present). Other important sites have been discovered near the town of Aq Kupruk, in Balkh province. The lithic assemblage includes flake blades and a sophisticated microblade technology. The site has been dated at 16,000 BP. There is evidence of heavy reliance on sheep and goat hunting. Little is known about the plant foods being exploited.

Limited as the archaeological evidence discussed above may be, it is clear that the human occupation of Afghanistan has considerable antiquity. Moreover, there are indications that the hunting-gathering populations in this area were adjusting to changing ecological circumstances by means of sociocultural adaptations, as evident in technological changes and the types of environments and repertoires of plants and animals being exploited. These adaptive strategies resulted in human interaction with wild ancestors of animal and plant species that comprise the basis of the farming economies that appear during the Neolithic period. This has important theoretical implications because it suggests the possibility that the Neolithic Revolution in Afghanistan may have been a local phenomena, rather than the outcome of diffusion from elsewhere, such as the Middle East.

The Neolithic Revolution represented the first major evolutionary transformation in human history. It was once believed that the Neolithic Revolution was centered in the Middle East from where the domestication of plants and animals subsequently spread to the rest of the world. This idea is no longer tenable. It is now believed that there were several Neolithic Revolutions that occurred virtually independently of one another. In this regard, further research in Afghanistan and Central Asia may add considerably to our understanding of the Neolithic transformation.

Data for the technological and sociocultural changes during the Neolithic come from cave sites in northeastern Afghanistan. Fully domesticated animals dating 10,000 years or more have been identified. These sites have also yielded processing tools found in association with plant domestication, such as sickle blades with the distinctive sheen on the edges produced by cutting grasses, as well as ground millstones and pounders, indicating that the groups possessing domesticated animals were also relying upon grasses. Pottery is the other addition to the cultural inventory.

Absence of associated architectural remains and location of the sites in caves is suggestive that the assemblage was associated with specialized pastoral nomads who used agricultural tools to process cereals obtained from farmers, or served as laborers for farming communities. If this interpretation is correct, it suggests that the present-day division of the Afghan population between sedentary agriculturalists and pastoral nomads is a continuation of a pattern that came into existence in very ancient times.

The last phase in the prehistory of Afghanistan was marked by the development of sedentary communities and the emergence of urbanization. Based on the limited number of sites excavated thus far, it is clear that the first farming villages appear in southern Afghanistan between 6,000 to 4,000 years ago, and perhaps earlier. The site was occupied until around 1500 BC. A much larger and more complex settlement that appears at around the same time period is Mundigak on the Helmand River. Associated artifacts included terracotta bull and human figurines, copper awls, stone hoes, stone seals, and flint projectile points. During this period we find a full-fledged town (urbanization), with mud brick ramparts, a palace complex with courtyards and a massive temple structure, with an inner sanctum and altars. Associate artifacts include terracotta male figurines; terracotta bull, goat, and dog figurines; bird figurine vases; bronze awls, lance heads, and seals; and pottery. Architectural and archaeological evidence suggests that since prehistoric times Afghanistan has had cultural linkages with its neighbors to the north, south, east, and west and possible cultural connections with the great civilizations of Mohenjo Daro and Harrapa in the Indus Valley to the south and Turkmenistan to the north, and with civilizations in Iran.

HISTORY

Since ancient times, Afghanistan's strategic location has made it the focal point of both regional and global power politics. Rule over Afghanistan has been a prerequisite for any power wishing to exercise control over Central Asia and India. Hence for millennia Afghanistan has experienced successive waves of invaders and colonizers. The first of many such invasions took place around the mid-second millennium BC, with the arrival of Indo-European-speaking people from the north, roughly corresponding with a time when a degree of urban life, occupational specializations, and trade networks with surrounding areas had already developed in Afghanistan and the Iranian plateau.

Prior to Western colonialism, various imperial policies of the major agricultural empires and local developments within the region of Southwest Asia have influenced the direction of political circumstances within Afghanistan. Geo-political competition among the major agricultural empires of Persia, Greece, India, and China had a major impact on internal developments in Afghanistan. Dramatic social and political transformations in the region followed the invasions of Turco-Mongolian nomads and the expansion of the Islamic dynasties from the Arab world. In addition, the increasing consolidation and expansion of power centers among the tribal populations, especially the Pashtuns, Uzbeks, and Tajiks, accelerated various local political tendencies that were in conflict with more global imperialistic developments within Afghanistan.

Afghanistan first appears in the historical record during the sixth century BC, by which time it had been incorporated into the eastern part of the Achaemenid Empire of Persia. Two centuries later, another invader appeared, Alexander the Great and his Graeco-Macedonian army.[5] Alexander crushed Achaemenid military might in 331 and marched into Afghanistan to subdue Persia's eastern provinces. Facing stiff military resistance, Alexander built a series of 10 to 12 colonies manned by Greeks as he marched from Herat to Seistan and then eastward to the Kabul Valley. Alexander conquered the entire region including the Kabul valley before crossing the Hindu Kush into Bactria in northern Afghanistan. Over the course of the next two years the Graeco-Macedonian army conducted difficult operations against Scythian horsemen in Turkmenistan, Uzkbekistan, and Tajikistan, and established additional fortified Greek colonies in the region. Following Alexander's death in Babylon, in 323 BC his domains fell to his generals who entered into a fierce power struggle over their master's empire. Eventually, Seleucus, one of Alexander's commanders, attained control of the eastern portion of the empire, which included what is now Afghanistan. More Greeks came to the east during the Seleucid period and established themselves in the colonies in Iran, Bactria, and the Kabul valley. Hellenistic culture took root in the region as a result of the presence of a large number of Greek settlers and would continue to have an effect for several centuries.

Subsequently, southern and eastern Afghanistan fell under the control of Chandragupta (326–302 BC), founder of the Mauryan Empire centered in northern India. From this early date the people of Afghanistan thus found themselves between contending imperial powers, a situation that has often repeated itself up to the present time. The Mauryan Empire reached its apogee under Ashoka (269–232 BC), a ruthless warrior king said to have slaughtered 100,000 people in his campaign in Kalinga (eastern India), but who gave up his violent ways and converted to Buddhism and established a series of rock edicts throughout his domain urging peace and nonviolence.

One of Ashoka's rock edicts, written in Greek and Aramaic, was discovered in the city of Kandahar in 1958, which was the headquarters of the religiously uncompromising Taliban during the end of the twentieth century. Ashoka's edict contains a message of peace and compassion, calling his subjects to desist from violence, and urges tolerance and respect for other people and their religious beliefs. It was at this time that Buddhism was introduced into Afghanistan, although it would not reach its apogee for several hundred years.

By around 246 BC, the Bactrian Greeks broke away from the Seleucids and established an independent kingdom, centered around Bactria and encompassing parts of Turkmenistan, Uzbekistan, and Tajikistan in the north and northwest, and Herat (Aria) in the west. The Graeco-Bactrians expanded their territory over the course of the next 130 years to incorporate most of present-day Afghanistan, northwest Pakistan, and possibly territories beyond the Indus. Greek Bactria became the hub of commercial traffic between east and west and as a result grew rich and powerful. During this turbulent period the Hellenistic culture radiating from Bactria merged with Asian cultural traditions. For example, the reign of the Greek king Menander (160–145 BC), who is

Early Buddhist statue in Afghanistan.

referred to in the Buddhist philosophical text *Milindapanha* as Milinda, marked the beginning of a fusion of Hellenistic and Indian cultural traditions that culminated in the development of the remarkable Gandharan artistic style.

Sometime around 140–130 BC, the Bactrian Greeks were overcome by horsemen from Central Asia, to the north. By the start of the present era, one clan, the Kushan, began to forge an empire that would extend from the Caspian and Ural seas, to present-day Uzbekistan, Tajikistan, part of China's Xinjiang province (Kashgar, Yarkand, Khotan), Afghanistan, the lower Indus valley in Pakistan, and northern India. This would be the first series of cavalry-based nomadic empires established by successive waves of people coming from Central Asia. The Kushan Empire reached its full extent of power under the Kushan king Kanishka, who ruled sometime around AD 128.

The Kushans adopted many elements of the Hellenistic culture still strong in the area, including the Greek alphabet, and were instrumental in the fusion of Hellenistic, Persian, and Indian influences, which had its beginnings with the Indo-Greeks, resulting in the efflorescence (blossoming) of the remarkable Gandharan artistic tradition in painting, sculpture, and architecture, which would dominate the region until the middle of the fifth century AD.[6] It is also during this time that artists began depicting the Buddha in human form. Kanishka vigorously spread Buddhism throughout his domain and constructed numerous sanctuaries and stupas along the major trade routes. Under Kanishka, Buddhism reached its zenith and spread westward across Central Asia to China. The religious complex in Hadda, near Jalalabad, has yielded numerous statues and images in the Hellenistic-Gandharan style. Another expression of the Gandharan culture was the magnificent Buddhas carved in the cliffs of the Bamiyan valley around the fourth and fifth centuries AD, which was connected to the spread of Buddhism along the Silk Road to China, Korea, and Japan. Bamiyan was a major center of Buddhism. Even as late as the seventh century there were numerous monasteries with thousands of monks in residence.[7]

Another important development during the Kushan period was political stability and the ability of rulers to protect trade routes and encourage commerce. This resulted in the emergence of the Silk Road linking India, China, and the Roman Empire, in which Balkh (Bactra, the capital of Bactria) served as an important commercial hub. The passage from Balkh through Bamiyan and the Shibar Pass provided access to the Indus Valley and the Indian Ocean, an important route during times when overland travel through Persia was blocked. The Kushans were engaged in a thriving commerce with Rome and China. Excavations of their capital at Kapisa have yielded artifacts manufactured in Rome, Alexandria, China, and India. The Kushan Empire held together until around AD 220, when it fragmented into a number of independent principalities to the north and south of the Hindu Kush.

For a brief period the Sasanians, a Zoroastrian tribe from the Zagros Mountains, emerged as a new political and military power in Iran. The Sasanians overran the Kushan states from Tajikistan (Sogdiana) to the Punjab. The Sasanian Empire (AD 224–561) emerged as the most powerful enemy of the Byzantine Empire and began a series of wars in the west with the Romans that would diminish both powers.

Then a new powerful, expansive group of Turco-Mongolian nomads, known as the Hephthalites (the White Huns), emerged in Central Asia and Afghanistan.[8] They defeated the peoples in the region and sacked and burned cities, slaughtered local inhabitants, and caused massive destruction. The Hephthalites ruthlessly persecuted Buddhist peoples in Kabul and Gandhara, demolished stupas and monasteries, destroyed works of art, and more or less obliterated the 500-year-old Graeco-Buddhist civilization.

The Hephthalite Empire, which lasted from around AD 450 to 565 were engaged in warfare with their principal antagonists, the Sasanians to the west. During the second half of the sixth century, the Hephthalites came under attack on two fronts, from the Western Turks who had appeared in Central Asia around AD 565, and the Sasanians in Iran. As a result, the Hephthalites were completely crushed. By the start of the seventh century most of Afghanistan was once again under Sasanian hegemony.

It is at this point that Islam began its eastward expansion. The Arabs defeated the Sasanids and the Sasanid king Yazdajird III fled to the east, where he was assassinated. Shortly after AD 642 the Arabs were in control of eastern Iran. They then captured regions in northern Afghanistan.[9] From bases in these areas the Arabs began launching military raids north across the Amu River, and in the east against the Turks. The Arabs marched through Seistan and conquered Sind; however, their advance deeper into Afghanistan was rather slow.

At this time, the Sasanids sought military assistance against the Arabs from China, which was attempting to extend its control over the Silk Road. Taking advantage of the political troubles and civil war in the Arab world during the caliphate of Ali (AD 656–661), eastern Iran became a Chinese province for a short time. Yet again this illustrates Afghanistan's strategic position that has made it the focal point of competing empires. However, Chinese hold was ephemeral and the Arabs reasserted their power in Iran but were unable to dislodge the Turks. Around AD 850, the latter were displaced by another Hindu dynasty, called the Hindu Shahi, based in the Kabul valley, which became the center of resistance against the Muslim invaders.

During the time that the Abbasidian empire emerged (AD 750–945) a number of semi-independent local dynasties appeared throughout the Muslim world. A powerful dynasty, the Saffarids, emerged in Seistan around AD 861 under a native named Yaqub bin al Laith. Yaqub attracted zealous men from the heartlands of Islam who came to fight the nonbelievers, much in the same way that in the 1980s zealous jihadis were attracted to the frontiers of Afghanistan to fight the "infidel" Soviet invaders.

Yaqub launched a military campaign against eastern Afghanistan, conquered Bamiyan, demolished a major Buddhist sanctuary there, and captured Ghazni and Kabul, where Hindu temples were razed and idols smashed. Saffarid forces next marched north, taking Herat and then northern Afghanistan, for the first time uniting northern and southern Afghanistan after many centuries. Persian language and culture thus started to spread to Afghanistan. The spread of Islam to eastern Iran and Afghanistan was not accompanied by the spread of Arabic language and culture. Instead the ninth century witnessed a revival of Persian language and culture and eastern Iran and Afghanistan became the centers of this cultural efflorescence. The numerous Turkic peoples migrating into the area from Central Asia also adopted Persian language and culture.

The Saffarids were defeated in AD 900 by another Iranian dynasty, the Samanids, put in place by the Abbasid Caliph, whose centers of power were in the cities of Samarkand and Bukhara in Uzbekistan. Their territory comprised Saffarid lands, including most of Afghanistan. Like the Saffarids, the Saminids propagated Iranian culture and the Persian language, and Bukhara and Samarkand became the centers of Persian scholarship and arts ranking alongside Baghdad, the intellectual center of Islam, as centers of culture and learning. In this way Persian soon became the *lingua franca* or universal ethnic language of eastern Iran and Afghanistan. The Samanids exercised direct rule over the heartland of their domain, but the remainder of their territory was governed through local chieftains or military governors, mostly Turkish slaves, large numbers of whom were imported into the Islamic world. Some of these Turkish slaves broke off from their masters and founded their own dynasties.

In AD 962, one of these slaves, the commander of the Samanid garrison in Nishapur, Iran, fled to the highlands of eastern Afghanistan after a failed palace revolution. There he gained control of the city of Ghazni and founded the Ghaznavid dynasty (AD 977–1186). A successor, Mahmud of Ghazni (AD 998–1030), became an independent ruler when the Turks descending from the north defeated the Samanids. Mahmud permanently vanquished the Hindu Shahi rulers of Kabul and Gandhara, forced his subjects to convert to Islam, and established the first major Islamic empire in Afghanistan. With the dual objectives of plunder and forcible conversion of infidels, Mahmud led 17 military expeditions to India, smashing idols and looting Hindu temples of their riches, efforts for which he earned the title of *Butt shekan* or "idol-breaker." He added northwest India and the Punjab to his domain. The period witnessed the conversion of a significant number of people in northwest India to Islam, ensuring the ascendancy of Sunni Islam both in Afghanistan and India. Mahmud was also a great patron of the arts and his court at Ghazni became the home for hundreds of scholars and poets, among them the great Persian poet Firdowsi who composed the epic of *Shahname*, which in some respects is comparable to Homer's *Iliad*, and represents the culmination of medieval Persian literature.

The Ghaznavid Empire endured for 125 years after the death of its chief architect. But by the twelfth century its power had declined and was ended by the Tajiks who lived in the mountains. By the end of the twelfth century the Tajiks conquered all Ghaznavid territories. This entire region was dramatically altered with the invasion of the Mongols from the steppes north and northeast of the Gobi desert in the year AD 1218.

The whole region of Southwest Asia changed radically with this invasion.[10] The Mongols swept upon northwestern Uzbekistan and sacked the cities of Samarkand and Bukhara and slaughtered their inhabitants. Muslim sources provided figures in the hundreds of thousands of people slaughtered. The Mongols also systematically demolished the sophisticated irrigation systems that were the basis of the agrarian economies of this region. During the assault against Bamiyan one of Genghis Khan's grandsons was killed and the Mongols exacted revenge by razing the cities and killing every living creature. Kabul was spared the worst, but Peshawar was ravaged. The plunder, depopulation, economic collapse, and social disorganization that resulted from the fury of the Mongols would affect these regions for over a century. The Mongol conquests not only destroyed the thriving major cultural centers, and centers of agricultural production in Afghanistan and Central Asia, but they also disrupted the long-distance trade that linked Central, West, and South Asia to northern Europe and the Mediterranean region. As a result, the entire region went into an economic and cultural decline that would have long-term effects.

Genghis Khan returned to Mongolia where he died in AD 1227. His empire fell to his sons and grandsons. Iran was passed to Hulague, his grandson, who founded the Il-Khan dynasty of Persia. Afghanistan became the domain of Genghis's second son, Jaghatai, whose heirs chose Kabul and Ghazni as their seats of power. The Mongol assault on the Islamic civilization of eastern Iran and Afghanistan was devastating, but Islam did not disappear. Instead, by the fourteenth century, Mongol warlords converted to Islam as well as adopting the local languages and customs of the people they had vanquished.

Toward the end of the fourteenth century Jaghatai's domains were in a state of political and economic decline and on the road to fragmentation and anarchy. Around AD 1364 a local ruler of Samarkand, a warlord named Timur (Tamerlane), began to extend his power and embarked on a career of pillage, conquest, and empire building. In 1384 he attacked Seistan, where he demolished the extensive irrigation system, transforming a wealthy and heavily populated region into a barren desert, where the eroded ruins of large settlements and fortress may still be seen today.

Timur also captured Kandahar, Ghazni, and Kabul and attacked Kafiristan ("land of the unbelievers"), a stronghold of non-Muslims to the northeast of Kabul, which was renamed Nuristan, or "land of light," after its people were forcibly converted to Islam in the nineteenth century. In 1398 a Timurid army marched on India, sacking along the way the lands of tribespeople in the Sulaiman Mountains who were known in Persian sources as Afghans (i.e., the Pashtuns). Timur's invasion of India culminated in the sacking of Delhi. Within 14 years, Timur forged an empire that included all of Afghanistan and northeastern Iran and extended from northern India to Turkey. Despite his ruthlessness in war, Timur was a patron of the arts and scholarship and his capital Samarkand became an important intellectual center.

After Timur's death in AD 1405, his empire began to collapse as a result of an ensuing power struggle among his sons and relatives. Within a few years Timurid holdings had receded, to consist only of northeastern Iran (Khurasan) and Afghanistan, a territory ruled by Timur's youngest son, Shahrukh, from his capital in Herat. Despite territorial losses, this was a period of great prosperity and relative stability. Under Shahrukh, who was a patron of the arts, Herat underwent a cultural renaissance, with great accomplishments in calligraphy, music, and miniature painting. The Timurids are especially known for their architectural greatness.

During the fifteenth century a new group of people, the Uzbeks, migrated from the steppes of Central Asia into Transoxiana. Under their leader Shaibani Khan they took Samarkand and Bukhara in 1500. The Uzbeks crossed the Amu River into northern Afghanistan, and by 1507 they ended Timurid rule. The Uzbeks continued to dominate until the start of the seventeenth century. Northern Afghanistan fell under Uzbek control. Their descendants still live in northern Afghanistan. The Uzbeks emerged as major contenders for the lands of Afghanistan. However, they soon found themselves confronted with competition over Afghan territories by two new forces, the Moghuls and the Safavids.

Uzbek and Pashtun tribes would become key players in the subsequent struggle over Afghanistan between the Moghul Empire, established by Babur in India, and the Safavid state, which arose in Persia. The Moghuls were able to maintain control over Pashtuns through a combination of bribery and coercion aimed at isolating them and fostering internal discords. At the same time the Pashtun tribes attempted to exploit the situation to their advantage by obtaining dispensations from the two rival powers. Eventually, Afghanistan became a northern province of the Moghul dynasty based in Delhi (see Chapters 3 and 4).

The Safavid dynasty (1499–1736) in Iran was established by Shah Ismail. He made Shi'a Islam the official religion of his state by forcibly converting the primarily Sunni population and put into place the geopolitical foundations of modern Iran. Shah Ismail stopped the Uzbek advance in AD 1510. Herat fell to the Safavids and remained under Persian control through the seventeenth century.

During the sixteenth and seventeenth centuries, therefore, Afghanistan was at the center of three rival powers, the Uzbeks in the north, the Safavids in the west, and the Moghuls in the south. Afghan tribes rebelled against the Moghuls periodically during the seventeenth century. These tribes became more and more independent as Moghul power began to wane. By 1648 the Moghuls gave up their efforts to control northern Afghanistan and Kandahar as they contended with Pashtun rebellions from 1658 and 1675. By the start of the eighteenth century Safavid power also began to wane. Two major contenders emerged to fill the vacuum, the rival Pashtun Ghilzai and the Abdali tribes.

By 1749 Delhi fell and the Moghul king ceded all lands west of the Indus to the Afghans. Once more India would provide the revenue to underwrite the invader's political enterprise. In 1750 a Pashtun leader, Ahmad Shah, captured Herat.

Although militarily successful, Ahmad Shah was never able to bring India under permanent control. This is because they were raiders seeking booty, and not effective administrators. They extracted tribute from those they conquered and the idea of permanent occupation or the shifting of the capital to India was never seriously entertained. Later, Ahmad Shah declared a jihad against the Hindus to the north.

Ahmad Shah is associated with an important religious and political symbol in Afghanistan. He signed a treaty to resolve a boundary dispute. As a symbol of their treaty the Islamic ruler presented Ahmad Shah with the *Kirqa-i-Mubarak*, or the mantel worn by the Prophet Muhammad, one of Afghanistan's most sacred relics. Ahmad Shah constructed a mosque in Kandahar where the Kirqa-i-Mubarak is enshrined. When the Taliban captured Kandahar, their leader Mullah Omar took out the cloak and held it before the gathered crowds as a way of uniting the different factions and to legitimize his position as "the Commander of the Faithful."

What Ahmad Shah forged was a Pashtun tribal confederacy, not a centralized state. The allegiance of tribal chiefs who provided the military force had to be paid for by means of revenue generated elsewhere, principally in India and Kashmir. Ahmad Shah had no means of asserting his power over his tribal constituency, aside from the Durrani. The other groups remained independent under their own chiefs, who supported Ahmad Shah as long as he could pay them. As such, his power was limited as was the durability of his empire.

Ahmad Shah's success in achieving tribal unity and his creation of a seemingly glorious Afghan Muslim empire, headed by a brave and just leader whose mandate to govern was based on election by an grand assembly, or *Loya Jirga*, of tribal elders, purportedly representatives of the country as a whole, thereafter became the mythical archetype of the ideal system of governance and statehood. Subsequent rulers, from the monarchs to the Marxists, attempted to employ this myth to legitimize their own positions. After the death of Ahmad Shah in 1772, his empire began to slowly collapse.

Afghanistan was becoming more isolated and impoverished. Ahmad Shah's successors no longer had India from where he had obtained the revenues to underwrite his political enterprise.[11] This severely curtailed the ability of subsequent dynasties to exercise effective political control. Also, the emergence of Shi'a Persia, which lay between Sunni Afghanistan and the Sunni Ottoman Empire, effectively isolated Afghanistan from the socioeconomic changes affecting Islamic culture in Western Asia. The situation was exacerbated by Ahmad Shah's sons and grandsons, who were involved in a violent power struggle resulting in a protracted period of disorder, conspiracies, and intertribal violence that would last over a generation.

The Great Game and Colonial Intervention

At the start of the nineteenth century new threats to Afghanistan emerged when Russian expansion into Central Asia and British expansion in India set the two nations on a collision course. The growing rivalries between these imperial powers, referred to as the "Great Game" of espionage, intrigue, and periodic warfare in which Afghanistan was the center stage,[12] would establish the parameters that would determine the subsequent political evolution of the Afghan state and the future patterns of outside intervention.

The British were concerned over the security of their Indian possession in light of a possible Tsarist invasion. For proponents of what was referred to as the "forward policy" direct control over Afghanistan and the natural barrier between South and Central Asia, the Hindu Kush and its passes leading to the south, was the key to the defense of India.

In 1838, the Russians encouraged the Persians to lay siege to the city of Herat. This convinced the British that it was time to act. They threatened the Persians into a withdrawal and in 1839 invaded Afghanistan, beginning the first of three Anglo-Afghan wars. At the time political authority was in the hands of a Pashtun warlord, Dost Muhammad, who had ended the region's political chaos in 1826 after bringing eastern Afghanistan under his control.[13] Rather than deal with Dost Muhammad, who the British suspected of collusion with the Russians and hence a threat to the security of India, they decided upon a formula very much in the forefront of early twenty-first-century global politics, namely "regime change."

The British army of the Indus entered Afghanistan from Quetta and quickly captured major cities, including Kabul. Dost Muhammad fled north. In his place the British installed Shah Shuja, the son of Timur, who had previously ruled Kabul in 1803–1809, before fleeing to India under pressure from rivals to the throne. In return for being reinstated, Shah Shuja relinquished all claims to Durrani-held territories in the Punjab. Keeping Shah Shuja in power required the deployment of British garrisons. The amir's power extended only over Kabul, Kandahar, Jalalabad, and Bamiyan. The rest of the country was under the control of tribal chieftains.

Soon tribal chiefs joined forces against the British and their protégé amir. Dost Muhammad attempted a return to power, and won a major battle, but subsequently surrendered and was sent into exile in India. Uprisings continued leading to the death of the British envoy and officers stationed in Kabul. In January 1842 the British were forced to withdraw from Kabul in what turned out to be one of the greatest British military catastrophes. On a poorly coordinated retreat to Jalalabad the British convoy of 16,500 people was massacred, with only a handful of survivors reaching India. The British army returned to Afghanistan the same year, installed Dost Muhammad on the throne, conducted punitive expeditions, and departed.

Dost Muhammad's followers subsequently murdered the hapless Shah Shuja, left behind by his foreign sponsors and was forced to take refuge in the Bala Hisar Fortress in Kabul. Afghans and some Western writers have often drawn parallels between the debacle of the British and their puppet Shah Shuja and the regime change implemented by the Soviet occupying army in 1979 and the subsequent war that ended with the withdrawal of the Soviets in 1989, and the Taliban execution of Najibullah, the last communist ruler of Afghanistan, who had taken refuge in the United Nations compound in Kabul.

Dost Muhammad consolidated his power and by 1855 brought northern Afghanistan and Kandahar under his control. Subsequently, Anglo-Afghan relations improved somewhat. This is because the Afghans and the British perceived a common threat by Russia and Persia. For the next three decades the British opted to support Afghan rulers, but without a military presence, with the idea of Afghanistan as a neutral zone or buffer state between Russian and British interests. However, Russian advances into Central Asia, which had extended up to the northern bank of the Amu Darya by 1868, led to renewed alarm and a return to the forward policy.

In 1878, Sher Ali Khan, the son and successor of Dost Muhammad, received an uninvited Russian diplomatic delegation in Kabul, but rejected a British envoy. The British army invaded in a three-pronged attack from Quetta, Kurram, and the Khyber Pass. Kabul was occupied and the amir was forced to flee north to take up an offer of assistance by the Russians that never came. Sher Ali died in Mazar-i-Sharif shortly thereafter. His son Yaqub Khan signed the Treaty of Gandamak in 1879, which allowed the British control over the Khyber Pass and the authority to place a diplomatic representative in Kabul, as well as control over Afghanistan's foreign relations. In return, the British would provide an annual subsidy and aid against outside attack. A mutiny by Afghan troops three months later brought the British back to Kabul and Yaqub Khan abdicated.

Realizing that direct military intervention in Afghanistan was costly and perhaps futile, the British sought a candidate who had the ability to create a stable state that would both transform Afghanistan into an effective buffer state against the Russians and one that would not himself become a political or military threat to India. The person who fit the criteria was Abdul Rahman (1880–1901), the grandson of Dost Muhammad, who for the previous ten years had lived in exile in Samarkand. With money and weapons supplied by the Russians he crossed the Amu Darya and in 1880 was crowned and proclaimed the amir in Kabul by the British.

The permanent boundaries of the Afghan buffer state were demarcated by the late 1890s through treaties between Tsarist Russia and British India. The demarcation of Afghanistan's boundaries was highly arbitrary from an ethnographic and geographical point of view and reflected late-nineteenth-century geopolitics. With the exception of the northeast, where the border coincides with the Panj River and Amu Darya, and a section of the Hari Rud, which makes up part of the Afghan–Iranian border, the frontiers of Afghanistan do not correspond to any geographical or geological features and arbitrarily cut through culture areas. The northern and northeastern borders divided populations of Tajik, Turkmen, and Uzbeks into separate countries. The Durand Line, imposed by the British in 1893, arbitrarily bisected Pashtun tribal areas between Afghanistan and British India. Today it marks the border between Afghanistan and Pakistan. The line was the cause of considerable frustration among the Pashtuns and generated a heated border dispute between Afghanistan and Pakistan during the twentieth century.

DEMOGRAPHIC PATTERNS

Superimposed upon the landscape, prehistory, and history as described above is Afghanistan's human population. There are broad territorial associations between various ethnic groups and particular regions of the country.[14] For example, Pashtuns are found primarily in the eastern, southwestern, and western sections of the country. However, many Pashtun communities are to be found in the north as well because of forced relocations and colonization during the nineteenth century. The Tajiks live mostly in the northern territories and also in the major cities. The Uzbeks and Turkmen are to be found in the north central region, and the Hazara are primarily found in central Afghanistan.

Towns and cities are generally located along major commercial lanes in agricultural areas located in fertile plains near perennial rivers. Areas of highest agricultural productivity and commercial interactions are the most densely populated areas of the country. These include the city of Kabul and the river valley plains to the north, east, and southwest. The most sparsely inhabited parts of the country are the central highlands and the western deserts.

To date no systematic comprehensive demographic survey has been conducted in Afghanistan. Therefore, reliable population figures for Afghanistan as a whole or for any of the different ethnic groups are absent. The problem has been compounded by the fact that successive governments have manipulated figures for political and economic reasons. Overall population figures were inflated to secure foreign economic aid. The numerical strengths of various ethnic groups were under- or overestimated for political reasons, with the Pashtun ruling elite consistently inflating the total number of Pashtuns inside Afghanistan, while at the same time underestimating the numerical strength of the other ethnic groups. The figures given here are therefore commonly cited estimates found in various sources and must be treated with caution. The pre-Soviet invasion estimates placed the total population of Afghanistan at around 14 to 15 million. Most recent estimates range from 22.3 million to 28.7 million, but the actual figures are probably much lower.

Between 80 to 85 percent of the population is rural and engaged in agro-pastoralism while the remainder lives in urban settings, which includes 10 cities and several hundred towns. Kabul is the largest, most ethnically diverse city and is the center of government, commerce, and educational institutions. According to a 1999–2000 United Nations–supported survey, Kabul had an estimated population of between 1.5 to 1.7 million people, but these figures have probably increased significantly in the post-Taliban period.

The other major urban centers include Kandahar, with a mainly Pashtun population of over 226,000; Herat with a primarily Tajik, Turkmen, and Uzbek population of over 180,000; Mazar-i-Sharif with a population of 131,000 consisting mostly of Uzbeks, Tajiks, and Turkmen; and Jalalabad with a mostly Pashtun population of around 60,000. These demographic figures are based on a 1988 U.N. estimate and actual numbers are probably much higher. Although all cities are multiethnic to a degree, their populations generally reflect the regional ethnic characteristics.

Effects of the War on Demographic Patterns

Afghanistan's population and demographic patterns have been heavily disrupted by political circumstances and the incessant warfare over the last 24 years. The centuries-old migratory cycles of pastoralists were interrupted, forcing many to settle down and others to flee the country. Many towns and villages were destroyed. Most cities have been affected by the war with considerable damage to their basic infrastructures, with many buildings in ruins and disrepair. Between 1.5 and 2 million people died during the years of conflict that began in the late 1970s.

Migrations from rural to urban areas began during the 1960s, facilitated by the country's new road system constructed with Soviet and U.S. aid. The rural–urban migration escalated drastically during the Soviet occupation, as people sought refuge from the violence in the countryside, which was the focus of most of the fighting, by fleeing to the relative safety of the urban centers. The populations in cities such as Kabul, Ghazni, Jalalabad, and Mazar-i-Sharif began to swell dramatically. According to some sources, by the mid-1980s the population of Kabul had increased to more than two million people, an increase of over 100 percent in less than a decade.

Population shifts (increase and decrease) relative to levels of security and violence created over five million refugees who fled either to Pakistan or Iran and displaced a million or more, who sought refuge from the war-ravaged countryside and associated breakdown of law and order by moving to the cities. During the 1980s, Afghans comprised the largest refugee population in the world. Some of the refugees returned during the 1990s, but a renewed cycle of violence, forcible recruitment of young men and boys into militias, and one of the worst droughts in 30 years resulted in another surge of refugees and internally displaced persons (IDPs). In the year 2000 over four million Afghan refugees lived in Pakistan and Iran. About two million returned following the defeat of the Taliban in 2001.[15]

Repatriation has been slow because of ongoing internal conflicts, banditry, and absence of civil security. Factors hampering repatriation include inaccessibility and difficulties associated with internal travel and transport; poor condition of houses in the villages, many of which are uninhabitable; destruction of irrigation systems and wells; and the threat of landmines strewn about the country in large numbers that cause frequent casualties.[16] Studies indicate that the productive capacities of the countryside were drastically reduced during the years of warfare and these areas may not be able to support returning refugees without rehabilitation of the agricultural systems through inputs of irrigation, seeds, fertilizer, and building construction. The likely demographic pattern for the moment seems to be continual settlement in cities as in the previous 20 years.

At present, some 200,000 pastoral nomads live as displaced persons in refugee camps inside Afghanistan. An equal number are refugees in Pakistan, and many more who lost their herds as a result of the drought from 1998 to 2002—one of the worst in living memory—have been forced to live as beggars in dire and impoverished conditions in urban or rural areas in Afghanistan.

The war did not affect all nomadic groups in the same way. Some used the flexibility of their mobility to benefit from the war environment by providing transportation for the massive quantities of arms being sent to Afghanistan. The leaky arms pipeline set up by the United States to funnel weapons to the Afghan resistance against the Soviets provided access to military hardware and created heavily armed groups whose participation resulted in increased political power. It also gave greater advantage to armed groups when dealing with sedentary populations and the new wealthy militarized elite.

ECONOMIC PATTERNS

Before the current wars Afghanistan was a preindustrial society. There was a limited amount of mining and manufacturing (coal, natural gas, textiles) involving only a small portion of the labor force. A small number of people worked for the state government and some were engaged in handicraft production (carpet weaving, etc.). But nearly 80 to 85 percent of the population lived in rural areas and subsisted on agro-pastoral production. However, because of Afghanistan's inadequate transportation infrastructure much of this economic activity was of local and regional scale only.

Pastoralism

Approximately 45–47 percent of the total surface area of the country consists of desert, semidesert, and high-mountain grazing grounds. Afghanistan's herders, called *kuchis*, have traditionally exploited this resource base. Kuchis and their distinctive tent encampments and large, ferocious guard dogs were once a ubiquitous part of the Afghan landscape. The nomad population is made up mostly of Pashtuns, but also includes Baluchis and Kirghiz. The Aimaq, Turkmen, and Uzbeks also have groups that subsist as nomads. The exact size of Afghanistan's nomad population is unclear and estimates from the 1960s and 1970s range anywhere from as low as 500,000 to as much as 2.5 million.[17]

Only a few groups were fully nomadic, a strategy that involved the movement of the entire human group, usually made up of nuclear families connected to each other by descent, and their mixed herds of sheep and goats in an annual migratory cycle sometimes over distances up to 500 or 600 kilometers. The principal pastoral animals are sheep and goats, usually in a ratio of four sheep for every goat, but herd composition is adjusted to suit local environmental conditions and types of vegetation and market prices for the different species. Pack animals including camels, horses, and donkeys transport family possessions as well as women, children, and older people.

A specialized herding system in northern Afghanistan is based upon the herding of *karakul* sheep, a breed introduced by the Uzbeks and Turkmen. These animals are raised solely for their pelts and the enterprise is geared to meet high demand in the world fur trade market. Karakul pelts were one of

Afghanistan's major export commodities before the Soviet invasion.

Fully nomadic groups would spend fall and winter in encampments in the lowlands and move with their herds to the highland pastures in the spring, where they remained through the summer months. Pastures are located between 1,000 and 3,000 meters in altitude to which nomads have traditional grazing rights. Durrani nomads follow a cyclical pattern of migration from their winter camps in the lower elevations to the summer pastures in the western part of the central highlands, home of the Hazaras. Historically, the encroachment of Pashtun nomads upon Hazara territory was supported by the Pashtun-ruled Afghan state, which granted the nomads grazing rights in Hazara territory. The migratory cycle of the Ghilzai nomads took them to winter grazing lands across the Durand Line into Pakistan as well as to the central highlands.

Many of the pastoralists in Afghanistan are seminomadic and engage in limited seasonal migrations involving only part of the group and rely upon farming and other subsistence strategies, such as trading or seasonal wage labor. These groups depend upon upland pastures for livestock herding in the summers. One part of the community stays in permanent settlements all year and farms or engages in wage labor. Another part undertakes herding activities, accompanying the livestock to the upland pastures in the summer and returning to the settlements in the winter. Groups employing this pattern are found in high alpine valleys where they live in small, dispersed hamlets. This pattern is referred to as *transhumant pastoralism* in the anthropological literature.

Pastoralism is a very flexible adaptive pattern that enables the exploitation of multiple resource bases by taking advantage of the mobility associated with herding activities and economic opportunities in other sectors as they presented themselves. There is a continuum between farming and livestock herding, which makes it difficult to categorize subsistence patterns based on these strategies into neat classifications (e.g., nomadic versus transhumant). Traditionally, the degree of emphasis upon each subsistence strategy has varied in relation to the specific environmental and sociopolitical and economic circumstances confronting particular groups.

Afghanistan's nomadic population was an important part of a broader socioeconomic system that included mixed farming and cash market components. Pastoralists provided essential items such as hair, wool, skins, and dairy goods in exchange for farm foodstuffs as well as manufactured consumer commodities sold in the cash markets. Pashtun and Baluch nomads who engaged in long-range annual migratory cycles began to specialize in caravan transport and sale of merchandise in the 1930s, and facilitated interregional trade and the flow of and access to locally unobtainable commodities.

Nomadic groups were involved in various economic relationships with sedentary farmers. Poorer nomads sought seasonal wage labor as farmhands, while the more affluent ones served as moneylenders to farmers, a process through which they sometimes acquired arable land from creditors because of defaulted loans. Social and political arrangements between nomadic and sedentary populations were also necessary to gain access to grazing grounds in territories controlled by others.

As with other Afghans, international and internal political conditions have sharply affected the nomadic populations. Throughout the nineteenth and twentieth centuries state authorities have tried to establish political control over the ethnic nomad groups in Afghanistan. The closure of the Afghan–Pakistan border in 1961 during the Pashtunistan dispute had a similar impact upon some groups. Drought and economic problems during the 1970s led many previously nomadic groups to settle down as farmers.

The Soviet invasion and the civil war greatly disrupted the traditional migratory cycles of the nomads and it is unclear how many still pursue this mode of subsistence. Some groups lost access to traditional grazing grounds as local and regional power relations shifted during the political chaos caused by the Soviet invasion and warfare. For example, Pashtun nomads whose traditional grazing grounds were located in Hazarajat were unable to use them due to assertion of political authority by the Hazaras. The preferential treatment of Pashtun kuchis in northern Afghanistan, who were given grazing rights well beyond their traditional territory by the Taliban, was also reversed when the latter were ousted from power. Some areas became inaccessible due to the millions of landmines scattered by government forces and the mujahideen and Taliban. As a result some nomads were compelled to seek other opportunities, such as opening shops in urban centers. Groups, like the Kirghiz, fled the country out of fear of persecution by the communist government.

Agro-Pastoral Production

Another subsistence strategy in Afghanistan involves operating sedentary crop-livestock farming systems. Farmers live in small, single-ethnic fortified villages adjacent to irrigated fields in the major river valleys. Often such villages are clustered around towns. The main limiting factor on agricultural production is water from rainfall, underground, or rivers. According to some estimates, roughly 5.1 percent of the land is under irrigation farming and about 7 percent is under rain-fed farming. Arable lands are therefore in very short supply. Before the Soviet invasion most farmers were heavily indebted to local landlords and worked the fields as sharecroppers, receiving under half and sometimes less than a quarter of the harvests. Some members of the family had to seek income outside the village or engage in handicraft production for local markets to enable the family to survive. Land reforms implemented by the communist regime to address such inequalities, and the reaction by the landed elite, were in part the cause of the rebellion that provoked the Soviet invasion.

The primary crop is wheat. Other crops include barley, legumes, and corn. Some farmers also grow alfalfa and clover for fodder, and plant fruit and nut trees and maintain a vegetable garden. All farmers own some livestock: large cattle necessary for traction, and sheep and goats to obtain dairy produce and meat. Farmers strive to increase their herds, which are a good source of income. Chickens are kept as well for eggs and meat. Some farmers may also keep a donkey or horse as a pack animal.

Because arable land is in short supply and areas around most villages do not have sufficient vegetation to sustain the livestock herds for the whole year, farmers place their sheep and goats under the care of shepherds, who take them to upland pastures during spring and summer. This enables them to tap otherwise unusable grass resources beyond the villages, allowing them to maintain more livestock than is possible on village-grown fodder resources alone, which can be stored and used to sustain the animals during winter months when they are kept in stalls.

The war and the political turmoil over the past two decades have had a significant impact upon the agricultural production, cropping patterns, trade networks and the prewar social and political relationships. Soviet antimujahideen retaliatory military offensives—which included the indiscriminate placement of antipersonnel mines, artillery strikes, and aerial bombardment, causing the destruction of irrigation systems, villages, granaries, and livestock herds and draught oxen—devastated the rural economy throughout the country.[18] Seeking to escape the destruction and forcible recruitment of males into the Afghan military or mujahideen militias, a large portion of the rural population fled to urban centers as internally displaced refugees and to Pakistan and Iran, becoming dependent on international humanitarian aid.

War Economy: Drugs and Contraband

The war against the Soviets created a new and highly militarized elite inside Afghanistan whose power and authority derived from their control of the means of destruction rather than means of production. The mujahideen leaders in Pakistan became wealthy by diverting large portions of the foreign military aid and massive cash subsidies without any accountability for their own use. The flow of weapons and cash subsidies from party leaders in Pakistan to mujahideen commanders inside Afghanistan made these new power holders somewhat independent of support from local populations. Party leaders and commanders inside Afghanistan emerged as key political and economic players, displacing the prewar landed elites, whose power derived from their control of agro-pastoral production and relationships to the state.

As their power grew these would-be "warlords" sought greater autonomy from party leaders in Pakistan by various means, such as obtaining direct funding from humanitarian agencies, setting up local markets in rural areas far from Soviet control for the sale of goods smuggled from Pakistan and Iran, and in the post-Soviet period, charging customs duties (i.e., selling protection) to the trucking convoys smuggling goods between Pakistan, Iran, and the Central Asian republics, passing through their respective domains.

The massive flow of hard currency and monetization of the economy, along with the decline of the subsistence economy, further fueled the need for cash-generating operations. Commanders began to rely upon the extraction of gemstones, such as emeralds, rubies, and lapis lazuli from Badakhshan, as well as the illegal export of timber from eastern Afghanistan, which contributed to a massive deforestation.

The defeat of the Kabul regime in 1992 meant the demise of the state itself. This created a deregulated environment transforming Afghanistan from a buffer state with defined borders into what it had been during various earlier periods, an uncontrolled land corridor connecting Central Asia and South Asia. The end of superpower patronage and the drying up of foreign revenues accompanied the fall of the communist regime. Competing and heavily militarized and predatory factions controlled by commanders, warlords[19] in Western sources, filled the power vacuum, each one seeking to promote its own economic and political interests rather than to rebuild a state apparatus.

From 1992 onward, the war in Afghanistan metamorphosed from an ideologically based insurgency backed by the United States and Saudi Arabia into an economically motivated conflict characterized by warlordism and banditry, in which nonstate collectives fought with one another over control of resources and territories. The absence of other sources of income for the warlords resulted in the development of a new phenomenon, a criminalized war economy based on high-value commodities, such as opium, with linkages beyond Afghanistan through illegal and quasi-legal transborder economic networks.[20] This made it possible for goods such as opium produced in areas on the periphery of the global economy to reach wider regional and international markets through parallel and illicit channels.

Opium proved the most profitable commodity, thus commanders forced farmers to grow opium. This was a highly a lucrative cash crop that could be marketed with ease, provided income for local power holders, pumped cash into the rural economy, and provided a source of income for the farmers and field hands working to harvest the opium. The opium economy enabled local commanders to maintain their militias and expand their patronage networks.

Opium production increased on a massive scale and Afghanistan became the world's largest producer. Laboratories established in southern Afghanistan and along the Afghan–Pakistan border converted the raw opium into morphine and heroin. The associated narcotic trafficking network extends into Pakistan, Iran, and the Central Asian republics, reconfirming Afghanistan's historical position as a crossroads of nations. Opium production increased following the rise of the Taliban, reached an all-time high in 1999, and has since increased even more.

The direction of the flow of trade goods in Afghanistan was also altered under these conditions. The illegal regional economies that emerged were based on the shipment of resources, not from rural areas to urban centers inside Afghanistan, but to regions in neighboring countries. Timber from eastern Afghanistan was shipped to the North-West Frontier of Pakistan; opium from Kandahar went to Quetta, Pakistan, while the flow of goods from Herat went to Iran, and those around Mazar-i-Sharif in the north went to Uzbekistan; and opium from Badakhshan in the northeast was shipped to Tajikistan and to Chitral, in Pakistan.

An ethnically diverse Kabul street scene.

ETHNIC GROUPS

The criteria used to define ethnic groups are fuzzy and problematic and the exact ethnic composition of Afghanistan is unknown.[21] Estimated numbers of ethnic groups vary considerably, ranging from 22 groups, to 54, to as many as 200. Absence of reliable criteria for determining ethnic affiliation therefore poses problems in the current process of state building and the issue of political representation. According to one estimate, the ethnic composition of Afghanistan is as follows: Pashtun 40 percent, Tajik 25.3 percent, Hazara 18 percent, Uzbek 6.3 percent, Turkmen 4 percent, and "other" (Aimaq, Arab, Baluch, Brahui, Farsiwan, Kirghiz, Nuristani, Qizilbash, Wakhi) 7.9 percent. As none of the ethnic groups comprise more than 50 percent of the population, Afghanistan has been called "a nation of minorities."[22] A brief survey of Afghanistan's ethnic groups clearly illustrates its incredibly complex sociocultural mosaic.

The Pashtuns are the largest ethnic group. The original homeland of the Pashtuns was in the Sulaiman Mountains along the Afghan–Pakistan frontier with equal numbers living in the frontier areas of Pakistan.[23] Pashtun tribes in Afghanistan occupy the mountainous territory extending from eastern Afghanistan to the fertile plains in Kandahar and the Helmand river valley. Pashtun-held territory stretches into southwestern and western Afghanistan and throughout eastern Afghanistan through Jalalabad. Pashtun enclaves are to be found in northern Afghanistan where they occupy prime agricultural lands, as well as across the country, the result of forcible relocations and colonization during the nineteenth century and more recent demographic shifts. Following the defeat of the Pashtun Taliban, many Pashtun communities in the north have been subjected to increasing acts of violence and pressure to relocate.

Occupation of prime agricultural lands has traditionally enabled the Pashtuns to operate subsistence economies based upon intensive irrigation agriculture, placing them at an advantage over other ethnic groups that survive on the basis of a combination of rainfall and irrigation agriculture. Geography and terrain have also allowed the Pashtuns to operate lucrative smuggling operations between Pakistan and Afghanistan. The Pashtun are primarily Sunni Muslims and operate agricultural and pastoral economies.

Historically, as mentioned above in the historical section, the Pashtuns are divided into two major tribal confederacies, the Durrani and the Ghilzai. Traditional animosities existed between the two confederacies, with the Ghilzai often exploited and subjected to much discrimination by the Durrani. There are other smaller tribal confederacies, such as the Yusufzai and other unaffiliated tribes that live in eastern Afghanistan, northeast and southwest of the Khyber Pass. These are the tribes that gave the British armies considerable difficulties in the nineteenth century during their violent campaigns along the North-West Frontier. They include the Afridi, Khatak, Orakzai, Waziri, Jaji, Mangal, Safi, Wardak, Massoud, and Shinwari tribes.

Historically the Pashtuns have had considerable political influence in Afghanistan. Members of the Durrani confederation ruled the country from the middle of the eighteenth century until 1978. The rulers of the Communist Democratic Republic of Afghanistan from 1978 to 1992 were Pashtuns as well, although they were drawn mainly from the Ghilzai confederation, centered in eastern Afghanistan. Many of the mujahideen resistance leaders were either Ghilzai Pashtuns or belonged to one of the unaffiliated tribes in eastern Afghanistan. The Taliban leadership was drawn from the Durrani Pashtuns.

The Tajik comprise the second largest ethnic group. A much larger Tajik population lives across the border in Tajikistan. The Tajiks of Afghanistan live in the Panjsher valley and the city of Kabul, which was once a wholly Tajik city, as well as in the northern and northeastern sections of the country. Some Tajiks live in the eastern part of the central highlands. They are predominantly Hanafi Sunni Muslims and speak a dialect of Dari, called Tajiki. They are non-tribal in social organization and identify themselves in reference to where they live, or their place of birth, such as Panjsheri, Andarabi, or Samangani. However, other Tajiks living in the eastern regions are Ismaili Shi'as. Tajiks operate an agro-pastoral economy and engage in transhumant pastoralism. In the cities they are engaged in commerce and civil service jobs. In the context of the national political scene, they are the second most powerful group. The only gap in continuous Pashtun rule over Afghanistan was when the Tajik rebel, Bacha-i-Saqaw, forced the Durrani king Amanullah out of Kabul in 1929 (see below). The Tajik military commander of Panjsher, Ahmad Shah Massoud (1953–2001) emerged as the major power holder during the Soviet period. Burhanuddin Rabbani, a Tajik from Badakhshan, occupied the office of president of the coalition government that ruled Afghanistan from 1992 to 1996.

The Hazaras live in Hazarajat, in the central mountains of Afghanistan. Some live in Badakhshan and western Afghanistan as well.[24] They speak a dialect of Dari, called Hararagi, which has many Mongol words in its lexicon. Some believe that the Hazaras are descendants of Mongol or Turkic hordes organized in units of one thousand (*hazar*) who were settled in central Afghanistan by the Timurids during the fourteenth and fifteenth centuries. The Hazaras adopted Shi'a Islam when central Afghanistan was under the control of the Persian Safavids during the sixteenth and seventeenth centuries. They have close ties with fellow Shi'a in Iran and Iraq; however, some Hazaras are Ismailis. Because of religious and racial prejudices the Sunnis have generally discriminated against them.

The Hazara seem to have had a tribal social structure headed by chiefs called *mirs*, but their tribal institutions were demolished when the

Pashtun king Abdul Rahman conquered their territory in 1891. The conquest of Hazarajat, a campaign that Abdul Rahman transformed into a jihad, or holy war, by playing upon long-standing Sunni prejudice against the Shi'a, was brutal and bloody and led to the death of thousands of Hazara men and the enslavement of their women and children. As a result of Pashtun encroachment, the Hazaras lost their prime agricultural lands and pastures, which were allotted to Pashtun clans. As a result of the Pashtun aggression many fled to Iran or to Quetta, Pakistan. Those who remained were forced to settle the barren highlands, where they lived as impoverished farmers and herders. The Hazaras have historically been politically and economically marginalized. During the 1960s many Hazara men moved into the cities, such as Kabul and Mazar-i-Sharif, where they engage in menial jobs, such as porters and construction workers.

In 1979 the Hazaras declared independence from the communist regime in Kabul and one of their first political acts was to prohibit Pashtun nomads access to central Afghanistan. A number of Hazara political parties formed during the war years, with substantial support from Iran. The mujahideen refused to form alliances with the Hazaras primarily because of religious prejudice and excluded them from political negotiations after the capture of Kabul. The civil war that began in 1992 led to a further sense of political unity among the Hazaras. The most important political party was the *Hizb-i-Wahdat* (Party of Unity), which conducted a number of successful military operations against the Taliban in the late 1990s. The Hazaras were subjected to great atrocities at the hands of the Pashtun Taliban when they captured Mazar-i-Sharif in 1998 and during their military operations in Hazarajat in 2000. Like many other ethnic minorities in the post-Taliban period, the Hazaras are seeking to prevent a return to their previous subordinate political status.

The Uzbeks live in the area extending east of Badghis in the northern plains of Afghanistan. The majority of Uzbeks live north across the border in Uzbekistan. The Uzbeks are Sunni Muslims and speak a Turkic language called *Uzbeki.* They operate an agricultural and trade economy. The Uzbeks came to Afghanistan from Central Asia during the sixteenth century and established control over much of northern Afghanistan. Additional Uzbeks came to northern Afghanistan during the late nineteenth century to escape Russian invaders. More Uzbeks came in the 1920s and 1930s during the Muslim uprisings in Soviet Central Asia. The main Uzbek power holder is Rashid Dostum, who controlled much of northern Afghanistan in the post-Soviet period and was a member of the non-Pashtun coalition that controlled Kabul from 1992 to 1996.

The Turkmen live in northwestern Afghanistan, in Badghis. They are Sunni Moslems and speak a Turkic language. They came to Afghanistan as refugees from Turkmenistan north of the border when the Russians invaded their homeland in the late nineteenth century. Some Turkmen migrated to Afghanistan after the Soviets crushed the Muslim Basmachi uprising in the 1920s and 1930s.[25] They settled in the territory between Balkh and Herat. The Turkmen brought with them karakul sheep, which they raise for their prized pelts, and their carpet weaving industry. Both economic activities are geared for export. The Turkmen also operate a mixed farming economy.

Other smaller ethnic groups in Afghanistan include the Aimaq, the Baluch, the Brahui, the Farsiwan, the Kirghiz, the Nuristani, the Qizilbash, the Wakhi, and the Arabs. Some of these groups are involved in nomadic pastoralist economic activities while others are engaged in more sedentary agricultural developments. Within these smaller ethnic groups most of them are Sunni Muslims. However, the Qizilbash and Wakhi are Shi'a Muslims.

Finally, one must mention the Kabuli, a designation for the ethnically mixed urban population of the capital city. Many Kabuli men and women were educated in secular schools and have a modern Western and cosmopolitan outlook on life, with a preference for Western-style clothing, music, and movies. Many Kabuli have traveled to the United States, Russia, Europe, and South Asia either for schooling or business. The Kabuli speak Dari and some are also fluent in English, French, German, or Russian. Before the collapse of the Afghan state in 1992, Kabulis were employed as civil servants, teachers, and health-care workers, ran private businesses, or were engaged in specialized occupations. Large numbers of Kabulis fled the country after the Soviet invasion. Others remained behind and led fairly uneventful lives until their city became the battle ground for the mujahideen factions in the 1990s. Thousands were killed and many more were maimed and crippled. Large numbers fled as refugees or as internally displaced persons (IDPs).

The Kabulis suffered outrageous atrocities at the hands of the mujahideen liberators. Matters became worse under the Taliban, which chose to make examples out of them by forcing them to abide by draconian religious codes of conduct and dress and strictures prohibiting women from working and girls from receiving education.

ETHNICITY

There is disagreement among Western scholars and Afghan intellectuals and political leaders over the importance of ethnicity in Afghanistan before and after the Soviet occupation and in the subsequent ongoing conflict. The categories of identity through which Afghans have traditionally related to one another include tribal affiliations, religion, occupational specialization, and gender. The degree to which each of these categories is emphasized in relation to others depends largely upon tactical choices under particular circumstances.

It is certainly the case that ethnicity became an important factor during the civil war that erupted after the departure of the Soviets and the collapse of the Pashtun-dominated state, when the vast array of armaments at everyone's disposal made it possible for some groups to seek greater autonomy from central authority, such as by Hazara and Uzbek elites, or to acquire more control over it, such as by Tajik elites. Increased political awareness leading to a rejection of Pashtun domination of national politics, and even the Soviet-inspired nationality policies of the communist government, have been suggested as reasons for increasing ethnic divisions. For example, in order to build ties of solidarity with rural communities, the communists assigned "nationality" statuses to various groups and created ethnic militias, such as the well-known Uzbek militia of Rashid Dostum.

Ethnicity was a major factor during the rule of the Taliban, whose policies polarized the country between the Pashtun east and south and the non-Pashtun center and north. This, however, was the ethnicization of war, not the ethnicization of the Afghan masses. To emphasize Afghanistan's ethnic diversity or ethnicity alone as a factor in the conflict, however, does not account for the innumerable shifting opportunistic alliances between various factions that characterized the conflict. For example, at various points during 1992–1993, when the mujahideen occupied Kabul, Sunni Tajiks, Uzbeks, and Pashtuns fought one another, Uzbeks formed an alliance with Pashtuns, other Pashtuns formed an alliance with Tajiks, and Shi'a Hazaras fought Pashtuns and later joined Uzbeks and yet another Pashtun faction. One must factor in personal ambition and continued interference by neighboring countries and other foreign powers, such as Pakistan, Iran, and Saudi Arabia, in addition to ethnic, religious, and regional considerations.

LANGUAGE AND LINGUISTIC PATTERNS

There is considerable linguistic diversity in Afghanistan, a reflection of the historical circumstances that led to the incorporation of diverse ethnolinguistic groups within its national boundaries and the relative isolation of many groups due to the difficult terrain, which enabled certain groups to retain their linguistic distinctiveness. Forty-five languages have been identified in Afghanistan.[26] The two official major languages are Pashtu and Dari/Farsi. Both belong to the Indo-Iranian branch of the Indo-European language family, although they are mutually unintelligible. The difference between Pashtu and Dari has been compared to the difference between English and German.

Pashtu is a grammatically complex language that is written from right to left in a modified Arabic script in which Dari is also written, but with some modifications to accommodate certain phonemes not found in either Dari or Arabic. It has many loan words from Persian and Arabic. As a written medium it dates back only to the sixteenth century, lacks an extensive literature, and the majority of Pashtu speakers are nonliterate.

In the 1930s, there were efforts to promote the growth and spread of Pashtu over all other languages as part of a broader program equating Pashtun ethnic dominance with national unity. Pashtu was declared the national language and fluency in it was required of all high school students and government employees. Despite this, there was considerable resistance among non-Pashtuns. These circumstances necessitated dual publication of government documents, dual educational systems, and created the necessity for translations and cross-translations of government communiqués. Moreover, it proved quite difficult to operate in this linguistic medium in the north of the country, where Dari and Turkic languages are spoken by the majority of administrators, bankers, and entrepreneurs. The communist leaders also attempted to promote Pashtu as the interethnic language of Afghanistan after taking power in 1978, but were unable to displace Dari. The new constitution of Afghanistan stipulates government support for the development and strengthening of all the languages of Afghanistan, although Pashtu and Dari remain the official national languages. This is in marked contrast to the 1964 Constitution that committed the state to strengthening Pashtu as the national language.

Dari, or Farsi, is a form of Persian and is the other major language spoken in Afghanistan. Farsi was the language of the court in Afghanistan, Mughul, India, and some of the former princely states in northern Pakistan, such as Hunza. Farsi underwent a major revival in eastern Iran and Afghanistan beginning in the ninth century. It has been the main language of commerce and principle literary medium, which may explain its preeminence. There is an extensive Persian literature that is familiar to most Farsi speakers, even those who are nonliterate. Farsi is written in a modified Arabic script and incorporates many Arabic words in its lexicon. Farsi is considered the *lingua franca* of Afghanistan and most speakers of other languages know some Farsi. The Hazaras, Aimaq, and Tajik all speak different dialects of Farsi. The Farsiwan in western Afghanistan speak Iranian Farsi, while the people of Herat speak a distinct dialect of their own, as do the residents of Kabul. All of these dialects are mutually intelligible despite considerable lexical variations.

Baluchi, another member of the Iranian languages, is spoken in southwestern Afghanistan next to the Pakistani and Iranian borders. Nuristani (or Kafari), another Indo-Iranian language group, is spoken in Nuristan in eastern Afghanistan, although Nuristani is considered by some to represent a third subgroup of the Indo-Iranian group, alongside the Iranian and Indic. Many Baluchi and Nuristani speakers also know some Pashtu or Dari.

The 2004 Constitution of Afghanistan stipulates Turkic languages as "the third official language" in majority speaking areas. These belong to the Uralic-Altaic language family and are spoken mostly in the area north of the Hindu Kush

Mountains. They include Uzbeki, Turkoman, and Kirghizi. Dialectical variations occur among different groups, but most are mutually intelligible. Speakers of these languages also speak some Dari as a second language.

The Dravidian language family spoken in southern India is represent by small numbers of Brahui, who live among the Baluchi population in southwestern Afghanistan. Punjabi and Sindhi, spoken by the 30,000 or more Hindu and Sikh merchants and moneylenders living in Kabul and other major cities in the eastern Afghanistan before the Soviet Invasion, represent the Indic branch of the Indo-European language group. Most of the Hindu and Sikhs left the country when the mujahideen captured Kabul in 1992, but very small numbers have returned in the post-Taliban period.

Semitic languages are not really spoken in Afghanistan. Before the war there was a small Jewish community in Kabul, but its members used Hebrew only in the context of rituals. Small communities of people calling themselves Arabs were reported in parts of northern Afghanistan prior to the Soviet invasion, but only a few actually spoke Arabic. Arabic is the ritual language of Islam; people utter the profession of faith, say their prayers, and recite the Koran in Arabic. However, very few understand Arabic, including the majority of the religious leaders and mullahs, most of whom are nonliterate.

Afghanistan has been called "a literate culture and non-literate society."[27] This characterization is to a large degree accurate. The literacy rate before the Soviet invasion was estimated at 11.4 percent of the total population. There were marked variations between urban and rural settings and in terms of gender and socioeconomic status. Urban–rural literacy rates were 25.9 percent among city dwellers versus 8.8 percent among those living in the countryside. Literacy rates in terms of gender in urban settings were 35.5 percent male and 14.8 percent female, and 15.6 percent male and 0.6 to as low as 0.1 percent female in rural settings.

FAMILY AND SOCIETY

The basis of interpersonal relationships and collective identities in all contexts in Afghanistan are family and extended family groups (*khanadan* and *khanawada*). These define not only individual identities within social groups but also the boundaries between groups. Associated with the family is a strong ideology that emphasizes group cohesiveness and solidarity and differentiates it from other similarly organized groups in the wider social context. The most important, resilient, and pervasive solidarity units in Afghan society upon which social continuity is based are the family and extended family organizations.[28]

Extended families typically consist of the male head of the household, his wife, unmarried sons and daughters, and married sons, their wives, and children. Polygyny is permitted (according to Islam a man may take up to four wives), but the practice is found among those who are wealthy or in cases where specialist female labor, such as carpet weaving, represents an economic asset. Postmarital residence rule is patrilocality, meaning that women upon marriage live with their husband's father's family. Afghan families are patriarchal, which means that authority is in the hands of the senior male head of the household, and patrilineal (agnatic descent), which means that inheritance is through the male line. These family units are linked through bonds of marriage and kinship to a larger web of kinship networks that traditionally serve as the principle support and social security system and the context for the enculturation of children. Family and kinship networks, in other words, are the basis of group formation.

Other recognized solidarity units beyond the family and extended family, commonly known as *qawm*, are organized along similar principles. The term *qawm* refers to any solidarity group or social network, which could be based upon common descent, patronage, occupational specialization, linguistic identity, sectarian affiliations (such as Sufi orders), place of residence (village or valley), or a combination of these, which serve to differentiate its members from others. A mosaic of "microsocieties" represented by these qawn networks characterized traditional Afghan society.

The primary frameworks of identity and social mobilization emanate from such small-scale communities and may be described as sequences of overlapping or concentric circles of loyalties and obligations of solidarity. Traditionally, power and social control resided primarily within such solidarity networks. The qawm is a source of support and protection, facilitates cooperative effort, and is the means of resistance to the intrusion of the state.[29] Interpersonal relationships within the localized qawm communities are hierarchical and are based upon sets of kinship, moral, religious, and political solidarity obligations and loyalties and reciprocal ties of patronage-clientalism between leaders and followers. These relationships are reinforced by Islamic religious beliefs and a code of honor, *nang*, which hinges upon the defense or protection of "women, riches/gold, and homeland" (*zan, zar, zamin*), collectively called *namus*, which along with linguistic and sectarian affiliations and loyalties constituted the basis of traditional society.

Such local, kin-based clientelist solidarity groups in which social networks beyond the family, lineage, village, and valley sometimes did not exist, and which resisted the intrusion of central authority, were insulated from the penetration of the state by the harsh terrain of rural Afghanistan and were more or less self-sustaining and politically autonomous units. They embodied a paternalistic model of community, which served to safeguard the collective interests and integrity of the group through local leadership. Local leaders called *khans* among the Pashtuns (*begs, arbabs*, and *maliks* in other areas) worked to shield and defend their qawm's interests and preserve its autonomy by mediating its interactions with other institutions and with the state, which existed as an entity external to society. Khans owned or controlled local resources, such as arable land, and commanded respect from the farmers to whom they leased land and provided credit, as well as offered protection. This pattern of clientelist organization created "survival networks" in traditional society and were reproduced in other spheres of Afghan society, including military organizations associated with warlords, after the collapse of the state.

Throughout the twentieth century, the traditional structure of rural society remained undisturbed, while the state at various times attempted to extend its influence over rural areas and introduce change and modernization, but not with a lot of success. During the twentieth century the government began to increasingly rely upon foreign aid and confined its efforts to modernize the country to urban areas, which resulted in the bifurcation of society between an urban modernizing sector and a traditional agrarian rural sector. This structure proved to be very fragile.[30] When groups of educated urban elites, who were influenced by 1960s political movements and who organized themselves into Western-style political parties, seized government control and attempted to impose change from above by force, the sociopolitical structure of Afghanistan collapsed and the country slid into rebellion and chaos.

THE TRIBAL SYSTEM

Tribal identity is based upon the idea of shared descent from a common ancestor through the male line, or patrilineal descent, and a sentiment of loyalty to the group defined in this way. The idea of tribe defines group boundaries as well as establishing the basis for relations between groups. The principle of patrilineal descent determines membership in family and lineage, and inheritance of property. Closely related individuals make up households.

Groups of households linked together by a common ancestor two or three generations back constitute lineages. Members of lineages may share a common name and have a strong sense of common identity and collective responsibility. Usually they have close interpersonal relationships and marriage ties. The preferred marriage partner for a man is his father's brother's daughters; however, this pattern is usually influenced by political, economic, and social alliances with outside groups in a pattern called hypergamy, in which a man from a dominant group obtains a wife from a socially subordinate and, in some cases, even different ethnic group to cement patron–client relations between two families. A cluster of lineages tracing their descent through a more distant common ancestor forms a clan, and a cluster of similarly related clans forms a tribe.

The main characteristic of a tribal society is the existence of several levels of more inclusive social groupings that can theoretically be mobilized for corporate action for political or military reasons. In the anthropological literature this has been referred to as the *principle of segmentation.* Segmentary organization (which is an idealized model or construct) constitutes a pattern in which descent-based units such as households, lineages, clans, and tribes are linked to other households, lineages, clans, and tribes through sets of common ancestors over past generations to make up large inclusive groupings, creating a kind of pyramid structure, with the named founding common ancestor at the top. This ideology of common descent is like a blueprint that can theoretically facilitate the unification of different tribes under charismatic leaders, creating large but short-lived confederations of many tribes. The capacity for mass mobilization for military or political purposes of a large number of distinct descent-based groups is what distinguishes tribal societies from societies that are simply based upon agnatic descent for the organization of social relations. Many tribes, however, are not political or corporate entities, although they possess the blueprint of common descent.

Although segmentary organization contributes to unity, at the same time because of the differences between segments that make up the larger whole, this pattern of organization is prone to fragmentation along segmentary lines. Not infrequently, tribal leadership is based upon individual charisma, aptitude for leadership, and patronage, rather than on heredity. A successful leader is one who is able to convince others to follow him on the basis of talent, ability to acquire and distribute resources from outside the tribe forming patron–client networks, and his ability to provide security in times of danger. There is considerable competition for leadership and leadership tends to be temporary. For these reasons tribes do not have permanent paramount chiefs who provide centralized authority.

Afghanistan is not entirely tribally organized. Tribal organization is found only among the Pashtuns and among nomadic non-Pashtun Turkmen, Baluch, Kirghiz, and the sedentary Nuristanis. However, there are also detribalized Pashtuns, such as some groups in the north of the country. Also, there are exceptions to the rule of patrilineality as the basis for inclusion into the tribe. Often outsiders, such as a holy man and his family, may be allowed to live among a tribe and follow the tribal code of behavior. Usually after a few generations the family may be accepted as a member of the tribe. Another exception is when some individuals are incorporated into a tribe through a female rather than a male link.

Tribal Pashtuns conceive of themselves as being members of one large super-family with a common language and a tradition or ideology of a shared common ancestor, a man named Qais who is said to have been one of the Prophet Muhammad's Companions (although there is disagreement on the identity of this common ancestor), and whose male offspring—sons, grandsons, and great-grandsons—were the ancestors of the different Pashtun tribes, subtribes, clans, lineages, and families. Tribalism is an ideology that defines genealogical rather than territorial boundaries. However, some tribes have distinct territories, whereas others do not.

The distinctive feature of Pashtun tribal organization include decision making by means of egalitarian community councils called *jirgas* (called *shuras* during the mujahideen period) in which all adult men are allowed to participate and speak, and the idea that group honor and vengeance are the collective responsibility of members of the tribe. Jirgas are used even in places where strong, wealthy khans or powerful military commanders have emerged.

For Pashtuns, interpersonal relationships within the group and relationships between subsections of the tribe are regulated through a tribal code of honor and conduct known as *Pashtunwali*, which specifies personal rights and obligations pertaining to *badal* (revenge), *nanawati* (giving asylum), *melmastia* (hospitality), *tureh* (bravery), *sabat* (steadfastness), *imandari* (righteousness), *isteqamat* (persistence), *ghayrat* (defense of property and honor), and *namus* (defense of the honor/chastity of female relatives). The notion of honor and disgrace are heavily vested in women's chastity.[31] Non-Pashtuns also share many of these values.

Pashtunwali is an ideology that also embodies customary law. Except in cases involving sexual crimes, such as adultery, which is a capital offense, Pashtunwali is based in general on "restorative justice," the objective of which is not retribution but restitution by the offender and his family. The offender pays damages in an amount determined through arbitration or consulation by a jirga, and involves payments of cash (blood money), services, livestock, or the transfer of women to be wedded to a family member of the victim. Although *badal*, or revenge, is a prerogative of every adult male in nearly all cases where an individual's honor is perceived to have been diminished, most often cases are settled through restitution, which is preferred whenever possible over the outbreak of a blood feud.

The restorative basis of Pashtunwali is at variance with the severe penalties under Islamic (*sharia*) law, called *hudud* and *qisas*, which require amputation of limbs for theft and infliction of identical harm ("eye for an eye") upon the perpetrator for murder or criminal physical injury. There are other noteworthy variations between tribal and sharia law. Under Pashtunwali, in cases of adultery hearsay is sufficient to condemn the accused to death by stoning or burial alive, while sharia requires evidence from four credible witnesses to the act of adultery. Another difference is that under Pashtunwali women are not entitled to inheritance, whereas under sharia women are entitled to half the share of men. Also, Pashtunwali does not allow for divorce, while under sharia a man may divorce his wife. In the tribal regions, sharia takes second place to Pashtunwali. This contrasts with the position of the Taliban, whose membership was drawn from among tribal Pashtuns, but whose obsession with the implementation of sharia was quite un-Pashtunlike.

GENDER ISSUES

Traditionally Afghans adhere to the custom of *purdah* (*pardah*, literally "curtain"), which involves the segregation and seclusion of women. Related to this is the custom of women wearing the *chadari*, or veil while in public. The Western media refer to the veil as *burqa*, which is a term used in the some parts of the Middle East to refer to the veil, but not in Afghanistan. The indigenous word is *chadari*, from the Persian word *chadar*, meaning "veil." *Purdah* delineates two categories of males: those with whom social interaction is permitted, such as father, brother, husband, and son, and those with whom interaction is forbidden. As a result, the two sexes are consigned to different domains. Women are assigned to private domestic roles—motherhood and the nurturing of children and taking care of their family's domestic affairs. Men are assigned to public roles: those of ensuring the family's economic well-being and maintaining social relationships with outsiders. The custom of secluding women greatly circumscribes and restricts the range of activities that are deemed permissible, including school attendance and working outside the domestic sphere. However, women are not totally bereft of social standing and acquire considerable authority within the family as a result of the support, loyalties, and respect from their grown sons.

The basis for the restriction of women's role in society is the idea that the honor, reputation, and social standing of a family, especially its male members, are dependent upon the reputation of its female members. The notions of honor and disgrace, as noted before, are heavily vested in women's chastity. For this reason, women are obligated to maintain the family's honor by conforming strictly to the culturally accepted norms of appropriate behavior and attire. The constraints imposed upon women and their appropriate roles are the prerogatives of males. The veil therefore symbolizes male control over women.

The status and role of women in Afghanistan are highly affected by socioeconomic circumstances and whether they live in the cities or rural environments. For example, before the war, women from affluent families in Kabul had achieved a considerable degree of autonomy and a wider range of social interactions, traveled about the city on their own, and asserted their right to higher education and a variety of career opportunities. Women also had some flexibility in terms of mode of dress. For example, when the Islamist Gulbuddin Hekmatyar and his associates threw acid on female university students for wearing miniskirts, there was a massive demonstration in the streets of Kabul in which over 5,000 angry women participated. However, women from the less privileged sectors of the city were confined to the domestic sphere, adhered to the custom of veiling in public, and seldom ventured out without male escorts.

The controversy surrounding gender issues, focused on the debate over what constitutes acceptable behavior for women, is primarily restricted to the urban settings, where marked contrasts are to be found as well as considerable social tensions. In the 1920s King Amanullah asked women to come out of seclusion and discard the veil, but the tribesmen who overthrew the king forced women back behind the purdah or veil. Things remained unchanged until 1959, when the Daoud government declared the veil and seclusion as voluntary. Urban Afghan women made considerable headway toward emancipation during the period of constitutional monarchy (1964–1973) and the second Daoud regime (1973–1978), and benefited substantially under the communist regime. It was the modernizing state, then, that bolstered the public role of women. With the collapse of the state, Afghan women lost support for their public role and were once again subjected to stern patriarchal strictures.

Conditions in the countryside were considerably different. Remote rural villages were often comprised of kinship-based communities (*khanadan* and *khanawada*) in which members were related by marriage or descent that created a safe environment for male–female interactions. Therefore, rural women had considerable freedom of movement in comparison to women living in large cities. However, they had little or no access to education and career opportunities available to their urban counterparts. Rural women did not wear chadari, except when traveling to the cities and entering environments where they would encounter strangers.

Effects of the War on Gender Roles

The status of women was drastically affected by the war and the changing sociopolitical conditions. Under the communist regime, the government stressed education and vocational training for women. During this period, fighting was confined to the rural areas and the cities were fairly secure and there were a wide range of educational and employment opportunities for women, such as jobs in the civil service, health care, education, the airline industry, the police and military forces, as well as in manufacturing industries.

In the countryside, which was subjected to heavy bombardment, the war had dramatically adverse effects upon the lives of rural women as a result of the destruction of rural agricultural infrastructure, massive population dislocations, and the breakdown of the secure descent-based communities. The breakdown of extended family and kinship-based communities, which comprised the principle support networks in the countryside, was particularly devastating. Life in the overcrowded refugee camps was associated with considerable restrictions on movement for rural women. Uncertainties associated with life as refugees in alien environments and crowded camps led to the imposition of strict patriarchal strictures upon women, including the adoption of veiling. However, life in the camps brought access to some health-care facilities and opportunities for education, unknown in the rural communities back home. For urban women, refugee life also resulted in drastic changes in the crowded neighborhoods of Pakistani cities where many families settled down, resulting in the adoption of traditional modes of dress and lifestyles.

During the mujahideen period, Kabul became the focus of heavy fighting and competing warlords who were fighting for political power and economic control destroyed much of the city. The destruction of factories, closing down of schools, and bombardment of government ministries meant loss of employment for women and restrictions on their movement. The mujahideen imposed severe restrictions upon women and enforced the veil. Women suffered great indignities during this period at the hands of mujahideen militia. Countless women were kidnapped from their homes, raped, and murdered. As a result of the violence many families fled to the countryside where they joined the ranks of internally displaced persons.

The Taliban pushed the idea of purdah, which they combined with their own extremely narrow view of the social role of women based upon the precepts of the Deobandi madrassas, to its logical and, by the standards of many Afghans, absurd conclusions by implementing the total seclusion and segregation of women from the public sphere.

Islam

Afghanistan is a predominantly Islamic country and Islam was the basis for the mujahideen's jihad against the Soviet invasion and the communist government in Kabul. Groups such as the Taliban and al Qaeda, which emerged as major power holders in Afghanistan at the close of the twentieth century, and who espouse jihadi agendas of their own, also employed the metaphors of Islam. The relationships are complex and an overview of Islam is necessary before a discussion of religion in Afghanistan and the rise of the Taliban and al Qaeda.

Islam is the religion of more than 1.2 billion people,[32] of which less than one-fifth live in the Arab-speaking Middle East. It is the second largest and currently the fastest growing major religion on the planet. The Muslim world, with Mecca as its spiritual center, encompasses and extends from Indonesia and Malaysia to Bangladesh, Pakistan, Afghanistan, Iran, Turkmenistan, Uzbekistan, Tajikistan, Kyrgyzstan, Kazakhstan, Turkey, Iraq, Syria, Jordan, Saudi Arabia, the Gulf states, Egypt, Somalia, Sudan, Libya, Chad, Tunisia, Algeria, Morocco, Mauritania, Mali, Niger, Senegal, and Guinea. Large numbers of Muslims also live in the Philippines, India, and Nigeria, as well as in Europe and North America.

Although it is true that those who profess Islam have a sense of membership in a universal community of believers worldwide, called the *ummah*, who share a common Islamic identity that transcends national, cultural, tribal, or linguistic differences, there is tremendous variation in its expression. It is also true that for fourteen centuries Islam has been expressed in a dynamic and ever-changing manner in the context of a wide range of societies with different patterns of political authority and social organization, ranging from peasant and pastoralist communities to urban communities with diverse historical and cultural traditions. Within these societies, groups that vary in terms of class, ethnicity, literacy, and political orientation have employed the key concepts, universalistic principles, and metaphors of Islam as a basis of custom, law, and political resistance. These often find expression through local institutions and in terms of individual perceptions and existing sociocultural, political, and economic realities.

There is therefore considerable variation in the expression of Islam from place to place and through time. As such, the anthropological study of Islam poses particularly difficult problems, as a number of scholars have acknowledged.[33] Given this range of variation, framing the complex local, regional, national, and international political relationships within the Islamic world, and those between it and the West in such terms as "a clash of civilizations," is rather simplistic and not particularly informative. A brief historical survey of Islam can serve as the general framework within which we might better understand the meaning of Islam to its adherents and its relationship to the radical ideological movements that have harnessed the metaphors of Islam toward their respective political agendas.

Early History of Islam

Like Judaism and Christianity, the birthplace of Islam is the Middle East. Islam began with the prophecy of Muhammad ibn Abdullah (ca. 570–632), a member of the Hashim clan of the Quraysh tribe of Mecca, in western Arabia. The Quraysh dominated commercial life in the town and were also the guardians of an important religious sanctuary known as the Kaaba. The central feature of the sanctuary was a cube-shaped structure, said to have been built by the Prophet Abraham, which contained numerous idols that were worshipped by different Arab tribes. The sanctuary was considered a consecrated place where bloodshed was prohibited. Associated with it was a famous and thriving market that operated under the sacredness of the sanctuary, where members of different tribes could meet and conduct business in safety, and from which the Meccan elite obtained considerable income.

Not much is known about Muhammad's early life. He was orphaned at a young age and was raised by his paternal uncle Abu Talib, a rich and respected member of the Quraysh tribe. According to tradition, Muhammad was a capable young man who took part in his uncle's caravan trade, which allowed him to travel outside Arabia and brought him into contact with other groups. He was also known to have periodically sought the solitude of a nearby mountain cave called Hira, where he would retreat to meditate. On one such occasion in 610 CE, when Muhammad was 40 years old, he heard voices and saw the apparition of the Archangel Gabriel, who commanded him to recite (*iqra*) the word of God, and called on him to become God's messenger. Terrified at first, Muhammad eventually accepted the message and his role as the Apostle of God. The revelations, which spanned a period of 22 years, were transmitted orally and over time were written down and compiled in the Qur'an (Arabic for "recitation"), Islam's sacred scripture. For Muslims, the Qur'an contains the literal word of God transmitted verbatim to Muhammad.

Muslims believe that God's message was revealed to a number of prophets before Muhammad, such as Abraham, Moses, and Jesus. These revelations are contained in the sacred texts of the Jews and the Christians, who are referred to by Muslims as *ahl al-kitaab*, "people of the book." However, the revelations to Muhammad, they believe, represent the final and most complete reiteration of the message from the same omnipotent God. The truths of Islam are therefore self-evident and everyone, including the people of the book, is invited to accept and live in accord with them. It is for this reason that the Qur'an (2:256) states: "Let there be no compulsion in religion: Truth stands out clear from error."

For Muslims, the final and most complete reiteration of God's eternal message, presented to Muhammad in lucid form in Arabic, is contained in the Qur'an. It is for this reason that Muslims feel that the Qur'an must be read and taught in the original Arabic and it is not to be translated into other languages because translations fail to capture the true essence of the divine words. This is why Muslims in non-Arab countries, such as Afghanistan, learn and memorize the Qur'an phonetically but do not necessarily understand Arabic.

Muhammad began to preach publicly from 613 CE. He espoused the oneness of God and denounced his tribe's polytheism as false and sinful. He condemned members of the Quraysh for their profiteering from the pilgrimage business and their greed, lack of piety, and absence of charity toward the poor. Muhammad called for social reform and asked people to submit to the will of the one true God. The Quraysh were outraged. At first Muhammad's followers were few and from the poorer social strata and could be mocked and ignored, but as their numbers grew and they posed a more tangible threat, the tribe reacted with determined hostility. Muhammad was safe so long as he had the protection of his influential uncle Abu Talib. However, Abu Talib died in 619 CE. The new head of the Hashim clan was ill-disposed toward Muhammad, who thus lost the protection of his kinsmen. Members of the Quraysh tribe now began to subject the small community of believers to increasing harassment.

In 622 Muhammad and his beleaguered followers were forced to move to an oasis 400 km (250 miles) to the north, called Yathrib, later known as Medina (from *medinat al nabi*, "the city of the Prophet," in Arabic), where he had been invited to come as peacemaker between the local Arab and Jewish tribes. Here Muhammad reorganized political life to create a community in terms of the divine laws and duties that God had entrusted him to pass on to humankind. The move to Medina is known as *hijra* (from *hijrat*, to escape) and marks the beginning of the Muslim calendar. Among the repertoire for collective action in Islam is the idea of hijrat, refuge to protect one's religion, which was employed by the Afghans who sought safe haven in Pakistan and Iran, and who were referred to as the *muhajereen*, those undertaking hijra.

The shift to Medina was the beginning of a new stage in the formation of Islam because it resulted in the transformation of the religious movement started in Mecca into a religiopolitical community, or the *ummah*, comprising a unified, divinely inspired community of believers for whom Islam superceded ethnic and tribal ties and other allegiances under the direction of a righteous leader. It is for this reason that Islam does not recognize the separation of the spiritual and religious dimensions of life from the secular and mundane, but instead sees them as united under the sacred laws set forth in the Qur'an.

The idea of ummah or community requiring Muslims to work in unison has historically played a central role in the spread of ideas and the alteration of the worldviews in elements within the Islamic world and has been the basis of overt political movements. It appeals to transnational Islamic identity expressed in pan-Islamist politics in Saudi Arabia, Libya, and Iran, as well in the discourse of radical Islamists, such as Osama bin Laden.

For Muslims the establishment of the ummah was a significant event in human history because this time members of the community to whom God had spoken would not consider the divine laws as applicable only to themselves, as the revelations to Moses had been misconstrued. Instead they would invite all others to take part in this momentous enterprise that took shape with the establishment of the nascent Muslim community in Medina. Nor would the Muslims make the mistake of worshipping the messenger instead of heeding the message, as had the followers of Jesus. Muhammad was emphatic that what was important was the message, and that he was merely a man. Although the Prophet could through his own actions and deeds set the examples of how the injunctions of the Qur'an could be applied to aspects of ordinary life, the message itself was of divine origins and primary importance.

The example set by this original and pristine Islamic community became the archetype for the ideal Islamic community that underlies Islamic politics and is something to which some subsequent reformers have aspired. Allusions to the original community of believers, or to the golden age of Islam, when the ummah was under the leadership of first four righteously guided caliphs (see below) is often used by present-day Islamic revolutionaries and would-be reformers espousing their own particular visions of Islam as justification for by-passing the accumulated corpus of Qur'anic scholarship and interpretation of the law to oppose traditional elites and Islamic religious hierarchies rooted in the more recent past, and cast doubt upon the Islamic credentials of opponents.

Islam began and continues to be at once both a faith and a polity. The importance of this event is reflected in the fact that the Muslim calendar is based upon the date of the hijra and the establishment of the ummah in Medina, rather than with the date of the first revelation of the Qur'an, or the birthday of the Prophet. Being a Muslim therefore entails simultaneously adherence to a faith (submission of the self to the will of Allah; *Islam* means "submission") and membership in a political community. It was in this form that Islam united the Arabian tribes and quickly spread beyond Arabia.

Muhammad consolidated his position in Medina and began to increase the membership of the ummah by spreading his message to surrounding tribes. In 630, after a long struggle and several battles, Muhammad brought Mecca and the Quraysh under his sway.

The military struggle for survival against the Meccans would become the prototype of *jihad*, or holy war, in subsequent Islamic discourse. In the Qur'an (e.g., 22:78, 8:60–61) the word appears as the verb *jahada* (from the Arabic meaning "to strive" or "to make an effort") in conjunction with "the cause of God." A much later juristic development led to the notion of jihad as an armed struggle for the faith, or holy war. Jihad is part of Islam's repertoire for collective action. For instance, in Afghanistan it was used against British intervention in 1838–1842 and 1878–1880; King Abdul Rahman Khan used jihad against local tribal chiefs and ethnic groups to consolidate central authority, whereas King Amanullah declared jihad against the British in 1919 to gain independence. Amanullah himself was overthrown during a jihad against his reforms, and jihad was the basis for resistance to the communist regime in Kabul and the Soviet invasion in 1979.

The term *jihad* is complex and has been attributed with various meanings, ranging from an inward struggle to attain spiritual perfection, to an external struggle to ward off injustice, warfare in defense of the faith, and holy war to propagate Islam. According to tradition, Muhammad made a distinction between the "lesser" jihad (*al-jihad al-asghar*), which is to fight a holy war in defense of the faith, and the "greater" jihad (*al-jihad al-akbar*), which is more important and refers to an inner spiritual struggle, as exemplified by the actions of the Prophet himself, whereby believers endeavor to become better Muslims by living according to rules, duties, and ritual obligations set forth by God. It was the Sufis, adherents of mystical Islam, who emphasized the importance of inner jihad over that of the external jihad. Radical Islamists, however, question the authenticity of the passages on which the idea of jihad as inner struggle is based, stressing the concept exclusively as holy war.

For the Muslims in Medina, their jihad bore fruit and Mecca capitulated without a fight. Upon taking the city, Muhammad had all its idols destroyed. However, the Kaaba was retained and the shrine was converted into the focal point of pilgrimage for all Muslims. Thus Mecca, along with Medina, became one of Islam's holy cities and Saudi Arabia the sacred land and preserve of Islam, the reverence for which among many Muslims is evident in the widespread outcry following the stationing of U.S. troops in Saudi Arabia during the 1991 Gulf War.

By the time of the Prophet's death in 632, most of the tribes in Arabia had converted to Islam. Muhammad named no successor and the community of Muslims had to address the question of succession. There could be no more prophets because Muhammad, "the Seal of the Prophets," was the last human in a long succession of prophets to be given a direct divine imperative. There could only be a secular successor whom the earliest documentary sources called Amir al-Momineen, or "the commander of the faithful," a title that was later replaced by the word *khalifa*, or caliph. It is noteworthy that Mullah Omar, the leader of the Taliban, whom we shall discuss later in this chapter, chose to call himself Amir al-Momineen, making allusions to the original Muslim community and the legitimacy and authority residing therein.

The Muslim community was not unanimous over the choice of candidate. At issue was the question of whether political legitimacy is inherent in the will of the community or in the right of descent from the Prophet. The majority chose Abu Bakr (reigned 632–634), Muhammad's father-in-law and closest Companion (*sahabah*), and a member of the Meccan elite, while a minority selected Ali ibn Abu Talib, the Prophet's paternal cousin and son-in-law, husband of his daughter Fatima, and the father of his grandsons Hasan and Husayn. Supporters of Abu Bakr later became known as the Sunni, or "people of tradition," while the proponents of Ali were called *Shi'at-i-Ali*, or "partisans of Ali," and later simply the Shi'a.

Abu Bakr confronted tribal uprisings under false messiahs, in a period referred to as the *riddah*, or "apostasy," which he crushed with extreme vigor. He then undertook a phase of expansion that led to the conquests of Iraq and Syria. This expansion necessitated the elaboration of an Islamic legal code. Abu Bakr thus devised a political and legal system for the administration of his realm, which became the system of governance adopted by subsequent Islamic polities. This eventually led to the formulation of a comprehensive legal system based upon the legal and ethical principles found in the Qur'an and *hadith*, the record of the examples set for by the Prophet's own actions.

The next caliph Omar (reigned 634–644), a close associate of Abu Bakr, transformed the Islamic state into an empire with its boundaries extending from Morocco to Afghanistan. Omar was assassinated in 644 and was succeeded by Uthman (reigned 644–656), a member of the elite Meccan Umayyad family. He is credited for centralizing the administration of the caliphate and compiling the official version of Qur'an. Uthman was murdered and the people of Medina elected Ali (reigned 656–661) as the fourth caliph. He was challenged by Muawiya, the nephew of Uthman and governor of Syria, whose rebellion led to a civil war, called the *fitna*, or "time of trial." This was a crucial period in the history of Islam because the violent struggles gave rise to the major sectarian divisions present in the Islamic world today.

A battle that ended in arbitration failed to confirm Ali as the rightful caliph. This badly weakened his position and a faction among his followers, called the Kharijites, or "seceders," broke away from his camp. The Kharijites, who were the first Islamic dissent group, repudiated Ali's recourse to arbitration on the basis of the injunction in the Qur'an that "judgment belongs to God alone," which became their battle cry, and deemed Ali's actions as counter to the Qur'anic directive that "If one party rebels against the other, fight against that which rebels." The seceders sought a return to the ideal consensual governance of the original Muslim community, based on the principle that legitimate power resides with the ummah. Moreover, they declared Muslims who deviated from their vision of true Islam and literalist interpretation of the Qur'an to be guilty of apostasy, or *riddah*, and thereby excluded from the ummah.

The Kharijite thus set a precedent used by subsequent radical Islamic groups, such as the Taliban in Afghanistan, to dismiss the legitimacy of other religious authorities and to declare jihad against Muslims who do not espouse their vision of Islam, even though the Qur'an states that Muslims must not kill other Muslims. The Kharijite declared a jihad or holy war both against Ali, who was assassinated by one of their agents in 661, and Mu'awiyah, who then claimed the title of caliph. Under the Ummayads the seat of government was relocated from Arabia to Syria and the caliphate became dynastic.

The passing of Caliph Ali marked the end of the golden age of Islam, the end of the reign of *al-khulafa'ar-rashidun*, the first four "righteously guided caliphs," when leadership was based upon the will of the ummah. As noted before, calls for a return to this idealized period in the history of Islam are often made by Islamic revolutionaries to legitimize their own particular visions of Islam over those of their opponents.

Muawiya's victory did not resolve the issue of succession and upon his death a second civil war broke out. The rebels rallied around Ali's son Husayn, who was tragically killed along with his family in 680 by Ummayad forces in Karbala, Iraq. Following this, the Shi'at Ali was transformed from a political movement into a religious sect based on the doctrine of a divinely appointed leadership, or *imamate*, in which legitimate leadership is restricted to Ali and his lineal descendants (called Sayyids) through his marriage with Fatima, the daughter of the Prophet. The ummah would thereafter remain divided between the Shi'a and Sunni.

The belief in a divinely appointed leadership, or imamate, beginning with the Caliph Ali and continuing through his descendants is one of the distinctive theological characteristics that set the Shi'a apart from the Sunni. Another distinction is the central importance of the martyrdom of Husayn, the second Imam, who was slain in Karbala.

Disagreements within the Shi'a over the order of succession to the imamate from among the various descendants of Ali resulted in further sectarian divisions. Two such sects that emerged include the Imami or Twelvers (also called Ithna Ashariya) and the Isma'ilis, or Seveners. The Imami recognize a succession of 12 imams, beginning with Ali and ending with Imam Muhammad al-Mahdi, who disappeared as a child in 874. It is believed that the 12th imam is in a state of "occultation" (out of sight and hearing of humankind), and will at some future date return as the *Mahdi*, a messianic figure, or righteously guided leader, to restore true Islamic order and justice on earth.

The Isma'ilis broke off from the Imamis over the question of the candidacy of the seventh imam. They chose Isma'il the eldest son of the sixth Imam Jafar al Sadiq (702–765), who they claimed to be the *Mahdi*, while the Imamis accepted Musa-i-Kazim, the designated successor.

This brief synopsis of the early history of Islam is relevant to the present discussion not only because it sheds light on today's major sectarian subdivisions within the Islamic world, but also because the events described have been perpetually evoked in the centuries that followed up to the present as means of explaining and legitimizing sociopolitical actions and socioeconomic circumstances.

The Practice of Islam

Islam is all at once a religion, a way of life, a moral and judicial system, and the basis of politics and cultural identity. Muslims are required to live their lives according to the moral precepts and observe a series of obligations and prohibitions necessary for righteous conduct in public and private life. These obligations and prohibitions are specified in the Qur'an and the hadith, a corpus of authenticated texts comprising the collected accounts of Muhammad's deeds, actions, and examples, or the *sunna*. For the devout, Islam permeates the whole of their lives and it is not possible to separate the spiritual from the mundane aspects of day-to-day living.

Muslims must fulfill a set of ritual obligations known as the Five Pillars (*arkan*) of Islam, which represent the public expression of the believer's religiosity. These are: *al-shahada*, the profession of faith in the one God; *salat*, five daily prayers; *al-zakat*, religious tax; *al-saum*, fasting during the month of Ramadan; and *hajj*, the pilgrimage to Mecca.

The first and primary tenet is the shahada, or the declaration of faith, which is *la-illaha illa Allah wa-Muhammed rasul Allah*, "there is no God but God and Muhammad is the messenger of God." Reciting the shahada with sincerity three times in public is all that is required for a person to convert to Islam. The two parts of the shahada contain important doctrinal points. The first stresses the oneness of God who is all-compassionate, omnipresent, and omnipotent. The second part emphasizes that Muhammad is considered the last prophet in a long line of messengers, whom God has sent to humankind. To acknowledge this in public is to acknowledge the truth of the revelations in the Qur'an.

The second pillar of Islam is prayer five times each day—at dawn, noon, afternoon, evening, and at night. Prayer is the tangible, observable public expression of submission to God and as such its importance cannot be underestimated. One may pray anywhere, but men are encouraged to do so in a congregation in a mosque, or else to join a prayer line that forms in a public place. Women, on the other hand, are expected to pray in the privacy of their own homes. In some Muslim countries, mosques have segregated areas where women may pray. The Friday noon prayers are especially important, and most men try to attend the mosque at this time. This is the occasion when religious leaders give their weekly sermons, or *khutba*.

The third pillar of Islam is al-zakat, or almsgiving, an obligatory sharing of one's wealth with those less fortunate. It is required each year from Muslims who can afford it. The rate of zakat is set at about 2.5 percent of an individual's annual income. Such donations are used for the general welfare of the community to provide social services for the needy. Many give an additional zakat in the form of food and money to the poor during religious holidays.

The fourth pillar of Islam is fasting during the holy month of Ramadan. It commemorates the time when Allah revealed the first verses of the Qur'an to Muhammad. The fast begins on the first day of Ramadan, which takes place in the ninth month of the Muslim lunar calendar. In some countries, the start of Ramadan is officially announced by the government and signaled with the firing of a cannon. Then, every day from sunrise to sunset, for the entire month, people abstain from eating, drinking, smoking, and engaging in sexual intercourse. Young children, those who are ill, pregnant or nursing mothers, and travelers are exempted from fasting. But adults who are unable to observe the fast during Ramadan for the reasons noted must make up the days missed at a later date. The fast is an expression of self-discipline, sacrifice of bodily desires, and obedience of God's directives. It instills a sense of common purpose and equality among members of the community. The end of Ramadan is marked by the festival Eid al-Fitr (called Eid i Ramazan in Afghanistan), the "Festival of Breaking Fast."

The fifth pillar of Islam is the hajj, or the pilgrimage to Mecca. Every Muslim who is physically, mentally, and financially capable must undertake the pilgrimage once in a lifetime. Circumambulating the Kaaba seven times in a counterclockwise direction, kissing the sacred black stone *al-hajar al-aswad* in the eastern wall of the Kaaba (retained from pre-Islamic times), and running between the hills of Safa and Marwa, located adjacent to the Great Mosque, seven times are among the principle rituals of the hajj. These two activities are called *umra* and are the opening rituals of the hajj, known as "the greater umra." The highlight of the hajj is the *wuquf*, or "standing" on the plain near mount Arafat—the location of the cave of Hira, where the Prophet Muhammad received the first divine revelation.

The annual pilgrimage to Mecca where Muslims from around the globe converge to demonstrate their religious oneness and identity, which transcend national, cultural, tribal, or linguistic differences, expresses Islam's nature as a transnational belief system and community.

Beyond these ritual obligations, Muslims are required to observe a strict code of conduct that stresses modesty in dress, honesty, kindness, justice, and partaking of actions for the betterment of the community. Muslims are forbidden from shedding human blood, stealing, prevarication, adultery, gambling, and taking usury. Strict dietary guidelines prohibit the ingestion of alcoholic beverages and other intoxicating substances, pork, and the flesh of animals that have been improperly slaughtered.

Islamic Law and Its Sources

The ummah was organized according to the divine laws pertaining to all aspects of human conduct. From its inception, there has been little distinction in Islam between the legal and religious aspects of life. Islamic law is based upon the moral principles and commands for human conduct, called sharia, set forth by God and revealed to humankind through the Prophet.[34] The sharia is the basis for the ideal civil society, the ummah, conceived as a universal social order that transcends ethnic and cultural differences.

Law is conveyed through two infallible sources. The first source is the Qur'an, which is the literal word of God, and provides the basic principles used to render legal decisions. The second source is the sunna, or "tradition," of Muhammad recorded in the hadith. This comprises the authenticated accounts of the conduct, teachings, and interpretations of Qur'anic injunctions by Muhammad, as witnessed by those who accompanied him and transmitted to subsequent generations through a chain of reliable narrators, validated through systematic appraisal of the sources by scholars. The Qur'an (4: 80) establishes the sunna of the Prophet as a source of sharia. Sharia specifies what is lawful (*halal*) and what is unlawful (*haram*). On issues where the injunctions are clearly specified in the Qur'an and sunna, they are considered revealed and the exercise of human reason is disqualified.

Situations where the application of the sharia injunctions to unprecedented cases is not explicit gave rise to a scholarly discipline that deals with sharia, known as *fiqh.* It provides practical rules, such as analogical reasoning (*qiyas*), to discover the unknown from a known precedent, and guidelines for correct interpretation (*ijthihad*), alongside consensus (*ijma*) among religious scholars or jurists (*ulama*). The process entails reading the relevant texts in light of the institution of scholastic commentary and the rereading of commentaries on commentaries, and producing additional commentaries. These commentaries are therefore another source for religious law. Rules derived in this way, however, are not immutable because they are not revealed and may be subject to alternative rulings if the revised juristic opinion and human reasoning receive ijma, or general consensus of the ulama. The importance of the interpretive methodologies based upon a process of legal reasoning in the context of the practices of particular legal schools has been the means through which Islamic law has adapted to local cultural traditions and changing sociopolitical conditions.

Within Sunni Islam, four major schools of jurisprudence emerged during the eight and ninth centuries, each named after the prominent jurists who founded them. These survive today and include the Hanafi, Maliki, Shafi, and Hanbali schools. The differences between them stem from disagreements on methods and judicial opinions and do not indicate divergence on matters of doctrine.

The Hanafi School, which has the greatest numbers of followers, predominates in Jordan, Lebanon, Turkey, Pakistan, and Afghanistan. It is named after Abu Hanifa (699–767), who emphasized the role of rationality through analogical reasoning and juristic preference, which provides space for pragmatic moderation.

The Maliki School predominates in Morocco, Algeria, Tunisia, northern Egypt, Sudan, Bahrain, and Kuwait. It was established by Malik ibn Anas (715–795), and it avoids reliance on human reasoning and emphasizes strict adherence to the Qur'an and the established precedence or sunna of the Companions of Muhammad in Medina. The Companions, or *sahabah*, of the Prophet Muhammad, were individuals who had personal contact with him and were eyewitnesses to his actions, but the term also extends to anyone who was alive and observed the Prophet during his lifetime. The Medinian Companions include those who went with the Prophet to Medina, called the *muhajirun* (those on the hijra), and the original converts in Medina, called *ansar*. The accounts of these individuals, who saw the deeds and heard the words of the Prophet during his lifetime, are considered to be the most reliable sources of the hadith by proponents of the Maliki School.

The Shafi School prevails in southern Egypt, Yemen, East Africa, Indonesia, and Malaysia. It was founded by Muhammad ibn Idris al-Shafi (767–820), who synthesized Hanafi rationalism and Maliki traditionalist approaches by combining analogical reasoning and the primacy of Medinan legal opinions.

The Hanbali School predominates in Saudi Arabia, Qatar, and Oman. It was founded by Ahmad ibn Hanbal (780–855), whose work on the sunna represents an effort to base legal doctrines exclusively on the Qur'an and hadith. This school of Islamic jurisprudence found its greatest appeal among the followers of the reformist Wahhabi movement that began under the impetus of Muhammad ibn Abd al-Wahhab (1703–1792) and is the predominant form of Islam in Saudi Arabia. (Western scholars refer to the form of Islam practiced in Saudi Arabia as Wahhabi, but adherents rarely use this term, referring to themselves as Salafiyyah.)

The Shi'a developed their own school of Islamic jurisprudence, called Jafari, based on the teachings of Imam Ja'far al-Sadiq (699–765). This school of jurisprudence, which predominates in Iran, involves ongoing and systematic reappraisal on the basis of reason by the religious leadership in each generation. In addition to the Qur'an, hadith, and human reason in the development of legislation, this school also gives considerable weight to the deeds and examples of the 12 divinely inspired Shi'a imams, who are deemed infallible as the descendants of the Prophet and his legitimate successors. The Jafari School considers the deeds of these imams as part of the hadith. In the absence of the Imam (who is hidden or absent and is said to return one day) it is the collective, ongoing intellectual effort of the ulama, who are the representatives of the Imam, that comprise the means of attaining the most relevant interpretations of the Qur'an and sunna.

Among the Sunnis the determination of religious law and practice are the tasks of religious scholars called ulama. Their training includes classical Arabic, theology (*kalam*), interpretation of the Qu'ran (*tafsir*), and the tradition of the Prophet (hadith), and Islamic law (fiqh). There is no organized religious hierarchy or ordained clergy and those who interpret the law and offer sermons do so on the basis of their qualifications as scholars of law, called *mufti*, who issue legal edicts or opinions, or *fatwas*. Individuals lacking these qualifications cannot issue fatwas. Therefore, from the standpoint of Islamic jurisprudence, the anti-American fatwas issued by Osama bin Laden are illegitimate.

In contrast to the Sunni, the Shi'a possess an organized hierarchy of religious leaders. Their authority is based upon their status as representatives of the absent Imam.

During the course of the last century a number of factors have contributed to the decrease in the status of the Sunni schools of law. These include the introduction of Western ideals of justice and democracy as a result of colonial rule, the emergence of authoritarian governments that have circumvented the judicial process, modernization, and the increasing emphasis upon secular education. Islamists such as Osama bin Laden and the Taliban reject traditional schools of Islamic jurisprudence and the vast corpus of Qur'anic scholarship and interpretation and interpretive methodologies of fiqh. Their argument is that rulings based upon analogy are extrascriptural and therefore invalid. Instead they wish to restrict sharia strictly upon the literal reading of Qur'an and sunna. Although groups like the Taliban rebuff the legitimacy of the interpretive tradition, they read and interpret the texts as well, according to their own political agendas and objectives. This deprives Islamic law of its capacity to adapt to changing conditions and in practice makes a travesty of justice.

Sufism

Sufism represents the inner spiritual or mystical dimension of Islam and is characterized by considerable religious tolerance and the free expression of religiosity. Sufism offers the means for individuals to find their own spirituality or spiritual path (*tariqa*) through selfless and unconditional devotion to God.[35] The path has many stages that one must travel to reach the ultimate goal of union with God. Sufism is an ongoing, thousand-year-old tradition that encompasses a wide range of beliefs and rituals as well as formal organizations, the Sufi orders.

Sufism developed in response to the increasing worldliness and political repression of Ummayad caliphs and the rigidity of the legalistic formulations or casuistry of the ulama. The early Sufis stressed spirituality over obedient conformity to doctrine. Sufi philosophical and spiritual discourse, often expressed in poetry, has had an immense impact on Islamic literature and is represented in the works of such writers as Abdullah Ansari of Herat (eleventh century); Sanayi of Ghazni (twelfth century), author of the first mystical poetry in Dari; and Rumi of Balkh (thirteenth century), founder of the Mawlayiya order of whirling dervishes based in Turkey, whose book *Mathnawi*, comprising more than 25,000 verses, is considered to be among the greatest works of poetry written in Persian. Maulana Nuruddin Jami (fifteenth century) of Herat is regarded as the last great Persian mystical poet.

The word *Sufism* comes from the Arabic word *suf*, meaning "wool" (*tasawwuf*, literally "to dress in wool" in Arabic), in reference to the rough woolen garments worn by early Muslim ascetics, following the example set by the Prophet, as a demonstration of their detachment from the material world and bodily pleasures.

Sufism offers a means of devotion through deeply personal, intuitive, and subjective experiences rather than by means of the traditional devotional activity based upon the scholarly scrutiny of religious texts or mechanical performance of rituals. The Sufi, however, does not necessarily depart from official doctrine, although some groups developed extremely heterodox practices, but instead strives to attain piety through deep personal commitment to the rigorous fulfillment of the injunctions of the Qur'an and sunna through long hours of prayer, unceasing meditation upon verses of the Qur'an, exceptional reverence for the Prophet, and repetition or intoning the names of God, or *ziker*.

Sufis are unvaryingly committed to the inner struggle against one's body or desires (*nafs*), or *al-jihad al-akbar*, the greater jihad, to attain spiritual enlightenment and moral perfection that comes through the loss of the self in the Ultimate. The emphasis upon the personal, intuitive, and experiential aspects of religion over sacred texts and law has made Sufism receptive to other belief systems and highly accommodating to local customs and beliefs in comparison with legalistic ummah-oriented perspective of the orthodoxy. This has made Sufism highly tolerant of other forms of religious expressions and other truths, which accounts for its widespread popularity and appeal among ordinary people. Sufism has had a profound influence upon Islam and has millions of adherents throughout the world. The nature and widespread popularity of Sufism historically has had a moderating effect upon Islamic beliefs and attitudes.

Sufism began on the basis of intense personal mystical experiences among early Muslim ascetics based upon the ecstatic love of God, and this individual dimension still remains an important aspect of Sufi spirituality. Some of the key principles of early Sufism included tawakkul, or the unconditional faith in God, *fana fil haq*, the complete loss of one's self in God, and the idea of divine love. Later on, various devotional practices and techniques were added to the Sufi repertoire, including music, dancing, whirling, special breathing, and other ecstatic techniques. Considered outside the sacred texts and law, to the fundamentalist ulama these accretions were viewed with suspicion and hostility, as innovations contaminating the faith. Therefore, at various times the relation of the ulama with the Sufis has been one of overt hostility.

Over time Sufism acquired considerable popular following and organized fraternal orders developed based on specific paths of spirituality, or *tariqa*, set forth by renowned sheikhs, or masters (*pirs* in Afghanistan). Many Sufi teachers are regarded as saints (*wali*) because they have attained personal contact with God and are therefore endowed with *karamat*, or charisma, and *baraka*, or holiness or grace. As such they are considered intermediaries between humans and God and command considerable social prestige.

Baraka is hereditary and runs in certain families, such as the Sayyids, who claim descent from Muhammad through his daughter Fatima and his cousin and son-in-law Ali, and the Hazrats, who are descendants of the Caliph Omar. Saints acquire an ongoing devotional allegiance from disciples called *murids*, creating solidarity groups, or qawm. As such, the pir and his followers may exercise considerable local political influence.

In some cases a family of saints receives the collective allegiance of a tribe, a phenomenon known as Maraboutism, as described by anthropologists working elsewhere in Central Asia and in the Middle East. In this type of Sufism, the pir is not a member of the ulama and bastion of sharia orthodoxy, who do not accommodate tribal law, and his position depends upon his spiritual (*ruhani*) capacities. The connection between the tribe and the saint is not one of pir-murid, but is based upon devotion to the person of the pir, who is lavished with offerings, and whose barakat sanctifies the tribe. This type of Sufism is found in the Pashtun tribal areas of southern Afghanistan in connection with the Qadiriyyah order, headed by Sayed Ahmad Gailani. Among the southern Pashtuns, the pir overshadows the mullah and ulama. This is thought to be a way of reconciling the necessity for religion with the need to assert tribal identity with respect to sharia law. Nomadic Pashtun groups are also linked to Sufi pirs in a Marabout relationship. A different situation holds true in the nontribal areas north of the country, where Sufi orders are orthodox and pirs are also members of the ulama.

Sainthood is not a status conferred after death, although someone who has been martyred in the cause of Islam may be recognized as such, and differs from the idea of sainthood found in Christianity because it is not based on institutional recognition by a church or formal organization. It is based on recognition by the local community. The murids are intensely loyal to pirs and this devotion does not dissipate upon the saint's death. Instead the tombs of Sufi saints become shrines and centers of pilgrimage drawing people seeking supernatural intercession. The countryside in Afghanistan is covered with such shrines, called *ziarat*, which attract considerable numbers of pilgrims. For this reason many Islamists and the Taliban in Afghanistan, who consider these developments as non-Islamic accretions, are hostile to and have attempted to suppress Sufism and ziarat pilgrimages. Followers of Osama bin Laden often clashed over this issue with the ziarat-oriented Afghan fighters with whom they associated.

The Sufi orders functioned in parallel with the orthodoxy, without trying to displace it. Nevertheless, charismatic Sufi masters who often attracted larger numbers of followers and who promised to guide the initiates toward attaining personal spiritual insights have sometimes posed a threat to political authorities and evoked hostility from the ulama, the guardians of orthodoxy. The latter also viewed the Sufi doctrine of unity of man and God, called *wahdat al wujud*, with suspicion as contrary to the sharia because it conflicts with the absolute unity of God, which is central to Islam. A number of Sufi teachers were executed over this doctrine.

The hostility by the orthodox ulama had by the tenth century made it necessary for Sufi masters to set down the basic tenets of Sufism in writing to demonstrate that it was not counter to orthodox practice. The Persian-born Muslim scholar Abu Hamid al-Ghazali (1058–1111), who taught Islamic law in Baghdad, reconciled Sufi doctrine and sharia law, thereby making Sufism acceptable as a legitimate expression of Islamic piety. By the thirteenth century Sufism had spread throughout the Muslim world.

Later on, some Sufi teachers adopted the doctrine of the separation of created and creator, *wahdat ash-shuhud*, first espoused as part of an effort to purge Sunni Islam of non-Islamic accretions by Shaykh Ahmad Sirhindi (1564–1624) in India, who became known as Mujaddid-i-Alf-i Sani (Renewer of the Second Millennium of Islam). Sufi orders that developed around this principle, such as the revitalized Naqshbandiyah, which has a strong presence in Afghanistan, are considered orthodox brotherhoods, fully within the parameters of sharia of the orthodox ulama. Called *tariqat-i shariati*, "paths that adhere to the sharia," their leaders, or pirs, while still believed to be endowed with baraka, are orthodox ulama, who teach fiqh or sharia as well as the esoteric Sufi doctrine. These orders, such as the Kabul-based Naqshbandiyah order associated with the Mujaddidi family, tend to be more conservative and fundamentalist in their outlook.

Sufi orders were heavily involved in missionary work and are responsible for the spreading of Islam in India and Southeast Asia during the thirteenth century, where large numbers of Hindus and Buddhists converted to Islam, moved by Sufi teachings on divine love and social equality. Sufi missionaries were also highly active in Central Asia during the seventeenth and eighteenth centuries. Sufi missionaries are still active around the globe, spreading their ideas of piety and message of religious tolerance and emancipated religiosity. Sufism's popularity is based on its openness and religious tolerance, enabling it to integrate local customs and traditions and thus serving as the framework for the formation of popular Islam and a means of integrating Islam into local communities. Saint cults and the notion of baraka are among the pre-Islamic beliefs incorporated into Sufism and preserved in popular Islam. Although from the point of view of the sharia ideologues popular practices, such as pilgrimage to the tombs of saints and devotion to pirs might appear blasphemous, for those who partake in such activities they are as much acts of devotion as adhering to the dictates of sharia.

Sufism has also inspired mass mobilization of society and political resistance. The Sufi orders are loosely associated with one another in extensive networks tying together communities ranging from nomadic camps to villages, towns, and cities and some Sufi orders have lodges (*khanqah*) in many countries throughout the world. Their membership cuts across ethnic and territorial divides. This lends itself for the mobilization of mass movements during times of crisis. The leader of the Naqshbadiyah order in Kabul, the Hazrat-i Shor Bazar, of the Mujaddidi family, who claims descent from Shaykh Ahmed Sirhindi, inspired the tribal uprisings against King Amanullah Khan's secular reforms that led to his abdication in 1929. Hazrat-i Shor Bazar supported Bacha-i-Saqaw, who reversed Amanullah's reforms, before shifting his support for Nadir Khan, another contender for the throne.

It is thought that the large following and political influence wielded by the Mujaddidi family was the reason the communist Taraki government had the patriarch and 79 male members of the family killed in Kabul in January 1979. A surviving member of the family, Sibghatullah Mujaddidi established the Jabha-i Nijat-i Milli Afghanistan party (National Liberation Party of Afghanistan), and later held the office of president of the failed muhajideen government that took power in 1992. During the anti-Soviet jihad the Sufi orders in Afghanistan offered a network of alliances outside the Islamist parties and ethnic groups. Sibghatuallh Mujadedi leader of the Naqshbaniyah order and the Sayed Ahmad Gailani head of the Qaderiyah order founded moderate nationalist Islamic parties, but were excluded from the flow of arms and money supplied by the CIA-ISI (Pakistan's Military intelligence, Directorate of Inter-Services Intelligence) in favor of the radical Islamic groups.

Political Islam

Political Islam (or Islamism, radical Islam, militant Islam) is a postcolonial phenomenon in the Muslim world. Islamists did not arise from among the conservative elements of society or the traditional ulama. Their social origins are the modern institutions of higher learning of the twentieth century, schools and universities in urban centers. The development of political Islam has been facilitated through the spread of literacy, electronic media, mimeographed texts, secret "lessons" on cassettes, and high-tech communication channels. This is how the key Islamist ideologues disseminate their message, bypassing the mosque and state apparatus, the traditional means of establishing religious authority and knowledge. Such access to religious knowledge has enabled recipients of secular education aspiring to political power to assert their own religious authority and definition of what is "Islamic," or "correct knowledge" in opposition to existing state powers and established religious authorities.

For the Islamists, Islam is a political ideology rather than just a religion. The objective of political Islam is not the reform of existing society, but the establishment of an Islamic state in which all political and social relations are modeled after the original Muslim community of the time of the Prophet and the first four caliphs. For this reason some Islamists refer to themselves as *salafi*, those who follow the example of the true ancestors. Islamists are utopian, not just fundamentalists wishing to impose strict religious practice or implement sharia as the only legal system. They wish to create an ideal society and claim that they alone have the blueprints for such a society.[36]

Islamists perceive the Qur'an and sunna as having ascendancy over other sources of law, thereby circumventing the long tradition of scholarly interpretation through rational analysis and Islam's tradition of scholastic commentary, which has often permitted pragmatic moderation. For the Islamists, sharia law is to be implemented not for the sake of establishing social justice, but to regulate personal behavior and modes of dress by instituting punishments stipulated in sharia criminal code called *qisas*, or retaliation in kind, and *hudud*, which prescribes stoning to death for adultery, the amputation of limbs for theft, and whipping for drinking alcohol.

Among the principle sources of inspiration for the Islamists are the works of Sayyid Qutb (1906–1966), the chief ideologue of the Muslim Brotherhood[37] in Egypt, and Abul Ala Mawdudi (1903–1979), founder of the Jamaat-i Islami[38] party in Pakistan. These writers asserted that in a truly Islamic society, every facet of human existence, not just the spiritual domain of life, must be subordinated to the moral principles set forth by God. For this reason, from the point of view of the Islamists, the idea of social justice is not compatible with the democratic principle of rule of the majority on the grounds that moral principles are preordained by God and must be obeyed—they cannot be shaped according to ballot counts.

As such, according to Qutb and Mawdudi social justice is restricted to those who abide by God's law. Islamists therefore vehemently denounce Western ideals of secularism (the separation of religion and politics), comingling of the sexes, nationalism, and democracy as contrary to Islam. They believe that these Western ideals are the principle cause of the decadence of Muslim society. Islamists regard these ideals and principles as emanating from *jahiliyaa* (a term associated with the pre-Islamic period, meaning a time of ignorance to be rejected). For the Islamists, nationalism is nothing more than the road to the cult of the nation, democracy constitutes the dictatorship of the majority, and secularism, which eschews God's sovereignty over everything, results in atheism. Therefore, any Muslim who upholds the ideals of Western democracy, secularism, or nationalism is in reality eschewing Islam and renouncing God.

For Qutb and Mawdudi it is mandatory for every believer to renounce Western ideologies and modernity and overthrow governments that uphold them. The goal is to establish a truly Islamic state, under God's law, or sharia, applied to all aspects of society. A true Islamic state, by virtue of being a moral polity, would be free of all the problems vexing the world today.

A true Islamic society can only be accomplished by means of jihad, which is obligatory for every Muslim, so that power may be seized from immoral and atheistic rulers. Jihad is the Islamist's theory of social transformation. They interpret the concepts of jihad as an "armed conflict," directed against un-Islamic regimes and enemies of the faith. For the Islamists jihad is a mandatory religious duty binding on the individual (*fard 'ain*), rather than in the traditional sense of the meaning, as an exceptional duty, required of the whole community (*fard kifayah*). By no means necessarily shared by all Muslims, such a construal of the concept of jihad has contributed to the allegation that Islam is a violent religion. The emphasis on jihad and call for a return to a community based upon the example set by the Prophet and his Companions is the reason why Islamist are sometimes referred to as salafi-jihadis. Moreover, for the Islamists, Muslims who live in non-Islamic societies who do not undertake jihad to establish an Islamic state are apostates, or unbelievers, which is akin to the views of the Kharijites. In this sense, jihad can be extended to include fellow Muslims, who by the Islamist's definition are unbelievers. This enables Islamist to bypass the injunction in the Qur'an (4:92–93) that Muslims must not kill other Muslims. Ideologues such as Mawdudi also espoused an extreme anti-Shi'a bias, a sentiment shared by most Sunni Islamists. Moreover, Mawdudi held a narrow and uncompromising stance regarding the social role of women and advocated the veil and strict gender segregation.

Qutb and Mawdudi had a considerable impact upon radical Muslims throughout the Arab world, especially following the 1967 defeat of the Arabs in the war against Israel. Their ideas were also a source of inspiration for Islamists in Pakistan, and the Muslims who joined the jihad against the Soviets in Afghanistan. The Taliban's uncompromising stance toward the West, extreme anti-Shi'a bias, willingness to kill fellow Muslims, and their radical views on the segregation and seclusion of women have also been shaped by the works of ideologues such as Qutb and Mawdudi.

This does not mean, however, that all Afghans or all Muslims everywhere subscribe to such radical Islamic perspectives or share the agendas of those who espouse these ideas. The important point to bear in mind is that although radical militant Islamic groups employ the metaphors of Islam as the basis of their respective political agendas, they are not representative of the Muslim world. Islam is also about coexistence and a vision of a global community striving for the betterment of humanity as a whole.

ISLAM IN AFGHANISTAN

Islam came to Afghanistan with Arab armies during the middle of the seventh century. However, Islam did not become entrenched among the local population for several hundred years. Sunni Islam became fully established in Afghanistan under the Ghaznavids (962–1186 CE), who forged the first great Islamic empire in Afghanistan by the middle of the tenth century and launched numerous military campaigns into India. Shi'a Islam was introduced much later, when part of Afghanistan fell under the control of the Persian Safavid dynasty (1499–1736).

Today the majority of Afghans are Muslims. However, there is little reliable information on Afghanistan's religious demography. According to estimates, some 85 percent of the population follows the orthodox Sunni Hanafi School of jurisprudence. The remaining 15 percent of the population subscribes to the Shi'a Islam (Imamis and Ismaillis).

In some ways Islam pervades every aspect of Afghan life.[39] Most Afghans observe the basic Islamic ritual obligations, code of conduct, regulations pertaining to relationships within the family, and customs associated with major life-cycle events, such as birth, marriage, and burial. References to Allah permeate practically all conversations. Religion structures daily life and provides a common Islamic identity and worldview. Afghans are also versed in Islamic lore concerning the life and deeds of Muhammad, accounts of saintly figures and Sufi masters, *malangs* (itinerant mendicants), and tales associated with holy shrines, or *ziarats*.

Western folk stereotypes equate Islam as a conceptual or normative system with culture, the totality of all the beliefs, values, norms, practices, and behaviors characteristic of any particular society. It is as if Muslim people lack nonreligious ideas, concepts, and behaviors. However, religion does not constitute everything. Afghans were never "puritanical" in their appreciation of art, music, and poetry. Moreover, Islam did not play a major political role in Afghanistan before the jihad against the Soviet occupation. Also, major sectarian conflicts were almost nonexistent until the war against the Soviets, the politicization of Islam, and the failure of the Islamic state following the collapse of the communist regime in Kabul in 1992, which brought these divisions to the forefront.

There is considerable variation in religious expression between cities and rural areas. The Islam of the educated urban elites derives from scholastic tradition and focuses upon theological subtleties. Rural populations are more concerned with the correct performance of religious rituals and obligation. In the villages the communal mosque, called *masjid*, is the center of religious activities and communal worship. Sunni Islam does not have an organized priesthood or ecclesiastical hierarchies, as noted before. Any believer may lead group prayers. However, before the war state-appointed *mullahs*, chosen with the consensus of the local communities, led prayers at local mosques. Mullahs have traditionally been supported in part by state subsidies and in part by their local communities, which provide room and board as well as a portion of their annual crops.

The task of the mullah is to instruct members of the community in the proper performance of rituals and appropriate conduct as Muslims. Most mullahs have only a slight amount of religious training, usually under another mullah in a mosque school. Their knowledge of the principle religious texts (most know parts of the Qu'ran by memory) and Islamic law allows them to function both as arbiters in village disputes as well as religious teachers who instruct village boys in reading the Qu'ran and the correct performance of rituals. The mullah also oversees the rituals associated with initiation of newborn children, marriage, and death.

Other religious specialists include the *muezzin*, individuals who call the faithful to prayer. Individuals who are able to recite the

Qur'an, are called *qari*, and those who have committed the entire sacred text to memory, are known as *hafiz*. The services of both are sought during times of crises, such as funerals. Another religious figure is the *Sayyid*, an individual who claims descent from the Prophet, thereby commanding a degree of religious esteem. In addition, there are a variety of religious mendicants, such as the malang, who are sometimes associated with the Sufi brotherhoods.

Finally, there are the learned religious scholars or ulama. By virtue of their specialist training members of the ulama serve as judges, called *qazi*, and canonical lawyers, called *mufti*. Before the implementation of secular law codes, beginning with the reign of Amanullah Khan, legislation was based upon the opinions and rulings of the ulama. The power of the ulama was greatly undermined by Abdul Rahman Khan who incorporated them into the state administrative structure and put them on salaries. The state also took over the education of judges and lawyers. The king himself adopted the role of ultimate arbiter in cases where sharia law was unclear. However, the religious and political authority of the ulama varied during different regimes and events in Afghanistan. For example, opposition by mullahs to the voluntary unveiling of women in 1959 was easily put down. In 1964 the Constitution transformed Afghanistan into a secular state by declaring Islam the state religion, but stressing the primacy of secular law over sharia law, with the latter applicable only in cases where secular laws failed to apply or appropriate secular legislation did not exist. The 1977 Constitution declared Afghanistan an Islamic state, but the Penal Code of 1976 and the Civil Law of 1977 both stressed the primacy of secular law, with the stipulation that sharia be applied where secular legislation failed to apply or appropriate secular legislation did not exist.

In Afghanistan Islam has generally served as a unifying force that, despite sectarian variations, has overridden the many ethnic, cultural, and linguistic differences among the Afghan people. Muslim identity was the basis of the popular opposition to the Soviet invasion. Muslim identity did not, however, serve as the basis of a pan-Afghan constituency in the period following the Soviet withdrawal, when factionalism, interregional competition, ethnic polarization, and sectarian rivalries plunged the country into a bloody and debilitating civil war leaving the already war-torn nation in ruins.

One of the major effects of the anti-Soviet jihad was the Islamization and Talibanization of Afghanistan as a result of the introduction of hitherto alien strands of highly politicized Islam into the country. Talibanization is characterized by an emphasis upon the reconstitution of the ummah, a call for jihad to liberate Muslim countries from the grip of nonbelievers (hence militancy), and a simplistic sharia-based view of Islam, which is reduced to a ready-made code of behavior, such as mode of dress, specific length of beard, enforced compliance of rituals, segregation of women, and an extreme anti-Shi'a and anti-West perspective.

POLITICAL EVOLUTION OF THE MODERN AFGHAN STATE

The foundation of the modern Afghan state is credited to the reign of Abdul Rahman Khan (1880–1901), who accepted the frontiers imposed upon Afghanistan by the British and Russians and began to consolidate his hold over the country. The amir used foreign military aid to create a professional national army and put into place the bureaucratic instrumentalities of state, tasks beyond the resources of traditional tribal leaders and power holders.[40]

The coercive powers with which the British endowed the amir enabled him to conduct a series of ruthless and bloody military campaigns over the course of 16 years, during which he crushed local warlords, shattered tribal strongholds, played tribe against tribe, and extended the power of the central government over local peoples. As part of this process he relocated

Pashtuns among non-Pashtun populations. To make up for shortfalls in state expenditures not covered by the annual subsidies from the British, the amir used his coercive powers to extract taxes from local landlords. The rule of Abdul Rahman Khan, who became known as the "Iron Amir," was marked by terror and was among the bloodiest in the country's history.

Abdul Rahman portrayed himself as the defender of the faith engaged in war against infidels, thereby employing religion to legitimize his activities. He claimed to rule by divine mandate, rather than tribal affiliation. Toward this end, he constructed an Islamic state and made sharia the law of the land to be administered by state-appointed judges. The religious leadership, or ulama, was inducted into the state bureaucracy and put on government salaries. Religious endowments, called *waqf*, that traditionally supported the spiritual leaders reverted to the state. The ulama were compelled to recognize the divine source of the king's authority and the Friday sermon, or *khutba*, was read in his name. The amir could use the ulama to ratify state actions, which elevated their prestige, but at the same time curbed the influence of these traditional power holders. With the religious establishment thus harnessed to his cause, the amir could denounce all opposition, whether tribal elders, mullahs, or aristocrats as enemies of Islam who were to be punished accordingly.

While Abdul Rahman established the essentials for a modern state, at the same time he adopted an isolationist policy and opposed the introduction of modern means of transportation and communications. This hampered economic development and linkages to the outside world, thereby setting limits on the extent to which the state could expand further. Intent upon maintaining Afghan independence, the amir was determined to preserve the fastness of his mountain domain as a barrier against outside intervention. Thus, the railroad, the very icon of modernity that stretched toward Afghanistan from British India and Russian Central Asia, terminated before crossing its borders. This not only hindered the development of a national market system, crucial to state building, but it also relegated Afghanistan to the hinterlands of the developing global economic system during the late nineteenth century.

The effect of these circumstances was that nation building and the continued existence of the Afghan state itself became dependent to a considerable degree upon revenues supplied by external sources. This not only resulted in a particular type of state structure and institutional pattern, but also affected the nature and development of state apparatus and its articulation or interface with society at large. The result was the emergence of what has been termed a "rentier state," a polity that depends primarily upon foreign aid, rather than on earnings generated through the extraction of taxes or the economic output of its own citizens. Under these conditions, no particular level of internal economic development or level of industrialization is necessary before state formation can occur. A powerful bureaucratic apparatus can be forged in the absence of state constituencies in civil society and institutionalized negotiating mechanisms between the ruling elites in urban centers and those they govern. Nor do these circumstances warrant the need to dismantle traditional social groups, tribal and clan structures in rural areas that are potential rivals for power and sources of resistance to state interests.

In a rentier state, the state's capacities to penetrate society and exercise its extractive and regulatory powers—such as taxation, the appropriation of resources for state purposes, regulation of social relations, and delivery of services—are not fully operative. The interface of the state with traditional communities that comprise the basis of society, whether in legislative, extractive, or service delivery sectors, is minimal at best. Under these circumstances the state's success in achieving compliance depends upon two factors: the resources at its disposal either to placate or coerce compliance; and the type of solidarity groups present within society and their capacity for mounting resistance against state policies.

Such were the characteristics of the state instrumentalities with which Afghanistan entered the twentieth century. The Great Game ended with the signing of the 1907 Anglo-Russian Convention in which both parties agreed on noninterference in Afghanistan's internal affairs. The 1917 Bolshevik Revolution and the emergence of the USSR altogether ended the imperial rivalries in Central Asia that gave rise to the Afghan state.

Abdul Rahman died in 1901. His eldest son, Habibullah Khan, succeeded him and ruled until he was assassinated in 1919. Habibullah was more secure in power and less inclined to rule by terror and repression. He eased the tight controls his father had imposed upon religious leaders and allowed them to exercise greater influence upon the state polity. Thus the accumulated capital of fear generated by Abul Rahman dissipated and this considerably weakened the monarchy, which became evident during the reign of Habibullah's son. At the same time, the king encouraged what would be the start of a reform and modernization program.

Habibullah's son Amanullah Khan (1919–1929) became the new king upon his father's death. Amanullah had a far-reaching vision of modernizing the country and instituting major social reforms.[41] A few months after ascending to the throne he took advantage of political unrest in the Punjab and Britain's post–World War I weakness, proclaimed independence, and invaded British India, starting the Third Afghan-Anglo War, called *Jang-i Istiqlal* (War of Independence). This move created a coalition of supporters that included tribal leaders, nationalist and modernist elements, and the ulama, who declared the war a jihad against the infidels and proclaimed the king the defender of Islam.

Although the Afghans were defeated militarily, they won a political victory. The brief war led to an armistice and the new king obtained independence from the British. This meant that Afghanistan now controlled its own diplomatic affairs. However, Amanullah was unable to gain the control Afghanistan greatly sought over the Pashtun tribal areas on the British Indian side of the Durand Line. Independence also marked the termination of British subsidies with which Amanullah's grandfather had founded the Afghan state.

Amanullah attempted to transform Afghanistan from a rentier state to a modern nation state. In order to do this he attempted to create effective mechanisms for taxation, stimulate a cash-based economy, set plans for a national railway system, and implement other necessary socioeconomic and political changes. Isolationism was ended with the signing of the Russo-Afghan Friendship treaty with the Bolsheviks in 1921 as well as the establishment of close diplomatic relations with France, Germany, Italy, Turkey, and Iran.

In 1923 the king introduced the country's first constitution that set forth the legislative basis for the government, the first effort toward the development of a constitutional monarchy. In contrast to the position of the previous dynasts, under Amanullah the monarchy was to be based on a national mandate, rather than supernatural sanctions, or agreements among tribal chieftains. According to the constitution all subjects of the king, regardless of ethnic and tribal affiliations or religion, were citizens of the state of Afghanistan and entitled to equal rights under the law. The power of the ulama was curbed by the imposition of secular ordinances over sharia law, as well as placing limitations upon religious education and the madrassa system. In addition, slavery was abolished and all citizens were guaranteed free universal education through a national school system with a modern secular curriculum. Amanullah also established schools for girls. Moreover, the new constitution prohibited child marriages and gave women equal rights in marriage, divorce, and inheritance, as well as the right to vote. Under the law it was now legal for women to give up the veil, or chadari, in favor of Western-style clothing.

The ideals and values driving the administration's modernization efforts were intended to strengthen Islam against the forces of colonial domination and were in line with pan-Islamic reform movements inspired by the examples set by Turkey and Iran. However, these values were incompatible with the traditional values and interests associated with tribal affiliations and they jeopardized Pashtun dominance. For Afghanistan's parochial and conservative religious establishment and traditionalist tribal interest groups the duty of the king as defender of Islam was to forge a community of Muslims, or ummah, a community governed by sharia law, not to steer the country toward modernization and westernization, which they deemed inimical to the precepts of Islam. Pashtun tribal chiefs and the religious orthodoxy were therefore equally antagonized by the proposed reforms.

The social and political capital Amanullah had accrued as defender of the faith and unifier of tribal groups when he secured independence from British hegemony was spent. He was now seen as a kafir, or infidel, an enemy of Islam. Amanullah's financial resources were inadequate for dealing with the type of responses his policies evoked. Also, his government did not have broad-based civil constituencies or well-developed institutionalized negotiating mechanisms (characteristic of the rentier state inherited from Abdul Rahman Khan) to ameliorate the resistance to its policies.

In 1928, tribal uprisings broke out in the east and north of the country, stirred up by mullahs calling for a jihad against Amanullah's modernist government, which they declared anti-Islamic. Success or failure in imposing change from above depended upon the cohesiveness of the administrative apparatus and its monopoly over the instruments of coercion to squelch opposition, circumstances remarkably similar to those encountered by the communist regime that came into power in 1978. For Amanullah, state instrumentalities failed because he had neglected to ensure the strength and loyalty of his military, which was in disarray because of budget cuts and bad council from Turkish military advisors. The underpaid and demoralized national army did not take action. Some units defected.

Amanullah was forced out of Kabul in 1929 by a "brigand" force from the Kohistan region to the north, led by a Tajik named Habibullah Kalakani, popularly known as *Bacha-i-Saqaw*, or "the water carrier's son." He had the strong backing of the ulama in the north and initially those in the capital city, especially the Hazrat of Shor Bazar, who headed the Naqshbaniyah Sufi order. Saqaw portrayed himself not as a tribal leader, but as a defender of Islam. He was crowned by the Pir of Tagao, the spiritual leader of Kohistan, rather than by tribal elders, and assumed the title of Amir Habibullah *Khadim-i-Din-i-Rasul-i-Allah* ("he who serves the religion of the prophet of Allah"), an epithet that appeared on coins minted during his brief reign, signifying his religious mandate.

Habibullah immediately overturned all of Amanullah's reforms. In scenes foreshadowing the capture of Kabul by the antimodernist Taliban in 1996, the amir implemented sharia law and restored Muslim clerics to their previous roles as judges and religious teachers. Secular schools were shut down, Western clothing was banned, and women were forced to don the chadari. The remaining relatives and followers of the king were executed, houses were looted, and the people of Kabul were subjected to unspeakable cruelties. Finally, museums and libraries, the icons of modernity, were sacked. After a failed attempt to regain power Amanullah left for Italy, never to return.

What followed were nine months of complete anarchy and bloodshed, when central authority collapsed and the country fell under the control of bandits and local tribal warlords. Pashtun tribes, although opposed to the Tajik usurper, were hopelessly divided and were unable to act in unison. Eventually Pashtun unity formed around the leadership of Nadir Khan, a Durrani aristocrat and a former general of Amanullah, who at the time was living in France. His political capital was the distinction he had earned during the Third Anglo-Afghan war. Nadir Khan and his brothers entered Afghanistan with help from the British in India, who were alarmed over the anarchy in the country, raised a *lashkar*, or tribal army, and attacked the forces of Saqaw. This was not a religious war—Saqaw had in fact overturned all the policies that had antagonized the mullahs—but rather an effort to reestablish Pashtun rule over the country. Kabul fell and Saqaw was deposed and executed late in 1929 along with his brothers and inner circle of supporters.

Some writers have drawn comparisons between the fall of the Tajik bandit Habibullah under the attack of Pashtun tribesmen and that of Tajik President Burhanuddin Rabbani and his military commander the Tajik Ahmad Shah Massoud in 1996, who were driven out of power by the Pashtun Taliban. The main difference was that Nadir Khan restored the monarchy, whereas the Taliban set up their version of a theocracy.

Following his victory, Nadir Khan was proclaimed king and Durrani rule was restored under the Musahiban dynasty, whose members would govern Afghanistan as king until 1973, and president until 1978. Nadir Khan sent Pashtun tribal armies to squelch the remaining Tajik rebel holdouts, thus restoring a semblance of order. The new ruler of Afghanistan took control at a time when state power had collapsed and tribal and religious leaders had reemerged as major power holders. Moreover, since the Musahiban came to power with the help of tribal Pashtuns, they were forced to compromise rather than contest the political power of these groups. This is evident in the 1931 constitution, which made Nadir Khan's family the ruling dynasty. A consultative body, the Loya Jirga, composed of tribal leaders, to be called upon regarding major policy changes, was established. This in effect reincorporated back into Afghan politics tribal leaders who had been excluded from administrative power by Abdul Rahman and his son and grandson. Nadir Khan also rewarded the particular tribes that had helped him come to power by exempting them from taxation and service in the military.

The constitution stipulated that Hanafi Islam was the official religion, and sharia the law of the land. The ulama were granted representation in the Loya Jirga to evaluate legislation and religious judges were given considerable independence. Secular courts, however, were allowed to operate in parallel to religious courts and the drastic punishments, hudud and qisas, prescribed under sharia law became progressively rare. The king attempted to placate religious leaders further by rescinding Amanullah's policies regarding veiling, polygyny, education for girls, and voting rights and equality of women.

Although the constitution specified the role of both tribal leaders and the religious orthodoxy in Afghan politics, it granted them symbolic roles, with no real authority. In reality it was the king and his brothers who were in complete control over the implementation of policy and they basically ruled Afghanistan as a family oligarchy.[42]

The Musahiban's strategy was to superimpose an administrative structure centered in Kabul upon traditional society, enveloping it without directly challenging traditional power holders or reconfiguring society from above. Tribal chiefs and ulama were allowed to exercise great autonomy over their local affairs. This created a bifurcation between an urban-based modernizing state structure, and a rural society that loosely articulated with state apparatus. The weakness and fragile and unstable nature of such a state structure became clear in how quickly Cold War rivalries shattered the Afghan state.

Nadir Shah, in a pattern to be followed by his successors, sought ways of tapping the global system and interstate relations for the resources with which to rebuild state power. He established diplomatic relations with major European powers and signed the Soviet-Afghan Treaty of Neutrality and Mutual Non-Aggression in 1931. To balance this, he accepted a cash and arms subsidy from the British with which he began to recreate a military. The Kabul University was established in 1932. The king also undertook the task of rebuilding the economy, established a national bank, and encouraged the development of export goods, such as cotton, dried fruit, and karakul lambskins. The Musahiban rulers began increasingly to rely upon revenues generated from taxes imposed upon international export of these commodities, and on the monopolies the state established on the import of petroleum and tobacco.

Nadir Khan's monarchy came to a sudden end when he was assassinated in 1933. His nineteen-year-old son Mohammad Zahir succeeded him, but real political power remained in the hands of Nadir's brothers, Hashim Khan, Shah Mahmud, and Shah Wali. Efforts at state building continued over the next 20 years, the bureaucracy expanded and the national army was slowly bolstered. However, the strength of the armed forces relative to tribal power was still uneven, preventing the central government from imposing upon tribal leaders a state-controlled system of military conscription.

The Afghan State and Foreign Aid

During the 1930s foreign economic aid came from Germany, France, Italy, and Japan for the development of a modern infrastructure. The educational system was expanded with assistance from France, Germany, and Britain in order to train a new generation of civil administrators necessary to operate the expanding state bureaucracy.

German assistance increased dramatically during this period with cash subsidies and the deployment of a large number of technical experts to supervise the construction of dams, bridges, governmental buildings, and hydroelectric plants. These efforts generated considerable pro-German sentiment within the Afghan government. Nevertheless, with the outbreak of World War II, Afghanistan declared neutrality. The British and Soviet governments, however, were wary of the close Afghan–German relationships and the presence of several hundred Germans between their respective territories and issued an ultimatum demanding their expulsion from Afghanistan. Refusal of a similar ultimatum had led to military action against Iran, and the Afghan government had to comply.

The international threats during World War II enabled the Musahibans to obtain tribal support for a centrally coordinated system of military conscription, something they had long sought, but were wary of implementing earlier. This, along with efforts to improve equipment and training, made the royal army a more effective fighting force compared to any potential internal armed force.

The post–World War II period was marked by major shifts in global political and military patterns that would impact Afghanistan in a number of ways. Several events were of particular significance: the withdrawal of the British from India in 1947, the emergence of the victorious Soviet Union as a superpower that began tightening its control over Central Asia, and the ensuing Cold War between the United States and the USSR.

Cold War Rivalries and Afghanistan

During the partition of British India in 1947, the Afghan government questioned the legitimacy of the Durand Line as an international boundary and called for the establishment of an autonomous tribal state of Pashtunistan, in what is now Pakistan's North-West Frontier province. The rationale was that just as Pakistan was allowed to gain its independence from India, so too the Pashtuns should be granted independence from Pakistan to form their own homeland, to be called Pashtunistan, "land of the Pashtuns."[43] Such an entity, it was assumed, would ally itself with Pashtun-ruled Afghanistan to create a greater Pashtunistan.

Afghanistan's objections went unheeded by the British and Pakistan was created with the disputed tribal areas within its national boundaries. The Afghan government's support for Pashtun independence became the major point of contention between the two countries. A propaganda war ensued to which Pakistan reacted by delaying the flow of Afghan exports. The Pashtunistan issue continued to worsen diplomatic relations between Afghanistan and Pakistan. The dispute became embedded in the Cold War competition between the United States, which allied itself with Pakistan, and the Soviet Union, which took up the Afghan cause regarding Pashtunistan.[44] The Afghans turned to the Soviet Union, their neighbor for favorable trade agreements that allowed the exchange of wool and cotton for petroleum, cement, cotton cloth, and other supplies previously obtained via Pakistan.

It was at this time that Soviets began oil exploration in northern Afghanistan, eventually leading to the discovery of natural gas deposits, which, between 1967 and 1973, the Soviets purchased for under half the world market price. The Soviets also constructed military airports in the north of Kabul at Bagram, the airfield now being used by the United States military, and in Jalalabad. The Kabul international airport was also built by the Soviets.

Afghan rulers also turned for help to the United States, the other superpower, which they saw as a counterbalance to the USSR. However, at the time the United States had little interest in Afghanistan, which it viewed as being strategically insignificant. The United States did assist in minor construction projects including an international airport and two major dams; however, the Americans denied Afghan requests for military aid. By the early 1950s, when America entered into regional power rivalries it was Pakistan that became the chief recipient of U.S. economic and military assistance. Afghanistan continued to look toward the Soviet Union.

In 1953 Muhammad Daoud Khan, the king's cousin, became the prime minister. He turned to the USSR for military and economic aid. After 1956 Afghanistan became completely dependent militarily upon the Soviets, who supplied firearms, tanks, warplanes, and helicopters. They also established an officer-training program in the USSR for Afghan candidates and Soviet military personnel took up advisory roles in Afghan military academies. By the late 1950s, the bulk of the Afghan military officer corps was Soviet-trained.

By the mid-1950s the Americans also began to offer aid, in a strategy of "containing communism," so that Afghanistan would not become an exclusive Soviet preserve. For a time the United States and the USSR actually entered into a kind of help-the-Afghans competition providing aid for different types of projects in different regions of the country. For example, the Soviet Union funded road-building projects north of the Hindu Kush, an area bordering its Muslim republics. One road extended from the Soviet border along western Afghanistan to Herat and Kandahar, across some of the stretch of land in which in the mid-1990s the American oil company UNOCAL wanted to construct an oil and gas pipeline with the help of the Taliban regime. The other road went to Mazar-i-Sharif and across the Hindu Kush Mountains through the Salang Tunnel onto Kabul, which offers the fastest passage across the mountains.

The United States constructed roads in the south of the country, linking Afghanistan to Pakistan and Iran, the major U.S. allies in the region. One of these roads connected Kabul to Kandahar; the other linked the capital to Jalalabad up to the Pakistani frontier.

The Daoud period marked the beginning of social and economic reform programs that had been put on hold since the disastrous outcome of Amanullah's efforts. Daoud had built a strong and loyal military force and secret police with the help of the Soviets and used them as instruments of repression to bolster his reforms. Among these reforms was to make veiling by women voluntary. Daoud challenged the delegation of religious leaders who raised objections to provide him with evidence in the sharia for the veil, which they could not. Riots followed nonetheless, stirred up by the religious leadership. These were swiftly crushed by military force and the way was opened for women to enter the urban workforce. Daoud's economic reforms were only mildly successful and foreign aid still constituted the bulk of the government's revenue.

Daoud also continued to push the issue of Pashtunistan. Escalating tensions between Pakistan and Afghanistan over the matter nearly led to war on several occasions and resulted in Pakistan breaking diplomatic links with Afghanistan in 1961 and sealing its borders. A propaganda war continued over the issue for the next two years. The crisis ended when Dauod was forced by the royal family to resign as prime minister in 1963, and mediation by the Shah of Iran led to reestablishment of diplomatic relations. For the time being Dauod was out of the political picture, but he would subsequently make a dramatic comeback.

The issue of Pashtunistan eventually died out, although thereafter the Punjabi (i.e., non-Pashtun) rulers of Pakistan and their military continued to perceive Afghanistan as a serious threat. These perceptions greatly affected Pakistani policies regarding Afghanistan during the war against the Soviets, during the formation of the post-Soviet government, and were among the reasons for Pakistan's financial and military backing of the Taliban.

During his time in office, Daoud had energetically pursued foreign funding from both the Americans and the Russians. But the flow of external aid into Afghanistan from these two sources was highly disproportionate. From the mid-1950s to 1978, the Soviet Union poured in roughly over a billion dollars in economic aid and an equivalent amount in the form of military aid. The United States' contribution was roughly half a billion in economic assistance.

During this period the United States perceived the growing Soviet influence in Afghanistan as irritating, but not particularly threatening as long as Afghanistan remained a sovereign neutral state. At this point, Soviet Afghan policies were thought to be merely defensive given the long border shared between the two countries. The United States' primary interests lay in the Persian Gulf and its oil reserves, which it was able to safeguard through the shah of Iran, who provided all the necessary operational bases and intelligence facilities. Besides Iran, the United States had Pakistan as its other significant South Asian ally in the region. The Soviet Union and India, Pakistan's archrival, formed a competing alliance system. Afghanistan fell between these two alliance systems. Thus, geopolitically Afghanistan continued in the position of a kind of buffer state through the mid-twentieth century, hemmed in between the competing alliance systems, which pulled developing countries into webs of economic and military dependency. Round two of the Great Game was thus under way.

The New Democracy and the Nature of the Afghan State

Following Daoud's resignation, King Zahir Shah finally assumed direct political power. In 1964 he unveiled a new constitution, marking a period called the "New Democracy." The constitution stipulated the primacy of secular law over sharia law, the equality of men and women, freedom of the press, and the legality of political activism, as long as it did not violate Islamic law. Although Islam was declared the state religion and sharia law admitted in cases where secular legislation was inapplicable, the constitution transformed Afghanistan into a secular state. It also called for the establishment of an elected parliament. Members of the royal family could no longer hold key political offices, such as prime minister, member of parliament, judge in the supreme court, or head a political party.

The foreign aid that flowed into Afghanistan enabled the state to extend its organizational bureaucratic apparatus, modernize and expand the national army, and extend its influence. However, it still lacked local political support from tribal, clan, and ethnic leaders in the countryside. Although rural populations in Afghanistan were armed and only under indirect control of the central government, many groups had been disarmed and most of the firearms still in the hands of local tribesmen were antiquated or handmade and the capacity of rural people to wage war was very limited. In contrast, the state now possessed strong coercive instrumentalities and a well-equipped modern army and police force, and it was able not only to effectively repress political opponents and squelch tribal rebellions, but also to ensure law and order throughout most of the country. Thus, the state was insulated from the tribal power holders that had toppled earlier dynasts and dynasties. The threat to the state's political stability did not emanate from the rural areas, but rather from the new social strata created by the needs of the expanding administrative apparatus made possible by massive foreign aid, namely an educated elite trained by state-supported institutions funded by foreign subsidies and scholarships to foreign countries, whose members were to serve as administrative and military personnel. They represented a new social phenomenon brought into being by the needs of the modern Afghan state, and whose identities, statuses, and fortunes became vested in the continued increase of the power of the state at the expense of the interests of other groups.

The New Urban Elite and the State

The long-term objective of Afghan rulers was that the new educated elite would not only assist in the administration of the government, but also penetrate and bring about social transformation of rural society. However, as the numbers of individuals flocked to urban areas to take advantage of new educational opportunities and the number of educated elites increased, so did their expectations, ambitions, and frustrations over the lack of opportunities for employment and advancement. Such opportunities were not available because of elitism and widespread corruption and nepotism in which patron–client relations outweighed aptitude and talent as the means of success both in the administrative bureaucracy and in the military. Foreign aid had decreased during this period and the bureaucracy could not absorb any more personnel. As a result there was growing dissent and political discontent. Expanded freedom of the press and political activism led to the formation of unofficial political parties, including communist and Islamist ones.

The king's experiment in democracy encountered serious problems that wore away at the state's legitimacy. In 10 years five successive governments, each with a different political vision, rose and fell. There were widespread calls for reform and student protests in the capital. One of the most violent student demonstrations to take place occurred on October 25, 1965, when the Afghan military upon opened fire upon the protesters, killing several students, in what became known as the incident of the third of Aqrab, *hadisa-i sehum-i Aqrab.* Ideological alternatives were sought. The leftist People's Democratic Party of Afghanistan (PDPA) attracted some of the educated people seeking a quicker pace in social and political reform. Others, alarmed at the sociopolitical changes already in progress, which they saw as the cause of all problems, sought answers in religion and advocated a return to an Islamic society based upon sharia law. The Islamic opposition group was called the Muslim Youth, *Jawanan-i Musulman*, or more commonly the Muslim Brotherhood, *Ikhwan al-Muslimin*. Both communists and Islamists were highly critical of the ruling elite and pushed for revolutionary change, but with drastically different visions.

The PDPA was established in 1965, headed by Marxist–Leninist ideologues Nur Mohammad Taraki (1917–1979), Hafizullah Amin (1929–1979), Babrak Karmal (1929–1996), and Mrs. Anahita Ratebzad (b. 1928). It won four seats in the 1965 parliamentary elections. The party split into two factions in 1967, the *Khalq* (People) under Taraki, which was supported by Pashtuns from the rural areas, and the *Parcham* (The Flag) led by Karmal, which attracted followers from the urban educated elite. The two factions shared the same set of objectives, which included implementation of an ambitious set of socioeconomic and political reforms, reordering gender relations, and a commitment to end the disparities in landholding and wealth. The main doctrinal difference between the two was a strategic one, with Khalq's stressing class warfare by any means to secure power, while Parcham emphasized the use of existing democratic political avenues and operating within the existing system to achieve its political objectives. However, deep-seated personal animosities between Amin and Karmal, which extended down the rank and files of both groups, also contributed to the rift between the two factions.

Professors from the Sharia Faculty of the Kabul University led the Islamists. Some were the product of the government-sponsored higher education, rather than the traditional religious schools, or madrassas. They considered themselves intellectuals, *roshanfiker*, rather than part of the traditional ulema. Their advanced training was at the renowned Al-Azhar University in Cairo, where they were exposed to the ideas of Sayyid Qutb and to members of the Egyptian Muslim Brotherhood, the Islamist movement whose aim is to create Islamic states throughout the Muslim world. Recruiting from the Muslim Youth, the professors formed a movement called *Jamiat-i Islami*, or "Islamic Society." Gulbuddin Hekmatyar, an engineering student and a person of considerable notoriety (known for throwing acid on female university students for wearing miniskirts and other crimes such as murder), was put in charge of political activities. The Jamiat-i Islami operated underground and its members sought to spread Islamist ideology among the student body at the university and to refute the Marxists on campus. Their main activities included organizing demonstrations against the government and the Marxists. The Islamists sought to overthrow the Musahiban rulers, who they accused of corruption and for subverting Islam.

Compounding the political unrest of the period, between 1971 and 1972 Hazarajat and northern Afghanistan suffered a devastating drought and widespread famine to which the government failed to respond adequately, revealing its ineffectiveness. Finally, in July 1973 Mohammad Daoud, the king's cousin and brother-in-law and former prime minister, overthrew the monarchy while the king was in Italy for medical treatment.[45] The coup was nearly bloodless and the majority of Afghans welcomed the shift in political power. This was the key event that would transform the remote, landlocked, impoverished Afghanistan into the central battlefield of the Cold War, sparking off one of the most destructive conflicts of the twentieth century. Daoud's coup d'état was achieved with the backing of the Soviet-trained military officers and the moderate wing of the Afghan communist party (PDPA), the Parcham faction.[46]

Daoud abolished the constitution of 1964, declared Afghanistan a republic, and named himself the president. Although he came to power with the support of the communists, many of whom were initially given posts in his cabinet, in time Daoud began replacing them with loyalists and members of his own family.[47]

He also began to take increasingly repressive measures to consolidate his grasp on power. Daoud constructed the massive Puli Charkhi Prison just outside the capital, where many of his political opponents perished while incarcerated. It was soon evident that the new ruler of Afghanistan was not steering a course to the left or right, but was in the pursuit of personal power. He alienated not only the Marxists but also the moderates and the Islamists.

Daoud's effortless coup, proclaimed as *inqilab*, or "revolution," set a dangerous precedent in Afghan politics. First, it destroyed the symbolism of the monarchy that had for so long served as a source of legitimacy. Second, it inspired and mobilized other political contenders, Islamists and Marxists alike, to contemplate bigger and better revolutions of their own as an easy shortcut to political power.

The first overt antigovernment activities came from the Islamist party, the Jamiat-i Islami. The Islamists rebelled against what they perceived to be Daoud's "atheistic reforms." In 1975 they launched a failed uprising, called the Panjshir Valley Incident. Similar Islamist efforts were met with popular hostility and were easily crushed. The state's reservoir of legitimacy had not yet been depleted. Daoud responded by imprisoning many members of the Islamist party, forcing its leadership, Rabbani, Hekmatyar, and Sayyaf, to flee to Pakistan. There, Hekmatyar and other Islamist groups developed. Pakistan's government began to support the Islamists in anticipation of using them in case Daoud rekindled the Pashtunistan issue.

Meanwhile the purge of communists in the government continued. By year's end they had all been removed from office. Daoud also started purging the military of communists and dismissed 40 Soviet-trained Parcham officers and exiled others to remote posts in the countryside. He also arranged for new military training for Afghan officers in Turkey, India, and Egypt.

Daoud began to distance himself more and more from the Soviets and attempted to expand his international support by establishing closer ties with the West and other Muslim countries, such as Saudi Arabia, Egypt, Pakistan, and Iran.[48] In 1975 the shah of Iran, acting as a proxy for the United States, offered Daoud a massive economic aid package amounting to $2 billion and established plans for the construction of a railroad linking Kabul, Khandahar, and Herat to Iranian railway lines that would give access to the Persian Gulf, which would end Afghanistan's dependence on Soviet trade. Daoud also tried to resolve the difference with Pakistan over the Pashtunistan issue, which he had rekindled when he assumed power, and reached some tentative agreements.

Daoud's 1977 constitution ratified by a Loya Jirga, from which PDPA members were excluded, outlawed the PDPA, and made Afghanistan into a one-party state under Daoud's own National Revolutionary Party. By this time Daoud's relations with Moscow had become extremely strained. Still, it appeared the Soviets were willing to tolerate Daoud's regime for the time being; the PDPA was not.

The PDPA picked up its efforts to recruit members among the armed forces. Amin, who established widespread ties with junior officers converted to his cause, directed these activities. Daoud's purges drove many disaffected officers still in the military to the ranks of the Khalq faction. In 1977 the two factions of the PDPA agreed to join forces against Daoud and initiated plans for a coup. This unification was partly the result of Daoud's actions and partly because of Soviet pressure.

Marxist Revolutionaries and Popular Uprisings: The Road to War

The event that precipitated the coup that brought the PDPA into power was the assassination of a leading Parcham ideologue on April 17, 1978. The PDPA accused the government of complicity in the assassination and organized a massive demonstration in the streets of Kabul.

Some 10,000 to 15,000 people took part in the demonstration. Startled by the turnout, Daoud ordered the arrest of the PDPA leaders. However, PDPA elements set a coup in motion, which began on April 27, 1978, in the lunar month of *Sawr*, after which the coup leaders dubbed their seizure of power. By nightfall, Daoud and his entire family had been executed.

Many Afghans suspected that the Soviets played a part in orchestrating the coup, and there were reports of Soviet advisors accompanying the troops during ground operations. However, there is no conclusive proof that the Soviets participated in either the planning or implementation of the coup.[49]

The PDPA came to power as a result of what amounted to a small mutiny in the capital, dubbed "the Sawr Revolution," *Inqilab-i Sawr*, with the help of mid-level Soviet-trained Marxist officers in the Afghan military. The PDPA did not have a significant social constituency outside the capital, nor was it swept into power as a result of a mass uprising. Its membership was drawn from the social actors created by the state's own foreign-funded schools and government scholarships to foreign universities for training as future functionaries in the state bureaucratic apparatus and national military. Its ideological orientation was Marxist-Leninist and many party members looked toward Moscow for inspiration.

The revolution allowed the PDPA to seize control of the old rentier regime's administrative apparatus. Like those they displaced from power, the revolutionaries sought support from foreign sources, rather than from social constituencies inside the country. Thus, as the political analyst Rubin has put it, "a rentier state produced rentier revolutionaries." The Democratic Republic of Afghanistan (DRA) was born, with Taraki as president, and Amin and Babrak as deputy prime ministers.

The communists attempted to harness the state apparatus that they seized in order to implement their program of social reform, a function for which the state institutions were unsuited. The outcome was not social reform, but the disintegration of a fragile state apparatus that had been painstakingly created over the better part of a century. The continuity of the type of state apparatus the PDPA inherited was almost entirely dependent upon its internal cohesiveness and monopoly over the instruments of coercion. The course of action the new leadership embarked upon very quickly disrupted the state's administrative cohesiveness and led to a loss of control over the military.

This process began within a few months after the PDPA seized power, when the long-standing hostilities between the Khalq and Parcham factions reemerged and a serious power struggle erupted. Khalq's close ties with the military gave it the advantage. Leaders of Parcham were removed from key offices and sent on ambassadorial exiles. The leaders of the radical Khalq faction, Taraki and Amin, having emerged victors of the internal power struggle, attempted to solidify their hold on power and create "party unity" by physically exterminating their rivals on charges of sedition. Toward this end thousands of Parchamis at all levels were rounded up, imprisoned, tortured, and secretly executed. The degree and scale of violence and bloodshed was unlike any other in Afghan history, including the mass killings under Abdul Rahman Khan.

Given the fact that the PDPA did not have a broad social constituency among the Afghan population, and altogether its total membership was only a few thousand (3,000 to 4,000 according to Western observers; 15,000 according to postwar Soviet sources, and an implausible 50,000 according to PDPA's own estimate), the elimination of the Parchamis, which reduced the total number of cadres by more than half, seriously weakened the party and its ability to carry out its policies.

The Khalqis also executed ministers of the former regime, as well as scholars and religious leaders, including over 70 male members of the

Mujaddidi family of Sufis, the many Islamists jailed by Daoud, and other perceived opponents. Thousands of trained civil servants were killed or removed and replaced by unqualified PDPA members. According to a list later released by the government, 12,000 people were executed in Kabul jails during this period.

The military high command was virtually wiped out and the Parcham officers, many of them coup leaders, who replaced those purged were subsequently purged as well. By the end of 1979, more than half of the entire officer corps had either been purged, executed, or had deserted, and the Afghan army fell from a high of 90,000 to 40,000 as a result of desertions. Thus, the coherence of the military institution as a whole was badly undermined and contributed to the disintegration of the state apparatus.

The Khalqis, having eliminated the moderate wing of the party, proceeded to implement social and economic reforms from above by decree reinforced by the use of brute force. The goal was to demolish the old order and with it eliminate the "backwardness of past centuries" in a single generation through sweeping land reform, a massive literacy campaign, and a reordering of gender relations. The reforms involved cancellation of peasant debts to landlords, equitable redistribution of land, the opening of hundreds of schools and clinics in the countryside, implementation of a large-scale literacy program, a ban on child marriages, and most of all, the touchy issues over which Afghan society continues to tussle back and forth since the 1920s—schooling for girls, equality for women, and freedom of choice in marriage. The true nature of the struggle, in particular the struggle over women's rights, which was a central issue, was obscured in the West by Cold War rhetoric and geopolitics.

To ensure compliance the government used excessive force and this sparked the uprisings. The accepted pattern of interaction between the state and the local community, which developed over the course of one hundred years, was one in which local leaders, khans, maliks, and arbabs, worked to shield and defend their qawm's interests and preserve its autonomy by mediating its interactions with the state, which existed as an entity external to society. The Marxist seizure of power and the abrupt efforts to implement revolutionary transformations of Afghan society by force represented a deviation from expected norms, which provoked a violent society wide reaction. Because Afghanistan was a mosaic of microsocieties, the rebellion was disorganized with multiple foci and there were no rebel strongholds to be conquered. The government responded by increasing the levels of violence. The ruthlessness with which the Khalqis dealt with resistance was demonstrated in the village of Kerala, in the eastern province of Kunar, when government soldiers killed over one thousand unarmed villagers in a single act of reprisal.

Analysts have attributed the failure of the reforms to different factors such as the lack of rural party members in the ranks of the PDPA for grassroots campaigning; the disruption of patron–client relationships, which formed the basis of political life in rural Afghanistan; excessive use of force; or simply a cultural clash between Marxists and a resolute Islamic rural population. However, internal dynamics alone do not explain the development and the progression of the resistance. Suprisingly, anthropologists working in Afghanistan and writing about the rebellion and the war afterward invariably noted Soviet interference, but were oblivious to the massive invovement of other foreign powers that commandeered and directed the rebellion.

Poorly thought out and rapidly and incompetently implemented policies that totally disregarded the sociopolitical and economic complexities and cultural and religious sensitivities and local traditions of rural Afghanistan evoked a widespread hostile response among the rural population, just as they had during the time of Amanullah Khan. Over the course of the next several months the popular uprisings spread and there were antigovernment demonstrations in the cities and mutinies and defections in nearly all the major garrisons, including Herat and Kabul. There is evidence of U.S. support for the anti-DRA demonstrations.

The insurrection in Herat, which began in March 1979, was brutally crushed, causing 5,000 deaths, including Soviet personnel. The breakdown of units of the military further fueled the uprising. The government responded to the rising opposition with increasing brutality by escalating the scale and intensity of violence against the countryside. Taraki and Amin repeatedly began urging Moscow to send troops to help quell the uprising. The Afghan leadership made altogether 20 requests for Soviet troops in 1979. Moscow responded by sending military aid and advisors, but refused to deploy troops.

As early as April 1979 the United States began to investigate which rebel group in Pakistan should receive covert aid. At the very same time the U.S. State Department was warning the Soviets not to intervene, while the Russians were accusing the CIA of arming Afghan exiles in Pakistan, and the Afghan government was pointing the finger at Pakistan and Iran for helping rebels launch military raids inside Afghanistan. The shift in U.S. policy regarding Afghanistan was due to the fall of the shah of Iran in 1979, and with it the loss of U.S. military bases and the main obstacle to Soviet advances toward the Persian Gulf and Indian Ocean.

Meanwhile, the Soviet leadership was urging the Khalqis to slow down the pace of their reform and widen their political base by incorporating noncommunists, but to no avail. Amin, who was by now wielding complete power in Kabul, had no patience for Soviet advice. Moscow went as far as contacting members of the former monarchy and other noncommunist leaders and urged them to join the DRA government and even informed the U.S. Embassy in Kabul of their activities. With conditions rapidly deteriorating inside Afghanistan, the Soviet leadership turned to Taraki, as the more moderate of the Khalqis, to eliminate Amin and adopt a more balanced political course. Amin struck first and had Taraki arrested and executed.

SOVIET MILITARY INTERVENTION: HOW AFGHANISTAN BECAME A COLD WAR BATTLEFIELD

The situation looked grim. Moscow was intent on preventing the rise of an anticommunist state in Afghanistan. Having failed to stabilize the situation through political efforts, which demonstrated the limitation of their influence, the Soviets began to entertain a military solution, "a regime change," a concept that would become familiar to us in the context of the U.S. war in Iraq in 2003. In late December 1979 the Soviet Union invaded Afghanistan. Hafizullah Amin was overthrown and killed by Soviet Spetsnaz commandos and a new government was installed, headed by the exiled Parcham leader Babrak Karmal. The Soviet objective was to replace Amin with Karmal, end the strife within the PDPA, and remain long enough for the new regime to stabilize. The Soviets rapidly became bogged down and what was supposed to be a quick surgical operation ended up becoming a military occupation that would last for almost a decade. Very shortly Soviet forces deployed in Afghanistan increased to 85,000 and later went up to as many as 150,000 soldiers.

Proxy Wars, Jihad, and Islamization in Retrospect

The next 20 years following the Soviet invasion were brutal and traumatic and the war went through a number of transmutations: jihad during the Cold War, 1979–1989; jihad among the Afghans, 1989–1992; factional war among Afghans, 1992–1996; regional proxy war and the Taliban, 1996–2001; Osama bin Laden and the war against terrorism, October–December 2001 to the present.

In the first phase, the war oscillated between mujahideen hit-and-run strikes, assassinations of government officials, car bombings in the cities, urban sabotage, sniper attacks, rocket strikes on military installations and towns, and Afghan–Soviet response by massive aerial bombardments, helicopter gunship attacks, mine-sowing operations, razing of entire villages, infliction of massive civilian casualties, and bribes and civic action campaigns from Kabul. Helicopter gunship attacks were used to depopulate strategically valuable terrain and in punitive assaults against villages and their civilian inhabitants. One consequence of such violence was the dislocation of millions of civilians, the muhajereen, or refugees, who fled to Pakistan and Iran. As the fighting progressed, each side and its external sponsors escalated the scale and intensity of the violence.

The ideological and material conditions for the conflict were created by the interaction of regional and global powers (often with conflicting agendas and strategic designs) that not only provoked the Soviet invasion of Afghanistan, but also cast the conflict solely in terms of a religious or holy war, and created an international alliance of countries to facilitate the recruitment, arming, and training of radical militant jihadis from around the world to fight it. This alliance was led by the United States with the help of Saudi Arabia, Pakistan, Egypt, the Gulf states, Britain, France, and China.

The true nature of the roles played by external super and regional powers in escalating the scale and intensity of the violence and destruction in Afghanistan has recently come to light and provides insight into the role of the interstate system and its web of interdependencies on the nature of modern war. Several things are now certain.[50] Contrary to the "official version" of events, the United States began its intervention in Afghanistan, authorized by President Jimmy Carter July 3, 1979, *six months* before the Soviet invasion on December 25, 1979. As Zbigniew Brzezinski, National Security Advisor to Jimmy Carter, acknowledged in 1998, the CIA aid was directed to support the mujahideen to provoke an inevitable Soviet military response. Brzezinski also stated that the aim was "to give the USSR its own Vietnam," by drawing them "into the Afghan trap." Soon the Islamist resistance movement found itself the beneficiary of masses of weapons and money from the United States and its allies.

While actively fueling the Afghan jihad with guns and cash, the United States refused to merge its massive support to the mujahideen with United Nation peace initiatives that could have resulted in an earlier Soviet withdrawal. No one in the U.S. government was advocating diplomacy as a means of resolving the conflict. When Ronald Reagan took office in 1980 he adopted an aggressive hard-line policy, which amounted to making the Soviet occupation costly and untenable by "fighting to the last Afghan."

Afghanistan thus became the battlefield in which the United States would fight a proxy war with its Cold War rival using an army of Muslim mercenaries recruited from around the globe in the name of Islamic solidarity. This attracted men like Osama bin Laden, who came with large bank accounts to join the jihad and would go on to establish a global terrorist network. The Afghan jihad attracted radical Muslims from over 50 countries, including Muslim communities in Europe and the United States. These recruits included many unsavory characters who were violent extremists and others were hardened criminals freed from jails in their home countries such as Egypt, Algeria, and Jordan, on the condition that they fight in the Afghan jihad.

These men trained and fought with the Afghan mujahideen and received religious training in the Deobandi madrassas set up on the Afghan frontier by the Pakistanis with the financial backing of donors from the Middle East. Afghanistan and Pakistan became the wellsprings of militant Islamic radicalism, where recruits from the Middle East, Africa, and South Asia were indoctrinated, trained to fight, provided logistical support, and were linked together in a transnational network. The Cold War agenda distracted many in the West from assessing the long-term implications of facilitating an international coalition of radical Islamists in the cause of the Afghan jihad.

A related phenomenon was the politicization of the refugees in Pakistan. Aid from the United States and its allies to the Afghan refugees was channeled through the Islamic parties supported by the Pakistan's military intelligence (ISI). Eligibility for aid was contingent upon membership in one of the seven Islamist political parties officially recognized by Pakistan, which led to the politicization of the aid distribution process by forcing men to join the parties and agree to take part in the jihad. To do otherwise would lead to the cancellation of party membership and the end of rations. The refugee population in Pakistan, which at the peak of the emigration numbered four million, thus became a sizable captive reservoir of manpower from which the mujahideen could recruit fighters.

Madrassas in Pakistan soon began teaching children in the refugee camps mujahideen ideology. The United States also contributed to energize and direct this effort. The Education Program for Afghanistan at the University of Nebraska, Omaha, funded by a $50 million grant from the United States Agency for International Development (September 1986 to June 1994) produced textbooks that were designed to stir up Islamic fervor and drive home the jihadi message of "violence for the sake of Islam." The books were filled with illustrations of bullets, landmines, grenade launchers, and mujahideen bearing Kalashnikovs (the main automatic rifle supplied by the United States). These textbooks remained at the core of the curriculum in Afghanistan long after the Russians left.

A whole generation was brought up absorbing the messages contained in these texts, which extol jihad against atheist oppressors and exhort little children to pluck out the enemy's eyes, cut off the enemy's legs, and kill the enemy wherever he is found. To cite a few examples, the Persian alphabet is taught in a first-grade textbook in the following form: "A is for Allah, J is for Jihad, R is for our religion of Islam and the Russians are the enemies of the religion of Islam." A third-grade mathematics book includes the following kind of problems:

> One group of mujahideen attack 50 Russian soldiers. In that attack 20 Russians were killed. How many Russians fled?

A fourth-grade mathematics book includes the following:

> The speed of a Kalishnikov bullet is 800 meters per second. If a Russian is at a distance of 3,200 meters from a mujahid, and that mujahid aims at the Russian's forehead, calculate how many seconds it will take the bullet to strike the Russian in the forehead.[51]

These texts inculcated a culture of violence.

The University of Nebraska program coordinator defended the decision to use the violent jihadi images in the schoolbooks, by stating that he did not want to impose American cultural values on Afghan education. The Taliban leaders endorsed these textbooks and adopted them for their madrassas and reprinted them for use in schools in Afghanistan once they seized power.

Disregarding the massive foreign intervention that animated and energized the Afghan war, some observers have attributed the duration and intensity of the conflict in Afghanistan to the country's internal ethnic sociopolitical dynamics, "the warrior tradition" of the Pashtun tribesmen, or Islamic fundamentalist "obsession" with jihad, or religious war. These are not credible or sufficient explanations because the Afghans were caught in circumstances over which they had little or no control. Moreover, traditional warfare in Afghanistan took the form of the feud, which was limited in nature for a number of reasons. First, it took place during spare time and not as a full-time occupation. Second, it rarely extended beyond a particular group's territory. Third, it was predicated upon mutually shared sets of rules based upon mutual knowledge.[52] Fourth, it did not result in the destruction of infrastructure. Fifth, casualties were restricted to specific individuals, and rarely involved women or children. Sixth, traditional warfare was based on antiquated locally made weapons of inferior quality, available in finite quantities, which limited the scale of destructive firepower. The type of warfare and destructive firepower that the Soviet Union and the United States fueled in Afghanistan was unprecedented.

Attributing the conflict in Afghanistan to militant Islamic fundamentalism is also erroneous. The antigovernment uprisings did not begin as an Islamist revolution, but as isolated outbreaks primarily in response to poorly thought-out and incompetently and brutally implemented social reforms imposed by the government. The nascent civil war, which was commandeered by the external forces, was over deep-seated social reforms and modernization and the response of ultratraditional patriarchical tribal chieftains and Muslim clergy, most affected by the new policies, who wanted to stop such reforms.

The Afghan Islamist parties, which the CIA and Pakistan's ISI transformed into the mujahideen, were a failed force inside Afghanistan. Their two coup attempts against the government of Dauod were utter failures. Islam as a political force in general was insignificant in Afghanistan until the United States and its allies focused and quickened it to life by creating a multi-billion-dollar arms pipeline and an international network that brought together zealous men from all over the Islamic world to fight in the Afghan jihad. In other words, Islamic militants were a *product* of the Afghan war, not its cause. The force that fought Afghanistan's rentier communist revolutionaries was itself a rentier resistance movement.

Likewise, attributing the destruction of Afghanistan solely upon the imperialistic ambitions of the Soviet Union, whose leaders it is said were intent on expanding their control over South Asia "heading for the warm-water ports of the Indian Ocean," and undertaking draconian measures to achieve their objectives, is incorrect.[53] The Soviet invasion it turns out was not part of an imperialist enterprise set into motion for the domination of the Persian Gulf. Minutes of the Politburo released after the Cold War indicate that Soviet officials repeatedly denied pleas from the Kabul government to send troops in the months before the invasion. The decision to intervene, which seems to have been a desperate attempt to prevent a perceived threat of a fundamentalist Islamic state emerging along the Soviet Union's Central Asian republics, home to approximately 40 million restless Muslims, was taken with great trepidation and was strongly opposed by several senior military and political leaders. Moreover, it now seems that the repeated Soviet claims[54] that it was combating covert U.S. intervention in Afghanistan, dismissed at the time, had much more than a grain of truth.

The implementation of what some writers have termed "the CIA's jihad"[55] involved compelling Saudi Arabia to match U.S. cash subsidies, obtaining Soviet-made weaponry from President Anwar Sadat of Egypt to establish "plausible deniability" for U.S. involvement, and making a deal with General Zia ul Haq, the military ruler of Pakistan, who would act as coordinator and conduit for the distribution of arms and money to the jihadi fighters. In charge of the secret war was Pakistan's military intelligence, the ISI, which used the massive foreign funding and logistical and technical support from the United States to establish an international jihadi infrastructure. The United

States and its allies in part supplied the Kalashnikovs that created the "Kalashnikov culture" of Afghanistan, so frightening to many in the West at the end of the twentieth century.

By the mid-1980s the Soviets began to adopt very effective and highly aggressive counterinsurgency tactics by relying on Spetsnaz special forces and heavily armored Hind Mi-24 helicopters for aerial search-and-destroy missions, with the objective of winning the war in two years. The United States responded by providing the mujahideen with American-made Stinger missiles, the world's most effective shoulder-held antiaircraft weapon. Plausible deniability was no longer a concern and for the first time advanced U.S. weapons made their way into the Afghan theater. The violence was thus increased to yet another level.

Pakistan became the staging ground for the jihad against the Soviets.[56] This translated into a massive windfall for Zia ul Haq, who was granted large U.S. cash and arms subsidies for his services. As large shipments of U.S. dollars and weaponry and other military equipment began flowing in, Zia ul Haq siphoned a significant portion of the money and materials flowing through the CIA's pipeline for Pakistani use. This enabled Zia ul Haq to consolidate and increase his power and prestige. Altogether, between 1986 and 1990 the United States and Saudi Arabia had poured in $5 billion in weapons to the mujahideen, and the Soviets $5.7 billion for arms and equipment to the Afghan government.

There were no centralized institutional controls over the weapons being passed on to the mujahideen inside Afghanistan. This resulted in an uncontrolled distribution of arms. Some of the weapons were resold, others stockpiled. As more and more weapons become available, market prices dropped and soon nearly all groups acquired large-caliber automatic weapons. Estimating the number of weapons on a per capita basis, Afghanistan became the most highly armed nation on earth.

The CIA's pipeline leaked terribly at many stages, flooding the entire region with massive quantities of arms. The CIA's arsenal was divided up in various ways before reaching the intended recipients. Some of the hardware ended up in the hands of Pakistani military. Some went to mujahideen leaders in Peshawar, who grew wealthy by selling millions of dollars' worth of the CIA's antiaircraft guns, missiles, rocket-propelled grenade launchers (RPGs), Kalashnikov AK-47 automatic rifles, thousands of landmines, and eventually Stinger missiles to criminal elements, heroin kingpins, and radical Islamic Iranian militants. This produced the phenomenon of *Kalashnikovization*, the creation of a culture of lawlessness and violence, named after the ubiquitous automatic weapon flooding the region.

Bolstered by the bounty of cash and weapons coming from the CIA-led coalition of jihad sponsors, Zia ul Haq was able to further Islamize Pakistani society and the Pakistani military, and especially the ISI, an organization that has virtually controlled Pakistan's foreign policy, including support for the Taliban and the Islamic insurgency in Kashmir.

The Islamization of Pakistan was fueled by various factors. First, it was evident that Islamic identity did not prevent independence of East Pakistan as Bangladesh in 1971, which prompted a radical fundamentalist stance by the Pakistani Islamic parties who construed this to mean that accommodation or deviation from the strictest interpretation of Islam leads to the weakening of the faith and the ummah. The perceived threat of Ayatollah Khomeini's revolution in Shi'a Iran in 1979 also contributed to radicalization of Sunni Pakistan.

Given these factors, the jihad was not going to end anytime soon—not because of the zeal for war among the Afghans, but because of the agendas of its key sponsors. The war in Afghanistan would continue as long as the enterprise remained lucrative and Zia ul Haq and ISI knew a good thing when they saw it. The Americans were also not interested in seeing an early end to the Soviet occupation because their strategic aims were being met and, unlike Vietnam, in this conflict there were no American casualties. Few in the United States, aside from the intelligence and military operatives involved in the grand orchestration of the jihad, even knew that the CIA was engaged in the largest covert operation in its history. No one among the U.S. public became aware of the conflagration taking place inside Afghanistan funded in part by their tax dollars.

Pakistan was given complete discretion regarding the deployment of the funds and arms. Zia ul Haq and the ISI ensured that only Islamist parties, who in fact represented the interests of only a small fraction of Afghans, would be beneficiaries of the largess. This strategy enabled Pakistan to divide the resistance movement and render it more prone to outside control. The chief recipient of the military aid was Hekmatyar's Hizb-i Islami party, the most radical and anti-American group, whose members were responsible for killing more fellow mujahideen than Soviet soldiers. Excluded were the supporters of the royal family, secular nationalist parties, and moderate, nationalistic Islamic groups, of which there were a number, also committed to driving the Soviets out of Afghanistan. Finding no support, these parties died out. Pakistan's objectives were to establish an Islamic client government in Afghanistan and forge an Islamic block encompassing Soviet Central Asia, thus obtaining "strategic depth" against India. None of the external players involved in the creation and perpetuation of the anti-Soviet jihad in Afghanistan ever bothered to consider the interests of the majority of Afghans who did not ask or desire this horrendous conflict brought upon them.

In addition to war, the anti-Soviet operation also brought large-scale drug trafficking to the region. The discretionary manner in which arms and weapons were being dispensed led some jihadi groups to supplement their revenues by searching for alternative sources of funding. One way of generating revenue was the production of opium and drug trafficking, which began in earnest during this period. The CIA helped establish a massive production infrastructure, making Afghanistan one of the principle sources of heroin in the world.[57] This created a burgeoning narcotics economy for the Kalashnikov culture developing in the region.

The Mujahideen in Retrospect

Washington's clients in the Afghan jihad, the mujahideen, require discussion. Western anthropologists praised them. Ronald Reagan called them "freedom fighters," and gave them U.S. dollars and weapons. Who were these "holy warriors"? This is a question that one can answer in retrospect. The mujahideen fought a holy war in the name of Islam to liberate Afghanistan. The actions of some of these individuals and their eventual victory, however, were not very holy. To achieve their objective the jihadi fighters routinely burned schools, killed school teachers, bombed health clinics, tortured and murdered unarmed civilians, persecuted religious minorities, and terrorized and brutalized whole communities through indiscriminate killing sprees.

By all accounts, many of these freedom fighters, whom Ronald Regan declared to be "the moral equivalent of our own Founding Fathers," were guilty of blatant acts of terrorism and crimes against humanity. Yet no American policy maker ever mentioned the word *terrorist* in connection with the Afghan jihadis, although that term was frequently used in reference to Khomeini's Iran. Washington was willing to overlook all of the mujahideen's unfortunate shortcomings and continued to lavish them with cash and weapons so long as they fulfilled their roles as proxy warriors against the Soviets. This Cold War mentality is well illustrated by Zbigniew Brzezinski, who when asked in 1998 whether he had any regrets about the covert war in Afghanistan and its broader consequences replied:

> Regret what? That secret operation was an excellent idea. It had the effect of drawing the Russians into the Afghan trap and you want me to regret it? What is most important to the history of the world? The Taliban or the collapse of the Soviet empire? Some stirred-up Moslems or the liberation of Central Europe and the end of the cold war?[58]

And so the war raged on through the 1980s without showing any signs of abating.

The Soviet Union withdrew its troops from Afghanistan in 1989 after signing the Geneva accords the year before.[59] The communist government under Najibullah, who succeeded Karmal in May 1986, continued to repel mujahideen attacks for another three years after the Soviets pulled out. Kabul fell in 1992, a year after the Soviet Union collapsed and all aid ceased. The rentier communist regime was no more. Najibullah resigned and took refuge in the United Nations compound and the mujahideen forces entered Kabul.

The Afghan resistance now controlled the ruins that once were Afghanistan. The Afghan people had paid a terrible price for the resistance's jihad in which literally every known modern conventional weapon of war was used. It cost the lives of one-and-a-half to two million Afghan civilians, the displacement of many more millions as refugees, and resulted in the destruction of buildings, schools, roads, dams, agricultural fields, and irrigation works, the reduction of the countryside to landmine-infested killing fields, and a surviving population living in squalor, maimed and mutilated. The destruction extended to the fragile ties that once held together the ethnolinguistically heterogeneous society, causing a breakdown of social order and a humanitarian catastrophe of massive proportions.

The refugee camps outside the country still held several million people and an entire generation of Afghans had been raised and socialized in the camps outside their homeland, products of a culture of war and a legacy of violence, never having learned the skills necessary to resume the agrarian lifestyle of their parents' generation.

The mujahideen factions faced the task of reconstituting a state. However, the war had changed Afghan society in ways that made their failure inevitable. There were no legitimate political institutions left. The norms governing violence had eroded in the context of full-scale, all-out warfare and the intensity of violence that the Afghan communists, the Soviets, and the Americans had unleashed upon Afghan society. As a result entirely different forms of military organizations, which have been called clientelistic "survival networks,"[60] had emerged. The mujahideen organizations were larger in scale than the traditional solidarity groups, included full-time permanent skilled personnel, and possessed massive destructive force. The introduction of advance military equipment in unprecedented quantities, which were widely available, endowed even small military organizations with the capacity to cause massive destruction and loss of life and contributed both to violence and criminal enterprises in Afghanistan.[61]

With the withering away of centralized authority and absence of alternate sociopolitical roles created by the destruction of traditional society and the development of a sociopolitical environment in which political contestation was determined solely by the greatest amount of military firepower, the mujahideen organizations were resistant to demobilization because of the threat of arbitrary violence, predatory behavior, and dispossession. In the postcommunist period, it was military power and the infliction of violence (control over the means of destruction) rather than any kind of broad social constituency that determined political ascendancy. Moreover, because the military capabilities of these organizations and their continuity depended upon subsidies obtained from external donors and cash derived from criminalized economic activities, these clientelistic networks were able to operate without accountability to the general population. Maintaining monopoly in the war economy contributed to ongoing violence between competing groups. Mujahideen organizations thus acquired predatory characteristics. Legitimate, nonviolent groups without access to external resources or alternate economic networks were barred from a role in politics and the exercise of power.

The continued availability of weapons and possession of considerable arsenals by competing groups meant also that no single entity could establish monopoly over the means of coercion. This presented an obstacle for the reconstitution of national centralized institutions of governance. Attempts to create a functioning government under these conditions were bound to fail.

Soon fighting that had been confined to the countryside during the previous decade broke out in the capital, as mujahideen factions began vying for power. Between 1992 and 1993, during roughly a one-year period, the mujahideen not only reduced the city into rubble block by block but also killed an estimated 30,000 Kabulis, wounded up to 100,000, and forced an even greater number to flee to refugee camps. During the fighting, civilians were deliberately targeted with mortar and rocket attacks and rival factions celebrated victories by abducting and raping women and young girls in their rivals' territories.

Thus Afghanistan plunged into "warlordism," which refers to circumstances where a state has collapsed and there is no one able or willing to recreate it, and a slide into regionalism, sectarianism, and the imposition of violence and extortion upon civil society. The result was the fragmentation of the country into myriad "fiefdoms" controlled by various warlords. The jihad or holy war thus devolved into a ghastly civil war (*jang-i dakhili*).

THE TALIBAN

The Soviet withdrawal from Afghanistan marked the end of U.S. involvement. The Americans and other Western powers that supported the jihad against the Soviets backed off and disengaged completely. Afghanistan was left in ruins, politically fragmented, and its traditional institutional mechanisms for the management of violence eroded. Left without any functioning political, administrative, law enforcement, or security structures, Afghanistan was abandoned by the international community to the ambitions of Pakistan and other foreign powers. This was the context in which the Taliban first appeared.[62]

Taliban is the plural of the word *talib*, meaning "religious student." The Taliban drew their religious inspiration from Deobandi teachings. The Deobandi School, *Dar-ul-Uloom* (House of Learning), a Sunni Muslim organization, was first instituted in 1867 in the town of Deoband in British India, north of New Delhi. The Deobandis were a reactionary reform movement who sought to revitalize Islamic society in the context of colonial domination. The Deobandis took an uncompromising and purist theological stance, opposed non-Islamic accretions and innovations (*bida*) in the practice of Islam, stressed the importance of a literal interpretation of the Qu'ran and sunna, advocated strict gender segregation and a narrow social role for women, and regarded the Shi'a as non-Muslims. Above all, the Deobandis opposed all accommodations to Western influences, which they viewed as a threat to Islamic societies. Some Western writers have referred to Deobandi Islam as South Asia's version of Wahhabism.

After its establishment, the Deobandi Dar-ul-Uloom in India grew in size and soon earned a reputation as a major center of Islamic learning with high academic standards. It attracted students from around the Islamic world. The standard course of study was 10 years and the graduates were qualified as religious scholars. Following the partition of India in 1947, a number of madrassas were established in Pakistan by a Deobandi organization called *Jami'at-e 'Ulema-e Islam* (JUI), which became a political party in the 1960s. In contrast to the original school, the Pakistani madrassas were small, poorly funded, and operated by nonliterate or semiliterate mullahs. They offered a three-year instruction program that emphasized the rote memorization of the Qur'an in Arabic, upon the completion of which the students, or talibs, were qualified to become village mullahs. The Deoband madrassas remained peripheral until the Afghan jihad brought foreign subsidies from the United States and Saudi Arabia.

The United States and Saudi Arabia lavished these schools with money and textbooks to produce a new generation of jihadi fighters against the Red Army in Afghanistan. During the 1980s the JUI established hundreds of Deobandi madrassas in the rural Pashtun belt along the Afghan frontier, offering students free education, room and board, and military training. The madrassas thus experienced a widespread resurgence, became highly militant and radicalized, and in the 1990s the Pakistani government organized students from these schools into Taliban units to fight in Afghanistan and mujahideen units to wage war in Kashmir.

In the post-Soviet period, considerable funding was provided to the madrassas by Saudi Arabia because the schools were sympathetic to the Wahhabi creed. Many of the Taliban leaders were trained in the Dar-ul-Uloom Haqqania in Akora Khatak, in the North-West Frontier province, set up by a JUI faction, where they were exposed to an extreme form of Deobandi ideology that had developed in the context of Pakistan which was more militant, uncompromising, and radical than the original Deoband School in India. This included an absolute puritanical and literalist view of Islam and sharia, a belief in the total segregation of women and their exclusion from public life, and militant anti-Shi'aism, coupled with an intense hatred of the West and modernity.

The Taliban movement was portrayed as an agglomeration of pious religious pupils, the so-called orphans of war, out to do a good deed. They first appeared in the political landscape in southern Afghanistan in the fall of 1994, when the government of Pakistan sent a trade convoy to Turkmenistan by way of Kandahar and Herat, ostensibly with the intention of reestablishing the overland trade route to the newly independent post-Soviet Central Asian Republics to compete with Iran for the export trade from the region. Once inside Afghanistan a local militia seized the convoy hoping to extort a ransom. The Taliban came to the rescue.

Once the convoy was sent on its way, so the story goes, the Taliban went on to easily capture the city of Kandahar. They disarmed the local population and declared that their mission was to end the anarchy and criminal behavior, purge all communists and mujahideen warlords who had become thieves and drug traffickers in the name of Islam, punish the guilty, and establish a true Islamic society through pious reconciliation.

The birth of the movement is steeped in mystery and a number of unverifiable origin myths were circulated. One such myth relates how the movement emerged after its spiritual leader, a previously unknown figure Mullah Omar, was inspired into action by a dream in which the Prophet Muhammad appeared to him and commanded him to lead an invincible army of pious religious students on a jihad to put an end to the corruption and depravity of the rapacious mujahideen warlords. Another account traces the origins of the movement to an incident in which an outraged Mullah Omar musters a group of disciples to rescue young women abducted and raped by a local mujahideen commander. Omar and his disciples freed the women and in retribution righteously hanged the rapist from the turret of his own tank. Soon appeals for help came pouring in from all over the area and the Taliban movement was under way.

Another account, for which there are no outside witnesses, relates the miraculous good fortune of the Taliban, who happen to come across a munitions depot at Spin Boldak containing 18,000 AK-47 assault rifles, grenade and rocket launchers, artillery, and ammunition from the period of the Soviet war, all in mint condition, in sufficient amounts to allow them to conduct operations for years to come. Another story circulated was that the Taliban were welcomed everywhere with open arms because they brought peace and security.

The underlying theme in these accounts is that the Taliban were a spontaneous, religiously inspired force. Establishing the autonomy of the movement from foreign influence was important to its spiritual legitimacy because the mujahideen factions that fought in the name of Islam but under the patronage of foreign sponsors had been totally discredited after 1992, when jihad had became merely a pretense for killing in pursuit of personal political ambitions. These stories strike all the right cultural and emotional chords—honor of women, bravery, piety, and so on. However, they have the attributes of origin myths fabricated to legitimize the existence of a military force that was created for altogether different reasons.

In reality the Taliban were a foreign occupation force. The capture of the ammunition depot, which was by many accounts emptied a long time ago, was a good cover story to account for the increase and circulation of arms that were being shipped into Afghanistan by the Pakistanis. The convoy that the Taliban "rescued" was actually carrying arms and ammunition, senior ISI commanders, and Taliban leaders, and was part of the military operation to capture Kandahar. The Taliban invincibility against battle-hardened mujahideen fighters, who in a number of cases capitulated without a fight, was bought by substantial bribes to local commanders from the ISI and later from Osama bin Laden, who joined the Taliban in 1996. The security that the invincible army of God brought was beneficial, not to ordinary people much in need of civil security, but to the smugglers and drug traffickers, who found the roads safer for the transport of their contraband.

The Taliban were a Pakistani-contrived proxy force.[63] Most Afghans regarded them as a foreign movement whose ideology had no basis in traditional Afghan Islamic or cultural values. As Ahmad Shah Massoud, senior commander of the forces that later became known as the Northern Alliance, stated about the Taliban in a letter to the U.S. Senate Committee on Foreign Relations, dated October 8, 1998: "For many Afghans, regardless of ethnicity or religion, Afghanistan, for the second time in one decade, is once again an occupied country." The pejorative term used by Afghans to refer to the Taliban was *Paki-Talibs*, designating them as foreigners.

Pakistan supplied manpower, diplomatic assistance, international representation, military training, ammunition and fuel, weapons, military transport planes, and direct combat support. Saudi Arabia, which sought leverage against Iranian influence in the region and an opportunity to spread the fundamentalist version of Islam practiced at home, provided money. In addition, support for the Taliban came from the Quetta and Chaman-based trucking mafia and Afghan drug barons who profited from the safer roads.

Within a few months of their initial appearance as a purported spontaneous indigenous movement of young acolytes, the Taliban acquired a complex command structure, 200 tanks, artillery, 400 brand-new Japanese-made four-wheel pickup trucks with tinted windows shipped from the Gulf states, which served as the Taliban's distinctive rapid troop transport vehicles during field combat, an air force of six MiG-21s and a dozen MiG-23 jet fighters, and six transport Mil-17 helicopters and fuel and specialist manpower to operate them. In an odd way, while the Taliban rejected modernity and all-things Western—for example, television sets and video and cassette players, which they confiscated and destroyed—they were willing and able to use Western instrumentalities for destruction with no misgivings whatsoever.

Remarkably, the Taliban ranks had swollen from a few hundred to between 20,000 and 25,000 men, with a crack infantry of 5,000 and thousands of madrassa acolytes and others as expendable foot soldiers. The Taliban militia was in part made up of recruits from the madrassas run by the Jamiat-e Ulema-i Islam party in the North-West Frontier province of Pakistan. Most of these recruits did not even speak any Afghan languages, as often pointed out by citizens of Kabul. However, the movement also included fighters from mujahideen parties, Khalqi communists (contrary to the Mullah Omar's declaration that he would purge these criminal elements), veterans from the Pakistani army, Pakistani soldiers dressing up as seminary students, and royalist Pashtuns who joined in the false hope that the Taliban would restore the former king Zahir Khan to power. The Taliban were able to cloak their membership by assigning their new collaborators religious titles (e.g., *mullah, mawlawi*), thereby concealing their origins from among the ranks of the detested communists or mujahideen fighters.

It is estimated that 80,000 to 100,000 Pakistani recruits fought as part of the Taliban in Afghanistan between 1994 and 1999. The Taliban force also included an estimated 8,000 to 15,000 non-Afghans—citizens of Saudi Arabia, the Gulf states, and other Middle Eastern countries, the so-called Afghan-Arabs (Arabs who trained and fought in Afghanistan). An estimated 3,000 to 5,000 of the foreign fighters belonged to Osama bin Laden's al Qaeda organization.

The revered leader of the movement was the reclusive Mullah Omar, a Kandahari Pashtun from the Ghilzai tribe and veteran of the Soviet jihad. In 1996, just before the Taliban's final assault on Kabul, Omar assumed the title of *Amir al-Momineen*, "commander of the faithful," a title first used during the early Islamic period, and renamed the country "The Islamic Emirate of Afghanistan." This constituted a claim to absolute and uncompromising authority. In this system of government, which was ostensibly modeled after the early caliphate, obeying the decrees of the amir is a directive from God. To legitimize his authority Omar appeared before his followers with the *Khirqa-i-Mubarak*, the "Cloak of the Prophet Muhammad," one of Afghanistan's most sacred relics enshrined in Kandahar. Most Afghans viewed such handling of the Prophet's cloak as an outrageous act of blasphemy. Henceforth the khutba, or Friday sermon, was read in Omar's name, the new amir of Afghanistan.

The Taliban leadership also included a *shura*, or council of elderly ultraconservative Kandahari ulama, a select core of madrassa-trained jihadis who envisioned a global role for their movement, ISI field commanders, Deobandi ideologues, and bin Laden, who acted as advisor on foreign and domestic policy, with his role increasing over time.

The Taliban, therefore, did not represent a spontaneous, indigenous movement of inspired "orphans of war." This movement was not a manifestation of some aspect of Afghan cultural tradition, but was a force created out of an alliance between the ISI, a Pakistani-trained core militia, bin Laden and his Afghan-Arab mercenary force, Pakistani trucking mafias and drug lords, and radical Pakistani and ultraconservative Afghan religious leaders.

The creation of the Taliban was yet another effort by Pakistan to manipulate circumstances inside Afghanistan. The Taliban movement has been called a "creeping invasion."[64] This refers to an intermediate power employing a proxy force that interferes with or endangers the political independence of another state, while denying any involvement in any military operations. Throughout the jihad against the Soviets, Pakistan's policy was to ensure its own internal security by achieving "strategic depth." This required the establishment of a pro-Pakistani government in Kabul that would not pursue the Pashtunistan issue. With the Afghan frontier thus secured, Pakistan could shift its military efforts toward India, its long-standing hostile neighbor to the east.

It is for this reason that during the jihad in Afghanistan, Pakistan channeled the resources it obtained from the CIA arms and cash pipeline to Hekmatyar's radical Islamist group, which was concerned with establishing an Islamic state, rather than creating an independent Pashtunistan along the Afghan–Pakistan border. Also, a client government in Kabul after the collapse of the Soviet Union would enable Pakistan to establish economic ties with the newly independent Central Asian republics. Hekmatyar's dismal military performance and his inability to gain ground against the mujahideen government in Kabul compelled the Pakistanis to search for an alternative. That alternative was the Taliban movement, whose ideologues were more concerned with implementing sharia law, the ummah, and establishing moral order, rather than pursuing a nationalist agenda. The Taliban seemed the perfect vehicle for the creation of a compliant puppet regime in Kabul.

The United States sanctioned Pakistan's effort to fill the power vacuum that arose when it disengaged from Afghanistan after the Soviet withdrawal. Washington displayed a lack of serious concern when bin Laden returned to Afghanistan in 1996 and joined forces with the Taliban, placing al Qaeda's resources at their disposal, even though he had been implicated in a number of terrorist attacks against U.S. targets. Bin Laden, whose personal financial assets have been estimated to be around $300 million (the *9–11 Commission Report* estimates less), supplied the Taliban with millions of dollars and thousands of trained Arab mercenaries and was the principal financier of the militia's final successful assault on Kabul. Al Qaeda's Brigade 055, which contained zealous and highly trained Arab mercenaries with bases in Kabul, Khost, Jalalabad, Kunar, and Kandahar and munitions depots in Tora Bora, constituted the most powerful branch of the Taliban military.

Washington's reaction to the rise of the Taliban was the announcement that it found nothing "objectionable" about the movement and extended support through its allies from the jihad days, Pakistan and Saudi Arabia.[65] Shortly after the Taliban takeover of Kabul in September 1996, the United States announced (but later retracted) that it would explore the possibility of reopening the U.S. embassy in Kabul. Zalmay Khalilzad, an Afghan-born Pashtun neoconservative in the U.S. State Department during the Reagan and Bush administrations, one-time UNOCAL advisor, and George W. Bush's special envoy to Afghanistan in 2002 (later U.S. ambassador), wrote an article in *The Washington Post* urging the United States to reengage the Taliban, whom he portrayed as not being anti-United States. Other U.S. officials depicted the Taliban as pious and decent guys with a good sense of humor. There are also reports of U.S. diplomats traveling to Kandahar, the Taliban headquarters, and senior Taliban leaders attending a conference in Washington in mid-1996.

The United States assumed that the Taliban were a pro-Western movement, constituting an unstoppable force capable of bringing peace to Afghanistan, that they would put a stop to opium production, that they would invite the former king to return, and that they would voluntarily relinquish power once they achieved these objectives. Especially appealing to Washington was the Taliban's anti-Shi'a and anti-Iran stance, since at that time Washington did not want to engage Teheran. Moreover, the Taliban's purported ability to secure and maintain a corridor through Afghanistan linking Pakistan to the oil-rich Central Asian republic of Turkmenistan would prove highly profitable to the American oil company UNOCAL and its

Saudi partner Delta Oil, which had already made plans to construct an oil pipeline to export gas from Turkmenistan to Pakistan and had entered into negotiations with the Taliban leadership.

To secure swift "Pax Talibana," which would enable the pipeline project to go ahead, UNOCAL hired senior American officials involved in the Soviet jihad as consultants, as well as procuring the services of Thomas E. Gouttierre's Center for Afghanistan Studies at the University of Nebraska, the same organization that published jihadi textbooks for Afghan children in the 1980s and early 1990s. The pipeline project was attractive to the U.S. government because it would eliminate Iran as a possible alternate route for a pipeline and break Teheran's monopoly on the southern trade routes from Central Asia. Believing that the Taliban would achieve all of these objectives, Washington supported the movement from 1994 to 1998. By the end of this period, the Taliban had captured, so they claimed, all but 5 to 10 percent of the country in the north, which remained under the control of Ahmad Shah Massoud.

The Taliban foot soldiers and ISI officers were no match for Massoud's tactical skills and his highly trained and fiercely loyal troops. Total victory upon which the pipeline deal depended did not happen. The Taliban were able to maintain their line against Massoud in the north only because of the presence of seasoned al Qaeda fighters stationed on the frontline by bin Laden, which made the Afghan-Arabs indispensable for the Taliban regime. By 1998 the Taliban's military stalemate, escalation of violence, growing evidence of ethnic cleansing in their territories, their involvement in opium production, appalling gender policies, and alleged connections with terrorism led to a change of heart in Washington.

What the United States failed to grasp at the beginning was the true nature of the Taliban regime and the kind of stability it brought. What the Taliban accomplished was martial law under the cloak of sharia law, which amounted to brutal repression and rule by terror in the pretext of stabilizing the country. The Taliban had no agenda for nation building. Their emirate was hardly a state, consisting of a loose political hierarchy, a radio station to announce decrees, and roving bands of religious police who acted as enforcers, beating women for being obtrusive in public and men for not wearing beards of a sufficient length or for having missed prayers at the mosque. The Taliban's main source of income, aside from the monies supplied by Arab princes and the $10 million provided by Pakistan for expenses, was the revenue generated through the taxation of the illicit cross-border transit trade and opium production.

The Taliban lacked administrative skills (most of the basic services in Kabul were being run by nongovernmental organizations or NGOs), they did not have economic or foreign policies, they were oblivious to international law and the international community, and they functioned like an occupying military force with no accountability to the people they ruled. They failed to achieve any of their objectives, such as securing a pipeline deal with UNOCAL, gaining recognition by the U.N. and the international community, or finding allies among the Muslim countries, aside from Pakistan and Saudi Arabia and the United Arab emirates. The Taliban responded to international pressures with respect to human rights issues and their gender policies with increasingly provocative countermeasures to demonstrate that compromise with the international community was out of the question.

When the Taliban captured Kabul, one of their first acts was to break into the U.N. office where Najibullah, the former president of the communist regime, had sought sanctuary in 1992. They seized Najibullah and his brother who was there on a visit, tortured and killed them, and left their battered and mutilated bodies hanging for three days. This violation of international standards turned out to be one of a long list to highlight the Taliban's human rights record.

The Taliban's program to solve the pressing sociopolitical needs of the shattered Afghan society was to enforce moral behavior. This required the strict and literal application of sharia law. Their version of law, however, excluded a premise central to Islamic jurisprudence, which is the idea of law as a complex process of interpretation, or *ijtihad*, and enunciation of evolving principles that capture the spirit of Islam applicable to prevailing sociopolitical and economic circumstances. For the Taliban, sharia as encapsulated in Mullah Omar's various decrees were God's laws, which all true Muslims were obligated to obey without question. Those who disobeyed were therefore non-Muslims and it was obligatory that they be punished. The Taliban thus dismissed the accumulated corpus of Qur'anic scholarship and interpretation of the law and discredited the legitimacy of other religious authorities and the Islamic credentials of their opponents.

The Taliban's own brand of Islam had no manifesto, no tradition of scholarly analysis of Islamic law and history, and admitted no debate. Their vision of Islam, a radicalized version of Deobandi precepts that rejected all accommodation with modernity, had no basis in the Islamic traditions of Afghanistan, or parallels anywhere else. It, like the Taliban themselves, was an anomaly in the context of Afghanistan. Nor was their behavior an expression of Afghan values. For example, beating women in the streets is something unthinkable in the context of Afghan society. It is important to keep in mind that the Taliban's vision of Islam was largely the product of a culture of war and a legacy of violence and their edicts were an embodiment of this culture of war rather than Islamic religious principles.

The Taliban considered sharia as a divinely ordained and fixed set of rules and punishments to be rigorously and dutifully implemented without question. Likewise violators had to be subjected to criminal punishments stipulated in sharia law called hudud, which includes stoning to death for adultery and amputation of hands and feet for theft, and qisas, or law of retaliation in kind (e.g., "eye for an eye") meted out by a member of the aggrieved family in public. Such measures had not been implemented by the state government in Afghanistan since the days after the reign of Nadir Khan and were not applied in the context of Pashtun tribal law.

For the Taliban, however, establishing sharia law was contingent upon applying hudud and qisas. Stoning to death, amputations, executions, and qisas punishments were carried out in public at the Kabul sport stadium and other venues, as object lessons for spectators. The Taliban would not heed the complaints of human rights organizations. For them, divine edicts were beyond question and not subject to change in terms of majority votes or because they did not correspond to some set of "human rights" established by Western institutions like the United Nations. On this issue they would not compromise, as illustrated by their refusal to engage the United Nations or the international community on their policies.

The Taliban imposed what they saw as measures to protect women's honor and what the Western media described as misogyny, "gynaeophobia," and "gender apartheid."[66] All schools for girls were closed. Women were forbidden to work outside the home or interact with male shopkeepers and vendors. Women were forbidden from venturing into the public unless completely covered with the chadari and accompanied by a male relative as a chaperon. While in public women were forbidden to speak or laugh loudly so that men would not hear their voices. In addition to these restrictions, the Taliban also banned cosmetics, brightly colored clothing, high-heeled shoes, or shoes that made a noise when walking, as these attracted undue attention to the feminine presence.

The Taliban mistreating a woman.

Finally, the Taliban ordered that exterior glass panels in windows be painted black in houses with female residents so that men outside might not catch a glimpse of the female occupants. Those who failed to observe these restrictions were punished on the spot by public beatings and imprisonment.

The impact of the Taliban's restrictions upon women was the loss wages for families with no male income. Particularly affected were Kabul's estimated 30,000 to 40,000 widows who were the only source of income for their families. The bulk of Kabul's health-care professionals, an estimated 40 percent of all doctors, 70 percent of all teachers, and 50 percent of all civil servants were women, which meant that what little medical care was available was drastically hampered and nearly all schools were no longer operational.[67]

With respect to their gender policies, the Taliban claimed that they were acting in the cause of social justice, fulfilling their Islamic obligation of protecting the honor and dignity of women and preservation of Islam. According to Taliban logic, to permit women freedom in public would certainly result in adultery and that would spell the annihilation of Islam. However, their own behavior fell short on this issue given that hundreds of women were abducted, forcibly married, raped, or sold into sexual slavery by higher echelon Taliban militiamen.

For the Taliban, the inhabitans of Kabul symbolized all the terrible things that had befallen rural Afghans since the Soviet occupation. Kabul was the den of atheist communists, and later the base of the corrupt and rapacious mujahideen warlords, and by exerting maximum control over the aspect of social life of its inhabitants that symbolized male honor, namely women, the Taliban were broadcasting the message that they controlled all aspects of social life in the city and that Kabuli men had no honor.

Restrictions were also imposed upon men, who were forbidden to wear Western-style clothing and were ordered to cut their hair short, wear turbans, grow full beards of a specified length, and pray at mosques five times a day. Neighborhood councils were set up to record the names of offenders who did not attend mosque prayers. All forms of entertainment, including music, singing, dancing at weddings, cigarettes, card games, chess, marbles, gambling, pigeon flying, and kite flying (favorite Kabuli pastimes) were declared illegal. Movie theaters were shut down. Portraits and the possession of photographs of people were forbidden. The traditional Afghan new-year celebration, called *Nauroz*, was abolished as pagan and un-Islamic. Western products, such as books, television sets, and video and audio cassettes, were banned. Radios were permitted, but only for listening to the programming on the Taliban's "Radio Sharia," which consisted of prayers and official announcements.

The Taliban's security service, their only highly organized and coherent institution, was "The Ministry of Enforcement of Virtue and Suppression of Vice" (*Amr bil-Ma 'ruf wa Nahi 'An al-Munkir*), modeled after a similar organization in Saudi Arabia and funded by Saudi money. Far more extreme than its Saudi counterpart, the Taliban Ministry was a religious police, the function of which was to enforce Taliban decrees and deter resistance by means of intimidation and terror. Roving bands of armed enforcers from the Ministry ensured compliance and delivered swift summary punishments, which included public beatings and whippings.

In addition to their gender policies, which received considerable media coverage in the West, the Taliban's human rights record, which included sectarian killings of Shi'a minorities, killing civilians, torture, arbitrary detentions, and destruction of cultural property,[68] contributed to their international isolation and failure to be recognized by the United Nations, and earned them condemnation from the West as political pariahs and from the Islamic world as a reactionary and anachronistic force out of touch and out of place in the modern world.

Osama bin Laden.

OSAMA BIN LADEN AND AFGHANISTAN

The most controversial policy of the Taliban, one that eventually brought about their downfall, was to play host to Osma bin Laden and his operatives.[69] Afghanistan's downward spiral into a hub and sanctuary for international terrorism began in the 1980s, when the CIA, ISI, and *Mukhabarat*, the Saudi Ministry of Intelligence, poured in large sums to finance the jihad against the Soviets by bringing Arab volunteers to fight alongside the Afghans after receiving military training in camps run by Pakistan's military intelligence. These mercenaries, nicknamed Afghan-Arabs, came to Afghanistan with the assistance of a facility called *Maktab al Khidmat ili-mujahideen al-Arab*, run by the wealthy Arab entrepreneur named Osama bin Laden. The operation was based in Peshawar, Pakistan, worked closely with the ISI, and was bankrolled by bin Laden and Arab princes. At the time, bin Laden was considered a prime CIA "asset" in that he shared the same objectives as the CIA. In Pakistan and Afghanistan bin Laden developed contacts with mujahideen leaders, the ISI, and the Afghan-Arabs from around the world, which he later harnessed toward his own objectives. In 1988, utilizing the financial resources and technical expertise put in place for the war against the Soviets, bin Laden formed al Qaeda (The Base), an organization with an international scope. The following year the Soviet army departed from Afghanistan.[70]

For bin Laden the defeat and collapse of the atheist superpower and triumph of the Afghan jihad was a defining moment in Islamic history, a triumph that could be repeated against other superpowers. Bin Laden returned to Saudi Arabia in 1989 as a hero, but had a falling out with the Saudi royal family over its alliance with the United States, when Iraq invaded Kuwait in 1990. In 1992 he established himself in the Sudan, but by 1996 he was back in Afghanistan when Sudan expelled him under international pressure by the United States and Saudi Arabia. During this time the Saudi government took away bin Laden's citizenship and his family allegedly disowned him.

Bin Laden and his associates became vehemently anti-American and anti-Western because of the Gulf War and the stationing of U.S. troops in Saudi Arabia, preserve of Islam and the location of "the two most holy places" of Islam—Mecca and Medina. Never in history had a Western army occupied the Arabian peninsula, where these sacred cities are located, and for bin Laden the presence of U.S. troops there was a catastrophe and humiliation for all Muslim people. He denounced members of the Saudi royal family as nonbelievers for their subservience to the Americans and for betraying the ummah and predicted their downfall. Bin Laden and his associates viewed the stationing of U.S. troops as part of a larger scheme by the Americans and their Western allies involved in the bombing of Iraq during Operation Desert Storm. U.S. support for Israel and attack upon the Muslim nation of Iraq were construed as part of a plan to control the holy land of Islam and rule the Muslim world. Bin Laden described these efforts as a declaration of war by the West "on God and the Prophet" and called upon all Muslims to rise up in a jihad to defend Islam.

The Afghan-Arab jihadis had thus found a new global mission: to defend the ummah from incursions by nonbelievers everywhere. Hailed up to that time as heroic holy warriors and freedom fighters in the Western media, the jihadis would henceforth be referred to as "terrorists." The Cold War battleground in Afghanistan thus produced a generation of Islamist militants, emboldened by their encounter with the Soviet army, and ready to expand their jihad beyond the Afghan theater to the international scene against new enemies—the United States, Israel, pro-Western Arab governments, and India in Kashmir. The weapons that the United States and its allies shipped into Afghanistan at a time when jihad directed at the Red Army was deemed a commendable battle cry was now redirected against their donors. Some analysts call this "blowback," a term that means the unintended consequences of covert U.S. policies abroad that result in retaliation against unsuspecting U.S. citizens.[71]

From 1993 onward, bin Laden's camps in Afghanistan, nicknamed "terrorist universities" by U.S. officials, became the training grounds for a new generation of jihadi recruits. Attacks against U.S. targets were carried out by trainees of these camps—including the World Trade Center in 1993; the attacks at Dhahran, Saudi Arabia, in 1996 that killed 19 American soldiers; the bombing of the U.S. embassies in Kenya and Tanzania in 1998 that left 258 dead and 5,000 injured; and the attack on the *USS Cole* in Aden, Yemen, in 2000, killing 17 U.S. service members. These attacks demonstrated al Qaeda's capacities for globally coordinated operations. By 1998, bin Laden had shifted his focus to the United States as the main enemy of Islam and in a fatwa issued that year he called on his followers to kill Americans, military or civilian, anywhere in the world. He justified targeting civilians by stating that any American who pays taxes is supporting the U.S. military machine against Islam and is therefore a legitimate target.

Bin Laden's organization played an important role in the success of the Taliban and their capture of Kabul. However, his presence in Afghanistan became a particularly pressing international problem for the Taliban after car bombs destroyed the U.S. embassies in Kenya and Tanzania in August 1998. The United States responded by missile strikes against training camps where bin Laden was believed to be, which failed to kill him, but because of the international media coverage made him into an instant celebrity in the Muslim world. The attacks allowed bin Laden to consolidate al Qaeda's jihadi network in preparation to strike at other American targets.

Thereafter, al Qaeda's influence in Afghanistan grew and the Taliban began to adopt an even greater radical stance toward the West. The bin Laden–Taliban merger transformed

Afghanistan into a magnet for radical Islamic dissidents and mercenaries from around the world, including Arabs, Kashmiris, Filipinos, Bangladeshis, Chechens, Uyghurs from the Xinjiang region of China, and Australians, and western Europeans, including Johnny Walker Lindh, the so-called American Taliban who came to Afghanistan on June 1, 2001.

The Taliban's new level of radicalization was expressed in a range of responses, including the destruction of pre-Islamic statues in the Kabul and Herat museums, demolition of the giant Buddhas of Bamiyan (two of Afghanistan's greatest archaeological treasures) in March 2001, decrees that non-Muslims must wear yellow identity patches, the closing down of U.N.-operated bakeries that supplied bread to the needy, and the arrest of Christian NGO aid workers on the charge of spreading Christianity. Observers also noted a dramatic increase in the number of foreign fighters in Afghanistan closely linked with the al Qaeda network who were assisting the Taliban in carrying out massacres of civilians in Hazarajat and acting as "shock troops" for the Taliban military offensives against the United Front. At the same time the tone of Mullah Omar's decrees underwent a transformation from concern with just Afghanistan to one in support for bin Laden's global jihad.

The United States and the United Nations responded by unleashing a barrage of sanctions against the Taliban to hand over bin Laden, which they dismissed. The reason this approach failed was because of the close connection between al Qaeda, the ISI, and the Taliban. Bin Laden provided the Taliban indispensible Afghan-Arabs, who formed their most effective fighters as well as large cash subsidies. It would not be possible to take on one without dealing with the others in the three-way alliance. The Taliban failed to relinquish bin Laden despite international pressures because they could not do without his seasoned mercenary force. In the end, bin Laden's presence in Afghanistan would be the Taliban's undoing, although it is unlikely that they fully comprehended their predicament.

The Taliban's destruction of a major Buddhist sculpture.

On September 9, 2001, suicide terrorists on orders from bin Laden assassinated Afghanistan's military leader Ahmad Shah Massoud, the senior military commander of the Jamiat-i-Islami party during the Soviet war, minister of defense in the mujahideen government in Kabul, and head of the United Front (Northern Alliance), who had resisted the Taliban for years. Such a suicide attack had no precedent in Afghanistan and marked a crucial event in recent Afghan history. It was eclipsed internationally, however, by what happened two days later. On September 11, bin Laden's suicide terrorists struck once more, this time at the Pentagon and the World Trade Center in New York City.[72] Ironically, Massoud had warned of such a possibility in his 1998 letter to the U.S. Senate Committee on Foreign Relations. He wrote: "Illegal drug production, terrorist activities and planning are on the rise." He spoke of the "dark accomplishment" that has given Afghanistan over to "fanatics, extremists, terrorists, mercenaries, drug Mafias and professional murderers," and warned of "three major concerns—namely terrorism, drugs and human rights—[originating] from Taliban-held areas but . . . instigated from Pakistan."

The United States reacted not only by pursuing bin Laden, who was identified as the mastermind behind the dreadful events of September 11, but also those who harbored him. The massive attacks by the United States began on October 7. Once more the Afghan people were under fire.

RECENT TRENDS: AFTER THE TALIBAN

Taliban rule ended quickly under U.S. bombardment and ground assaults by American Special Forces and soldiers of the United Front (Northern Alliance).[73] On December 5, 2001, Afghan elites met in Bonn, Germany, under a U.N. initiative and signed an agreement that would serve as a blueprint for rebuilding the collapsed Afghan government under an interim administration. Following the Bonn agreement, Hamid Karzai, an ethnic Pashtun from Kandahar, was appointed head of a 30-member government with a timetable for transition to a democratic government.

In June of 2002 Karzai was elected as head of an interim government by an emergency Loya Jirga. In April 2003 the initial draft of a new constitution endorsing a system of government was completed and the Loya Jirga approved the constitution on January 4, 2004. National elections in Afghanistan scheduled for June 2004 were held in October 2004 due to security concerns. Costing approximately $200 million (U.S.) in international contributions, the outcome of the election was never in doubt. Karzai emerged as the victor.

The difficult task facing the new government is to build a stable state, the legitimacy of which is widely acknowledged, and which is capable of guaranteeing security, justice, and freedom from persecution on the basis of gender, ethnicity, and religion in local communities outside Kabul. Security remains an important issue, as does the presence of regional power holders, commonly referred to as warlords. The U.S. military strategy in its War on Terror has been to rely upon regional power holders, which has contributed to a resurgence of warlords and warlordism. While the Taliban were defeated, most of their leadership and a large number of their followers are at large, and the movement remains viable with a base of operations in Pakistan. The Taliban continue to be potential challengers for state power as long as their foreign sponsors continue to push their own political and strategic agendas and interfere in Afghanistan's internal affairs.

The circumstances confronting the people of Afghanistan were not entirely of their own making, or a manifestation of their cultural traditions, religious fundamentalism, or warrior ways, but were created by the manner in which Afghanistan has been and is embedded into the global system and web of interstate competition. The responsibility for the horrors that befell the Afghans over the last 20 years, and the repercussions of short-sighted policies that contributed to the tragedy of September 11, falls largely upon the international community, as does the responsibility for undoing the tragic circumstances in Afghanistan.

The Soviet Union's invasion, the way the United States chose to fight the Soviets by supplying arms and money to political parties representing the interests of a minority of the population rather than a centralized political structure, and the involvement of regional powers such as Pakistan, Saudi Arabia, and Iran contributed to the factionalism, warlordism, militarization, and the introduction of radicalized and alien ideologies, Marxist-Lennist and Islamist. There has never been a mass popular demand among Afghans for a fundamentalist Islamic government. Instead there has been a powerful insistence that they be allowed to practice their own religion as individuals, free from the impositions and interference of communists, atheists, Arab extremists, or Pakistani and Iranian fundamentalists. Whether the

Afghan people will succeed in their efforts to restore their country depends largely on the commitment of the international community to respect the integrity of the country, provide the assistance it promised, and ensure peace so that the reconstruction process can proceed.

NOTES

1. Willem Vogelsang, *The Afghans* (Oxford, England: Blackwell, 2002), ix.

2. A number of useful bibliographic references exist for Afghanistan. See George Grassmuck, Ludwig W. Adamec, and Frances H. Irwin, *Afghanistan: Some New Approaches* (Ann Arbor: Center for Near Eastern and North African Studies, University of Michigan, 1969); Louis Dupree, *Afghan Studies: An Overview* (Hanover, NH: American Universities Field Staff, 1976); M. Jamil Hanifi, *Annotated Bibliography of Afghanistan* (New Haven, CT: HRAF Press, 1982); Keith McLachlan and William Whittaker, *A Bibliography of Afghanistan: A Working Bibliography of Materials on Afghanistan with Special Reference to Economic and Social Change in the Twentieth Century* (Cambridge, England: Middle East & North African Studies Press, 1983); Schuyler Jones, *Afghanistan* (Oxford, England: Clio Press, 1992); Cary Gladstone, *Afghanistan: History, Issues, Bibliography* (Huntington, NY: Novinka Books, 2001). For anthropological overviews of Afghanistan see Louis Dupree, *Afghanistan* (Princeton, NJ: Princeton University Press, 1973); Peter Blood, ed. (1997), *Afghanistan: A Country Study*, retrieved from the Federal Research Division, Library of Congress Web site: http://lcweb2.loc.gov/frd/cs/aftoc.html; Bernt Glatzer, *Afghanistan* (London: Routledge, 2002). Other general works from a variety of disciplinary perspectives include Martin Ewans, *Afghanistan: A New Story* (London: Routledge-Curzon, 2002); Willem Vogelsang, *The Afghans* (Oxford, England: Blackwell, 2002); Ralph Magnus and Eden Naby, *Afghanistan: Mullah, Marx, and Mujahid* (Boulder, CO: Westview Press, 1998). Excellent studies focusing on political and military factors include Amin Saikal, *Modern Afghanistan: A History of Struggle and Survival* (London: I.B. Tauris, 2004); Angelo Rasanayagam, *Afghanistan: A Modern History: Monarchy, Despotism or Democracy? The Problems of Governance in the Muslim Tradition* (London: I.B. Tauris, 2003); William Maley, *The Afghanistan Wars* (New York: Palgrave Macmillan, 2002); Barnett Rubin, *The Fragmentation of Afghanistan: State Formation and Collapse in the International System* (New Haven, CT: Yale University Press, 2002); Stephen Tanner, *Afghanistan: A Military History from Alexander the Great to the Fall of the Taliban* (New York: Da Capo Press, 2002); Eric Margolis, *War at the Top of the World: The Struggle for Afghanistan, Kashmir, and Tibet* (New York: Routledge, 2000).

3. For scientific geographic descriptions see Johannes Humlum, *La Géographie de l'Afghanistan: Étude d'un Pays Aride* (Copenhagen, Denmark: Gyldendal, 1959). See also Sophia Bowlby, "The Geographical Background," in *The Archaeology of Afghanistan: From Earliest Times to the Timurid Period*, ed. F. R. Allchin and Norman Hammond, 9–36 (London: Academic Press, 1978). For a more recent work based mostly on secondary sources, see Eugene Palka, ed., *Afghanistan: Geographic Perspectives* (Guilford, CT: McGraw-Hill/Dushkin, 2004). On Afghanistan's strategic geographical location at the crossroads of civilizations see Arnold Joseph Toynbee, *Between Oxus and Jumna* (London: Oxford University Press, 1961); John Griffiths, *Afghanistan: Key to a Continent* (Boulder, CO: Westview Press, 1981); Arnold Fletcher, *Afghanistan: Highway of Conquest* (Westport, CT: Greenwood Press, 1982). On the ecological degradation of forests and pasturelands see Ali Azimi and David McCauley, *Afghanistan's Environment in Transition* (Manila, Philippines: Asian Development Bank, 2002); and the report by the Asian Study Group, *The Destruction of the Forests and Wooden Architecture of Eastern Afghanistan and Northern Pakistan: Nuristan to Baltistan* (Islamabad, Pakistan: Asian Study Group [Afghanistan Circle], 1993).

4. For an overview of the prehistorical archeology of Afghanistan see Louis Dupree, ed., *Prehistoric Research in Afghanistan (1959–1966)* (Philadelphia: Transactions of the American Philosophical Society, 1972). For an overview of archaeological sites see Warwick Ball and Jean-Claude Gardin, *Archaeological Gazetteer of Afghanistan: Catalogue des Sites Archéologiques d'Afghanistan* (Paris: Éditions Recherche sur les Civilisations, 1982). For general overviews of archaeological research in Afghanistan see Walter Fairservis, *Future Archaeological Research in Afghanistan* (Albuquerque: University of New Mexico Press, 1953); Louis Dupree, "Archaeology: Recent Research in Afghanistan," *Explorers Journal* 47, no. 2 (1969): 84–89; Nadia Tarzi, "Renaissance of Afghan Archaeology," *The SAA Archaeological Record* (January 2003): 34–37. To date, the best comprehensive set of articles in English extending from prehistoric to historic times is the edited volume by F. R. Allchin and Norman Hammond, *The Archaeology of Afghanistan: From Earliest Times to the Timurid Period* (London: Academic Press, 1978). Another excellent compilation of articles is A. H. Dani and V. M. Masson, eds., *History of Civilizations of Central Asia* (Paris: UNESCO Publishing, 1992). Another good general overview is Edgar Knobloch's *The Archaeology & Architecture of Afghanistan* (Charleston, SC: Tempus, 2001). See also the series *Mémoires de la Délégation Archéologique Française en Afghanistan* which covers the Graeco-Bactrian through the Kushan periods. An overview of French archaeological research in Afghanistan is found in Joseph Hackin et al., *Diverses Recherches Archéologiques en Afghanistan (1933–1940)* (Paris: Presses Universitaires de France, 1959).

5. On Alexander and the Greeks in Afghanistan see A. B. Bosworth, *Conquest and Empire: The Reign of Alexander the Great* (Cambridge, England: Cambridge University Press, 1988). For Alexander's campaigns in Afghanistan, his cities, and the rise of the Graeco-Bactrian kingdom, see H. Sidky, *The Greek Kingdom of Bactria* (Lanham, MD: University Press of America, 2000); Frank Lee Holt, *Alexander the Great and Bactria: The Formation of a Greek Frontier in Central Asia* (Leiden, the Netherlands: Brill, 1989); A. H. Dani and P. Bernard, "Alexander and His Successors in Central Asia," in *History of Civilizations of Central Asia: Vol. 2. The Development of Sedentary and Nomadic Civilizations, 700 B.C. to A.D. 250*, ed. Janos Harmatta, 67–98 (Paris: UNESCO Publishing, 1992).

6. There are a number of excellent volumes on the cultural fusion resulting in the Gandharan artistic tradition. See Raymond Allchin, Bridget Allchin, Neil Kreitman, and Elizabeth Errington, eds., *Gandharan Art in Context: East-West Exchanges at the Crossroads of Asia* (New Delhi, India: Regency Publications, 1997); Elizabeth Errington, Joe Cribb, and Maggie Claringbull, *The Crossroads of Asia: Transformation in Image and Symbol in the Art of Ancient Afghanistan and Pakistan* (Cambridge, England: Ancient India and Iran Trust, 1992); Kurt A. Behrendt, *The Buddhist Architecture of Gandhara* (Leiden, the Netherlands: Brill, 2004); Bérénice Geoffroy-Schneiter and David Wharry, *Gandhara: The Memory of Afghanistan* (New York: Assouline, 2001). On Kushan art see G. A. Pugachenkova, S. R. Dar, R. C. Sharma, and M. A. Joyenda, "Kushan Art," in Harmatta, *History of Civilizations of Central Asia*, 331–398.

7. On Buddhism in Afghanistan see Si Esa Upasaka, *History of Buddhism in Afghanistan* (Sarnath, Varanasi: Central Institute of Higher Tibetan Studies, 1990); Pierre Herman Leonard Eggermont and J. Hoftijzer, *The Moral Edicts of King Asóka (King of Magadha): The Greco-Aramaic Inscription of Kandahar and Further Inscriptions of the Maurian Period* (Leiden, the Netherlands: Brill, 1962); Simone Gaulier, Robert Jera-Bezard, and Monique Maillard, *Buddhism in Afghanistan and Central Asia* (Leiden, the Netherlands: Brill, 1997); Nagendra Kumar Singh, *International Encyclopaedia of Buddhism: Vol. 1: Afghanistan* (New Delhi, India: Anmol Publications, 1996). On Bamiyan see P. H. B. Baker and F. R. Alchin, *Shahr-i Zohak and the History of the Bamiyan Valley, Afghanistan* (Oxford, England: Tempus Reperatum, BAR International Series 570, 1991).

8. On the nomadic invasions see Luc Kwanten, *Imperial Nomads: A History of Central Asia, 500–1500* (Philadelphia: University of Pennsylvania Press, 1979); Walter Fairservis, *Horsemen of the Steppes* (Cleveland, OH: World, 1962); Thomas Barfield, *The Perilous Frontier: Nomadic Empires and China* (Oxford, England: Blackwell, 1989). On the Hephthalites see Muhammad Usman Sidqi [M. Osman Sidky], *Yaftaliyan* (Kabul, Afghanistan: Pashto Tolanah, 1947). See also Y. A. Zadneprovskiy, "The Nomads of Northern Central Asia After the Invasion," in Harmatta, *History of Civilizations of Central Asia*, 473–484; see also Fairservis, *Horsemen of the Steppes*.

9. On the Sasanians see John Curtis and Vladimir Lukonin, *Mesopotamia and Iran in the Parthian and Sasanian Periods: Rejection and Revival c. 238 BC–AD 642* (London: British Museum Press, 2000). For the Arab invasions of the region and the Saffarids see Clifford Edmund Bosworth, *Sistan Under the Arabs, From the Islamic Conquest to the Rise of the Saffarids (30-250/651-864)* (Rome: IsMEO, 1968). On the Saminids see Jürgen Paul, *The State and the Military: The Samanid Case* (Bloomington: Indiana University, Research Institute for Inner Asian Studies, 1994). For the Hindu Shahis see Yogendra Mishra, *The Hindu Shahis of Afghanistan and the Punjab, A.D. 865–1026: A Phase of Islamic Advance into India* (Patna, India: Vaishali Bhavan, 1972). Comprehensive studies of the Ghaznavids are the two volumes by Clifford Edmund Bosworth, *The Ghaznavids: Their Empire in Afghanistan and Eastern Iran, 994–1040* (Edinburgh, Scotland: University Press, 1963), and *The Later Ghaznavids: Splendour and Decay: The Dynasty in Afghanistan and Northern India, 1040–1186* (New York: Columbia University Press, 1977).

10. On the Mongol invasion see Henry Wiencek and Glenn Lowry, *Storm Across Asia: Genghis Khan and the Mongols, the Mogul Expansion* (London: Cassell, 1981); Stephen Turnbull, *Genghis Khan & the Mongol Conquests, 1190–1400* (New York: Routledge, 2004). An accessible account of Timurlane is Harold Lamb's *Tamerlane: The Earth Shaker* (Garden City, NY: Garden City Publishing, 1928). See also Terry Allen, *Timurid Herat* (Wiesbaden, Germany: Reichert, 1983). On the Moghuls and Babur see Jean-Paul Roux, *Histoire des grands moghols: Babur* (Paris: Fayard, 1986); Fernand Grenard, *Baber: First of the Moguls* (New York: McBride, 1930). There is also the account by Babur himself, *The Baburnama: Memoirs of Babur, Prince and Emperor* (New York: Modern Library, 2002).

11. For the rise of the Afghan empire under Ahmad Shah see Ahmad Ali Kuhzad, *Men and Events through 18th and 19th Century Afghanistan* (Kabul, Afghanistan: Afghan Books, 1972); Ganda Singh, *Ahmad Shah Durrani: Father of Modern Afghanistan* (London: Asia Publication House, 1959).

12. Among the more accessible studies of "the Great Game" is the volume by Karl Ernest Meyer and Shareen Blair Brysac, *Tournament of Shadows: The Great Game and Race for Empire in Central Asia* (Washington, DC: Counterpoint, 1999); see also Peter Hopkirk, *The Great Game: The Struggle for Empire in Central Asia* (New York: Kodansha International, 1994). For original documentary sources on the Great Game see Barbara Harlow and Mia Carter, eds., *Imperialism & Orientalism: A Documentary Sourcebook* (Malden, MA: Blackwell, 1999). A related study to be consulted is William Habberton, *Anglo-Russian Relations Concerning Afghanistan, 1837–1907* (Urbana: University of Illinois Press, 1937). For a general treatment of British policies contributing to the Anglo-Afghan wars see Jeffery Roberts, *The Origins of Conflict in Afghanistan* (Westport, CT: Praeger, 2003); Malcolm Yapp, *Strategies of British India: Britain, Iran, and Afghanistan, 1798–1850* (Oxford, England: Clarendon Press, 1980); John H. Waller, *Beyond the Khyber Pass: The Road to British Disaster in the First Afghan War* (Austin: University of Texas Press, 1993).

13. For background materials for the emergence of the modern Afghan state see Christine Noelle, *State and Tribe in Nineteenth-Century Afghanistan: The Reign of Amir Dost Muhammad Khan (1826–1863)* (Richmond, England: Curzon Press, 1997). Less accessible, but useful sources include Munshi Mohana Lala, *Life of the Amir Dost Mohammed Khan of Kabul* (Karachi, Pakistan: Oxford University Press, 1978 [original work published 1846]). On Shah Shuja, king of Afghanistan, consult the general works on Afghanistan, such as Dupree, *Afghanistan*, and Vogelsang 2000. Also see Muhammad Husayn Hirati, *Waqi'at-i Shah Shuja* (Kabul, Afghanistan: Anjuman-i Tarikh-i Afghanistan, 1954). On the disastrous British retreat from Kabul see the account by Lady Florentia Wynch Sale, *A Journal of the Disasters in Afghanistan, 1841–2* (London: J. Murray, 1843). Contemporary accounts include Tim Coates, *The British War in Afghanistan: The Dreadful Retreat from Kabul in 1842* (London: Tim Coates, 2002); Vincent Eyre, *The Military Operations at Cabul: Which Ended in the Retreat and Destruction of the British Army, January 1842—With a Journal of Imprisonment in Afghanistan* (London: John Murray, 1843). On the Anglo-Afghan wars see H. W. Bellew, *Afghanistan and the Afghans: Being a Brief Review of the History of the Country and Account of Its People, with a Special Reference to the Present Crisis and War with the Amir Sher Ali Khan* (New Delhi, India: Shree,

1879); Leigh Maxwell, *My God-Maiwand!: Operations of the South Afghanistan Field Force, 1878–80* (London: Cooper, 1979). Charles Metcalfe MacGregor, *War in Afghanistan, 1879–80: The Personal Diary of Major General Sir Charles Metcalfe MacGregor* (Detroit, MI: Wayne State University Press, 1985).

14. On demographic patterns see Dennis Cowher, "Population Geography," in *Afghanistan: Geographic Perspectives*, ed. Eugene Palka, 74–86 (New York: McGraw-Hill, 2004); Brandon Herl, "Urban Geography," in Palka, *Afghanistan: Geographic Perspectives*, 64–74. No reliable, systematic demographic census has been conducted in Afghanistan since the early 1970s. The 1972–1974 demographic survey conducted by the State University of New York (SUNY) for the United States Agency for International Development (AID) placed the total population of Afghanistan at around 11 million. A 1979 figure released by the Afghan government put total population at 14 million. Other estimates range between 16 and 18 million. The 28 million figure is given in the *CIA World Factbook 2004*, http://www.cia.gov/cia/publications/factbook/geos/af.html, and the U.S. State Department, *Bureau of South Asian Affairs*, November 2004, http://www.state.gov/r/pa/ei/bgn/5380.htm. The 22 million figure is given by the Population Division of the Department of Economic and Social Affairs of the United Nations Secretariat, *World Population Prospects: The 2002 Revision* and *World Urbanization Prospects: The 2001 Revision*, retrieved November 16, 2004, from http://esa.un.org/unpp. On the impact of the war on demographic patterns see Noor Ahmad Khalidi, *Demographic Consequences of War in Afghanistan* (Canberra, ACT, Australia: International Population Dynamics Program, Division of Demography and Sociology, Research School of Social Sciences, Australian National University, 1990); James Spitler and Nancy Frank, *Afghanistan: A Demographic Uncertainty* (Washington, DC: U.S. Department of Commerce, Bureau of the Census, 1978). See also Marek Sliwinski, *Afghanistan 1978–87: War, Demography and Society* (London: Society for Central Asian Studies, 1988).

15. On the Afghan refugees see Audrey Shalinsky, *Long Years of Exile: Central Asian Refugees in Afghanistan and Pakistan* (Lanham, MD: University Press of America, 1994). See also *Refugees from Afghanistan: A Look at History, Culture and the Refugee Crisis* (Washington, DC: United States Catholic Conference, Migration and Refugee Services, 1984); Tom Rogers and Anthony Hyman, *Afghans in Exile* (London: Centre for Security and Conflict Studies, 1987). Also see the U.S. Department of State, Bureau of South Asian Affairs, *Background Note: Afghanistan* (January 2004).

16. See *Human Rights Watch Backgrounder: Landmine Use in Afghanistan* (October 2001). Antipersonnel mines have been indiscriminately placed throughout Afghanistan, in both rural and urban areas, including pastures, farmlands, irrigation systems, roads, footpaths, and residential areas. In 2000 alone, there was an average of 80 recorded landmine casualties per month, with the totals for all such casualties estimated to be 50 to 100 percent higher. See also Stuart Maslen and Richard Lloyd, *Mine Action After Diana: Progress in the Struggle Against Landmines* (London: Pluto Press, 2004).

17. On the nomads of Afghanistan see Bernt Glatzer, "Afghan Nomads Trapped in Pakistan," in *The Tragedy of Afghanistan: The Social, Cultural and Political Impact of the Soviet Invasion*, ed. Bo Huldt and Erland Jansson, 240–247 (London: Croom Helm, 1988); Thomas Barfield, *The Central Asian Arabs of Afghanistan: Pastoral Nomadism in Transition* (Austin: University of Texas Press, 1981); Grom Pedersen, *Afghan Nomads in Transition: A Century of Change Among the Zala Khan Khel* (New York: Thames and Hudson, 1994); Birthe Frederiksen, *Caravans and Trade in Afghanistan: The Changing Life of the Nomadic Hazarbuz*, ed. Ida Nicolaisen (London: Thames and Hudson, 1996); M. Nazif Shahrani, *The Kirghiz and Wakhi of Afghanistan: Adaptation to Closed Frontiers and War* (Seattle: University of Washington Press, 2002). See also Larry Thompson, "Forgotten People: The Kuchis of Afghanistan," *Refugees International Bulletin* 17 (December 2003).

18. For a description of Afghan village life before the war, see A. P. Barnabas, *Farmer Characteristics in the Koh-i Daman Pilot Area Kabul* (Afghanistan: Programme on Agricultural Credit and Cooperatives in Afghanistan, 1970); A. P. Barnabas, *A Village in Afghanistan: A Descriptive Account, Kabul* (Afghanistan: Programme on Agricultural Credit and Cooperatives in Afghanistan, 1969). For the impact of the war on Afghan farmers see the report by the Swedish Committee for Afghanistan, *The Agricultural Survey of Afghanistan: First Report* (Peshawar, Pakistan: Swedish Committee for Afghanistan, 1988); Terje Skogland, "Ecology and War in Afghanistan," in Huldt and Jansson, *The Tragedy of Afghanistan*, 175–196. On the impact of the war in the post-Soviet period see Barnett Rubin, "Afghanistan: The Last Cold-War Conflict, the First Post-Cold-War Conflict," in *War, Hunger, and Displacement: The Origins of Humanitarian Emergencies: Case Studies*, ed. E. Nafziger, F. Stewart, and R. Vayrynen, Vol. 2, 23–52 (Oxford, England: Oxford University Press, 2000). On economic conditions during the Taliban and post-Taliban period, see Sue Lautze, E. Stites, N. Nojumi, and F. Najimi, *Qath-E-Pool "A Cash Famine": Food Insecurity in Afghanistan 1999–2002* (Boston, MA: Feinstein International Famine Center, Tufts University, 2002). For more recent developments see Adam Pain and Jonathan Goodhand, *Afghanistan: Current Employment and Socio-Economic Situation and Prospects*, InFocus Programme on Crisis Response and Reconstruction, Working Paper 8, Recovery and Reconstruction Department, Geneva, 2002.

19. On the concept of warlordism see J. A. G. Roberts, "Warlordism in China," *Review of Political Economy* 45/46 (Summer 1989), no. 16: 26–34.

20. On the criminalized war economy see Jonathan Goodhand, "From Holy War to Opium War? A Case Study of the Opium Economy in North Eastern Afghanistan," *Peace Building and Complex Political Emergencies* (Working Paper No. 5, IDPM, University of Manchester, 1999). Also see *The Opium Economy in Afghanistan: An International Problem* (New York: United Nations Office on Drugs and Crime, 2003); and see the report *Access to Labour: The Role of Opium in the Livelihood Strategies of Itinerant Harvesters Working in Helmand Province, Afghanistan: Final Report*, United Nations International Drug Control Programme; UNDCP Afghanistan Programme, 1999. On the regional implication of war economies see Michael Pugh, Neil Cooper, and Jonathan Goodhand, *War Economies in a Regional Context: Challenges of Transformation* (Boulder, CO: Lynne Rienner Publishers, 2004). On cross-border smuggling activities see Zafar Mahmood, *A Study of Smuggling on Pak-Afghan Border* (Islamabad, Pakistan: Pakistan Institute of Development Economics, 1998).

21. On ethnicity and ethnic groups in Afghanistan see Conrad Schetter, "Die Schimäre der Ethnie in Afghanistan," *Neue Zürcher Zeitung* 249 (2001), http://www.nzz.ch/dossiers/2001/afghanistan/2001.10.26-al-article7QTQF.html; Conrad Schetter, "Ethnicity and the Political Reconstruction in Afghanistan" (paper presented at the State Reconstruction and International Engagement in Afghanistan Organized by the Centre for Development Research, Bonn University [ZEF], and the Crisis States Programme, Development Research Centre, London School of Economics [LSE], Bonn, May 30–June 1, 2003), http://bglatzer.de/arg/arp/schetter.pdf. See also Bernt Glatzer, "Afghanistan on the Brink of Ethnic and Tribal Disintegration?," in *Fundamentalism Reborn? Afghanistan and the Taliban*, ed. William Maley, 167–181 (New York: New York University Press, 2001). On Afghan ethnic groups see Erwin Orywal, *Die Ethnischen Gruppen Afghanistans: Fallstudien zu Gruppenidentität und Intergruppenbeziehungen* (Wiesbaden, Germany: L. Reichert, 1986); Dupree, *Afghanistan*, 57–65; V. M. Masson and V. A. Romodin, *Istorija Afganistana*, Vols. 1–2 (Moscow, 1964–1965); Nassim Jawad, *Afghanistan: A Nation of Minorities* (London: Minority Rights Group International, 1992); Peter Marsden, *Afghanistan: Minorities, Conflict and the Search for Peace* (London: Minority Rights Group International, 2001). On the phenotypic characteristics of the Afghan population see G. F. Debets, *Physical Anthropology of Afghanistan* (Cambridge, MA: Peabody Museum, 1970).

22. Nassim Jawad, *Afghanistan: A Nation of Minorities.*

23. For historical background on the Pashtuns see Kirkpatrick Caroe, *The Pathans, 550 B.C.–A.D.* (Karachi, Pakistan: Oxford University Press, 1983); Richard Ridgway and Malik Munir Ahmed, *Pashtoons: History, Culture and Traditions* (Quetta, Pakistan: Sales and Services, 1997). For an anthropological study of the Ghilzai Pashtuns see Jon Anderson, *Doing Pakhtu: Social Organization of the Ghilzai Pakhtun* (Ann Arbor, MI: UMI Research Press, 1979). On the Pashtun tribes in the Khyber area see James Spain, *The People of the Khyber: The Pathans of Pakistan* (New York: Praeger, 1963). On Pashtuns in Pakistan see Charles Lindholm, *Frontier Perspectives: Essays in Comparative Anthropology* (Karachi, Pakistan: Oxford University Press, 1996); S. Iftikhar Hussain, *Some Major Pukhtoon Tribes Along the Pak-Afghan Border* (Islamabad, Pakistan: Area Study Centre, Hanns Seidel Foundation, 2000); Robert Wirsing, *The Baluchis and Pathans* (London: Minority Rights Group International, 1981); David Hart, *Qabila: Tribal Profiles and Tribe-State Relations in Morocco and on the Afghanistan-Pakistan Frontier* (Amsterdam, the Netherlands: Het Spinhuis, 2001). On the broader political impact of Pashtun tribal rivalries see Rahimullah Yusufzai, "Influence of Durrani-Ghalji Rivalry on Afghan Politics," in *Afghanistan: Past, Present and Future* (Islamabad, Pakistan: Institute of Regional Studies, 1997), 76–116.

24. On the Hazaras see Robert Canfield, *Hazara Integration into the Afghan Nation: Some Changing Relations Between Hazaras and Afghan Officials* (New York: Afghanistan Council of the Asia Society, 1970). See also Hassan Poladi, *The Hazaras* (Stockton, CA: Mughal, 1989); Klaus Ferdinand, *Preliminary Notes on Hazara Culture: The Danish Scientific Mission to Afghanistan 1953–55* (København: I kommission hos E. Munksgaard, 1959). See also Franz Schurmann, *The Mongols of Afghanistan: An Ethnography of the Moghôls and Related Peoples of Afghanistan* (The Hague, the Netherlands: Mouton, 1962); Sayed Askar Mousavi, *The Hazaras of Afghanistan: An Historical, Cultural, Economic and Political Study* (New York: St. Martin's Press, 1997). On the impact of the Soviet war on the Hazaras see Kristian Berg Harpviken, *Political Mobilization Among the Hazara of Afghanistan, 1978–1992* (Oslo, Norway: Institutt for Sosiologi og Samfunnsgeografi, Universitetet i Oslo, 1996). For the political/sectarian killings of the Hazaras during the Taliban period see Human Rights Watch, *Massacres of Hazaras in Afghanistan* (New York: Human Rights Watch, 2001).

25. On the Turkmen see William Irons, *The Yomut Turkmen: A Study of Social Organization Among a Central Asian Turkic-Speaking Population* (Ann Arbor: University of Michigan, 1975). On the Afghan Arabs see Thomas Barfield, *The Central Asian Arabs of Afghanistan: Pastoral Nomadism in Transition* (Austin: University of Texas Press, 1981). For the Baluch see Robert Wirsing, *The Baluchis and Pathans* (London: Minority Rights Group International, 1981). For an ethnographic account of the Nuristani see Schuyler Jones, *Men of Influence in Nuristan: A Study of Social Control and Dispute Settlement in Waigal Valley, Afghanistan* (London: Seminar Press, 1974); Karl Jettmar, Adam Nayyar, Schuyler Jones, and Max Klimburg, *The Religions of the Hindukush* (Warminster, Wiltshire, England: Aris & Phillips, 1986); Lennart Edelberg and Schuyler Jones, *Nuristan* (Graz, Austria: Akademische Druck- u. Verlagsanstalt, 1979. For a description of Nuristani culture written during the nineteenth century before the Afghan conquest see George Scott Robertson, *The Káfirs of the Hindu-Kush* (Karachi and New York: Oxford University Press, 1974).

26. On the languages and linguistic patterns in Afghanistan see Barbara Grimes, ed., *Ethnologue: Languages of the World* (Dallas, TX: Summer Institute of Linguistics, 2000); D. N. MacKenzie, "Pashto," in *The World's Major Languages* ed. B. Comrie, 547–565 (New York: Oxford University Press, 1987); MacKenzie, "Pashto," in *International Encyclopedia of Linguistics*, ed. W. Bright, Vol. 3, 165–170 (Oxford: Oxford University Press, 1992); H. G. Raverty, *A Grammar of the Pukhto, Pushto, or Language of the Afghans* (New Delhi, India: Asian Educational Service, 1987 [original work published 1860]); Herbert Penzl, *A Grammar of Pashto: A Descriptive Study of the Dialect of Kandahar, Afghanistan* (Washington, DC: American Council of Learned Societies, 1955); A. G. Raven Farhadi, *Languages* (Kabul, Afghanistan: Kabul Times Publishing Agency, 1967); Jadwiga Pstrusinska, *Afghanistan 1989 in Sociolinguistic Perspective* (London: Society for Central Asian Studies, 1990). On Dari/Farsi see J. R. Payne, "Iranian Languages," in Comrie, *The World's Major Languages*, 514–522.

27. Dupree, *Afghanistan*, 74.

28. On family and gender issues see Dupree, *Afghanistan*; Blood, *Afghanistan: A Country Study*; M. Nazif Shahrani, "The Future of the State and the Structure of Community and Governance in Afghanistan," in Maley, *Fundamentalism Reborn?*, 212–242; M. Jamil Hanifi, "Cultural Diversity, Conflicting Ideologies, and Transformational Processes in Afghanistan," in *The Nomadic Alternative: Modes and Models of Interaction in the African-Asian Deserts and Steppes*, ed. Wolfgang Weissleder, 387–396 (The Hague, the Netherlands: Mouton, 1978); Ruth Einsidler Newman, *Pathan Tribal Patterns: An Interim Study of Authoritarian Family Process and Structure* (Ridgewood, NJ: Foreign Studies Institute, 1965); Sarah Safdar, *Kinship and Marriage in Pukhtoon Society* (Lahore, Pakistan: Book Empire, 1997).

29. On the relationship between tribe and state see Richard Tapper, *The Conflict of Tribe and State in Iran and Afghanistan* (New York: St. Martin's Press, 1983); Christine Noelle-Karimi, Conrad Schetter, and Reinhard Schlagintweit, *Afghanistan: A Country Without a State?* (Frankfurt, Germany: IKO, 2002). See also Einsidler Newman, *Pathan Tribal Patterns;* Safdar, *Kinship and Marriage.* On the segmentary model see Steven Caton, "Power, Persuasion, and Language: A Critique of the Segmentary Model in the Middle East," *International Journal of Middle East Studies* 19, no. 1 (1987): 77–102; Dale Eickelman, *The Middle East and Central Asia: An Anthropological Approach* (Upper Saddle River, NJ: Prentice Hall, 2002), 120–126.

30. Rubin, *The Fragmentation of Afghanistan.*

31. On gender issues and tribal ideologies see Asta Olesen, *Islam and Politics in Afghanistan* (Richmond, England: Curzon Press, 1995), 33–34; Mark A. Drumbl, "Rights, Culture, and Crime: The Role of Rule of Law for the Women of Afghanistan," *Washington & Lee Public Law and Legal Theory Research Paper Series* (Working Paper No. 03-15, January 2004); Nancy Dupree, "Afghan Women Under the Taliban," in Maley, *Fundamentalism Reborn?*, 145–166; see also Valentine Moghadam's chapter "Afghanistan: Revolution, Reaction, and Attempted Reconstruction," in *Modernizing Women: Gender and Social Change in the Middle East* (Boulder, CO: Lynne Rienner, 2003), 227–297; Olesen, *Islam and Politics in Afghanistan,* 33–34; Nancy Tapper, *Bartered Brides: Politics, Gender, and Marriage in an Afghan Tribal Society* (Cambridge, England: Cambridge University Press, 1991). On human rights abuses and women see Amnesty International, *Women in Afghanistan: A Human Rights Catastrophe* (London: Author, 1995). On women and economic development see Sultan Barakat and Gareth Wardell, *Capitalizing on Capacities of Afghan Women: Women's Role in Afghanistan's Reconstruction and Development* (Geneva, Switzerland: InFocus Programme on Crisis Response and Reconstruction, 2001); Hafizullah Emadi, *Politics of Development and Women in Afghanistan* (Karachi, Pakistan: Royal Book Company, 1997); International Crisis Group, *Afghanistan: Women and Reconstruction* (International Crisis Group Report no. 48, Kabul and Brussels, 2003).

32. On Islam, a good general work to consult is John Esposito, ed., *The Oxford History of Islam* (Oxford, England: Oxford University Press, 1999). On the history of Islam see Gustave E. Von Grunebaum, *Classical Islam: A History, 600–1258* (Chicago: Aldine, 1970); G. E. Von Grunebaum, *Islam: Essays in the Nature and Growth of a Cultural Tradition* (London: Routledge and Kegan Paul, 1961); Jonathan Berkey, *The Formation of Islam: Religion and Society in the Near East, 600–1800* (New York: Cambridge University Press, 2003). For an overview of the caliphate see William Muir, *The Caliphate: Its Rise, Decline, and Fall (From the Original Sources)* (Edinburgh, Scotland: John Grant, 1924). An excellent introduction to the religion may be found in Montgomery Watt, *A Short History of Islam* (Oxford, England: Oneworld, 1996); Daniel Brown, *A New Introduction to Islam* (Malden, MA: Blackwell, 2004); Wilfred C. Smith, *Islam in Modern History* (New York: Mentor Books, 1957). See also Henry Corbin, *History of Islamic Philosophy* (London: Kegan Paul International, 1993). On the faith outside the Arab-speaking Middle East see David Westerlund and Ingvar Svanberg, *Islam Outside the Arab World* (New York: St. Martin's Press, 1999); John Miller and Aaron Kenedi, *Inside Islam: The Faith, the People, and the Conflicts of the World's Fastest-Growing Religion* (New York: Marlowe, 2002).

33. On the anthropological study of Islam see Gregory Starrett, "The Anthropology of Islam," in *Anthropology of Religion: A Handbook,* ed. Stephen Glazier, 279–304 (Westport, CT: Praeger, 1999); Dale Eickelman, "The Study of Islam in Local Context," *Contribution to Asian Studies* 17 (1982): 1–16; D. Eickelman, *The Middle East and Central Asia: An Anthropological Approach* (Upper Saddle River, NJ: Prentice Hall, 2002), 242–245; Richard Martin, "Clifford Geertz Observed: Understanding Islam as Cultural Symbolism," in *Anthropology and the Study of Religion,* ed. R. Moore and F. Reynolds (Chicago: Center for the Scientific Study of Religion, 1984), 11–30. See also Ernest Gellner, *Muslim Society* (Cambridge, England: Cambridge University Press, 1981).

34. On Islamic law see Mohammad Hashim Kamali, "Law and Society: The Interplay of Revelation and Reason in the Sharia," in Esposito, *The Oxford History of Islam,* 107–153; Vincent Cornell, "The Relationship Between Faith and Practice in Islam," Esposito, *The Oxford History of Islam,* 63–106. On Wahhabism, see Ayman Al-Yassini, *Religion and State in the Kingdom of Saudi Arabia* (Boulder, CO: Westview Press, 1985).

35. For overviews of Sufism see Corbin, *History of Islamic Philosophy,* 197–204; Brown, *A New Introduction to Islam,* 154–174; and Watt, *A Short History of Islam,* 126–130. See also Victor Danner, *The Islamic Tradition: An Introduction* (Amity, NY: Amity House, 1988); Arthur Arberry, *Sufism: An Account of the Mystics of Islam* (London: Allen and Unwin, 1950). On Sufism in Afghanistan see Bo Utas, "Scholars, Saints, and Sufis in Modern Afghanistan," in Huldt and Jansson, *The Tragedy of Afghanistan,* 93–105; see also Bo Utas, "Naqshbandiyya of Afghanistan on the Eve of the 1978 Coup d'état," in *Naqshbandis in Western and Central Asia: Change and Continuity: Papers Read at a Conference Held at the Swedish Research Institute in Istanbul, June 9–11, 1997,* ed. Elisabeth Özdalga (Richmond, England: Curzon Press, 1999). On Maraboutism see Dale Eickelman, *Moroccan Islam: Traditional Society in a Pilgrimage Center* (Austin: University of Texas Press, 1976); see also V. N. Basilov, "Honor Groups in Traditional Turkmen Society," in *Islam in Tribal Societies: From the Atlas to the Indus,* ed. A. Ahmed and D. Hart (London: Routledge and Kegan Paul, 1984), 220–243. On popular Islam see Vernon Schubel, "Devotional Life and Practices," in *The Muslim Almanac: A Reference Work in the History, Faith, Culture, and Peoples of Islam,* ed. Azim Nanji (New York: Gale Research Group, 1996), 223–231. On the role of Sufis in the antigovernment resistance see Robert Canfield, "Islamic Coalitions in Bamyan: A Problem in Translating Afghan Political Culture," *Revolutions and Rebellions in Afghanistan: Anthropological Perspectives,* ed. M. N. Shahrani and R. Canfield (Berkeley: University of California Press, 1984), 211–229. See also Robert Canfield, *Faction and Conversion in a Plural Society: Religious Alignments in the Hindu Kush* (Ann Arbor: University of Michigan, 1973).

36. On political Islam and the meanings of the concept of jihad see Olivier Roy, "Islamists in Power," in *The Islamist Debate,* ed. Martin Kramer (Tel Aviv, Israel: Tel Aviv University Press, 1997), 69–85; John Esposito, ed., *Political Islam: Revolution, Radicalism, or Reform* (Boulder, CO: Lynn Rienner, 1997). On theological issues and the Islamists see Majid Fakhry, "Philosophy and Theology," in Esposito, *The Oxford History of Islam,*

269–303. See also John L. Esposito, *Unholy War: Terror in the Name of Islam* (New York: Oxford University Press, 2002); James Turner Johnson, *The Holy War Idea in Western and Islamic Traditions* (University Park: Pennsylvania State University Press, 1997). On the concept of jihad see Sohail H. Hashimi, "Jihad," in *Encyclopedia of Politics and Religion*, ed. Robert Wuthnow (Washington, DC: Congressional Quarterly, Inc., 1998), 425–426; Lew Ware, "A Radical Islamist Concept of Conflict," in *Terrorism: National Security Policy and the Home Front*, ed. Stephen Pelletiere (Carlisle Barracks, PA: Strategic Studies Institute, U.S. Army War College, 1995), 31–60, http://www.carlisle.army.mil/ssi/pubs/1995/terror/terror.pdf. On the Islamists' use of high-tech communication channels see Gary Bunt, *Islam in the Digital Age: E-jihad, Online Fatwas and Cyber Islamic Environments* (London: Pluto Press, 2003). Other studies of radical Islamism include Olivier Roy, "The Transnational Dimensions of Radical Islamic Movements," in *Talibanisation: Extremism and Regional Instability in South and Central Asia* (Brussels, Belgium: Conflict Prevention Network, 2001), 75–88. See also Gilles Kepel, *Jihad: The Trail of Political Islam* (Cambridge, MA: Belknap Press of Harvard University Press, 2002); Malise Ruthven, *A Fury For God: The Islamist Attack on America* (New York: Granta, 2002).

37. The Muslim Brotherhood, *Jamiat al-Ikhwan al-Muslimin*, is a *salafi* Islamist organization that was created in 1928 by the Egyptian religious leader and ideologue Hasan al-Banna (1906–1949). The objective of the organization is to rid Islam of Western influences and all secular accretions and a return to the original precepts of the Qur'an. During the two decades after its creation, the Muslim Brotherhood increased in size and established economic, political, and educational components. It also became increasingly militant and established a military infrastructure. The movement's militancy and political violence led to crackdowns by the Egyptian government, which banned the Brotherhood in 1948. From that point onward, the Muslim brothers more or less functioned clandestinely. During the late 1980s the Egyptian government lifted the ban on the Brotherhood, but cracked down again in the late 1990s. The organization has a powerful presence in Egypt, Syria, Sudan, and many other Arab states in the Middle East. A number of militant groups that advocate political violence have splintered off from the Muslim Brotherhood, such as *Hamas, Gama'a al-Islamiya*, and Islamic *Jihad*. Among the members of the Muslim Brotherhood is Ayman Al-Zawahiri, Osama bin Laden's lieutenant and strategist for al-Qaeda and the founder of the Egyptian Islamic *Jihad*. On the Brotherhood see Carrie Rosefsky Wickham, *Mobilizing Islam: Religion, Activism, and Political Change in Egypt*, (New York: Columbia University Press, 2002); see also Quintan Wiktorowicz, *The Management of Islamic Activism: Salafis, the Muslim Brotherhood, and State Power in Jordan* (Albany: State University of New York Press, 2001); Christina Harris, *Nationalism and Revolution in Egypt: The Role of the Muslim Brotherhood* (Westport, CT: Hyperion Press, 1981); Johannes J. G. Jansen and Muhammad 'Abd al-Salam Faraj, *The Neglected Duty: The Creed of Sadat's Assassins and Islamic Resurgence in the Middle East* (New York: Macmillan, 1986). On Qutb see William E. Shepard, *Sayyid Qutb and Islamic Activism: A Translation and Critical Analysis of Social Justice in Islam* (Leiden, the Netherlands: Brill, 1996).

38. The Jamiat-i-Islami is very similar to the Egyptian Muslim Brotherhood in terms of its overall objectives and goals. It was established in 1941 by Abul Ala Mawdudi as an organization dedicated to enhance Islam in India. Following the partition of India, Jamiat-i-Islami committed itself to establish an Islamic state in Pakistan based upon the implementation of sharia law and under the leadership of the ulama. Among its activities was the eradication of non-Islamic beliefs and practices and heterodox Muslim religious sects, such as the Shi'a, and other lesser known groups, such as the Ahmadiyya movement. Like other salafi groups, the Jamiat-i-Islami strongly opposes Westernization and democratic ideals, and advocates the segregation of the sexes. The Jamiat has played an active role in Pakistani politics since the 1950s. See Seyyed Vali Reza Nasr, *The Vanguard of the Islamic Revolution: The Jama'at-i Islami of Pakistan* (Berkeley: University of California Press, 1994). On Mawdudi's ideas see his book, Sayyid Abul Ala Mawdudi, *Towards Understanding Islam* (Leicester, England: Islamic Foundation, 1980).

39. On Islam in Afghanistan see Olivier Roy, *Islam and Resistance in Afghanistan* (Cambridge, England: Cambridge University Press, 1986); Jon Anderson, "How Afghans Define Themselves in Relation to Islam," in Shahrani and Canfield, *Revolutions and Rebellions in Afghanistan*, 170–184. See also Graham Fuller, *Islamic Fundamentalism in Afghanistan: Its Character and Prospects* (Santa Monica, CA: Rand, 1991). On shrine worship and related practices see H. Sidky, "Malang, Sufis, and Mystics: An Ethnographic and Historical Study of Shamanism in Afghanistan," *Asian Folklore Studies* 49, no. 2 (1990): 275–301.

40. For a discussion of state structure during this period see Hasan Kakar, *Government and Society in Afghanistan: The Reign of Amir' Abd al-Rahman Khan* (Austin: University of Texas Press, 1979). For contemporary accounts of the amir see Frank A. Martin, *Under the Absolute Amir* (New York: Harper & Brothers, 1907); John Alfred Gray, *At the Court of the Amir: A Narrative* (London: Darf, 1987). For an overview see Vartan Gregorian, *The Emergence of Modern Afghanistan: Politics of Reform and Modernization, 1880–1946* (Stanford, CA: Stanford University Press, 1969).

41. On the rise and fall of Amanullah see Leon Poullada, *Reform and Rebellion in Afghanistan, 1919–1929: King Amanullah's Failure to Modernize a Tribal Society* (Ithaca, NY: Cornell University Press, 1973); Rhea Talley Stewart, *Fire in Afghanistan, 1914–1929; Faith, Hope, and the British Empire* (Garden City, NY: Doubleday, 1973). On the conflict between the state and the religious establishment over modernization see the study by Senzil Nawid, *Religious Response to Social Change in Afghanistan, 1919–29: King Aman-Allah and the Afghan Ulama* (Costa Mesa, CA: Mazda Publishers, 1999); Ikbal Ali Shah, *The Tragedy of Amanullah* (London: Alexander-Ouseley, 1933). On relations with the British see G. N. Molesworth, *Afghanistan 1919: An Account of Operations in the Third Afghan War* (Bombay, India: Asia Publishing House, 1962). On Bacha-i-Saqaw see Habibullah Khan (amir of Afghanistan), *My Life: From Brigand to King: Autobiography of Amir Habibullah* (London: Octagon Press, 1990).

42. On the nature of the Afghan state under the Musahiban see Richard Newell, *The Politics of Afghanistan* (Ithaca, NY: Cornell University Press, 1972); Barnett Rubin, *The Fragmentation of Afghanistan: State Formation and Collapse in the International System* (New Haven, CT: Yale University Press, 2002). On the ideological effects of the bifurcated structure of the

Afghan state and society see David Edwards, *Heroes of the Age: Moral Fault Lines on the Afghan Frontier* (Berkeley: University of California Press, 1996).

43. On the Afghan perspective on the Pashtunistan issue see Abdur Rahman Pazhwak, *Pukhtunistan: The Khyber Pass as the Focus of the New State of Pukhtunistan* (Hove, England: Key Press, 1952); see also the discussion by Louis Dupree, "*Pushtunistan:" The Problem and Its Larger Implications* (New York: American Universities Field Staff, 1961).

44. On the relations between the United States and Afghanistan up to the end of the monarchy see Leon Poullada and Leila Poullada, *The Kingdom of Afghanistan and the United States: 1828–1973* (Lincoln: Center for Afghanistan Studies at the University of Nebraska at Omaha and Dageforde, 1995); see also Leon Poullada, "The Road to Crisis 1919–1980—American Failures, Afghan Errors and Soviet Successes," in *Afghanistan: The Great Game Revisited*, ed. Rosanne Klass (New York: Freedom House, 1987), 37–69. On Afghan relations with Russia, Britain, and Germany see Ludwig Adamec, *Afghanistan's Foreign Affairs to the Mid-Twentieth Century: Relations with the USSR, Germany, and Britain* (Tucson: University of Arizona Press, 1974). For Afghan–Soviet relations see Anthony Hyman, *Afghanistan Under Soviet Domination, 1964–81* (New York: St. Martin's Press, 1982).

45. On Daoud's revolt see Hasan Kakar, "The Fall of the Afghan Monarchy in 1973," *International Journal of Middle East Studies* 9 (1978): 195–214; Louis Dupree, *A New Decade of Daoud?* (Hanover, NH: American Universities Field Staff, 1973). On military and political conditions during this period see Ralph Magnus, "The Military and Politics in Afghanistan: Before and After the Revolution," in *The Armed Forces in Contemporary Asian Societies*, ed. Edward Olsen and Stephen Jurika, 325–344 (Boulder, CO: Westview Press, 1986). See also Amin Saikal and William Maley, *Regime Change in Afghanistan: Foreign Intervention and the Politics of Legitimacy* (Boulder, CO: Westview Press, 1991), which covers the period between 1973 and 1989.

46. See Raja Anwar, *The Tragedy of Afghanistan: A First Hand Account* (London: Verso, 1988).

47. On the Marxist regime and its agenda see Anthony Arnold, *Afghanistan's Two-Party Communism: Parcham and Khalq* (Stanford, CA: Hoover Institution Press, Stanford University, 1983); see also the report by the PDPA itself, *A Short Information about People's Democratic Party of Afghanistan* (Kabul, Afghanistan: People's Democratic Party of Afghanistan, 1978). On the regime see Louis Dupree, "The Marxist Regime and the Soviet Presence in Afghanistan: An Ages-Old Culture Responds to Late Twentieth-Century Aggression," in *Revolutions and Rebellions in Afghanistan: Anthropological Perspectives*, ed. M. N. Shahrani and R. Canfield, 58–73 (Berkeley: University of California Press, 1984). See also Louis Dupree, "Red Flag Over the Hindu Kush. Part II: The Accidental Coup, or Taraki in Blunderland," *American Universities Field Staff Reports*, Asia, No 45, 1979. Other useful studies on the communist takeover and its consequences include Henry Bradsher, *Afghan Communism and Soviet Intervention* (New York: Oxford University Press, 1999); Thomas Hammond, *Red Flag Over Afghanistan* (Boulder, CO: Westview Press, 1984); Raja Anwar, *The Tragedy of Afghanistan: A First-Hand Account* (London: Verso, 1988). See also Hafizullah Emadi, *State, Revolutions, and Superpowers in Afghanistan* (New York: Praeger, 1990). On the Afghan resistance see Abdul Rashid, "The Afghan Resistance: Its Background, Its Nature, and the Problem of Unity," in Klass, *Afghanistan: The Great Game Revisited*, 203–227; Grant M. Farr and John G. Merriam, eds., *Afghan Resistance: The Politics of Survival* (Boulder, CO: Westview Press, 1987); Olivier Roy, *Islam and Resistance in Afghanistan* (Cambridge, England: Cambridge University Press, 1986); Jan Ovesen, "A Local Perspective on the Incipient Resistance in Afghanistan," in Huldt and Jansson, *The Tragedy of Afghanistan*, 148–154. On human rights during the Soviet period see Helsinki Watch Committee, *"Tears, Blood and Cries": Human Rights in Afghanistan Since the Invasion 1979–1984* (New York: Helsinki Watch Committee, 1984); Barnett Rubin, *To Die in Afghanistan: A Supplement to "Tears, Blood and Cries," Human Rights in Afghanistan Since the Invasion, 1979 to 1984* (New York: Helsinki Watch Committee, 1985); Amnesty International, *Afghanistan, Torture of Political Prisoners* (New York: Author, 1986).

48. On how the Soviets implemented regime change in Kabul see Lester Grau, *The Take-Down of Kabul: An Effective Coup de Main* in *Urban Operations: An Historical Casebook* (Fort Leavenworth, KS: Combat Studies Institute, 2002), http://www.globalsecurity.org/military/library/report/2002/MOUTGrau.htm. A revealing work on the Soviet invasion and its consequences is Douglas MacEachin, *Predicting the Soviet Invasion of Afghanistan: The Intelligence Community's Record* (Washington, DC: Center for the Study of Intelligence, Central Intelligence Agency, 2002). See also Anthony Arnold, *Afghanistan: The Soviet Invasion in Perspective* (Stanford, CA: Hoover Institution, 1981); Henry Bradsher, *Afghanistan and the Soviet Union* (Durham, NC: Duke University Press, 1983); Joseph Collins, *The Soviet Invasion of Afghanistan* (Lexington, MA: D.C. Heath, 1986); M. Hasan Kakar, *Afghanistan: The Soviet Invasion and the Afghan Response, 1979–1982* (Berkeley: University of California Press, 1995); Giustozzi, *War, Politics and Society in Afghanistan*. See also Huldt and Jansson, *The Tragedy of Afghanistan*; Joseph Collins, *The Soviet Invasion of Afghanistan: A Study in the Use of Force in Soviet Foreign Policy* (Lexington, MA: Lexington Books, 1986); Roger Reese, *The Soviet Military Experience: A History of the Soviet Army, 1917–1991* (London: Routledge, 2000); Edgar O'Ballance, *Afghan Wars, 1839–1992: What Britain Gave Up and the Soviet Union Lost* (New York: Barssey's, 1993); Douglas Borer, *Superpowers Defeated: Vietnam and Afghanistan Compared* (Portland, OR: F. Cass, 1999); Mark Galeotti, *Afghanistan, The Soviet Union's Last War* (London: Frank Cass, 1995). Studies from a military perspective include Mohammad Yousaf and Mark Adkin, *The Bear Trap: Afghanistan's Untold Story* (London: L. Cooper, 1992); Lester Grau and Michael Gress, *The Soviet-Afghan War: How a Superpower Fought and Lost* (Lawrence: University Press of Kansas, 2002). On Mujahideen tactics see Ali Ahmad Jalali and Lester Grau, *The Bear Went Over the Mountain, The Other Side of the Mountain: Mujahideen Tactics in the Soviet-Afghan War* (Quantico, VA: U.S. Marine Corps, Studies and Analysis Division, 1999). On the evolution of the Afghan jihad see David Edwards, *Before Taliban: Genealogies of the Afghan Jihad* (Berkeley: University of California Press, 2002). On Soviet casualties in Afghanistan see G. F. Krivosheev, *Soviet Casualties and Combat Losses in the Twentieth Century* (London: Greenhill Books, 1997). On the social effects of Soviet casualties sent home in zinc coffins see Svetlana Aleksievich, *Zinky Boys: Soviet Voices from the Afghanistan War* (New York:

W.W. Norton, 1992); see also Vladislav Tamarov, *Afghanistan: A Russian Soldier's Story* (Berkeley, CA: Ten Speed Press, 2001).

49. Useful primary sources on U.S. policy regarding Afghanistan during this period are available in Steve Glaster, *Afghanistan: The Making of U.S. Policy, 1973–1990,* National Security Archive, George Washington University, 2001, http://nsarchive.chadwyck.com/afintro.htm. For an overview of Cold War relations between the United States and the Soviet Union see Raymond Garthoff, *Détente and Confrontation: American-Soviet Relations from Nixon to Reagan* (Washington, DC: Brookings Institution, 1985). On how the Soviets were lured into invading Afghanistan see Selig Harrison, "How the Soviet Union Stumbled into Afghanistan," in *Out of Afghanistan: The Inside Story of the Soviet Withdrawal,* ed. Diego Cordovez and Selig Harrison, 13–49 (New York: Oxford University Press, 1995). On Reagan's strategy to use Afghanistan as a means of destabilizing the Soviet Union see Peter Schweizer, *Victory: The Reagan Administration's Secret Strategy That Hastened the Collapse of the Soviet Union* (New York: Atlantic Monthly Press, 1994). Some analysts disagree that the Soviet Union collapsed as a result of the war in Afghanistan; see Cordovez and Harrison, *Out of Afghanistan,* 2–16.

50. See the discussion of U.S. and Pakistani interference inside Afghanistan by Anwar, *Tragedy of Afghanistan,* 229–236. See also John Cooley, *Unholy Wars: Afghanistan, America, and International Terrorism* (London: Pluto Press, 2002); Kristian Harpviken, "'War and Change' in Afghanistan: Reflections on Research Priorities," in *Return to the Silk Routes: Current Scandinavian Research on Central Asia,* ed. Mirja Juntunen and Brigit Schklyter, 167–186 (London: Kegan Paul, 1999); Diego Cordovez and Selig Harrison, "Overview: Afghanistan and the End of the Cold War," in Cordovez and Harrison, *Out of Afghanistan,* 2–16. On the role of foreign powers see Amnesty International, *International Responsibility for Human Rights Disaster* (London: Author, 1995).

51. Craig Davis, "'A' is for Allah, 'J' is for Jihad," *World Policy Journal* 19, no. 12 (2002): 90–94.

52. On the tribal feud see J. Black-Michaud, *Cohesive Force: Feud in the Mediterranean and the Middle East* (New York: St. Martin's Press, 1975). For ethnographic material on tribal feuds see L. Keiser, *Friend by Day, Enemy by Night: Organized Vengeance in a Kohistani Community* (Orlando, FL: Holt, Rinehart & Winston, 1991).

53. The idea of the Soviet's master plan for global domination by trying to get to "warm water ports" from where they would threaten everyone else in South Asia, which was part of the United States' Cold War rhetoric, seems to be the underlying theme in the work of most of the anthropologists and other Western writers of the period. The Soviets had no such plans. See G. M. Kornienko, "The Afghan Endeavour: Perplexities in the Military Incursion and Withdrawal," *Journal of South Asian and Middle Eastern Studies* 17, no. 2 (1994): 2–17. For primary sources see Svetlana Savranskaya, ed., *The Soviet Experience in Afghanistan: Russian Documents and Memoirs,* National Security Archive, George Washington University, 2001, http://www.gwu.edu/~nsarchiv/NSAEBB/NSAEBB57/soviet.html.

54. On covert operations by the United States in Afghanistan see the report compiled by V. Ashitkov, Karen Gevorkian, and Vladimir Svetozarov, *The Truth About Afghanistan: Documents, Facts, Eyewitness Reports* (Moscow: Novosti Press, 1986); also see R. Galiullin, *The CIA in Asia: Covert Operations Against India and Afghanistan* (Moscow: Progress Publishers, 1988); the pamphlet issued by the Afghan government, *The Secret War of CIA Against Afghanistan* (Kabul, Afghanistan: Government Printing Press, 1984); and *Afghanistan: The Target of Imperialism* (Kabul, Afghanistan: Party Printing Press, 1983). On the role of Iran see *White Book: The Role of the Islamic Republic of Iran in the Undeclared War Against the Democratic Republic of Afghanistan* (Kabul, Afghanistan: DRA, Ministry of Foreign Affairs, Information and Press Department, 1986). There are a number of general studies of covert U.S. intervention in Afghanistan. See Steve Coll, *Ghost Wars: The Secret History of the CIA, Afghanistan, and Bin Laden, from the Soviet Invasion to September 10, 2001* (New York: Penguin Press, 2004); John Prados, "Notes on the CIA's Secret War in Afghanistan," *Journal of American History* 89, no. 2 (2002), available from the History Cooperative, http://www.historycooperative.org. See also Charles Cogan, "Partners in Time: The CIA and Afghanistan Since 1979," *World Policy Journal* (Summer 1993); Phillip Bonosky, *Afghanistan: Washington's Secret War* (New York: International Publishers, 2001); Peter Harclerode, *Fighting Dirty: The Inside Story of Covert Operations: From Ho Chi Minh to Osama Bin Laden* (London: Cassell, 2001); Edward Alexander Gibbs, *Agency Without an Adversary: The CIA and Covert Actions in the Nineteen-Eighties and Beyond* (dissertation, University of Nevada, Las Vegas, 1996); George Crile, *My Enemy's Enemy: The Story of the Largest Covert Operation in History—The Arming of the Mujahideen by the CIA* (London: Atlantic, 2002); Tim Weiner, *Blank Check: The Pentagon's Black Budget* (New York: Warner Books, 1990); William Blum, *Killing Hope: U.S. Military and CIA Intervention Since World War II* (Montreal: Black Rose Books, 1998).

55. Robert Friedman, "The CIA's Jihad," *The New York Times,* March 27, 1995, pp. 36–47.

56. On Pakistan's role in the war in Afghanistan see Frédéric Grare, *Pakistan and the Afghan Conflict, 1979–1985 (With an Afterword Covering Events From 1985–2001*) (Karachi, Pakistan: Oxford University Press, 2003). On the radicalization of Pakistani society because of the Afghan jihad see Larry Goodson, "Foreign Policy Gone Awry: The Kalashnikovization and Talibanization of Pakistan," in *Pakistan 2000,* ed. Charles Kennedy and Craig Baxter, 107–128 (Lanham, MD: Lexington Books, 2000). See also Charles H. Kennedy, "Islamization and Legal Reform in Pakistan, 1979–89," *Pacific Affairs* 63 (1990): 62–77; Anita Weiss, ed., *Islamic Reassertion in Pakistan* (Syracuse, NY: Syracuse University Press, 1986); Afzal Iqbal, *Islamisation of Pakistan* (Lahore, Pakistan: Vanguard Books, 1986). See the article by Seyyed Vali Reza Nasr, "The Rise of Sunni Militancy in Pakistan: The Changing Role of Islamism and the Ulama in Society and Politics," *Modern Asian Studies* 34, no. 1 (2000): 139–180; S. V. R. Nasr, "International Politics, Domestic Imperatives, and Identity Mobilization: Sectarianism in Pakistan, 1979–1998," *Comparative Politics* 32, no. 2 (2000): 171–190; and S. V. R. Nasr, "Islam, the State and the Rise of Sectarian Militancy in Pakistan," in *Pakistan: Nationalism Without a Nation,* ed. Christophe Jaffrelot, 85–114 (New York: Zed Books, 2002). See also Mary Anne Weaver, *Pakistan: In the Shadow of Jihad and Afghanistan* (New York: Farrar, Straus and Giroux, 2002).

57. On the role of the CIA and ISI in drug trafficking see Weiner, *Blank Check,* 151–152; Alfred W. McCoy, *The Politics of*

Heroin: CIA Complicity in the Global Drug Trade, Afghanistan, Southeast Asia, Central America, Colombia (Chicago: Lawrence Hill Books, 2003); Alexander Cockburn and Jeffrey St. Clair, *Whiteout: The CIA, Drugs, and the Press* (New York: Verso, 1998); and Cooley, *Unholy Wars*, 105–134. See also Peter Dale Scott, *Drugs, Oil, and War: The United States in Afghanistan, Colombia, and Indochina* (Lanham, MD: Rowman & Littlefield, 2003). On the development of the Afghanistan–Central Asia drug trade see Tamara Makarenko, "Crime, Terror and the Central Asian Drug Trade," *Harvard Asia Quarterly* 6, no. 3 (Summer 2002).

58. Zbigniew Brzezinski, "Some Stirred Up Muslims: Reflections on Soviet Intervention in Afghanistan," in *The Middle East Reader*, ed. Marvin Gettleman and Stuart Schaar, 273–274 (New York: Grove Press, 2003).

59. On the Soviet withdrawal see Sarah Elizabeth Mendelson, *Changing Course: Ideas, Politics, and the Soviet Withdrawal from Afghanistan* (Princeton, NJ: Princeton University Press, 1998); Tom Rogers, *The Soviet Withdrawal from Afghanistan: Analysis and Chronology* (Westport, CT: Greenwood Press, 1992); Amin Saikal and William Maley, *The Soviet Withdrawal from Afghanistan* (Cambridge, England: Cambridge University Press, 1989). See also Cordovez and Harrison, 2–16. On the aftermath of the collapse of the Kabul regime see Rasul Bakhsh Rais, *War Without Winners: Afghanistan's Uncertain Transition After the Cold War* (Karachi, Pakistan and New York: Oxford University Press, 1994); Barnett Rubin, *The Search for Peace in Afghanistan: From Buffer State to Failed State* (New Haven, CT: Yale University Press, 1995); also see Rubin, *The Fragmentation of Afghanistan*; Kurt Lohbeck, *Holy War, Unholy Victory: Eyewitness to the CIA's Secret War in Afghanistan* (Washington, DC: Regnery Gateway, 1993); Charles Howard Norchi, *Afghanistan After the Soviets: Time, Culture and Chaos* (Geneva, Switzerland: Modern Asia Research Centre, 1995); William Maley and Fazel Haq Saikal, *Political Order in Post-Communist Afghanistan* (Boulder, CO: Lynne Rienner, 1992); Olivier Roy, *Afghanistan: from Holy War to Civil War* (Princeton, NJ: Darwin Press, 1995).

60. Schetter, "Die Schimäre der Ethnie in Afghanistan."

61. On the political and economic effects of the weapons flooding the region see Chris Smith, "The Impact of Light Weapons on Security: A Case Study of South Asia," in *Yearbook 1995: Armaments, Disarmament and International Security* (Oxford, England: Stockholm International Peace Research Institute, 1995), 583–593; see also Bobi Pirseyedi, *The Small Arms Problem in Central Asia: Features and Implications* (Geneva, Switzerland: United Nations Institute for Disarmament Research, 2000).

62. For general background of the Taliban movement see Larry P. Goodson, *Afghanistan's Endless War: State Failure, Regional Politics, and the Rise of the Taliban* (Seattle: University of Washington Press, 2001). Useful general works on the Taliban's nature, origins, and rise to power include Michael Griffin, *Reaping the Whirlwind: Afghanistan, Al Qa'ida and the Holy War* (London: Pluto Press, 2003); Neamatollah Nojumi, *The Rise of the Taliban in Afghanistan: Mass Mobilization, Civil War, and the Future of the Region* (New York: Palgrave, 2002); M. J. Gohari, *The Taliban: Ascent to Power* (Karachi, Pakistan: Oxford University Press, 2000); Kamal Matinuddin, *The Taliban Phenomenon: Afghanistan 1994–1997* (Karachi, Pakistan: Oxford University Press, 1999); Peter Marsden, *The Taliban: War and Religion in Afghanistan* (New York: Zed Books, 2002); Maley, *Fundamentalism Reborn?* On the Taliban agenda see the article by Julie Sirrs, "The Taliban's International Ambitions," *Middle East Quarterly* 8, no. 3 (2001): 61–71. For background on the Deobandi roots of the Taliban consult Barbara Daly Metcalf, *Islamic Revival in British India: Deoband, 1860–1900* (Princeton, NJ: Princeton University Press, 1982). For the story of the "American Talib," or "Johnny *Jihad* Walker" of the U.S. media see Mark Kukis, *"My Heart Became Attached:" The Strange Journey of John Walker Lindh* (Washington, DC: Brassey's, 2003). On the events surrounding Walker's capture and the massacre that ensued at Qala-i-Janghi prison in Mazar-i-Sharif see Richard Mahoney, *Getting Away with Murder: The Real Story Behind American Taliban John Walker Lindh and What the U.S. Government Had to Hide* (New York: Arcade, 2003).

63. On the role of Pakistan in the creation of the Taliban movement see Ahmed Rashid, "A New Proxy War: Foreign Powers Again Feeding Arms to Factions," *Far East Economic Review*, February 1, 1996; Ahmed Rashid, "The Taliban: Exporting Extremism," *Foreign Affairs* 78, no. 6 (1999): 22–35; see also M. Rubin, "Who Is Responsible for the Taliban?" *Middle East Review of International Affairs* 6, no. 1 (2002): 1–16; Gilles Dorronsoro, "Pakistan and the Taliban: State Policy, Religious Networks, and Political Connections," in *Pakistan: Nationalism Without a Nation*, ed. Christophe Jaffrelot, 161–179 (New York: Zed Books, 2002); Anthony Davis, "How the Taliban Became a Military Force," in Maley, *Fundamentalism Reborn?*, 43–71. An interesting article on the same subject is Robert Kaplan, "The Lawless Frontier: Tribal Relations, Radical Political Movements and Social Conflict in Afghanistan-Pakistan Border," *The Atlantic Monthly*, September 1, 2000, and his book *Soldiers of God: With Islamic Warriors in Afghanistan and Pakistan* (New York: Vintage Books, 2001). See also Barry Shlachter, "Inside Islamic Seminaries, Where the Taliban Was Born," *The Philadelphia Inquirer*, November 25, 2001. For an overview of Pakistan's interference in Afghan affairs see Human Rights Watch, *Afghanistan: Crisis of Impunity: The Role of Pakistan, Russia, and Iran in Fueling the Civil War* (New York: Author, 2001); Olivier Roy, "The Taliban: A Strategic Tool for Pakistan," in Jaffrelot, *Pakistan: Nationalism Without a Nation*, 149–160; William Maley, "Talibanisation and Pakistan," in *Talibanisation: Extremism and Regional Instability in South and Central Asia* (Brussels, Belgium: Conflict Prevention Network, 2001), 53–74. For primary sources on the Taliban movement see Sajit Gandhi, ed., *The Taliban File Part III: Pakistan Provided Millions of Dollars, Arms, and "Buses Full of Adolescent Mujahid" to the Taliban in the 1990's*, National Security Archive Electronic Briefing Book No. 97, http://www.gwu.edu/~nsarchiv/NSAEBB/NSAEBB97/index.htm.

64. Maley, *Afghanistan Wars.*

65. On the U.S. diplomatic stance on the Taliban see the article by Zalmay Khalilzad, the neoconservative State Department employee and UNOCAL advisor currently the U.S. Ambassador to Afghanistan, "Afghanistan: Time to Reengage," *The Washington Post*, October 7, 1996; Brisard and Dasquié, *Forbidden Truth*; Maley, *Afghanistan Wars*; Amin Saikal, "The Afghan Tragedy and the US Response," in *The Day the World Changed? Terrorism and World Order*, ed. S. Harris, W. Maley, R. Price, C. Reus-Smit, and A. Saikal, 9–17 (Canberra,

Australia: Department of International Relations, 2001); Richard Mackenzie, "The United States and the Taliban," in Maley, *Fundamentalism Reborn?*, 90–103. On U.S. efforts to negotiate an oil pipeline deal with the Taliban see Ahmed Rashid, *Taliban: Militant Islam, Oil, and Fundamentalism in Central Asia* (New Haven, CT: Yale University Press, 2000), Brisard and Dasquié, *Forbidden Truth*; Scott, *Drugs, Oil, and War.*

66. On Taliban policies on women see N. Dupree, "Afghan Women Under the Taliban." See also the report by Amnesty International, *Women in Afghanistan: Pawns in Men's Power Struggles* (New York: Author, International Secretariat, 1999). For a general account of life under the Taliban, bin Laden, al Qaeda, and Mullah Omar, see the volume compiled by the staff of Reuters, *Afghanistan: Lifting the Veil* (Upper Saddle River, NJ: Prentice Hall, 2002); Vincent Iacopino, *The Taliban's War on Women: A Health and Human Rights Crisis in Afghanistan* (Boston: Physicians for Human Rights, 1998); and Chris Johnson, *Afghanistan: A Land in Shadow* (Oxford, England: Oxfam, 1998). Other insightful accounts include Rosemarie Skaine, *The Women of Afghanistan Under the Taliban* (Jefferson, NC: McFarland, 2002); Sally Armstrong, *Veiled Threat: The Hidden Power of the Women of Afghanistan* (New York: Four Walls Eight Windows, 2002); Deborah Ellis, *Women of the Afghan War* (Westport, CT: Praeger, 2000).

67. These statistics are provided in the report by Human Rights Watch, *Humanity Denied.*

68. On Taliban violations of international law, human rights, and sectarian killings see Human Rights Watch, *Massacres of Hazaras in Afghanistan* (New York: Human Rights Watch, 2001); Amnesty International, *Human Rights Defenders in Afghanistan: Civil Society Destroyed* (London: Author, International Secretariat, 1999); Amnesty International, *Afghanistan: Detention and Killing of Political Personalities* (London: Author, International Secretariat, 1999). See also the report by Rahimullah Yusufzai, "Taliban Enforce Islamic Justice," *The News* (Pakistan), March 1, 1995. On the genocidal attacks by the Taliban and the Arab Afghans on religious minorities see U.N. Security Council, "Report of the Secretary-General on the Situation in Afghanistan and Its Implications for International Peace and Security" (report S/2001/1157, December 6, 2007, p. 13). On the murder of Najibullah, the last communist leader, by the Taliban see Phillip Corwin, *Doomed in Afghanistan: A UN Officer's Memoir of the Fall of Kabul and Najibullah's Failed Escape, 1992* (New Brunswick, NJ: Rutgers University Press, 2003). On the destruction of Afghanistan's cultural property at Taliban hands see Nancy Dupree, *Status of Afghanistan's Cultural Heritage* (Peshawar, Pakistan: Pakistan Society for the Preservation of Afghanistan's Cultural Heritage, 1998); see also K. Warikoo, ed., *Bamiyan: Challenge to World Heritage* (New Delhi, India: Bhavana Books & Prints, 2002).

69. On bin Laden see Yossef Bodansky, *Bin Laden: The Man Who Declared War on America* (Rocklin, CA: Forum, 2001). See also Peter Bergen, *Holy War, Inc: Inside the Secret World of Osama Bin Laden* (New York: Free Press, 2001); Alex Woolf, *Osama bin Laden* (Minneapolis: Lerner Publications, 2004). Additional information on bin Laden is provided in the following articles: Mary Anne Weaver, "The Real Bin Laden," *New Yorker*, January 24, 2000; John Miller, "Greetings, America. My Name Is Osama bin Laden. Now That I Have Your Attention," *Esquire* 131 (February 1999): 96–103. See also *The 9–11 Commission Report: Final Report of the National Commission on Terrorist Attacks Upon the United States, Official Government Edition*, http://www.gpoaccess.gov/911/. On bin Laden's political views and declarations see Benjamin Orbach, "Usama bin Laden and *al-Qaeda*: Origins and Doctrines," *Middle East Review of International Affairs*. 5, no. 4 (2001): 54–68; "Osama bin Laden v. U.S.: Edicts and Statements," *Frontline*, http://www.pbs.org/wgbh/pages/frontline/shows/binladen/who/edicts.html. On the fatwas see Bernard Lewis, "License to Kill: Usama bin Laden's Declaration of Jihad," *Foreign Affairs* (November/December 1998); Peter Bergen, "Terrorism's Dark Master," *Vanity Fair* (December 2001); Magnus Ranstorp, "Interpreting the Broader Context and Meaning of Bin-Laden's 'Fatwa,'" *Studies in Conflict & Terrorism* 21 (October–December 1998): 321–330. On the relationship between al-Qaeda, bin Laden, and the Taliban see Kenneth Katzman, *Afghanistan: Current Issues and U.S. Policy Concerns, Congressional Research Service* (Washington, DC: Library of Congress, November 15, 2001), 18–19. See also the report by Bob Woodward, "Bin Laden Said to 'Own' the Taliban," *The Washington Post*, October 11, 2001: and Steve Le Vine's article "Helping Hand," *Newsweek*, October 14, 1997. On pre-September 11 U.S. efforts to neutralize bin Laden see Ryan Hendrikson, "The Clinton Administration's Strikes on Usama Bin Laden: Limits to Power, in *Contemporary Cases in U.S. Foreign Policy*, ed. Ralph Carter (Washington, DC: CQ Press, 2002), 196–216; Anthony Davis, "Targeting Bin Laden," *Asiaweek*, September 4, 1998; Richard Newman, "America Fights Back," *U.S. News & World Report*, August 31, 1998; Barry Watson and John Barry, "Our Target Was Terror," *Newsweek*, August 31, 2000. On efforts to neutralize bin Laden following September 11 see Robin Moore, *The Hunt for Bin Laden: Task Force Dagger* (New York: Random House, 2003). On the Afghan Arabs see Barnett Rubin, "Arab Islamist in Afghanistan," in Esposito, *Political Islam*, 179–206. On bin Laden's complicity in the assassination of the Afghan military commander Ahmad Shah Massoud see Alan Cullison and Andrew Higgins, "Computer in Kabul Holds Chilling Memos," *The Wall Street Journal*, January 1, 2002; see also Joseph Fitchett, "Did Bin Laden Kill Afghan Rebel?" *International Herald Tribune*, September 17, 2001.

70. On al Qaeda see Simon Reeve, *The New Jackals: Ramzi Yousef, Osama Bin Laden and the Future of Terrorism* (Boston: Northeastern University Press, 1999); Montasser Zayat, *The Road to al-Qaeda: The Story of Bin Laden's Right-hand Man* (London: Pluto Press, 2004). On the global terror network see Roland Jacquard, *In the Name of Osama bin Laden: Global Terrorism & the Bin Laden Brotherhood* (Durham, NC: Duke University Press, 2002). For a general overview see Katzman, *Terrorism: Near Eastern Groups.* On the organization's ideological stance see Christopher Blanchard, *Al Qaeda: Statements and Evolving Ideology* (Washington, DC: CRS, 2004). For other recent studies see Phillip Margulies, *Al Qaeda: Osama bin Laden's Army of Terrorists* (New York: Rosen Publishing Group, 2003); Jason Burke, *Al-Qaeda: The True Story of Radical Islam* (London: Penguin books, 2004); Bruce Hoffman, *Al Qaeda, Trends in Terrorism and Future Potentialities: An Assessment* (Santa Monica, CA: Rand, 2003); Jane Corbin, *The Base: Al-Qaeda and the Changing Face of Global Terror* (Oxford, England: ISIS, 2003).

71. Chalmers Johnson develops the concept of "blowback" in his book *Blowback: The Cost and Consequences of American Empire*

(New York: Henry Holt, 2000). See also Mary Anne Weaver, "Blowback," *Atlantic Monthly* (May 1996), http://www.theatlantic.com/issues/96may/blowback.htm#Weaver. There are a number of studies relating to Afghanistan on the blowback theme: Charles H. Norchi, "Blowback from Afghanistan: The Historical Roots," *International Security Studies at Yale University*, February 1996, http://www.ciaonet.org/wps/noc01/; Richard Labévière, *Dollars for Terror: The United States and Islam* (New York: Algora, 2000); Cooley, *Unholy Wars*; Coll, *Ghost War*; Crile, *My Enemy's Enemy*; Harclerode, *Fighting Dirty*; Tom Lansford, *A Bitter Harvest: US Foreign Policy and Afghanistan* (Burlington, VT: Ashgate, 2003); Mark Zepezauer, *Boomerang!: How Our Covert Wars Have Created Enemies Across the Middle East and Brought Terror to America* (Monroe, ME: Common Courage Press, 2003); Mahmood Mamdani, *Good Muslim, Bad Muslim: America, the Cold War, and the Roots of Terror* (New York: Pantheon Books, 2004); Mariam Abou Zahab and Olivier Roy, *Islamist Networks: The Afghan-Pakistan Connection* (London: Hurst & Company in association with the Centre d'Etudes et de Recherches Internationales, Paris, 2004).

72. A useful place to begin is Fredrik Logevall, ed., *Terrorism and 9/11: A Reader* (New York: Houghton Mifflin, 2002). On the September 11 attacks see Joanne Meyerowitz, *History and September 11th* (Philadelphia: Temple University Press, 2003); Fred Halliday, *Two Hours That Shook the World, September 11, 2001: Causes and Consequences* (London: Saqi Books, 2002). See also *The 9-11 Commission Report*; Tamara L. Roleff, ed., *The World Trade Center Attack* (San Diego, CA: Greenhaven Press, 2003). On the failure of the hunt for al Qaeda in Afghanistan see Philip Smucker, *Al Qaeda's Great Escape: The Military and the Media on Terror's Trail* (Washington, DC: Brassey's, 2004).

73. For analysis of the U.S. operations in Afghanistan see Carl Conetta, *Strange Victory: A Critical Appraisal of Operation Enduring Freedom and the Afghanistan War* (Cambridge, MA: Commonwealth Institute Project on Defense Alternatives, research monograph 6, 2002); Norman Friedman, *Terrorism, Afghanistan, and America's New Way of War* (Annapolis, MD: Naval Institute Press, 2003). On U.S. human rights abuses see Human Rights Watch, *"Enduring Freedom": Abuses by U.S. Forces in Afghanistan* (New York: Human Rights Watch, 2004). See also the controversial documentary film *Massacre in Mazar*, by Irish director Jamie Doran (2002). On U.S. policy in the post-Taliban period see Kenneth Katzman, *Afghanistan: Post-War Governance, Security, and U.S. Policy* (Washington, DC: CRS, 2004). On the reconstruction of Afghanistan see Barnett Rubin, Ashraf Ghani, William Maley, Ahmed Rashid, and Olivier Roy, *Afghanistan: Reconstruction and Peacebuilding in a Regional Framework*, Koff Peacebuilding Reports, Report 1, 2001, Bern, Switzerland: Center for Peacebuilding (KOFF), Swiss Peace Foundation (SPF), 2001. See also William Maley, "Terrorism, Freedom, and Institutions: Reconstructing the State in Afghanistan," *Aakrosh: Asian Journal on Terrorism and Internal Conflicts* 5, no. 15 (2002): 22–36. On the problem of warlords see United States Institute of Peace, *Unfinished Business in Afghanistan: Warlordism, Reconstruction, and Ethnic Harmony*, Special Report 105, April 2003. See also Human Rights Watch, "Human Rights Watch Briefing Paper: Afghanistan: Return of the Warlords," June, 02, 2004, http://www.hrw.org/backgrounder/asia/afghanistan/warlords.htm. On the resurgence of the Taliban see B. Raman, "The Fall and Rise of the Taliban," *Asia Times* online, October 23, 2003, http://atimes.com/atimes/Central_Asia/EJ23Ag02.html; David Rohde, "Taliban Raids Widen in Parts of Afghanistan," *The New York Times*, September 1, 2003; U.N. Security Council, "Report of the Secretary-General on the Situation in Afghanistan and Its Implications for International Peace and Security" (report A/57/850–S/2003/754); Christopher Langton, "Instability Threatens Reconstruction," Institute for War and Peace Reporting, No. 13914, June 13, 2003, http://www.iwpr.net/index.pl?archive/arr/arr_200306_64_2_eng.txt. See also Antonio Donini, Norah Niland, and Karin Wermester, *Nation-Building Unraveled?: Aid, Peace and Justice in Afghanistan* (Bloomfield, CT: Kumarian Press, 2004).

3 INDIA

Anne Hardgrove

GEOGRAPHY

The region known as India is often referred to as a subcontinent, a reference to the peninsular shape of the landmass jutting into the Indian Ocean, and to the diversity of peoples and cultures that have inhabited its lands. It is one of the oldest and most complex civilizations in the world. This chapter discusses the peoples and cultures of India, addressing issues about land and environment, religious traditions and diversity, and history and politics.

To what does the term *India* refer? Use of the term may cause confusion because of the fact that in 1947 the Indian subcontinent was divided into two separate countries, India and the new nation of Pakistan. (Later, in 1971, East Pakistan separated from Pakistan to become the new nation of Bangladesh.) When speaking of India it is important to be clear about whether one is referring to the entire geographical subcontinent of India, or specifically to the modern nation-state of India. This chapter will use the term *India* to refer to the politically undivided Indian subcontinent before 1947. If the chapter makes reference to events or people or institutions before 1947, we will be talking about undivided India. If the chapter refers to events or people or institutions dating after 1947, then it is about the present country of India, exclusive of Pakistan and Bangladesh.[1] Chapter 4 on Pakistan in this book details this nation's peoples, history, and culture after 1947. Some of the pre-1947 topics discussed in this chapter, such as the archaeological sites of the Indus river valley, are technically located in the modern nation of Pakistan.

One other important term that comes up in reference to the Indian subcontinent is *South Asia. South Asia* or *southern Asia* refers to India, Pakistan, Ceylon, Nepal, Bhutan, and sometimes Afghanistan. The rather new term *South Asia* was coined after World War II by American policy makers who hoped to coin a neutral geopolitical term to refer to the entire region, as distinct from the newly independent nation of India.

Geologically, the region of India was created as the northeastern section of the Australian tectonic plate began to move northward and pushed into the large Eurasian tectonic plate. The gradual collision of these gigantic land masses, a very slow process that continues to this day, caused the overlapping land to buckle upon itself, creating the largest mountains on Earth, the Himalayas. The tallest of these mountains is located in the modern nation of Nepal. This 29,028 foot giant is known as Mount Everest, and has long been a spiritual

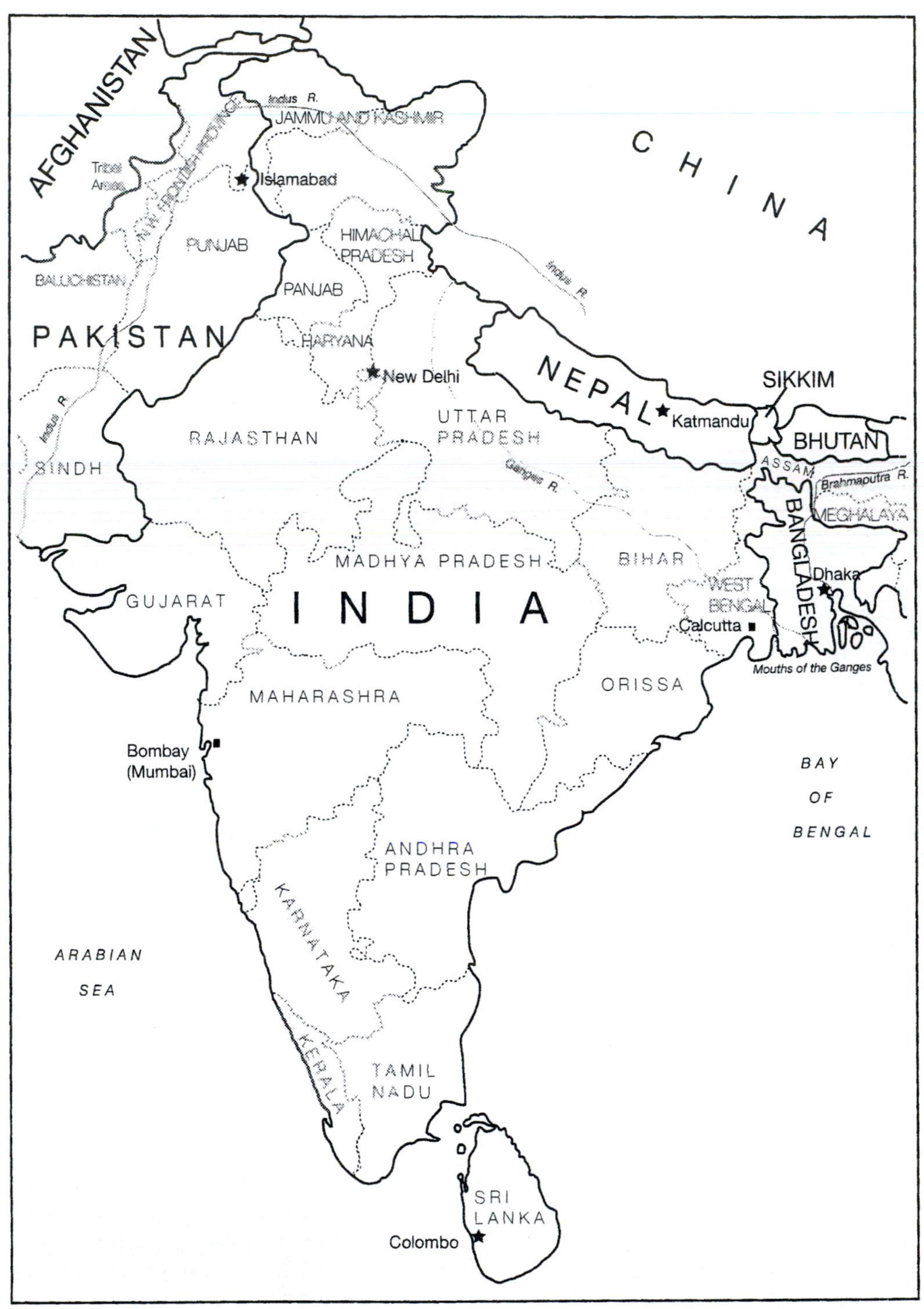
AFGHANISTAN
Indus R.
JAMMU AND KASHMIR
CHINA
Tribal Areas
Islamabad
PUNJAB
HIMACHAL PRADESH
BALUCHISTAN
PANJAB
PAKISTAN
HARYANA
New Delhi
NEPAL
SIKKIM
Katmandu
BHUTAN
Indus R.
RAJASTHAN
UTTAR PRADESH
SINDH
ASSAM
Ganges R.
Brahmaputra R.
MEGHALAYA
BANGLADESH
MADHYA PRADESH
BIHAR
WEST BENGAL
Dhaka
GUJARAT
INDIA
Calcutta
Mouths of the Ganges
MAHARASHRA
ORISSA
Bombay (Mumbai)
BAY OF BENGAL
ANDHRA PRADESH
KARNATAKA
ARABIAN SEA
KERALA
TAMIL NADU
SRI LANKA
Colombo

site of local Hindu and Buddhist peoples, as well as posing one of the most intensive physical challenges for mountain-climbing enthusiasts from all over the globe. Hundreds of people have attempted to climb this mountain in the last half-century, with nearly one out of three losing their lives at some point during the summit and descent.[2] Due to the continuing pressure of the colliding tectonic plates, such towering mountain peaks, including Mount Everest and Pakistan's K2, continue to grow. Occasional earthquakes in the northeastern part of the region are evidence of these continuing geological changes.

There are several major land features in the Indian subcontinent. First are the impressive mountain ranges of the subcontinent, as discussed. The tallest of these are in the northern part of the region, the Himalayas. Though we tend to think of mountain ranges as natural barriers separating groups of people who may live on either side, there has been a significant amount of trans-Himalayan trade across this region.[3] The hill areas tend to be cooler in temperature than the plains regions, and offer a break from the heat and humidity of climates at lower altitudes. There are also smaller hill systems, such as the eastern and western Ghats. These hills run roughly parallel to eastern and western coastlines, and culminate in the state of Tamil Nadu in the Palni Hills. One major geographical division in India is the divide between North India and South India, and many geographers cite the Vindhya range as the dividing point between north and south, running east from the Gulf of Cambay. However, the north–south divide is arguably more related to the dramatic linguistic differences between north and south, between the Indo-European languages and the Dravidian languages, respectively, rather than being geographically determined.

A second major feature is the river valleys of the Ganges, Indus, and Brahmaputra. The starting points of these rivers are the melting glaciers of the Himalayan mountains. There is recent scientific evidence that these glaciers are melting at rates more rapid than normal, and could eventually dry up completely, which would cause massive ecological and human destruction. These river systems have deposited rich soils in an arclike shape extending from the western Arabian Sea to the eastern Bay of Bengal. Most of the major world civilizations sprung up around river systems, and the river valleys of South Asia are no exception. A large majority of the population of India lives along the river banks of the Ganges and Brahmaputra in India and the Indus in Pakistan. The rivers have played an important role in the religious practices of the population. Places where certain rivers cross each other, namely, the confluence, are important holy sites to pilgrims who travel long distances to bathe in the waters.

A third notable feature is the deserts of Rajasthan, the Punjab, and Central India, where sandy soil composition and hot weather create an arid climate, presenting challenges to cultivation. Other major topographical features include the swampy lowlands in Bengal, Orissa, Andrha Pradesh, and the Malabar and Konkon Coasts on the east and west coasts, respectively.

The climate of India is generally tropical. The region is entirely north of the equator and thus in the earth's Northern Hemisphere. The warm climate is amenable to agriculture, which is the mainstay of the economy and India's agricultural self-sufficiency. The wet climates produce rice, and the drier areas produce wheat, millet, corn, lentils, spices, sugarcane, cotton, tea, tobacco, and jute. The success of the crops, however, depends on the yearly rains, known as the monsoon. The word *monsoon* comes from the Arabic word for season.

One of the most prominent features about the climate, affecting both culture and economics, is the monsoon. These yearly rains that are expected in the months of June, July, and August follow the hot "summer" months of

April and May. The arrival of the monsoon brings relief from the relentless heat of summer. Some historians have gone so far as to say that one can define "Asia" as being the countries where the monsoon flourishes.[4] Both the timing of the monsoon and the amount of rain that falls are important in determining whether or not the monsoon is a success. Inadequate rainfall or late arrival can mean insufficient crop production and potential famine, but an overabundance of rain may lead to torrential flooding with tragic loss of human life.

The monsoon is considered one of the three seasons in the Indian climate, in addition to summer and winter. The monsoon is eagerly awaited, bringing its cooling and rejuvenating rains, and the storm systems have acquired an enormous symbolic value in Indian culture. After all, a good harvest is dependent on having a good monsoon, and a weak monsoon, or the failure of the monsoon to arrive at all, can mean disaster and even starvation for many people. The monsoon has had a massive impact on the local cultures. For centuries people have sung folksongs to beckon or to welcome the rain. The enormously popular Indian movies almost always feature scenes of the monsoon, more often than not depicting the sultry heroine dancing in the rain in a sopping wet sari, drawing connections between sensuousness and the renewal of life through the annual rains.

The width of India would normally justify dividing the country into two separate time zones. But for convenience, the country occupies one time zone, which is either 10½ or 11½ hours ahead of the Central Time Zone in the United States (depending on daylight savings time). Nepal, to the north and east, sets its national clock 15 minutes ahead of India.

PREHISTORY

South Asia has been inhabited by people for at least the past half-million years. This section will discuss two periods of ancient Indian history: the Stone Ages and the Indus Valley Civilization. We might first start out by addressing the question of how the experts know about these oldest civilizations. Scholars have learned about these ancient societies by two methods. The first is in the study of archaeology: The primary evidence comes from stone tools that they used. Archaeology has provided us with tangible, three-dimensional facts in the material remains discovered through survey and excavation. These facts not only corroborate the second method, literary evidence, but they also help fill in the gaps, particularly in the earliest period of Indian history. Archaeology has been the most important tool in learning about the Stone Age and the Indus Valley. What is described in the following sections is a general summary—the prehistoric periods of various regions and societies differ; there is no single chronology for the subcontinent.

The so-called Stone Age peoples date back from 400,000 BC to 3500 BC. The earliest traces of human activity in India, so far discovered, go back to the second Interglacial period between 400,000 and 200,000 BC. These show evidence of the use of stone implements. Over time these people gradually refined their tools, and the sophistication of their tools helps scholars further classify the Stone Age peoples into three periods.

The first period is the Early Stone Age, also known as the Paleolithic period. The earliest tools date back to 400,000 BC. In this early Stone Age there was a hand-ax industry similar to that found in western Asia, Europe, and Africa. They had quartzite hand axes, cleavers, chopping tools, and flake tools. Note that these early axes differ from modern-day axes because they are not hafted. Experts believe that these tools spread from Africa and the Near East into India. No axes have been found in the Himalayas or near the Ganges, which were probably heavily forested and considered unfavorable places to live.

The second period of the Stone Age is known as the Middle Stone Age, also referred to as the Mesolithic period. This period is characterized by quantities of flake-blade artifacts. The hand axes gave way to these flake tools. The flakes are made into a variety of tools such as scrapers and borers. They are made on jasper, hert, agate, and other fine-grained stone. These were first found in the western state of Maharashtra. The people from this era may represent a transitional stage between early food-collecting cultures and later agriculturalists and herders. This age thus might also be called the wood age. The scrapers and other tools were used for fashioning projectiles and wooden implements. They made projectile points out of bamboo or wood to make hunting spears.

The third period is the Late Stone Age, also called the Neolithic period. This period includes ground, polished stone tools, agriculture, domesticated animals, and pottery. There is also evidence of bows and arrows. This is the precursor to the development of the Indus Valley or Harappa Civilization that came next. We still have many unanswered questions about cultural contact with other groups. We do not know about the different tribes or even what these people looked like.

Archaeologists have even found some human remains from this period. Humans were buried with their knees drawn up to their chins, and there was a dog buried with one man. Gujarat is the only area that provides a clear picture of concepts such as the afterlife. Archaeologists have found burial sites with ornamentation of the body and the presence of small animals, fish, and grains.

One brief comment about the periodization of the three periods of the Stone Age is pertinent here. Of course, there is some variation and overlap among these periods. For example, there is not a smooth transition from the use of one type of tool to another. Some people were using older tools when others were using newer ones. It is clear that peoples living in the late Stone Age hunting and gathering mode persisted into periods that were characterized by more advanced technologies. In this respect they were probably no different than many contemporary Indian tribal groups who in their remote villages persist in a way of life significantly different than their more "modern" neighbors.[5]

After the Stone Ages, the second major period of ancient India is the Indus Valley Civilization, also called the Harappa Civilization. The discovery of the Harappa Civilization had great intellectual significance for the understanding of Indian society. In modern times, nobody realized before the 1930s that a widespread primary civilization stretched out over most of Pakistan and parts of western India. This civilization in its mature period lasted from 2400 to 1750 BC, and it petered out around 1300 or 1500 BC. From the Hindu texts, we had thought that the Aryans were the oldest civilization.[6]

There are two major sites of the Indus Valley Civilization. Technically the cities of Mohenjo-Daro and Harrapa are located in Pakistan, and Harappa is located where the modern Punjab is. Mohenjo-Daro is located along the Indus River in modern Pakistan. Unlike the later Aryans, the Harappa civilization was predominantly urban. Evidence of elaborate city planning shows how important the organization of the city was to this civilization. The cities were very uniform. This suggests a centralized political organization—there were orderly streets, sanitary facilities, and fortifications. Each city was divided into the citadel area, where the essential institutions of civic and religious life were located, and a residential area where the urban population lived.

Harappa was the first site to be discovered in modern times. Clues to the existence of an early civilization were discovered in 1872 at the site of Harappa in the Punjab. But, at the time, the excavator believed that the finds (stone tools and a seal) were non-Indian and discontinued the explorations since it was generally assumed Indian civilization had begun with the Aryans (1000–8000 BC).

Mohenjo-Daro was discovered in 1921 and was immediately recognized as being prehistoric and of great importance. Its connection with Harappa over 400 miles away was established by the discovery of seals in the Harappan style. Over an eight-year period of excavation, this discovery extended knowledge of civilization in India to 3000 BC. One of the major finds at Mohenjo-Daro was evidence of fortification and weapons, which disproved an earlier idea that the occupants were all pacifists. Now experts believe that Mohenjo-Daro was a provincial capital in a network of such cities.

Until this discovery in the early twentieth century, most experts believed that the Aryans were the earliest inhabitants of India, as mentioned. It is hard to pinpoint when the Harappa civilization began, but some experts think as early as 3000 BC. The anthropologist Stephen Tyler gives the dates of 2150 BC to 1750 BC as the time span of the Indus Civilization in the Indus Valley. Tyler chose these dates on the basis of radiocarbon dating tests.

Archaeologists have found evidence of extensive trading networks. The presence of the seals reflects trade with Mesopotamia—extended to the Deccan, Tibet, and Central Asia.

An example of Indus Valley seals.

There is also evidence of subsistence production: grains were cultivated, including wheat, barley, and rice. There was also extensive use of domesticated animals. The use of metal appears to be common as well—there many recovered artifacts including copper spears, a bronze ax, and a famous image of a dancing girl.

The discovery of physical evidence has led experts to speculate on social and religious organization. First of all, this civilization was organized by classes, or what anthropologists call a stratified society. Harappa society probably included priests, merchants, nobles, agriculturalists, and crafts workers (metal workers, sculptors, seal engravers, carpenters, potters, and brick makers). The culture also included practices of fertility worship. There is evidence of mother goddess worship, animal worship, ritual bathing, tree worship, and phallic worship. A figure that looks like an early version of the god Shiva was also discovered. Some of these elements were absorbed into later Hindu culture, including worship of the phallus by Saivites, the followers of Shiva, and the eventual emergence of mother goddesses in the male-dominated Vedic pantheon.

Whether or not the Indus civilization is the essential paradigm of all subsequent Indian civilization is an interesting debate for modern Indians. One of the major questions is to determine who these people were. Were they Aryans? Were they Dravidians? What is the overall significance of the Indus Valley Civilization for modern India? In one sense, present-day Indian society and culture are the result of 5,000 years of Indian history stretching back to the Indus Valley cities of Harappa and Mohenjo-Daro (300–1500 BC). The first prime minister of independent India, Jawaharlal Nehru, wrote,

> Who were the people of the Indus Valley civilization and whence had they come? We do not know yet. It is quite possible, and even probable,

> that their culture was an indigenous culture and its roots and offshoots may be found even in southern India. Some scholars find an essential similarity between these people and the Dravidian culture of south India. Even if there was some ancient migration to India, this could only have taken place some thousands of years before the date assigned to Mohenjo-Daro. For all practical purposes we can treat them as the indigenous inhabitants of India.[7]

As Nehru wrote, many now believe that the Indus Valley peoples were the ancestors of the Dravidian speakers and that the invading Indo-Aryan speakers were actually not the carriers of higher civilization into the subcontinent, as nineteenth-century Europeans tend to argue.

Material evidence reveals complex patterns of life. This was an agricultural society and had wheat, barley, peas, melon, sesame, and cotton. Indus valley peoples used flood irrigation. They also had domesticated animals, including cattle, buffalo, goats, sheep, pigs, and dogs. There was extensive overland trade through caravans and river and sea routes. They imported gold, copper, and ornaments that show their links with civilizations in the west. The Indus seals found in Mesopotamian sites stand as evidence of these trade links. Cities were built with elaborate planning principles and reflect centralized authority, social stratification, and craft specialization. The planning of cities was particularly sophisticated and there was nothing like it anywhere else in the world. They had wells, piped water, and bathrooms with waste pipes and drains. In America and western Europe these innovations were not widespread until the late nineteenth century—about 2,500 years later! This emphasis on water suggests an origin of the Indian civilization's emphasis on bathing, washing, and ritual purity. There were early representations of Shiva (Creator and Destroyer); the god of harvest; the cycle of birth, life, death, and rebirth (reincarnation); the mother goddess; phallic images; and worship of cattle.

There was a "citadel" mound dominating the cities. The people had written records on seals used for trade and administration, although we have not deciphered them. There are inscriptions in pictographic script—which represent proper names of gods, high officials, institutions, and individuals. There are also iconographic pictures with animals and anthropomorphic figures that may be early forms of Hindu gods. Sculpture included works of high artistic quality, with stone torsos, priest-king busts, and bronze dancing-girl figures. There is evidence that pottery and tools and weapons were mass produced.

Why did the Indus Valley Civilization decline? Two major theories exist. The first theory is that there were significant geographical changes, including coastal uplift and abnormal flooding. The resulting erosion of the land led to economic decline, lower civic standards, and cultural collapse. In short, this theory says that floods destroyed the civilization to the extent that it could not be rebuilt. The second theory is that the civilization of the Indus Valley was destroyed by invaders, probably the Aryans. The weakened cities may have been overcome by waves of Aryan invaders from the northwest. The archaeological evidence for Indo-Aryans in the Punjab includes graves, pottery, and copper hoards. In the Rg Veda, one of the oldest Hindu texts, there are condescending references to Punjab rivers and to battles with dark-skinned, snub-nosed people who are phallus worshippers, cattle keepers, and city dwellers. It is possible that these describe the collision of cultures between the Indus Valley dwellers and the Aryan invasion.

LANGUAGE

One of the most remarkable things about the people of India, at least from an American perspective, is that it is typical for Indians to speak at least two languages fluently, if not more, as part of their everyday routines. It would not be uncommon, for example, for a professional urban woman to speak in a regional language such as Marathi with the domestic help, to speak Hindi with the driver who takes her to work, and to speak and write in English at the office. In the evening, on the telephone, she might call her parents and speak to them in their family's mother tongue of Kannada. Her husband and children, away visiting cousins in Canada, send emails in English and French. A popular television movie in Tamil plays in the background. Later, at a religious function with her friends, she might hear or recite prayers in Arabic or Sanskrit.

The Constitution of India officially recognizes 17 national languages in India, and within each of those major languages there are innumerable dialects. Yet, it is estimated that 35 different languages are used by at least one million people. Many people wonder how Indians are able to communicate with each other in the midst of such diversity. Contrary to what some foreigners might think, there is no language called "Indian." Even the English language, which was originally foreign to India, is spoken by about 6 percent of the population, and can provide only a limited "link language" among the middle classes and elite. Even though the government of India has declared Hindi to be the Official Language of the Central Government, outside northern India, where Hindi is locally found, there has been resistance in adopting Hindi as the language of government administration, let alone in everyday life.

Language plays an important role in how South Asians choose to identify themselves as part of particular communities of speakers. The identification of language and region became strong enough to form the basis of the linguistic reorganization of Indian states. The language that one learns as a child, and speaks with the family at home, is called the "mother tongue" and becomes a primary marker of one's community. The mother tongue may be different than the local regional language, especially when one's parents live away from their linguistic homeland. For example, a Tamil boy growing up in the provincial capital city of Lucknow, an Urdu-speaking city in the state of Uttar Pradesh, may consider Tamil to be his mother tongue, even though his family may have lived outside the state of Tamil Nadu for several generations. A number of social movements have formed on the basis of language identity. For instance, the decision to create a new nation of Bangladesh in 1971 came about on the insistence of the Bengali-speaking people of East Pakistan. Even though these Bengalis shared a religious identity with the Pakistanis, through Islam, to them the issue of language played a more important role.

In addition to the nation of Bangladesh, the separate states of the independent country of India have been drawn largely on the basis of linguistic boundaries. Hindi is the official language of several northern states, including Uttar Pradesh, Bihar, Rajasthan, Haryana, Madhya Pradesh, and Himachal Pradesh. Hindi speakers may understand the "modern standard" Hindi taught in schools and found in the workplace, but are likely to speak one of many dialects, and be able to understand many others. Maharashtra is defined by the regional language of Marathi, Bengal by Bengali, Punjab by Punjabi, and Orissa by Oriya, to cite a few examples. Urdu has been the mother tongue to many in India's large Muslim community, along with north Indians in general, and as a spoken language is nearly identical to Hindi, although it is written in a different script. In the south, state boundaries were also defined by local regional languages: Tamil Nadu by Tamil, Kerala by Malayalam, Karnataka by Telugu, and Andhra Pradesh by Kannada.

These languages of southern India are called Dravidian, and the major ones include Tamil, Kannada, Malayalam, and Telugu. There is evidence to suggest that an early form of Dravidian languages was the language of the Indus Valley Civilization and in western India, and speakers of these languages were pushed southward with the migration and settlement of the Aryans from the north. The many Sanskrit words found in these languages suggest the influence of the Indo-Europeans on their vocabulary. Each of the Dravidian languages has a separate vocabulary and grammar, and is written in a different script, or alphabet. These languages are not at all related to the languages of northern India. The speakers of the Dravidian languages have considerable pride in their own mother tongue, and object strongly to the imposition of Hindi as both the language of government and a language of everyday use. Visitors to South India often comment that they have been better off trying to communicate in English than in Hindi, for fear of offending local sensibilities.

Another family of languages spoken by tribal peoples are those known as Munda. Speakers of Munda dialects live in remote areas of India. These languages have been shown to be related to the languages spoken by aboriginal peoples of Australia in the southeast portion of that country.

The languages of northern India are part of the Indo-European family, a linguistic chain that includes many of the languages of Europe. They are even distantly related to the languages of Greek and Latin. It is probable that the Aryans spoke an early prototype of Indo-European language, and that this gradually developed into the language of Sanskrit, which is one of the classical languages of India, and the language of many important epics and poems. The languages of northern India evolved from Sanskrit, and these languages still draw upon Sanskrit for much of their vocabulary, in particular Bengali. The northern languages also derive many vocabulary words taken from Persian and Arabic, as a result of long-standing trade relationships with people from those regions, as well as Muslim migrations and Muslim rule in northern India from about AD 700 to the eighteenth century. Even the name *India* is rooted in these origins.

By 1000 BC, the Aryans had conquered as far as the Deccan, but the Aryan languages have never prevailed in the south. The south resists what it still refers to as Aryan pressures or influences. South Indians tend to reject Hindi as the national language—they feel that they are being forced to study it, and they do not like to speak it as a point of pride. Some of the tensions among speakers of languages have become enveloped in the tensions among ethnic identities. This is the case in the island nation of Sri Lanka (formerly known as Ceylon), off the southeast coast of India, which was settled by both Aryan language speakers who speak Sinhala and by Dravidians from South India who speak Tamil.

The film industry in Bombay—called Bollywood (*Bombay* + *Hollywood*)—is the biggest in the world, and has had an important impact on the dispersal of Hindi throughout the subcontinent and beyond.[8] The language of Bollywood films is an accessible form of Hindi mixed with Urdu, and many people who grew up outside Hindi-speaking regions have learned to understand Hindi by watching these movies in cinema halls or at home on VCRs and DVD players. Even in the largely anti-Hindi south, audiences thoroughly enjoy the latest hits. Bollywood films are watched all over the world, and have a particularly strong following in Africa and in the Persian Gulf. There is also a film industry in the south of India that makes films in Tamil. Like the Hindi films, these films are shown in theaters, but also there is an explosion in the videocassette industry. The filmmakers increasingly incorporate Western motifs and travel scenes when the characters travel abroad, implying the cosmopolitan nature of Hindi as a language that links Indians overseas. Tamil-language films are also very popular within India, with a film industry on par with the Hindi-language film studios, but do not yet have the global circulation of their Hindi-language competition.

HISTORY AND POLITICS

Throughout history, India has been the home of a diverse people. The nation of India has many reasons to be proud. India is a vibrant, sovereign, independent nation that boasts the largest democracy in the world. India is a major player in world trade, and known for its nuclear capacities, scientific and technical achievement, leadership in the sports world in cricket, and leading role in international affairs. Increasingly the global high-tech sector has relied on Indians' professional expertise and employs large numbers of English-speaking graduates from Indian universities. Through satellite technology, it is increasingly likely that an American corporate or bank representative handles its customer care operations through the metropolis of Mumbai (formerly known as Bombay). Doctors' clinics in the United States have begun to transmit physicians' dictations on patients' symptoms over Internet or satellite links at the end of the business day—which, because of the 11½ hour time change, arrive just at the start of the workday in India. The notes are transcribed and sent back to the United States by the start of the next workday, ready to be cataloged in the patient's files. Since the mid-1960s a number of South Asians have emigrated to the United States, and it is likely that the average American would encounter a person from the subcontinent as a doctor, engineer, computer programmer, or professor, or as a worker in the service sector. People today proudly identify themselves as Indians, taking pride in the accomplishments of the nation and its peoples.

But as recently as three hundred years ago, the situation was different. The land mass of India was there, the diversity of its languages, cultures, and religions was there, but the modern Indian nation did not exist as such. Instead, the region was comprised of separate territories, and people identified themselves as being part of a particular village or princely kingdom—not a whole "nation." No one would have thought of himself or herself as being "Indian." In fact, that concept can apply for many peoples of the world. But, in spite of this diversity there was a concept of a broader landscape unified through cultural practices. However, this recognition of sameness came largely from outside the region. Foreigners ranging from the Persians and the Arabs to the British spoke of the region as India or Hindustan (Land of the Hindus), but the term carried no meaning for the local inhabitants.

So how did India get its name? The Aryan word for the Indus River and its valley was *Sindhu*, which also meant "sea." The term gradually referred to the land across from the Indus River. In later years the Persians changed the name *Sindhu* to *Hind* to refer to the river valley. The Greeks—Alexander the Great—called the land "India," which they took from the Persian Hindu. During the millennium of Muslim rule in the subcontinent, *Hindu* referred to anyone living in the river region and beyond who had not converted to Islam. One legacy of this is that in the Spanish language, Indians are referred to as Hindu.

The history of India is typically organized into chronological periods, depending on the origins and identity of the rulers. The first historical record comes with the rule of the Aryans, and our discussion starts there. Then follows the rise of various kingdoms, including the Guptas, Mauryas, Muslims, Mughals, the British, and finally independent India.

When scholars talk about Aryans, they are talking about a group of people who spoke Indo-European languages. They are not referring to an ethnic group. The term *Aryan* refers to a group of nomadic tribes bound by closely related dialects of parent languages. *Aryan* is a linguistic term—but has been misused to mean a people or a race. After 2000 BC there were a series of migrations from Iran—both to the west and to the east to India. These people spoke an early form of Sanskrit. This Aryan language was a proto Indo-European language. There is also archaeological evidence that their homeland was in the southern Russian–Ukrainian steppes as well as Iran. They called themselves Aryan, a term denoting their superiority. *Aryan* also meant "noble" and "respectable," in distinction to the preexisting people of India. The Aryans had domesticated horses and used light war chariots. There is inscriptional evidence of Indo-European names, gods, and terminology in Asia Minor by 1800 BC. The Aryans (or Indo-Aryans as they are sometimes called) entered the northwest of India. They were the descendents of the Indo-Europeans. By about 1700 BC they migrated into northern India through the passes in the Hindu Kush Mountains.

The superior military tactics of the Aryans, especially the domestication of horses and the use of light war chariot, were probably the main factors behind the spread of the Aryan languages across such a vast geographic space. The introduction of bronze weapons and war chariots from Mesopotamia may have encouraged nomadic Indo-European tribes to loot or conquer advanced societies. The Aryan expansion was generally an eastern movement and settlement around the Ganges River, accompanied by a gradual shift from nomadic to sedentary life. Archaeologists have found the remains of pottery that suggest settlement. They also colonized south into the Indian peninsula where they were a minority.

When the Indo-Aryan–speaking peoples entered India around 1500 BC, like their counterparts on the Iranian plateau, they were loosely divided into three orders of society: warriors, priests, and common people. By the sixth century BC the social ideology of the Indo-Aryan peoples was being influenced if not shaped by their contacts with non-Indo-Aryan agriculturalists and town dwellers. By the third century BC there was a social ideology that divided society into four major orders (*varnas*): the priests (Brahmans), warriors (Kshatriyas), traders (Vaishyas), and cultivators (Shudras).

The burgeoning civilization inspired by Aryan culture became marked by these class distinctions. Education was limited to upper classes, and there was a general high caste or Brahmanic dominance of the society. In education, there was a guru system whereby a teacher worked with students to transmit knowledge by memory. As such, there was stress on elaborate rituals and the cultivation of memory. The Aryans had no written language but spoke an early form of a language known as Sanskrit. Sanskrit was codified in 500 BC by the grammarian Panini. This became the official literary language of the educated, and became a high status language.

The Mauryan Empire began around 321 BC. The most famous Mauryan leader was Ashoka, who reigned from 269 to 232 BC. Ashoka was known at first for his aggressive military tactics—he built an empire stretching across the north and central portions of India. What followed was one of the most radical royal personality transformations in history. He embraced Buddhism, particularly the elements of nonviolence, and expressed great sadness for the war and bloodshed his campaigns had caused. He resolved not to pursue conquests by war, and funded Buddhist missionaries to spread the cause of peace. He even abolished hunting. Ashoka's obsession with righteous living did not help build a lasting legacy, however. The military had been made inactive, and morale was low. Provincial leaders were not well supervised and had become corrupt. After Ashoka's death, the empire was weakened and individual princes had little power.

From Graeco-Roman times until about AD 1820 India was considered a wealthy country, and was an important producer and exporter of luxury items. India had a favorable balance of trade—more exports than imports—and its trading partners often complained about the cost of importing Indian items that drained the treasuries of the Romans and the Greeks. India was famous for medicines, ivory, diamonds, pearls, spices, silk, and colorfast cotton textiles that were especially prized commodities.

The Gupta period (320–647) is thought of as the "golden age" of Indian civilization, and is sometimes referred to as classical India. Military leaders such as Samudragupta (335–375) and Chandragupta II (375–415) launched military campaigns in the north and on the Deccan plateau, annexing these areas and taking tribute. Earning revenue from land holdings was at the heart of the administrative structure. Culturally, the Sanskrit language had a major revival. The Gupta kings were patrons of Sanskrit literature, and great works such as Kalidasa's play *Sakuntala* were composed during this period. Scientific knowledge became among the most advanced of its time. In mathematics, the use of the decimal system and the first use of the zero sign were achieved. In painting and sculpture, numerous Buddhist cave paintings were produced at Ajanta and at Sarnath.

In South India, the Tamil people were political and cultural leaders from 500 to 1300. The south was somewhat isolated from the north of India, up until the Muslim unification of the subcontinent. There were numerous powers who rivaled each other for power. Some of these groups included the Pandya, the Chola, the Chera, and the Pallava. This culture left archeological evidence in the form of coins and inscriptions, and a number of well-known epics and poetry. The Tamil kingdoms of Madras were especially powerful, the Pallava dynasty followed by the Chola kings. The kings claimed divine origin and the kingship was hereditary. At this stage there was an extensive sea trade with Southeast Asia. In religion, Hinduism was centered in temples that had royal patronage. Female dancers, known as *devadasis*, were common features at the temples. The British later disapproved of such dancers, seeing them as mere prostitutes.

Between 650 and 1200 there were a number of strong regional states of North India. There were great and lesser kinds, known as maharajas and rajas. One might think of this period as Indian "feudalism" because there was no overarching centralized state, and the political and economic structure was built around kings who commanded regional loyalty. One example of these major groups of rulers is the Rajputs (literally, sons of princes) from present-day Rajasthan. The Rajputs prided themselves on their military prowess, and were considered just under the priestly class in terms of social structure.

The religion of Islam arrived in the northwestern part of the Indian subcontinent in AD 712, when people from the Arabian peninsula in the Middle East traveled eastward not long after the Prophet Muhammad's death. Local Muslim kingdoms competed for power with Hindu royals. The Mughal Empire—established in 1526—was to become the most powerful and centralized of the various Muslim kingdoms that ruled the subcontinent. The Mughals deserve the credit for the unification of India as a modern region. The single largest commodity of Mughal India was cotton textiles, including piecegoods, calicos, and muslin, either unbleached or in a variety of colors. Early modern Europe was a major importer of cotton textiles, pepper and other spices, indigo, and silks. There was an enormous European demand for Indian products, but the demand for European products in Mughal India was very small. In the early eighteenth century the formal Mughal Empire declined—due to imperial disintegration, internal rebellions, and external invasions. Once opulent treasuries were drained. Huge market cities decayed. High agricultural taxes led people to avoid risk and also innovation.

British Colonialism in India

The period of British influence, beginning with trading companies and escalating through military conquest and colonization, from 1600 to 1947, was a formative period for the development of the modern Indian nation. But the rise of an independent nation of India came about despite the great damage that the British ultimately wreaked on Indian society in many areas of life, both economic and social. Colonial rule and the systematic extraction of raw materials impoverished India, and prevented the possibility of an agricultural and industrial revolution such as in the West. The lack of agricultural revolution, little technological advancement, and reliance on animal power all held India back. India's poverty–which is actually quite recent in origin—was much exacerbated by colonial lack of scientific and commercial innovation.

The economic and political colonization of India by the British began in the form of economic trade. This period of mercantile trade occurs between 1600 and about 1750. At the end of the year 1600, British traders were authorized by the Crown to set up a trading company known as the East India Company. Along with the founding of this company, the British also set up an administration. Judges, missionaries, and administrators began to come to India to work for the administration that handled this trade. These administrators worked closely with the Mughal rulers and Mughal administration. Many high-level British needed to learn Persian, Arabic, and Sanskrit to fulfill their job duties. A few of them, such as Sir William Jones, became accomplished translators and were instrumental in giving English-language readers access to important ancient texts that had been written in Persian and Sanskrit.[9] At this point in history, these administrator-scholars were quite passionate about learning about Indian society, and admired the culture that had produced these great works.

At the same time, while the British administration grew more and more complex and developed, the European colonists needed to be able to justify their administration. This period of conquest and colonization starts in the middle of the eighteenth century, roughly around 1750. They promoted the idea that India's progress under their golden age had been destroyed by Muslim rule in the subcontinent, and believed that they could help restore India to its former glory. Military conquest accompanied trade and a number of key battles were fought, such as the battle of Plassey in Bengal, in which the British defeated local Muslim rulers. After these battles, the British began to solidify their hold over the subcontinent. Three important cities—Calcutta, Bombay, and Madras—grew from tiny villages to major metropolis under British rule. The British established three regional centers of administration, known as presidencies, called Bombay, Bengal, and Madras. The purpose of the East India Company began to shift from purely trading interests to that of governing and administration by about 1790.

From 1757 to 1813, the East India Company held a monopoly over India's foreign trade. Exports were cotton piecegoods, raw silk, indigo, sugar, rum, opium, and raw cotton. Imports were restricted due to low Indian demand, and exports exceeded imports. But the Charter Act of 1813 changed all of this—it abolished the company's monopolistic trading rights and allowed private individuals to invest directly in Indian development. After the Charter Act passed, the rise in imports was striking: By 1817–1818, imports had risen over 80 percent from their 1813–1814 levels. Indians were able to import large numbers of relatively inexpensive manufactured goods. Now, imports grew faster than exports.

The general impact of the Industrial Revolution hit India hard. The British started to invest in selected industries for processing local raw materials and agricultural products into commodities mainly for overseas markets. In the early nineteenth century, the deindustrialization process destroyed the traditional cotton and cloth industry. The Charter Act of 1833 opened the door for unrestricted British mercantile and missionary activities in India. As Britain became the industrial workshop of the world, demand for Indian cloth diminished rapidly in London and Lancashire, and cheaper machine-made cloth from England became more popular in Calcutta, Patna, Bombay, and Madras. The East India Company's cloth factories in Dhaka were abolished by 1820, and before 1833, British cloth swept Dhaka muslin cloth from the Bengal market. The period 1813 through 1833 marked the collapse of Bengal's vast home-spun cotton industry, and millions of Indians, men and women, were thrown out of their jobs by "machines half the world away." Bengal's unemployment reached unusually high levels as the Industrial Revolution destroyed India's peasant economy. India became dependent on Britain for industrialized products. There was a great decline in the number of people who did hand spinning of cotton yarn. The 1881 census recorded only 200,000 spinners for the entire state of Bengal. In 1812–1813, there had been 300,000 spinners just in the two districts (counties) of Patna and Gaya alone. By 1901, the total number of women of Bengal presidency working in the cotton textile industry had dropped to 135,000.

The most important form of transportation was the railroad.[10] In India, the construction of railways had a huge impact on the overall development of the subcontinent. The railroads were planned in the 1850s, and by 1900 made a network covering almost all of the subcontinent. They made British factory goods available everywhere so that people in remote villages began using Western technology including matches, cloth made by mill, paper, and kerosene. Although railroads helped prevent famine through the redistribution of food, they also spread diseases such as malaria. On the other hand, local people took advantage of the increased opportunities of transportation and, for example, were able to travel longer distances for pilgrimage and trade.

Railway construction took place primarily for economic reasons—routes were laid and rates developed to make the export of Indian food grains and other agricultural products cheaper and more efficient and to provide for the inexpensive delivery of coal to markets. There were military advantages as well: The new railways provided a means for speedily transporting soldiers anywhere in India or the world they might be needed. Just as in other countries with railways, rail development in India was not without adverse economic consequences. There was a decrease in the cost of goods and an increase in the availability of new consumer items that turned India into one large market. The introduction of the railroads helped complete the undermining of India's small-scale cotton textile industries, created high unemployment, and converted India into an exporter of raw cotton. Some of the traditional trade centers were bypassed by the early rail network and experienced a marked decline. The positive side to railroads was that they helped create a sense of unity among the diverse regions of the subcontinent. At Partition in 1947, India had the best railway system of any non-Western country in the world.

The high costs of rail development were criticized then and later, especially for the lack of benefit to Indian workers. In contrast to national railway developments in Britain, the Indian people achieved few of the advantages of the new technology. Apart from employment as unskilled laborers, Indians gained neither money nor experience in modern engineering from the building of locomotives and rolling stock, for these came from Britain and benefited owners and workers there. Very few advanced technical skills were imparted, since Indians held a mere 10 percent of superior posts in the railways by 1921, and only 700 locomotives were made in India over the century before independence. British firms exported 12,000 engines to India during the same period, benefiting British workers who built the trains.

Roads, canals, and railways all hastened the tempo of commercialization in British India, and a burst of export expansion during the 1860s led to prosperity, especially where cotton could be grown. In the early 1860s, cotton expanded quickly in response to a fivefold increase in cotton prices as supplies dwindled due to the American Civil War. When the war ended, the price of cotton went down. Also, the price of wheat export had gone down. The railways were carrying a large proportion of cheap food grains to distant markets. Small farmers had to finance their debts through risky export trade or else lose their land. The export of food through the railways contributed to the terrible series of famines to which the British imperial government was slow to respond.

Prior to the introduction of the railways, transportation, except in the major river valleys of the Ganges and Indus and along the coastal regions, was very expensive, undependable, and difficult. Few roads existed and many of these had fallen into disrepair. In many regions commodities could be moved only by oxen. Internal transportation was very slow and spoilage of perishable goods was common. They also restricted the size of manufacturing enterprises to small-scale, often cottage, industries. There were a couple of exceptions. The high value of handloom textiles had made India a major exporter of cloth until the early nineteenth century when protective tariffs in Britain and the competition of foreign textile mills brought this trade to an end. Similarly, the international value of cotton during the Civil War in America stimulated the export of Indian cotton in spite of the risk of spoilage and the high cost of transport. Apart from these few exceptions, however, the high cost of transport usually made it unprofitable to ship goods far from the regions in which they were produced.

The impact of railways was felt in all sectors of the Indian economy. Both people and goods began to make extensive use of the railways. Contrary to early predictions that they would not travel on railways in large numbers, there was a total of 19 million passengers in 1871, 183 million in 1929–1930, and by 1945 the number of passengers buying tickets had exceeded one billion. The volume of freight moving around the subcontinent also rose dramatically in the railway era. Railways helped Indian agricultural commodities become competitive internationally and made possible an enormous expansion in the export of wheat, rice, jute, leather, oilseeds, and cotton. There was also a huge expansion in imports—including cotton textiles, yarn, and capital goods. By the 1880s Britain had become both India's largest customer and the source of fully three-quarters of the subcontinent's imports. Railways not only reshaped the pattern of India's foreign trade but also helped tie India to the British economy.

Railways also promoted India's internal trade, and had a major impact on prices. Previously, different regions had large price differences. But with the railroad, the prices came more in line with each other, and were evidence that India was becoming one national market. From a country of many segmented markets, separated from each other by the high costs of transport, India became a nation with its local centers linked by rail to each other and to the world. Railways, by establishing these links, had an impact throughout the Indian economy.

In the Industrial Revolution in Britain, children and women became an important part of the workforce. In India, however, there was a very different outcome for women. Female workers formed only a small part of the workforce in large-scale industries and in the service sector that developed as part of this modern economy. Ultimately, the only expanding occupation for women in the modern sector came to be domestic service—working as maids and cleaners in homes. A significant section of women's nonagricultural occupations in the traditional sector was destroyed. As a result, female workers increasingly came to crowd into agricultural occupations. Their share in the urban population fell steadily during this period. So why did the Industrial Revolution in India have a different impact on Indian women compared to Indian men, and also different from the model set by Britain in its early phases of industrial revolution? The British showed little inclination to invest in or modernize the vast bulk of traditional economic activities that continued to serve the needs of the ordinary people. That women's economic activities were relatively more affected in this entire process appears to be the result mainly of the traditionally assigned role of women in this society that limited their mobility and confined them to skills and occupations susceptible to swift obsolescence.

Cotton spinning was one of the traditional occupations for women of all castes and income levels. But by the middle of the nineteenth century spinning, as a cash-earning occupation for women, had lost its preeminence. For women, the process of the British Industrial Revolution meant a permanent shift toward the periphery of the economy. Their nonagricultural occupations in the traditional sector suffered a setback mainly because of the intervention of the modern sector in the village economy. Women had neither the skills nor the capital to resist these changes, and were reluctant to join the local mills as unskilled labor. The traditional society had imposed stringent constraints on their mobility between regions and occupations.

The desire to drive the foreign British rulers from the land eventually became one of the primary unifying features of Indian society. But this is not to say that the process was easy. A number of local Indian rulers and business groups had a stake in the rule of the British, for it helped them maintain their own power, albeit under the auspices of a more powerful central colonial power. Business groups like the Parsis and the Marwaris established trade routes among British trading posts, and were able to profit handsomely from the trade they conducted under foreign rule.[11] About one-third of the land mass of India was never formally colonized by the British—these smaller landholdings were known as princely states, and the local princes held power over their kingdoms with the British consent. Of course, they owed paybacks and loyalty to the crown. It took time for the British to consolidate their power on the subcontinent, but Indians formed an anticolonial nationalist movement to earn their right to independence.

At the same time as the agricultural and Industrial Revolution occurred in the eighteenth and nineteenth centuries, the British conquered a global colonial network to extend their markets. The British merchant could sell more, if only more could be produced. He had customers, he had ships to transport goods all over the world, and he could get capital to finance new ideas. Using hand methods, Europe could not compete with the competition from the East and the traditional Indian textile production, which was a major export. But if cotton could be spun, woven and printed with less labor, such as by machines, the market for British cloth could be endless.

Europe required many material goods, many of which could come from only tropical regions. Working classes began to drink only tea or coffee sweetened with sugar every day. After the American Civil War, Europe relied on Africa and the East for its cotton. Industrial countries also attempted to sell their own products and one of the primary reasons given for imperialism was the need to find new markets. It was argued that each industrial country must develop a colonial empire dependent on itself, in which the home country would supply manufactured goods in return for raw materials. This would create a self-sufficient trade unit, guaranteeing a market for all its members and wealth and prosperity for the home country. This expansion of trade allowed for periods of overproduction and depression, which would lead people to seek distant markets for their goods. The goal was to establish colonies that would be politically submissive, but economically profitable. Cotton cloth that had been manufactured in Manchester was sold throughout India for one-half or one-quarter of the cost of handwoven Indian cloth. This put millions of Indian spinners, weavers, and other craftspeople out of work in just a few decades. One could say that at exactly the same time that Britain was making itself into a more urbanized, industrialized, and modern society, India was becoming more backward because the artisans were unemployed and lost their skills in artisan manufacturing, and millions of unemployed craftspeople had to go to farming to earn a livelihood directly from the land. So by the end of the nineteenth century, India was actually less urbanized than it had been at the beginning, with 90 percent of the population directly depending on the land for support.

The colonization of India was not merely economic; there were far-reaching implications for changes in social life, particularly for women. Europeans had internalized the idea that civilizations of the East were once great, but had now fallen into decay and were in need of Western domination. The British took it upon themselves to make a number of changes in Indian society, particularly to stop cultural practices that they found abhorrent and which they believed kept India from progressing as a modern society. The British tended to focus their attention on the cultural practices of the elite—and paid particular attention to the rites practiced by the upper castes. One of the first practices that they put a stop to was the seldom-practiced rite of sati, whereby an upper-caste widow was burned alive on her deceased husband's funeral pyre.[12] Indian reformers such as Ram Mohan Roy took up the British side, and fought conservatives in the society that did not want their traditions criticized by the foreign rulers. The British made the status of Indian women a primary target in their campaign to improve the overall society. They attacked cultural practices like the seclusion of women, the lack of female education, and the prohibition against widow remarriage by elite Indians. What the British failed to understand was that these customs were designed to designate a certain elite status among particular castes of women, and their laws against it did not apply to the vast majority of Indians, for whom women had to work in the fields out of economic necessity, and for whom schooling for anyone, let along women, was a luxury far out of reach for the common family.

Although economic considerations and the civilizing mission were paramount in the British conquest of the Indian subcontinent, political factors also had a major impact on Indian society. In order to rule over India more effectively, the British tried to learn as much as about the colony as they could. British officials started a massive effort to enumerate, classify, and control 250 million Indians. The census was begun in 1872 to collect facts. The census made a ranked list of castes derived from classical Hindu texts. They asked people which caste they belonged to. This had a major impact on how Indians saw their relationships with one another, and made caste divisions very rigid. These divisions became uniform across India, whereas before they had varied from place to place. In their attempt to codify law, the British exacerbated the differences for Hindus and Muslims. The process of doing the census, and specifically of counting relative numbers of Hindus and Muslims, established a Hindu majority and a Muslim minority. Of course, the division between Hindus and Muslims was not entirely a colonial invention. But to count the relative numbers of these communities and to have leaders represent them was something new, and had an impact on the development of religious nationalism. British rule thus contributed significantly to the rise of a heightened sense of religious identity, which ultimately led to the Partition of India at the time of independence. The British strategy of hanging on to their power in India can be described as "divide and rule." By exploiting minor differences between Hindus and Muslims, the British promoted a rise of violence between Hindus and Muslims, thus justifying their own presence to keep the peace. Some of the contentious issues included whether Hindus should be allowed to make music in front of mosques, disrupting Muslim worship, and whether the Hindu desire for cow protection could prevent Muslim butchers from slaughtering cows for human consumption.

At times, however, religious sentiment and resentment of British rule worked together to ferment anticolonial action. The year 1857 marks the date of the Indian Mutiny, one of the most major revolts against the British. A number of factors were behind this first war of independence, including resentment about the cheap imports of British cloth that ruined the domestic textile market. In addition, taxes on landownership and the seizure of the lands of rulers contributed to the widespread discontent. A rumor spread from the city of Meerut that the British had greased bullets with the animal fat from cows and pigs, upsetting the sentiments of the Hindu and Muslim communities. The Meerut regiments shot their commanding officers and went to Delhi, which they held for four months. In Lucknow, rebellion troops held the British Residency buildings for five months before being defeated. The following year, 1858, British domination of India was official, and Queen Victoria became empress of India.

The Indian National Congress was formed in 1885 to begin to demand limited political representation in the Indian government. But one of the most important developments under colonial rule was the development of identity based on religious affiliation to the exclusion of other potentially unifying factors, such as region, language, or class. The 1905 Partition of Bengal by Lord Curzon was an early important step in the development of communal sentiments. The result was an anticolonial movement for *Swadeshi* (self-rule) and an economic boycott of British goods to help strengthen local nationalism. The rise of religious sentiment prompted the idea of separate nationalisms. At this time, there was the early recognition by Muslims that the Congress could not be a national organization, and the Muslim League was formed in 1906. The Government of India Act 1909, known as the Morley-Minto reforms, established a system whereby there were nominated and elected legislative bodies. In 1911, the British moved the capital to Delhi, a more central location, and away from the local politics of Bengal. Starting in about 1919, there was tremendous disillusionment by the experience of World War I. Over one million Indian soldiers fought in the war on the side of the British with about 10 percent casualties, and cynicism arose among Indians from such losses, in recognizing that they were helping Europeans fight for freedom in Europe, while their own freedom was not secured. Colonial control tightened in the wake of anti-imperialist sentiment. The Rowlatt Acts of 1919 imposed even stricter control of press. Violent attacks on political meetings reinforced the cruelty of colonial oppression. In the Jallianwala Bagh Incident, an officer named General Dyer ordered soldiers to shoot into protesting crowds in Amritsar, leaving at least 1,000 dead, with no justice for victims.

Mahatma Gandhi and Indian Nationalism

These acts helped inspire a widespread movement to decry the injustices and racism of British rule. A lawyer named Mohandas Karamchand Gandhi (1869–1948) became the figurehead for Indian nationalism.[13] After training in law in London, he spent many years in South Africa between 1893 and 1914. His work there focused on the conditions of the Indian people who labored in that nation under discriminatory conditions. He returned to India in 1914 to work on the nationalist movement, and was the intellectual architect of nonviolent tactics to fight the oppression brought on by British rule. By 1919, Gandhi became a national leader. Gandhi developed the concept of *satyagraha* (truth force) that depended upon the use of nonviolent resistance to injustice, and civil disobedience in the face of unjust laws. Gandhi took his inspiration from a variety of sources, and was inspired by Thoreau, Tolstoy, and the Sermon on the Mount. Gandhi preached that obeying an unjust law makes you party to injustice. One of his most unique actions was to discard Western clothing and wear clothes of peasants (such as homespun cloth, or khadi, and a traditional wrapped loincloth known as a dhoti). This was a far cry from the Western-style suits and top hats that he had worn as a lawyer. His motivation to dress simply was to make people aware of India's poverty brought about by British exploitation. India needed to rely on Indian goods and Indian cloth, and stop buying British goods.

Gandhi made a conscious choice to dress simply to identify with the peasantry of the country.[14] He chose to favor the clothes of the Indian peasantry above those of Europeans. This move was very deliberate, since Gandhi was not from a peasant family and had spent little of his adult life in an Indian village. But Gandhi's decision was also intrinsically linked to his desire to restore the Indian handweaving and hand-spinning industries. He began to experiment with weaving and later spinning. He wanted Indians to boycott foreign goods and to wear khadi cloth made from yarn they had spun themselves by hand. It was very difficult for Gandhi to find people who still knew the art of hand-spinning, then almost in total decline. Why did Gandhi wear this loincloth? He was addressing the comments of people who argued that they could not afford to discard their foreign cloth in favor of the more expensive Indian khadi cloth. Gandhi was sometimes criticized for encouraging people to burn foreign cloth while others were dying from starvation and nakedness. Gandhi's goal was to get every Indian in the country to wear khadi and have a complete boycott of foreign cloth. The homespun cloth should be woven from handspun yarn.

In Gandhi's own perception, the loincloth was a sign of India's dire poverty and of the need to improve its wealth through the freedom struggle and through a wholesale rejection of European civilization. It was a rejection not only of the material products of Europe, but also of the European value system. It was better for the poor to wear scanty loincloths than to clothe themselves in garments from abroad. Gandhi hoped to expose Indian poverty while simultaneously suggesting its resolution through hand-spinning, weaving, and freedom from British rule. He never obtained his objective of clothing the entire Indian nation in khadi and reestablishing a self-sufficient craft-based society. So even after the attainment of independence, he had no reason to return to normal dress. This choice affected the clothing of politicians. The first prime minister of independent India, Jawaharlal Nehru, made the shift from once dressing like a perfect English gentleman to wearing homespun khadi cloth. Politicians today in India still wear the homespun khadi cloth as a symbol of their nationalism. It attempts to send the message that they are loyal to Indian-made products and will not wear the cloth that symbolizes the tyranny of foreign rule.

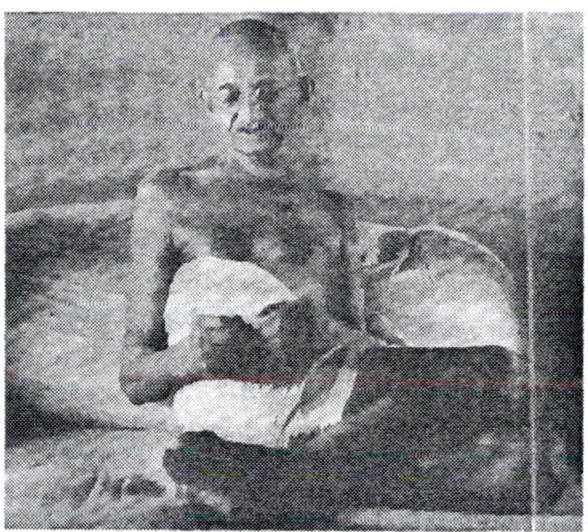

Mahatma Gandhi in a loincloth.

Gandhi's symbolic investment in cloth greatly helped shape the movement, but other acts of defiance against British rule came in the areas of unfair taxes levied against Indian-made products. One of the most famous moments of the 1930s civil disobedience movement was Gandhi's protest against the British tax on common salt, which prompted him to lead a march and walk 241 miles to Dandi to manufacture salt out of ocean water in direct defiance of the British law.[15]

The End of British Rule

Muhammad Ali Jinnah (1876–1948) was an ardent member of the Congress, who at first refused to join the Muslim League because it was not nationalist enough. But he later joined the Muslim League in 1913 as a "suitable form of self-government." His primary goal in the quest for independence was unity between Hindus and Muslims, Congress and the Muslim League. The Lucknow Pact came about from a joint conference of League and Congress in 1916. It represented a joint demand for political reform and for making India a dominion. Most importantly, it would give a certain percentage of seats to Muslims through a separate electorate, therefore ensuring that Muslims would have some Muslim representatives in government. Pan-Muslim movements impacted on the identity of Indian Muslims to see themselves as a group with some unique aspirations. Muslims increasingly grew convinced that their fate as a religious minority in Hindu-majority India would not be good, and that the Congress would be unlikely to share power.[16]

The British saw rebellions as law and order problems, and not as a revolution against injustice. The Government of India Act in 1919 divided government between center and provinces, elected members of provincial legislatures, and extended communal representation to Sikhs, non-Brahmins, Europeans, Anglo-Indians, and Indian Christians. This divisive policy of the British to separate Indians into different groups and emphasize their differences in their political aspirations exacerbated the rifts between various sectors of society. The founding of the right-wing organization the Hindu Mahasabha in 1906 was indicative of this divide and rule tendency. Led by Madan Mohan Malaviya (1861–1946), the Hindu Mahasabha established the goal to preserve and spread Hindu culture at the expense of the rights of religious minorities. The 1920s were marked by communal riots between Hindus and Muslims, with great bloodshed, anger, and trauma.

The 1931 Gandhi-Irwin Pact was a momentary truce in the struggle for justice. In this agreement, Gandhi called off the civil disobedience movement, Congress agreed to participate in the next round table conference, and Irwin released political prisoners. Indian cloth boycotts had hurt Lancashire textile industry back in Britain. Whereas there was 26 million pounds sterling revenue from cloth sales in 1929, there were only 5.5 million pounds revenue in 1931. In 1932, the arrest of political workers prompted Gandhi to restart his disobedience movement against the British. In addition to the Muslims, other groups such as the untouchables also clamored for representation. During the1930–1931 First Round Table Conference of negotiations between the British and Indian leaders, the untouchable leader Ambedkar accepted reservations for lower castes within general elections. In the Poona Pact, Ambedkar eliminated the demand for a separate electorate in exchange for larger representation through reserved seats.

The Government of India Act 1935 had many consequences. The nation of Burma split from India, and the new states of Orissa, Sind, and North-West Frontier province were formed. The franchise (right to vote) was extended from 6 million to 40 million (2.8 percent to 18 percent), but the British still did not grant dominion status to India. At this point, the nationalist movement called for complete independence. The Quit India Movement in 1942 relied on mass civil disobedience and called for an immediate end of British rule. A horrible calamity known as the Bengal Famine in 1943 saw three million people die.[17] The British even rejected American humanitarian offers of grain.

The final collapse of the empire came about in a number of ways. In Britain, Prime Minister Churchill was replaced by the Labor Party. The bombing of Hiroshima and Nagasaki, effectively ending the war, meant that the British could no longer use war as an excuse for extending their empire. But still there was the question of how to solve the religious minority problem. The Union of India would embrace British India and the princely states, with regional provinces being highly autonomous. But Jinnah refused the offer of a "moth-eaten Pakistan" which was not to be given total sovereignty. August 16, 1946, was Direct Action Day, when Muslims began their final struggle for Pakistan. Other groups tried to establish states on the basis of religious identity—there was also a call for a Sikh nation of Khalistan. On Independence Day, August 15, 1947, the subcontinent was divided into three parts: India in the center of the subcontinent, with East and West Pakistan on either side. The states of the Punjab and Bengal were split into East and West, and the most turmoil occurred in these regions.

Over 10 million refugees fled across the new borders in one of the largest mass migrations in human history. Families that had once lived side by side now pulled up their roots, packed up as much as they could, and set out for a new life that they could not imagine. No one could be sure what the drawing of new political boundaries would mean for life as they had known it. The people of Punjab and Bengal were the most directly affected, since their states had literally been cut into two separate pieces. Many people were confused about whether they should stay in the homes and on the land their families had lived on for generations, or embrace a religious identity and move on. Many hundreds of thousands of women on both sides of the border were kidnapped and raped. The problem of the identity of these women and their children became a crisis for governments of India and Pakistan, whose national honor had been tarnished by the bodily violation of "their" women.[18] Thousands of families were divided and lost contact with each other. This was the first time in human history that the Indian subcontinent had been divided on the basis of religious identity. For Pakistan, the Partition of the subcontinent is more widely understood as part of their country's original liberation—freedom from the British, and a new country where a Muslim majority could rule itself. But for India, independence was scarred by the experience of losing territory to a rival nation.

Post-Colonial India

The first prime minister of independent India was Jawaharlal Nehru. As the United States developed closer ties with Pakistan, and as Indian–Chinese tensions intensified, India began to ally itself more closely with the Soviet Union. Five-year plans to chart economic industrialization and national development were based on democratic socialism. Military conflicts with neighboring countries became more frequent. Good relations with Pakistan waxed and waned. Wars with Pakistan over the disputed province of Kashmir—which had a Hindu king but Muslim subjects—in 1965 and the 1990s intensified problems with Pakistan. A border dispute with China in 1962, which occurred over the Himalayan areas of Ladakh and the North-East Frontier area, remains unsolved to the present day.

After Nehru died in 1964, his daughter Indira Gandhi was elected prime minister in 1966. Indira had married Feroze Gandhi and taken his last name in 1942, but Feroze was no relation to Mahatma Gandhi. Her political support withered away over the years, and she called for a State of Emergency between 1975 and 1977 to retain her hold on power. During this period, the national government, led by initiatives of her son Sanjay, took a draconian approach to population control. Forced sterilizations, violence against the poor masses, the jailing of political opponents, and the censorship of the press caused one of the biggest threats to Indian democracy.[19] Even though she managed to turn around the Indian economy during this period, Indira was voted out of power for her abuses. Only a few years later, however, with widespread inflation and political unrest, Indira was reelected in 1980 by a huge majority. Her biggest challenge in the 1980s was from Sikh radicals in the Punjab, who made demands to separate from India and form the independent nation of Khalistan. Indira used harsh means to crush the movement, invading the Sikh's holiest temple at Amritsar, which further set off the passions of Sikhs. Though her advisers had warned her to choose bodyguards of another faith, Indira was committed to the values of democracy and would not dismiss her Sikh bodyguards. They assassinated her in 1984, setting off widespread mass murder of Sikhs in retaliation. These riots reminded people of the violence they had suffered at the time of Partition in 1947.

Indira's son Rajiv took over his mother's position as head of the Congress Party, and he was elected prime minister of India. He favored economic liberalization, and India began to open itself up to foreign investment and global trade. He was assassinated by Sri Lankan separatists called Tamil Tigers. His Italian-born widow, Sonia, became the head of the Congress Party in 1997. After the collapse of the Soviet Union, India began to move even further away from democratic socialism and developed closer ties with the United States. Right-wing Hindu parties, particularly the Bharatiya Janata Party (BJP), began to dominate the political scene in 1989, first forming a coalition with Congress, and then gaining national control from 1998 onward. Nuclear explosions in 1998, conducted by their respective governments, brought India and Pakistan into a nuclear arms race. In 2004, a national election brought the Congress Party back into power. Analysts credit the politicization of rural voters who felt left out of the benefits of India's globalizing economy. Though the head of the Congress Party was Sonia Gandhi, the widow of Rajiv, the fact that she was Italian by birth dissuaded her from assuming the position of prime minister. Instead, Manmohan Singh, often credited as the founder of Indian liberalization, was sworn into the highest office, reassuring the business community of their continued support. Additionally, as the first Sikh to hold this office, his presence may help reduce ethnic and religious tensions between religious groups within India and in India's relationships with adjacent nations.

DEMOGRAPHY, ECONOMY, AND RURAL–URBAN DIFFERENCES

India prides itself on being the largest democracy in the world today. With a population of over one billion people, the practice of democracy and capitalism is a model for other nations in the world. In fact, India is the only democratic country in the world that gave universal citizenship to all adults at the moment of its founding in 1947. That is, no other democracy in history has allowed all adults to vote for its political representation, without imposing qualifications of gender, property ownership, class, or race. Because a good deal of the population of India is nonliterate, each political party is designated by a symbol, to be recognized by people who do not read or write. Using various pictures to identity each party—for example, the Bharatiya Janata Party is represented by a lotus flower—voters can choose their party affiliation without being hindered by literacy requirements. It is a novel way to practice citizenship for people who might otherwise be excluded in other democratic societies.

The economy of India is that of capitalism, albeit with a heavy dose of government controls, checks, and balances. The first prime minister of India, Jawaharlal Nehru, had a vision of industrial development built similarly to the Soviet model of socialism. He instituted various five-year plans to develop infrastructure to ensure India's self-sufficiency. This was quite different than the plan envisioned by Gandhi, who held an ideal of village life based on environmentally sensitive living and simple technologies.

Typical agriculture in India.

The rural–urban differences in Indian society are immense. So much so, in fact, that upper-middle-class urban Indians living in one of the major metropolitan cities probably have a lifestyle quite similar to their counterparts of European and American cities. Life in rural India—where about three-quarters of the Indian population still lives—is quite different. People live and work in villages without the conveniences of the modern cities. There, basic necessities like clean and easily accessible drinking water are still unequally distributed and unevenly available. Migration from rural areas to the urban cities in search of better jobs and living conditions has caused the populations of Indian cities to swell, and immense slums with unsanitary conditions have become the permanent homes of people from rural origins.

Emigration and the presence of millions of Indians overseas has had an impact on the way that Indians perceive their global presence.[20] One common public perception of the expatriate Indian community is dominated by an image of highly educated, professional elite of doctors, engineers, scientists, and college professors, all of whom but the last category earn high salaries. They live in comfortable suburban houses, drive luxury cars, and send their children to Ivy League universities. As immigrants, they were not necessarily poor, like many immigrants in the past. They are generally not refugees who are fleeing from political oppression at home. They do not reside in ethnic ghettos; for the most part these elite live in suburban neighborhoods and have successfully climbed the economic ladder. But this is not the entire story. At the other end of the spectrum are still-struggling working-class Indian immigrants who lack language and professional skills, need basic job training, and suffer in the clutches of a depressed economy. About half a million Indians were admitted to the U.S. as immigrants between 1961 and 1990, according to figures of the Immigration and Naturalization Service (INS). Unlike the agricultural workers who mostly hailed from Punjab that came to California during the first half of the twentieth century, the post-1965 wave came from all over India and were well educated.[21] Unlike other Asian Americans, such as Koreans and Vietnamese, many Indian immigrants learned English in grade school and spoke English fluently long before coming to the United States. These Indians attended convent schools or public schools modeled on the British system. This legacy of colonialism has given them an enormous advantage and helped them gain a foothold in America. The second generation is somewhat different than their parents. They are sometimes called the one-and-a-half generation—half in Indian culture and half in American. In particular, they have different concerns about finding a marriage partner, dating, and sexuality.[22] There are also considerable numbers of South Asian immigrants from working-class backgrounds, who work in the service sector and struggle to make ends meet.

SOCIAL LIFE, FAMILY, DESCENT GROUPS, KINSHIP, AND GENDER

The family is one of the most important social structures in the Indian subcontinent. Though two-generation "nuclear" families consisting of parents and their children have become more

An Indian family.

common, particularly in urban areas, mentally most Indians imagine themselves as part of a much larger kinship structure. The tradition ideal is that of the extended or joint family, where multiple generations of grandparents, uncles and aunts and their children all live together in a large house or adjacent to each other. In this model, it is assumed that sons will stay with their parents forever, and continue to support and care for them into their old ages. The daughters will move away from their parents and join their husbands in the extended household. Daughters, therefore, are expected to marry and move out of the family when they reach adulthood. Their inheritance is received at the time of their marriage as a dowry given to their in-law family, whereas the sons would inherit at the time of their parents' death.

The extended family has both advantages and drawbacks. Cooperation between brothers can mean cooperative arrangements for the care of children and the elderly, family businesses, and the pooling of financial resources. But daughters-in-law sometimes feel caught under the thumb of controlling mothers-in-law, and push their husbands to leave the nest and establish a separate and joint residence. Marriage is understood less as the relationship between a couple, than a relationship built between two families. About 95 percent of marriages in India are "arranged," meaning that the parents and families have met and approved of each other—although it is common for the prospective bride and groom to participate in the selection and exercise veto power. But these stereotypes of domineering mothers-in-law are only one side of the story. For some women, and men too, marriage also brings independence and autonomy, and in some cases is less restrictive than their upbringing by parents. Being married gives a woman status, and the birth of a child, particularly a son, also helps cement her place as a respected member of the family and of society.[23]

One of the more difficult things to understand about the status of women, at least from an American perspective, is how people in India understand practices of veiling. Purdah refers to the practices of female seclusion and veiling among the higher economic classes, and exists among both Hindus and Muslims. It is part of a status marker of women not having to work outside the home, not so dissimilar from the role of "trophy wives" in the United States. Among some orthodox Hindus, purdah is related to relations of respect between affines, or kin, where women veil in front of senior male family members. Among Muslims who practice purdah, modesty is related to unity of one's own kinship group vis-à-vis the outside. Veiling and privacy involves seclusion from the public sphere. Families that can afford to keep women in seclusion and uninvolved in economic activity have a relatively high status—in some ways similar to elite Western families where women don't work outside the home. The forms of body concealment go beyond the wearing of a veil, and there are many possibilities. Baggy trousers, loose dresses, dupattas or shawls, a cap or veil (*burqa*) worn in a variety of combinations create respectable clothing styles. To a certain extent, politics comes in: The politics of nationalism has created a sense that the modesty of women signifies the honor of the nation. The similarities between Hindu and Muslim traditions include the ideas of patriarchal control over the female body, where women are sacred objects that have to be protected against outsiders. Protection is offered by the state, husband, or male relatives.

The Indian household, especially the kitchen area, is seen as a very auspicious place for the Indian family. People generally remove their shoes before entering the household, out of deference to the symbolic boundary of the space demarcating inside and outside. There are certain things that household members might do outside the house—such as eat meat, drink alcohol, smoke cigarettes—that they would not do within the boundaries of their home, out of respect for family members who do not share those practices, and to maintain the sacred space of the domestic hearth. The process of keeping house in India is quite elaborate, including the preparation of food that is painstaking and delicious. A very large number of people in South Asia work as the domestic help of households, cleaning, preparing meals, doing laundry, running errands, and taking care of children and the elderly. Unlike in the West, a much greater percentage of the population hires daily household help. Lower middle class families will hire sweepers to clean floors and toilets on a daily basis, whereas middle- and upper-class families may have round-the-clock domestic assistance. The household servants work for very low wages and sometimes flit from job to job, although some servants have remained with a particular family for generations.[24]

Outside the family, people in South Asia might identify themselves as being part of a particular community, which could be regional, but also include caste. Caste, like the sacred cow, is one of the major curiosities but least understood aspects of Indian society. People have studied it and more than 5,000 books have been written about it. It is at once very complex and unwieldy, and varies from place to place. Anthropologist Clarence Maloney writes that practically any statement made about caste may be valid for one region but not for another, for one village but not for the next village over, for an urban setting but not for its suburb, for one religious group but not for some other sect, for one individual but not for his brother or sister.

People in South Asia have a hard time talking openly about caste. Many people see it as a "social evil." The Constitution of India has abolished the practice of untouchability, and says that caste discrimination in public places is forbidden. Still, like racism, it must be acknowledged that caste discrimination exists everywhere, even though officially it is illegal. Pakistanis tend to deny that caste exists in their country, for it goes against the Islamic ideal of brotherhood. If they do admit to it, they blame it for being a relic of the earlier Hindu civilization. Yet, most of the people who decry it still continue to marry off their daughters and sons within their own castes.

Changes in caste ranking and ritual status generally follow changes in power, ritual status, and wealth. A common misconception is that caste is the only criterion of social status in India and that it explains all hierarchy and interaction.[25] Some people in Western countries assume that it is stagnant and unchanging. British administrators in the nineteenth century found it simpler to deal with social units presumed to be discrete and stable, rather than deal with social change. In fact, all aspects of caste are indeed found elsewhere in the world, though they have become more institutionalized in South Asia. After all, every society has hierarchy and its own forms of social segmentation.

So what is caste? *Caste* comes from the Portuguese word *castas*, meaning "breed, race, kind." Caste society can be described as being segmented, hierarchically arranged, and endogamous (i.e., one generally marries within one's group). Caste is not a tribe, which is an independent and complete social system. In any village the 5, 20, or 40 castes within it make up the cultural system. What are the criteria of the castes? Usually we talk about each caste being a separate occupation, but this fails to explain the difference between farmers and laborers; and among the artisans, many do not follow their traditional occupations. Kinship and lineage are also mentioned, but most castes are far larger than a kin group and many contain clans. Muslims and Hindus both invent lineages that tend to support rather than determine caste distinctions. A man can take a concubine from a lower caste or a widower a second wife from an unusual source.

The four varnas—Brahman (priest), Kshatriya (warrior), Vaishya (merchant), and Sudhra (servant)—differ from castes in that they are not observable groups in the villages of India. In fact, the untouchables are considered so low that they are completely outside the varna ranking. Instead, people talk about having or belonging to a particular *jati.* Within these castes, there are subcastes. A *gotra* is like a lineage except that it is a ritual or mythical one, going back to some holy person. *Gotras* are exogamous, meaning one marries outside one's own *gotra.*

When Hindus and Muslims live in the same region, the Hindu castes tend to have their Muslim counterparts. Though contrary to original Islam, caste is now tacitly supported by this religion. Christianity too has developed caste-like sectarian groups. Converts to Christianity retain their caste identity, especially if they were untouchables.

Caste is reinforced by the idea of purity and pollution, acquired in the practices of daily life. Lowest castes are literally not to be touched, while high castes are born with an inherent purity that has to be maintained by avoiding the pollutants, by frequent ablutions and purifying ceremonies, and by worship of the pure and high gods. Among the pollutants are body secretions such as blood, dung, hair, leather, dirty clothes, a corpse, or street dirt.[26] Anyone who handles these things, such as a sweeper, barber, washer-man, or leatherworker, carries the effects of them. Foods fried in oil or enriched by ghee do not transmit pollution, but foods cooked in water do. One of the difficult things to understand about the rules of caste is that there are different rules for people of different castes; the rules of purity and pollution vary. At many levels, this would seem antithetical to democratic society. Some castes are allowed to drink alcohol and have meat, and engage in different kinds of professions without a loss of caste status. Most Indians eat meat and think that it is fine for them to do so. People belonging to vegetarian castes, however, would see such actions as polluting, especially when doing so in the home. For the highest castes, acts contrary to Brahmanic behavior cause pollution, including eating meat—especially beef—as well as killing things, drinking liquor, and crossing the sea. A person of any caste might pollute himself or herself by taking drinking water from the hand of a person of a lower caste. The outward signs of caste affiliation typically include a person's surname, profession, and style of dress. Progressive Indians who object to the hierarchy of caste sometimes drop their surnames as a way of protesting this kind of authority, and have social lives that include friendships—even marriages—with people from different groups.

Considered so low as to be outside the "caste-Hindu" varna system, and the victims of countless generations of caste discrimination, the ex-untouchables, or Dalits as they prefer to be called, are an important demographic group in India. There are many hundreds of millions of untouchables. The largest occupational category is leatherworkers, called chamars. Gandhi called untouchables the *harijans,* God's people. During colonial times they were put at the bottom of a ranked list, called a schedule, and are still referred to as scheduled castes and tribes.

In the1930s, the government changed legislation to force temples to open their doors to all untouchables, but still, most worship from afar without going in. Among untouchables, both Buddhist and Christian missionaries have historically had some success in conversion. In recent times, Hindu officials have sought to bring Indian Christians back into the Hindu fold by a process they refer to as "reconversion." There have been efforts to exclude school children from government schools unless they renounce their religion.

Outsiders tend to think of caste as something very fixed and set in stone, but caste mobility is part of the experience of caste. Therefore, it is untrue that you cannot change your caste. A caste may try to rise up within the orthodox system, through changing habits according to beliefs about purity and pollution. Often, this involves emulating the habits of higher castes. These can include practicing religious piety and vegetarianism, avoiding alcohol, and forbidding widows to marry. This process is referred to as *Sanskritization.*

The consumption of food and drink has particular practices associated with it. Food is never eaten by taking a bite from the whole, as Americans eat bread. A fragment of bread is ripped off and dipped to avoid polluting the rest of the piece. When you drink water, you hold the cup above your face to drink—and do not touch your mouth to the bottle. Generally, Indians do not traditionally use a handshake; instead, they fold their hands together and say "namaste" (literally, I bow to you). Muslims also have practices of ritual purity: In Pakistan and Bangladesh, sweeping streets and cleaning bathrooms is sometimes done by Hindu untouchables.

RELIGION

The Indian subcontinent is the birthplace of many of the world's great religions—including Hinduism, Buddhism, Jainism, and Sikhism. During the Middle Ages, Islam traveled here from the West and became an inspirational force in its own right, attracting millions of followers, particularly in Bengal, and especially among the lower castes, who embraced the Islamic idea of equality. Practitioners of all religions, including "Western" religions like Christianity and Judaism, have all found homes in the subcontinent at one time or another. Early Christian saints such as Saint Thomas ventured to South India, and very old communities of Christians and Jews can be found in the subcontinent, dating back hundreds of years.[27] India was also the birthplace of Buddhism, which spread to China and Southeast Asia, and is still widely practiced in those regions, although it has only recently reemerged in India. The spread of religions from India to other places is a legacy of the widespread cultural influence that the subcontinent has had on world history and civilization.

Most important, the religions that developed and were nurtured here interacted with each other—sharing ideas and responding to the challenges that other co-religionists posed.[28] Though one would certainly question the Western stereotype of Indians being mired in religious thought to the exclusion of everything else, there is no doubt that the way religion has been understood and practiced has been a truly formulative part of the region's history and culture.

Hinduism in Modern Times

The majority of inhabitants of India today would describe themselves as being Hindu. But *Hinduism* is a recent term to describe an ancient conglomeration of connected beliefs and practices in the Indian subcontinent. As a religion, Hinduism is somewhat difficult to describe in the conventional monotheistic terms that we often use to define religion. There is no one founder (such as Muhammad, the Buddha, or Jesus), there is no one book (like the Bible or the Qur'an), there is no one set of beliefs that all Hindus share. Furthermore, there is no centralized "church" hierarchy, such as popes or bishops or rabbis or lamas, that give it organization. On one hand, then, we might be tempted to think about Hinduism in terms of what it lacks—such as lacking one founding figure, prophet, or leader, a centralized hierarchy, and one defining creed. It is perhaps most useful to think of Hinduism in terms of the tremendous local religious diversity that exists in the subcontinent, and replace the word *one* with *many*. In fact, there have been many important saints and religious leaders throughout history, a large number of important texts that elaborate a variety of religious messages, and a variety of beliefs and practices of worship that are found among Hinduism's adherents. Thus, Hindu co-religionists might profess devotion to different forms, manifestations, and images of God, visit and pray at different temples, and worship on different days of the week, but still consider each other to be part of a larger religious culture.

Hinduism is the religion of the majority of people in India and Nepal, as well as being an important cultural force in all other continents. The 2001 census lists 1 billion 27 million inhabitants. About 82 percent of the population is Hindu, and Muslims comprise 12 percent. The rest are Sikhs, Christians, Jains, Buddhists, Parsees, Jews, and followers of tribal religions. There are also sizable Hindu communities in South Africa, East Africa, South America, the West Indies, the United States, Canada, Europe, Australia, New Zealand, Bali, and Java. Any visitor to South Asia from the West is struck by the vibrancy of daily ritual observances, and by the centrality of religion in people's lives. There are innumerable wayside shrines to local goddesses or divine ancestors, majestic temples to the great deities such as Vishnu or Siva, festivals, pilgrimages to rivers and sacred places, and pictures of saints garlanded in flowers located in buses, shops, and homes. Taxi drivers pray at the beginning of the route, and when passing shrines and temples.

What is Hinduism? This is a complex issue, since the term *Hinduism* is of relatively recent origin. *Hinduism* denotes the religion of people who call themselves "Hindu." Difficulties in defining Hinduism arise when we try to understand what this means, because there is great diversity within Hinduism and its history is very long and complex. Some might claim, both from within the tradition and from outside it, there is no such thing as Hinduism because of its diversity. Others claim that despite the diversity, there is some essence that structures its many patterns. After all, the differences between Hindus can vary a great deal. As a category, Hinduism has very fuzzy edges. Some people call Hinduism a way of life rather than a religion. What we understand by Hinduism as a religion depends upon what we mean by religion. Our understanding of Hinduism has been mediated by Western notions of what religion is and the projection of Hinduism as an "other" to Christianity. The category *religion* has developed out of a Christian, largely Protestant understanding which defines it in terms of belief. Thus the word *faith* is interchangeable with religion.

Before launching into a chronological discussion of the development of different religious traditions, and their impact upon one another, it is perhaps most useful to begin with some of the basic features of the religion that Hindus have in common.[29] One basic way to understand what Hinduism is all about is to consider that practice takes precedence over belief. At the same time that Hinduism affirms worldly life and social values on one hand, there is rejection of worldly life and value placed on renunciation (*samnyasa*). One of the most basic aspects of Hinduism is karma, which can be defined as the inevitable consequences of action. Good actions lead to rebirth as a higher being. Samsara is the cycle of rebirth. Moksha (release) is liberation from the cycle of rebirth and the achievement of salvation.

In the Hindu tradition, the social order of castes emerged from a divine source. The idea of dharma has reference not only to one's caste, but also to the particular stage of one's life, including those of student, householder, retiree from domestic duties, and ascetic. Dharma is the most significant concept in Hindu tradition and the basis of the status of the individual in Hindu society. To act according to the rules of his dharma means that a man must accept his position and role in society on the basis of the caste into which he was born and the norms that have been enunciated for that caste by the authors of the law books or sacred texts. Every individual should recognize the duties he is expected to perform and act accordingly. An individual is born into a particular caste and cannot acquire the status of any other caste. Karma maintains that one's deeds and activities in one's present birth determine one's status and activities in the life to follow. A person's caste status is entirely of his or her own making and one is in a position to improve it by conforming to dharma and being reborn at a higher status in the next birth. This serves as a check on nonconformity through the threat and fear of worsening one's condition in future births. A ban on commensality—sharing food and socializing with members of a lower status—helps impose religious discipline on Hinduism adherents.

So what does *religion* mean in India, when no exact Indian word can be substituted in translation? The notion of dharma is derived from the root word *dhr-*, to sustain; *dharma* refers to religiously ordained duty, morality, right conduct, or the rules of conduct. The rules of dharma are considered to be revealed by the Veda, the sacred collections of hymns and prayers. Dharma also refers to custom, law, or ordinance. Although *dharma* has no exact meaning in English, it usually gets translated into English as *religion* or sacred laws. The nineteenth-century Hindu reformers referred to Hinduism as *sanatana dharma*, a term used today to define an orthodox strain of Hinduism. Different phases of the lifespan require different practices. Most Hindus accept four basic life stages. The first is the Brahmacarin or "student" phase. The next is the Grhastha—householder stage—in which a person's focus is on the home and the family. Vanaprastha—forest dweller—can be loosely characterized as "retirement," when the person slows down on daily activities. The final stage is that of the Sannyasin—ascetic.

Having a sense of sacred geography is integral to the experience of religion in the subcontinent. Pilgrimage is a practice followed by people of all religions, and involves a journey from one's village or city to a sacred center and back. Performing pilgrimage reinforces the notion of a wider community of believers. Hindu pilgrimage is also known by the term *tirtha-yatra.* Tirtha is a crossing place on a river, but in the religious context it means to cross to the other side, the other world of ancestors and gods. Many pilgrimage centers are constructed for Vishnu and Shiva and their avatars. Rama—the incarnation of Vishnu—has his birthplace in Ayodhya. The birthplace of Krishna is the Mathura, and his youthful adventures with cowherd girls is in nearby Brindavan. The word *yatra* refers to "the journey." The significance of pilgrimage actually increased in the colonial and postcolonial periods, due to increased transportation networks, such as the railroads. Pilgrimage is also important to Muslims. Hajj—pilgrimage to Mecca—is one of the main pillars of Islamic faith, and like Hindu shrines, enables a sense of a sacred geography. In India and Pakistan, people also visit shrines where Sufi saints are buried.

Often outsiders will associate Hinduism with peace, but Hinduism is actually not characterized by pacifism. Nonviolence is an opposition to animal sacrifice. It provides an ideology for vegetarianism, but not pacifism generally. Saints and sadhus have always been soldiers as well as traders. Their pilgrimage routes were also used as a trading network. Hindu "saints" are organized into a number of different monastic orders. Their major cults are around the two deities Vishnu and Shiva. Those cults are organized around the worship of images of a personal savior-god. Every guru has his followers without being answerable to a higher authority.

Religion in Historical Perspective

For ease of reference, the chronology of religion in India can be divided into five basic periods. First is the Indus Valley Civilization which lasted from 2500 to 1500 BC. Second is the Vedic period from 1500 to 500 BC. The rise of Aryan, in contrast to Dravidian, culture occurs during this period. At this point, the Veda was formulated. Third is the Epic and Puranic period, 500 BC to AD 500. This period saw the composition of the epic poems *Mahabharata* and *Ramayana*. Traditions of Vaisnavism, Saivism, and Saktism begin to develop. Fourth is the Medieval period from AD 500 to AD 1500. This period saw the development of devotion to Visnu, Siva, and Devi. The fifth basic era, called the Modern period, began in 1500 and lasts up to the present. The Modern period witnessed the rise and fall of two great empires—Mughal and British—and was the origin of India as a nation-state, and the loss of royal patronage for traditions. It also saw the development of Hinduism as a major world religion.

Indus Valley Period (2500–1500 BC)

During the Indus Valley period we find the development of Aryan culture interacting with non-Aryan or Dravidian and tribal cultures. There is much debate over how much the Aryans have influenced modern India. Anthropologist Stephen Tyler takes the position that these elements were part of Indus Valley. Two views represent the basic spectrum of theories about early Indian society. The first is the Aryan migration thesis. According to this theory, people of the Indus Valley spoke Dravidian languages and the society declined in 1800 BC. Aryan migrations or invasions occurred from 1500 BC and Aryans became dominant. Evidence that the Indus script belonged to the Dravidian language group supports this theory. Tyler's variation of this theory says that the basic elements of Indian culture were already in place with the Indus Valley, and Aryans did little to change it. The second theory, supported by Hindu nationalists with a political agenda, states that Hinduism was inherent in the subcontinent all along. This theory, which we call cultural transformation, posits that Aryan culture is a development of Indus Valley; that the Indus Valley itself is an early Aryan or Vedic culture.

The quest for origins is relevant in the contemporary politics of Hinduism, which traces continuity between an ancient past and the present. It is of course problematic to trace the origins or roots of Hinduism. When we do so, we are making a hypothesis about some kind of essence or durable continuity to the religion that has more to do with contemporary politics and is highly problematic. The origin is always the consequence of something that has gone before, and the origin cannot be regarded in a uniform pattern, with hindsight, as pointing toward that which follows. We have to remember that a culture was complete in itself rather than in some sense preliminary, lived by people who experienced the fullness and contradictions of human life.

Vedic Period (1500–500 BC)

What we know about the Vedic period and about the Aryan-speaking peoples comes from three written sources: the Vedas, the epic *Mahabharata*, and the epic *Ramayana*. These latter two texts were oral epics that were written down many centuries later in Sanskrit, which is the oldest written language in South Asia and is considered the ancestor of the languages of modern North India. Vedic literature represents earliest records of Aryan culture in India. These consist of sacred oral tradition, maintained in an exclusively oral form for about 30 centuries (1400 BC to AD 1400). This literature was transmitted by memory from Brahman teacher to pupil. The modern last names of some Brahman families reflect this oral tradition. For example, the surname Trivedi—literally, "three Vedas"—implies that an ancestor could recite by memory three of the Vedas.

Sacrifice was the central religious practice of the Vedic Aryans. There were no fixed places of worship and no images or sacred texts to be carried around, which suggests a nomadic lifestyle. This is very different than modern Hinduism. Interestingly, some of the Hindu traditions revere a body of sacred literature, the Vedas, though some do not. There are two main classes of writing from this period. First are the verse collections, consisting of the Rg Veda, Yajur Veda, Sama Veda, and Atharva Veda. The second class of literature is that of expository prose: including the Brahmanas, Aranyakas, and Upanishads.

The Rg Veda is the basic anthology of hymns, mainly composed while Aryans were in the northwest, and was completed by 1000 BC. These include epic chants, hymns of praise, prayers to gods, and magic spells, and feature elaborate language and structure. Hymns describe pastoral culture, which has been substantiated by and is compatible with archaeological evidence. Both the hymns and the physical evidence suggest that this society had wagons and chariots; domesticated horses, sheep, goats, and cattle; barley and wheat; and copper-bronze tools and weapons. The social organization included warriors, priests, householders, servants, and laborers.

The rich mythology of the Rg Veda includes three important deities. First is Indra, the thunder and monsoon god, who drinks intoxicating soma. Indra is a consummate cattle-raider and barbarian battle-leader, who destroys enemy strongholds. Agni is the god of fire, a divine priest who is an intermediary between humans and gods. Domestic sacrifice, which needs to be performed by priests, promotes universal order and secures the wealth and well-being of the householder. Varuna represents the sky, and is an upholder of moral and cosmic order. The idea of *vrata*, a personal vow, and *rita*, the cosmic order, are associated with Varuna.

As the Aryan society transitioned from a nomadic society to a more settled, agricultural one, it developed a number of social divisions reflecting the new social order. Rg Veda 10.90 contains a creation myth in which the Brahman class emerges from the mouth of the primordial male Purusha. This hymn of the Rg Veda presents the mythological charter for the establishment of the four orders, or varna, of ancient Indian society:

> When they divided the Man, into how many parts did they divide him?
>
> What was his mouth, what were his arms, what were his thighs and his feet called?
>
> The Brahman was his mouth, of his arms was made the warrior.
>
> His thighs became the vaisya, of his feet the sudra was born.

The specialization of society into different social orders created a special class of priests who alone could offer ritual sacrifice to the gods. Sacrifice became the basic element of Vedic religion. The hymns that accompany fire cult discuss domestic hearth rites, seasonal and special public sacrifices (*yajna*), and priests who officiate on behalf of warriors. These hymns suggest that the society was materialistic, with a focus on wealth, health, sons, and victory in war. The hymns invoke gods and are considered to have magical potency, especially Brahman. There is a bit of esoteric ritual involved in the rites, including fire, the consumption of intoxicating plant juice (*soma*), and animal sacrifice.

After the Vedas, the second type of Vedic literature is the expository literature. The first type of such literature are the Brahmanas, composed between 1000 and 800 BC. They include a huge prose collection of guidelines to and discussions of principal great rituals such as the soma sacrifice. In essence this literature is priests talking to priests. It suggests that rites sustain the universe, and shares some ideas with later Upanishads. The Aranyakas are forest treatises dating from 800 to 600 BC. The Aranyakas contain ritual material from the forest that are considered too dangerous for the village.

The Upanishads, dating from the seventh to fifth centuries BC, represented a new tradition of thought that rejected the authority of the Vedas, denied superiority of the Brahman caste, denigrated ritual, and challenged the orthodoxy. The Upanishads were composed from 700 BC onward. The name literally means "secret communications" and is also called Vedanta (end of the Veda). The Upanishads do not accept the idea of sacrifice as the motivating principle of the universe. Instead, they are concerned with search for mystery of the cosmos and humans' relation to it, and are not a systematic philosophy. One can think of the Upanishads as a type of pantheistic mysticism: The individual (*atman*) is the universe (*brahman*). They carried the idea that the individual was the same as the universe and that knowledge brings immortality and limitless mystical power. Therefore, there is no need for esoteric rituals. The individual does not acquire the power of the universe through ritual manipulation, but becomes identical with it.

Challenges to Vedic Religion from Jains and Buddhists

In the sixth century BC, society was divided up into four varnas—Brahmans, Kshatriyas, Vaishyas, and Shudras. Each varna had its own well-defined function. Varna was based on birth and the two higher varnas were given some privileges. The Brahmans were priests and teachers and had the highest status. They demanded sexual privileges, receiving gifts and exemption from taxation and punishment. The Kshatriyas (warriors) ranked second in the hierarchy. They fought and governed, and lived on the taxes collected from peasants. The Vaishyas were agriculturalists and traders. They were the principal tax payers. The fourth varna category was comprised of Sudras, who were agricultural laborers or any low profession. To these four were later added the untouchables who were in fact outside the caste system. In the sixth century many religious teachers preached against Vedic religion. The new anti-Vedic and anti-Brahman ideas were tied to the rise of lower social groups in conjunction with a new agricultural economy. At the same time, the use of coins facilitated trade and commerce—adding to the importance of the Vaishyas. They also looked for a religion that could help them improve their position.

The religions of Jainism and Buddhism arose in part as a challenge to the caste-based order of Vedic religion, which empowered ritual specialists of priests and denied the ability of the average person to access God. They were alike in their opposition to the varna system, and both championed a gospel of nonviolence. These religions are perhaps more easily grasped than one like Hinduism, having historical origins, founding leaders (Buddha and Mahavir), and a system of prescribed beliefs.

Buddhism, the earlier of the two movements, was a vibrant religion in India from sixth century BC to twelfth century AD, and has made a comeback in the twentieth century. In 300 BC, the Mauryan king Ashoka embraced Buddhism and it spread to many countries—Central Asia, West Asia, and Sri Lanka—and made Buddhism into a world religion. Today many countries in Asia profess Buddhism as a major faith, including Sri Lanka, Burma, Laos, Cambodia, Thailand, Tibet, parts of China, Korea, Mongolia, Vietnam, and Japan.

Siddhartha Gautama, the Buddha, was born in the foothills of the Himalayan Mountains in 566 BC. He left home at age 29, became an ascetic, and gained enlightenment under a pipal tree at Gaya. He said that he would not get up from the tree until he had gained enlightenment. That night he attained nirvana and became a Buddha. He died at age 80 in 544 BC. According to Buddhist philosophy, the only way to end the process of rebirth is to achieve nirvana (bliss) through moral conduct and meditation. Like Mahavir and the early Jains, the Buddha considered that the most effective way for his disciples to work toward individual salvation was in small monastic groups. Renunciation from society was good, but one should also avoid the isolation of being a hermit. Buddhists are those who follow the way of the Buddha; beings who have fully "awakened" to the true nature of things. Buddha criticized the idea that Brahmans came out of the mouth of Purusha. He claimed that they come out of the same female bodily organ as everyone else. He also questioned Brahmanic claims that the Vedas were revealed texts, not human in origin, as well as their claims to a special inborn religious authority. During the Buddha's "enlightenment" he developed sophisticated powers of perception, and grasped the essence of what became the four noble truths.

The eightfold path outlines the lifestyle that Buddha developed for people who accepted his teachings and wanted to pursue nirvana. One could escape the terror of aging, sickness, and death by withdrawing one's concerns for or anxieties about them—by no longer desiring youth, health, or even life itself. By withdrawing in this manner, one could lessen the bad effects of karma, since desire was the means by which karma kept the personality on the wheel of dying and rebirth. Removing desire took away karma's poison. The eightfold path includes (1) right views, namely, the knowledge of the four noble truths; (2) intention—dispassion, benevolence, and refusal to injure others; (3) speech: no lying, slander, abuse or idle talk; (4) action: not taking life, or stealing; (5) livelihood: taking an occupation that does not harm living things; (6) effort: avoiding thinking evil thoughts; (7) right mindfulness: awareness is disciplined so that it focuses on an object to know its reality; and (8) concentration: focusing on a worthy object of meditation.

Jainism arose alongside Buddhism as a challenge to Vedic religion. The religion of Jainism was founded by Mahavira (the great hero), who lived from 502 to 468 BC. Born of royal parents, Mahavira left his family and home at age 30. He abandoned all of his possessions, stripped off his clothes, and pulled out his hair by the roots. He began 12 years of severe austerity, and at the age of 42 he attained moksa (release) and became a jina. Mahavira preached for ahimsa—nonviolence—and criticized the Vedic animal sacrifice. One of the primary teachings is that the soul (*jiva*) needs to be freed from its immersion in karmic matter. A Jain should avoid meat, wine, and snacking at night. One should give up lying, stealing, and especially violence. Jain texts also recommend fasting to strengthen one's resolve. Five virtues include nonviolence, truth-speaking, nonstealing, chastity, and nonattachment to worldly things. Jains can either be lay followers or renouncers, who live as nuns or monks. In monastic life, they might pull out their hair, give up their own names, and take five vows: abstaining from violence, dishonesty, theft, sexual intercourse, and personal possessions. Lay Jains must earn a living from activities that don't involve violence. Many of them are traders and are concentrated in the western state of Gujarat. Many Jains nowadays consider themselves to be Hindu, as well as Jain, and do not make strict distinctions between the two religious identities.

Hinduism Responds to the Challenges

How did these new coterminous religious movements change Hinduism? Buddhism and Jainism provided challenges to Vedic religion, with its primary emphasis on sacrifice and priestly interventions. The rise of two major deities—Vishnu and Siva—provided a focus for parishioners of Hinduism to follow. Even today, most Hindus will identify themselves as followers of either Vishnu or Shiva. The worshippers of Vishnu are called Vaishyas. Vishnu is considered to be Indra's younger brother. As a supreme being, he has had the largest following. Vaisnavism saw the composition of epics, the *Mahabharata* and the *Ramayana*. These epics show that the Vedic gods are unable to contend with the demons and chaos of a new age, and introduce a new deity, Vishnu. But Vishnu is not entirely new. He appears in the Rg Veda. The epics present Vishnu as a divinity with heroic qualities, who takes over Indra's role as the primary vanquisher of demons.

Krishna is an incarnation of Vishnu. He is the great lover who has endless relations with the cowherd girls (*gopis*). This love is interpreted not as sexual gratification, but as selfless devotion. The emotion of love is sublimated into devotional worship, known as *bhakti*. One no longer needs the Vedic-style religion with priestly intermediaries to have a relationship with God—personal devotion can be its own path to liberation. In the Ramayana, Vishnu comes embodied in the form of Rama, the young prince of Ayodhya, whose mission is to rid the world of Ravana and other demons. The Ramayana deals with the sacred marriage of Rama and his wife, Sita. Rama is the ideal of the detached husband, of chastity within marriage, and Sita is the ideal loyal wife.

The other major god, Shiva, appears in the late Upanishads and in the epics. Some claim that seals found in Harappa and Mohenjo-Daro were interpreted as Siva. The Nataraja symbolizes the creative and destructive functions of Siva. Saivism has inspired its followers to magnificent temple buildings and poetry. The city of Varanasi (Benaras) is Siva's abode. Shiva is a grandiose, self-sufficient ascetic whose erect phallus (*linga*) is the symbol of chastity and erotic life-giving power. His mythology centers around the tension between his asceticism and the claims of domestic life with wife and child.

Epic Period (500 BC to AD 500)

The Vedas and the epics tell the story of Aryan victories over alien peoples. The Aryans are portrayed as godlike heroes and the conquered as irreligious, inferior people. They describe South India and Sri Lanka as inhabited by savages and demons. But unlike the sacrificially oriented Vedic religion, which depended upon the actions of priests, the composition of epic poetry of the *Mahabharata* and the *Ramayana* suggest that professional minstrels appealed to the popular taste. The *Mahabharata* describes the epic war between the Kauravas and Pandavas. As a story, it is a timeless encyclopedia of moral teaching. The main action revolves around the famous struggle between the Kauravas and the Pandavas over land rights. The Kauravas were the cousins of the Pandavas. There were five Pandava brothers. The Kauravas were the hundred sons of Dhritrashtra. Dhritrashtra hoped to avoid conflict so he divided the kingdom and gave half to the Pandavas. But the Kauravas did not like this and challenged the Pandavas to a gambling match. The latter lost and had to go into exile for 13 years before they could regain their kingdom. After 13 years the Pandavas reclaimed their kingdom, but the Kauravas were unwilling to let them rule. So the Pandavas declared war and fought a long battle which resulted in the annihilation of the Kauravas. The Pandavas ruled long and peacefully.

The *Ramayana* is a relatively homogeneous work of art and ornate poetry. It is an ancient Sanskrit epic ascribed to the poet Valmiki, considered the first poet. This epic has idealized characters: hero-prince Rama, faithful wife Sita, and demon Ravana. It received its present shape perhaps as late as the second century CE, but contains much older materials. It tells the life of Rama from before birth to after death. It is divided into seven sections: (1) Balakanda—the birth and boyhood of Rama; (2) description of the capital city Ayodhya and the banishment of Rama; (3) Rama's wanderings in the forest during his 14-year exile and the abduction of Sita by Ravana; (4) Rama's sojourn in the capital of the monkey-king Sugriva; (5) Rama's efforts to recover Sita and his winning of allies to invade Lanka; (6) the war with Ravana, his defeat and the recovery of Sita, his return to Ayodhya, and the coronation of Rama; and

(7) Sita's banishment, the birth of her two sons in the forest, her ordeal and reunion with Rama, Sita's death, and Rama's merging with Vishnu. The *Ramayana*, both in Sanskrit and in its vernacular recreations such as Tulsidas's Hindi *Ramcaritmanas*, has remained extremely popular in India and parts of it are performed in the yearly Ramlilas, theatrical recreations especially of the battle between Rama and Ravana and Rama's entry into Ayodhya.[30] The epic is generally based on the kingdom of Kosala and its capital Ayodhya in the seventh century BC. The campaign against Ravana reflects the contemporary penetration by the Aryans into the Dravidian stronghold of South India and their victory over the darker races.

Medieval Period

In the early thirteenth century, the Delhi Sultanate was established. There was a succession of rulers and courts of Afghan, Turk, and Persian origin, which later gave rise to independent Muslim dynasties in many parts of the north. The Mughals founded their dynasty in the sixteenth century. The most famous of the Mughals was Akbar, who developed his own syncretistic religion, a fusion of Hinduism and Islam. In the seventeenth century the Mughal ruler Shah Jahan built the Taj Mahal as a mausoleum for his wife. The five centuries of Muslim rule from Delhi saw the conversion to Islam of most people in the Indus and western Punjab plains and the Ganga plains, the Deccan, the west coast, and most of the people of eastern Bengal. One quarter of the entire population of South Asia took up this religion. It is interesting to note that the regions where the greatest numbers of people converted to Islam, the Punjab and Bengal, were the regions where Buddhism lasted longest and was never replaced by the reformed Hinduism, Brahmanism. There were some practical advantages in converting: a head tax on non-Muslims, for example. But Islam provided a sense of equality in the context of a divisive caste society, even though socially other forms of hierarchy emerged in its place.

A further challenge to the caste order of Hinduism in the fifteenth century began with the rise of Sikhism. The word *Sikh* means "spiritual discipline" and Sikh followers form a *panth*, spiritual path. At its heart, Sikhism is an anticaste movement. It was originally founded by Guru Nanak (1469–1539), who accepted the Hindu idea that the ultimate goal is absorption into God. Guru Nanak was influenced by both Islam and Hinduism, and most Sikh converts came from Hinduism. The Adi Granth is the holy book of the Sikhs, and there is a copy of it in all Sikh temples, where it is revered and worshipped like puja. At the heart of being a Sikh man is the Sikh code of conduct, often called the "Five Ks." These practices include having a beard and uncut hair, wearing a turban, wearing a steel bangle, wearing a sword, and wearing a particular kind of shorts or breeches. All Sikhs take the last name of Singh, and men are to be addressed as "Sirdarji." The impact of European rule created some changes in Sikh self-identity. The British saw the Sikhs as a martial race, and preferred to recruit Sikhs into the military.

Non-Hindu Movements in the Modern Period

The rise and fall of the Mughal dynasty and the British empire are the major events of the modern period, and have already been discussed. One of the important developments in modern India is the return of Buddhism to the Indian subcontinent, the place of its birth. There are two ways by which the Buddhist tradition has returned to India. The first is Dr. Bhim Rao Ambedkar, who was born in 1891. He was the first law minister of independent India and the author of India's Constitution. Ambedkar grew up as a member of a Maharashtrian untouchable community and spokesman for untouchables nationwide. Ambedkar fought for rights for the untouchables, and was unhappy with the way Gandhi handled the untouchable question.

Buddhist sculpture from North India.

After a lifetime of fighting for social justice, Ambedkar decided that Hinduism as it existed would never allow full status to the lowest orders of society, and at a huge public ceremony in 1956 he converted to Buddhism. As described earlier, caste was opposed by the Buddhist tradition; Buddha said that all castes are equally pure and are equal before the law. The Buddhist tradition stressed the equality of human beings, equality of all before the law, disapproval of slavery, and higher status for women, and placed greater value on empirical thinking. Toward the end of his lifetime, Ambedkar led a mass conversion of untouchables to Buddhism in the 1950s. Many of his followers also converted. The last census estimates that there are four million Buddhists in Maharashtra alone.

The second important reason for the resurgence of Buddhism in the Indian subcontinent leads us to the Dalai Lama, the spiritual Tibetan leader of Buddhism now living in exile in India. He is a world spokesperson on peace and nonviolence. The term *Dalai Lama* is Mongolian for "Teacher (dalai) like the Ocean." The 14th Dalai Lama is the god king of Tibet, a reincarnation of the Buddha, supreme spiritual leader for Buddhists around the globe. When he is not traveling around the world promoting peace and nonviolence, the Dalai Lama lives in Dharamsala, a hill station in India. He was forced to flee China in 1959 when the Chinese invaded their country. Since that time he has run the Tibetan government in exile from India. During the same period as Ambedkar's conversions, the Chinese takeover of Tibet forced many Tibetan monks and lay Buddhists to flee south. The Dalai Lama, the spiritual head of the Tibetan people, established his new home in exile in India, where he leads a substantial community of Buddhist refugees.[31]

CURRENT TRENDS

With a population that has surpassed one billion, and soon poised to overtake China to become the most populous nation in the world, India has fared well as the world's largest democracy. Its strong system of capitalism has encouraged private investment and entrepreneurship for its inhabitants. There are some major areas of concern for the nation that impact every citizen, however. Some of the most pressing include poverty elimination; more equitable distribution of resources; public health campaigns to halt the spread of the HIV virus and to provide vaccinations against diseases such as polio; clean drinking water and adequate food distribution; development of infrastructures such as roads and telecommunications; and educational opportunities. Technological innovation has revolutionalized the links between the urban well-to-do, leaving the majority of Indians, the rural and the poor, lagging far between in the information divide. The rise of right-wing Hindu sentiment is perhaps the most worrisome development, and threatens further religious discrimination against Muslims, Christians, and low castes. The growth of global anti-Muslim sentiment after the events of 9/11 has only encouraged the Hindu fundamentalists to be even bolder and more discriminatory against religious minorities.

At the center of these issues is an ongoing and at times violent debate about the essential religious character of Indian society. This chapter ends with some discussion of how the epic *Ramayana* has taken on new meanings that are interspersed with Indian politics and culture. This epic—dramatizing the contemporary fight over a religious site that has been both a mosque (now destroyed) and a Hindu temple—has become the battle cry of right-wing Hindu nationalists in the country, who threaten traditions of acceptance and tolerance in the name of a Hindu nation. This dispute has fueled anti-Muslim sentiment and generated communal rioting several times since the 1990s, with the Indian government only looking the other way and not defending the rights of religious minorities. In particular, the Vishwa Hindu Parishad, or VHP (a world Hindu organization), has emerged as a powerful organization, whose activities are regarded with suspicion by religious minorities.

The VHP proclaims that there was a golden age of a just society, followed by a long period of oppression, first by Muslims and then by the British. According to its doctrine, such decline must be stopped and Hindu society redeemed, at the expense and exclusion of other religious groups. The VHP was founded in Bombay on August 29, 1964 (the date is considered the birthday of Lord Krishna). The VHP wants to create a modern Hinduism that is the national religion of India. Naturally, this has sparked resentment by non-Hindus who fear oppression and exclusion from their nation. This religious movement has been characterized by its transnational character—representatives from Kenya and Trinidad and the United States and probably every nation in the world have been involved. In order to attract local participation, the organizers combined VHP conferences with religious festivals, called *melas*. In the 1970s the VHP focused on missionary work among tribals to "reconvert" them to Hinduism and on organizing Hindus abroad.

It is important to point out, however, that the Hindu nationalist reading is not the only way that Indians interpret the *Ramayana*. In the south the *Ramayana* played a significant role in the development of the Dravidian movement, developed from the 1920s onward. They argued that the *Ramayana* was a text of Brahmanical hegemony. The leader Naichekr attacked the worship of Rama, whom he depicted as a depraved character, while defending the demon king Ravana as a Dravidian hero. In this view the *Ramayana* story of the march of the North Indian Rama on Lanka, the capital of the South Indian Ravana, tells of the Hindu subjugation of Dravidian culture. This interpretation allowed him to promulgate a cultural separation and mount an attack on Brahman privilege in the south. In 1956, this campaign burned images of Rama as part of the propaganda for the cause.[32]

The development of visual technology of television in the subcontinent, and its widespread distribution in the 1970s and 1980s, played a prominent role in the reimagination of the *Ramayana* on a national level. There is a close relationship between politicians and movie actors, especially in South India. It has become popular for politicians to use the cinema to cultivate certain kinds of popular movements, particularly religious. In the late 1980s, the Indian government–run television network, Doordarshan, broadcast a serialized version of the *Ramayana*.[33] It had over 300 actors and was extended to 78 episodes, thereby being broadcast over about a year and a half. The audience that it drew was enormous—never before had so many people in the subcontinent been united in the same activity. Was this from the age-old popularity of the *Ramayana*? Or was it the mesmerizing influence of television? I quote from a news report:

> Sunday mornings will probably never be the same. Most of the nation comes to a grinding halt at 9:30 am as multitudes drop whatever they are doing to watch the Ramayana. People put telephones off the hook, cancel appointments. Factories cannot find workers for urgent jobs even if they offer double pay. In Nasik pilgrims can't get a priest to do worship. Timings of social gatherings, political meetings and religious functions are changed to suit the timings of the Ramayana. Otherwise attendance is so poor that meeting have to be cancelled. It is reported that at least 50 per cent of those who work in hotels and hospitals don't show up for work during the telecasting of the serial.[34]

In comparing the popularity of the television broadcast of the *Ramayana* to the American television shows *Dallas* or *Dynasty*, history Peter van der Veer argues that this program "has done more than anything else to make a standard version of the epic known and popular among the Indian middle class. Moreover, it greatly enhanced the general public's knowledge of Ayodhya as Rama's birthplace and therefore as one of the most important places of pilgrimage in Uttar Pradesh."[35]

The rise of the Rama cult, centered around the site Ayodhya, has been very controversial. For several decades there was a desire to tear down the mosque, which happened in 1992, with no government interference to protect the mosque. The question now at hand is whether the state should build a temple where the mosque once stood. For Muslims, the mosque is sacred space. The first Mughal emperor, Babur, was involved in building of the mosque. Muslims in fact refer to the site as the Babri Masjid, Babu's Mosque. Having the mosque torn down is a slap in the face to religious minorities, in the sense that the state has sent a message that it will not necessarily protect minorities over majority sentiment.

The dispute over Ayodhya also has implications for the impact of globalization on Indian society. What the dispute over the mosque or temple at Ayodhya suggests is that modern technologies—print, radio, television, film, railroad—can actually reinforce the importance of the basis of religious communities. Religion provides particular imaginations of the world and particular ways (rituals) of communicating them. Technological innovation in the subcontinent does not necessarily mean a move from a religious culture to a secular culture, and may in fact be contrary to the diversity that has characterized India since its early times.

As we have seen, the country of India has had a rich, deep civilization that has endured for many centuries. The indigenous civilization was influenced by many outside migrations and penetrations by people from other regions of Asia and the Middle East, such as the Aryans and the various Muslim groups. Eventually, British colonialism had dramatic consequences on the demography, the economy, social life, politics, and religious developments in India. During the post-colonial period, India has had technological and economic changes that have brought forth political and religious movements that provide the cultural touchstones for the many diverse groups that are coping with these traumatic and wrenching cultural transformations. Yet, as is obvious, people have adjusted to the many broad-scale changes throughout their history and more contemporary periods. Undoubtedly, the rich cultural fabric of this civilization will continue to provide the sustenance for these people to endure during this rapid and more fluid process of globalization.

NOTES

1. For an excellent historical and geographical overview of South Asia, see Karl Schmidt, *Atlas and Survey of South Asian History* (Armont, NY: ME Sharpe, 1997).
2. Sherry Ortner's *Life and Death on Mount Everest* (Princeton, NJ: Princeton University Press, 2001) is an accessible and fascinating account of the history of Himalayan mountaineering. It is an ethnography both of the climbers who attempt the feat, along with a discussion of how mountaineering has affected the local culture and society. For a popular account of climbing Mount Everest, see Jon Krakauer, *Into Thin Air* (Garden City, NY: Anchor, 1999).
3. James Fisher, *Trans-Himalayan Traders* (Berkeley, CA: University of California, 1986) advances this point.
4. See Rhodes Murphey, *A History of Asia* (Upper Saddle River, NJ: Pearson Addison Wesley, 1999).
5. Clarence Maloney's *Peoples of South Asia* (New Delhi, India: International Thomson Publishing, 1974) has excellent detail on the archaeological discovery of ancient India. This text, along with Bernard Cohn's *India: Social Anthropology of a Civilization* (Upper Saddle River, NJ: Prentice Hall, 1971) remain the classic textbooks on the subcontinent. The material they both present on ideas of race is no longer current, but the majority of each text presents an outstanding and clear narrative of the South Asian past. Leonard Gordon and Barbara Stoler Miller published *A Syllabus of South Asian Civilization* (New York: Columbia University Press, 1971) which presents a comprehensive chronology of the major events and social movements of the subcontinent.
6. Stephen Tyler's *India: An Anthropological Perspective* (Pacific Palisades, CA: Goodyear, 1973) presents a good, if somewhat dry, discussion of the Indus Valley and early civilizations.
7. Jawaharlal Nehru's *Discovery of India* (Oxford, England: Oxford University Press, 1990) is a classic narrative of ancient Indian history.
8. Bollywood produces more films than one could ever hope to watch, and a number of them are available for rent at local American video stores. These films are a terrific introduction to the imaginative sensibilities of modern India. I recommend *Monsoon Wedding* and *Lagaan* for starters.
9. Thomas Trautmann's *Aryans in British India* (Berkeley, CA: University of California, 1997) contains a clear account of Jones and his contemporaries.
10. Headrick's *Tools of Empire* (Oxford, England: Oxford University Press, 1981) gives insight into the development of technology and infrastructure as an important part of colonial rule.
11. Anne Hardgrove's *Community and Public Culture: The Marwaris in Calcutta* (New York: Columbia University Press, 2002) discusses the complicated identity of middlemen traders in modern Indian society.
12. Lata Mani's *Contentious Traditions* (Berkeley, CA: University of California, 1998) is a pioneering work on this subject.
13. Lloyd and Suzanne Rudolph's *Gandhi: Traditional Roots of Charisma* (Chicago: University of Chicago Press, 1983) is an excellent text to teach in class. See also Richard G. Fox, *Gandhian Utopia: Experiments with Culture* (Boston, MA: Houghton Mifflin, 1989).
14. Emma Tarlo's *Clothing Matters* (Chicago: University of Chicago Press, 1996) contains a good discussion of the meaning of homespun cloth to the Indian nationalist movement.
15. Jim Masselos's *Indian Nationalism: An History* (New Delhi, India: Sterling, 1985) is one good starting point on the major personalities, events, and motivations of the anticolonial nationalist movement.
16. Aishya Jalal's account of Jinnah, *The Sole Spokesman* (Cambridge, England: Cambridge University Press, 1994) is a classic.
17. Mike Davis, *Late Victorian Holocausts* (New York, NY: Verso, 2002) discusses colonial manipulation of "natural" disasters to benefit the colonizers.
18. Urvashi Butalia, *The Other Side of Silence* (Durham, NC: Duke University Press, 2000) is a beautifully written and moving study of Partition and its repercussions on families in the subcontinent.
19. Emma Tarlo's *Unsettling Memories* (Berkeley, CA: University of California, 2003) represents recent scholarly research on the Emergency. Rohinton Mistry's enchanting novel *A Fine Balance* (Vintage, 2001) details the abuses of Indira Gandhi's regime.
20. Arjun Appadurai's *Modernity at Large: Cultural Dimensions of Globalization* (Minneapolis: University of Minnesota Press, 1996) highlights the Indian experience of globalization.
21. Karen Leonard's fine study, *Making Ethnic Choices* (Philadelphia, PA: Temple University Press, 1992) is an insightful account of the forging of community among the Punjabi workers in California.
22. A number of anthologies discuss aspects of sexuality and gender among diasporic South Asians. Rakesh Ratti, ed., *Lotus of a Different Color* (Allyson Publications, 2000) highlights the gay and lesbian experience.
23. Stern's *Changing India: Bourgeois Revolution on the Subcontinent* (Cambridge, England: Cambridge University Press, 1993) contains an excellent discussion of change among Indian families. A collection of essays by Diane Mines and Sarah Lamb, eds., *Everyday Life in South Asia* (Bloomington, IN: Indiana University Press, 2002) presents contemporary views of Indian society. The film *Dadi's Family* presents a rural family undergoing generational upheaval, and the film *Caste at Birth* by Filmakers Video is also quite revealing.
24. Swapna Bannerjee presents a unique account of servant life in India in *Men, Women and Domestic Workers* (Oxford, England: Oxford University Press, 2004).
25. Nicholas Dirks has written much about the social construction of caste in colonial India. See his book *Hollow Crown on South India* (Cambridge, England: Cambridge University Press, 1988) as well as his collected essays, *Castes of Mind* (Princeton, NJ: Princeton University Press, 2001).
26. Mulk Raj Anand's novel *Untouchable* (London, U.K: Penguin Books, 1990) portrays a day in the life of a sweeper boy. Bama's *Karukku* (South Asia Books, 2000) is an autobiographical account of caste oppression in the Indian Catholic Church.
27. Jael Silliman's *Jewish Portraits, Indian Frames* (Waltham, MA: Brandeis University Press, 2003) documents four generations of Jewish women of her family and their lives in Calcutta.

28. The best summary of the historical unfolding of Indian religions is in Richard Davis's Introduction in *Religions of India in Practice* edited by Donald Lopez (Princeton, NJ: Princeton University Press, 1995).
29. Diana Eck's *Darsan: Seeing the Divine Image in India* (Columbia University Press, 1988) is a classic book on Indian worship. See also Gavin Flood, *An Introduction to Hinduism* (Cambridge, England: Cambridge University Press, 1996).
30. Philip Lutendorf's *The Life of a Text* (Berkeley, CA: University of California, 1991) outlines these performances.
31. There have been a number of popular films, including *Seven Years in Tibet* and *Kundan.*
32. Paula Richman, *Many Ramayanas* (Berkeley, CA: University of California, 1991) discusses the varied appropriations of this epic at various junctures in history.
33. Arvind Rajagopal's *Politics After Television* (Cambridge, England: Cambridge University Press, 2001) explores these fascinating developments in Hindu nationalism.
34. Lavina Melwina, "Ramanand Sagar's Ramayan Serial Re-Ignites Epic's Values." *India Worldwide,* February: 56–57. Quoted in Philip Lutgendorf, "Ramayan: The Video." *The Drama Review* 4(2): 136, 1990.
35. Peter van der Veer, *Religious Nationalism* (Berkeley, CA: University of California, 1994).

4 PAKISTAN

Anita M. Weiss

INTRODUCTION

Pakistan's sociocultural and historical importance is often neglected in the United States, either because much of what is known about South Asia is either India based or India biased, or else people inaccurately associate the whole country with Islamic zealots and extremists. For the most part, few people know much about Pakistan, India's neighbor to the northwest, and what they know is often based on sensationalized news reporting. This is a country as culturally diverse as any in Asia, though the vast majority of the population shares a common religion, Islam.

In the northwestern part of the Indian subcontinent, Pakistan was formed as a state in the partition of British India that took effect on August 14, 1947. This division was the result of demands by the Muslim League, led by Muhammad Ali Jinnah, which was seeking a homeland for Muslims where they would not be at risk of discrimination or persecution by a Hindu majority in postindependence India. Based principally on where Muslims were in the majority, the new country had initially included the northeastern sector of the subcontinent as well as the northwestern. The name of the new country, which in Urdu (the national language) also means "land of the pure," is actually an acronym and was formulated to represent what were its component parts:

- P Punjab (the populous eastern province)
- A Afghania (now referred to as the North-West Frontier Province, NWFP)
- K Kashmir (i.e., from the outset, perceived as a component part of Pakistan)
- I (short vowel that doesn't exist in Urdu)
- S Sindh (the southern province)
- T
- A Final part of Baluchistan (the southwestern province)
- N

What is missing from this acronym is a *B* for Bengal, whose eastern half comprised East Pakistan from 1947–1971. Separated from West Pakistan by about 1,600 kilometers (992 miles) of Indian territory and a great deal of linguistic and cultural differences, East Pakistan became the independent state of Bangladesh in December 1971. Importantly, too, when Kashmir was *not* included as a part of Pakistan in 1947, Pakistan set out to liberate the area in the 1948 war with India and hence annexed the now quasi-autonomous Azad ("Free") Kashmir and parts of what now comprise the Northern Areas.

Through most of its political history, Pakistan's government has been controlled by the military. Muhammad Ali Jinnah, the Quaid-e-Azam

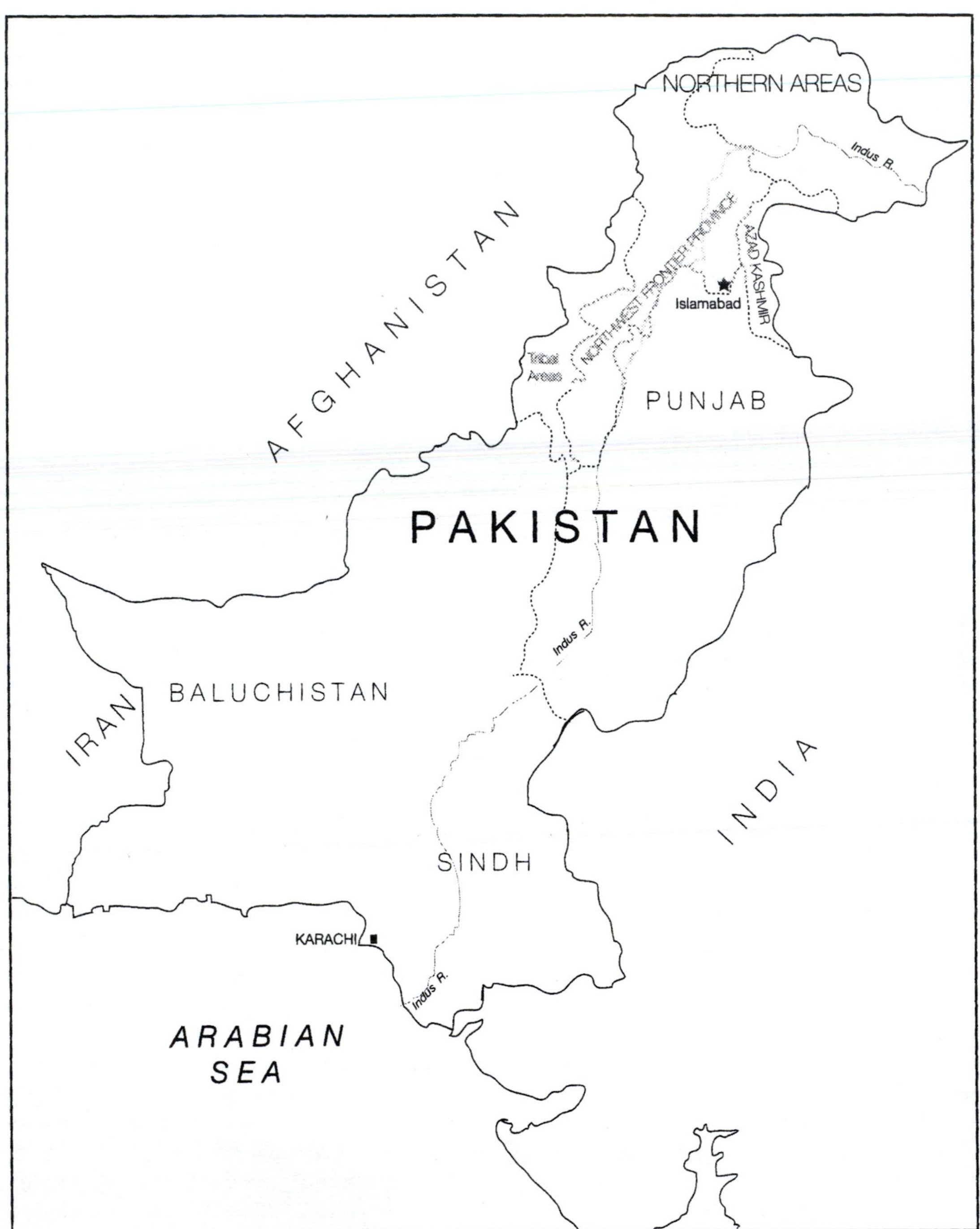
NORTHERN AREAS
Indus R.
AFGHANISTAN
NORTHWEST FRONTIER PROVINCE
AZAD KASHMIR
Islamabad
Tribal Areas
PUNJAB
PAKISTAN
Indus R.
BALUCHISTAN
IRAN
INDIA
SINDH
KARACHI
Indus R.
ARABIAN SEA

(founding father) of the country, envisioned that a secular democracy would take root in the country, but the influence of parliamentary processes remain limited. Jinnah died of cancer a year after the new country was born and his successor, Liaqat Ali Khan, was assassinated three years later. The ensuing political chaos combined with the absence of a charismatic civilian leader with strong national standing and the military threat from India, created an opening for military rule to be widely condoned, at least for a while. The influence of the military in governing Pakistan remains potent today. Hasan-Askari Rizvi, a Pakistani political scientist who has researched the military extensively, contends that its influence extends far beyond the barracks in Pakistan:

> The long years of direct and indirect rule have enabled the military to spread out in the civilian administration, semi-government institutions, the economy and the major sectors of the society. Its clout no longer depends on controlling political power. It is derived from its organizational strength and its significant presence in the polity and the society. The military has acquired a formidable position and role over time. It is the crystallization of the importance and centrality it has enjoyed in the state structure from the beginning. . . . the survival of the state became the primary concern of the rulers of Pakistan who equated it with an assertive federal government, strong defense apparatus, high defense expenditure and a state-directed monolithic nationalism. The imperatives of state security and survival gave primacy to state building over nation building.[1]

These "imperatives of state security" resulted in four instances of direct military rule (1958–1962, 1969–1972, 1977–1985, and 1999–present) and two phases of indirect "civilianized" military rule following martial law (1962–1969 and 1985–1988).

The nagging legacy of the dispute over Kashmir has contributed to the military's political power as it remain the critical antagonist in Pakistan's problematic relationship with neighboring India. This defining dispute about where jurisdiction for Kashmir's governance lies has prompted a wide range of rethinking of Pakistan's historical legacy and contemporary place in the South Asian subcontinent and the wider global economy.

Pakistan's most obvious feature on a map is its strategic placement in the global system. Nestled between India on the east, China on the northeast, Afghanistan on the northwest (with just a thin piece of land separating it from Tajikistan, due north), Iran on the west, and the Arabian Sea to the south (leading to the nearby Arab emirates), it has to exist alongside very powerful neighbors in a fairly tumultuous region of the world.

Pakistan is politically divided into four provinces: Baluchistan, the North-West Frontier Province (NWFP), the Punjab, and Sindh In addition, there are a number of other political entities that are federally administered but which enjoy a great deal of local autonomy: FATA, the Northern Areas, Azad Jammu and Kashmir (AJK), and the capital city area of Islamabad.

Along Pakistan's northeastern border with Afghanistan lies a legacy of the British colonial enterprise, the seven tribal agencies and six frontier regions that comprise the somewhat autonomous FATA, Federally Administered Tribal Agencies.[2] Here, federal institutions and laws are by in large irrelevant; the federally appointed political agents are essentially a liaison between the state and distinct tribal leaders. The Northern Areas, comprising Baltistan, Gilgit, and Hunza, are small, remote princely states that had acceded to Pakistan at the time of independence. Azad Kashmir (as AJK is commonly called), consisting of those parts of the princely states of Jammu and Kashmir which Pakistan annexed in the 1948 war with India, shares some features with the federally administered areas in that their external relations are under the protection and control of the government of Pakistan while their internal affairs enjoy a great degree of political autonomy. However, Azad Kashmir has its own constitution and prime minister and, unlike FATA and the Northern Areas, does not send its own representatives to the federal parliament (National Assembly) in Islamabad. The federal capital, Islamabad, is an autonomous district.

Pakistan, whose land area is 32nd in size in the world, is the 6th most populous country with a 2001 population of 146 million, which is expected to rise to 205 million by 2015. In mid-2003, the government of Pakistan estimated its population was 148.4 million. With one of the world's highest population growth rates, Pakistan has a very young population with two-fifths of the population below the age of 15.[3] Pakistan's population, however, is not evenly distributed throughout the country, ranging dramatically from sparsely populated Baluchistan to some of the highest densities in the world in parts of Karachi and the old city of Lahore. Two-thirds of the population still lives in rural areas, though this is higher in Baluchistan (three-quarters) and NWFP (five-sixths).

Lifestyles in rural areas for many Pakistanis remain physically similar to those of their grandparents and great-grandparents: living in mud huts, sleeping on charpais (string beds), walking to work in the fields, getting stoneware from the village potter and cloth from one of the village weavers, and cooking over an open fire. But what often *is* different is the paved road that leads from the main road to most villages, the buses and trucks that can transport people and goods long distances, smaller families (4 or 5 siblings, down from 9 or 10), and the electric fans that make life in the hot season just a bit more endurable. Today, the vast majority of villages have been "electrified," though as in cities, brownouts remain frequent. Few people can afford to purchase or run a refrigerator, allowing for icemen to retain their professions. The "hoo hoo hoo" of tube wells, a legacy of the British, traverse the countryside, enabling water to irrigate what would otherwise be unfertile desert in many parts of the country.

Less than a fifth of Pakistan's land area has the potential for intensive agricultural use. Nearly all of the cultivable land is actively under cultivation, though outputs are low by world standards. While cultivation is sparse in the northern mountains, the southern deserts, and the western plateaus, the Indus River basin in Punjab and northern Sindh enables Pakistan to feed its population under usual climatic conditions.

The name *Indus* comes from the Sanskrit word *Sindhu*, meaning "sea" (from which also come the words *Sindh, Hindu* and *India*). Each of the country's major rivers—Kabul, Jhelum, Chenab, Ravi, and Sutlej—flow into the Indus, one of the great rivers of the world. The large alluvial plain formed by silt from the Indus River and its tributaries created the large, fertile Indus Basin. This area has been inhabited by cultivating civilizations for at least five thousand years. The Upper Indus Basin consists of the Punjab, whereas the Lower Indus Basin begins at the Panjnad and extends south to the coast of the Arabian Sea.

Punjab literally means "the place where five rivers meet": the Indus, Jhelum, Chenab, Ravi, and Sutlej. The latter, however, is mostly on the Indian side of the Punjab. In the southern part of the province, the British had attempted to harness the irrigation power of the water over a hundred years ago when they established what came to be known as the Canal Colonies. This facilitated the emergence of intensive cultivation despite arid conditions, resulting in important social and political transformations.

ETHNIC AND LINGUISTIC LANDSCAPES AND POLITICAL FOUNDATIONS

Little remains, ethnically or linguistically, from the Indus Valley Civilization that was situated in southern Punjab (located around present-day

Harappa) and northern Sindh (in the Mohenjo-Daro area) and which dominated much of Pakistan and northwestern India from 2600 to 1900 BC.[4] Controversy has existed over the political, economic, and religious practices of the region ever since excavations in the 1920s were started, particularly over how the civilization disintegrated. A major reason behind the controversies is that the script from the Indus Valley, often found on seals, remains undeciphered. Previously, most scholars had conjectured that an invasion of Indo-Aryans hailing from the eastern steppes of contemporary Iran had destroyed the cities and pushed the area's indigenous peoples, Dravidians, to the south. J. Mark Kenoyer, co-director of the Harappa project, contends that current thinking on the demise of this once great civilization is due to a variety of complex factors, and that it occurred over a considerable period of time:

> Contrary to the common notion that Indo-Aryan-speaking peoples invaded the subcontinent and obliterated the culture of the Indus people, we now believe that there was no outright invasion: the decline of the Indus cities was the result of many complex factors. Overextended economic and political networks, the drying up of major rivers as well as the rise of new religious communities all contributed in some way to the creation of a new social order. More than one thousand years later, between 600–300 B.C., as new cities grew up in the Ganga and Yamuna river valleys and peninsular India, the classical Hindu and Buddhist civilizations of ancient India were established. Many of the technologies, architectural styles, artistic symbols and aspects of social organization that characterize these later cities can be traced to the earlier Indus culture.[5]

The cities of the Indus Valley—Harappa and Mohenjo-Daro—are considered the first in the world to be built on a grid pattern, and were formidable economic and political entities in their time. Ancient cloistered settlements have also been discovered as far north as Swat and the Potwar valley and southwest in Sukkur and Quetta. Relics from ancient Buddhist times and the Gandharan civilization remain in various sites in northern Pakistan, notably in Swat and Taxila, though little cultural influences from that era persist. Small subcultures or linguistic groups have been able to retain a great degree of cultural cohesiveness with little external influence, such as the Kalash in the Hindu Kush and the Brahuis (of Dravidian origin) in the Quetta-Kalat part of contemporary Baluchistan.

Sufis are credited with having brought Islam to Pakistan shortly after the death of the Prophet Muhammad. Shrines acknowledging the local popularity of such sufis have been built throughout the country. The most important of these spiritual pioneers were Data Ganj Baksh, buried in Lahore, and Shahbaz Calandar, buried in northern Sindh. These and other tombs of Sufi saints and local *pirs* remain important sites of religious pilgrimage throughout the country.

The historical period that most significantly contributed to the shaping of contemporary Pakistan is that of the Mughal dynasty.[6] North India had long been the scene of Muslim penetration and conquest, with the invasions of Mahmud of Ghazni (in contemporary Afghanistan) who extended his dominions east of the Indus in the eleventh century and the establishment of the Delhi Sultanate (1206–1556) with the crowning of Sultan Aibak in Lahore.[7] As discussed briefly in Chapter 3 on India, Muslims in the Indian subcontinent were a minority ruling a vast Hindu majority. While quite powerful, Muslim dynasties never ruled the whole of India. Local Muslim kingdoms became rivals with one another for political power and authority with Hindu and later Sikh kingdoms.

The zenith of Islamic civilization in India occurred during the Mughal Empire (1526–1857), which became the most powerful and centralized of the various Muslim kingdoms that had ruled in northern India; John Richards considers the Mughal Empire to have been one of the largest states in the early modern world.[8] We know that many residents became Muslims, but what is less clearly understood is whether they converted due to preference, belief, or compulsion, or had never previously identified with a distinct religion, particularly with Brahmanical Hinduism. Richard Eaton argues that while there is no single explanation for the expansion of Islam in South Asia, one pattern stands out:

> In the regions of the heaviest growth—e.g., eastern Bengal, western Punjab, and Kashmir—a deepening of Muslim identities in the pre-colonial period often coincided with the integration of non-agrarian communities into agrarian economies . . . [Islam gradually] became perceived as a "civilization-building" ideology.[9]

The cultural, religious, and political legacy of the Mughal Empire has had enduring influence on northern India, particularly on the areas that later became Pakistan. Babur (1483–1530), the founder of the Mughal Empire, was a descendant of Timur and Genghiz Khan of Central Asia. His reign was followed by those of his son Humayun (1530–1556), then Humayun's son the great Akbar (1556–1605), Akbar's son Jehangir (1605–1627), Jehangir's son Shah Jehan (1627–1657), and then the last great Mughal emperor, Shah Jehan's younger son Aurangzeb (1658–1707).

During the long reign of Akbar, considered the greatest of the Mughal emperors, he significantly extended Muslim rule into major areas of the South Asian subcontinent through both conquest and diplomacy. Importantly, his reign laid the foundations not only for greater political centralization but also for the social integration of his Muslim, Hindu, and other subjects. Religious learning, tolerance, harmony, and syncretism were hallmarks of Akbar's reign. Royal patronage sponsored the building of schools and libraries, a practice that was expanded under the rule of his son, Jehangir.

Akbar's political and social innovations were by no means without controversy. A policy of religious tolerance and encouragement of all faiths fostered loyalty among Hindus, who constituted the majority of Akbar's subjects. He had decreed that he was "the final authority in matters of interpretation and application of religious law" based on *hadiths* (traditions of the Prophet Muhammad) that define the position of a "just ruler."[10] Shortly afterward, in 1581, Akbar promulgated the *Din-i Ilahi* (also referred to as *Tauhid-i Ilahi*), which is often misconstrued as Akbar's attempt to create a new religion (a claim that is tantamount to apostasy in Islam). The actual beliefs and practices of this order for a new brotherhood, according to Annemarie Schimmel, "are nowhere expressly stated," though they resembled a Sufi initiation; there were never many members and few visible traces remained after Akbar's death.[11] Regardless, the cultural synthesis that he encouraged between Islam and other religions, stressing similarities rather than differences, was decried by the *'ulama* (Muslim religious scholars) and other advocates of Islamic orthodoxy, such as Shaykh Ahmad Sirhindi (1564–1624). A member of the Naqshbandi Sufi order, Sirhindi rejected Akbar's claims for religious assimilation and pluralism and advocated a more pronounced emphasis on the Islamic basis and character of state and society.

An even stronger reaction against the legacy of Akbar's tolerant religious, social, and political policies erupted during the reign of his great-grandson, Emperor Aurangzeb (1658–1707). Aurangzeb systematically dismantled Akbar's pluralistic system of governance and replaced it with one that emphasized implementation of Islamic *sharia* (law). He brought in a state taxation system in line with Islamic jurisprudence, ceased the patronage of court astrologers, and introduced prohibitions on intoxicants, extravagant pilgrimages to Hindu religious sites, and music and dancing. Aurangzeb came to be seen as a champion of orthodox Islam in India. Alan Guenther, in his analysis of the application of Hanafi *fiqh* (a distinct codified system of Islamic jurisprudence) in Mughal India, argues that Aurangzeb "invoked Islamic symbols to legitimatize his power, putting forth his orthodox credentials to demonstrate his claim to the throne."[12]

The legacy of these two forms of Islamic religious and political authority—represented by the pluralism of Akbar and the orthodoxy of Aurangzeb—has influenced Pakistan's (and India's) ethnic and religious developments today. The Mughal Empire began its decline with the death of Aurangzeb in the early eighteenth century and the rise of internal rebellions and external forces as the British moved into incorporating India into their imperial realm. Although influential reform movements emerged in the nineteenth century, many of the religious and political leaders in contemporary Pakistan draw on the legacies of these two very different emperors as a means of motivating, mobilizing, and justifying contemporary religious interpretations and political policies in Pakistan today. What Guenther wrote about Aurangzeb's use of Islamic symbols to justify his political power could certainly also be argued about Zia ul-Haq's implementation of an Islamic legal system in Pakistan in 1979.

The political and religious accomplishments of Akbar and his successors were accompanied by the efflorescence of Mughal art and architecture.[13] Mughal art reached great heights in manuscript illustration and miniature paintings as well as the design and building of religious and public monuments, notably grand mosques, forts, palaces, and tombs. The most famous product of this era is the Taj Mahal (built in Agra by the Mughal emperor Shah Jahan as a memorial to his beloved wife, Mumtaz, who died bearing his eighth child), though other Mughal edifices are equally spectacular: the Red Fort in Delhi, Shalimar Gardens in Lahore, and the great Badshahi mosque and Fort on the Ravi River side of Lahore.

The Taj Mahal of the Mughal dynasty.

The single largest manufacturing item of Mughal India was cotton textiles. Early modern Europe became a major importer of these textiles along with pepper, other spices, indigo, and silks from the region.

Language, Ethnicity, and Social Life

The Mughal legacy has also played an important role in creating a sense of community among many South Asian Muslims through the medium of the Urdu language. Urdu, with its origins in the Mughal period, literally means "a camp language," as it is said to have been spoken by the imperial troops who, originally Persian speakers (as were the Mughals), gradually mixed with the local Hindustani-speaking population in northern India and began to combine their own language with the local one. However, they never adopted the Devanagari script (in which Sanskrit and contemporary Hindi are written) but instead retained the Persian script for the new hybrid language, Urdu. Hindi and Urdu, essentially dialects of a single language, have changed considerably since 1947 as they have become the national languages of hostile states. In India, Hindi has incorporated more Sanskrit-based vocabulary while in Pakistan, Urdu now includes more Persian and Arabic terms. Today, whereas vernacular Hindi and Urdu remain mutually intelligible to both populations, most news broadcasts—a key medium of the state, respectively—are no longer so.

Christopher Schackle writes that during the colonial period, "Urdu was the main literary vehicle of the Muslim elite of India" and it was used to link the educated Muslim population together.[14] At Independence, the Muslim League supported elevating Urdu to be Pakistan's national language, one with which the new state could build an identity. However, since so few people actually spoke it, English was retained as the de facto national language as most elites were fluent in it. The adoption of Urdu as a national language, however, was not a popular decision in East Pakistan as most of its population spoke Bengali and identified instead with its literary heritage. Language riots in Dacca ensued in the early 1950s, finally culminating in Bengali being elevated to the stature of a second national language until the secession of East Pakistan in 1971.

Social patterns fall into four general groups in Pakistan: tribal, feudal, rural, and urban. These overlap with each other as they are interwoven with provincial norms and social relations. Individuals in Pakistan identify with a tribe (*qawm*), although this identification is generally more meaningful and salient to daily life in the westernmost parts of the country. Agricultural areas are the most significantly affected by feudalism, which was strengthened when the British instituted the *zamindar* landholding or taxation system in the Punjab. This system allotted large landholdings to individuals who were to be responsible to the Crown for both loyalty and payment of taxes. The resultant feudal system of patronage is in marked contrast with the indigenous tribal systems (whose particulars are discussed below in sections on Pashtun and Baluch social structure).

Marriages are nearly universally arranged, ideally with paternal first cousins. This has significant social implications for alliances. Distinct priorities concerning marriage exist among different communities and are undergoing important transformations (as discussed below in the section on gender relations).

Language often accentuates social values. Language remains an important marker of ethnic identity in Pakistan, where more than 20 languages are still spoken. The most common—Punjabi, Seraiki, Sindhi, Pashto, and Urdu—as well as most others belong to the Indo-Aryan branch of the Indo-European language family. While Urdu is the national language, it is spoken as a native tongue by only 8 percent of the population. People who speak Urdu as their native language generally identify as being *muhajirs*, immigrants from India (often from Uttar Pradesh in the northeast) at the time of Partition in 1947. Their descendants generally still identify as *muhajirs* and have mobilized around a political party in Karachi, the Muhajir Quami Movement (MQM) to achieve various socioeconomic goals. A greater proportion of people from educated backgrounds (and who aspire for upward mobility) now speak Urdu in their homes, as opposed to their regional language, usually to facilitate their children learning it.

The public school system was based on the British model that prioritized early specialization in arts (which includes social sciences) or science. After completing 10 years of schooling, students received a Matric degree, followed by an F.A. or F.Sc. (Intermediate) degree 2 years later, and a B.A. or B.Sc. degree after 2 additional years. Outlying rural areas in Pakistan have long had "open-air" schools as funding constraints have often limited constructing buildings for schools. Traditional religious education—provided either through mosques, individual *maulvis* (religious teachers), or other individuals—existed alongside the formal education system throughout the country.

Instruction in the best government schools in Pakistan continued to be in English until the early 1980s. Indeed, being well versed in English facilitated many Pakistanis to acquire admission to good universities in Britain, the United States, Canada, and Australia. However, in a move to promote nationalism, the government of Zia ul-Haq (1977–1988) declared the medium of instruction in government schools to be Urdu, the national language. The government also actively promoted other vehicles for the dissemination of Urdu to a wider population such as educational facilities and its proliferation on television and radio. Private schools (where many children of elite study) could retain English, while smaller rural schools could continue to teach in the respective provincial language. Some of these private schools have expanded and have branches throughout the country, including Beaconhouse, Esena Foundation, and the Grammar schools.

Nearly half of all Pakistanis speak the provincial language Punjabi, while over two-thirds identify with it as their ethnic group. The next most populous language group is Sindhi (12 percent) followed by the Punjabi variant Seraiki (10 percent), Pashto (8 percent), Baluchi (3 percent), Hindko (2 percent), and Brahui (1 percent). Other languages, which include native speakers of English, Persian, Balti, and Burushaski among others, account for 8 percent.

Punjabi is an old, literary language whose early writings consist chiefly of folk tales and Sufi poetry and romances, the most famous being Waris Shah's version of *Heer Ranjha.* While Sikhs had written down Punjabi in the Gurmulki script, it is only relatively recently that Muslims have been writing down the language in the Urdu script. Punjabi has a long history of being mixed with Urdu among Muslims, especially in urban areas. Numerous dialects exist, some associated more with Sikhs while others associated more with regions. However, while linguists generally consider Seraiki, common in Pakistan's southern belt of Punjab, to be a variant of Punjabi, most Seraiki speakers assert that they speak a distinct language that has its own literary traditions and culture, though they agree they share a common system of social organization.

Perhaps the most poignant description of the Punjabi language was written by Prakash Tandon, himself a Punjabi who captures its unique sociocultural qualities in his literary history of the province, *Punjabi Century*:

> Punjabi is a quaint language, slow, indelicate and lusty. . . . [It] excels in love and abuse. Its abuse is of the genealogical kind which can trace one's family history in the most revealing and incestuous terms. . . . vivid in quarrel, Punjabi can equally convey its vigour in love, whether in the ballads, the improvisation of the peasant in the field or the women quarreling in the *muhallas* (neighborhoods), its purple passages are those tinged with the facts of life. They are earthy and direct.[15]

Tandon is underscoring, in this passage, the lack of affectation or pretense in this language; it is an earthy language of farmers. Indeed, unlike inhabitants of other areas who often remained isolated from outside influences, the very diversity of origins of Punjabis facilitated their coalescence into a coherent ethnic community which has historically placed great emphasis on farming and fighting. Tribal affiliation, based on descent and occupational specialization, tend to merge in the Punjab into a qawm identity.

Most indigenous Punjabis trace their ethnicity to Hindu Jat and Rajput castes (prior to conversion to Islam) or to external invaders to the area. As they intermarried with other ethnic groups, certain qawms (tribal groups) came to predominate, most prominently Jats, Gujjars, Awans, Arains, and Khokkars among the peasant classes as well as Gilanis, Gardezis, Qureshis, and Abbasis. Pashtuns and Baluch have also been settled throughout the Punjab for many generations, a testament to the indigenous fluidity of provincial borders only later demarcated by the British.

An important aspect of Punjabi ethnicity is the notion of reciprocity at the village level. This makes sense, as the Punjab has a long history of settled agriculture and age-old alliances within agrarian communities are essential. Within the Punjabi family, there is an intensively doubled kinship: A man's brother is his friend; his friend is his brother; and both enjoy equal access to his resources. In a traditional context, there is virtually free access to a kin's resources without a foreseeable payback. This results in social networks based on local solidarities of (kinship-based) group necessity as opposed to self-oriented ones. These reproduce not only friendly relations but also a local community structure. There is, consequently, a great deal of social pressure on an individual to share and pool resources (e.g., income, political influence, personal connections).

Such kinship obligations remain central to a Punjabi's concerns.[16] While distinctions based on qawm remain significant social markers, particularly in rural areas, they continue to remain important in urban areas as well:

> As the expansion of capitalism in Western Europe was accompanied by the breakdown of traditional forms of the family, so too do we see changes occurring in the physical forms of the family in the Punjab, especially in urban areas. What has not occurred, however, is a substantial change in the notion of kinship. This is understandable in the context of the realities of Punjabi culture where jobs are acquired through kinship ties and everyone involved is well aware of the obligations which press on all participants.[17]

Punjabis, therefore, often perceive their actions in which they use their influence to benefit other Punjabis as a component part of the cultural requirement of mutual obligation and reciprocity. This notion of intensively doubled kinship, however, leaves some non-Punjabis to perceive certain kinds of actions as showing favoritism toward other Punjabis, thus fueling anti-Punjabi sentiments in the country.

Throughout the province, power has been held by *zamindars*, landlords who owned and controlled large tracts of land for centuries. When the British set out to document land ownership in the region, zamindar families were granted additional land by the British in return for favors for having served the Raj. Zamindars continue to exercise considerable influence in rural areas and provincial politics, although those families that have not diversified into industrial or commercial ventures have witnessed a decreasing power base in past decades. In the past, ties between a zamindar and local villagers were pivotal to social organization: neither group could function without the other. Local villagers largely consisted of (1) tenants, who worked distinct parts of a zamindar's land in return for a set percentage of the crop; (2) farm laborers, who earned a set annual wage paid in kind (e.g., wheat, rice, etc.); and (3) craftspeople and others who provided goods and services to the zamindar and to the larger local populace, paid in kind or cash annually or piecemeal, respectively. The latter group still consists of barbers, drummers, potters, weavers, and owners of nearby *tandoors* (ovens) who supply bread on a daily basis. The zamindar, conversely, couldn't function in his fields, in his household, or in his travels outside his immediate village without his entourage of loyal helpers. While such relationships have broken down to some extent, especially in the past decade, they still remain intact by and large. Villagers avidly campaign for "their saheb" to win. If he—or in rare cases, she—wins an election, villagers will regularly come to them imploring a water supply be connected, a job be found for a relative, or a promised (or implied) gift be given to help pay for a daughter's wedding. Such ties take generations to build, and both sides—zamindars and villagers alike—distrust those who shift allegiances for temporary gain.

Sindh, situated due south of the Punjab, spent much of the era of the British Raj as the nearly forgotten hinterland of Bombay. The social order was dominated by relatively few families, *waderas*, who owned large tracts of land and regarded them as personal fiefdoms. Most of the population consisted of tenants who faced terms of contract that were a scant improvement on outright servitude; a middle class was virtually nonexistent in this rural landscape of unremitting poverty. Hindus played a significant economic role in most parts of pre-Partition Sindh, and most remained afterward given how well entrenched they were in the province's commerce. The port city of Karachi grew from a sleepy fishing village into the fourth British port city (following Calcutta, Bombay, and Madras) during the Raj.

Systems of patronage in rural areas of Sindh resemble those in Punjab except they tend to be even more impervious to shifting allegiances. The only way Sindhi villagers opt out of the wadera patronage system is to flee to cities (generally Karachi) in search of work; but the most effective way for them to find housing and employment in the city is through the largesse of the patronage system.

Sindh suffered a great deal of social, economic and political upheaval in the years following Partition. Millions of Hindus and Sikhs left the major cities for India to be replaced by roughly seven million muhajirs, immigrants from India. Generally better educated than most native Sindhis, these refugees filled a vacuum in the province's commercial life left by the departing Hindus and Sikhs, and later provided the political basis of the MQM, noted earlier.

Sindh has emerged as an ethnic battlefield within Pakistan, pitting indigenous Sindhis against muhajirs aligned with the MQM and, more recently, Sunnis against Shi'as. It continues to witness repeated kidnappings throughout the province, some with political provocation, others without. Fear of dacoits has given rise to the perception that the interior of Sindh is unsafe for road and rail travel. The provincial capital of Karachi, which had been the country's capital until 1962 (when administrative offices shifted to the new capital city of Islamabad), remains Pakistan's commercial center, but it is repeatedly wracked by sectarian, ethnic, and class violence.[18]

The provinces of Sarhad, generally referred to in English as the North-West Frontier Province (NWFP), and the Federally Administered Tribal Areas (FATA) are closely identified with Pashtuns, who now also account for the majority of population in Baluchistan. It is difficult to ascertain an accurate figure of the Pashtun population as questions about women in a household are, in the Pashtun view, an invasion of privacy and numbers of men in a household are often overstated as sons and brothers are a source of strength. By whatever count, Pashtuns constitute one of the largest tribal groups in the world.

The Pakistan–Afghanistan boundary, the Durand Line, was drawn in 1893 by Sir Mortimer Durand for the British Empire. While the actual boundary between the two countries has not been in contention, its legitimacy has been questioned by many Pashtun tribespeople (often supported by the government of Afghanistan) who have advocated the establishment of a new country, Pashtunistan, west of the Indus River.

The NWFP provincial capital, Peshawar, is a quintessentially Pashtun city: The crowded commercial center is constantly in motion, propelled by bearded, turbaned men with nary a woman in sight. Compelling archways reveal bazaars where goods and currencies from throughout the world are traded. Commercial transactions, consistent with all forms of transactions among Pashtuns, are negotiated through tribal and clan lenses.

Tribes and clans are composed as patrilineally related lineages. These lineages eventually tend to fragment, which, over the centuries, has given rise to larger groupings of clans and tribes. Social variation between Pashtun tribes—despite what Pashtun tribes themselves may contend—is relatively minor. At every level of Pashtun social organization, groups are split into a complex and shifting pattern of alliance and enmity. Tribe is also an important designator regarding the variation of Pashto or Dari (or, in fewer cases, Persian) members of a group speak. Most Pashtuns are pious Sunni Muslims and effective religious leaders often acquire a substantial following.

An intensely egalitarian ethos exists among Pashtun men in a clan; the tribal leader is considered as the first among equals. No man will willingly admit himself less than any other's equal hence, only under the direst circumstances will a Pashtun put himself in a position of subservience. This sense of equality is evident in the structure of the men's council, comprised of lineage elders who deal with matters ranging from disputes between local lineage sections to relations with other tribes or the Pakistan government. Although the council can make and enforce binding decisions, within the body itself all are considered equals. The attempt at coercion—even simply the appearance of such an attempt—is considered a serious insult and risks precipitating a feud.[19] Today, however, many Pashtuns are frustrated by what they perceive as a creeping "Punjabization" of social hierarchies that has been growing in the NWFP in the past 20 years; the Pashtun concept of a leader being "first among equals" has been eclipsed by Punjabi practices of elites considering their constituents as inferiors who should serve *them.* This has elicited noticeable resentment against many incumbent politicians.

Pashtuns are irredentists: Traditionally, they acknowledge only the legitimacy of their own group's *khan* or *malik* (small-scale chief), not of others. This irredentism has contributed to a reluctance to have contact with or to trust members of other groups, resulting in apprehension regarding the Pakistan government and contributing to the perception of Pashtun conservatism. Agreements in which Pashtuns have acceded to an external authority—be it the British or later the Pakistani government—have been tenuous at best. By way of comparison, while Punjabi ties are based on mutual reciprocity and obligation, Pashtun ties are impenetrable as they are grounded in insider–outsider sensibilities and notions of legitimacy.

Much of the Pashtun ethos is focused on the Pashtun code of honor, *pashtunwali.* The tenets of the code are virtually omnipresent throughout Pashtun social life.[20] Pashtunwali demands that the individual offer hospitality to guests consisting of food, shelter and the provision of security under all circumstances. Some people have argued that the relatively minimal tension which initially existed between Pakistani Pashtuns and the large number of Pashtun refugees from Afghanistan following the Soviet invasion of Afghanistan in 1979 can be attributed to a heightened sense of kinship with their fellow tribes people along with the deeply felt obligation of Pashtuns to obey the customary dictates of hospitality. An extension of the norms of hospitality implies that even if the person seeking shelter is an enemy, he must be well treated. However, to receive hospitality consistently from someone implies that the recipient is under his protection, a subservient relationship that Pashtuns shun. The level of frustration among Pakistani Pashtuns with the refugees escalated after the former Soviet Union withdrew from Afghanistan in the early 1990s and many felt the internecine violence resulting from warring clans in the conflict was overflowing into their borders.[21] Following the U.S. attack on the pashtun-dominated Taliban government in Afghanistan in 2002, many Pashtuns once again sought shelter under the mandate of pashtunwali from their fellow tribespeople on the other side of the Khyber Pass, in Pakistan.[22]

Vendettas and feuds are an endemic feature of social relations and often span many generations.

A popular perception among Pashtuns is that if the vendetta is not successful this generation, it will be successful in the next. In tribal areas, where government control only erratically contains violence and the level of wealth is generally limited, perennial feuding remains persistent. The proliferation of guns—including clones of AK47s, Uzis, and Kalishnikovs made in the town of Dara Adam Khel—has exacerbated much of the violence. Once a feud becomes resolved, a common practice has been that the aggrieved clan is given a female for marriage, under the assumption that the children of that union will ensure peaceful, long-lasting ties between the clans. This practice of *swara,* however, has been criticized for having girls as young as six years old taken away, and a female given in swara—in actuality a sentence she must pay because of a crime committed by a male family member—is essentially condemned to a life of mental and physical torture. In 2003, the NWFP provincial government outlawed swara on the grounds that there is no basis within the religion of Islam for the practice.

Honor also demands that sexual propriety be maintained. Complete chastity among a man's female relatives is essential as it is through the purity and good repute of his mother, daughters, sisters, and wife (or wives) that a man ensures his honor and that of his clan. In the case of women, even the suggestion of impropriety may result in an "honor killing." Those involved in illicit sexual liaisons are killed if they are found out. While men may often be able to escape to other regions (where they may well be tracked down by a woman's kin), women, almost without exception, are killed by a close male relative. Killings associated with sexual misconduct—honor killings—are the only ones that do not demand revenge or result in a vendetta.[23]

Some women have been organizing against so-called honor killings so that the courts consider such acts as akin to any other form of murder. A highly publicized event in Lahore has further prompted the federal government in Pakistan finally to declare, in May 2000, that honor killings would be treated as murders from then on, although little evidence exists to show that this is now the case. What happened was that a 29-year-old woman from Peshawar, Samia Sarwar, contacted a lawyer in late March 1999 and asked for assistance in divorcing her husband of 10 years. She alleged that she had been physically abused and tortured by her addict husband, her maternal aunt's son, and had moved into her parents' home 4 years earlier. Her parents, however, refused to help her get a divorce on the grounds that this would bring disgrace to their family. She finally fled to Lahore and moved into DASTAK, a shelter set up by the law firm, AGHS, to aid victims of domestic violence. She did not want to meet anyone from her family as she feared for her life. But her family countered her claims and said that they wanted to avoid a court case. She finally consented to meet with her mother—but only if she came alone—in the safety of the office of her lawyer, Hina Jilani, a well-known human rights activist. Her mother, however, did not arrive alone: Samia's paternal uncle and Habibur Rehman, her driver, accompanied her. When Samia's lawyer tried to get them to leave, the driver pulled out a gun, shot Samia through the temple, and nearly killed Jilani as well.

Samia's family claimed the murder was justified on the basis that it is a tribal custom to kill female family members who dishonor their families, and that lawyers who take up such cases should instead be regarded as criminals for "showing Pakistani women a western path." Such occurrences notwithstanding, murdering a woman because she is seeking a divorce is against Pakistani civil law and Islamic sharia (religious law).

Indeed, marriage is a highly structured aspect of Pashtun social life. While parallel-cousin marriage (father's brother's child) is a norm throughout Pakistan, it remains a compelling one among Pashtuns. Relations between a husband

and wife (or wives) tend to be quite formal, as there is little contact aside from the wife serving food to and engaging in sexual relations with her husband.

Pashtuns are disproportionately represented in the police force, civil services, and the military, perhaps due to their historic designation by the British as being "a martial race."[24] In addition to Sikhs, the British encouraged enlisting Pashtuns to service the British Empire, especially to police the Straits Settlements and Hong Kong. This heritage of identifying with the police or armed forces remains potent today among Pakistani Pashtuns.

The government of Pakistan has established numerous schools—including ones devoted exclusively to girls—in an effort to imbue Pashtuns with a sense of Pakistani nationalism and to ward off separatist movements, as well as to promote development and alleviate poverty. Numerous development projects in the past two decades have sought to provide diverse employment opportunities for Pashtuns in the NWFP given limited prevailing economic and commercial options. In particular (and with ample support from international donor agencies), the government has attempted to develop comprehensive development projects in areas of opium poppy cultivation that include roads, schools, as well as incentives for industrial investment.

The final significant ethnic group in Pakistan are the Baluch, of which some 70 percent in the world are said to reside in Pakistan, and the majority in its province of Baluchistan.[25] Baluch tribes claim to have originated near the Caspian Sea along with the Kurds.[26] They then migrated to Aleppo, Syria, and sometime between the sixth and fourteenth centuries, to the region of present-day Baluchistan, which is now divided between the states of Pakistan, Iran, and Afghanistan. Some Baluch claim descent from Hazrat Amir Hamza, the uncle of the Prophet Muhammad, the founder of the Islamic religion. However, it is more likely that they fought under his banner after converting to Islam while living in Arabia.

Baluchistan has long served as a crossroads, with fluid borders until the British Raj and later the government of Pakistan demarcated distinct boundaries. For example, Dera Ghazi Khan (now in Punjab) and Dera Ismail Khan (in southern NWFP) are said to have been founded by Baluch cousins, though neither is located within the contemporary province of Baluchistan. Visiting foreign geologists have characterized the landscape as similar to that found on Mars. The province of Baluchistan itself is an exceedingly inhospitable habitat despite being rich in natural resources, especially natural gas. However, it was only in September 2004 that gas lines finally made this resource—which is ample elsewhere throughout the country—available in rural areas of this province as well.

Baluch tribal structure, as irredentist as that of Pashtuns, concentrates power in the hands of

A Baluchi family.

local tribal leaders, *sirdars*. Baluch society is highly stratified, in marked contrast to that of the neighboring Pashtuns. Significant social ties are between the sirdar, *hakim* (lower level tribal leader) and clan members, who are further stratified as farmers and herdsmen followed by a lower level of tenant farmers and former slaves. Supra-family groups formed through patrilineal descent are significant mostly for the sirdars and hakims. The basic exchange traditionally underlying this elaborate system was the leader's offer of booty or property rights in return for support in battle. In more recent years, various favors are generally traded for votes, but the structure of the system—the participation of the lower echelons through patron–client ties—remains essentially the same.

As with the Pashtun tribes to the north—and virtually throughout the subcontinent—the British played local rivals against each other in a policy of indirect rule. In essence, they exchanged local autonomy and subsidies to rulers for access to the strategic border with Afghanistan. Local leaders today maintain this policy to a large extent, continuing to exploit the endemic anarchy be it regarding local, provincial, or national affairs. Governments change and natural resources are commodified (e.g., *sui* gas, petroleum, and precious minerals), but the key players—or their descendants—remain the same.

Pastoral nomadism, dry-land and irrigated agriculture, and fishing are the principal means of subsistence. Most Baluch eke out a living herding as well as some by farming, especially among many seminomadic herders. Sheep and goats are the main herd animals as the meat and wool can be sold while the dairy products are consumed within the family. Extended families organize themselves around water sources since wells are the property of specific groups. Kinship and social relations reflect the exigencies and realities of dealing with the harsh physical environment. Like other Pakistanis, Baluch reckon descent patrilineally. Lineages, however, play a comparatively minimal role in the lives of most Baluchis. They are notably flexible in arrangements with both family and friends. Ideally, a man should maintain close ties with relatives in his father's line, but in practice most relations are left to individual discretion and there is wide variation. The norm is that lineages split and fragment, often over disputes concerning inheritance and bad relations within marriages. Most Baluch treat both their paternal and maternal kin as a pool of potential assistance to be called upon as the occasion demands (in contrast to Pakistanis elsewhere in the country who would rarely call on maternal kin). Again, the precariousness of subsistence favors having the widest possible circle of friends and relatives. Actual marriage patterns embody this kind of flexibility. As in many parts of West Asia, Baluch say that they prefer to marry their parallel cousins though in actuality, marriage choices are more commonly dictated by pragmatic considerations. The plethora of land tenure arrangements tends to limit the value of marrying one's cousin, a marriage pattern that functions to keep land in the family.

In common with the neighboring Pashtuns, Baluch are deeply committed to maintaining their personal honor, showing generous hospitality to guests and giving protection to those who seek it of them. In contrast, though, is the pronounced relationship between leaders and their followers. While competition for scarce resources (water and land) characterize social relations, this coexists with a deeply held belief in the virtues of sharing and cooperation, the foundation of existing networks of obligation. Indeed, there is no indigenous Baluchi term for "thank you," as things given and received (goods, assistance, hospitality, etc.) are regarded as a right, not a favor or privilege. Such mutual aid is a virtual insurance policy in the face of a precarious livelihood.

There have been sporadic separatist movements in Baluchistan since independence. Baluch have been long accustomed to indirect rule, a policy that leaves local elites with a substantial measure of autonomy, where decisions were made by the sirdar in consultation with elders in a tribal *jirga* (a form of local court). Such decisions were absolutely binding. The federal government, however, abolished the jirga system in the 1970s in a bid to have more control over the population through its judiciary.

The violent confrontation between Baluch insurgents and the Pakistani government in the mid-1970s was particularly brutal and has had long-lasting repercussions. The conflict touched the lives of most Baluch and politicized those long accustomed to accepting the status quo. Original demands for greater regional autonomy escalated into a full-scale movement aimed at restructuring the government along confederal lines. By the mid-1980s, traditional cleavages had declined in importance as Baluch increasingly thought of themselves as a unified group in opposition to Pakistani or Punjabi hegemony. Today, many Baluch, in contrast to the vast majority of Pakistanis, are relatively ambivalent over the matter of Kashmir. Many consider the government of Pakistan's stance on Kashmir to be a convenient ploy to deflect attention away from its exploitation of their province. They cite that while Baluchistan supplies the rest of country with natural gas and other valuable resources, there has been little development in Baluchistan outside its capital city, Quetta.[27]

Many in Baluchistan welcomed Zulfiqar Ali Bhutto's overthrow by Zia ul-Haq in 1977, in contrast to popular sentiment in the rest of the country which was appalled by yet another military takeover. Just as relations with the central government began to improve, the Soviet Union invaded Afghanistan, engendering nearly the entire northern border of Baluchistan to be placed on alert as a front-line area. Baluchistan's landscape in the 1980s changed markedly as Afghan refugee camps were established throughout the northern parts of the province. Eventually, temporary mud housing became transformed into cement structures in many instances. This has also caused the demographic balance to change as ethnic Pashtuns, many being refugees from Afghanistan, have settled in Baluchistan and, through their political party Pashtunkhwa, have been demanding a political voice in the province.

In the 1980s, a new ethnic group was added to the social environment in Pakistan: Afghan refugees. As mentioned above in the discussion of the Pashtun ideology of pashtunwali, these refugees who fled to Pakistan following the December 1979 Soviet invasion of Afghanistan were initially welcomed and granted safe refuge. However, the effect of over three million Afghan refugees on Pakistan has had a weighty impact on the demographics of the country. Areas of NWFP and Baluchistan that had been previously uninhabited were settled by refugees in the 1980s. Aside from the environmental effects of populating desert areas, the social impact has been profound. The escalation of animosity between refugees and Pakistanis, particularly in the Punjab, caused the government of Pakistan to restrict the refugees' free movement in the country in the mid-1980s. While Pakistan had tried to extend assistance to its neighbors at a time of need, many Pakistanis, hurt by the resultant inflation, lack of lower paying jobs that had been taken by refugees, and the proliferation of weapons especially in urban areas (which many felt had been smuggled by refugees to pay for the war effort in Afghanistan) felt their friendship had gone far enough.

The United Nations High Commissioner for Refugees (UNHCR) facilitated the Pakistan government's efforts to keep the refugees separate from the local population by placing restrictions on disbursements of food and other goods from its refugee camps in the NWFP and Baluchistan. Following the October 2002 attack by the United States against the Taliban-led government in Afghanistan, the UNHCR, the Pakistan government, and an array of NGOs (nongovernmental organizations) have encouraged the refugees to return to Afghanistan. However, until internecine fighting stops and substantive rebuilding in Afghanistan commences, chances for this to occur at any significant rate are slim.

Instead, an unusual alliance seems to have emerged in recent years with the ascent of the Muttahida Majlis-e-Amal (MMA), a coalition of various Islamist political parties that won the October 2002 provincial elections in NWFP and also has considerable influence in Baluchistan.[28] The influence of separatist provincial political parties appears to have receded as Pashtuns and Baluch alike are responding receptively to the more religious and socially orthodox message of the MMA. In the NWFP, where the MMA holds a majority of seats in the provincial legislature since the October 2002 elections, the government is seeking to purge non-Islamic traditions and practices as it asserts it is bringing provincial laws into conformity with the dictates and edicts of Islam. Importantly, too, has been its rhetoric—and practice—to support Pashtuns and Baluch seeking shelter in Pakistan from American troops in Afghanistan. Whether aligned with the former government of the Taliban in Afghanistan or not, the defining relationship between groups in the eastern part of Pakistan is tribal affiliation, and no government, national or foreign, can supercede that potent affinity.

Azad Jammu and Kashmir, an autonomous region within Pakistan, today is known more for its political predicament than for any other reason. While the origins of the conflict are clear, the subsequent history and ongoing violent encounters that resulted in two wars (1948 and 1965) and nearly escalated into a nuclear confrontation in the high mountains of Kargil in July 1999 are highly contested.[29] The state of Jammu and Kashmir was one of 584 princely states that, in August 1947, were given the option of joining either India or Pakistan. While the population was overwhelmingly Muslim, the state's Hindu prince, Maharaja Hari Singh, opted to become a part of India. Kashmir was subsequently annexed into the Indian Union on October 27, 1947, despite objections by many of its Muslim citizens as well as by the government of Pakistan. The Pakistan government, soon after, took its complaint to the United Nations which decreed that India was to hold a referendum in Kashmir to ensure the right of self-determination for the people of Kashmir. What follows—from Pakistan's "liberation" of parts of northwestern Kashmir in 1948, the 1965 war, the escalation of the war with India over East Pakistan's secession in 1971 into Kashmir, and the militant uprising in the province that has escalated in the past decade—has resulted in the widespread assertion within Pakistan that resolution of the territorial boundaries of Kashmir is central both to the integrity of the republic of Pakistan as well as to Muslims throughout the world as well as to improving political, economic, and social relations with India.

There are a number of other ethnic minorities in Pakistan. Despite their small numbers, they have received a great deal of attention from nineteenth-century British civil servants and anthropologists from around the world. Areas where significant ethnic minorities live include Chitral and Nuristan,[30] Hunza, Gilgit, and Baltistan.[31] Much has also been written about Swat Pashtuns in particular.[32]

FAMILY AND GENDER RELATIONS

Pakistani social life revolves around family and kin. For most people, family loyalty overrides other obligations; the overwhelming importance of family ties retains its significance even among the most Westernized members of the elite. The family is the basis of social organization and provides its members both identity and protection. The honor or shame of individual members—particularly of female members—affects the general standing of a family in the greater community.[33] The isolated individual living apart from relatives is uncommon; even male workers who have migrated to cities will tend to live with a relative, or a friend of a relative. Adults who do not have their own households usually join that of a relative.

Two perceptions characterize the basic understanding of gender relations: Women are subordinate to men, and men's honor resides in the actions of the women of his family. Throughout the country, gender relations differ more by degree than by type.

The household is the primary kinship unit. In its ideal form, it includes a married couple, their sons, their sons' wives and children, and unmarried offspring. Daughters live with their parents until marriage; it is expected that sons will live with their parents their whole lives in the joint family system. Sons often establish separate households upon their father's death, though this depends on circumstances. Whether or not an extended family persists depends on the preferences of the individuals involved and financial circumstances. Limited resources, quarrels, and divisiveness are the main reasons behind the premature dissolution of a household.

Descent is considered patrilineally, and the *biradari* (patrilineage) plays a significant role in social and political relations. The biradari is not an economic entity as its members neither hold property in common nor share earnings. Biradari members often live in close proximity in rural areas, although land fragmentation and generations of out-migration have led to the dispersal of many members. Patrilineally related families continue to maintain ties with their natal village, and enjoy the legal right of first refusal in any biradari land sale.

Members of a biradari celebrate life events together. Patrilineal kin are expected to contribute food and help with guests in the ceremonies accompanying birth, marriage, death, and major religious holidays. The patrilineage has traditionally served as a sort of mutual aid society-cum-welfare agency, arranging loans to members, assisting in finding employment, and contributing to the dowries of poorer families. An important social change that has occurred as Pakistan moves from a culture based on ascribed status to one based on achievement is that close kin from one's mother's family also actively participate in the above to the extent that individual members urge them to consider themselves as close kin.

There is considerable pressure for patrilineal kin to maintain good relations with one another so as to present a unified public front. Those with sons and daughters of marriageable age feel intensely the necessity to maintain good relations because a child whose family is at odds with his or her biradari is considered a poor marriage prospect.

Marriage serves as a means of cementing alliances between two extended families. There remains a preference for marriage to one's patrilineal cousin, otherwise to a kin from within the biradari. Some groups allow for marriage of cousins related through one's mother, although all Pakistanis do not accept this practice. One is also restricted from marrying a "milk" brother or sister, someone who suckled milk from the same woman's breast as a baby. The pattern of continued intermarriage coupled with the occasional marriage of nonrelatives creates a convoluted web of interlocking ties of descent and marriage.

Social ties are defined in terms of giving away daughters in marriage and receiving daughters-in-law. To participate fully in social life, a person must be married and have children, preferably sons. Women overwhelmingly get married and have children in Pakistan; 98 percent of all women in 2002 between 35 and 49 had been married. However, fertility rates are finally declining. Two generations ago, an average family consisted of 8–10 children; a generation ago, it was 6–8 children; and today, the norm is 2–4, even among many rural families.[34]

Parents and their siblings become actively involved in arranging marriages for their children. The assumption is that elders are more worldly and experienced, and that they know the temperament of their own child very well, hence are in a better position to decide a good match than their child. Older siblings arrange marriages for younger ones in the event of their parents' early deaths or if the older becomes particularly successful in business or politics. Traditionally, a husband and wife would meet each other only after they signed the *nikah nama,* the Muslim marriage contract, unless they were already related and knew each other. Even then, in most families, once the marriage had been agreed upon, a female cousin would no longer meet with her male cousin or fiancé, until the marriage. Today, the vast majority of marriages are still arranged, though among some elite and some highly educated families (still a minority of both of these, however), a son may suggest with whom he would like for the parents to arrange his marriage. In research I conducted on women's life histories in working-class communities in the Walled City of Lahore, I never met any woman who had met her husband prior to her marriage:

> No woman [whom] I interviewed had any say in who she married, and no woman advocated her daughter having any say in her marriage either. . . . the implication here is that a male as well as a female lose respectability if they have any input into judging the qualities of their prospective spouse. . . . That arranged marriages continue to be accepted as the norm is no surprise in this collective-oriented culture.[35]

An extreme form of arranged marriage, referred to as an exchange marriage—*watta satta*—is also common in parts of the Punjab and Sindh: A sister and brother are married to a brother and sister, respectively. Traditionally, this is thought as being a kind of "insurance" for daughters, in that her brother would know that if he mistreats his wife, his wife's brother will in turn mistreat his sister (the brother's wife), hence the women would be better cared for. However, this practice has been raised repeatedly in recent years as a human rights abuse, for women are often victimized or divorced not because of their own actions, but because of something that has happened in some other marital unit.

In wealthy families, the process of arranging a marriage (i.e., securing an agreement between two families for a male and female to be married), having an engagement ceremony, and all of the functions leading up to the actual wedding celebration take a lot of time and entail numerous gifts be exchanged between the two families. In the majority of families, however, while such processes are a bit shorter they still require the exchange of relatively expensive gifts, which many families find financially unbearable. The financial hardship of marrying off a daughter, in particular, leads some poor families to agree to a match with a much older man, often a widower, that would not require as many gifts or as much dowry.

Dowry—*jahez*—is the gift a family gives to their daughter when they marry her off. There is no association between dowry and Islam, as the religion calls for a bride price (*haq mehr,* discussed below) but not for a dowry. Instead, this is a cultural tradition common in the Punjab and most parts of Sindh, but practiced far less in the NWFP and Baluchistan. Families save up their entire lives for their daughters' dowries, and both the daughter and other female family members sew, knit, and embroider various goods she will take with her to her in-laws' home. In addition, it is expected that the dowry will include a bedroom set (bed, dresser, etc.), cooking utensils, clothes, and extra *charpais* (string beds) for guests. The government of Pakistan has variously tried to restrict the cost of marriages (e.g., banning serving a meal at functions; restricting the extra lighting used), and has outright banned dowries, but with little practical success. These cultural traditions run deep, and while people may discuss the various merits of less grandiose functions or eliminating dowries, no one wants their own daughter to have to be demeaned that her family did not adequately provide for her at the time of her marriage. A rich dowry confers prestige on the young married woman, and its contents—household goods, furniture, clothing, jewelry, and a car or motorcycle, if at all possible—are to remain the property of the bride.

Marriage is also to contain a dower established under Islamic law, the *haq mehr*, a stipulated figure between the two families that would be paid to the wife in the event of divorce or her husband's early death. While some families set a symbolic *mehr* of 32 rupees—in accordance with the traditions of the Prophet—it is usually instead a substantial figure. Elites may demand hundreds of thousands of rupees.

A married woman's lot is often difficult in the early years of marriage. The young bride has very little status in her husband's household. She is subservient to her mother-in-law, and has little influence on her husband's activities. A wife gains status and power as she bears sons. Sons will care for her in her old age, while daughters are a liability, to be given away in marriage with their virginity intact. Therefore, mothers favor their sons, often nursing them longer than daughters. In later life, the relationship between mother and son remains intimate, with the mother retaining far more influence over her son than most wives ever have.[36]

Space is allocated to and used differently by men and women in Pakistan. Traditionally, a woman was seen as needing protection from the outside world where her respectability—and therefore that of her family's—is at risk. Women in many parts of the country live under traditional constraints associated with *purdah*, which necessitate the separation of women from the activities of men, both physically and symbolically, thereby creating very differentiated male and female spheres. Most women spend the bulk of their lives physically within their homes; they go outside only when there is a substantive purpose. The culture outside the home generally revolves around the actions of men. In most parts of the country—perhaps Islamabad, Karachi, and wealthier parts of a few other cities to the exception—people consider a woman (and by extension, her family) to be shameless when there are no restrictions placed on her mobility.

Purdah is practiced in various ways, depending on family tradition. There is less of an urban–rural divide among purdah practices of wealthier classes. Rather, family traditions have more to do with whether or not women observe purdah and, if they do, the kind of veil they might wear. In some cases, women will simply observe "eye purdah," in which they tend not to mix with men and when they do, they avert their eyes when interacting with them. Bazaars in wealthier areas of cities in Punjab differ from those in poorer areas by virtue of the greater proportion of unveiled women shopping in them. Bazaars in cities throughout NWFP, Baluchistan, and the interior of Sindh are markedly devoid of women in general; when a woman does venture out into a bazaar in these areas, she will always wear some sort of veil. The most extreme forms are found in remote parts of NWFP and Baluchistan, where a woman essentially never leaves her home except at the time of her own marriage and never meets with unrelated men. Restrictions also exist regarding male relatives: In the most conservative families, females often may have no contact with maternal first cousins (as they are considered outside the family), and an adult woman will have formal relations with virtually all men except when she is alone with her own husband. While gender relations are somewhat more relaxed among most people in Punjab and Sindh, nowhere (traditionally) do unrelated men and women mix freely.

As in other orthodox Muslim societies, the onus of responsibility for adhering to respectable norms of conduct and limiting contact between the sexes, thereby ensuring a family's honor, is placed on women. This is achieved by limiting her mobility and placing restrictions on acceptable behavior and activities.

Two important factors differentiate the degree to which women's mobility is restricted: class and rural or urban residence. Poor rural women in Punjab and Sindh have traditionally enjoyed a great degree of mobility if for no other reason than sheer necessity. These women characteristically are responsible for transplanting seedlings and weeding crops, and are often involved in activities such as raising chickens (and selling eggs) and stuffing wool or cotton into local blankets (*razais*). When a family's level of prosperity rises and it begins to aspire for a higher status, often the first social change that occurs is putting a veil on its women and placing them into some form of purdah.

Poor urban women in close-knit communities, such as the old cities of Lahore and Rawalpindi, will generally observe some form of purdah and wear either a *burqa* (fitted body veil) or *chadar* (loosely draped cotton cloth) when they leave their homes. In such localities, large living areas had originally been constructed so as to accommodate many levels of extended kin living together. For purposes of economy today, these former *havelis* have been sectioned off into smaller living units, so now there is often one family—with an average of seven members—living in one or two rooms on each small floor. In areas of lower density where people generally do not know their neighbors, there are fewer restrictions on women's mobility.

The common perception that women are to remain confined within their homes so that neighbors don't begin to gossip about their respectability has important implications for women's productive activities. As with social life in general, work openly appears to be a domain of men. Census data and other official accounts of economic activity in Pakistan support such conclusions. For example, the 2002 Pakistan Integrated Household Survey assessed that only 9.3 percent of all women participated in the labor force in 1999–2000. However, rural women are generally engaged in production for exchange at the subsistence level, not earning a countable wage, while urban women often engage in piecework production in the informal sector. In both urban and rural contexts, women's economic contributions are often counted as part of the total family's labor, with government data crediting it to the male earner. Research reveals that women are often engaged in piecework labor at home for considerably lower wages than the equivalent work done by men.[37]

The traditional concept of the gendered division of space continues to be perpetuated in broadcast media. Women's subservience is consistently shown on television and in films, while popular television dramas raise controversial issues such as women working, seeking divorce, or even having a say in family politics. What is often depicted, however, is the image that when a woman strays from traditional norms, she faces insurmountable problems and becomes alienated from her family.

The past century has witnessed various attempts at social and legal reforms regarding Muslim women's lives in the subcontinent. Such attempts began as an offshoot of two separate kinds of movements: the larger social reform movement in British India and the growing Muslim nationalist movement. In the post-Partition era, the issue of the changing status of women in Pakistan largely has been associated with the discourse of the role Islam can or should play in a modern state. Importantly, it addresses the extent to which civil rights common in most Western democracies are appropriate in this context and whether they should override Islamic injunctions in the realm of family law, or vice versa. Other areas include the promotion of female education, integration of women into the labor force, and increased participation in the political process.

Muslim reformers in the nineteenth century had an uphill struggle in introducing female education, easing some of the extreme restrictions on women's activities associated with purdah, restricting polygamy, and ensuring women's legal rights under Islamic law. Sir Syed Ahmad Khan's Mohammedan Educational Conference, which began promoting modern education for Muslims in the 1870s, included many of the earliest proponents of female education and of raising women's social status in the wider society. As tended to be the case in many other parts of Asia at the time, these advocates for social reform were men. The intent was to advance girls' technical knowledge (evidenced in sewing and cooking classes) within a religious framework and thereby reinforce Islamic values. However, progress in promoting female education was slow: By 1921, only four out of every thousand Muslim females were literate.

The promotion of female education was a first step in moving outside the bonds stipulated by traditional views of purdah. The nationalist struggle also tore at the threads in that curtain as women's roles were being questioned and their empowerment was being linked to the larger issues of nationalism and independence. The demand for Muslim women to inherit property as well as other rights Muslims had lost with the Anglicization of certain civil laws was rectified somewhat in 1937 with the enactment of the Muslim Personal Law. In the lead-up to independence, it appeared that the state would prioritize empowering women as Pakistan's founding father, Quaid-i-azam Muhammad Ali Jinnah, said in a speech in 1944:

> No nation can rise to the height of glory unless your women are side by side with you; we are victims of evil customs. It is a crime against humanity that our women are shut up within the four walls of the houses as prisoners. There is no sanction anywhere for the deplorable condition in which our women have to live.[38]

After Independence, elite Muslim women in Pakistan continued to advocate women's political empowerment through legal reforms and promote social welfare projects largely through the All Pakistan Women's Association (APWA). APWA leaders, among others, mobilized support that eventually resulted in the passage of the Muslim Personal Law of Shariat (1948) which recognized a woman's right to inherit all forms of property, and were behind the futile attempt to have the government include a Charter of Women's Rights in the 1956 Constitution. The most important sociolegal reform was the 1961 Family Laws Ordinance, regulating marriage and divorce, which is still widely regarded in Pakistan and Bangladesh as empowering to women. It requires the registration of all marriages, the written permission of a man's wife (or wives) before an arbitration council decides if he may marry again, the abolition of divorce by simple repudiation (*talaq*), and other safeguards for women in the event of a divorce, thereby providing economic and legal protection to women by regulating divorce and restraining polygamy.

Two issues—promoting women's political representation and finding some accommodation between Muslim family law and civil, democratic rights—came to define the discourse regarding women and sociolegal reform in Pakistan in the years following the 1971 war. The latter became particularly prominent during the era of the Zia ul-Haq government (1977–1988), as women's groups emerged in urban areas in response to the promulgation of an Islamization program that many feared would discriminate against women.

It was in the highly visible territory of law that women were able to articulate their objections to the Islamization program initiated by the government in 1979. Protests against the 1979 "Enforcement of *Hudood* Ordinances" focused on its lack of distinguishing between adultery (*zina*) and rape (*zina-bil-jabr*) and that its enforcement was discriminatory against women: A man could be convicted of zina only if he was actually observed committing the offense by other men, but a woman could be convicted more easily as pregnancy became admissible evidence.

The Women's Action Forum (WAF)—*Khawateen Mahaz-e-Amal*—was formed in 1981 in response to the implementation of the above penal code and to strengthen women's general position in the society. Members feared that many of the proposed laws being forwarded by the martial law government of General Zia ul-Haq were discriminatory against women and hence would compromise their civil status. Women, most from elite families, banded together on the principal of collective leadership in the three major cities of Karachi, Lahore, and Islamabad to formulate policy statements and engage in political action to safeguard women's legal position.

In its Charter, WAF asserts that it is "committed to protecting and promoting the rights of women by countering all forms of oppression" by being a consciousness raising group as well as a lobby cum pressure group to create a heightened awareness of women's rights and mobilize support for promoting these rights, as well as "counter adverse propaganda against women." WAF has played a central role in publicly exposing the controversy regarding various interpretations of Islamic law, its role in a modern state, and ways in which women can play a more active role in political matters. WAF members led protests in 1983–1984 against the public flogging of women and the promulgation of the Law of Evidence, which many felt did not give equal weight to men's and women's legal testimony. The final adopted version of the Law of Evidence restricted the testimony of two women being equal to that of one man to financial cases; in other instances, acceptance of a single woman's testimony has been left to the discretion of the judge. Even though the final evidence law was modified substantially from the initial proposal, WAF held the position that the state's declaring a woman's evidence in financial cases as not equal to that of a man's would constrain women's economic participation and was symbolic of an ideological perspective that could not perceive women as equal economic participants with men. They argued that for the first time in Pakistan's history, the resultant laws regard men and women as having different legal rights, and despite the rhetoric that such laws were being promulgated to protect women they were indeed constraining women's power and participation in the larger society.

An important debate, beginning in August 1986, was led by WAF members and their supporters over the passage of the Shariat Bill and the Ninth Amendment—that all laws in Pakistan should be in conformity with the sharia, Islamic law. Opponents argued that passage of the Shariat Bill would negate principles of justice, democracy, and fundamental rights of citizens, and give rise to sectarianism. Some were concerned that Islamic law would come to be identified solely with the relatively conservative interpretation of Islam that had been supported by General Zia's government. Most also felt the Shariat Bill and the Ninth Amendment had the potential to withdraw many of the rights women in Pakistan had already won. In April 1991 under the Nawaz Sharif government, a compromise version of the Shariat Bill was promulgated, but the debate over the issue of which kind of law—civil or Islamic—should prevail in the country remains unresolved.

Discourse about the position of women in Islam and women's roles in a modern Islamic state was sparked by the Pakistan government's attempts to formalize a specific interpretation of Islamic law and exposed the controversy surrounding its various interpretations and role in a modern state. While the issue of evidence became central to the concern for women's status, matters such as mandatory dress codes for women and whether females could compete in international sports competitions underscored the reality that Zia's Islamization program was having a comprehensive effect on women's lives.

Despite numerous commissions' and political leaders' recent calls to repeal the laws implemented under Zia's Islamization program, no action has yet been taken to this effect. It is a highly nuanced position for a government to articulate that they are being supportive of Islam—which Pakistani popular culture by in large requires—and are therefore repealing Islamic laws, even if those laws are often regarded as being discriminatory toward women.

The means by which poor urban women have been able to act outside their mandated roles traditionally have been very limited. In the past, only the very poorest of women would actually leave their homes and labor for someone else for a cash payment, often as a midwife, sweeperess, or nanny. Despite the economic exigencies of Pakistan's industrializing, changing environment, restrictions on women's mobility have resulted in the most common way for urban women to earn money being to manufacture something at home for a middleman. Such items include making ready-made clothes, artificial earrings, scrub brushes, *sehras* to be worn by bridegrooms around their necks at weddings, and embroidered goods.[39] Given the dissolution of extended families concomitant with higher female literacy levels and considerable inflation, more and more urban women are engaged in such activities. However, while there are greater chances for urban women today to earn an income than in the past, concerns over traditional notions of propriety still prevent women and their families from admitting that women engage in such work and that a family is living off the labor of its women. In working within their own homes, they are able to retain their family's respectability. Lack of official recognition of the labor that women already engage in has prompted past governments to articulate priorities to increase women's labor force participation rates, instead of enabling a greater economic return for the work that women actually do or to ensure legal support for their rights to work.

A melding of the women's movement's traditional social welfare activities and its more recent political activism has occurred. Groups with such diverse class basis as WAF, APWA, Pakistan Women Lawyer's Association (PWLA), and the Business and Professional Women's Association, as NGOs, are supporting small-scale projects throughout the country that focus on women's empowerment. Different women's groups have been involved in such activities as instituting legal aid cells for indigent women, opposing the gendered segregation of universities, and playing an active role in condemning the growing incidents of violence against women and bringing them to the attention of the public.

By the 1990s, the women's movement had regrouped from being a force reacting to the state's actions and shifted its focus to three primary goals: to secure women's political

Benazir Bhutto.

representation in the parliament; to work to raise women's consciousness, particularly in the realm of family planning; and to counter suppression by taking stands and issuing statements on events as they occur to raise public awareness. Benazir Bhutto's government played a major role in the 1994 UNDP Population and Development conference in Cairo, followed by the 1995 U.N. Fourth Women Forum for Women in Beijing. Six months after the Beijing Forum, Pakistan became a State Party to the United Nations CEDAW Convention (Convention on the Elimination of All Forms of Discrimination against Women), in March 1996. We can review the role Pakistan has played in other international negotiations in the 1990s to understand how this finally came to fruition. When the 1993 United Nations' Conference on Human Rights in Vienna declared that women's rights were unequivocal human rights, Pakistan was at the forefront of the Muslim states that declared that this should be judged on the basis of equity, not equality. The following year, discussions at the UNDP Population and Development Conference in Cairo connected the question of engendered human rights with women's participation in family planning decisions.

Pakistan's *National Report*, prepared for the Beijing Conference under the auspices of the PPP government's Ministry of Women's Development, took uniquely powerful stances toward empowering women within the 12 categories addressed in the *Platform for Action*. Bhutto's government had turned to activists, scholars and representatives from various NGOs in the country to assist her government in writing the *National Report*. Each of the 12 chapters candidly reviewed women's circumstances in that area, what the state had done thus far to rectify identified problems, and outlined what the state might do to further improve conditions for women. Importantly, in the report, the state vowed to "repeal discriminatory laws, bringing personal laws in line with universal standards of human rights, and working towards uniformity of rights" as well as to sign, ratify, and implement CEDAW without any reservation(s), which finally occurred the following February (1996).

Indeed, all of these challenges emerge from the "culture wars" under contestation between various groups and communities today in Pakistan, all of which revolve around the place and role of women.[40] Are women the *responsibility* of men and, as such, cannot make decisions without male consent and need to be protected by them in whatever ways men determine? Are women the *property* of men, to be traded in marriage as male guardians see fit? Are women to be *encouraged to be mobile*—walk out of their homes to become educated or whatever—but which, conversely, may put a woman's honor at risk? What roles are *appropriate* for women to play in public life? Where is *the balance* between poverty alleviation and improving women's living conditions and local values, between maintaining cultural integrity and outright Westernization, each of which has its own empowering and discriminatory features?

We can identify five critical challenges that now confront women in Pakistan: (1) recognition of changing perceptions regarding women's roles and status in the country, which consistently results in a great deal of social confusion and outright conflict; (2) increasing females' access to practical literacy; (3) creating viable employment opportunities for women in the formal sector of the economy; (4) identifying laws and social practices or attitudes that discriminate against women; and (5) enabling women to gain a public voice both within and outside the political process.

While such concerns had been the domain of the Ministry for Women's Development for over a decade, in 2002, the president of Pakistan established a permanent National Commission on the Status of Women to further promote dialogue between groups grappling with such issues. The debate continues.

RELIGIOUS LIFE

Founded as an Islamic republic with 97 percent of its population professed Muslims, Pakistan still seeks to find an appropriate role for Islam in civic life. This debate also continues—and has escalated in the past decade—over the role that Islamic law should play in the country's affairs and governance.

Two major divisions exist in Islam, between the Sunnis and the Shi'as. They are differentiated by the former's acceptance of the temporal authority of the Rashudin Caliphate ('Abu Bakr, Omar, Usman, and 'Ali) after the death of the Prophet, and the latter's acceptance solely of 'Ali and his descendants. Over time, the Sunni sect has divided into four major schools of jurisprudence (*fiqh*); the Hanafi school is the most prominent in Pakistan. The Shi'a sect later split over a matter of succession, resulting in two major groups: the majority Twelver Shi'as, and the numerically smaller community devoted to following the Aga Khan. Over three-quarters of Pakistanis are Sunni Muslims. Shi'as comprise an additional 20 percent. The remaining 3 percent consists of Christians, Hindus, and members of other religions.

Islam was spread to the South Asian subcontinent by wandering Sufi leaders, pirs. Local sensibilities derived from pre-Islamic influences combined with deep reverence for these religious leaders resulted in practices that veered from the orthodoxy common in the Arab Muslim world and a religion traditionally more flexible.[41] Even in the NWFP, where more orthodox religious parties were voted into office in October 2002, the practice of pilgrimage to pirs' shrines remains strong.

The two most influential sects of among South Asian Sunnis are the Barelvis and the Deobandis. Each has had an important influence in shaping religious practices, influencing the nationalist movement that led up to the creation of Pakistan and political activism in contemporary Pakistan. There has been a great deal of discord between the two sects over time. Some adherents refuse to pray with members of the other sect and many regard the other in pejoratively, akin to non-Muslims.[42]

Muslims adhering to the Barelvi Sunni tradition constitute somewhat half of the population of Pakistan; their strongest concentration is in the Punjab. Initially founded by Sayyid Ahmad Barelvi in the early nineteenth century, members of the Barelvi sect are the direct descendants of the Sufi tradition in South Asia and espouse a pir-focused, populist understanding of Islam. The priority is more on communal practices rather than reading texts.

The Deobandi sect emerged as a nineteenth-century Islamic reform movement in part as a reaction to the populist traditions of Barelvi Islam. Sunni Muslims opposed to British rule in South Asia established a *madrasa* (religious school), the Dar-Ul-Ulom, in 1867 in the North Indian city of Deoband. Here, followers elaborated on the notion that the Qur'an itself provides believers with explicit guidelines for living and that these should be followed explicitly. In addition to this very literal interpretation of Islam, followers of the Deoband school contend that being a Muslim is their first identification (far superceding national or ethnic identity), and that they have an obligation to assist other Muslims anywhere they may need help. Given the importance of literal interpretations of the Qur'an, Deobandis have heavily prioritized religious learning. Hence Deobandi madrasas account for over two-thirds of all the religious seminaries in Pakistan, despite their adherents comprising only about a fifth of the country's population. The Deobandi legacy remains compelling in the ideology of the present-day Jamaat-i-Islam (JUI), its political successor, which continues to promote a rigid, literal interpretation of Islam.[43]

Deobandi teachings are also at the foundation of the Taliban movement in both Pakistan and Afghanistan, which decries Western influences and values. The most famous Deobandi madrasa in Pakistan today, the Dar ul Uloom Haqqaaniyah at Akora Khatak, is closely associated with the Taliban movement.

A third Islamic reform movement is the Ahle Hadith, which relies directly on the sunnah of the Prophet Muhammad for guidance as opposed to the teachings that emerged from the four major schools of Sunni jurisprudence. While less than 5 percent of Pakistan's population, the Ahle Hadith have enjoyed a political influence far greater than their numbers reflect.

The most basic belief in Islam, which *all* Muslims adhere to regardless of sect, is that there is only one God, Allah, and the Prophet Muhammad (PBUH)[44] was his final messenger. *Islam* means "submission," particularly in reference to the blueprint for humanity which Allah has created and outlined in the Qur'an. A believer—a *Muslim*—is one who submits to this plan. The person who submits achieves peace is *salaam*. God, the creator, is invisible and omnipresent; to represent God in any form is a heresy.

Islam is derived from the Judeo-Christian tradition, and recognizes the validity of the Old and New Testaments. However, it claims that Allah's message had become somewhat confused and corrupted over the ages, and that the revelation by Muhammad was to be the final one for all time, the seal of prophecy. While other sects have emerged claiming a new prophet—Bah'ais in Iran and Ahmadiyahs in northern India—these have been controversial and declared to be non-Muslim minorities.

Ahmadiyahs, in particular, have had a difficult time in Pakistan, especially in the past quarter century. They are members of a religious group that originated in central and eastern Punjab founded by Mirza Ghulam Ahmad (1835–1908). Today, they are estimated to number between two and three million persons in Pakistan, less than 1 percent of the total population. This is a group that has undergone persecution and discrimination from Muslims since its founding, though this has further intensified in four recent stages:

1. In the early 1950s after its headquarters had moved to Pakistan and the Ahmadiyahs founded the city of Rabwah (in Punjab) to be its headquarters
2. In the mid-1970s after the Pakistan state declared Ahmadiyahs to be a non-Muslim minority
3. In 1984 after Zia ul-Haq's government ordained that Ahmadiyah religious practices were punishable offenses
4. In the 1990s with the passage of the Blasphemy Law

Details of this heightened discrimination are noted in the *Oxford Encyclopedia of the Modern Muslim World*:

> A messianic movement in modern Islam, the Ahmadiyah has been one of the most active and controversial movements since its inception in British India in 1889. . . . Claiming for its founder messianic and prophetic status, the Ahmadiyah movement aroused the fierce opposition of Sunni Muslims and was accused of rejecting the dogma according to which Muhammad was the last prophet. While India was under British rule, the controversy remained a doctrinal dispute among private individuals or voluntary organizations, but when the Ahmadiyah headquarters moved in 1947 to the professedly Islamic state of Pakistan, the issue became a constitutional problem of major importance.[45]

The key point here is that by stating a foundational belief of the Ahmadiyahs, who believe that Mirza Ghulam Ahmad is a prophet, they are claiming that the Prophet Muhammad was *not* the last of the prophets, which is counter to a foundational belief of Islam. It was on this basis that Ahmadiyahs were declared to be a non-Muslim minority in Pakistan in 1974 and their religious practices were declared to be punishable offenses in 1984. The town of

Rabwah, the spiritual center for Ahmadiyahs, was recently renamed Chenab Nagar as a way to disassociate it from its Ahmadiyah past.

There are five pillars of Islam, certain beliefs and acts to which a Muslim must adhere to affirm membership as a believer in the community. The first is the *shahadah* (testimony), the affirmation of the faith that succinctly states the central belief of Islam: "There is no god but God (Allah), and Muhammad is his Prophet." To become a Muslim, one needs only to recite this statement. Mosques throughout the country bellow out the shahadah when they call Muslims to pray. Indeed, in most rural and some urban parts of the country, the call to prayer is so regular that it makes a watch redundant.

The second pillar of Islam is *salah*, the obligation for a Muslim to pray at five set times during the day as follows: *fajr*, before sunrise; *zohar*, after sunrise; *asr*, midday; *maghreb*, just at sunset; and *isha*, after sunset. Muslims value prayers recited communally, especially the midday prayers on Friday, the Muslim sabbath. Mosques have emerged as important social and political centers as a byproduct of this unifying value. The most famous mosque in Pakistan is the Badshahi, built by the Mughal emperor Shah Jehan across from his palace. Nearby is the tomb of the local Sufi saint Data Ganj Baksh, whose recently reconstructed mosque is one of the largest in Asia. The architecturally modern Faisal Mosque in Islamabad has become a visual symbol of the nation's capital.

The Badshahi Mosque in Lahore, Pakistan.

The third pillar is *zakat*, the obligation to provide alms for the poor and disadvantaged. Zia's government formalized the system in Pakistan whereby the federal government administers collection of the zakat, though its distribution is administered provincially. It is the most significant kind of social welfare system operative in Pakistan today.

The fourth pillar is *siyam* (*sawm*), the obligation to fast from sunrise to sunset during the holy month of Ramadan (pronounced *Ramzan* in Pakistan), in commemoration of the commencement of the Prophet receiving Allah's revelations that comprise the Qur'an. The month itself is considered to be a time of spiritual renewal. Sunnis begin the fast when the sun is first seen over the horizon and end it at the end of the day when it drops beneath the horizon; Shi'as begin the fast about 15 minutes earlier, when light first appears in the sky, and end the fast about 15 minutes later, when the last bit of light from the sun disappears. The morning meal prior to the fast, the *sehri*, is usually shared with immediate family members. The evening meal, on the other hand, has become an opportunity for socializing throughout the country. *Iftari*, the food imbibed to break the fast, generally consists of dates, salads, and tea or sweet drinks. Then after everyone completes the *maghreb* prayers, people will eat and drink long into the night. Very pious Sunnis, during this month, will add a sixth prayer, *taravi*, late at night.

Travelers, non-Muslims, pregnant and menstruating women, and children are exempted from the obligation to fast. Curiously, however, virtually *all* restaurants are closed throughout the country until sunset, making it essentially impossible for a traveler to purchase food, regardless. At the height of government-sanctioned religious fervor during the Zia ul-Haq and Nawaz Sharif periods, the so-called food police would arrest anyone eating (or even chewing gum) in public.

The final pillar is the requirement for every adult Muslim physically and financially able to perform the *hajj*, the pilgrimage to Mecca at least once in his or her lifetime. The pilgrimage occurs during the last month of the Muslim lunar calendar, just over a month after the end of Ramadan. Its social importance as a unifier of the greater Muslim *ummah* (community of believers) has led to the establishment of Hajj committees for its regulation in every Muslim country, including in Pakistan. Elaborate preparations for sea and air transport begin to be made for the next *hajj* period soon after the hajj season ends each year. It is customary in Pakistan for many pilgrims who have completed the hajj either to shave off their hair or to dye it red with henna.

If a Muslim wishes to travel to the sacred places at any other time of the year, this is referred to as *umra* (visitation); at various times of political crises in Pakistan, virtually every major leader has left for Saudi Arabia to perform umra. This may—or may not—increase the politician's moral standing among his or her followers.

Pakistani Shi'as also like to embark on an additional pilgrimage, termed *ziarat*, if they can. This is a journey to the sacred shrines in Karbala (the tomb of Imam Hussain, one of the Prophet's grandsons) and Najaf (to the tomb of Hazrat 'Ali, the Prophet's cousin and son-in-law as well as the fourth Rashudin Caliph) in Iraq and various sites in Iran. Following the first Gulf War in 1991, many Shi'as started to defer traveling to Iraq because of safety considerations. They still retain deep emotional bonds with the sacred sites at Karbala and Najaf.[46]

There are a few other elements that are important in Islam. They contribute to a sense of social membership whereby Muslims see themselves as separate from non-Muslims. These elements include food taboos restricting pork and alcohol (the sale of both is banned in Pakistan), the requirement that animals be slaughtered in a ritual manner to make them *halal* (clean) before consumption, and the obligation to circumcise sons. Another element is *jihad*, "striving." Jihad is often misunderstood in the West, where people think of it as a fanatical holy war. The origins of that concept lie in the European view popularized during the Crusades; what the crusaders did not know nor seek to understand was that there are two kinds of jihad: the more important inner one, the battle each Muslim wages with his or her lower self; and the outer one, which each Muslim has a responsibility to wage for the preservation of the religion and its followers. Someone who fights the outer jihad is a *mujahiddin*.[47] The Afghan rebels waging an insurrection against the Soviet-backed government in the 1980s deftly used this term to identify themselves and hence include a moral dimension to their struggle. Kashmiris fighting against the Indian government today do so as well.

The concept of predestination in Islam is rather different from that in Protestantism. Instead, the Islamic belief lies in the existence of an all-powerful force (Allah) that rules the universe and knows all things. Something will happen—*insha'allah*—if it is God's will. It is not purely fatalistic, for although people are responsible to God for their actions these actions are not predecided. Instead, Allah has shown the world the right way to live as revealed through his blueprint, the Qur'an, and then it is up to individual believers to choose how to live. Yet for a visitor to Pakistan, it does become a bit unsettling when traveling by air within the country on a domestic PIA flight and the flight attendant announces that the flight is scheduled to arrive at its destination at a certain time, "Insha'allah."

Pakistan was initially envisioned as a Muslim homeland, one in which Muslims would not have to live under the threat of Hindu hegemony. Allama Iqbal, considered the "Father of the Country," elaborated what is known as the Two Nations theory: That there existed two distinct nations based on religion (Muslim and Hindu) in the Indian subcontinent. They had different historical backgrounds, traditions, cultures, and social orders.

However, while Islam was envisioned as a unifying link within the country, Pakistan's founder, Muhammad Ali Jinnah, made his commitment to secularism in Pakistan clear in his inaugural address when he said:

> [Y]ou will find that in course of time Hindus would cease to be Hindus and Muslims would cease to be Muslims, not in the religious sense, because that is the personal faith of each individual, but in the political sense as citizens of the State.[48]

This vision of a Muslim majority state in which religious minorities would share equally in its development came under question shortly after independence, and the debate continues amid questions of rights of Ahmediyas, issuance of identity cards denoting religious affiliation, government intervention in the personal practice of Islam, whether the Hudood Ordinances should be repealed, or if the Sharia Bill should be strengthened.

In Pakistan, what it means to be a Muslim is intrinsically tied to local cultural traditions which, to many adherents, are inextricably intertwined. Indeed, there exists substantial confusion over where the lines are drawn between what is Islamic, what is codified tradition, and how (if at all) to delineate their separate jurisdictions. For example, members of the *Sipah-e-Sahaba*, the *Jamiat-i-ulema* and of many *madaris* (residential religious schools) experience their identity as Muslims as inseparable from other component parts of their culture, and often confuse those things that are not in accordance with cultural norms, values, or practices as being in contradiction with Islam. Alternatively, various women's rights groups such as AGHS, the Aurat Foundation, Bedari, Pattan, Shirkat Gah, and Simorgh—engaged in activist research addressing such themes as the rise in domestic violence, female education, and women's political participation—question Islam's jurisdictional space in the contemporary political sphere and whether women's rights need necessarily be limited at all by Islamic injunctions.

From the outset, Islam has been a politicized religion. By virtue of the fact that the Prophet established a government in Medina, precedents of governance, laws, and taxation exist. Through history, from the Ummayyad and Abbasid empires to the South Asian Mughals and later to the Turkish Ottomans, there has been no attempt to think of Islamic beliefs and practices as separate from the actions of the state. Indeed, the ideal purpose of the state is to provide an environment where a Muslim can properly practice the religion. If the leader of a state fails to do that, the people have a right to depose him. This is an aspect that extends back to the South Asian Islamic history.

Despite having been declared an "Islamic Republic" in its second Constitution in 1965, no substantive program of Islamic reforms existed in Pakistan prior to General Zia ul-Haq's implementation of his Islamization program in February 1979. Those reforms included the establishment of the zakat-based welfare or taxation system (mentioned above), a profit-and-loss banking option in accordance with Islam's prohibitions against usury, and an Islamic penal code that had far-reaching implications for women more than men. While Zulfiqar Ali Bhutto's government had outlawed alcohol and changed the "day off" from Sunday to Friday in 1977, General Zia's government further emphasized these features.[49]

However, the Islamization program under Zia ul-Haq was pursued in a rather complicated ideological framework. His stance contradicted popular culture in which most people are "personally" very religious but not "publicly" religious. An untoward outcome was that by relying on an Islamically based policy, the state fomented factionalism: By legislating what is Islamic and what is not, Islam itself could no longer provide unity as it was now being defined to exclude previously included groups. Shi'a–Sunni disputes, ethnic disturbances in Karachi between Pashtuns and muhajirs, increased animosity toward Ahmediyas, and the revival of Punjab–Sindh tensions can be traced to Pakistan having lost the ability to use Islam as a common moral vocabulary. Most importantly, the state had attempted to dictate a specific ideal image of women in Islamic society, which was largely antithetical to that existing in popular sentiments and in everyday life.

Madrasas and deeni madaris (schools founded by religious organizations) began to proliferate in the early 1980s as the government of Pakistan divested its support of public education. They sprang up as alternative venues where poor children could receive an education without the burden of their families' having to pay school fees or for school uniforms. In many instances, they provided students' families with basic foodstuffs and cooking oil. The Pakistan government encouraged them as then-CMLA Zia ul-Haq started patronizing religious groups to create a constituency for himself. He compelled the University Grants Commission (UGC) to recognize certificates issued by such schools as the equivalent of a Master's degree, despite the UGC having no practical control over their syllabi. A Pakistani journalist, Muhammad Ali Anwar, has written:

> Holy war against non-believers is one of the important teachings of the madaris, and this has indirectly led to the creation of sectarian hatred because each sect believes the other to be heretical. While it may be said that religious schools are meeting a need for education among lower-income families, that too is because the state has abdicated its role to educate the people. In the process, a lot of intolerance is being spread.[50]

The most recent major component in the Islamization program was passed by the government of Nawaz Sharif in April 1991, the Shariat Bill. During his tenure, General Zia ul-Haq had been unable to pass this bill which would require *all* laws in the country to be in conformity with Islam. While seemingly unpretentious, there are many ways in which such laws could be interpreted. Women's groups in particular were concerned that the reforms made in the Muslim Family Laws Ordinance of 1961 would be jeopardized if more conservative forces could convince the courts that it was not in conformity with religious precepts. The constitutionally mandated Council for Islamic Ideology has undertaken review of the Ordinance, but despite having had it for years, has not released its assessment. To do so would be taking a distinct position one way or other, something that may result in further polarizing Islamist and secular factions in the country.

A highly controversial law, section 295 C PPC, has drawn a lot of criticism. Introduced in 1986 by Zia ul-Haq, the Blasphemy Law—often referred to as "the blasphemy trap"—states that "whoever by words, either spoken or written, or by visible representation or by any imputation, innuendo, or insinuation, directly or indirectly, defiles the sacred name of the Holy Prophet (peace be upon him) shall be punished with death or imprisoned for life and shall be liable to fine." While the law extends to Muslims and non-Muslims alike, it has been indiscriminately used against members of minorities. A well-known case of the abuse of this law was a charge in 1992 against Akhtar Hamid Khan, the prominent social activist who founded both the Chittagong and Orangi Pilot Projects. He was accused by someone who alleged that he had said something disparaging about the Prophet, though there were no other witnesses. While Akhtar Hamid Khan eventually was released from prison, that he had to undergo the strain of being arrested merely on the statement of someone who wanted to settle a personal score against him was been seen by many as an abuse of human rights. Numerous cases exist against

Christians and Ahmediyahs who have been charged with blasphemy, only later to be discovered that enemies who had some sort of dispute with them had conveniently registered the case.

The provincial government in the NWFP that came to power in November 2002 is a coalition, the Muttahida Majlis-e-Amal Pakistan (MMA), consisting of six Islamist parties: Jamaat-i-Islam, Jamaat ulama-e-Islam (Fazlur Rehman group), Jamaat ulama-e-Islam (Sami ul-Haq group), Jamaat ulama-e-Pakistan, Markazi Jamaat Ahle Hadith, and Tehrik Nifaz Fiqah Jaferiya (a Shi'a party). In its first year in power, the MMA government passed a Shariah Act (June 19, 2003) that vowed to constitute distinct commissions to examine educational, judicial, and economic institutions in the province to ensure conformation to the requirements of Islam. In addition, it introduced a bill, still pending, that would ensure such implementation, termed the Hasba Act. This controversial bill would create a new ombudsman's office to "advocate virtue (*amar-bil maroof*) as it is in Qur'an and guidance from Sunnah" and ensure that "social evils, injustices and the misuse of powers could be checked properly." The controversy surrounding the bill is that advocates maintain it would eliminate non-Islamic practices from the province and bring "justice to people's doorsteps" while critics fear that it may result in an overwhelming vice squad that would compromise human rights in the process of requiring a rigid conformity to regressive practices considered to be "Islamic" by its advocates. In the event the Hasba Act is passed and effectively implemented in the province, it may provoke the culture wars in the country, mentioned earlier, to new extremes.

The most visible groups of non-Muslim minorities are Hindus and Christians. Hindus are found largely in the interior of Sindh and in the vicinity of Quetta, in Baluchistan. Christians are found throughout the country, and are largely engaged in menial tasks. Many Christians had once been Hindu untouchables who had converted during the time of the Raj. Other minorities include Zoroastrians (also referred to as Parsis), largely congregated in the city of Karachi, and members of groups only recently designated as non-Muslim, notably the Ahmediyahs.

The various minority groups have secured separate representation in the provincial and national assemblies, but still have had limited influence in affecting national policy. However, they finally were able to unite around a common issue in October 1992 when the government decreed that religion would be added as a column on identity cards. These cards are used for a range of reasons—to get admission into a school, open a bank account, register to vote and cast a vote, and get a passport. Members of minority groups organized excited demonstrations to protest this discrimination which they argued would demote them to the ranks of second-class citizens. They argued that safeguards existed for them both within Islamic law as well as in the promises that were made to them at independence in 1947. The state finally concurred that the designation of religion on identity cards would be an unnecessary expense.

By the late 1990s, the effects of the proliferation of deeni madaris began to be felt throughout the county. Pakistan had enjoyed a fairly good public education system in its first three decades, albeit it remained plagued by limited attendance from poor communities, especially in rural areas. In the early 1980s, Zia's government declared that the medium of instruction in all public schools would be the national language, Urdu; wealthier Pakistanis began to send their children to the English medium private schools that were becoming established in urban areas. However, a crisis of confidence ensued: It was still expensive to send a child to a government school as families were still required to purchase school uniforms and books, and would also have to do without the benefit of the labor a child might contribute. However, many people ascertained that there would be a limited return (by way of a child being able to get a well-paying job later on) by attending government school. Meanwhile, many deeni madaris were being established throughout the country, often with funding from Saudi Arabia or from expatriate Pakistanis now working in the Gulf region. Many of these religious schools would offer a student's family essential grains (rice, wheat, etc.), cooking oil or even money to help toward a sister's marriage. Families considered that at the least, their son would learn to read the Qur'an and lead prayers, which has a moral benefit. They also surmised, and appropriately so, that their son could earn a living later on by teaching children the Qur'an and their prayers, as many families have a *maulvi saheb* visit their house daily to do so. The Zia regime indeed encouraged their proliferation by approving their syllabi for degrees being granted at government schools.

One of the largest of these madaris is located on the Grand Trunk (G.T.) Road, a half-hour's drive east of Peshawar at Akora Khatak in NWFP. It is run by Maulana Sami ul-Haq, leader of his own faction of the JUI (the political successor of the Deobandi school discussed earlier) that is now a constituent part of the MMA coalition. A decidedly male enclave, the madari at Akoora Khattak's most famous alumnus is said to be Mullah Omar, the leader of the fallen Taliban in Afghanistan (though there is some controversy about this, and some claim he was only given an honorary diploma by the madari). The MMA Information Minister, Asif Iqbal Daudzai, contends that madaris throughout the province are undergoing internal reform and are introducing new subjects, and that both English and computer science are now being taught at Akoora Khattak.

But these madaris have noticeably changed the tone of Islam practiced in Pakistan today, particularly in Punjab and Sindh that had been historically less orthodox than the western parts of the country. It is a stricter Islam, one far removed from the pir- and shrine-centered practices of just a generation ago. Muslim communities worldwide became politicized in the 1990s; nowhere is this truer than in the Islamic Republic of Pakistan.

SOCIETY AND POLITICS IN FLUX TODAY

Social organization in Pakistan is not quite as static as it has been portrayed here. As noted earlier, industrialists in some locales, especially in Punjab and Sindh, have supplanted feudal landlords, though not as often as many journalists writing in Pakistan seem to believe. Where they have replaced the former groups, the essential relations of power remain in most contexts.

Social movements, particularly concerning women and the environment, that had been largely peripheral to the mainstream social order have, quite recently, moved closer to center stage in public life. Nongovernmental organizations (NGOs) committed to economic and social development have emerged essentially in the past decade and have began to take on important responsibilities as more formal official development assistance (ODA) has dwindled.[51]

While it was once imagined that development would improve everyone's life chances, few people subscribe to this notion any longer, particularly as economic prospects for many Pakistanis have become increasingly limited. Instead, a more self-focused approach—in large part emerging from the recognition of how many new elites have acquired wealth and power through unscrupulous means—is rapidly replacing the group-oriented outlook that had been a cornerstone of Pakistani social values for generations.

The loss of a social contract between Pakistanis has had major ramifications in all arenas of life throughout the country's infrastructure: in the economy, the educational system, the government bureaucracy, and even the arts. How people drive and the way related laws are enforced is both symbolic and symptomatic of this loss of a social contract, as size of the vehicle rules the road. Police will generally pull over an offender only when they perceive the driver has no political clout; upon affirming who one's relations are, well-connected offenders are generally let go without any repercussions.

Another example is evidenced in the poverty that remains prevalent resulting in about a third of the population living on less than $1 USD per day (85 percent live on less than $2 USD per day).[52] The World Bank's 2003 Country update on Pakistan states that while the "poverty headcount fell in Pakistan during the 1980s, from 47% in 1985 to 29% in 1995, more recently, it has been increasing (1999–2000, 32%), leaving 45 million people below the poverty line." Key social development indicators remain among the lowest in the world: Adult literacy is at a dismal 44 percent, with female adult literacy even worse at 29 percent (Pakistan's overall spending on education has fallen while that of other countries in the region has risen); over a third of the population (38 percent) does not have access to improved sanitation; and Pakistan's ranking in the 2003 United Nations' Human Development Index (144) places it among other countries with far lower gross domestic product (GDP) per capita rates. While life expectancy for a child born in 1960 was 43 years and today it is over 64, and rates of children dying before the age of one have plunged from a high of 162 per thousand in 1960 to 95 per thousand in 1998, still more than a third (38 percent) of all children in the country under the age of five are under weight for their age.[53]

The social implications of poverty and lack of emphasis on human development are vast. World Bank economists recognize the seriousness of the situation and the potential for prevailing inequities to result in political unrest:

> Poverty remains a serious concern in Pakistan. . . . more importantly, difference in income per capita across regions have persisted or widened. Poverty varies significantly among rural and urban areas and from province to province . . . Pakistan has grown much more than other low-income countries, but has failed to achieve social progress commensurate with its economic growth. The educated and well-off urban population lives not so differently from their counterparts in other countries of similar income range. However, the poor and rural inhabitants of Pakistan are being left behind.[54]

While it was only in the mid-1980s that World Bank experts were heralding Pakistan's crossing over into the ranks of middle-income countries, 20 years later few are even thinking of that as a possibility. Economic growth rates have been consistently high, but it has been Pakistan's failure to make significant progress in human development that is widely presumed to be the major cause of the economic impasse. Having a high population growth rate contributes further to social unrest as greater numbers of people are competing for diminishing resources.

A newspaper editorial once noted that three things came to symbolize Pakistan's material culture in the 1990s: videocassette recorders (for playing Hindi films), Suzuki cars, and Kalashnikov rifles (a byproduct of the struggle by the Afghan mujahiddin against the former Soviet Union). The rural population, still in the majority, is increasingly taking social cues from cities. Videocassette tapes can be rented in many small villages where residents now watch Cable News Network (CNN)—often censored through Islamabad—on televisions that are as numerous as radios were in the 1970s. The cities are more crowded than ever; parts of Karachi and Lahore are considered to be more densely populated than Dakka (in Bangladesh). Locally manufactured tiny Suzuki cars have replaced bicycles and motorcycles in many areas where merely a decade earlier the latter were in great demand. However, urban violence has escalated dramatically with a serious side effect: Anonymous violence is on the increase, as opposed to the more traditional violence that resulted from blood feuds.

Today, in the first decade of the new millennium, many of these issues have become even further exacerbated. Pakistan finds itself once again under military rule, wracked by sectarian conflicts and a declining economy. The most common aspiration of the majority of its people is that they can leave the country to earn a living elsewhere and repatriate those monies back to their families in Pakistan.

What are the factors behind the decline of a social contract among Pakistanis?[55] Many things have combined together to create the current situation that affects how Pakistanis think about themselves. We can trace the struggle to find an all-encompassing social contract in Pakistan to the origins of the state itself, in 1947. Pakistan was founded by Western-oriented professionals and bureaucrats to be a homeland for Muslims, a place where they would not have to be concerned about being a minority community in the Hindu-majority state of India. There was an overall enthusiasm within the new country that there would be a virtual renaissance for Muslims. They would build up new industry and a new ideology, and engage each other in parliamentary debate, all under the umbrella of Islam: That they held something in common that was distinguishable, profound, and moral. However, the most religiously oriented parties did not initially support the establishment of the state. Following Partition, many members of such parties, however, eventually migrated into Pakistan. Additionally, members of Baluch and Pashtun irredentist tribes in the northwest and southwest areas of the new country were not about to relinquish traditional authority to what they perceived as an outside power, the central state of Pakistan.

Partition was also responsible for creating an entirely new ethnic community in Pakistan, muhajirs (discussed earlier in the section on Sindh). While most Pakistanis remain tied, emotionally as well as politically and many even geographically, to a specific place in the country, muhajirs do not share this sentiment. The first clashes between resident Sindhis and Punjabis with muhajirs emerged when the new state gave the latter replacement housing and land for what muhajirs claimed to have left behind in India. Some questioned the parity involved when those who had fought for the country but remained within it were not compensated with abandoned property, although the new immigrants were. In the 1950s, the language riots in Dakka and anti-Ahmadiyah protests in Punjab began to question the principle of citizenship united under the rubric of Muslim Brotherhood.

In the 1950s and 1960s, the state was intent on establishing an industrial base. However, the bureaucracy that had been established by the British was not sufficiently modified to incorporate new technologies and innovations.[56] Establishing what the state stood for ideologically did not seem as important at the time as ensuring its existence and feeding its people. Different groups began contesting for the government's ear, but the ones being heard were the Western-educated professional and industrial classes that the late Hamza Alavi referred to as the *salariat*.[57] Those feudal landlords who had educated their sons also found a place in this scenario; those who had not saw their power deteriorate.

The 1965 war with India over Kashmir produced no definitive closure over the sovereignty of that province. Six years later, when the eastern portion of Pakistan sought to secede from the nation, the rift quickly erupted into yet another war between India and Pakistan as the former became an ally with the nascent state, Bangladesh. Once and for all, cultural and economic differences had superceded the notion that religion was sufficient to hold a very disparate nation together as Pakistan was dismembered, leaving only the western portion of the country intact.

Pakistan's new prime minister, Zulfiqar Ali Bhutto, educated at both Berkeley and Oxford, raised the campaign slogan of "Islamic socialism." It is unlikely that he was fully aware of the new force he was unleashing by elevating religion to the level of political discourse. Regardless, Bhutto was to ban alcohol and move the weekly holiday from Sunday to Friday. He implemented massive land reforms that resulted in the redistribution of land to the extent that some previously landless farm laborers were given parcels of land. In urban areas, he championed the cause of factory workers to the extent that the early 1970s was syncopated by constant strikes and factory closings. However, very importantly, such policies raised the expectations of the masses to an unparalleled level and many people believed that life under the Pakistan People's Party (PPP) with Bhutto as the country's prime minister would indeed be improved. In hindsight, when looking back to those six years, 1971–1977, we can see the divisions between groups becoming more prominent. On a class basis, the expectations of the lower and middle classes were raised, but there was little actual difference in their lives. The upper-class industrialists were alienated from the state by its nationalization policies; the upper-class feudal landlords were alienated by an ineffective land reform that served only to weaken Bhutto's own adversaries. Ethnically, his tenure was plagued by efforts in Baluchistan and the NWFP for increased autonomy. Muhajirs were not yet organized into a separate political group, but by all accounts effectively ran the city of Karachi. Non-Muslim minorities began to grow nervous as the state seemed increasingly intent to formalize its connection with Islam. In the bureaucracy, Bhutto's government revamped the civil service, alienating some men at the highest echelons of power while opening up opportunities for others previously left out. This, the first democratically elected government in 20 years, made full use of its power by giving jobs and privileges to supporters of the PPP.

However, Bhutto's tenure can only be considered as a sort of democratic interregnum, for he was to be overthrown in a bloodless coup d'etat on July 5, 1977, by General Zia ul-Haq. In February 1979, President Zia elevated Islam—or rather, a distinct interpretation of orthodox Islam—to a lawmaking capacity within the state. Non-Muslim minorities began to emigrate from Karachi in unprecedented numbers since 1947; Shi'as marched on Islamabad in 1982 in an effort to maintain their own system of social welfare within their community.

What one knew became dramatically supplanted by who one knew during the tenure of Zia ul-Haq's government (1977–1988). Jobs, contracts, and privileges were increasingly given to those whom the state felt were allies in the contest to diminish the PPP. What could have tied disparate groups together became subordinate to the means through which they gained an identity. Mother tongue, kinship ties, and area of family origin all became overwhelming indicators not only of ascribed status, but also of the potential most individuals could achieve. A common expression that Urdu and Punjabi speakers use translates as "the whole world knows (or believes) that . . ." when what is meant is that the majority of people in their small circle (generally defined by kinship or neighborhood) know or believe something in a certain way. This insular way of constructing a social world is not conducive, under the best of circumstances, to setting aside one's own kinship identity and ties in favor of a more abstract national one based on citizenship. This is particularly true when obvious material and social advantages can be gained from clinging to the former, as increasingly became the case—and remains so—in Pakistan.

The Soviet invasion into Afghanistan in December 1979 was a boon that the Zia government made full use of. Despite the rhetoric that it was searching for an Islamic base for the state's foundation, the reality was that it was a military dictatorship. As such, the large arsenal of weapons being dispatched to Pakistan through overt and covert means did not always find their way into the hands of the mujahiddin. Indeed, some experts argue that the explosion at the Ojhri munitions camp on the outskirts of Rawalpindi in April 1988 was a planned government coverup, that the military could declare that more explosives ignited than actually did, thereby never having to explain what had happened to the weapons that they had diverted.

The invasion also caused the opium pipeline from Afghanistan to the West to dry up. Iran was not an alternative, as Khomeini's government was cracking down hard on drug smuggling. Pakistan was indeed a superior option, especially since many of those who held power—either traditional power or derived from their position in the bureaucracy or military—would allow such smuggling for a small fee. Opium poppies have been grown in remote highland areas of the NWFP since the late nineteenth century, though their cultivation significantly increased after World War II. An entire village's annual yield can be transported out of remote and isolated areas on two donkeys, over high passes, through gorges, or by other simple means in areas with limited transportation facilities. Therefore, with its high labor demand at harvest and its value as a profitable and easily marketed and stored crop, opium poppy has remained important in the high plains and northern valleys, and is often the basis of local economic systems.

While the state cooperated with international agencies, most notably USAID in its opium poppy substitution programs, both cultivation and drug smuggling escalated in the mid-1980s, which resulted in Pakistan emerging as a front-line heroin production and transit route for the international drug market, which it remains today. Given Pashtun irredentist traditions and resistance to become integrated in the wider Pakistani socioeconomic networks, it is not surprising that they have largely resisted efforts to replace opium poppy crops with tomatoes or onions. In the mid-1990s, after the Taliban came to power in Afghanistan and banned opium poppy cultivation, it proliferated once again in the NWFP.

Concomitant with the growth of opium poppy cultivation in Pakistan came a phenomenal rise in its use within Pakistan. This dramatic increase is attributed to many things, including the ready availability of the drug, the breakdown of extended families in cities leading to greater alienation, high unemployment and underemployment rates, and a powerful ethos of consumerism permeating social life.

Despite that the late Mahbub ul-Haq, one of the founders of the UNDP Human Development Index, hailed from Pakistan, the state had consistently failed to promote human development. Instead, the government's priorities were in the political arena where it favored certain political leaders because of their ability to contain the PPP in their local areas. These leaders became virtual medieval lords themselves, hiring and firing people within the bureaucracy at will, making significant commissions from contractors on projects they approved, while all along declaring that democratic principles would have to remain in abeyance while the state's apparatus searched for the right Islamic guidelines.

In August 1988, Zia ul-Haq—along with then U.S. ambassador Arnold Raphael—died in a plane crash whose cause has never been established. That November, elections were finally held once again in Pakistan and Benazir Bhutto, the leader of the PPP, was invited to form a government. In December 1988, she became the first female prime minister of any Muslim country.[58] The ensuing years saw Benazir Bhutto and the PPP jockeying for power with Nawaz Sharif, scion of an industrial family who revived the Pakistan Muslim League (PML). Social conditions continued to deteriorate while each government was dismissed twice on charges of corruption, culminating in General Pervez Musharraf declaring martial law on October 12, 1999.

The Musharraf government had attempted to "clean things up," particularly deteriorating relations between sectarian groups—especially between Sunni and Shi'a extremist groups—that was resulting in increased acts of violence. Instead of becoming the chief martial law administrator (CMLA) as previous military rulers had become, he declared himself the chief executive (CE), in line with the idea that he would lead the country onto a more solid economic footing. In the first week of September 2001, Musharraf launched a new Task Force on Human Development initiative, whose goals were to undertake a universal primary education plan and an adult literacy program, primary health-care plan, skills training and microcredit programs, and the like.[59] Yet events of the following week—September 11, 2001—placed Pakistan squarely into a front-line position in U.S. efforts to thwart al Qaeda and other terrorist entities. The assistance offered to the United States in its war in Afghanistan put Musharraf into direct confrontation with many Pakistanis, especially those who opposed the U.S. invasion and the ensuing raids within Pakistan in search of Taliban and al Qaeda personnel. In January 2002, Musharraf banned a number of extremist Islamist groups for having terrorist connections, including Lashkar-e-Jehangir and Sipah-e-Muhammad. However, many of these banned organizations have reappeared with new names and have continued their vitriolic tirades against each other.

In general, however, most Pakistanis do not support the ongoing U.S. military presence in the region. A June 2003 study released by the Pew Research Center for the People and the Press found that while previously, in 2002, there had been a mixed reaction to "the U.S.-led efforts to fight terrorism" (20 percent favored them while 45 percent opposed them), by mid-2003 whereas 16 percent favored those efforts, a whopping 74 percent—three-quarters of Pakistanis polled—opposed U.S.-led efforts. Nearly half (47 percent) of Pakistanis polled were very concerned about a potential U.S. military threat, with a quarter somewhat concerned; in effect, 72 percent of Pakistanis in this poll feared their country could become a target of U.S. wrath as well.[60] Many Pakistanis assess that the United States has been very heavy-handed in its actions, and the implications of this view on public opinion are serious. This sentiment was echoed in early September 2003, when the MMA parliamentary leader Qazi Hussain Ahmed claimed, "the jihadi character of the Pakistan Army was being destroyed at the behest of the U.S." and that the armed forces should shun this policy. On the same day, several legislators in the NWFP (from the MMA) demanded that the Pakistan and U.S. forces hunting for Osama bin Laden and other al Qaeda operatives in Bannu district, 25 miles from the Afghan border, end their operations.

Yet there are some social movements that have been trying to move beyond such limitations and focus on substantive change. Popular concerns with sustainable, environmental concerns are relatively new entrants onto Pakistan's sociopolitical landscape. For over a decade, Pakistan has enjoyed three major success stories in community organizing leading to sustainable development that have only recently attracted efforts at duplication: the Aga Khan Rural Support Program headquartered in Gilgit, the Orangi Pilot Project located in a Karachi slum, and SUNGI in the NWFP. At the outset, each of these NGOs refused much external support, careful not to compromise their goals and principles. They are comprehensive in scope and include requirements for local participation in development projects, underscoring a philosophy of nonreliance on other entities to provide for community needs. In the Pakistani context, this is exceptional: No longer needing to rely on people with power or access to power opens up the potential to overturn existing priorities and implement development agendas that actually seek to improve people's lives.

A number of these new NGOs led by dynamic, charismatic founders have had uphill battles in breaking through existing patronage networks.

These new organizations generally fall into two groups: social advocacy NGOs or religious movements. The phenomenon that spurred their emergence is similar: an excessive state that sought to manipulate symbols and belief, to the point where many became alienated from its actions. Some reacted by calling for a return to the basics of Islam—and their followers by and large fed up with the unending corruption contended that "at least they're honest"[61]—while others developed into socially committed activists forming or joining advocacy-based organizations. The late Omar Asghar Khan, one of the founders of SUNGI (a social advocacy NGO in NWFP) and a scion of a well-connected, influential military family, argues that an overreaching state that ignored the concerns of the average citizen led to its loss of legitimacy (prior to October 1999):

> When ideology fails to homogenize populations, the state resorts to co-option and manipulation. When this fails, it resorts to the use of force. This is what we see happening in Pakistan. In an attempt to control the lives of an increasingly ungovernable polity, the state—while losing legitimacy—has become more oppressive. Both military and civilian rulers have resorted to patronage and authoritarian measures to perpetuate their rule over a people whose basic needs have largely been unfulfilled.[62]

Alternatively, Omar Asghar Khan argues that a key factor in the emergence of social advocacy NGOs in Pakistan since the latter half of the 1980s was "state control over the media, art and culture as well as the purge of universities" which resulted in many socially committed activists forming or joining advocacy-based organizations. He writes:

> The failure of a top-down, centralized approach to the planning and implementation of programs in Pakistan was an important determinant in catalyzing the formation of a number of groups which initiated a bottom-up and people-centred approach to development.[63]

Both kinds of organizations have undertaken numerous attempts at people-centered development, the former encouraging the formation of a "religious" society and the latter the formation of a "civil" society.

Pakistan today finds itself at a critical crossroads: To continue the path already traversed or to make fundamentally new transformations. Although the former captures the uniqueness and originality of cultural nuances, it also survives due to long-standing systems of power and patronage that have resulted in the poverty, inequity, and sectarianism that plagues the country today. The latter involves new ways of considering culture, of seeing all other citizens as members of one's tribe, clan, or kinship group. That is indeed a great challenge for the people of Pakistan.

NOTES

1. Hasan-Askari Rizvi "The Military" in *Power and Civil Society in Pakistan*, ed. Anita M. Weiss and S. Zulfiqar Gilani, 186 (Oxford, England: Oxford University Press, 2001).
2. The North-West Frontier Province (NWFP) also administers a provincial tribal area, referred to as PATA.
3. The Pakistan Integrated Household Survey conducted under the auspices of the Federal Bureau of Statistics in July 2002 estimated the current population growth rate at 2.16 percent. Pakistan's 1998 national census estimated the rate to be 2.7 percent. The UNDP estimated the population growth rate during 1975–2001 to have been 2.8 percent, while the current rate of growth, from 2001 to 2015, is predicted to be 2.4 percent. Regardless of official estimates, given most people's reluctance to discuss sexuality (hence also skewing the contraceptive usage prevalence rate) and the number of females in their household, it is likely higher. The 1998 Census determined that 43.4 percent of the total population was under age 15, broken down by province as follows: Baluchistan 46.7 percent; NWFP 47.2 percent; Punjab 42.5 percent; Sindh 42.8 percent; FATA 25.9 percent; and the federal capital area 37 percent.
4. Jonathan Mark Kenoyer, *Ancient Cities of the Indus Valley Civilization* (Oxford, England: Oxford University Press, 1998), 17. Kenoyer clearly lays out arguments covering various aspects of the Indus Valley Civilization including its origins, physical structures, trading systems, political and class issues, the rise and demise of the script, and so on. Other accessible, major texts on the Indus Valley Civilization include Gregory L. Possehl, ed.,

Harappan Civilization: A Recent Perspective (New Delhi, India: Oxford University Press and IBH, 1993); Richard H. Meadow, ed., *Harappa Excavations 1986–1990* (Madison, WI: Prehistory Press, 1991); J. Mark Kenoyer, ed., *Old Problems and New Perspectives in the Archaeology of South Asia* (Madison: University of Wisconsin, Department of Anthropology, 1989).

5. Kenoyer, *Ancient Cities of the Indus Valley Civilization*, 19.

6. There are a number of good sources on the Mughal dynasty, notably John Richards, *The Mughal Empire* (Cambridge, England: Cambridge University Press, 1993); Barbara Daly Metcalf and Thomas R. Metcalf, *A Concise History of India* (Cambridge, England: Cambridge University Press, 2002); Richard M. Eaton, *The Rise of Islam and the Bengal Frontier, 1204–1760* (Berkeley, CA: University of California Press, 1993). The most comprehensive work that details the historical contributions of the Muslim period in Indian history is Richard M. Eaton, ed., *India's Islamic Traditions, 711–1750* (Oxford, England: Oxford University Press, 2003).

7. For further elaboration of this early period of Islam in South Asia, see Annemarie Schimmel, *Islam in the Indian Subcontinent* (Leiden, the Netherlands: Brill, 1980).

8. John F. Richards, "The Mughal Empire," in *The Magnificent Mughals*, ed. Zeenut Ziad, with a foreword by Milo Beach (Oxford, England: Oxford University Press, 2002), 3.

9. Eaton, *India's Islamic Traditions*, 20.

10. Alan M. Guenther, "Hanafi *Fiqh* in Mughal India: The *Fatawa-i-Alamgiri*," in Eaton, *India's Islamic Traditions*, 211. For further elaboration of Akbar's religious policy, see Iqtidar Alam Khan, "The Nobility under Akbar and the Development of His Religious Policy, 1560–80," in ibid., 120–132.

11. Annemarie Schimmel, "Religion," in Ziad, *The Magnificent Mughals*, 63.

12. Guenther, "Hanafi *Fiqh* in Mughal India," 211.

13. Significant works that analyze how Mughal thought influenced architecture as well as the art forms that emerged during that period include Elizabeth B. Moynihan, *Paradise as a Garden in Persia and Mughal India* (G. Braziller, 1979); Catherine Asher, *Architecture of Mughal India* (Cambridge, England: Cambridge University Press, 1992); Milo Beach, *Mughal and Rajput Painting* (Cambridge, England: Cambridge University Press, 1992); Stuart Cary Welch, *The Emperors' Album: Images of Mughal India* (New York: New York Metropolitan Museum of Art, 1987).

14. Christopher Schackle, "Punjabi in Lahore," *Modern Asian Studies* 4, no. 3 (1970): 241.

15. Prakash Tandon, *Punjabi Century* (Berkeley: University of California Press, 1968), pp. 68–71.

16. This is elaborated further in Anita M. Weiss, *Culture, Class and Development in Pakistan: The Emergence of an Industrial Bourgeoisie in Punjab* (Boulder, CO: Westview Press, 1991).

17. Ibid., 22–23.

18. For a more extensive discussion about the development of ethnic politics in Sindh, refer to Hastings Donnan and Prina Werbner, *Economy and Culture in Pakistan: Migrants and Cities in a Muslim Society* (New York: St. Martin's Press, 1991); Stanley J. Tambiah, "Ethnic Conflict in Pakistan," in *Leveling Crowds: Ethnonationalist Conflicts and Collective Violence in South Asia* (Berkeley: University of California Press, 1996), 163–212; Oskar Verkaaik, *A People of Migrants: Ethnicity, State and Religion in Karachi* (Amsterdam: VU University Press, 1994).

19. The most comprehensive study of Pashtun social life can be found in Louis Dupree, *Afghanistan* (Princeton, NJ: Princeton University Press, 1980). Other important works on Pashtuns include Fredrik Barth, *Political Leadership among Swat Pathans* (London: University of London, Athlone Press, 1959); Akbar S. Ahmed, *Millennium and Charisma among Pathans: A Critical Essay in Social Anthropology* (London and Boston: Routledge & Kegan Paul, 1980).

20. For further elaboration of this, refer to Ahmed, *Millennium and Charisma*.

21. For further discussion, refer to Asif Ashraf and Arif Majid, *Economic Impact of Afghan Refugees in NWFP* (Peshawar: Pakistan Academy for Rural Development, 1988).

22. There is a great deal of literature on the subject of Afghan refugees in Pakistan. For example, consult Fiona Terry, *Condemned to Repeat? The Paradox of Humanitarian Action* (Ithaca, NY: Cornell University Press, 2002); Saba Gul Khattak, *In/Security: Afghan Refugees and Politics in Pakistan* (Islamabad, Pakistan: Sustainable Development Policy Institute, 2003); M. Nazif Shahrani, "Afghanistan's *Muhajirin* (Muslim 'Refugee-Warriors'): Politics of Mistrust and Distrust of Politics," in *Mistrusting Refugees*, ed. E. Valentine Daniel and John C. Knudsen, 187–206 (Berkeley: University of California Press, 1995).

23. Further elaboration of the unique conditions of Pashtun women can be found in Nancy Lindisfarne, *Bartered Brides: Politics, Gender, and Marriage in an Afghan Tribal Society* (Cambridge, England, and New York: Cambridge University Press, 1991). Benedicte Grima, *The Performance of Emotion among Paxtun Women: "The Misfortunes Which Have Befallen Me"* (Austin: University of Texas Press, 1992) powerfully reveals women's ethos in the Pashtun system of honor and shame.

24. Susan Bayly provides a lucid discussion of the British perception of race in colonial India. See "Case and 'race' in the Colonial Ethnography of India," in *The Concept of Race in South Asia*, ed. Peter Robb, 165–218 (Oxford, England: Oxford University Press, 1995).

25. Spelling of the tribe and province is also commonly *Baloch* and *Balochistan*, respectively.

26. A Baluch *sirdar* pointed out to me how the similarity in dress of Baluch and Kurds seems to justify this popular belief. Both wear baggy pants consisting of about 25 yards of material, and the cloth (*pushtee*) a Baluch drapes over his shoulder is worn as a sort of cummerbund by the Kurds. Both the Khosa and Mazari clans have tribal sections called the Kurds, though the latter pronounce it as "Kiird."

27. What rural programs exist in Baluchistan are mostly due to the efforts of the Agha Khan Rural Support Development Project which has expanded into rural Baluchistan based on its successes in the mountains of Gilgit. This NGO works on organizing disparate communities into local support groups, and has had particular success in its efforts to reach women in this remote, traditional area. Most other programs in the past two decades have been more concerned with Afghan refugees who migrated to the province.

28. The MMA consists of six distinct parties: Jama'at-i-Islam, led by Qazi Hussain Ahmed; the JUI (Jamiat-i-Ulema Islam),

Fazlur Rehman group; the JUI Sami ul-Haq group; the JUI Pakistan; the Markazi Jamiat Ahle Hadith Pakistan; and the TNFJ (Tehrik Nifaz Fiqah Jaferiya), a Shi'a political party.

29. For various interpretations of this conflict, see Sumit Ganguly, *Conflict Unending: India-Pakistan Tensions since 1947* (New York: Columbia University Press, 2001); Eric S. Margolis, *War at the Top of the World: The Struggle for Afghanistan, Kashmir and Tibet* (New York: Routledge, 2000); Sumantra Bose, *Kashmir: Roots of Conflict, Paths to Peace* (Cambridge, MA: Harvard University Press, 2003); Robert Wirsing, *Kashmir in the Shadow of War: Regional Rivalries in a Nuclear Age* (New York: M.E. Sharpe, 2003). An interesting exercise is to look at the international boundary line on a map of the region issued by India and a map issued by Pakistan: they're different! Even something as mundane as a map can speak volumes about political realities and orientations.

30. Works on the Kalash include Wynne R. Maggi, *Our Women Are Free: Gender and Ethnicity in the Hindukush* (Ann Arbor: University of Michigan Press, 2001); Jean Yves Loude and Viviane Littvre, *Kalash Solstice: Winter Feasts of the Kalash of North Pakistan* (originally published as *Solstice Pagen: Fates d'hiver chez les Kalash du Nord-Pakistan* (Paris: Presses de la Renaissance, 1984, and Islamabad, Pakistan: Lok Virsa, 1988); A. Sayeed Khan Qamar, *Kalash: The Vanishing Culture* (Islamabad, Pakistan: Agha Jee Printers, 1999); Mytte Fentz, *Natural Resources and Cosmology in Changing Kalasha Society* (Copenhagen, Denmark: Nordic Institute of Asian Studies, 1996).

31. Works in these areas include Kari Jettmar, "Northern Areas of Pakistan: An Ethnographic Sketch," *History of the Northern Areas of Pakistan*, ed. A. H. Dani, 59–88 (Islamabad, Pakistan: National Institute of Historical and Cultural Research, 1989); H. A. Rose, Sir Denzil Ibbetson, and Sir Edward Douglas Maclagan, *Lesser Known Tribes of NW India and Pakistan, Based on the Census Reports of 1883 and 1892* [by Sir Densil Ibbetson and Sir Edward Maclagan] (Delhi, India: Amar Prakashan, 1991); Hastings Donnan, "The Rules and Rhetoric of Marriage Negotiations Among the Dhund Abbasi of Northeast Pakistan," *Ethnology* 24 (1991): 183–196; Sabine Felmy, *The Voice of the Nightingale: A Personal Account of the Wakhi Culture in Hunza* (Karachi, Pakistan, and New York: Oxford University Press, 1996); Elena L. Bashir and Israr-ud-Din, *Proceedings of the Second International Hindukush Cultural Conference* (Karachi, Pakistan: Oxford University Press, 1996).

32. For example, refer to Charles Lindholm, *Generosity and Jealousy: The Swat Pukhtun of Northern Pakistan* (New York: Columbia University Press, 1982); Inam-ur-Rahim and Alain M. Viaro, *Swat, an Afghan Society in Pakistan: Urbanisation and Change in a Tribal Environment* (Karachi, Pakistan and Geneva, Switzerland: Graduate Institute of Development Studies, City Press, 2002).

33. Two interesting books for teenage audiences about Pakistani family life published in the United States are Ailsa Scarsbrook and Alan Scarsbrook, *A Family in Pakistan* (Minneapolis, MN: Lerner Publications, 1985); and Karen English and Jonathan Weiner, *Nadia's Hands* (Honesdale, PA: Boyds Mills Press, 1999), which follows a Pakistani American girl as she participates in her aunt's traditional Pakistani wedding.

34. The mean number of children born, in 2002, is shown by age and location as follows:

Age of Women	*Urban*	*Rural*	*Total*
Overall	2.4	2.8	2.7
15–19 years	0.1	0.1	0.1
20–24 years	0.7	1.1	0.9
25–29 years	2.1	2.6	2.5
30–34 years	3.7	4.2	4.1
35–39 years	4.8	5.7	5.4
40–44 years	5.8	6.4	6.2
45–49 years	6.5	6.7	6.7

Source: From the Federal Bureau of Statistics, *Pakistan Integrated Household Survey* (Islamabad, Pakistan: Author, 2002), x.

35. Anita M. Weiss, *Walls within Walls: Life Histories of Working Women in the Old City of Lahore* (Boulder, CO: Westview Press, 1992), 120.

36. For an interesting discussion of the social implications of relationships between sons and parents in Pakistan, refer to S. Zulfiqar Gilani, "Personal and Social Power in Pakistan," in *Power and Civil Society in Pakistan*, ed. Anita M. Weiss and S. Zulfiqar Gilani, 49–63 (Oxford, England: Oxford University Press, 2001).

37. For example, see the study by Farida Shaheed and Khawar Mumtaz, *Women's Economic Participation in Pakistan* (New York, NY: UNICEF, 1992); Weiss, *Walls within Walls.*

38. As quoted in Khawar Mumtaz and Farida Shaheed, *Women in Pakistan: Two Steps Forward, One Step Back?* (London, U.K.: Zed Press, 1987), 183.

39. For a more complete description of the lives of women who engage in such home-based work, see Weiss, *Walls within Walls.*

40. For more details on these challenges, refer to Anita M. Weiss, "Interpreting Islam and Women's Rights: Implementing CEDAW in Pakistan," *International Sociology* 18, no. 3 (September 2003): 581–601. Other valuable resources on women's issues in Pakistan include Government of Pakistan, Ministry of Women Development, Social Welfare & Special Education, *Report of the Commission of Inquiry for Women in Pakistan* (Islamabad, Pakistan: Author, 1997); Mahbub ul Haq Human Development Centre, *Human Development in South Asia 2000: The Gender Question* (Karachi, Pakistan: Oxford University Press, 2000); Farida Shaheed, S. A. Warraich, Cassandra Balchin, and Aisha Gazdar, eds., *Shaping Women's Lives: Laws, Practices and Strategies in Pakistan* (Lahore, Pakistan: Shirkat Gah, 1998); Shahla Haeri, *No Shame for the Sun: Lives of Professional Pakistani Women* (New York: Syracuse University Press, 2002).

41. There is not a great deal of literature readily available in English on most Sufi *pirs* of Pakistan. Some very useful sources include Sarah Ansari, *Sufi Saints and State Power: The Pirs of Sind, 1843–1947*, 2nd ed. (Cambridge, England: Cambridge University Press, 2002); Annemarie Schimmel, *Pain and Grace: A Study of Two Mystical Writers of 18th-Century Muslim India* (Leiden, the Netherlands: Brill, 1976); Inam Mohammad, *Hazrat Lal Shahbaz Qalandar of Sehwan-Sharif* (Karachi, Pakistan: Royal Book, 1978); Syed Dinal Shah Darbelevi, *Hazrat Shahanshah Lal Shahbaz Qalander* (Hyderabad, Sind: S.D.S. Darbelvy, 1984); N. Hanif, *Biographical Encyclopaedia of Sufis: South Asia* (New Delhi, India: Prabhat Kumar Sharma,

for Sarup & Sons, 2000); Simon Digby, "The Sufi Shaikh as a Source of Authority in Medieval India," in Eaton, *India's Islamic Traditions.*

42. For further discussion of the rise of the Barelvi and Deoband schools, see Usha Sanyal, *Devotional Islam and Politics in British India: Ahmad Riza Khan Barelvi and His Movement, 1870–1920* (Delhi, India, and New York: Oxford University Press, 1996); Barbara Daly Metcalf, *Islamic Revival in British India: Deoband, 1860–1900* (Princeton, NJ: Princeton University Press, 1982).

43. Vali Nasr's *Islamic Leviathan: Islam and the Making of State Power* (New York: Oxford University Press, 2001) includes a valuable discussion of the role various religious groups have played in Pakistan's politics. Other important works in this arena include David Gilmartin, *Empire and Islam: Punjab and the Making of Pakistan* (Berkeley: University of California Press, 1988); Barbara D. Metcalf, "Islamic Arguments in Contemporary Pakistan," in *Islam and the Political Economy of Meaning: Comparative Studies of Muslim Discourse,* ed. William R. Roff, 132–159 (Berkeley: University of California Press, 1987); Mumtaz Ahmad, "Islamic Fundamentalism in South Asia: The Jamaat-e-Islami and the Tablighi Jamaat of South Asia," in *Fundamentalism Observed,* eds. M. E. Marty and R. S. Appleby, 459–530 (Chicago: University of Chicago Press, 1991).

44. Whenever Muslims refer to the Prophet by name in English, they write *PBUH (Peace Be Upon Him),* following it as a sign of respect. Occasionally, they may transliterate the Arabic and write *SAW.*

45. John L. Esposito, ed., *Oxford Encyclopedia of the Modern Muslim World* (Oxford, England: Oxford University Press, 1995), 54–55.

46. For further elaboration of popular Shi'a practices in Pakistan, see Juan R. I. Cole, "Popular Shi'ism," in Eaton, *India's Islamic Traditions.*

47. John Esposito has written an accessible, comprehensive account of historical and contemporary understandings of jihad. See his *Unholy War: Terror in the Name of Islam* (New York: Oxford University Press, 2002). See also the eminent French scholar Gilles Kepel's *Jihad: The Trail of Political Islam,* translated by Anthony F. Roberts (Cambridge, MA: Belknap Press of Harvard University Press, 2002).

48. As quoted in C. M. Naim, ed., *Iqbal, Jinnah, and Pakistan: The Vision and the Reality* (Syracuse, NY: Syracuse University Press, 1979), 213.

49. In an effort to promote economic growth, the "day off" in the country reverted to Sundays in the late 1990s, so that the business week in Pakistan would be the same as in much of the world.

50. Muhammad Ali Anwar ("Mushroom Growth of Deeni Madaris," *Dawn* newspaper, May 24, 1997) writes that four sects have been the most prominent in creating such schools: Deoband, Barelvi, Ahle Hadith, and Ahle Tashi.

51. Since the U.S. war in Afghanistan began in October 2001, the United States has reinstated ODA to Pakistan, while multilateral aid has also increased.

52. World Bank, *World Development Indicators* 2003.

53. This data is based on the UNDP *Human Development Report 2003.*

54. World Bank, *Annual Report on Pakistan,* released September 3, 2003.

55. For further discussion of the decline of a social contract and its effects on the emergence of civil society in Pakistan, see Weiss and Gilani, *Power and Civil Society in Pakistan.*

56. An extensive discussion of the social, political, and economic forces that influenced industrial development in this time period can be found in Weiss, *Culture, Class and Development in Pakistan.* See also Lawrence J. White, *Industrial Concentration and Economic Power in Pakistan* (Princeton, NJ: Princeton University Press, 1974) as well as publications available through the Pakistan Institute of Development Economics (PIDE) at: http://www.pide.org.pk.

57. This class emerged dependent on the state for their survival (as well as for their salaries). Alavi argues that it was, therefore, in its class interests to maintain prevailing bureaucratic structures. Alavi's seminal works that further elaborate his theories on the nature of class structure in Pakistan include "The State in Post-Colonial Societies," *New Left Review,* no. 74 (1972); "Ethnicity, Muslim Society and Pakistan Ideology," in *Islamic Reassertion in Pakistan: The Application of Islamic Laws in a Modern State,* ed. Anita M. Weiss (Syracuse, NY: Syracuse University Press, 1986); and *South Asia: Sociology of Developing Societies* (co-authored with John Harriss) (London: Macmillan Press, and New York: Monthly Review Press, 1989).

58. The eldest of four children, Benazir was born in Karachi on June 21, 1953. Educated in Pakistan at various convent schools (where children of the elite generally studied), she went abroad to Radcliffe (in Cambridge, Massachusetts) in 1969 to pursue a BA. She went on to graduate school at Oxford where she was studying when the contentious March 1977 election was held in Pakistan which resulted in riots by the opposition to her father. She returned to Pakistan 10 days before her father was overthrown by Zia ul-Haq on July 5, 1977. For further reading about Benazir Bhutto, refer to her autobiography *Daughter of the East* (London: Hamish Hamilton, 1988).

59. Refer to http://www.hdtaskforce.com for further elaboration of the task force's goals and subsequent activities.

60. Data is from the PEW Global Attitudes Project, *Views of a Changing World,* June 2003, 12.

61. This phrase has been told to me repeatedly from the late 1980s through the 1990s by many people from a divergent cross-section of the population that supported Islamist political groups.

62. Omar Asghar Khan, "Critical Engagements: NGOs and the State," in Weiss and Gilani, *Power and Civil Society in Pakistan,* 278.

63. Ibid., 276. He elaborates on the range of social advocacy NGOs and related civil society groups contending for power in Pakistan.

CHINA

Pamela A. De Voe

Often when we think of China we visualize a country with a long, stable, unchanging history and a homogeneous ethnic population—that is, a people who share one culture and one language. What we will discover in this chapter, however, first, is that while there are definitely certain themes, ideologies, and practices that dominate the historical landscape, there was considerable range in the way these themes were manifested throughout China's prehistory, history, and contemporary periods. Second, the diversity of China's geography has had an influence on cultural developments. As will be seen, China's political structure and culture have been dominated by intra- and interethnic relations. In fact, all or parts of China were often governed by non-Chinese peoples, whose measure of success (i.e., the length of time they were able to remain the ruling power) was related to the degree they adopted the Chinese sociocultural and political system—in other words, how *sinicized* (becoming Chinese) they became. Third, we will discuss how having an ideology that was based on achieved social status, versus ascribed social status (although the dominance of one over the other altered through time), gave the Chinese social system enough flexibility to withstand dramatic sociocultural and political changes. Finally, critical to the success of China on its journey to becoming the third largest country in the world was how it managed to unite such disparate ethnic and linguistic populations through a common writing system and an official national language, while allowing individual groups to maintain and continue to use their home languages.

GEOGRAPHY

China's cultural, social, and political development has been intimately linked to its geography. The country covers 9.6 million square kilometers (5.9 million square miles) of fertile lowlands, inhospitable deserts, rolling plateaus, challenging mountain ranges, intimidating steppes, the highest tableland on Earth, and 18,000 kilometers (11,160 miles) of coastline (its land-based border is 20,000 [12,400 miles] kilometers). Historically, in spite of having such a long coastal border, the dominant Chinese ethnic groups were not oriented toward the sea. Having developed an agriculture-based society along the Yellow River in the central and eastern area, they remained land oriented.

Wet-rice agriculture allowed them to intensively exploit fertile lowland areas and foothills, produce populations in the millions, and support major cities with their non-food-producing populations. At the same time, other ethnic groups lived in the adjacent northern and

RUSSIA
MONGOLIA
KAZAKHSTAN
HEIONGJIANG
Harbin
JILIN
NEI MONGOL
LIAONING
Urumqi
XINJIANG
Yellow R.
NORTH KOREA
Beijing
GANSU
KYRGYZSTAN
Yellow R.
SHANDONG
SOUTH KOREA
JAPAN
QINHAI
Xi'an
HENAN
SHAANXI
SICHUAN
HUBEI
Chengdu
Yangtze R.
XIZANG
HUNAN
Lhasa
PAKISTAN
NEPAL
INDIA
YUNNAN
TAIWAN
INDIA
MYANMAR
VIETNAM
LAOS
HAINAN
PHILIPPINES
THAILAND

Chinese rice paddy agricultural fields.

western steppes and plateau areas that had proven to be unreceptive to intensive agriculture. These groups responded to their environment by developing a pastoral and nomadic culture. These nomadic cultures, with their domesticated horses, were often dominated by a warrior ethos. China's long history reflects the ongoing tensions and struggles between these two cultural types: the warrior nomadic culture and the assimilation-oriented, intensive agricultural culture. Where one strove to dominate through military power, the other strove to dominate through cultural assimilation. The goal for both groups was the same—control over an ever-expanding area.

The southern and southwestern mountainous areas proved to be a more complex environment and, therefore, presented a different range of issues. The Chinese were able to move into the valleys, but left the more mountainous terrain to horticultural ethnic groups whose less invasive subsistence style (using digging sticks and rotating their plots every several years) proved to be more environmentally acceptable. As horticultural societies, the many non-Chinese ethnic groups were compatible with the surrounding Chinese, yet could, if they desired, maintain a physical distance from them by remaining in their mountain villages. Therefore, over time, considerable diversity developed within any given ethnic group regarding its members' degree of assimilation or sinification.

Overall, the physical environment of China's border areas have been a two-edged sword. On one hand, because of their inherently inhospitable nature, they formed a broad protective area around China, making it more difficult for foreigners to attack the country. On the other hand, the various harsh environments made it difficult for China's rulers to maintain tight controls over the indigenous populations, creating continuous concern over border security. This historical tension remains salient today.

CHINESE PALEOANTHROPOLOGY AND PREHISTORY

China's prehistory reaches back to about one million years ago, when the hominid *Homo erectus* came into the area, traveling from Africa through Southeast Asia.[1] The most famous *Homo erectus* fossils (referred to as Zhoukoudian fossils) were found in a limestone cave 25 miles southwest of Beijing in the 1920s. The *Homo erectus* were foragers—taking advantage of what was easily available in the environment, whether it was fruit, vegetables, seeds, roots, or animals. Their material culture included tools, such as stone choppers, needles (of antler or bone), and other cutting tools.

Besides the very early time periods showing the presence of *Homo erectus* in China, the second most important finding was their use of fire. The earliest well-accepted date for the conscious use of fire is at Zhoukoudian around 500,000 years ago. Fire usage was noteworthy for several reasons: (1) it offered protection from wild animals; (2) it could be used for cooking—making meat more tender and easier to eat and digest; and (3) it provided light—allowing more time for communicating, socializing, and working.

There is good evidence, based on *Homo erectus* brain impressions from skulls and from the reconstruction of the vocal areas based on the anatomy of the cranial (head's) base, that these hominids may have been capable of language usage. *Homo erectus*, who probably existed as an identifiable group in China until about 250,000 years ago, can be considered a very successful species.

The earliest modern *Homo sapiens* fossils came from a cave in southern China at Liujiang with a date of 67,000 years before present. These *Homo sapiens* had fully modern features and brain. With modern *Homo sapiens'* appearance came an enormous variety of material culture and eventually plants and animals were domesticated. From about 20,000 to 10,000 years ago, people in the area began to shift from a foraging society to a food-producing society by domesticating plants, such as millet and soybeans, as well as animals, such as dogs and pigs.

Agriculture appeared about 10,000 years ago in northern China—about the same time that it appeared in the Middle East, although it was an independent development in China. As rice agriculture developed, it was able to support a larger population in a smaller geographic area than foraging had been able to support. Domestication of high-yielding varieties of rice set the stage for the future development of Chinese culture and society.

About 6,000 to 7,000 years ago, the Yang Shao culture appeared. It was characterized by villages with related cemeteries, semisubterranean houses, painted pottery, and millet, pigs, dogs, and silkworms. Following this, by about 5,000 BCE the Lungshanoid culture developed, showing even more refinement than the Yang Shao culture: pottery made on a wheel, the beginning of rice cultivation, signs of divination and ancestor cults, as well as the rise of social classes. These early cultural groups were probably the ancestors to the Chinese sociocultural system.[2]

CHINESE—A MATTER OF COMMUNICATION

To understand the Chinese people and their culture you must know something of their language—both written and spoken.

When Westerners use the word *Chinese* to refer to the language people from China speak, the linguistic complexity of China is masked.[3] All people within the area from northeastern Manchuria to northwestern Gansu and from southwestern Yunnan to southeastern Guangdong are said to speak the Chinese language. Yet, the speech in one region may not be understood by people in another region. For example, people in the southern area of Guangdong speak in a way that is not understood at all by people in the north around Beijing. Using the criteria of mutual unintelligibility to define two spoken systems as different languages means that the languages spoken by the Chinese in Guangdong and around Beijing are two different languages, not simply two different dialects.[4]

It is difficult to say how many languages are spoken in China; however, in 1955 China officially decided that there were eight major forms of speech (*fāngyán*) or separate languages. Table 5-1 indicates the percentage of people speaking various Chinese languages according to the mainland Chinese government at that time. These can be considered conservative

Table 5-1 Chinese Languages in Mainland China

Linguistic Division	Speakers (%)
Northern (Putonghua, Mandarin)	71.5%
Jiangsu-Zhejiang (Wu)	8.5
Cantonese (Yue)	5.0
Hunan (Xiang)	4.8
Hakka	3.7
Southern Min (Fukinese)	2.8
Jiangxi (Gan)	2.4
Northern Min	1.3

Source: Adapted from John DeFrancis, *The Chinese Language: Fact and Fantasy* (Honolulu: University of Hawaii Press, 1984), p. 58.

estimates. For example, Southern Min, which is also spoken by about 66 percent of the people in Taiwan, consists of several dialects, each of which in turn consists of subdialects. As one dialect is compared to another, the degree of intelligibility varies considerably so that in some cases cross communication is very difficult.

The Northern language, or Mandarin, is also called *pǔtónghùa*, which means "common speech." Both mainland China and Taiwan promote *pǔtónghùa* as Standard Chinese today. Hong Kong, however, while under British rule, used Cantonese (Guangdong hùa) as the standard language and it remains a dominant language in Hong Kong.

While there are eight separate "Chinese" languages, these are all a part of one language family because they all have certain elements in common. The Chinese languages belong to a language family called Sino-Tibetan, which are tonal languages. That is, the intonation of a syllable has the same impact on the meaning of a word as a vowel or consonant would have. For example, Mandarin has four tones: high level, high rising, low dipping, and high falling. As the following table shows, when a syllable such as *ma* is pronounced with a different tone, it has a different meaning.[5]

Mā	first tone	high level	"mother"	媽
Má	second tone	high rising	"hemp"	麻
Mǎ	third tone	low dipping	"horse"	馬
Mà	fourth tone	high falling	"scold"	罵

Development of a Standard Spoken Chinese

Historically, written Chinese has remained fairly constant since the Zhou dynasty (1028–500 BCE); however, spoken Chinese (the many languages and dialects such a term encompasses) is more complex.

The origin of contemporary Chinese is from Yinxu in western Henan province where the Shang dynasty capital was situated from 1324 to 1066 BC.[6] As successive governments took over larger and larger areas, this early language spread as the *yǎyán*, or elegant speech. From the Eastern Zhou period (771–249 BCE) the area was often the seat of government, adding to the status of the local language, which was also known as the dialect of the He Luo (Yellow River and Luo River) or Zhongzhou (Central China). Its status as the language of the literati and of the government ensured its place as the standard language and dialect. Confucius, the great Chinese philosopher who lived ca. 551–479 BCE, refers to yǎyán in his writings; and, while he spoke his own dialect, Lu, he was proficient in yǎyán, using it in formal settings.

Therefore, we see that while yǎyán was not used in everyday speech across China, it was the language of choice for the government and, most importantly, for the national examination system, adding considerably to its status vis-à-vis other Chinese dialects and languages. Even when non-Han ethnic groups took over China and its political authority, culturally they assimilated into the Han culture, acquiring yǎyán or the Zhongzhou dialect as their official Chinese language. In this way, Zhongzhou became the basis of standard spoken Chinese throughout the region. Eventually, dialectical changes occurred as the Zhongzhou people came into contact with other Chinese dialects and languages and non-Chinese languages. As a reflection of this ongoing intermingling, the writings from the early historical period often discussed accents, indicating that there was a strong impetus to move toward a standard spoken language. Critical to the development of a standard pronunciation was the refinement of the *kējǔ* or "imperial examination system" from the Sui and Tang (589–907 CE) dynasties. The kējǔ were used to select all government officials. It was the primary path to social as well as economic success until the end of the Qing dynasty (1644–1911 CE), the last dynasty before the modern political period.

It is important to note that while the Zhongzhou dialect represented the standard pronunciation of the country, it did not preclude the continuation of local Chinese languages and dialects as home tongues. Due to geographic isolation, limited mobility, and the dominance of oral communication, it is to be expected that outside the learned and business communities the local languages would remain dominant among the common people. It was not until the modern period that the Chinese people began to be concerned about everyone using a standard language. In the mid-nineteenth century a great push began to modernize the country and to make it equal to, or greater than, the Western powers. Some people looked to Japan, a fellow Asian country that appeared to successfully challenge the West. By creating a national language, Japan had begun to develop a new national consciousness among its people.

The process of deciding which dialect should be considered the national standard and of designing a system to implement the knowledge and use of this standard took a long time. In 1911, at the very end of the Qing dynasty, an "Act of approaches to the unification of the national language" was passed. Part of the act was to survey all the provinces and their various dialects. The goal was to choose a standard based on the Beijing dialect that reflected an "elegant, correct, and popular" *guóyǔ* or "national language." By 1919 a dictionary, the *Guóyīn zìdiǎn* [*Dictionary of National Pronunciation*] was published. This indicated that as China entered the modern era, and recognized the need to address global pressures, one of the first areas to be developed was bringing the people together with one national language. As in the past, standardization was encouraged through the education process. The spread of universal education encouraged the use of a national language. Recognizing the diversity of its people, the Chinese employed a common, standard language as a means of encouraging a sense of common nationality and, therefore, of national strength in the face of outside political, technological, and military pressures.[7]

Chinese Script

As noted previously, discussions of the Chinese language often reflect a confusion of Chinese script with spoken Chinese. This confusion is stronger in discussions of the Chinese language than with other languages that have a literate tradition. In part, the reluctance to distinguish between the spoken and written forms is due to the long unbroken written tradition going back to the second millennium BCE. Karlgren stated, "the day the Chinese discard [the Chinese script] they will surrender the very foundation of their culture."[8]

Central to understanding "Chinese" is acknowledging the role the written language has had as a symbol of a unified cultural tradition. Over the long span of history, whether politically divided into fiefdoms or unified in one empire, there remained an ideal of a single culture that tied people together. How could this be done? Unlike phonetic scripts, such as Latin, Chinese script is independent of phonetics. The disconnect between phonetics and script allowed for (1) the Chinese to believe their language was uniform and unchanging over time, and (2) speakers of different Chinese languages to use essentially the same writing system to express their ideas and to be understood by other Chinese language speakers.

The first evidence of written Chinese goes back to the Shang dynasty (1600–1028 BCE) where it appeared in an already developed form on turtle shells and bone. The materials were used in divination rites. Even more written texts were found from the following Zhou dynasty (1122–249 BCE) where it was written on bronze artifacts. This early language is thought to be the direct ancestor to all contemporary Chinese languages and dialects.

Although the ethnically Chinese people started out as a small group living in the Yellow

River plain, even during the Zhou period they had begun to spread out geographically, eventually assimilating the various ethnic groups living around them, leading to the assimilation of Chinese language and cultural traditions by an ever broadening geographic area. Texts, such as those of Confucius, Mencius, and Lǎozǐ (Lǎo Tzǔ),[9] were written in this early period and provide core philosophical concepts today. The texts probably reflect the learned speech of the time; and it was not until the Han dynasty (206 BCE–220 CE) that a real division between written and spoken Chinese began to develop. By the Qing dynasty (1644–1911 CE) the gulf between literary Chinese and the vernacular was significant.

Written Chinese consists of characters that individually or in combination with other characters represent a particular concept. Originally, as with most early writings, there was a pictographic connection between the character and what it represented. However, today pictographic words represent a very small part of written Chinese.

As noted earlier, Chinese characters are made up of a number of strokes—from 1 to 64—and are often placed in a dictionary by the number of strokes they contain.

一	*yī*	"one"
龍龍 龍龍	*tiè*	"verbose"

As a move to increase the literacy rate in China, the mainland Chinese government simplified many complex characters in the 1950s. This change was derived from the perception that people could learn to read and write more quickly if the more common characters had fewer strokes. For example,

mǎ	became	*mǎ* [meaning "horse"]
馬		马
9 strokes		3 strokes

Most Chinese characters are compound characters. That is, they are made up of recurrent elements. While there are various theories relative to character formation, one practical method of understanding them is through their use of radicals. Radicals are key characters that are combined with other elements to form another character. There are 214 radicals used today. A radical can represent a word itself or it can be used with other elements to indicate a sound or meaning. Some Chinese dictionaries arrange their words by their radicals, which are divided into groups depending on the number of strokes used to write it. Using this method the first radical consists of one stroke. All characters using a given radical are presented in the order of the number of total strokes used, along with their pronunciation. This continues through all 214 radicals.[10]

The fact that ordering words by sound was not used to organize a dictionary until 700 ACE, when such dictionaries as the *WǔFāng Yuán Yīn* [*The Original Sounds of the Five Regions*] were published, indicates how unimportant the pronunciation of a character was. The *WǔFāng Yuán Yīn* used a syllabic system and organized its words by the rhymes and tones of the characters. As a result, unless you knew how to pronounce a character, it was almost impossible to find it in the dictionary, therefore, an index using radicals was also included in these dictionaries.

As we have seen, the written Chinese character was developing in the Shang (1600–1028 BCE) and Zhou (1122–249 BCE) dynasties, and the diversity found in the writing system was almost chaotic. Certainly, the multiple and competing political states contributed to this linguistic disunity. However, when China unified under the Qin dynasty in 221 BCE, the government started standardizing the characters. The Han dynasty (206 BCE–220 CE) continued the standardization process and the system that developed during the Han dynasty remained until the mainland Chinese government's simplification program in the 1950s.

In many ways, written Chinese has taken on an importance of its own. For example, artists use characters as the sole decoration for pottery, porcelain, and clothing, where the design of the character itself was as relevant to the artwork as its meaning. Today, you have only to walk through department stores to see examples of contemporary designers using Chinese characters to decorate clothing and household accessories. In some circumstances, carrying a piece of paper with a word written on it gave spiritual power to the paper and the person carrying it, indicating that the character itself was imbued with spiritual power. Overall, we find that through time, the written character has come to communicate not only ideas, but also a sense of beauty and spirituality.

SOCIAL MOBILITY: EDUCATION AND ACHIEVED STATUS

While both ascribed and achieved status can be found within the Chinese social structure, the ideals of achieved status dominate and, except for the emperor and his immediate family, describe the Chinese social structure throughout much of written history. It is fair to say that ascribed status (where a person is born into his or her sociocultural position) defined the position of the emperor and his family. Traditionally, the Chinese believed that the gods determined who would be emperor. The emperor had a Mandate from Heaven to be the ruler of all China. As long as he obeyed the rules of propriety and followed the appropriate rituals vis-à-vis the gods and his ancestors, the gods would bring peace and prosperity to the country and its people. When the emperor died, the Mandate from Heaven fell to one of his sons (often after much political intrigue and murder), who followed the same rituals as his father, with ancestor worship being among the key rituals. Therefore, the emperor and his family were automatically at the top of the social structure, whatever their particular traits.

Ideally, everyone else, outside the emperor and his family, achieved their positions through personal ability and familial support. The Chinese social class hierarchy consisted of the literati, farmer, merchant, and artisan. Below these four classes were the lowly people (such as actors and actresses), and below these were slaves, although the last were not considered to be a real part of society.[11] While the rights and obligations of these different social groups were fixed by law, it was possible for people within the four classes to move up and down the social hierarchy through personal effort. Key to that personal effort was the examination system designed and set up by the government.

The literati or the gentry held the top position within the social hierarchy, and was made up of men who had studied the Confucian classics, passed a series of government examinations, and became government officials, running the large bureaucracy set up by the government. Since the government depended on the intelligence and ability of these men to run the country, their positions were dependent on their personal abilities, not necessarily on genealogy. However, as far back as the Han dynasty (206 BCE–220 CE), even if two men, one from a gentry family and one a poor farmer family, had the same abilities, the gentry member's son had a distinct advantage. During the Han period special state schools were created for the sons of officials, to teach them the Confucian classics and to prepare them for the examinations. Others had to rely on their lineage schools or personal family finances for a tutor. Nevertheless, although difficult, it was not impossible for a man to move into the gentry class and become an official. At the same time, a man who was born into the gentry class but who did not study, either because of a lack of talent or because of laziness, would not be able to maintain gentry status.

The state examination system, based as it was on the Confucian classics, provided a moral system with an ethical orientation and personal standard of behavior and integrity. The Confucian moral–ethical system became bedrock not only for the gentry, but for all members of the Chinese society. It provided a cultural value system with a moral compass that survived and even supported a series of ethnically diverse dynasties.

During the Han dynasty a bureaucracy was established to run the affairs of state on behalf of the emperor. The emperor's primary responsibility for the success of his administration and the security of his dynasty was to choose competent civil servants. Therefore, the imperial administration was intimately concerned with the selection and control of potential bureaucrats and other civil servants. The government developed a Confucian-based, imperial examination system to create a pool of potential officials. The officials were capable administrators who shared similar values and beliefs in a diverse country and who followed an official orthodoxy.

In the early Han period the classics included the Book of Changes (on divination); Book of History; Odes (ancient folk poems); Book of Ceremonies and Proper Conduct; Spring and Autumn Annals (stories of Confucius's home state); plus commentaries. Eventually, the commentaries on these books grew to about 120 volumes, increasing the difficulty for scholars.

In the Song dynasty (907–1279 CE) two changes brought about reform. First, to make the body of materials less unwieldy, Song scholars reduced the materials by basing the examinations on the Four Books: the *Analects* of Confucius, the *Book of Mencius*, the *Doctrine of the Mean*, and the *Great Learning*. Embedded within these books was the view of government as paternalistic and essential for social order and defense, along with a moral code of behavior not only for the gentry, but for all human relationships.

The second change was the introduction of printing. Printing, along with the use of paper made of plant fibers, made books cheaper and more available than handwritten books had been. As John King Fairbank in *China: A New History* noted, "Printed matter was the life-blood of the expanding Song educated elite."[12] By the 1020s, the government sought to encourage the development of a large pool of potential officials by sponsoring schools across the country. The ultimate aim was to have a school in every prefecture. From this time, until 1905, when the examination system was abolished, there was more opportunity for talented young men from outside the gentry to become educated, pass the examinations, and enter officialdom. At the same time the numbers of men who actually moved from peasant status to gentry status varied within the development of each dynasty,[13] with the best chance for mobility being in the beginning of a new dynasty, since the elite often found special ways to side-step the system and get their sons degrees through alternate means.

In 1905 the traditional Confucian-based examination system was abolished to make way for a more modern educational system. Elementary schools based on the Japanese model were established, and colleges opened across the country. By 1911, about 1 out of 40 children attended school.

While the Chinese wanted to modernize their educational system, at the same time they maintained the idea that the government should and would control the educational system. After Chiang Kai-shek and the Nationalists, fleeing from the mainland and the Chinese Community Party after World War II, set up a new government in Taiwan, they set a minimum of six years and then nine years of education for all students. Chiang Kai-shek and his government used the educational system to support the idea of one China by requiring the use of only Mandarin Chinese in instruction. In this way, the Nationalist government designated Mandarin Chinese as the language of all Chinese in Taiwan, even though the majority of Taiwanese spoke other Chinese languages.

In the People's Republic of China, the Chinese Communist Party (CCP) took over a country that already had a well-developed educational system, although it had been interrupted by war. In keeping with its ideology of the superiority of peasants and the inferiority of old elites, the communists used the educational system to encourage that image. During various periods, such as the Cultural Revolution, schools (particularly higher in education) accepted men and women from peasant and working-class backgrounds, excluding those from formerly elite families. As a result, they often had people attending who were not necessarily interested in scientific or scholarly training. The educational process had become a way to make a political statement, and no longer created a learning environment. From 1949 to the present, educational institutions, their students, and curriculum reflected the political ideology and needs of the time.

THE HISTORICAL PERIOD

From the Beginning: Continuity and Change

Early Chinese History

The Shang dynasty is thought to have existed from about 1600 to 1028 BCE. Shang culture introduced walled cities, which remained a ubiquitous feature of Chinese urban life down to modern times and was a symbol of Chinese administration. One of the earliest cities of the period had walls with a height of 10 meters (32.8 feet) and an average width of 20 meters (65.6 feet). A wall of this size would take at least 10,000 laborers 18 years to build and suggests that the Shang had a centralized, controlling leadership in a stratified society. The first written documents, oracle texts on tortoise shell and bone, were also found in the walled city of Yin near An-yang and from the later part of the Shang dynasty.

During the Shang period the people engaged in unrelenting warfare with neighboring tribes, such as the Ch'iang of Tibetan culture and the Ti tribes of the northern culture, the Hsien-yün, and other northwestern cultures. Many of these neighboring non-Chinese peoples had early state societies similar to the developing Chinese state societies. By the end of the Shang dynasty the Shang rulers controlled Honan, western Shantung, southern Hopei, central and southern Shansi, eastern Shensi, and parts of Kiangsu and Anhui. The population consisted of four or five million free men and serfs.

The ancestors of the Zhou dynasty (1122–249 BCE) came from central Shensi, an area that included many tribal peoples, such as Turkish ethnic groups. The Turkish groups forced the Zhou to move eastward toward the Shang peoples.

While the ruling family may have been from the Turkish ethnic groups, the Zhou subjects were probably mostly Tibetan tribal peoples. The Zhou noblemen-warriors had bronze weapons and used war-chariots with horses. The latter led to the introduction of roads, since foot paths could not accommodate the larger chariots. Although the Zhou culture had elements of Turkish and Tibetan cultures, it was also greatly influenced by the adjacent Shang dynasty.

Zhou society was an agrarian-based feudal system ruled by a hereditary noblemen-warrior elite. Other classes consisted of farmers, artisans, and slaves. The rulers governed through feudal lords, and both the rulers and the feudal lords were often from different ethnic groups than the indigenous rural populations they controlled. The towns were made up of the ruling families and their vassals, as well as the urban Shang noble families along with their bondsmen and serfs. The indigenous populations lived in smaller villages, further away from the administrative centers and towns.

In the areas of religion, society, and the economy the Zhou implemented several changes. They abolished human sacrifices and accepted the concept of the soul, bringing it into line with an early version of ancestor worship. They used

Chart of Chinese Dynasties

2200–1600 BCE Xia (Hsia) dynasty: first prehistoric dynasty

1600–1028 BCE Shang dynasty: first written records; agricultural-based society with some hunting and gathering

1122–249 BCE Zhou (Chou) dynasty: feudal period

1122–771 BCE Western Zhou: shared language and culture of Shang people
Zhou court destroyed in 771 BCE by northern invaders
771–249 BCE Eastern Zhou: fragmentation of kingdom increased

722–481 BCE Spring and Autumn Period (also called Eastern Zhou)
Laozi (Lao-tzu)
Confucius (Kongfuzi or K'ung-fu-tzu) (551–479 BCE)

403–221 BCE Warring States Period: seven states fight for dominance

221–206 BCE Qin (Ch'in): standardizes writing style and weights and measures

206 BCE–220 CE Han dynasty
111 BCE conquers Vietnam and the southwestern region
108 BCE establishes a colony in Korea
25–220 CE Eastern Han

220–581 CE Period of Division
220–280 Three Kingdoms Period: rule by warlords and an age of civil wars
220–265 Wei dynasty
221–263 Shu dynasty
229–280 Wu dynasty
265–316 Jin (Chin) dynasty: ended by invasion of Hsiung-nu
318–589 Eastern Jin (Chin): Chinese from Jin dynasty establish the Eastern Jin after fleeing to Nanjing in South China; sinization accelerated among non-Chinese in the north and south

589 CE–618 Sui dynasty: reunified China, but short-lived—too tyrannical
Completion of Grand Canal

618–907 CE Tang (T'ang) dynasty: golden age of literature and art
From mid-eighth century to 907 country divided into multiple dynasties

907–1279 CE Song dynasty: reunited China proper; spread of printing and education—emphasis on landed scholar-officials; growth in market economy
960–1127 Northern Song: lost North by 1127 to nomadic Mongol invaders
1127–1279 Southern Song

1280–1368 CE Yuan dynasty: under Mongol rule; first non-Chinese dynasty to rule all of China

1368–1644 CE Ming dynasty: founded by a Han Chinese

1644–1911 CE Qing (Ch'ing) dynasty: ruled by Manchus
Taiwan was brought under mainland government rule for first time

1911 CE– Republican China
Fled to Taiwan in 1949

1949 CE– People's Republic of China
1958–1960 Great Leap Forward
1966–1968 Cultural Revolution under Mao's leadership

Shang people and other slaves as domestic servants, and Shang serfs as farm laborers. They considered all land to be state land and divided it up among the feudal lords and sublords. Using a technique called shifting agriculture, which involved moving the fields every few years, they grew wheat and millet on the plains.

The period after the Zhou dynasty is called the Warring States Period (403–221 BCE). During this dynamic period more than 1,000 city states were collapsed into 14 large states. These 14 were further conquered until there was one ruling state: the state of Qin in 221 BCE. The population within the Warring States area was already substantial, about 25 million by 400 BCE.

Chinese peasants, using plows drawn by people and later by animals, pushed agriculture into new areas. The surrounding indigenous peoples, who used the simpler technology of digging sticks, were not able to compete with this ever expanding, land-hungry population. This was a period of great migration movements. Trade and agriculture expanded southward as merchants and peasants pushed into Guangdong (Kwangtung), Guangxi (Kwangsi), and Tonking. A shift in the concept of landownership also began at this time. In this era of weakened authority, and as new lands were opened up through agriculture, families began to think of the land as their own property. Also, assisting both the movement and unity of people was the invention of copper coins, which stimulated trade.

From this period on, the Chinese expansion into non-Chinese areas can most clearly be seen by the spread of Chinese walled cities as administrative seats where the local rulers and artisans lived. That some cities produced their own money further shows the independent power of these cities. And, as with the Zhou road-building tradition, roads continued to be built to support the military; in this case, to move armies and army supplies more easily.

Whether the Qin period begins in 256 BCE—when the last ruler of the Zhou dynasty stepped down in favor of the Qin ruler—or in 221 BCE—when the Qin actually ruled all of China—the important feature of this short dynasty is that it brought all of China under one rule. Although the Qin was a multiethnic state, containing Chinese, Turks, and Tibetans in its population and ruling class, it is most known for its centralization of government, language, economics (for example, in trade, nationalization of resources, unification of weights and measures, and taxes), and law. It was law that gave the Qin dynasty its notorious quality for future Chinese. Rather than base its law on Confucian morality, Shi Huangdi (Shih Huang-ti), the first emperor to bring all of China under one rule, followed the Legalist school. This created a society based on the rule of law, not on a moral code. As part of the move toward a rule of law and away from Confucianism, in 213 BCE Shi Huangdi destroyed all extant Confucian texts, except for one copy of each that was held in the State Library. Unfortunately, in the struggle to overturn the Qin, the State Library itself was burned down and many of these books were destroyed.

Shi Huangdi's dynasty marks the transition to the Chinese Middle Ages. At the same time, however, the shortness of this dynasty demonstrates both the lack of stability of his political system and the powerful gentry elite's rejection of the rule of law over Confucian morality. The following Han dynasty (206 BCE–220 CE) set into place a state based on Confucian principles and largely ruled through a bureaucratic meritocracy.

As we have seen, Chinese history is characterized by a tension between agricultural-based peoples and the nomadic and militaristic tribal peoples of the north and northwest.[14] Basically, the relationship among these groups was addressed through military power and political relationships, including intermarriage among the leaders. For example, the period between the Han (206 BCE–220 CE) and Sui-Tang dynasties (589–907 CE) left North China destroyed by nomad invasions, and South China, along the Yangzi (Yangtze), prosperous due to relative peace. The following Sui-Tang period is often seen as three centuries of the Chinese ideal of state unification. The Sui-Tang dynastic founders intermarried with the aristocratic families of nomadic tribal families in northwestern China. The founder of the Sui dynasty was from a part-nomad Yang family and the Tang founder was from a Li family of Turkic military origins. The nomadic rulers, however, were highly sinicized, having adopted Chinese ways in terms of language, dress, and methods of government. Thus, the Chinese capital was an international metropolis; foreigners came from Japan, Korea, Vietnam, Persia, and West Asia. One off-shoot of this multicultural interaction was a blossoming in China's literary and artistic traditions.

Another tension within early Chinese society was who would wield political power and authority. The final swing toward the educated gentry elite came in the Tang period. The third Tang emperor was a weak leader; however, he had a determined and intelligent wife, the Empress Wu (654–705 CE), who became China's only woman ruler. She ruled first through her husband, then through young successors to the throne, and finally as empress in her own right. At this time (in 657 CE), China's population was about 50 million people. During Empress Wu's rule, she managed to break the power of the mainly non-Chinese aristocratic clans of northwestern China who, during the period of disunity, had been the major source of officials controlling the central government. They achieved office through a recommendation system or *guan-xi* (personal connections). Under Empress Wu; the examination system became a critical path to government official status. The men who passed the government examination began to form an elite group. While the recommendation system continued, it did so as a weakened avenue for achieving status positions.

The transition from rule through aristocratic families to rule through a trained bureaucracy (with the training process and a renewal of Confucianism determined by the government) meant that the central government could dominate local regions in a way not possible when there was a powerful local aristocracy. As part of this shift, two long-lasting patterns were strengthened. First, the emperor was sacrosanct and therefore less involved in actual military movements, was remote from his people, and was more reliant on his counselors and the bureaucratic officials. Second, the rise of Tang civil service led to a growth of the Confucian-based scholar-elite class.

The Song Dynasty (907–1279 CE)

The Song dynasty is considered one of China's most creative periods, catapulting China ahead of the European Renaissance by two centuries. There were great technological inventions, for example, in ironworking, steelmaking, nautical technology, printing presses for books, paintings, the civil service examination system, and trade. At the same time, in spite of this rise in Chinese technology, education, and the arts, tribal invaders from inner Asia eventually became militarily dominant and took over the governance of the Chinese people.

The population was about 100 million at the beginning of the Song period and reached 120 million by the end of the twelfth century. Dynamic urban development was related to this population growth. In 1021 CE the capital of Northern Song, Kaifeng, had a population of about 500,000 within the city walls, and about one million when including its suburbs. An urban population of this size could exist because of agricultural surpluses that were cheaply transported on the Grand Canal, the Yangzi River, and other interrelated lakes, rivers, and canals.

Socially, the patrilineal clan (and its control over its members) increased in importance. To consolidate their status and authority, clans started developing genealogies for its members, so each clan would know exactly who belonged and who did not. In addition, clans took more responsibility for the daily life of their members by setting up strict standards of behavior and monitoring how well their members followed the established rules. Larger clans established clan-based welfare systems for their poor members and established clan schools, guaranteeing education for their young men.

When Northern Song fell to the Ruzhen (Juchên) northern invaders in 1126 CE, the Song dynasty moved south to establish a new capital at Hangzhou, where the population grew from an estimated 1 million to 2.5 million by the time of the Mongol conquest in 1279. Hangzhou, a walled city of seven square miles, had the world's largest urban population. Many southern Chinese families, including the Hakka, trace their ancestry back to the great migration from the north. The historian Wolfram Eberhard maintains that very few families in Fujian (Fukien), Guangdong (Kuangtung) and Guangxi (Kuangsi) can trace their southern roots past this period.

The desire for luxury goods led to an increase in foreign trade, such as spices via the Silk Route to the East Indies and even to Europe and an active sea trade with Islamic groups. The Chinese exported silks, porcelains, and copper cash. The increased commerce led to the revival of paper money, which had originated during the Tang dynasty, making it easier to carry out transactions without having to carry bulky copper coins as currency.

The Yuan Dynasty (1280–1368 CE)

Of the 631 years between 1280 CE and 1911 CE, when the dynastic period ended, China was under alien rule for 355 years, or 56 percent of the time. The Mongols established the Mongol dynasty (1280–1368 CE) and were the first non-Chinese to rule all of China. The Tungus Manchus ruled the Qing dynasty from 1644 to 1911 CE.

The Mongols were able to take over all of China because of their exceptional military organization and technology. Further, included in the Mongol invasion were Turks, Tunguses, and others, making about one million invaders living in China. The Mongols included among their auxiliaries the Uighurs, people from Central Asia and the Middle East, as well as Europeans, who were technicians in the Mongol court.

However, conquering China militarily was not the same as ruling such a vast agricultural area with a population in the tens of millions. Kublai Khan recognized this logistical problem and separated China from the rest of the Mongol realm, making it an independent unit within the Mongol Empire and designed the first nationality legislation ever implemented in the Far East, dividing the population into four groups: the Mongols, the Central Asian auxiliaries (Naimans, Uighurs, Turkish people, and Tanguts), north Chinese, and south Chinese. Naturally, the Mongols were the privileged ruling class and remained militarily organized. The auxiliary peoples worked in government (for example, as clerks), as soldiers, and as merchants (for example, the Uighurs and Hui Muslims). Since the Mongol rulers were not generally literate in Chinese, the government offices were bilingual (using both Mongolian and Chinese) with the indispensable Uighurs acting as bilingual clerks. In this ethnic division the south Chinese were in the lowest position and had almost no rights. They were forbidden to marry a Mongol, carry arms, and, for a while, were forbidden to learn Mongolian or any other foreign language, thereby keeping them outside the political and commercial arenas. In spite of these laws, which were to support the Mongol rule of China, their dynasty lasted less than one hundred years.

Chinese Rule Is Reestablished: The Ming Dynasty (1368–1644 CE)

The revolts against the Mongol dynasty were not revolutionary in character: The Chinese wanted to maintain the general social system but without alien rule. Because of the nationality laws, ethnic Chinese developed strong ethnonationalism sentiments. This ethnonationalism may have begun in the Southern Song period because of conflict with the Ruzhen and Mongols, but it was the discriminatory laws of the Yuan dynasty that accelerated the ethnonationalist movement.

Zhu Yuanzhang (Chu Yüan-chang), a commoner and former monk, established the last ethnic Chinese dynasty, the Ming dynasty, when he conquered Beijing (Peking) in 1368. In the beginning the new Chinese government was concerned with driving the Mongols out of China, to remain aloof from outside influence, and to maintain peace at home. Its goal was to revisit the Chinese models of the Han and Tang periods; however, many features of the Mongol Yuan dynasty remained; for example, militarily, Zhu followed the Mongol military system.

Zhu understood peasant needs, and carried out very practical changes: holding down land taxes, planting trees to keep the land from eroding, maintaining dikes on the Yellow and Yangzi rivers, keeping granaries stocked in case of famine, suppressing banditry, and encouraging the gentry to care for the poor. Yet, he also wanted to control people's physical and social movements; he believed that people should stay in or near their home area.[15] As a result, he mandated that people could move only with the permission of the state. Punishment for traveling without government permission was a flogging of 80 strokes. If a person went outside China without permission, he or she was to be executed upon return. Socially, the same lack of mobility was enforced. For example, the son of an artisan was to remain an artisan. Zhu appeared to want peace and prosperity for the commoners, but, at the same time, he maintained a high degree of centralized control over their lives.

Overall, while this was a great period of technological development and artistic growth it was also a period of anticommercialism and xenophobia, making the country look more and more inward. The sinologist Mark Elvin, in *The Pattern of the Chinese Past*, pointed out another change that had long-term effects on Ming advancement: the gentry's attitude toward nature.[16] That is, rather than demonstrating an interest in systematic investigations, and in science and technology generally, the gentry became introspective and intuitive, more interested in spiritual issues and the spiritual quality of nature. At a time when China had the technological ability to create an industrial revolution and a modern science, they did not. Instead, they stepped back and concentrated their efforts on discussions of the mind and the spirit. However, many other historians indicate that ecological, economic, and political developments had an enormous influence on underdevelopment in technology in China.[17]

The Qing Dynasty (1644–1911 CE)

Fairbank suggested that the Manchu conquest of China and their establishment of the Qing dynasty in 1644 demonstrated how it was easier for a non-Chinese than a Chinese ruler to combine the strength of a military with the strength of a civil administration. Living on the northern edge of China, the Manchus kept their nomadic, militaristic cultural traditions, and at the same time, learned Chinese culture without being subject to Chinese law.

Significantly, the Manchu rulers, as the Jin and Yuan before them, used Confucian ideas, forms, and terminology to support and maintain their political authority. They encouraged people to study the classics and continue ancestor worship; they implemented a state-sponsored cult of Confucius; they held up Confucian values and internalized the concepts involving the Mandate of Heaven in determining the ruler–subject relationship. They closed inner Mongolia to Chinese immigration, maintained northern Manchuria as a hunting land, and forbade the expansion of agriculture into the area. To maintain racial purity, the

Manchu (as the Mongols before them) banned marriage with the Chinese, and they recognized and encouraged the maintenance of distinct cultural traits to prevent interethnic mixing.[18] For example, Chinese women bound their feet and Manchu women did not. Another technique for maintaining control was to preserve the Manchu language, as did the Qidan, Ruzhen, and Mongol before them. Documents had to be in Manchu and Chinese.

Politically, the Manchu ruled through dual appointments, where both Chinese and Manchus were given important offices. Such a system is called synarchy, the joint administration by two or more parties. Essentially it involved the Chinese carrying out the duties of office and the Manchu supervising it. For example, both Chinese and Manchus were appointed governors-general and governors, who then reported jointly to the emperor.

Western Contact

From the late eighteenth century, Great Britain tried to find trade goods that China wanted to buy, but largely to no avail. In addition, as foreign merchants they were restricted to Canton and Macao, and were permitted to trade with only the Hong, who held a monopoly on foreign trade. Great Britain was interested in buying silk and tea, but had not yet found a desirable item to import into China. Finally, however, the British found that opium, grown in India, was the perfect commodity: The price was high and it took up very little cargo space. From 1800 on, opium became the chief trade item for the British and silver flowed from China to Great Britain. Recognizing the serious consequences of opium for its people and economy the Chinese government sent Lin Tsê-hsü to Canton to handle the situation. In 1839 Lin prohibited the opium trade and seized and destroyed illegal British opium. Using this situation as a pretext to attack China, British ships-of-war bombarded the southeastern coast of China in 1840. China soon found that it was defenseless against the superior military technology of the British and capitulated in 1842. Under the Treaty of Nanking, China ceded Hong Kong to Great Britain and paid a war indemnity. The British continued to encourage opium smuggling by letting Chinese junks fly the British flag, and protecting the smugglers with British ships-of-war. Nevertheless, in 1856 the Chinese stopped one of these vessels on suspicion of smuggling, ripped down the British flag, and arrested its crew. Great Britain reacted militarily. After a few years, China again capitulated. The result was the 1860 Treaty of Tientsin which included ceding Kowloon, near Hong Kong; allowing British subjects to buy land in China; holding the British accountable only to their own laws, and not to Chinese rules and courts; allowing missionary activity throughout the country; and no longer restricting foreigners to a few designated areas. Further, Great Britain forced the legalization of opium, with indemnity to be paid by China. All of this led to a more striking imbalance of trade between China and Europe. China's economic loss led to general impoverishment, widespread financial problems within the Chinese state, continuous financial crises, and inflation.

At the same time that the general population and the old upper classes were becoming more and more impoverished, a new group of rising capitalists was developing. They were growing rich working with Europeans, building capital, buying land from the impoverished gentry, and sending their sons abroad to foreign universities. Most of this rising class lived in and around the treaty ports from Shanghai south.

In such an environment—of uncertainty, impoverishment, unsettled social class relationships, and intrusion of foreigners—civil unrest was a natural development. Two great events were about to shake China's foundations even further: the uprisings in Sinkiang and the T'ai-ping Rebellion.

In Sinkiang, there were Turkish Muslims living under Qing rule. The government required every citizen to join the official form of civil worship, and they regarded this prescription as a pragmatic, political matter. Privately, people could believe in any other religion they wanted; it did not matter to the government. However, for the Muslims, it was intolerable that they should have to participate in a political religion that was not their own. They absolutely refused to take part in any other religious observances. The Qing government tried to apply the same rule of law that all other parts of China had to follow, but the followers of Islam were irreconcilable with most of their rules. There was a disconnect between the Chinese—who came into the area as soldiers, merchants, and administrators—and the local people. This disconnect led to a series of uprisings in the nineteenth century. An uprising in the 1870s led to the temporary loss of Sinkiang. While the exact number is unknown, it is possible that ten million lives were lost in the Sinkiang revolt.

In Guangzhou, a disaffected and frustrated Hakka named Hong Xiuquan (Hung Hsiuch'nan) fell ill and was bedridden for 40 days. While sick, he had a vision where the Christian God the Father told Hong that he was to save humankind and Jesus addressed him as his Younger Brother. After recovering, Hong took what he understood of Christianity—its morality, social equality, and traditions—merged it with Chinese values, and established the God-Worshipers' Society. His militant version of Christianity quickly inspired a dedicated army who fought to establish the Kingdom on Earth.

On January 11, 1851, Hong proclaimed himself Heavenly King of the Kingdom named Taiping (T'ai-Ping), or Supreme Peace. The civil war spinning out from the Taiping rebellion lasted from 1851 to 1864: At least six hundred walled cities were involved, many suffering horrendous massacres in the process. The Manchu government sent down armies of hereditary Manchu and Mongol solders, but their cavalry, unaccustomed to the southern climate, bogged down in the rice fields. Finally, it came down to Chinese against Chinese.

In 1853, the Taiping captured Nanjing (Nanking), making it their capital. They succeeded in much of their early push to take over territory, but within a short time the leadership watered down their newfound faith. They became corrupted by the total power they had over their people, and morality deteriorated. For example, while originally Hong had declared all marriages must be monogamous, supporting equality between men and women, eventually, he took 88 concubines; other leaders also maintained clusters of concubines.

In the end, by the time the Manchus exorcised the Taiping and reestablished control, the only significant impact the Taiping rebellion had on the area was massive depopulation due to the grisly wars that raged over the countryside and through the towns and cities.

The End of the Qing Dynasty

In spite of being able to put down these major rebellions and numerous smaller rebellions, and in spite of trying to make changes to accommodate the modern world, the Qing dynasty was unable to continue. The Empress Dowager, Tzŭ Hsi, who had held the ruling power in her hands at the end of the Qing dynasty, died on November 15, 1908. She designated the two-year old P'u Yi as emperor. He ruled for two years, from 1909 to 1911. Having a child emperor in the face of massive political and economic problems strengthened the growing revolutionary party and its leader, Sun Yat-sen.

Sun and his compatriots were young men who had been educated in Europe and America. As revolutionaries, they were determined to have a republic, and on December 29, 1911, they set up a provisional government at Nanjing with Sun Yat-sen as president. Meanwhile Yüan Shih-k'ai, a leading political figure who was interested in creating a new political system, convinced the Manchu government to issue an edict on February 12, 1912, renouncing the throne of China and declaring China a republic with a constitutional form of government. When Sun Yat-sen heard about the abdication, he resigned and recommended that Yüan Shih-k'ai be made president.

The Republic (1912–1948 CE)

The Republic period was marked by war, struggling over what kind of government would be established in China and who would rule. Sun Yat-sen and his group wanted a republic. Class solidarity of the gentry was dissolving, there were many new choices to be made, and the old status system no longer had any value. A new tripartite was developing in place of the old gentry class: the new middle class, who were against the dynastic system, but were also uncertain what should replace it; a very small group of capitalists, who were largely in Shanghai; and the massive peasantry, uninvolved in politics, uneducated, and ready to support anyone who promised to change their dire economic conditions.

Intellectually, China was also undergoing change. Confucianism was out: It did not seem able to move China into the modern, industrial world; technocrats were needed now. The May Fourth Movement demonstrated the changes that were taking place. On May 4, 1919, National University students in Beijing demonstrated against the government and their pro-Japanese stance. When the police attacked the students, more demonstrations and anti-Japanese boycotts took place. The students spoke out against the monarchy, Confucius, and old customs and traditions. They started using the vernacular to write rather than the classical language traditionally used, thus creating a literary revolution.

By the end of the First World War China was divided three ways. First, Japan had control over China and intended to make China its colony. Second, the Communist Party had been created in July 1921, following the Soviet model, and was trying to take the country back from the Japanese and to set up a communist system. Third, when Sun Yat-sen died on March 12, 1925, Chiang Kai-shek emerged as the natural leader of the People's Party. As he successfully moved north to bring the people together, he reached the gates of Shanghai on March 21, 1927, and had to make a decision: (1) to let the group's left wing dominate and to deprive the great capitalists of Shanghai of their possessions, or (2) to let the right wing dominate and form an alliance with the capitalists. Chiang, who was allied with one of the largest banking families in China, chose to turn against the left and to let the right dominate. He took Shanghai without a struggle and soon found Shanghai bankers and foreign capital to help him pay his troops and finance his administration.

The Historical Present

Chinese Communist Party—The People's Republic of China

Living in mainland China from 1949 to the present was not unlike riding a roller coaster in deep darkness.[19] You did not know when you would rise or drop precipitously, or when you would be jerked to the right or left as you rounded another corner. Because of the darkness, you were hurling toward an unknowable future through an unseen present political and economic environment. Yet, there was no way for you to get off the roller coaster—there was no out; there was only survival and hope.

When Mao Zedong (Mao Tse-tung) and the Chinese Communist Party (CCP) took over in 1949, people were euphoric. They trusted the new government, which promised to clean up their cities from the drains and streets to the beggars, prostitutes, and petty criminals.

As the CCP and the People's Liberation Army took over new areas, they set up military administrative regions, administered by military commissions. These remained in place until 1954. During this time, out of necessity the CCP kept the local Nationalists or GuoMinDang (GMD) (Kuomintang KMT) in office to fulfill government functions. There were not enough CCP cadres to take over the two million positions filled by the GMD. So, as with governments in the past, the CCP relied on the bureaucratic structure that was already in place.

By 1951, however, the CCP started replacing the old local administration with new personnel, who could be counted upon to not just perform governmental duties but to carry out the revolution. The Three-Antis Campaign against government officials (corruption, waste, and bureaucratism) and the Five-Antis Campaign against employers (bribery, tax evasion, theft of state assets, cheating in labor or materials, and stealing state economic intelligence) brought change in 1951–1952. Through these campaigns many employers and former government officials were exorcised in an atmosphere of terror.

Critical to the radical change in peasant China's sociocultural milieu was the collectivization of agriculture. Land had been a keystone of family and lineage identity for over two thousand years; the process of collectivization minimized and weakened that identity link. The CCP moved gradually in implementing the change from private land ownership to collectivization. The three stages were (1) putting peasants into mutual-aid teams; (2) establishing Agricultural Producers' Cooperatives where each peasant received a return according to his or her input; and (3) executing a true cooperative structure where all peasants worked for the same wages. The Agricultural Producers' Cooperative became production teams or the bottom of a three-tiered system: production teams → brigades → communes.[20] Each stage represented a significant transformation from the past, and was often accompanied by targeting former landowners as the enemy of the people—again, creating change through an atmosphere of terror.

Families were absorbed into the Agricultural Producers' Cooperative; they no longer owned their own land, product, or labor. Individuals were defined not by their family affiliations, but by their class status within the commune. Loyalty to one's family was replaced by loyalty to the commune. It was not unusual for a person to use betrayal of family members as a way of proving himself to the higher authority, the commune. Shifting loyalties became the only way to survive.

Gradually, ambitious and eager young people became CCP cadres and the new local elite. They used *guanxi*, ingratiation with superiors, and exploitation of inferiors in establishing their positions. In many ways, this was in keeping with the traditional Chinese style of authority—with a twist. Being politically oriented, they used ideology as a weapon against their enemies and a mechanism for establishing their own power base.

The Great Leap Forward (1958–1960) represents a time when (1) ideological enthusiasm dominated over practical, technical, and scientific expertise; and (2) when the leadership, under Mao's guidance, became monoclonal and unwilling to engage alternative ideas or strategies. The resulting tragedy of these two perspectives, hyperideological thinking and monolithic leadership, was that in the 1958–1960 period, 20 to 30 million rural Chinese died because of malnutrition and famine, making this one of the greatest human disasters known. Outsiders wonder: How could such a catastrophe happen? Why did people accept the economic principles that led to their own destruction?

In many ways, the Great Leap Forward rested as much on traditional Chinese sociopolitical customs as it did on new revolutionary ideas. The traditional elements that enabled peasants to follow this ruinous program were:

- Acceptance of Mao Zedong as the ultimate authority in China—In many ways, the people of China regarded Mao as a contemporary emperor with all that that implied.

- The sense of uncritical loyalty to the central hierarchy—Local officials (as did the gentry of the past) sought approval from their superiors as a way of improving their social positions.
- The Chinese peasants' acceptance of local and central authority figures—People believed that social order and security would emanate from their rightful leaders, beginning with Mao Zedong. Mao's personal cult status was undeniable: Hysterical masses listened to him and believed whatever he said.

Mao Zedong.

Out of devotion, loyalty, and uncritical acceptance, during the Great Leap Forward both cadres and the common people worked nonstop, even in the face of certain starvation, to meet the unrealistic quotas and standards set by the CCP.

The CCP and Mao Zedong believed that the path to national strength and independence was to decentralize: Each village would exist as a self-sufficient economic unit, while still producing enough food to support a growing urban population. Through this system, the benefits of health care, industrial production, and material goods, which had been mostly urban benefits, would be more equally distributed.

The "back yard" iron smelter is an example of the attempt to decentralize small-scale industry. In 1958 the CCP encouraged people to build iron-smelting furnaces in their backyards for steel production. By the end of the year, there were as many as one million backyard smelting furnaces. Unfortunately, the steel produced in these furnaces was substandard and almost totally unusable. At the same time, other essential areas, such as agriculture, suffered because of a lack of resources and labor. The latter had been diverted into decentralized small-scale industry, causing further food shortages and economic catastrophes.

Rather than develop a strong, independent China with a decentralized technological system, the unintended result of the Great Leap Forward was to create youth who were disengaged from the past and from their sociocultural traditions; to divide the formerly unified CCP (with the dissenting voices being labeled as disloyal to Mao); and to show that Mao Zedong could make serious leadership mistakes, thereby undermining his leadership credibility.

As with the Great Leap Forward, the Cultural Revolution (1966–1976), while shocking in its attack on former authority figures (such as parents, teachers, and local leaders) and institutions (educational and religious), nevertheless had its roots in traditional Chinese society. Mao Zedong and the party dictatorship were able to incite the Chinese youth to harass and demonize its citizens because the citizenry themselves were passive politically, uncritically obedient to authority, and without human rights, since to assert human rights was selfish, antisocial, and morally corrupt. Formerly, through the Confucian tradition (which ironically was also attacked at this time), people believed that they must subordinate themselves to the greater good. This value remained strong and was easily manipulated by Mao and the CCP.

After the Great Leap Forward, Mao believed that the new elite, built on the old top-down authority pattern, was reinstituting past social structures with the peasants at the bottom. At the same time, with the split in the CCP, he felt a challenge to his authority and wanted to consolidate his power. Therefore, he wanted a more decentralized administration, curtailing the Beijing bureaucrats' power. Government was to be concerned with the welfare and indoctrination of the masses. Anyone against this new perspective was called a revisionist or someone who abandoned the revolution's goals and accepted the evils of special status and capitalism. The Cultural Revolution became a radical transformation against revisionism.

To carry out the struggle, Mao mobilized urban student youths to attack the establishment, including leaders within his own party, and to purge China of revisionist elements. As the situation spun out of control and became more violent, Mao tried to slow it down; however, he was largely unsuccessful. The Cultural Revolution quickly took on a life of its own. After it was over, about 60 percent of the party officials were purged and another 400,000 people died.

Critical to the Cultural Revolution was the youth organization called the Red Guards. The Red Guards were formed in 1966 and were abolished in 1968; however, in this very short period of time they were extremely destructive. Energized by Mao through slogans such as "Bombard the Headquarters" and "Learn Revolution by Making Revolution," they became his destructive arm. Between August 18 and November 26, 1966, about 10 million youths from around the country poured into Beijing and volunteered to be Red Guards; they each carried the little red book of *Quotations from Chairman Mao* that had been compiled for indoctrinating them. School classes had been suspended and universities closed.

Red guards often humiliated people during the Cultural Revolution, 1966–1976.

Whatever terror people had experienced before as the CCP brought changes to Chinese social, political, and economic structure, they would not have been able to imagine what was to come. The Red Guards terrorized by breaking into the homes of intellectuals, officials, and people thought to be connected to the West (for example, they knew a foreign language) or to have capitalist leanings (such as having a relative living in the West), or who had a higher social status in the past. They destroyed books, manuscripts, religious artifacts, and ancestral tablets; and publicly humiliated, interrogated, incarcerated, beat, terrorized, and sometimes killed people. At times their victims seemed random: Why was one professor chosen and not another? Everyone lived in fear. All of this violence, carried out in support of the revolution and in an attack on the Four Olds (old ideas, culture, customs, and habits), was perpetrated by youths between 9 and 18 years of age. They roamed the streets in gangs wearing red armbands that marked them as having the moral authority to punish anyone they considered to be a revisionist and, therefore, a threat to the revolution. They were uncontrolled and uncontrollable.

In January 1967, Mao ordered the People's Liberation Army to help the antirevisionists in their fight against conservative counterrevolutionaries. However, political alliances were so complex and local power structures in such disarray that instead of clearly delineating lines of change, the addition of the army into the politicized mix brought China to the brink of a violent civil war. The Red Guards factionalized and fought with each other, while the army came in and took sides instead of providing security. By 1968 the People's Liberation Army was ordered to stop working with the Red Guards' factions and to undergo political training. However, the removal of the army did not stop the fractionalization of the Red Guards; therefore, Mao disbanded them and dispersed them throughout the countryside. Unfortunately, dispelling the Red Guards did not end the reign of terror, since the equally brutal Revolutionary Rebels replaced them.

Technically, the end of the Cultural Revolution came at the Ninth Party Congress in April 1969. A new party constitution was adopted, which stressed Mao Zedong's thought, the importance of class struggle, and limiting party membership by class origin. While this marked the official end of the Cultural Revolution, terrorism as a tool of rule continued. The military security personnel were ruthless in searching for counterrevolutionaries: People were interrogated and forced to confess to crimes they did not commit and to name others as associates; several thousand were said to be executed. Behind this brutalization was the idea that there were people conspiring to destroy the revolution and that "they" had to be stopped at all costs.

In the 1970s, the Cultural Revolution moved into the countryside. Peasants had to discontinue their petty capitalism enterprises—such as sideline businesses of raising and selling animals—leading to greater economic deprivation in their area.

Mao Zedong died on September 9, 1976. In keeping with the traditional belief that there is a link between the natural and human world, Mao's death was foretold in July of that year by a major earthquake, which killed 500,000 people east of Beijing. After a complex power struggle, Deng Xiaoping finally won the party leadership in late 1978, beginning a new period of reform. Nevertheless, an enduring legacy of the Cultural Revolution was a class system, which closely resembles a caste system, based on ascribed status. That is, a class or caste system where succeeding generations were marked by their families' former position, as described by the Four Bad Types (landlord, rich peasant, counterrevolutionary, and bad element).

The period from 1979 to the present signals the Chinese people's movement into a modern economy. The CCP tried to recover from the last years under Mao by encouraging rural production, industrialization, foreign trade and investment, and science and technology. Under Deng Xiaoping's leadership, China moved from class struggle to economic development. Ideology was being replaced by information, facts, and expertise. The Four Modernizations referred to agriculture, industry, defense, and science and technology. Political reform or modernization was not mentioned. The expectation was, and still is, that economic changes can occur without political change, that the Chinese society can embrace capitalism and its benefits without abandoning the so-called communist system of governance. That this expectation is out of sync with reality has lead to continuing socioeconomic–political problems.

There is a clear disjuncture between China's growing capitalism and its government's political conservatism. People are demanding more personal and political freedom as they become more involved with the global capitalist economy and have access to modern international communication systems with Fax machines, email, and other Internet technology. Contemporary disasters such as the 1989 Tiananmen Square massacre—where people demonstrated, demanding democracy and freedom—are part of China's ongoing socioeconomic–political disjuncture legacy.

SOCIAL STRUCTURE

The Glue of Chinese Life and Society: Lineage, Clan, and Family

The recognition of lineages as critical to one's place in society can be discerned at least as far back in Chinese history as the Shang dynasty (1600–1028 BCE).[21] Bronze inscriptions give an ancestor's honorific title, relationship (usually "father"), and the date, along with other information such as the purchaser's name and an admonition. During this period, an elaborate ceremonial system (a type of ancestor worship) was devised to give legitimacy to ruling lineages as well as to establish a social hierarchy among the lineages. An uneven distribution of wealth was also apparent by the Shang dynasty, based on intensified agriculture, a geographically dispersed commerce system, and transethnic interaction. The lineages helped solidify and maintain the developing power groups.

The great lineages and clans kept control over power and land through the Zhou dynasty (1122–249 BCE). Eventually, the role lineages and clans played in consolidating and maintaining power and resources, when there were literally thousands of contending states, was seen as a liability when one state finally emerged to rule over the others. Thus, while under the Zhou feudal system strict primogeniture was supported among the nobility, by the Han dynasty (206 BCE–220 CE) several laws were passed to weaken the political and economic strength of kinship groups.

The distribution of property was the key to changes in inheritance laws and primogeniture. Originally, the land went to the oldest son of the main wife, keeping the family's wealth intact. However, after the Zhou dynasty inheritance laws changed, dividing the family's land equally among all sons. Primogeniture was retained only in the ritual areas, where the oldest son represented the family in ancestor worship ceremonies. Daughters, who were considered temporary members of their natal families, did not inherit land. Women were raised within their natal family, but once married, they and their children belonged to their husband's family. In recognition of this process, the husband's family gave the woman's family a "bridal gift" (bride wealth) to compensate them for losing their daughter.

Even before the Han dynasty, however, the potential countervailing power of family units to the state system can be seen in laws that were developed in the fourth century BCE Qin dynasty. The state tried to limit the size of family units by

- Taxing families double if there were two or more adult sons living with their parents
- Prohibiting fathers, sons, and brothers from living in the same room

The first discouraged extended families and the second had the most effect on poor families where it had been common for the male members of a family to live in one room as a single economic and social unit. However, both the wealthy and poor family units were impacted. Under the new law, adult male members were forced to move out of the family home and earn a separate living.

The long-term effect of the tax and residential laws on family structure and size could be seen two hundred years later as Chia I, a contemporary writer, noted. He lamented that one consequence of these laws was a greater stress on individualism—that is, since families had to live on their own, there was a lack of subordination and politeness between family members, particularly in the daughter-in-law's behavior toward her husband's parents. He complained of the loss of Confucian defined behavior in families. Nevertheless, these family-oriented laws were kept for five centuries—until the Wei dynasty. From the Wei dynasty on, father and son were again able to own property together.

In later Chinese history, families rarely divided. Notably, from the Tang dynasty (618–907 CE) through the Qing dynasty (1644–1911 CE), the law became punitive in support of family unity. For example, if a son owned property separate from his parents the law considered him an unfilial son and, therefore, subject to punishment. Nor could a parent allow a son to own property separately. If a father gave his son permission to live independently, the father was subject to punishment under the law. Keep in mind that this requirement for the sons to live at home was not necessarily a physical requirement. For example, especially among merchants and government officials, the sons often lived for extended periods, even years, in houses in other parts of the country. However, economically, socially, and spiritually, their home was still considered to be with their parents.

An example of how critical lineages were to the social and political structures within China is Yuen-fong Woon's case study of the Kuan lineage in south China in the first half of the twentieth century. Patrilineal kinship was one of the major principles of social organization, along with ethnicity and socioeconomic class. Patrilineal kinship systems were actively promoted by the state as a mechanism of social control. No matter how well or how poorly the government was able to administer the local area, they could depend on lineages to maintain order and control. Woon noted that a magistrate and a small staff of ten men or less easily controlled a county (*xian* or *hsien*) administrative unit consisting of hundreds of villages. The local government's chief responsibility was to collect taxes and prevent rebellion. By law, none of the significant government workers were locals; they came from other geographic areas. The latter requirement prevented favoritism and the development of powerful warlords. Therefore, it was in the interest of the government to support a strong, traditional lineage system. The leadership within the lineage groups were usually elders or local gentry members. If they were gentry, the men had passed the traditional government examination system and were scholars or retired officials. The lineage leadership formed a bridge between the government and the people, helping explain and carry out governmental laws. Given the interdependence between lineages and the government, it is not surprising that the government has had, throughout history, a strong interest in the family system and inheritance. The government's interest has been expressed in laws which had, over time, encouraged, restrained, supported, or undermined the lineage system.

While small, powerless lineages with little or no ancestral property and consisting mostly of poor peasants existed, Woon's study of a large corporate lineage gives us a picture of the role lineages played locally and why the Chinese government was interested in them. Lineages provided ritual leaders, and, even more importantly to the government, they provided political leaders who were the wealthy elite within their family patriline. They maintained peace and order within their areas and worked closely with the government. Because they assisted and upheld the government and its policies, they, in turn, were given status, prestige, and financial benefits.

A Chinese peasant family.

A second technique for maintaining their position of power and status within their kin group was for the elite to donate land to their lineage. The poorer families within the patriline, who either owned very little or no land at all, farmed the lineage land. Such a system allowed for the distribution of wealth, while, at the same time, linking the interests of the rich and poor.

In areas where either the lineage was not rich enough to have lineage land that the poorer members could use to support their families, or where the lineage did not satisfactorily provide for their poorer members, the disenfranchised formed ties with others in a similar situation, regardless of their lineage ties. The Triad secret society in southern China is one example of the kind of political, economic, and social mobilization that occurred when the basic needs of the poor were not met. While the Triad was an antigovernment political group, its ability to attract peasants to the organization was based on the promise of assistance. Such non-kin-based groups were a threat to both the government and to the lineage power structure.

Family

Traditionally, the Chinese family was patrilineally based. But beyond that brief description lies a complex family system, which forms the primary basis for individual, social, legal, and political life:

> [W]e knew the family only as . . . the basis of human society. The system colors all our social life. . . . It very nearly takes the place of religion by giving man a sense of social survival and family continuity.[22]

In the Chinese patrilineal family system family members related by blood through the father's line are considered to be your blood relatives (i.e., they have a consanguineal relationship to you). All family members related to you through your mother's line are considered to be related through law and are referred to as *wài* meaning "outside" or "foreign." Thus, your grandfather on your father's side (your father's father) is called *zǔ fù (tsǔ fù)*, where *zǔ* means "ancestor" and *fù* means "father." However, your grandfather on your mother's side (your mother's father) is called *wài zǔ fù (wài tsǔ fù)*, indicating that he is outside the family line. Similarly, the term you would use for your grandmother, uncles, aunts, and cousins would vary depending on whether they were related to you through your mother's side or your father's side. A further distinction within the family is made by generation and relative age. For example, you would call your father's older brothers by a different term for "uncle" than you would use for your father's younger brothers; the same would be true of your older or younger siblings. This refinement in distinctions makes it clear to everyone just exactly how two people are related to each other in terms of blood, gender, and relative age vis-à-vis your parents.

Behind the kinship system of terminology are unstated, and unquestionably real, rights and obligations.[23] Historically, these rights and obligations were formalized in law; today they are largely informal in that the governments of mainland China and Taiwan do not officially recognize these relationships through law, yet family members have different expectations of each other depending on their exact relationship. Confucius constantly referred back to the family and family relationships when he gave examples of how people should behave socially and politically, thereby using the family to ground all other social relationships from the simplest to the most elite. Occasionally, as in the Tang (618–907 CE) and Sung (907–1279 CE) dynasties the government actively supported Confucian principles that promoted the primacy of the family through its educational system. The uneducated learned the correct procedures through their local teachers, lineage leaders, and community leaders, thereby ensuring the dominance of Confucian family ideals in popular culture. Bodde and Morris's book on the last dynasty (1644–1911 CE), *Law in Imperial China,* shows how one's exact relationship to another can determine (1) whether a crime has been committed; (2) how serious the crime was; and (3) what the punishment should be. For example, a daughter-in-law who accidentally caused the death of her father-in-law was condemned to death by slicing. In another case, the court maintained that if a father "unreasonably beats and thus kills a son or daughter who has violated his commands" he should be punished by receiving 100 blows of a heavy bamboo.[24] While laws today do not formalize the importance of exact personal relationships between potential litigants, the informal weight of these relationships remains, as contemporary work by several anthropologists testify.[25]

Given the critical nature of family in defining who one is and in providing security and a place in society, it is not surprising that marriage and children are every adult's primary goals. Traditionally, a marriage was not between two individuals; it was between two families. A go-between was used to match the families' backgrounds and the individuals' personal details, such as age and horoscope. The latter was to make sure the match was in keeping with the spiritual as well as the mundane. The first preference was for a cross-cousin marriage, for example, the father's sister's child and his own child. In other cases, the partner may have been chosen to solidify economic, political, or social relationships between families. Usually, unless the two were related, the couple met for the first time on their wedding day.

In contemporary China these patterns have changed.[26] Women cannot be forced to marry someone they have never met. Often love marriages are formed by couples who developed strong emotional ties independent of their families' intervention. In other cases, a family may still use a matchmaker, but with a twist: Once the go-between finds a likely candidate for a young woman or man, the couple meets to see if they are personally compatible. Essentially, they go on a "date," with the explicit purpose of determining their compatibility for marriage. If they decide that they are not compatible, they will not marry and the go-between will continue to look for other possible partners.

Traditionally, the newly married couple lived with the husband's family in a patrilocal arrangement. The ideal family living arrangement was where the parents, their married sons and their sons' wives and children all lived together in one house. This pattern is called a joint family and involves three generations of family members living together. Bernard Gallin found that in the Taiwanese village of Hsin Hsing only 5 percent of the households were joint families. The dominant pattern was the conjugal family, where the family consisted of a man, his wife, and his unmarried children: About 66 percent of the Hsin Hsing households were conjugal families. The remaining 29 percent of households were stem families—that is, they fell between joint and conjugal family patterns, consisting of one or both parents, their unmarried children, and one married son with his wife and children.

Two government policies in mainland China undermined the ideal of a joint family in contemporary society. One was that the individual's first responsibility and loyalty was to the country. Therefore, each individual should be willing to be sent to wherever the government deemed it was necessary. A person could be sent to the countryside far from their original home, and might never return. This program particularly affected the urban populations whose youths were sent out into the country.

The second, and perhaps the most important, was the one-child family policy. In 1981 as a response to a growing population and limited resources, the government developed, and strictly implemented, a one-child plan throughout the country. To carry out this policy, couples were not allowed to marry until they were older, thereby reducing the women's reproduction years in marriage. Once married, the couples were put on birth control until given official permission to become pregnant. Each couple was to have only one child, whether a male or female. While the government initiated this program to provide for its people, the laws also functioned to concomitantly undermine the powerful patrilineal loyalties that could be stronger than loyalties to the state. A negative side effect of the new laws, combined with the residual patrilineal values, was that the number of female infanticide cases went up. If a family was to have only one child and that child turned out to be a female, how was the family line, which was still determined through the male side, to continue? Due to internal and international pressures, the Chinese government eventually allowed those families whose first child was a girl to have a second child.[27]

Taiwan, which had more leeway in population growth and did not force a one-child policy on its people, had more success in curbing its population growth—without creating an increase in female infanticide—through a mass media campaign. They stressed that girls were equal to boys. In their economy, women were able to work and contribute to the family income, thereby adding to their status within the family. Therefore, while overall families were larger than one-child families, the total number of children was reduced when compared to traditional families.

What about the problem of not having your own biological male child? While in the past, Chinese condoned polygamous marriages of one husband and two or more wives, marriages are monogamous today. Even in the past, however, simply having multiple wives did not guarantee male off-spring. Therefore, there is a long tradition of adoption. The most acceptable form was to adopt a child with the same surname as your own, for example, a nephew or cousin from your father's line—that is, one of your brother's sons or one of your father's brother's son's sons.

The level of importance such relationships had in determining who one adopted is demonstrated in Chinese legal code. In Ann Waltner's study of adoption she noted that the earliest mention of adoption was in the Tang dynasty (618–907 CE).[28] The Tang code states that the child must be from the same lineage, that is, have the same surname and be related through the father's line. If a nonlineage related child was adopted, the adopting father could be banished for a year, the natural father could be beaten with 50 strokes, and the adoption would be annulled. These laws refer to male children, for as a Sung (in 963 CE) commentary states: "Adopting a male is serious; adopting a female is trivial."[29] The reason adopting a male child was serious (versus a female child who technically marries out of the family and therefore, had no rights within her natal family after marriage) rests in the economic and spiritual consequences of such a step. As the only male child, he would inherit his father's property and take care of his parents in their old age. Spiritually, the lineage would continue through the male child, creating an unbroken tie from one's ancestors through one's descendants. If the child were from another lineage, an adoption, which creates a parent–child bond, would be unnatural, an aberration, and as such would create a challenge to the entire society. From the Han period (206 BCE–220 CE) through the next two thousand years or so, there existed a belief that political order rested on a strong, solid patrilineal line of descent. Thus we see that political ideology, legal codes, and social relationships through family ties were bound together.

The term *ancestor worship* does not mean that people worshipped their ancestors in the same sense that one worshipped a god. What ancestor worship refers to is the fact that, although dead, ancestors nevertheless maintain a linkage with their living descendants. Both the living and the dead had rights and obligations to each other. As we will see in the Chinese idea of religion, dying is simply going to another plane of existence, without fully cutting off all ties with the living. A family's fortune—or misfortune—was related to the intervention of their ancestor in their lives. On their side, ancestors had needs in death that were very similar to their needs in life: for example, they needed money, food, and shelter. As a result, the living had to continually give offerings of food and money to their ancestors, thereby ensuring their comfort and their willingness to help the living succeed. If ancestors are not taken care of, are not fed and given money for their needs, they will become angry and vengeful, causing misfortune or even death in their earthly families. Those who die without anyone to take care of them, that is, without descendants, become dangerous ghosts and a threat to everyone.

As Yun Xiang Yan's study of the contemporary family in mainland China indicates, there has been a significant shift from the family reflecting the importance of the patrilineal line to the family reflecting the importance of the conjugal unit, or what Yan calls "the triumph of conjugality over patriarchy."[30] That is, as the dominance of the patrilineal line in determining behavior and beliefs has declined, the conjugal relationship between husband and wife has increased in importance. Yan discusses the move as a change from stress on the vertical parent–son relationship to the horizontal conjugal tie. The change resulted in a decline in the father's authority and power and a move toward independence for the mother and youth in the family.

Yan clearly shows how mainland China's patrilineal family, and its place as the social, cultural, legal, and political base, was caught in a three-way vise. First, the 1950 Marriage Law and its revision in 1980 gave men and women the legal right to choose their own partners and the right to divorce. Second, the government undermined the spiritual influence held by the family patriline by secularizing many community rituals, festivals, and family ceremonies including ancestor worship. Third, the state "privatized the family" by destroying its informal power within the community and replacing it with a formal administrative system and a group of cadres, or politically indoctrinated local leaders. These three policies destroyed the relationship which had existed for over two thousand years among power, authority, and the patrilineal system.

In mainland China, from the late nineteenth century onward, there has been a steady erosion of the control and power of the traditional patriline system through formal mechanisms, such as law. However, informally, women's position in society, as well as their ability to insist on their rights as citizens, has been consistently overshadowed by traditional, restrictive views. For example, in 1984 the number of male to female college graduates from Beijing Institute of Foreign Languages was equal, yet, 70 work units needing someone with this education specifically stated that they only wanted males and would not accept any females. This was one-third of the jobs offered to the graduating class.

Even though such gender discrimination is against the central authorities' policy, and is of great concern to the graduating institutions, it nevertheless continues, particularly in the countryside.[31] In part, such discrimination is so widespread and overt because the government, itself, is ambiguous in its position toward women's rights. An early study by C. K. Yang, *The Chinese Family in the Communist Revolution*, indicated that the Chinese central authorities were not consistent in their support of women's economic rights.[32] The government used women as a malleable labor pool. That is, when the government had an economic plan with great labor needs, the women were told they were selfish to stay home and care for their family; their place was out in the factory or farm, working for their country. On the other hand, when the government was downsizing economically, women were told their place was in the home, working for the betterment of the community through care of their family and the elderly. By tying women's economic rights to their economic decisions, the government gave a clear message: Women did not have the same inalienable rights to participate in the socioeconomic milieu that men had. Therefore, despite laws and lip service to the contrary, women and their rights were still considered secondary to men.[33]

Along with employment difficulties are issues of personal safety. Violence against women takes many forms.[34] Women are kidnapped and sold within China; raped; battered by their husbands and members of his family; and mistreated by their own parents if they assert their rights to marry a man of their own choice. Authorities believe that the incidence of abuse has risen since the Cultural Revolution, which caused a destruction of social order. Whether this is true or not is difficult to say because the government did not keep statistical data on crimes against women. However, given the frequency of this topic in both fictional sources and in nonfiction newspaper accounts, the fact of such violence is a part of the social landscape of contemporary China. Although, as in the past, the enforcement of controlling measures is uneven and inadequate, the government has started to address the issue of violence against women by reasserting its right to intervene in private domestic relations.

Non-Kin Interpersonal Relationships

As much as Americans value individualism, Chinese value social relationships. The critical nature of this social pattern has been consistently reaffirmed by anthropologists from very early village studies.[35] Fei Xiaotong, a Chinese social anthropologist who lived and worked in mainland China, studied Chinese social systems and concluded that they were a web of dyadic relationships. Anthropologist Robert Silin studied the role of relationships in Chinese thought and behavior in both Hong Kong and Taiwan, and he pointed out that Confucian thought assumes the impossibility of a person existing separate from other people.[36]

As the Chinese understand the universe, our human relationships guide and determine not only our humanity, but also our moral behavior. More specifically, our moral behavior is derived from our education, which we acquire through interaction with other people. To lose the linch pin of morality is to lose one's humanity and to devolve into a state of egocentricity, with its accompanying refusal to uphold one's social obligations. This latter state is to be absolutely avoided, if a person is to be considered a human being.

At the same time, we know that values, which may have been important historically, may not be viable today. That is, as society changes and enters the contemporary sociocultural global economy values are modified. To understand the importance of social relationships in Chinese culture and how the concept of relationships has changed, we will look at three related concepts: *rén-qìng (jén-ch'ìng)*, *gǎn-qìng (kǎn-ch'ìng)*, and *guan-xì (kuan-hsì)*.[37] Each of these concepts is a critical type of extra-kin relationship.

Rén-qìng (Jén-ch'ìng)

The Chinese have an expression, "*Tā bù shì rén*" or "She [or he] is not a person."[38] By this they mean that a person's behavior vis-à-vis other people is not correct. In this context, the concept *rén* (person) stresses interpersonal relationships, not the individual and his or her needs and desires. *Rén* refers to how one's behavior fits the Chinese social expectations of interpersonal relationships.

Similarly, *rén-qìng* means human feelings, in that it refers to dyadic relationships based on positive feelings between the people involved.

In other words, a rén-qìng relationship implies that the people involved share an emotional attachment. This is not a utilitarian or instrumental relationship; it is built on an expressive tie between two people. Such relationships epitomize the core dyadic relationship in Chinese culture with its emotional component being recognized as far back as two thousand years. Therefore, the basis of this extra-kin relationship is an expressive tie between two people, such as two villagers or two classmates.

Găn-qìng (Kăn-ch'ìng)

As with rén-qìng, *găn-qìng* also implies a relationship based on positive feelings between two non-kinspeople. Implicit in a găn-qìng relationship is a mutual attraction, or emotional attachment, between two people. However, an interesting addition to this concept is the asymmetrical nature of the relationship of the people involved. The anthropologists Morton Fried and Bernard Gallin both studied the hierarchical nature of this relationship. For example, a person would have a găn-qìng relationship with someone of another social class, such as a peasant with his land owner. Fried, in *Fabric of Chinese Society*, noted that in the mainland Chinese village he studied, the worst găn-qìng relationships were those which were considered "absent." That is, găn-qìng relationships were defined by the degree of emotional warmth and attachment that existed between a landlord and his tenant. It was a way of reducing the class differences between nonrelated people. The term was not typically used for a friend, because in a friendship situation the people are assumed to be social equals and would have a rén-qìng relationship. The strength and positive nature of a găn-qìng relationship was also correlated with the length of time of the acquaintanceship. Gallin found the same hierarchical relationship in Taiwan, where, for example, the tenant was able to maintain some sense of security in his relationship to his landlord through his găn-qìng relationship with him. He found that even a simple matter of borrowing a tool from another villager depended on one's găn-qìng relationship—one villager would not borrow a tool from a neighbor if he did not have a good găn-qìng relationship with him. Thus, we see that in both mainland China and on Taiwan, significant, non-kin dyadic relationships were defined in terms of the quality of their găn-qìng.

Guan-xi (Kuan-hsi)

As we have seen, both rén-qìng and găn-qìng involve dyadic relationships between two nonrelated people, have an emotional component, and are built over time. They are different because in găn-qìng the people are involved in an asymmetrical relationship. These dyadic relationships worked well in traditional and early modern China where most people still lived in the area where they were born and where mobility was not the norm. However, in today's China, as with the rest of the world, vast numbers of people move around for economic reasons. Individuals now find themselves in areas where they have no family or friends. As a result, one's daily contacts have expanded to include more instrumental relationships, while at the same time, one's expressive relationships have diminished in number. In spite of these changes, the cultural, social, and psychological pressure for developing and maintaining relationships continues. In such an environment, a more functional, instrumental form of dyadic relationship developed, called *guan-xi.*

Mayfair Yang, in her extensive work on guan-xi in mainland China, demonstrated how from the socialist period onward guan-xi was critical in the flow of favors, gifts, and everyday work. In other words, it involved doing favors for another person, thereby creating a linkage between that person and one's self. Guan-xi relationships can be between relatives, or nonrelatives of equal or asymmetrical status; they create a network of mutual dependence based on obligations and indebtedness; they are ubiquitous, expected, and the cultural norm. In other words, guan-xi comprises a fundamental part of everyday life in modern China. These relationships are what allow people to operate socially, politically, and economically.

Unlike rén-qìng and găn-qìng, guan-xi, while considered necessary in carrying out one's everyday activities, also has a pejorative connotation, like a two-sided coin. One side is positive because through guan-xi relationships work gets done and personal desires are met. The other side is more problematic: Guan-xi relationships are thought to be based on self-interest and reciprocity, and therefore, to be somewhat antisocial in nature. In Yang's study, one woman described it as representing the general turn toward "treacherousness in social relations."[39]

Yet, from the anthropologist's point of view, as Ambrose King pointed out, guan-xi can be seen as an instrumental relationship that is required in a changed economic and bureaucratic environment. That is, in a society which is traditionally relationship based, and is at the same time fully engaged in developing a modern economy, guan-xi functions as a tool. It allows people to create, to shape, their own social or economic successes. Each person develops a set of dyadic relationships based on a functional reciprocity. Emotional, long-term commitments need not be a part of the guan-xi relationship, although they are not excluded.

There are two basic types of guan-xi relationships: those involving economic exchange and those involving social exchange.[40] Economic guan-xi is content specific and largely controlled by impersonal market forces; social guan-xi, while still ruled by the principle of reciprocity, is more diffuse. Also, unlike economic quan-xi relationships, in social guan-xi rén-qìng is central to the relationship. At the same time, unlike the more traditional concept of rén-qìng discussed above, the rén-qìng of today is also considered to be a kind of resource or social capital that can be exploited or developed.

Overall, guan-xi appears to be a more market driven concept of relationships than rén-qìng or găn-qìng: Guan-xi is a consciously recognized mechanism and often involves short term relationships to achieve immediate and pragmatic goals such as buying a refrigerator. Thus, guan-xi is based on the principle of reciprocity and instrumental rationality.

ETHNICITY

In China, ethnic groups and ethnic boundaries are dynamic social constructs. Before we look at specific groups, however, let's consider three concepts: ethnic groups, ethnic boundaries, and ethnic nesting.

George DeVos defined an ethnic group as a group of people who see themselves as separate from others with whom they come in contact.[41] They base their perceived differences on such attributes as folk religious practices, language, sense of historical continuity, and common ancestry or place of origin. Ethnic identity is not only formed internally, or from within the group; the perceptions of those outside the group are also important in defining a community's ethnicity. While these defining characteristics appear static, ethnic groups themselves are in a constant state of flux. Fredrick Barth, in *Ethnic Groups and Boundaries*, discussed the persistence of ethnic groups—despite individual movement across ethnic boundaries. The perception of ethnic distinction depends on the dichotomization of ethnic status, based on a group's maintenance of specific processes of exclusion and inclusion. In fact, cultural differences, and therefore, group identification, exists precisely because there is interethnic contact and interdependence. Through interethnic contact, each group develops a definition of self and other.

Keep in mind two principles. First, the factors defining an ethnic group appear categorical and objective: purported racial uniqueness, territoriality, economic position (for example, a special occupation), religion, language, and other aesthetic cultural patterns (such as food, clothing, or dance). Second, ethnic identification of a group is subjective: Ethnicity is a feeling, a sense of continuity with one's past.

The subjectivity of ethnic groups reflects the existence, or lack thereof, of ethnic boundaries. In other words, there is no clear relationship between the existence of ethnic groups and cultural similarities and differences. Defining ethnic factors vary with what is being contrasted; they are not objective factors. That is, the individuals involved define the critical elements used to determine ethnic boundaries. Since these factors are subjective, they can change over time. For example, language may not be a critical factor at one point in time, but may become a defining factor at another time. In essence, ethnic boundaries are not real, physical boundaries; rather, they are social constructs that contain all the variation to which other social phenomena are subject.

Finally, the term *ethnic nesting* refers to one's identification with more than one ethnic group. Often these identities are hierarchical, although they need not be. For example, a person can identify herself as Chinese (from the country of China), Han (the dominant ethnic group in China), and Shanghaiese (that her home area is the city of Shanghai). She would stress one identity over the other depending on the circumstances. If traveling outside China, she would identify with being Chinese (versus French or American, or whatever other country she was visiting). If traveling within China, she would probably identify with her home region, Shanghai, versus other Chinese regions that vary culturally from her own.

Multiethnic China

Today when we look at China, we often think of only the dominant ethnic group, or the Han Chinese, who comprise about 94 percent of the people of China. Yet, historically they have not always been dominant in numbers or in power. Chinese history is a picture of dynamic interethnic contact.[42] In the comprehensive research on race and ethnicity by Frank Dikötter, it is obvious that the Chinese had strong folk notions of race that were related to family, blood relationships, and descent.[43] From the earliest centuries of Chinese civilization one's social identity revolved around membership within a particular family, a family that had deep historical roots. As mentioned earlier, in traditional China, a family was part of a patrilineage, or *zǔ*, a group of people who could demonstrate through written records or oral history that they were descended from particular ancestors. A group of patrilineages was referred to as a *clan*. Clans shared the same surname, such as *Li*, *Mao*, or *Chang*, and often shared property, such as an ancestral temple, cemetery, or common land. In some regions of China this emphasis on patrilineal clans led to villages where almost all the inhabitants shared the same surname.

Throughout much of traditional Chinese history these patrilineal clans were involved in competition and conflict over land, power, and status. They became militarized, and struggled with each other for leadership. Those patrilineal clans that attained leadership success and were able to rule over various regions gained higher status. To justify their claims to high status, various concepts of descent, blood ties, and kinship solidarity were developed. Cults and folk notions of patrilineal descent emphasizing specific families as superior "peoples" and "culture" were acknowledged. As expected, the Chinese emperor's patrilineal clan was superior to all.

Various people outside the confines of traditional Chinese civilization were classified as "barbarians," *yongxiabianyi*. The barbarians living beyond the realm of Chinese civilization were classified as nonhuman animals. The only people who were *rén*, "human beings," were the Chinese. Thus an ideology emphasizing the "purity" of the Chinese versus the "impurity" of barbarians emerged. One of the principal duties of the Chinese emperor was to keep the boundaries between these groups distinct.

Further, with Western penetration into Asia, European pseudo-scientific beliefs about race were diffused and integrated with indigenous concepts into China. In China, the Western pseudo-scientific category of "race" and the purported evolutionary superiority of specific races were fused with folk models of patrilineal descent. The term *zu* for patrilineage was eventually redefined as *minzǔ*, which integrated people (*min*) and descent (*zǔ*) to refer to the people, race, or nation of China.

The term *minzǔ* was introduced into China in the late nineteenth century when other Western concepts were translated into Japanese and transmitted to China. In particular, the "Han race" was identified with the purest race. The leader and first president of the Republic in China, Sun Yat-sen, promoted a racial nationalism as a basis for the nation-state in the early twentieth century. He wrote that the Han had common blood, common language, common religion, and common customs, and was a single, pure race. Sun believed that groups such as the Mongols, Manchus, Tibetans, and Mohammedan Turks were different minzǔ, or peoples or nationalities.

China's Minorities Policy

As the Chinese developed a strong sense of nationalism in the nineteenth century they also developed a deeper sense of the ethnic differences that existed within their borders. Again, the question came back to how the various ethnic groups could be brought into the state system. How much independence should these groups be given in terms of keeping their own languages and cultural practices; should they hold administrative office? With the takeover of communism these questions were considered moot. All people were seen as the same, as one in their class struggles, therefore, all groups would be raised together as one to higher social levels once communism was implemented. As Mao Zedong said, "what has been called nationality struggle is in reality a question of class struggle."[44]

Following Marxist–Soviet pronouncements on how to handle minorities, the Chinese Communist Party (CCP) originally promised self-determination and autonomy to their minority peoples. Nevertheless, the expectation was that once given the choice, the minorities would voluntarily join with China proper. So powerful was their faith that the minorities would want to join with a communist China that in 1930 the party gave the minority nationalities the right to secede or federate. However, by 1938 after the Long March, and after experiencing the hostility many minorities felt toward Han Chinese, Mao changed his mind. He no longer allowed them the right to an independent nation, although he continued to offer them the right to keep their own language, culture, and education. While even these rights were modified as the Chinese communists tried to encourage their minorities to join with the nation-state, the Chinese government remained sensitive to their interdependence with the nationalities.

Although the minorities constitute about only 6 percent of the total Chinese population, they are critical to the security of China. Most minority groups live in the border areas of China. Further, these groups often live on both sides of the Chinese border, making them a possible national security risk. For example, the Shan people in Thailand and Burma also live in neighboring southern China; the Mongols in Russia and the Mongolian People's Republic also live in northern China; and Muslim groups found throughout the Middle East are concentrated in western China. Because of the concentration of Han Chinese along the coastal areas and in the valleys, the majority of 94 percent live in 40 percent of the land area, leaving the 6 percent minorities dominating 60 percent of the land area, most of which is mountainous or desert. While this 60 percent may not be hospitable to an agricultural society, it is where China's major resources are found: mineral deposits, forests, and 80 percent of China's meat- and wool-producing animals.

The CCP took a structured approach in dealing with Chinese ethnic minorities. In the 1960s, following a Russian Marxist ideology, the People's Republic established guidelines defining Han Chinese and other ethnic groups. At that time, they decided there were 56 official ethnic groups, each having a different culture, language, race, and territory. The Chinese majority, one of the 56 ethnic groups, were no longer call *Zhong-guo-rén* (Chinese), but *Han-rén* (ethnically and racially Han). The impact of this political decision was broad and deep.

One of the new nationalities, the Bai, are the second largest ethnic group in Yunnan province and have about 1.2 million people. They now reside in an area designated the Bai Autonomous Prefecture. Other Bai people are scattered in eastern Yunnan province. What is remarkable about this group is that until 1958, when the government completed its official list of nationalities, the Bai did not perceive themselves as a separate ethnic group. They did not distinguish themselves from other Chinese and had been assimilated into Chinese culture for many centuries, if not a millennia. In fact, in the 1930s a Chinese anthropologist, Francis L. K. Hsu, carried out fieldwork among the Bai people, using them as a typical example of Chinese culture and tradition. Later, in the mid-1980s when Tu Wei-ming did fieldwork among the Bai, studying people in the Bai Autonomous district, he found that physically and culturally the Bai were indistinguishable from other Chinese. Yet, when he asked the Bai about their ethnicity, they now said that they were different, that they were Bai, although they were hard pressed to give any specific differences between themselves and ethnic Chinese. The change in the Bai people's self-perception seems to have come from their official designation as being a separate ethnic group. They now claim to be a minority and non-Chinese. This case demonstrates the impact political and state decisions have on ethnic identity.

Thus, due to such intervening factors as political ideology, concern for the secure borders, and desire to exploit natural resources, the minorities question remains highly inflammatory.[45] It is still referred to as *the nationalities problem*. Whatever rights or restrictions are put on the ethnic populations, the underlying assumption by the CCP government is that eventually all ethnic distinctions will disappear as class differences disappear. So, while there is recognition that there are ethnic minorities in China today, they are officially considered remnants of the past class system and not a natural distinction within human societies. Further, in observing the CCP's reactions to the minority question, we see the old patterns of either (1) expecting the minorities to assimilate voluntarily because of the superior Chinese social, cultural, and political system; or (2) perceiving the intransigent minorities as dangerous to the larger Chinese society and in need of confinement and control.

The Muslim Minority in China

Anthropologist Dru Gladney has been conducting ethnographic research on the Muslim minority in China, illustrating how ethnic relations between the national minorities and Han majority have evolved and persist.[46] As noted above, after the communist revolution in China, 56 different nationalities, including the Han majority, were recognized by government authorities to control and consolidate the nation-state. Within these 56 nationalities are 10 Muslim nationalities: Hui, Uygur (Uighur), Kazak, Dongxiang, Kirghiz, Salar, Tadjik, Uzbek, Baonan, and Tatar—consisting of over 17 million people.

The earliest Muslim groups in China were descended from Arab, Persian, Central Asian, and Turkish peoples who migrated into China and settled in the northwestern and southeastern coastal regions. Prior to 1949 the term *Hui* was a general term for "Muslims." However, following the communist revolution, the Muslims were separated into the 10 separate groups, based on language. The Hui, who are the largest Muslim group, have a population of over 8 million people and are widely distributed throughout China, residing in most of the counties and cities throughout China, including major cities such as Beijing and Shanghai. Unlike the other Muslim nationalities in China, the Hui speak whatever dialect is dominant in the areas in which they live, usually Mandarin Chinese. Some of the Hui, however, reside in areas such as Tibet or Mongolia, where they speak Tibetan or Mongolian.

One important expression of ethnic and religious identity does appear to cut across the dispersed Muslim population in China. The notion of belonging to the Islamic faith, the "pure and true" (*qing zhen*) religion, is emphasized by all Hui Muslims. This phrase *qing zhen* is found wherever Hui Muslims reside, and it refers to such Islamic dietary rules as the avoidance of pork consumption. To some extent, it is similar to Jewish notions of "kosher" and approximates the Arabic concept of "halal." For example, among the approximately 200,000 Hui Muslims in the capital city of Beijing, the most important expression of ethnic identity is based on their dietary restrictions, especially the absence of pork, which is maintained through their own ethnic restaurants. Pork is the staple meat of the Han majority in Beijing and throughout China, and many of the Han cannot fathom why the Hui do not eat pork. Thus, the pork taboo has become a critical ethnic marker for Hui identity within Beijing.

Gladney resided in the Hui rural community in Ningxia, which is representative of many of the Muslim communities of northwestern China. Ningxia is the Ningxia Hui Autonomous Region, one of the five minority autonomous regions in China (including Tibet, Uygur, Inner Mongolia, and Zhuang in Guangxi). The Ningxia Hui community has a completely different form of ethnic expression than that of the Beijing Hui. Within this community, the emphasis on qing zhen is sought through a close identity with the Islamic religious tradition. They maintain a rigid notion of qing zhen, which results in strict rules of pure and impure behaviours. These pure and impure regulations divide the Hui from the Han in the northwestern area. For example, Ningxia Hui Muslims cannot accept food from their Han neighbors because of pure–impure cultural norms. In addition, an Islamic resurgence movement has developed among these Hui Muslims. Increases in religious education, mosque attendance, traditional restrictions on male–female interaction, decreases in Hui–Han intermarriages, and extensive contact with other areas of the Islamic world are recognizable signs of an enhanced ethnic and religious identity among the Ningxia Hui Muslims.

Tibetan Minorities

Another example of the destructive ethnic relations that have emerged since the 1950s between the Maoist government of the People's Republic and other ethnic groups is the Tibetan minority's circumstances. Tibet was a traditional region in the Himalayan Mountains that had tributary and political relationships with China's government for many centuries. While Buddhist, the indigenous Tibetan people maintained a different religious tradition of Buddhism than the Chinese. Their language and culture were also unique. Traditionally, Tibet was ruled by the highest ranking Tibetan Buddhist monk, known as the Dalai Lama.

Following the establishment of the People's Republic of China, the Maoist government sent their military into Tibet to absorb this region into the PRC in the 1950s. In response, the Dalai Lama fled Tibet with thousands of his followers to the area of Dharmsala, in northern India. China took over Tibet and in the 1950s sent the Maoist Red Guards to destroy Buddhist temples, burn religious texts, and purge the so-called backward feudal theocratic regime and superstitious religious culture of the region. The PRC government orchestrated a mass migration of ethnic Han people into Tibet (known as Xizang to the Chinese) to foster its cultural assimilation and to control the area.

Many Tibetans resisted this political and cultural domination and were supported by the Dalai Lama's worldwide campaign to help restore Tibetan culture, ethnicity, and religion. Over the years, recognizing the political difficulties in resisting the PRC on developing independence, the Dalai Lama has only campaigned for a degree of cultural and religious autonomy for Tibet. A number of anthropologists including Melvin Goldstein, Marcia Calkowski, and others have been doing ethnographic work in this region for many years and have been consulting with the governments there and elsewhere on the ethnic, religious, and political tensions between the Tibetans and the PRC.[47]

THE CHINESE RELIGIOUS EXPERIENCE

To understand the Chinese religious experience—involving Daoism, Buddhism, and Confucianism—we should first consider the anthropologist Robert Redfield's classic theory on peasant-based (agricultural) societies.[48] His theory was an attempt to understand the interaction between the elite and the peasants. Within agricultural societies there were two interacting cultures that Redfield named the Great Tradition and the Little Tradition. The Great Tradition was based on a literate, rationalizing tradition, which also informed the society's art, philosophy, and institutions with a coded set of ideals and values. The Little Tradition was a folk tradition coming out of peasant villages, where the norms, values, and behaviors were passed down verbally from generation to generation. That is, it was an oral, not a written, tradition. Religion is an important institution that reflects these two interacting traditions. Although Redfield's classic theory of the Great and Little Traditions has been criticized as too exaggerated in its emphasis in polarizing the elite from the peasants, it offers a model for understanding the interaction between China's history and its religious developments.

Daoism (Taoism)

The Dào (Tao) of Daoism is a complex concept and a simple translation does not do justice to it, but essentially there are at least two significant meanings of Dào in Chinese thought.[49] One is a metaphor meaning a road, a path, or way. In this latter case, *Dào* often refers to behavioral, moral and religious truth. The second usage of *Dào* involves the Chinese worldview: that the world, involving both the natural and supernatural, is predictable and systematic; that there is a regularity of operations in the universe. At the same time, there is a reality behind appearances that is the ultimate metaphysical truth and that is unpredictable and unknowable:

> The unnameable is the source of the universe.
> The nameable is the originator of all things.[50]

Daoism comes from an ancient text, the *Dào Dě Jing (Tào Tě Ching)* [*The Canon of the Way and Its Attainment*]. As the basis of a philosophical and religious tradition, the *Dào Dě Jing* is quite short, around five thousand words. Traditionally, the *Dào Dě Jing* is attributed to the mythical philosopher sage, Lǎo-zǐ (Lao Tzǔ), who is said to be about 20 years older than Confucius (551–479 BC). While such a chronology is unproven, what is significant about this historical view is the claim that Lǎo-zǐ was older than Confucius, thereby giving him seniority and superiority.

A second seminal text is *Zhuang-zǐ* (*Chuang-tzŭ*) written by the fourth century BCE philosopher Zhuang-zǐ, who was thought to be a follower of Lǎo-zǐ. These two books, *Dào Dě Jing* and *Zhuang-zǐ*, have fascinated educated Chinese throughout history, right up to today.[51] Daoism can be viewed as producing two traditions: One is called philosophical Daoism and the other religious or mystical Daoism.

Philosophical Daoism was popular among intellectuals or literati, especially disaffected intellectuals who lived under corrupt governments. The literati were men whose entire educational experience had been devised to prepare them for participation as officials in the governmental bureaucracy. During periods when corruption or political alliances made it difficult for men of conscience to participate, they withdrew from office. Living nonpublic lives, they promoted the search for transcendental values through critical study and independent thinking. Seeking to escape the Confucian defined mundane world, they studied Daoism, searching for the ultimate reality.

Religious Daoism is a syncretic tradition drawing on ancient cultural practices: *wu*, who were shamans or spirit mediums, and *fang-shih*, who were ritual specialists, served as medical specialists and magicians. Appearing in early religious Daoism were the "hygiene school," where one learned how to achieve longevity through controlled breathing and exercise techniques; and alchemy, where Daoist specialists used chemicals to search for the elixir of life. In the quest for immortality, or at least longevity, Daoism stressed the importance of nourishing and maintaining one's innate life forces. Everyone was born with these life forces, but they could be lost through immoderate living, resulting in an early death.

Another underlying principle in Daoism was the natural connection between humans and the universe. By developing one's relationship with the universe people could gain spiritual prowess not only for themselves, but also for others. The popularity of religious Daoism and its practitioners rose and fell through history. Several emperors, going as far back as the first emperor, Qin Shi Huangdi (Ch'in-shih-huang-ti), in 221 BC, were enamored with the idea of immortality and supported religious Daoism.

Besides pursuing immortality, the hygienic school stressed practical concerns, such as the importance of acting virtuously by caring for orphans, the elderly, and sick, as well as maintaining public roads and bridges. Renunciation of wealth, living simply, and giving alms to the poor were also encouraged.

When Buddhism entered China, it brought new ideas such as the existence of a soul, life after death, and a world filled with gods, bodhisattvas, and spirits. These ideas merged with Daoism until eventually, in the folk religion of the Chinese people, it became impossible to separate one set of ideas, values and behaviors from the other. The spiritual world was a bureaucratic mirror image of the earthly world, which was ruled by a moral system supported by a series of rewards and punishments for correct and incorrect behavior.

There is one more dimension of Daoism that should be mentioned. That is its early linkage in the Han dynasty to religiopolitical mass movements. This linkage remained intact throughout China's long history, making Daoism a potential threat to the state in times of civic unrest. When the dynasties became weak and could no longer maintain social order, and when poverty with its attending misery and suffering spread throughout the land, new challengers to the state appeared. The challengers often built on religious Daoism's tradition by preaching millennarist and apocalyptic hopes, and promising to establish a new sociopolitical system that would bring peace and prosperity. The new millennium would be achieved through military means and be supported by supernatural powers. The leaders of these movements were thought to have magical powers and took on the aura of a theocratic ruler.

Buddhism

Buddhism has been a central component of the Chinese religious tradition for well over two thousand years, even though throughout this period it was also considered a foreign religion. From the Han dynasty (206 BCE–220 CE) to the Tang dynasty (618–907 CE)[52] missionaries from India and Central Asia came to China bringing various versions of the Buddhist traditions, along with sacred writings.

Relevant to the difficulty in understanding the original Indian Buddhist concepts and ideas, and adding to the sinification of Buddhism, was the simple act of translating scriptures from Sanskrit to Chinese. Modifications in the original scriptures came from at least two translation-related issues. First, as Arthur Wright, a sinologist, pointed out, values that were seen as inconsistent with Chinese values were modified. For example, the phrase '"Husband supports wife" became "The husband controls his wife,'" and the phrase "'The wife comforts the husband" became "The wife reveres her husband."'

Second, in trying to make the alien Indian ideas more comprehensible to the new Chinese audience, early Buddhist missionaries used Daoist terms and concepts. For example, the Daoist term *wúwéi* (nonaction) was used for *nirvana.* While this may have been a practical solution to the problem of translating such a new and alien idea, it was impossible for the *wúwéi* of Buddhism to avoid being invested with established Daoist meanings of the term. It took some time for people to understand the very different Indian ideas encapsulated in the original Buddhist scriptures. Nevertheless, eventually, Chinese intellectuals were drawn to Buddhist philosophy and concepts. At the same time, those of a conservative bent consistently criticized Buddhism throughout history as a "barbarian religion" because it was non-Chinese in origin and held certain central ideas that were anathema to the Chinese cultural tradition, such as putting the individual over the family.

The Chinese school of Buddhism is the Mahayana (The Broad Path) school. Both Hinayana (Theravada, The Narrow Path) and Mahayana texts were available to the Chinese in translation. The Hinayana school of Buddhism was considered a gradual approach to salvation, one's ultimate release from this world and into nirvana was developed through a long, arduous accumulation of good karma. Religious insight was built up through study, accumulating knowledge and, concomitantly, wisdom. Mahayana offered the religious follower more support through the help of several Buddhas and Bodhisattvas. One could even experience a single, sudden burst of enlightenment. Being more closely aligned with preexisting Daoist beliefs, Mahayana Buddhism found a more sympathetic intellectual and emotional environment than Hinayana did.

As Buddhism was accepted into Chinese life, its relationship with the state became critical. As with any organized religion, it could form a strong power base outside the government, even in opposition to the government. Therefore, besides adapting to the already existing Daoist concepts and ideas prevalent in Chinese society, Buddhism, as a potential nongovernmental power, also had to adapt to the needs of the Chinese state. Education is one example of this process. First, the national examination system was based on Confucian training; and second, the Confucian ethical tradition defined moral behavior for all Chinese. Since the novices were required to pass government-regulated examinations to become monks, and since Confucian education stressed moral behavior, the Buddhist training included countless rules of conduct based on Confucianism and its moral code. The community of monks, nuns, novices, and lay believers, known as the *sangha,* were to follow the code of behavior as well as to perform good works and charity. The latter is also a part of the Confucian tradition involving community concerns. Eventually, under the Tang dynasty, Buddhism, which was under the Ministry of Rites, became more bureaucratized through governmental control, giving titles, sale of ordination certificates, and the further development of clerical examinations.

The legacy of Buddhism is obvious in China. For example, there are many Buddhist proverbs found among the peasants today. But, even more important, are the popular ideas of karma, afterlife, folk-gods, and festivals with Buddhist symbols and observances, as well as artistic motifs of Buddhist origin. At the same time, Buddhism ceased to be an independent, separate religious tradition. It had become fragmented and sinicized, merging with Daoist and other folk cultural elements. As Arthur Wright noted in *Buddhism in Chinese History*, it was not until the modern period, in the late nineteenth and early twentieth centuries, that a few Chinese tried to revive Chinese Buddhism as a separate religious tradition. Yet, even as some Chinese tried to reconstruct a Chinese Buddhism, others, such as Hu Shih in 1937, continued to revile it, claiming that Buddhism represented a two-thousand-year period of cultural domination by India.

Thus, we see that over the course of two thousand years, Buddhism became sinicized and integrated into the Chinese folk, social, cultural, and political traditions. This acceptance in the Little Tradition and in much of the Great Tradition is in contrast to Buddhism's rejection by some Chinese intellectuals, and sometimes by state authorities where it is still defined as a foreign religion and as a form of intellectual colonialism and sought independence from government.

Confucian Traditions

Confucius (Kong Fu-zi or K'ung Fu-tzu) was a teacher in the state of Lu (ca. 551–479 BCE).[53] He lived in troubled times with warlords creating unrest everywhere. There was no peace. He and his followers contrasted the chaos of their world with the past, the golden age, when sage-like emperors ruled their people. Confucius and many of his contemporaries revered the legendary founders of the three dynasties: Xia dynasty (ca. 2200–1600 BCE); the Shang dynasty (ca. 1600–1028 BCE); and the Zhou dynasty (ca. 1122–249 BCE). These dynasties became the ideal, the moral gold standard for leaders and governmental systems to measure themselves against.

Interestingly, what we think of as Confucianism, that is, a distinct intellectual tradition, did not exist until the former Han dynasty (206–8 BCE). It was during the Han dynasty that the gentry elite were grappling with the problem of how to rationalize the new imperial order and their own place within that order. Much of the political system was beyond their control. It had, for example, already developed a hereditary monarchy. The newly emerging Han elite were functionaries of the previous feudal states who had land, wealth, and time for learning. They offered their skills to the new emperor and moved forward consolidating their power positions within the bureaucratic state. They also acted as guardians of their cultural heritage and the new social order. The peasants, in contrast, lived a precarious life: working the land, paying taxes, and enduring forced labor demands for military and public works programs.

At the same time, because the Han period was also a time of rapid economic expansion and development, merchants and traders became wealthy and often aligned themselves (and their interests) with the imperial family. In this social system, the merchant class with their increased wealth posed a threat to the power balance of the rising gentry functionaries. As a result, the gentry functionaries worked to control the social system—the relative status, prestige and position of the imperial line, merchant class, gentry, peasants, and others—by defining a hierarchy of values and behavior; moral and ethical standards; and the basic interconnection among humans, institutions, and natural phenomena.

Heaven, earth, and humans made a triangle. The three were indivisible. Whatever happened in one part had an impact on the other two. If humans behaved well and followed correct behavior, all would be well. If humans did not follow correct behavior, natural disasters could befall the entire country. The emperor, as the Son of Heaven, symbolized the link among these three, and carried out appropriate rituals and established and maintained a harmonious sociopolitical system. Such a sociopolitical system required programs for controlling land use and taxation, caring for the people, meeting people's basic needs, educating those who were capable, and ensuring that people knew and followed correct moral behavior.

The social class relationships, which were defined as natural (and therefore necessary for the health and well-being of all Chinese) by the gentry, were hierarchal and ranked in the following order: gentry, peasants, merchants, and artisans. The rationale behind giving peasants second place over the merchants in the class structure was that the entire society depended on agriculture and their labor was morally correct work. Merchants, on the other hand, lived off other people's labor, and therefore should not be given a higher status or position than those who do work that is critical for the country's existence. At the same time that class relationships were defined, the correct moral behavior of people was also defined. Confucianism set an ethical standard where the basic premise was that the behavior of each person was critical to the well-being of the entire Chinese society. That is, the health and stability of the country was in part dependant on everyone, no matter who they are, to obey and follow the rules required of their position.

Because of the practical needs of the Han gentry in their struggle to maintain primacy in the newly developed empire, Confucius

> was dehumanized and transformed into the prophet and patron saint of a united empire of which he had never dreamed. The old books were pushed, forced, interpolated, and 'interpreted' to give them a consistency which their differing ages and authorships belied. The *Book of Changes*, basically a primitive text for taking oracles, was associated with Confucius and made the authority for all manner of analogical constructs. The *Book of Poetry*, in which the people of an earlier day had sung of their hopes and fears, was tortured to provide authority for approved moral principles. New "classics" such as the *Classic of Filial Submission* (*Hsiao-ching*) went far to transform Confucius into what Granet called the patron saint of a conformist morality.[54]

Once put into place, Confucianism became an institution that supported the Chinese way of life by defining the only acceptable Chinese ethical system. In spite of periods when Confucianism was adjusted for changing problems, it remained a stable and essential element in traditional China. Confucianism and its ethical system have even played a role in supporting modern political systems and the status quo. Therefore, even though Confucianism does not involve the supernatural or spiritual beings, as an ethical system it is often considered a part of China's religious tradition.

Contemporary Religious Issues

Today the Chinese government recognizes five religions: Buddhism, Daoism, Catholicism, Protestantism, and Islam.[55] It does not recognize folk religious practices as a legitimate form of religion, although it is pervasive throughout China. Folk religion is considered a form of superstition. As a communist system the government does not advocate or encourage religious beliefs; however, since it recognizes the existence of these five religious groups, it has developed bureaucratic means to handle religious issues: the Religious Affairs Bureau and Public Security Administration.

When the Chinese Communist Party established itself and took over the government of mainland China, it discouraged religious ideologies as superstitious remnants created to control people's minds. During the Cultural Revolution the Red Guard attacked all things religious, causing serious harm: Monks and nuns were forced to abandon their religious life; temples, ancestor altars, books, and statues were destroyed. This was one of the darkest periods of religious persecution in Chinese history. A generation of Chinese was deprived of its spiritual roots.

However, at the cessation of overt persecution, there followed a ground swell of interest in traditional religious beliefs and practices.[56] By 1980, in a response to international pressure, the Chinese government relented on its religious repression of the previous 30 years and permitted a greater degree of religious freedom. Given this new freedom, religious activity quickly expanded, particularly in the southeastern area of the country. As local people became wealthy through capitalist enterprises and as recent overseas Chinese also began to be economically significant in the area, they enthusiastically began rebuilding and expanding Buddhist and Daoist temples as well as Christian churches.

New religious sects also developed in response to the vacuum created by the extreme religious persecution of the Cultural Revolution period. One such sect is the Falun Gong, which erupted onto the Chinese society in the late 1990s. At first the governmental authorities considered the Falun Gong to be a benign group, interested in health and physical development through exercise. However, it quickly recast the organization as a dangerous religious sect, which had too much control over its practitioners and could be a possible counterweight to the government. Shortly thereafter, the central authorities began to suppress Falun Gong leaders and activities. As Falun Gong has spread beyond the borders of China, its persecution has become a *cause célèbre* among many. While the government is actively attacking the unofficial Falun Gong, it is also allowing a religious rebirth and rapid expansion of ritual activity among the five officially designated and monitored religions, thus demonstrating the complex and tenuous relationship that exists between religion and government in mainland China.

The anthropology of Chinese history and culture as presented here does not simply give a backdrop for contemporary China and its issues. Rather, it provides the foundation and structure for understanding what is unique about these issues in the Chinese context. Therefore, wherever one's more refined interest may lead--and there are myriad possibilities, such as sports,[57] homosexuality,[58] prostitution, elder abuse,[59] migrant workers,[60] Internet technology, globalization,[61] law,[62] or environmentalism[63]--the materials in this chapter are foundations for developing a more complete knowledge base. China is one of the most populous countries in the world, with a highly diverse population, and a rapidly changing economy. In analyzing each exciting new area or interest and to truly appreciate and to understand them, one needs to understand how they are also influenced by China's geography, prehistory, language, ethnicity, social organization, as well as historical and contemporary changes in the economic, political, and religious institutions. This chapter provides the beginning of that intellectual endeavor.

NOTES

1. Good introductory information on the paleoanthropology of China can be found in Michael Alan Park, *Biological Anthropology* (St. Louis, MO: McGraw-Hill, 2002); Bernard G. Campbell and James D. Loy, *Humankind Emerging* (Boston: Allyn & Bacon, 2002). For more in-depth discussions of Zhoukoudian see L. Binford and K. Chuan, "The Cave Home of Beijing Man," *Current Anthropology* 26(5)(1985): 413–443; L. Binford and N. M Stone, "Zhoukoudian: A Closer Look," *Current Anthropology* 27(5)(1986): 435–476.

2. One of the classic sources on the prehistory and archaeology of China is Chang Kwang-chih, *The Archaeology of Ancient China*, 4th ed. (New Haven, CT: Yale University Press, 1986). A more current survey is Judith M. Treistman, *The Prehistory of*

China (New York: Doubleday, 1972). An excellent contemporary general source on the archaeology of China is Michael Loewe and Edward Shaughnessy, eds., *The Cambridge History of Ancient China: From the Origins of Civilization to 221 B.C.* (Cambridge, England: Cambridge University Press, 1999).

3. There are several excellent sources on Chinese script and spoken languages and dialects such as Leonard Bloomfield, *Language* (Chicago: University of Chicago Press); and John DeFrancis, *The Chinese Language: Fact and Fantasy* (Honolulu: University of Hawaii Press, 1984).

4. Examples of two different dialects would be southern American English and midwestern American English. Two different languages (which are related to each other, yet are mutually unintelligible) are English and German.

5. DeFrancis, *The Chinese Language,* xix.

6. A good source for work on spoken Chinese is Ping Chen, *Modern Chinese History and Sociolinguistics* (New York: Cambridge University Press, 1999).

7. The issue of whether one Chinese dialect should be the dominant, official language or whether there should be more than one is an ongoing discussion in both mainland China and Taiwan. In mainland China, for example, Mandarin is the official language, yet the people of Hong Kong use Cantonese as their home language. Under British rule, Cantonese was taught in the schools and functioned as the dominant Chinese language. Eventually Cantonese became another marker of a "national" Hong Kong identity versus a Chinese identity. For more information on Hong Kong's development of a national identity, note Ackbar Abbas, *Hong Kong: Culture and the Politics of Disappearance* (Minneapolis: University of Minnesota Press, 1997). This is an insightful examination of Hong Kong's sense of self as it became a part of mainland China. In Taiwan, Mandarin has been the official language since the mainland Chinese came over after World War II. The home languages of Taiwanese Chinese, Hokkien, and Hakka were actively discouraged by the government. However, today, as Taiwan struggles to define itself as a nation-state many people want Hokkien to be accepted and recognized as a legitimate Taiwanese language.

8. For good sources on Chinese script see Insup Taylor and M. Martin Taylor, *Writing and Literacy in Chinese, Korean and Japanese* (Philadelphia: John Benjamins, 1995); Jerry Norman, *Chinese* (New York: Cambridge University Press, 1988); DeFrancis, *The Chinese Language*; R. H. Mathews, *Chinese-English Dictionary* (Cambridge, MA: Harvard University Press, 1971); R. H. Mathews, *KuoYü Primer* (Taipei, Taiwan: Ch'eng Wen, 1971).

9. While the primary Romanization system used in this chapter is pinyin, for many words, concepts, and names alternative spellings using other Romanization systems, such as Wade-Giles, are also indicated. This is because the reader will find these alternative systems used extensively in other materials. Therefore, both pinyin and a dominate alternative spelling will be given initially to clarify that these terms refer to the same concept or person.

10. An excellent example of this is the *K'ang Hsi Dictionary* (Kang Xi) published in 1716.

11. Major resources for Chinese history include Wolfram Eberhard, *A History of China* (Berkeley: University of California Press, 1991); John King Fairbank, *The United States and China* (Cambridge, MA: Harvard University Press, 1983); John King Fairbank, *China: A New History* (Cambridge, MA: Harvard University Press, 1992); Joseph R. Levenson, *Confucian China and Its Modern Fate* (Berkeley: University of California Press, 1965). A good source on the ideals of achieved status and its influence on the quality of historiography in China (along with many other areas of the world) is Donald E. Brown, *Hierarchy, History, and Human Nature: The Social Origins of Historical Consciousness* (Tucson: University of Arizona Press, 1988).

12. Fairbank, *China: A New History,* 94.

13. Ibid., 95. Fairbank has some very enlightening statistics on how many were able to take and pass the examinations over time: "5 out of 10 were allowed to pass in 1023, 2 out of 10 in 1045, 1 out of 10 in 1093, 1 out of 100 in 1156, and 1 out of 200 in 1275. As more competed, fewer passed." These numbers reflect (1) an increasing number of men taking the examinations, and (2) the increasing ability of those in power to limit access to their power and status positions.

14. A very readable historical account of Chinese history can be found in both Fairbank, *China: A New History*; and Joseph R. Levenson, *Confucian China and Its Modern Fate* (Berkeley: University of California Press, 1965).

15. A detailed look at the Tai-ping rebellion can be found in Timothy Brook, *The Confusions of Pleasure* (Berkeley: University of California Press, 1999); Immanuel C. Y. Hsu, *The Rise of Modern China* (New York: Oxford University Press, 1990); Franz Michael, *The Taiping Rebellion* (Seattle: University of Washington Press, 1972); Vincent Y. C. Shih, *The Taiping Ideology* (Seattle: University of Washington Press, 1967).

16. Mark Elvin, *The Pattern of the Chinese Past* (Stanford, CA: Stanford University Press, 1973). This is a unique insight into the relationship between society and economic development.

17. A general source for evaluating the ecological, economic, and political factors that played a role in China's technological achievement and lack of development (and other civilizations) is Jared Diamond, *Guns, Germs, and Steel: The Fate of Human Societies* (New York: W.W. Norton, 1997).

18. The major source on "race" and ethnicity and their role in Chinese social life, history, and politics is Frank Dikötter, *The Discourse of Race in Modern China* (Stanford, CA: Stanford University Press, 1992); and his excellent edited survey *The Construction of Racial Identities in China and Japan: Historical and Contemporary Perspectives* (Honolulu: University of Hawaii Press, 1997). Another discussion of these topics of race and ethnicity in China is Dru C. Gladney, *Muslim Chinese: Ethnic Nationalism in the People's Republic* (Cambridge, MA: Harvard University Press, 1991); and his *Ethnic Identity in China: The Making of a Muslim Minority Nationality* (Orlando, FL: Harcourt Brace, 1997). A brief discussion of these issues is in the chapter on Asia in Raymond Scupin, ed., *Race and Ethnicity: An Anthropological Focus on the U.S. and the World* (Upper Saddle River, NJ: Prentice Hall, 2002).

19. As with earlier Chinese history, the most important works for this period come from Eberhard, *A History of China*; Fairbank, *The United States and China*; Fairbank, *China: A New History*.

20. There are three administrative levels in rural China under the CCP. The commune is the highest administrative level and its headquarters is usually in the largest village. Its average size is around 15,000 people or 3,000 families. A commune usually has 15 production brigades, and each brigade has about

100 teams. A team has 20 to 50 households or 100 to 250 people. Generally speaking, the commune shares land; economic rights and responsibilities; governmental, social, and political leadership; and educational functions. Often the brigade runs the primary school, has a local clinic with paramedics (called "barefoot doctors"), plays an intermediate role in agricultural production, and is the basic level for political activities. The team is responsible for the daily activities of its members, for example, in farming and political studies. See the Area Handbook Series *China: A Country Study*, ed. Frederica M. Bunge and Rinn-Sup Shinn (Washington, DC: U.S. Government Printing Office, 1981).

21. Good historical and anthropological materials are Kwang-chih, *The Archaeology of Ancient China*; T'ung-tsu Ch'ü, *Han Social Structure* (Seattle: University of Washington Press, 1972); T'ung-tsu Ch'ü, *Local Government in China Under the Ch'ing* (Stanford, CA: Stanford University Press, 1962); Eberhard, *A History of China*; Treistman, *The Prehistory of China*; Yuen-fong Woon, *Social Organization in South China, 1911–1949* (Ann Arbor: Center for Chinese Studies, University of Michigan, 1984).

22. Lin Yutang, *My Country and My People* (New York: John Day, 1939).

23. Two interesting books on these rights and obligations are Derk Bodde and Clarence Morris, *Law in Imperial China: Exemplified by 190 Ch'ing Dynasty Cases.* (Philadelphia: University of Pennsylvania Press, 1971); and Patricia Buckley Ebrey and Peter N. Gregory, *Religion and Society in T'ang and Sung China* (Honolulu: University of Hawaii Press, 1993).

24. Bodde and Morris, *Law in Imperial China*, 391.

25. There are several good anthropological works in this area: Maurice Freedman, *Chinese Lineage and Society: Fukien and Kwangtung* (New York: Humanities Press, 1966); Morton H. Fried, *Fabric of Chinese Society* (New York: Octagon Books, 1974); Bernard Gallin, *Hsin Hsing, Taiwan: A Chinese Village in Change* (Berkeley: University of California Press, 1966); Ruth Sidel, *Women and Child Care in China* (New York: Penguin Books, 1973); Margery Wolf, *The House of Lim* (Upper Saddle River, NJ: Prentice Hall, 1968); Margery Wolf, *Women and the Family in Rural Taiwan* (Stanford, CA: Stanford University Press, 1972); C. K. Yang, *The Chinese Family in the Communist Revolution* (Cambridge, MA: MIT Press, 1972); Yun Xiang Yan, *Private Life under Socialism: Love, Intimacy, and Family Change in a Chinese Village 1949–1999* (Stanford, CA: Stanford University Press, 2003).

26. This has changed in part because of contact with the Western world and the different view of marriage and women's place in society, which leads young people to want their individual interests and desires taken into consideration when choosing a spouse.

27. An insightful contemporary look at China's attempt to control its population through limiting family size is the 2004 *National Geographic* program "China's Lost Girls" by Lisa Ling.

28. Ann Waltner, *Getting an Heir: Adoption and the Construction of Kinship in Late Imperial China* (Honolulu: University of Hawaii Press, 1990). Another good source for information on children is Anne Behnke Kinney, ed., *Chinese Views of Childhood* (Honolulu: University of Hawaii Press, 1995).

29. Waltner, *Getting an Heir*, 49.

30. Yun Xiang Yan, *Private Life under Socialism.*

31. An excellent newspaper article by Yang Xingnan, "Rejection of Female College Graduates Must Be Stopped," in *Chinese Civilization, A Sourcebook*, ed. Patricia Buckley Ebrey, 482–483 (New York: Free Press, 1993).

32. Yang, *The Chinese Family.*

33. For insight into the ramifications of this view and for further discussion on contemporary women laborers, read Ching Kwan Lee's ethnographic work *Gender and the South China Miracle, Two Worlds of Factory Women* (Berkeley: University of California Press, 1998).

34. Information on this aspect of women's lives can be found in E. Honig and G. Hershatter, *Personal Voices* (Stanford, CA: Stanford University Press, 1988); and "Economic Liberalization and New Problems for Women," chapter 97, Buckley Ebrey, *Chinese Civilization.* An example of a fictional account is Yuan-Tsung Chen, *The Dragon's Village, An Autobiographical Novel of Revolutionary China* (New York: Penguin Books, 1980). Two good references showing how complex this topic is, however, are Goran Aijmer and Virgil K. Y. Ho, *Cantonese Society in a Time of Change* (Hong Kong: Chinese University Press, 2000); and Ellen R. Judd, *The Chinese Women's Movement, between State and Market* (Stanford, CA: Stanford University Press, 2002). One of the most current overviews of gender (both male and female) is Susan Brownell and Jeffrey N. Wasserstrom, eds., *Chinese Feminities, Chinese Masculinities: A Reader* (Berkeley: University of California Press, 2002). This volume contains state-of-the-art anthropological and historical essays on gender issues during various historical periods including the Maoist and post-Maoist period with discussions on marriage, law, gender identity, and homosexuality; and literature on gender, prostitution, sexuality, gender, and ethnicity. Brownell and Wasserstrom provide an excellent introduction and afterword summarizing the major generalizations and specifics of gender research in China.

35. Noteworthy work in this area includes Fei Xiaotung, *Xiangtu zhongguo* [Folk China] (Shanghai, China: Guancha Press, 1947); Robert H. Silin, *Leadership and Values: The Organization of Large-Scale Taiwanese Enterprises* (Cambridge, MA: Harvard University Press, 1976); Yunxiang Yan, *The Flow of Gifts: Reciprocity and Social Networks in a Chinese Village* (Stanford, CA: Stanford University Press, 1996). One of the earliest discussions of group-based versus individual-based relationships in China is Francis Hsu, *Under the Ancestor's Shadow: Chinese Culture and Personality* (New York: Columbia University Press, 1948).

36. This is why other anthropologists, such as Yun XiangYan, who also studied Chinese concepts involving relationships, maintained that China was neither individual nor group based, but rather relationship based.

37. Good sources for these concepts and how they are used in Chinese culture and society are Morton H. Fried, *Fabric of Chinese Society* (New York: Octagon Books, 1974); Bernard Gallin, *Hsin Hsing, Taiwan: A Chinese Village in Change* (Berkeley: University of California Press, 1966); Ambrose Yeo-chi King, "Kuan-hsi and Network Building: A Sociological Interpretation," in *The Living Tree: The Changing Meaning of Being Chinese Today*, ed. Tu Wei-ming (Stanford, CA: Stanford University Press, 1994); Silin, *Leadership and Values*; Yan, *The Flow of Gifts*; Mayfair Mei-hui Yang, *Gifts, Favors & Banquets: The Art of Social Relationships in China* (New York: Cornell University Press, 1994).

38. Silin, Leadership and Values, 43.
39. Yang. *Gifts, Favors, Banquets,* V51.
40. To read more on these two types of relationships refer to Tu Wei-min, ed. *The Living Tree.*
41. Defining early work on ethnicity are Fredrick Barth, *Ethnic Groups and Boundaries: The Social Organization of Culture Difference* (Boston: Little Brown, 1969); and George DeVos, "Ethnic Pluralism: Conflict and Accommodation" in *Ethnic Identity: Cultural Communities and Change,* edited by DeVos and Lola Romanucci-Ross (Palo Alto, CA: Mayfield Press, 1975). A good brief overview of the concept of ethnic groups is Charles F. Keyes, "Ethnicity," in *The Dictionary of Anthropology,* ed. Thomas Barfield (Oxford, England: Blackwell, 1997).
42. Good source material for this area is June Teufel Dreyer, *China's Forty Millions: Minority Nationalities and National Integration in the People's Republic of China* (Cambridge, MA: Harvard University Press, 1976); Arthur F. Wright, *Buddhism in Chinese History* (Stanford, CA: Stanford University Press, 1971); Tu Wei-ming, *The Living Tree*; Hsu, *Under the Ancestors' Shadow*; David Y. H. Wu, "Culture Change and Ethnic Identity among Minorities in China," in *Ethnicity and Ethnic Groups in China,* ed. Chien Chiao and Nicholas Tapp (Hong Kong: New Asia College, 1989); David Y. H. Wu, "Chinese Minority Policy and the Meaning of Minority Culture: The Example of Bai in Yunnan, China," in *Human Organization,* March 1990.
43. Frank Dikötter's book on race in China is *The Discourse of Race in Modern China* (Palo Alto, CA: Stanford University Press, 1992).
44. Teufel Dreyer, *China's Forty Millions,* 61.
45. Another example is the increasingly hostile relationship between the Han Chinese and the Uighurs, a Muslim minority found largely in Zinjian province. Where once they were intermediaries between the Yuan Dynasty's emperor and his Chinese subjects, they are now considered terrorists by the Chinese government. Using direct measures (arrest, imprisonment, and execution of Uighurs) and indirect (the forced migration of Han Chinese into Zinjiang Province) the Chinese government is using long-established techniques to control the area. For more information see John Derbyshire, "Hell, No, Uighur Won't Go," *The Weekly Standard,* December 5, 1999, and the Uygur.org Web site.
46. Dru Gladney's major book on Muslims in China is *Muslim Chinese.* Gladney's other more recent discussion of ethnic identity in China is *Ethnic Identity in China.* Another ethnographic study of the Islamic developments in China is Maris Boyd Gillette, *Between Mecca and Beijing: Modernization and Consumption Among Urban Chinese Muslims* (Palo Alto, CA: Stanford University Press, 2000).
47. A good overview of the Tibetan issue is David Maybury-Lewis, *Indigenous Peoples, Ethnic Groups, and the State,* 2nd ed. (Boston: Pearson Education, Allyn & Bacon, 2002). The most knowledgeable Western anthropologist of Tibet is Melvyn Goldstein. For a well-written overview of Tibetan religion and politics see Melvyn C. Goldstein, *The Snow Lion and the Dragon: China, Tibet and the Dalai Lama* (Berkeley: University of California Press, 1999). Also, for a recent discussion of religious and ethnic identity in Tibet see Melvyn Goldstein and M. Kapstein, eds., *Buddhism in Contemporary Tibet: Religious Revival and National Identity* (Berkeley: University of California Press, 1999). In addition, more recently Goldstein has collaborated with Dawei Sharep and William Siebenschuh to examine the role of a contemporary Tibetan revolutionary in *A Tibetan Revolutionary: The Political Life of Bapa Phuntso Wangye* (Berkeley: University of California Press, 2004). For a good overview on religious developments in Tibetan Buddhism and the anthropology of Buddhism see Marcia Calkowski's chapter titled "Buddhism," in *Religion and Culture: An Anthropological Focus,* ed. Raymond Scupin (Upper Saddle River, NJ: Prentice Hall, 2000).
48. Robert Redfield, "The Folk Society," *American Journal of Sociology* 52 (1947): 293–308; Robert Redfield, *Peasant Society and Culture* (Chicago: University of Chicago Press, 1967); Arthur F. Wright, *Buddhism in Chinese History* (Stanford, CA: Stanford University Press, 1971).
49. For an excellent discussion on Dao and Daoism see Laurence G. Thompson, *Chinese Religion: An Introduction,* 5th ed. (Belmont, CA: Dickenson, 1996); Chang Chung-yuan, *Tao: A New Way of Thinking* (Taipei, Taiwan: Chang Chung-yuan, 1975); Yen Ling-feng, *A Reconstructed Lao Tzu* (Taipei, Taiwan: Ch'eng Wen, 1976). For a discussion on philosophical Daoism (representing the Great Tradition) and folk Daoism (representing the Little Tradition) see D. Howard Smith, *Chinese Religions from 1000 B.C. to the Present Day* (New York: Holt, Rinehart and Winston, 1968); Christian Jochim, *Chinese Religions,* (Upper Saddle River, NJ: Prentice Hall, 1986); Donald S. Lopez, Jr., ed., *Religions of China in Practice* (Princeton, NJ: Princeton University Press, 1996).
50. Chang Chung-yuan, *Tao: A New Way of Thinking,* 3.
51. A good example of this is the charming work of Tsai Chih Chung (C. C. Tsai), a famous cartoonist who published *The Dao of Zhuangzi: The Harmony of Nature* as a comic book with the classic text put into modern Chinese.
52. For a discussion of Buddhism's historical development as a foreign religion that became sinicized see Thompson, *Chinese Religion*; Fairbank, *China: A New History*; and Wright, *Buddhism in Chinese History.*
53. For a good overview of Confucius and Confucianism see Jochim, *Chinese Religions*; Wright, *Buddhism in Chinese History.*
54. Wright, *Buddhism in Chinese History,* 16–17.
55. An excellent ethnographic study of the growth and viability of Chinese religions in the mainland as well as overseas is Kenneth J. Guests, *God in Chinatown* (New York: New York University Press, 2003). Another good source is Goran Aijmer and Virgil K. Y. Ho, *Cantonese Society in a Time of Change* (Hong Kong: Chinese University Press, 2000). Robert P. Weller addresses the issue of how religion can be used to threaten governments in "Matricidal Magistrates and Gambling Gods: Weak States and Strong Spirits in China," in *Unholy Gods, Divinity and Society in China,* ed. Meir Shahar and Robert P. Weller (Honolulu: University of Hawaii Press, 1996). Notable sources for religious revival in Taiwan are P. Steven Sangren, *History and Magical Power in a Chinese Community* (Stanford, CA: Stanford University Press, 1987); and Wang Mingming, "Shiding Village," *Chinese Studies in History* 34, no. 4 (Summer 2001): 12–83. For a discussion of both mainland China and Taiwan see Robert P. Weller, *Resistance, Chaos and Control in China* (Seattle: University of Washington Press, 1994); and Robert P. Weller, *Alternate Civilities* (Boulder, CO: Westview Press, 1999).
56. Studies to examine for further information on contemporary religion include Julian F. Pas, ed., *The Turning of the*

Tide: Religion in China Today (Hong Kong: Oxford University Press, 1989); Kenneth Dean, *Lord of the Three in One: The Spread of a Cult in Southeast China* (Princeton, NJ: Princeton University Press, 1998); and Mayfair Yang, "Putting Global Capitalism in Its Place: Economic Hybridity, Bataille, and Ritual Expenditure," *Current Anthropology* 41, no. 4 (2000) 477–495.

57. Susan Brownell's landmark work *Training the Body for China: Sports in the Moral Order of the People's Republic* (Chicago: University of Chicago Press, 1995); and her "Strong Women and Impotent Men: Sports, Gender, and Nationalism in Chinese Public Culture" in edited volume *Spaces of Their Own: Women's Public Sphere in Transnational China*, ed. Mayfair Mei-hui Yang Minneapolis: University of Minnesota Press, 1999).

58. For a discussion of contemporary homosexuality see John A. Wiggins, Jr., "'May I Talk to You?' Ethno-Sexual Encounters in Taipei's New Park—A Queer Ethnography," *East Asia* (Winter 2000).

59. This difficult topic is dealt with in Elsie Yan, Catherine So-kum Tang, and Dannii Yeung, "No Safe Haven: A Review on Elder Abuse in Chinese Families," *Trauma, Violence & Abuse* 3, no. 3 (2002): 167–181.

60. Nicole Constable has written a fascinating account of Filipina workers in Hong Kong: *Maid to Order in Hong Kong: Stories of Filipina Workers* (Ithaca, NY: Cornell University Press, 1997). A more recent article concerning Filipina workers was titled "An Anthropology of Happiness," *The Economist* 361, no. 8253 (2001): 42.

61. A good beginning book for this area is Henry Wai-Chung Yeung and Kris Olds, eds., *Globalization of Chinese Business Firms* (New York: St. Martin's Press, 2000); and Frank Jurgen Richter, ed., *Business Networks in Asia: Promises, Doubts, and Perspectives* (Westport, CT: Quorum Books, 1999).

62. See, for example, David C. Buxbaum, ed., *Chinese Family Law and Social Change in Historical and Comparative Perspective* (Seattle: University of Washington Press, 1978).

63. This is an area of great concern since by size alone China's negative or positive behavior will have a great impact on the environment. Excellent basic references are: for environmental history see Mark Elvin, *The Retreat of the Elephants: An Environmental History of China* (New Haven, CT: Yale University Press, 2004); for general introductions to China's challenges see Vaclav Smil, *China's Past, China's Future: Energy, Food, Environment* (New York: RoutledgeCurzon, 2004) and Richard Louis Edmonds, *Patterns of China's Lost Harmony: A Survey of the Country's Environmental Degradation and Protection* (London: Routledge, 1994); for non-Han regions see Dee Mack Williams, *Beyond Great Walls: Environment, Identity and Development on the Chinese Grasslands of Inner Mongolia* (Stanford, CA: Stanford University Press, 2000). An essential review of China's energy system is Michael McElroy, Chris P. Nielsen, and Peter Lydon, *Energizing China: Reconciling Environmental Protection and Economic Growth* (Cambridge, MA: Harvard University Committee on Environment, 1998); and Elizabeth Economy, *The River Runs Black: The Environmental Challenge to China's Future* (Ithaca, NY: Cornell University Press, 2004).

6 JAPAN

John L. McCreery and Ruth S. McCreery

What is Japan to you?

- Famous brands: Toyota, Nissan, Honda, Sony, Toshiba, Sharp. How many more can you name?
- Entertainment: *Manga, anime, idoru,* video games, a setting for science fiction novels or thrillers?
- Fashion: Issey Miyake, Kenzo, Comme des Garcons. Have you ever worn their clothes?
- Tradition: Zen, swords, shrines, temples, martial arts, tea ceremony. Does anything else come to mind?
- Exotic food: *sushi, sashimi, sukiyaki, tempura,* Cup Noodle. What else?
- The world's second largest economy: A market where brands like Coca-Cola, McDonald's, and KFC have been part of the landscape for generations and newcomers like Kinkos, Toys R Us, and Starbucks have done very well, indeed. Are there still opportunities there?
- A nation in search of a role: With a constitution that renounces war and the second largest military in Asia, what role should Japan play in global politics?

If you feel confused, you aren't alone. As consumers and scholars, business people and diplomats, individuals who deal with Japan see Japan (in Japanese, *Nihon* or *Nippon*[1]) in different ways. Japan is always changing, and so are the perspectives of the authors who write about Japan, including the anthropologists.

The resource titled *Doing Fieldwork in Japan* brings together chapters by 21 scholars.[2] The topics on which they did their research are as varied as the individuals who chose them. In the order in which they appear, they include Japanese teenagers who hang out in Harajuku, Tokyo's teen fashion Mecca; radical student movements; a rural community in Kyushu, the southernmost of Japan's four main islands; a new religion reinterpreting Buddhist belief and practice to meet the needs of modern believers; an ancient but still thriving pilgrimage on Shikoku, the smallest of the four main islands (think Chaucer in a tour bus); a bioscience institute located in Osaka, the commercial heart of Kansai, the southwestern part of Japan; the impact of JETs, participants in the Japan Exchange and Teaching Program, on English-language education; the prosecutors' office in Kobe, which along with Osaka and Kyoto is one of the three major cities in the Kansai; security policy making by the Japanese Defense Agency and Ministry of Foreign Affairs; NHK, Japan's public broadcaster; a quantitative study of women in the labor market and why men's wages are so much higher than women's; the impact of mine closure on a coal-mining community in Hokkaido, the northernmost of the four main islands; Japanese bureaucrats responsible for addressing the problems of the elderly,

RUSSIA
CHINA
Kanggye
SEA
OF
JAPAN
NORTH
KOREA
Wonsan
Demarcation line
and Demilitarized
zone (DMZ)
P'YONGYANG
KOREA
BAY
SEOUL
Wonju
SOUTH
KOREA
TAEGU
JAPAN
YELLOW
SEA
KOREA STRAIT

a rapidly growing segment of the Japanese population; Japanese foreign aid (Japan being one of the world's largest donors); modern Japanese social history, with a focus on the Japanese labor movement; *enka*, an old-fashioned but still popular music genre, whose role in Japanese popular culture resembles that of Country and Western in the United States; two corporations, a lingerie manufacturer and a foreign multinational in the financial services industry; the creation of tradition in a changing Tokyo neighborhood and Tsukiji, the world's largest seafood market; the betwixt-and-between lives of reverse immigrants, Japanese Brazilian workers in Japan; and a review of a long and distinguished career that began with a study of a rural community and has included an award from Japan's emperor.

This list is long, but it still contains only a sample of what it might. Where are the studies of bar hostesses and geisha, kindergartens, bikers and bankers, blue-collar workers, the homeless, the aging, the comics, the artists, the shamans, the celebrities who make up the *geinôkai* (the world of the *tarento*, "talents," performers and personalities who appear on TV, in movies, in ads), the potters, the fishermen, the cops, the gangsters, the juvenile delinquents, the baseball players, the sumo wrestlers, the account executives and art directors who work for advertising agencies, the women who get out the vote for local politicians, the mothers, the office ladies, the young women who travel overseas in search of handbags, love, new careers, and new selves? The list gets longer every day.[3]

Note, too, that when we study Japan, we do not have the luxury of studying the lives of people who inhabit an isolated corner of the globe and, so far as the rest of the world is concerned, have nothing to say about how we describe their behavior. We study the lives of people who are often as highly educated and may be wealthier and more powerful than the anthropologists who struggle to understand how they think, feel, and behave. No place on earth illustrates more vividly the anthropological predicament that Marcus and Fischer describe so well: "We step into a stream of already existing representations produced by journalists, prior anthropologists, historians, creative writers, and of course the subjects of study themselves."[4]

THE ROAD AHEAD

No chapter could ever be more than a taste of the vast, complex, and constantly changing reality of Japan. The taste this chapter offers combines three ingredients. The first is a prowl through Yokohama, Japan's second largest city, in search of things Japanese. As you read this part of the chapter, imagine that you have just gotten off a plane at Narita International Airport and taken the NEX (Narita Express) to Yokohama Station. Your friends meet you there, take you home for a rest, and then drag you off to see the city. Since you don't speak the language, you are looking, tasting, sniffing, touching, while keeping an ear open for what your guides have to say.

Like many of the Japanese among whom they have lived for more than two decades, your friends, the authors of this chapter, are history and archeology buffs. They are deeply committed to the idea that to know a place well, you need to know not only its history but its prehistory as well. That is why the prowl begins by stepping out on their balcony and having them talk your ear off about these two subjects. In the rest of section 1 we will examine Japanese cities and the homes in which the majority of Japanese now live. We will also look at their toilets and their baths, how they dress, and the food they eat, their religions, and their language.

Section 2 explores a suite of common ideas about Japan, what it is to be Japanese, and the nature of Japanese society. We will look at where those ideas came from, the issues being addressed when these ideas were formulated, and what has become of them since. Our approach will be highly selective, focused on the research of three remarkable anthropologists, who all happen to be women. One is an American forced to study Japan from a distance, one a Japanese who studied anthropology in Britain, did fieldwork in India, then brought her comparative perspective home, and one is a Japanese American whose fieldwork in Japan tests her understanding of her own, partly Japanese, identity. The first two attempted the impossible—to summarize Japan in one short book. While frequently criticized, the books they wrote were so powerful that they have shaped discussions of Japan ever since they were published. The third book illustrates a newer, more modest approach to the study of Japanese lives.

Our first author conceives of her research as the study of patterns of culture, habits of thought, behavior, and feeling. The second sees Japanese society through the lens of social structure, how groups and individuals relate to each other. The third focuses on stories and how stories are used to construct different kinds of Japanese selves.[5]

In section 3, we will look at the dramatic changes that have reshaped Japanese society since World War II. Our focus will be on the Japanese household and on how Japanese families have been affected by changing labor markets, the demographics of an aging society, and the growth of rampant consumerism. We will address them through four key topics: gender, generation, social class, and geography.

By the end of this chapter you will have had only a taste of Japan. If you wish to learn more, however, you will have a foundation on which to build as you study the topics of your choice: a sense of what you might experience if you travel to Japan, a set of ideas that are likely to appear in one form or another in whatever you read about Japan, a sense of their power and limitations, and, finally, some knowledge of the fundamental changes that are now reshaping Japan.

ENCOUNTERING JAPAN

To the authors of this chapter, Japan is, first and foremost, the High Town, the corner of Yokohama where we have lived since September 1980, where our daughter grew up and attended a local kindergarten and the local elementary school. Our home is one of 440 condominium units (ranging between 50 and 70 square meters [164 and 230 square feet] in floor space) that make up a complex that was, our neighbors tell us, an architectural marvel when it was built in 1970. Then it was seen as a symbol of a modern lifestyle to which many Japanese aspired. Now its plain ferroconcrete structures look and feel old-fashioned compared to the newer buildings that have sprung up around us. They offer larger apartments (80 square meters [262 square feet] is common). Their tastefully colored tile exteriors, bits of stained glass and landscaping, and the absence of rules against pets contrast with the modernist functionality that the High Town represents. Parking garages and broadband Internet connections enhance what are still at heart, however, high-density machines for living.

The High Town is built on one of several ridges that radiate toward the sea, creating a hilly landscape reminiscent of San Francisco. From our second-story veranda, we look down on a narrow road that winds down the hill to our local shopping street. On one side of the road is a small park equipped with swings, a jungle gym, and other play equipment that might be found in Omaha or London. Directly across from it, however, is a private cemetery. The distinctively shaped tombstones, the long wooden markers for each memorial service held for the dead whose ashes are buried beneath each stone, the scent of incense that sometimes permeates the air, and the standing Buddha carved into one slightly tipsy stone remind us that we are in Japan. A little further on, on the left, stands a lovely, now rare, example of a wood-frame house that a guidebook would label traditionally Japanese in style. Its garden, glimpsed over the wall that surrounds it, is one of the neighborhood's treasures.

A variety of small businesses line the shopping street below. There we encounter the liquor store and the butcher who, during the real estate boom of the 1980s, replaced his old two-story building with his display case open to and facing the street with a four-story building with a small supermarket on the ground floor.[6] The greengrocer and fishmonger still work out of old-fashioned open-front shops, though they too have rebuilt in ferroconcrete, with apartments above their shops.

A bit further down are a stationery shop that caters to the students at the local elementary school, a barber, and a drycleaner. Other businesses scattered along the street include a bakery, a florist, a lumberyard, a tea seller, two dentists, an orthopedic surgeon, three restaurants, two bars, and a shoe store. Where the shopping street Ts into a main four-lane road, what used to be another liquor store has become a Lawson convenience store, whose services include a 24-hour ATM as well as parcel delivery. At this and other convenience stores, customers can buy tickets to concerts, pay their utility bills, or pick up a quick meal. The Lawson is usually busy, but the other shops along the street are not doing so well. Like their counterparts in other parts of the world, they have been losing trade to large supermarkets and discount stores in nearby suburbs or urban shopping centers as well as to convenience stores like the Lawson.

According to real estate ads, we are located an 18-minute walk from Yokohama Station, where several major rail lines intersect. An estimated 1.7 million persons use it daily, making it, along with Shinjuku and Shibuya in Tokyo, one of Japan's busiest stations. The station complex is also, in effect, a huge shopping mall, anchored by four major department stores. In terms of sales per square meter, this complex is among the most profitable retail spaces in Japan.[7]

Those are huge claims, indeed. Yokohama is now Japan's second largest city, with a population of 3.5 million. Only Tokyo, with a population of 8 million, is larger. Together they account for about a quarter of the 40 million people who inhabit the seven prefectures that make up the Kanto region, or a bit less than 10 percent of Japan's total population of 127 million.[8]

Japanese often say that Japan is a small, crowded country with few natural resources. At rush hour in Yokohama, there is no disputing the "crowded" part. Geographically speaking, however, Japan is larger than Germany and Italy and nearly twice the size of Britain. Its population is larger than that of any country in western Europe.

According to World Bank statistics for 2002, Japan has the world's second largest gross domestic product (GDP), $3,978,782 million (US), a figure smaller than that for the United States but larger than that of Germany, Britain, France, and China.[9] Organisation for Economic Co-operation and Development (OECD) statistics for 2001 put Japan's per capita GDP at $32,800 (US), well above the $29,300 (US) G7 average.[10] Prices are somewhat high in Japan, so in terms of purchasing power Japan is slightly on the low side. By any standard, however, Japan is a rich country, and Yokohama shares in that wealth.

A Constantly Changing Landscape

From where we stand on our High Town veranda, our line of sight is interrupted by a tall cluster of trees at the end of the ridge that forms the other side of the valley in which the shopping street is located. These trees mark the site of our neighborhood Shinto shrine, which enshrines the deity that protects our area. Shortly after we moved to the neighborhood, it celebrated the nine hundredth anniversary of its founding.

Just beyond the ridge on which the shrine sits is a narrow street, a humble remnant of the old Tokaido, the main highway for travelers between Kyoto, the ancient imperial capital, and Edo, the city now called Tokyo that rose to prominence four centuries ago when the Tokugawa shoguns made it their capital.

But Japanese urban landscapes are restless. So much has changed since 1980. Then the blocks that lie between our shopping street and Yokohama Station were a mixed residential-commercial-industrial zone of mostly one- or two-story buildings. Now they are filled with office and high-rise apartment buildings. The *soba* (Japanese buckwheat) noodle shop from which we sometimes order lunch now has an "Italian Wine and Antipasto" bar next door that serves up elegant dinners designed to stimulate consumption of vintage Italian wines. A short distance away is a small lumber yard sandwiched between two office buildings, the last remnant of what was once a major local industry based on logs floated down the rivers that fed into the bay.

Rising above the trees that surround our neighborhood shrine—and actually located several kilometers beyond them, on Tokyo Bay—is Landmark Tower, Japan's tallest building and the centerpiece of Minato Mirai 21 (MM21), an urban reconstruction project conceived as Yokohama's vision of the ultramodern nation that Japan would become in the twenty-first century. The bottom five floors of Landmark Tower house a shopping complex with an atrium of epic proportions. The next 50 floors are an office building. The top 25 are a luxury hotel. The MM21 area also includes museums, parks, a convention center, a hospital, more hotels and office buildings, a concert hall, and, of course, more shopping.

Taking a Longer View

The earliest human inhabitants of the ridge where the High Town is located may have been Jômon hunters and gatherers, who lived in Japan as early as 13,000 BCE. A short walk takes us to a public park that sits on top of a late Jômon shell midden. The shells came from the sea that, in an earlier era of global warming, used to lap right at the foot of the ridges. "Late Jômon" means sometime before 300 BCE, when rice cultivation began in Japan, and a culture now called Yayoi emerged.[11]

Jomon pottery.

The first written mention of Japan occurs six centuries later. The historical records of China's Wei dynasty mention a land called Wa, with a female ruler named Himiko. These records describe Himiko as being skilled in magic and ruling by enchanting her people. Normally she remained concealed in her palace, while her brother governed on her behalf. This division of authority between a sacred chief and a governor who acts on behalf of the chief is one that echoes throughout Japanese history.

Precisely where Wa was located is a matter for scholarly dispute. Some authorities say Kyushu, the southernmost of Japan's four main islands. Others say Honshu, the largest of the four main islands, in the area now called Kansai, where the cities of Osaka and Kobe and the old imperial capitals of Nara and Kyoto are located.

According to historian Joan Piggott, the five centuries that followed Himiko saw

> an array of paramounts and kings variously styled King of Wa, Child of Heaven, and Heavenly Sovereign. They presided over first confederate chieftaincies, then expansive coalescent polities, and eventually the [Japanese] archipelago's earliest state formation.[12]

The state to which Piggott refers adapted its laws and rituals from those of China's Tang dynasty. The descendants of its Heavenly Sovereigns are Japan's imperial family today.

During the Nara and Heian periods (710–1185 CE), that first Japanese state flourished, then decayed. During this period, Buddhism imported from China established strong roots in Japan, complementing and influencing the native animism, now called Shinto. The Japanese language began to be written in a combination of Chinese characters and Japanese syllabaries based on simplified characters, the writing system still used today. Murasaki Shikibu wrote *The Tale of Genji*, the world's first great novel.

During the subsequent Kamakura (1185–1333), Muromachi (1333–1568), and Azuchi-Momoyama (1568–1600) periods, warlords fought for control of Japan, with alternating periods of centralized government control and collapse and civil war. The largely powerless emperors remained above the fray; their role was mainly ceremonial. They did, however, continue to provide the sacred validation required to legitimate the authority of the shoguns (chief warlords, literally "barbarian-subduing generals"). Like Himiko, these later emperors played a largely ceremonial role.

Over these centuries, the land under centralized control, the land that was called "Nihon," continued to expand northeastward, up the Japanese archipelago, a process not completed until the nineteenth century, when Hokkaido, the northernmost of Japan's four main islands, was finally absorbed. But the triumph of the Tokugawa, who ruled throughout the Edo period (1600–1868), marked a definitive shift in the center of political power, from the Kansai to the Kanto, where Edo, now Tokyo, is located.[13]

Edo Society

The Tokugawa shoguns created a political system similar in several respects to European feudalism. Japan was divided into domains governed by feudal lords, the *daimyô*. Society was conceived as made up of distinct hereditary social classes.

The *samurai* started out as warriors, the vassals who had fought for their lords, the shoguns and daimyô, although during the long Tokugawa peace they became more bureaucrats than warriors.[14] They continued to wear their swords; but with no wars to fight, they had to get by on the stipends that they earned as administrators.

Farmers were, in theory, next in importance and prestige. Agriculture was seen as the source of all wealth. In practice, however, farmers were heavily taxed peasants, legally forbidden to leave their villages.

There was one striking difference from medieval Europe, where lords continued to live on their manors and interact directly with the serfs who farmed the land. The samurai were separated from the land and concentrated in the towns that grew up around daimyô castles. As a result, the villages in which the farmers lived were largely self-governing, and individual samurai had no peasantry of their own to mobilize in time of war.

Craftworkers ranked third in the Edo caste system. Like farmers, they too were seen as productive members of society. Merchants ranked fourth, while the *eta*, whose livelihoods as executioners and leatherworkers involved dead bodies, were outcastes. Polluted by their occupations, they were society's negative pole—the antithesis of the pure and holy emperors, in relation to whom other classes were ranked. The outcastes' pollution defined society's bottom, as the emperors' transcendence defined the top.

In theory, merchants ranked low, for they were not seen as making an important contribution to society. But in practice they became increasingly wealthy. The Tokugawa creation of a stable society and a nationwide market created opportunities that the abler merchants seized upon to make themselves rich. They became moneylenders and bankers to the samurai, who, stuck with fixed incomes, found themselves increasingly impoverished as standards of living and prices both rose.

Japan was, moreover, no exception to a pattern found round the world, wherever impoverished aristocrats and moneyed merchants mingle. Marriage and adoption became mechanisms for converting merchant wealth into samurai status, economic into social capital. The new class created by these unions, samurai with merchant connections, would play a critical role in the next great stage of Japanese history, the Meiji Restoration of 1868.

The Meiji Restoration

In 1853 an American naval flotilla commanded by Commodore Matthew Galbraith Perry arrived in Japanese waters. Perry came to Japan seeking access to Japanese ports for American and other merchants excluded from Japan by Tokugawa Ieyasu's decision to close the country to foreigners in 1639. To a moribund shogunate, the modern cannon of Perry's steam-powered "black ships" were the last straw in a growing threat that included pressure from other foreign powers, reinforced by China's defeat by Britain in the Opium Wars. So, when Perry returned in 1854, the shogun signed a treaty that granted most of Perry's demands. Other treaties, with European powers as well as the United States, soon followed.

The shogun's capitulation to foreign demands did not, however, sit well with many outside the shogunate's inner circles. In 1868, after years of unrest and a brief civil war, the shogunate collapsed, replaced during the Meiji Restoration by a new government whose leaders proclaimed that they were restoring the authority of the emperor, to whom it rightly belonged.

In part, the leaders of the restoration were driven by long-standing resentment of Tokugawa dominance. Many came from domains that had been among the last to accept Tokugawa rule and remained outsiders in Edo corridors of power. But their motives included new aspirations as well. The ideas to which they appealed stressed Japan's uniqueness but included in that uniqueness the ability to accept and mold foreign influence, while Japan remained true to itself. Pointing backward to Japanese domestication of Chinese writing, Chinese Buddhism, and the Chinese-style imperial state, these ideas also pointed forward—to adopting European and American models while shaping them to fit what was seen as Japan's unique national essence.

Two critical factors reinforced their thinking. The West was both a threat and a source of legitimacy. The late nineteenth century was the heyday of imperialism, with British, French, Germans, Russians, and Americans all scrambling to seize control of as much of the world as they could conquer. This period also saw the flourishing of idealistic nationalism, the belief that nations are natural entities, each with its own blood, soil, and language. Rivalry with the imperialists drove Japan to seek its own place in the sun. At the same time, however, nationalistic philosophies justified its insistence on Japanese uniqueness. Together they formed a potent combination that would lead Japan to modernization, totalitarianism, and war.[15]

Transforming Japan

The post-restoration leaders (known to historians as the Meiji oligarchs) dismantled the rigid Tokugawa caste system that divided Japanese into warriors (samurai), farmers, craftsworkers, merchants, and outcastes and insisted that all Japanese share the same national identity. While reinforcing what they saw as the core of that identity, unstinting and sacrificial loyalty to the emperor, they embraced and domesticated what they saw as the best Western models for modern nation building. As Edwin Reischauer puts it, "They went to England to study the navy and merchant marine, to Germany for the army and for medicine, to France for local government and law, and to the United States for business methods."[16]

The Meiji oligarchs recognized that schools were not only essential to equip Japanese with the habits and skills that a modern economy would require; schools were also the ideal places to instill the Restoration's imperial and nationalistic ideals. In 1871, they created a Ministry of Education and embarked on a program of universal education that has made modern Japan one of the world's most thoroughly schooled societies.

Japan's success astonished the world. After defeating China in the Sino-Japanese War of 1895, the Japanese established themselves as successful imperialists by acquiring Taiwan as a colony. Next, in 1905, they won their first war against a European power, defeating Russia. European preoccupation with World War I, the Great Depression, and then the onset of World War II opened the way, it seemed, for Japan to create a Greater East Asian Co-Prosperity Sphere, a part of the world in which Japan would be the natural ruler. Fear that America would cut off vital supplies led to Pearl Harbor and a war of initial successes followed by crushing defeat—the firebombing of Tokyo, the atomic bombs dropped on Hiroshima and Nagasaki, the emperor's surrender, and the occupation by American forces from August 1945 to April 1952.

As John Dower writes, however, the Japanese were down but not out.[17] The postwar years, the decade following World War II, were a time of poverty, as a devastated Japan began to rebuild. Then Japan's economy began to take off. From 1955 to 1970, Japan's economic growth far outstripped that in Europe and America. Following the 1971 Nixon Shock (the end of a yen artificially pegged at 360 yen to the dollar) and the Oil Shock of 1973, when skyrocketing Organization of the Petroleum Exporting Countries (OPEC) oil prices sent economies around the world reeling, the pace slowed but growth continued. Then, in the 1980s it accelerated again. For a brief moment at the end of that decade, Japan's economy seemed almighty. The phrase "Pax Japonica" was bandied about. At the height of the "bubble economy" (largely a stock and real estate bubble that collapsed in 1991), the grounds of the imperial palace alone were said to be equal in value to the whole state of California.

The economic bubble's collapse has been followed by more than a decade of economic stagnation, compounded by demographics that Japan shares with other advanced, industrial nations: a rapidly falling birthrate and a rapidly aging population. Japanese aged 65 and older outnumber those aged 15 and younger. Some pundits bemoan the loss of national vitality. Others try to envision a quieter but more spiritually fulfilling future, still affluent, of course, but less obsessed with material goods and more in tune with natural (now conceived as ecological) rhythms.

Japan remains a wealthy nation, but what the future will bring is a source of deep anxiety. The economy has recovered from the post-bubble recession, but sustained growth driven by domestic demand remains elusive. Even relatively optimistic economists writing works such as *Japanese Phoenix: The Long Road to Economic Revival* suggest that there are structural problems that will take a long time to solve.[18]

The Japanese Urban Experience

According to Australian urban planner Barrie Shelton, Europeans who visited Japan during the seventeenth century found much to admire in Japanese cities.[19] They commented on their size, their cleanliness, and the size and number of bridges, as well as the sharp division between the areas inhabited by the warrior classes, where there were houses in gardens, with those where the merchants and artisans lived in houses aligned along the streets. One perceptive Spanish observer noted that while Spanish houses looked better from the outside, Japanese houses were more beautiful inside.

Nineteenth- and early-twentieth-century visitors had a far more negative impression. They

An aerial view of Tokyo.

found Japanese cities chaotic and monotonous. Japanese cities lacked, they reported, any semblance of clear city planning. Most buildings were similar, and only one or two stories tall. With no grand vistas, the landscapes they filled seemed boring and tedious. The buildings themselves seemed flimsy and shoddily constructed. These were, to be fair, the views of observers to whom the state of the art in city planning was a city like Paris, with a clear center and the Champs D'Elysees.

More recent observers, including Shelton himself, have begun to reassess these judgments. He cites, for example, the German author Gunther Nitschke, who suggests that the Japanese sense of urban space is not something created by compositional elements, with spaces defined by buildings and walls. Japanese places are defined by human activities; their character changes as the activities that fill them start and stop. He notes how English author Peter Popham describes the urban fabric of Tokyo as similar to a basket of eggs, with soft residential "yolks" surrounded by hard commercial "shells." Turning to Japanese authorities, he describes how architect Ashihara Yoshinobu contrasts Japanese and Western cities. Ashihara begins with traditional Japanese buildings, highlighting, for example, the Japanese focus on the floor instead of the wall, ambiguity instead of clarity in distinguishing inside and outside, an irregular and omnidirectional structure that contrasts sharply with Western emphases on symmetry and front. Inspired by Mandelbrot's fractal geometry, Ashihara suggests that Japanese cities embody a flexible, orderly structure that underlies their apparent chaos.

Shelton concludes his survey of basic ideas about Japanese cities by turning to the work of Maki Fumihiko, who contrasts two kinds of order. In one, called "clock," the relationship of the parts to the whole is systematic. In the other, termed "cloud," the relationships are shifting and never in more than temporary equilibrium. Where European cities are clocks, Japanese cities are clouds. Yokohama is a good example.

Space, Time, and Japanese Cities

Yokohama is now Japan's second largest city, but that is not a position it has held for long. Japan's first cities were built in the Kansai. Their design reflected Chinese ideas about urban design imported into Japan at the same time as Buddhism, Chinese writing, and the institutions of the emperor-centered state.

These cities were laid out on a rectangular grid. The imperial palace was located at the northern edge of the grid, facing south with its back to the north. A broad avenue running from the palace to the southern edge of the city bisected the rectangle. Other streets ran either parallel or perpendicular to it, dividing the city into smaller rectangular blocks. Nara, the imperial capital before the capital was moved to Kyoto, and Kyoto, which remained the imperial capital for most of Japanese history, are the two surviving examples. Kyoto is still regarded by many as the cultural capital of Japan, one reason why it was not bombed during World War II and so many of its ancient structures survive.

The warlords who fought for power after the decline of the emperor-ruled state created a new kind of city, the *jôkamachi* or castle town. Edo,

The famed Golden Temple in Kyoto.

now Tokyo, was by far the largest and most famous example. As "castle town" implies, these cities were built around the warlords' castles, the fortified residences from which they asserted and defended their power. The land closest to the castle was used for the residences of the warlord's most loyal and important retainers. Other parts of the town were parceled out to lesser retainers. One area was set aside for the homes and shops of commoners: merchants, craftsworkers, and laborers. Streets were deliberately left crooked to confuse those attacking the castle. (In contrast to medieval towns in Europe, or contemporary Chinese towns, the town had no walls of its own.)

In jôkamachi, the size of building plots was determined by the owners' rank. During the Tokugawa period, Edo, for example, occupied roughly seventy square kilometers (43 square miles). Seventy percent of this area was allocated to samurai residences. Commoners were allocated 15 percent. The castle itself, temples, and shrines accounted for the remainder. The samurai areas located in the hills to the north, west, and east of Edo castle became the *Yamanote*, the "High City" associated with rank and the refinements of samurai culture. The commoner quarter, squeezed onto reclaimed land to the east and northeast of the castle, became the *Shitamachi*, the "Low City" associated with a lively, if (as seen through High City eyes) frequently crude, street life. As Jinnai Hidenobu points out, these differences are still visible in Tokyo today.[20] While no longer a center of political power, the castle, now the imperial palace, is still the center of the city. The huge lots once allocated for daimyô residences are now the sites of government offices and educational institutions, and High City and Low City are still regarded by Tokyo residents as quite different places with different local cultures.

During the Tokugawa period, Edo became the seat of government. Osaka, a strategically located transportation nexus, became the business capital. Kyoto, the Japanese emperors' ancient capital, retained its special status as a sacred or cultural center. Focused on stability, Tokugawa policy restricted migration between the domains into which Japan was divided. Following the Meiji Restoration, these restrictions were eliminated. As Japan's industrialization began, impoverished farmers, no longer confined to their villages, poured into cities in four coastal regions where ports simplified the importation of raw materials and the export of finished products. The largest of these regions was the Keihin industrial belt that stretches between Tokyo and Yokohama. The others were the Hanshin region (the area between Osaka and Kobe), the Chukyo region (centered on Nagoya and Aichi Prefecture, later the home and manufacturing base of Toyota Motor Corporation), and Kitakyushu (the northern part of the island of Kyushu, including the city of Fukuoka that would later become a major center for precision machinery and electronics, especially microchip, production).[21]

Yokohama, however, was neither an ancient city nor a castle town. Before Perry's black ships arrived, it was a small fishing village far from the old Tokaido highway. Only after Perry's arrival were its fields and marshes converted into a treaty port opened to foreign settlement. To this day the city prides itself on its internationalism and its role in introducing new ideas to Japan.

A modern robotic factory in Japan.

To see something "typically Japanese," Japanese as well as foreign tourists travel a half-hour south to Kamakura, once capital of Japan during the Kamakura shogunate, to see the *Daibutsu* (Big Buddha), the massive Hachimangû Shrine dedicated to the Shinto god of war, and the handsome temples built as Zen took root among Kamakura-era samurai. They come to Yokohama to see the international and the new, in spots like Motomachi, where merchants catering to foreign residents introduced nineteenth century Japanese to the latest foreign fashions, the Hotel New Grand, where General Douglas MacArthur spent his first night in Japan after Japan's surrender, and now Minato Mirai 21, where Landmark Tower rises, a castle for captains of industry and a temple to consumerism.

But what is it like to live in this city? We begin with a look at Japanese homes.

The Japanese House

An Internet search for "Japanese house" will produce a list with several thousand entries. Those at the top of the list deal mainly with two topics: one particular type of Japanese house, which is now a rarity in Japan, and customs associated with visiting Japanese homes that are still very much the norm: removing your shoes before entering the Japanese house and washing off before you climb into a Japanese bathtub.

The "Japanese house" at the top of your search list is an idealized version of the samurai family house once found in great numbers in the areas of castle towns allocated to the retainers of the lord who lived in the castle. The typical description refers to a middle-ranking samurai home.

That house sits in a garden surrounded by a wall. It is, in effect, a smaller version of the castle whose lord the retainer serves. Typically the wall is made of wood or bamboo plastered with clay. Passing through the gate, a visitor traverses a path marked by stepping stones that lead to the front of the house. Stepping up onto a veranda under the overhanging roof, the visitor now finds himself facing sliding panels, which open revealing the interior, which is further subdivided by other sliding panels, either *fusuma* covered with heavy, opaque cloth or paper, which is sometimes lavishly decorated, or *shôji*, thin, translucent white paper glued to an exposed wooden lattice. The veranda is an extension of what is, in effect, a single, continuous, elevated floor, a space that can be rearranged at will by opening and closing the fusuma and shôji. The roof that extends over the veranda rests on a post-and-beam frame, with the posts set at fixed intervals.

A traditional Japanese house.

The floor inside the house is covered with *tatami*, rice-straw mats with woven-rush covers held in place by cloth edgings. The tatami is the unit in which room sizes are measured, and two tatami equal one *tsubo*, the unit in which land and house sizes are measured.

This is the house to which Ashihara Yoshinobu refers when he talks about Japanese focus on the floor. Because of the overhanging roof, natural light that enters the house falls on the tatami but leaves the ceilings in shadow. Because the tatami are fragile and hard to clean, visitors must remove their shoes before stepping up onto them.

In this type of traditional house, the tatami are where you sit and sleep. Furniture is minimal. This is also the house that illustrates Ashihara's assertion that in contrast to the clarity with which Western walls divide inside from outside, traditional Japanese architecture leaves this division ambiguous. With the panels thrown open, the house becomes a pavilion, overlooking the garden. Paintings on fusuma frequently depict birds, trees, flowers, and other natural motifs, sustaining a sense that house and garden are one. In the main room where guests are received, the *tokonoma*, an alcove containing a seasonal painting and seasonal flower arrangement, further reinforces this theme.

Western interest in Japanese gardens preceded interest in Japanese houses. Nineteenth-century visitors found in Japanese gardens the use of miniaturized trees and artificial mountains to create seemingly expansive spaces in compact places similarities to the formal gardens that had long been popular in Europe. It was only in the twentieth century—when Frank Lloyd Wright, Bruno Taut, and other modernist architects visited Japan and discovered in the samurai house a forerunner of modular structures, multifunction spaces, and minimal furnishing and decoration—that the houses standing in those gardens became a focus of interest. It was these modern architects who made that samurai house the archetype of "the Japanese house," instead of one type among many.

Varieties of Japanese Housing

Relatively few Japanese were samurai; the majority were peasants, with commoners in the cities the second largest group. They did not live in samurai houses.

The farmhouses in which peasants lived are found in many local variations, but the basic pattern was similar. The roof would cover both a *doma*, a space with an earthen floor that functioned as both kitchen and work area, and an area with an elevated wooden floor for sleeping, living, and storage. Long after tatami became popular, it was customary in all but the wealthiest farm households to store them away and to get them out only for special events, when guests were invited to the house.

In northern Japan, the domas might include a stable for farm animals and the floored space a sunken hearth over which a table would be placed, with a quilt over it to keep in the heat. The descendent of this heating system is the *kotatsu*, the low table to the underside of which an electric heater is attached, found in Japanese homes today. Family members gathered around this table for social as well as physical warmth, which is why, to this day, it remains an important symbol of family unity.

In Japanese cities, traditional commoner (merchant, artisan, and laborer) housing combined the same basic elements, compressed to fit deep and narrow urban spaces. Merchant townhouses lined major streets. The doma became a shop-front and workspace. Rooms on the elevated floor would be reached by a path running between them and leading, if the merchant were prosperous, to a miniature garden tucked into a courtyard toward the back. The rooms backed onto the outer walls, which were plastered with clay to guard against fire and thieves. Since these townhouses typically occupied the whole lot on which they sat, successful merchants expanded their residences by adding a second or third story, reached by narrow, steep wooden stairs.

The most basic form of traditional urban housing was, however, the *uranagaya* (literally "long houses in back"), the rental housing in which artisans and laborers lived. Individual units, sharing the same roof, lined the alleys branching off the main streets along which the merchants' townhouses were arrayed. The units themselves were generally only two to three tatami (4–6 square meters) (13–20 square feet) in size. A third of the space was a tiny doma, where cooking was done on *hibachi*, small charcoal-fired stoves. The alleys, where shared toilets and wells were located, were narrow, from 1.0 to 1.9 meters in width. Construction quality was typically poor and privacy nonexistent. This was the style of housing in which the majority of Japanese city-dwellers lived even long after the Meiji Restoration.

From Postwar Devastation to "Mansions"

The first reinforced concrete apartment building in Japan was built in 1920. But wood-frame, post-and-beam construction remained the norm in Japanese housing. The predominance of wooden housing was one reason for the terrible effectiveness of the firebombing of Tokyo and other Japanese cities during World War II. More than half of Japan's 160 cities were burned and 2.1 million houses destroyed by the fires resulting from the bombing. Another 550,000 were torn down in attempts to create firebreaks.[22] That is why so many Japanese who lived through the immediate postwar years remember living in shacks thrown together from whatever could be salvaged from the rubble. As recovery began, 470,000 new houses were built in 1947. In 1948, the number of new houses constructed rose to 740,000. Still, barely a third of the houses destroyed during the war had been replaced. Then, in 1949, the number of new dwellings fell to 330,000. The reason was diversion of building materials and craftworkers to construct dependents' housing for the occupation forces.

Contrasted with the poverty in which most Japanese were living, those big (by Japanese standards), modern appliance-equipped, American-style houses were a potent symbol of the American lifestyle to which growing numbers of Japanese would aspire as economic recovery began.

As urban planners and architects grappled with Japan's postwar housing crisis, they embraced new democratic ideals, equality between the sexes and respect for the individual, both seen as essential for modern living. Two new types of housing emerged from their efforts to blend these ideals with traditional expectations: ferroconcrete apartment blocks and suburban housing tracts, both mass-produced using prefabrication and other industrial production techniques. Those techniques made it possible to produce large numbers of units quickly but also reduced demand for the specialized skills of the master carpenters and clay workers required to build traditional Japanese-style houses.

In 1955, the Japanese government created the Japan Housing Corporation to provide inexpensive apartments for workers in districts with inadequate housing. In the *danchi* (public housing complexes) built by the corporation, the standard apartment was the 2DK (two-room, dining-kitchen) type. In a typical example, the apartment door opens on the *genkan* (entrance). In effect a miniature doma, this is where visitors stand before they remove their shoes to step up on the modestly elevated floor (we are talking inches instead of feet) to enter the apartment proper. To the right of the entrance are the toilet and bath. To the left are the DK, the dining-kitchen area, from which sliding doors open onto a veranda. Directly behind the DK is a six-tatami (12 square meter) (39 square feet), tatami-floored room. Beside it, straight ahead from the *genkan* is a 4.5-tatami, tatami-floored room. An additional 1.5-tatami space is taken up by the *oshiire*, the closet where the family's bedding and other possessions are stored.

Glancing around the illustration on which we base this description, we see several signs of modern living, as conceived when the first danchi were built. The mother faces a built-in kitchen sink, chopping vegetables for dinner. She is wearing a Western-style blouse and skirt. The pot to the right of her sits on a gas burner fed gas through a hose emerging from the wall. On the veranda we see a washing machine, clothes hung out to dry on the clothes line, a *futon* hung over the balcony to air, and the TV antenna. A closet at the opposite end of the veranda provides a bit of extra storage space. The spaces in this apartment may seem cramped, but compared to the uranagaya, they represent a gigantic improvement. Occupying a 24-tatami space, this apartment is 8 to 12 times bigger than the basic uranagaya unit.

Turning to how the idealized, mother-and-father-with-two-kids family that lives in this apartment is envisioned, we see that the mother's back is to the father, who sits in a chair at the kitchen table reading his newspaper. Baby is asleep on a futon in the 4.5-tatami room. Older brother is watching TV in the 6-tatami room. Each has achieved a measure of privacy.

"Mansion" is the Japanese term for the privately constructed equivalent of Housing Corporation danchi apartments. They now come in a variety of sizes, from 1DK for singles, to 2, 3, and 4LDK and larger versions for couples and families. The *L* in *LDK* stands for "living" and marks the addition of space for a separate, typically Western-style, living room to the basic design described above. Thus, for example, the High Town apartment in which the authors live started out as a 4DK. From the genkan, visitors would first pass two 4.5-tatami rooms on either side of the hall. At the end of the hall, they would come to the 8-tatami-size DK on the left and a sink and laundry room, toilet and bath on the right, before reaching another 8-tatami and a 6-tatami room. When we bought the place (the High Town is a condominium), both the 8-tatami and 6-tatami size rooms at the back, facing on to the veranda, were Japanese-style, tatami-floored rooms.

There are two points worth noting about the apartment's design. The first is the two 4.5-tatami rooms on either side of the hall from the genkan. Separated by the DK and laundry-toilet-bath complex from 8-tatami and 6-tatami rooms at the back, they give, in our neighbors' families, the children private spaces of their own, separated from the spaces in which the parents sleep. This sort of spatial arrangement allows a clearer separation between parents and children, providing for the children, in particular, a degree of privacy impossible in 2DK or traditional Japanese houses.

The second is that like many of our High Town neighbors, we have since remodeled, taking advantage of the fact that our ferroconcrete box retains the modular flexibility that Frank Lloyd Wright and Bruno Taut found so attractive in the classic samurai dwelling. We have turned the DK, 8-tatami, and 6-tatami rooms into a single wood-floored space, one of the 4.5-tatami rooms into a walk-in closet, and the other into a tatami-floored room. Many of our neighbors have also combined the DK and 8-tatami space to create a single large room but retained a 6-tatami room, separated from it by sliding fusuma panels.

The Suburbs

In 1894, English author Ebeneezer Howard published a book titled *Tomorrow: A Peaceful Path to Social Reform*, later republished under the title *Garden Cities of Tomorrow*. Howard advocated the creation of "Garden Cities" that, by combining the best of urban and country living, would avoid the drawbacks of both big city and rural life and lay the foundation for a bright and prosperous future. In Howard's book we catch the first glimpse of one of the twentieth century's most influential ideas—the suburbs.

In 1909 the book was translated into Japanese under the auspices of the Ministry of Home Affairs; but at this point in time, both Tokyo and Osaka were just beginning to develop into modern cities. It was a decade later, after World War I, that Japan's first city planning law was passed and Howard's ideas were hotly debated at architectural conferences. Then, in 1922, Denentoshi K.K. (Garden City, Inc.) was formed. The new company set out to realize Howard's dream in Japan. It bought up land along the Mekama and Ikegami (later Tokyu) private railroad lines in what is now the southern part of Tokyo and built 400 European-style homes that it sold to company executives and high-ranking government officials and military officers. Sales of its new houses were spurred by the Great Kanto Earthquake of 1923, which destroyed much of central Tokyo and occasioned the city's first great twentieth-century rebuilding. (The second would be after World War II.)

In 1952 and 1953 Gotô Keita, head of the Tokyu Group of companies—a real estate, retailing, hotel and resort, advertising and entertainment conglomerate built around what is now Tokyu Corporation, the operator of the Tokyu railways—led fact-finding missions to America. Like other Japanese business leaders who made similar trips (Matsushita Kônosuke, founder of Matsushita Corporation, Honda Sôichiro, founder of Honda Motor Corporation, and Ibuka Masaru, one of the founders of Sony Corporation, are other prominent examples), Gotô was not only awed by what he discovered, but he was also determined that Japan would equal or match it. As head of a group of companies developing land along its parent company's railway lines, Gotô was especially impressed by American suburbs and determined to build their Japanese equivalents. Years later, for eight months in 1970, the Tokyu Group and Levitt and Sons, the builders of Levittown, concluded a tie-up under which Levitt and Sons contributed its expertise in mass production of suburban housing in return for the Tokyu Group's exploration of the possibilities of Levitt and Sons selling their materials and technologies in Japan.

Miura Atsushi observes that the postwar development of suburbs in Japan lagged that in the United States by roughly a decade.[23] The first Levittown was built in 1948. The expansion of Japanese suburbs began during the high-growth years from 1955 to 1970 and then took off in the seventies as Japan's baby boomers started new families.

We shall return to Miura's thesis later in this chapter. For the moment, let us note that in terms of their layout, Japanese suburban houses are largely free-standing versions of layouts similar to those in danchi and condominium apartments. The commonest architectural differences lie in having two stories, with one or more bedrooms upstairs, a more clearly defined Western-style living and dining room downstairs with the kitchen and laundry-toilet-bath facilities, and a bit of garden as well (though these are often minute, since even suburban houses tend to fill the lots on which they are built). Newer suburbs, built further away from rail lines, are also car country. They are reachable by train and bus, but most suburban families own cars and use them to drive to the family restaurants, discounter outlets, and shopping malls that are now an integral part of Japanese suburban life.

A typical modern Japanese house.

The Japanese Bath and Toilet

We turn now to the second topic that pops up in an Internet search for "Japanese house." Internet sites that offer advice to foreigners visiting Japan typically focus on the following customs:

- Visitors remove their shoes in the genkan before stepping up on the elevated floor that marks the entrance to the private spaces inside the home. The door to a modern apartment or house is the functional equivalent of the gate in the wall of a traditional samurai dwelling. It serves as a barrier between the private property inside and the public spaces without. The invitation to enter the home is "*O-agari kudasai*" ("Please step up").
- Guests are offered slippers. These are worn on floors that are not tatami covered and must be removed before stepping onto tatami, where only bare feet or socks are allowed. (The conventional explanation is that tatami are easily damaged. It is also apparent, however, that tatami have become markers for spaces generally reserved for family or special guests.)
- Those slippers are, however, replaced with other slippers when entering the toilet. Toilet slippers stay in the toilet room and should not be worn outside it. (Again, if we ask why, we hear a practical-sounding reason, to avoid tracking filth from the toilet into other rooms. As anthropologists, however, we instantly think of cultural issues, purity and pollution, that arise when cultural categories have sharp and strongly defended boundaries and things must be kept in their proper places.)

To visitors from Europe or North America, one of the most unexpected features of Japanese domestic architecture is the separation of the toilet and bath. In modern Japanese residences, no matter how small, bath and toilet are clearly separated by their own walls and doors, although they may be adjacent to each other, the lavatory area, and the laundry room in a layout that simplifies the plumbing. Japanese tourists traveling abroad may thus be uncomfortable with Western-style "bathrooms" in which tub and toilet sit directly beside each other.

Which brings us to more advice concerning the Japanese bath:

- In contrast to Western bathtubs, which are typically long and narrow, allowing the bather to stretch out, Japanese tubs in private homes are typically short and deep. The bather is expected to sit and soak in the typically very hot water.
- Soaping, rinsing, and washing are done outside the bathtub, which should be entered only with a clean body. Getting into the tub to scrub off is a huge faux pas.

The historical reason for this practice is that baths were shared. In the countryside, water for the bath was heated once and family members took their baths in strict order of seniority, starting with father, the head of the household. Clean first, then soak was the rule, with the most senior getting the hottest water and the most junior the coolest. In cities, private baths were rare. Baths, like toilets and wells, were public facilities. The public bath was, in effect, a community center where a neighborhood's residents socialized and enjoyed skinship at the end of the day. Here, too, clean first, then soak was the rule.

Now, however, the public bath experience has become increasingly rare. Built-in private baths are a standard feature of modern Japanese housing, and public baths are going out of business. To experience public bathing, most Japanese must, like foreign tourists, travel to hot-spring resorts.

Who, Then, Are the Japanese?

As we start our walk down to Yokohama Station, we look at the people we pass and ask ourselves this question: What is it to be Japanese? The official answer is a simple one: A Japanese is a Japanese citizen, an individual entitled to carry a Japanese passport.

Japanese citizenship includes a small number of people who are not ethnically Japanese. It excludes far larger numbers who may have been born and raised in Japan but remain foreign nationals, not Japanese citizens. According to the 2000 census of Japan, 528,904 Koreans (born in Japan or in Korea) comprised the largest group of foreign nationals (40 percent), followed by 252,680 Chinese (19.3 percent), 188,190 Brazilians (14.4 percent), and 93,352 Filipinos (7.1 percent).[24]

But Japanese citizenship, the right to a Japanese passport, leaves unanswered a question that Japanese and foreign pundits both worry about: What is it to be a "real" Japanese?

Can a real Japanese be an Ainu, a Japanese citizen who belongs to an ethnic group of roughly 24,000 people whose ancestors were pushed northeastward into Hokkaido, whose status in Japanese society resembles that of Native Americans in the United States?

Can a real Japanese be a member of a group called Burakumin, descendants of Edo period outcastes? About 2 percent of Japan's population, they are both physically and behaviorally indistinguishable from other Japanese but continue to face discrimination in employment and marriage prospects.[25]

Can Japanese who have lived and worked overseas for long periods be real Japanese? Have they been contaminated by foreign influences and lost their Japaneseness? What about the "returnees," their children, who may have grown up overseas and display habits at odds with those acquired by children who grow up in Japan? What about "halfs" (some of the bolder ones call themselves "doubles"), children of mixed marriages?

And what about members of the younger generation, offspring of Japanese citizens, born and raised in Japan, who speak, dress, and behave in ways that seem alien to older Japanese? Have they, too, lost whatever it is to be "real" Japanese?[26]

Is It What They Wear?

When we think of Japan, the first image that comes to mind may be a woman dressed in *kimono,* a garment made by cutting fabric in straight lines and sewing them together into robes held together by *obi,* fabric sashes knotted in the back. Kimono vary from the simple cotton *yukata,* worn to fireworks or festivals during the summer and supplied to their guests by Japanese inns, to elaborate garments with layers of undergarments beneath kimono of lined silk in exquisitely woven, dyed, or embroidered designs.

An elegant and, in many ways, practical garment, the kimono is now worn mainly on ceremonial occasions like *shichi-go-san* (seven-five-three), when girls aged seven and three and boys aged five are dressed up and introduced to the gods at Shinto shrines. They appear again on *seijin no hi* (Coming of Age Day), when young Japanese become legally adult. Couples who select Japanese-style weddings may wear special wedding kimono for the Shinto ceremony but switch to Western-style clothing for the reception and the parties that follow the reception.

Outside of ceremonial occasions, kimono are mostly confined to special settings: restaurants that specialize in traditional Japanese cuisine as well as Japanese inns. Practitioners of traditional arts such as the tea ceremony or playing the bamboo flute wear kimono in public performances. Actors wear kimono in traditional theater (*Kabuki* or *Noh*) performances, and in historical dramas on film or TV.

Kimono have, that is, ceased to be daily wear for virtually everyone who does not have a special ceremonial or professional reason to wear them. Everyday wear is Western-style clothing not unlike that found in New York, London, Paris, Hong Kong, or Singapore, in a full range of fashion statements from zero style to haute couture.

In the 1980s, foreigners often commented on the way in which Japanese dressed. They expected to see police officers and train conductors wear uniforms, but not factory workers or students attending junior high and high schools. Construction worker jodhpurs (baggy pants cut tight from the knee down) and split-toed rubber boots—those seemed truly exotic. What attracted the most notice, however, were Japanese at play. On ski slopes, hiking trails, and golf courses, everyone seemed perfectly outfitted, as if they had just stepped off the pages of product catalogs. Even counterculture was fashion, and rebellious teens had to be properly costumed to play the parts they had chosen. Even when dressing down, Japanese seemed to be dressing up. An argument could be made that their costuming was evidence of the way in which Japanese divide their lives into neat compartments—and dress and act appropriately. From traditional theater (*Noh* and *Kabuki*) to street theater (punks, bikers, fashion statements), dressing the part and dressing to perfection seemed part of being Japanese.

In 2003, however, the proliferation of consumer choice, the endless advertising messages that stress the importance of individuality, the easy access to global trends, and the casual tastes shared by Japan's baby boomers and their children, the boomer juniors, have all shaped new realities. In what they choose to wear, Japanese seem as varied as any population in the world.

What remains perhaps most visibly Japanese is the care with which fashion-conscious women attend to every detail of the looks they are striving for. Makeup is heavy and artfully applied, but is normally not as bold and flashy as that observed in China, Korea, or Latin America. It is commonplace to see a woman whose hair is dyed a brown that precisely complements the rest of her outfit.

But even this kind of detail is becoming less distinctively "Japanese." Japan has become the epicenter of new styles that spread at the speed of television, especially in East and Southeast Asia. Fashion-conscious young people in street scenes shot in Shanghai, Seoul, or Taipei are increasingly hard to distinguish from those in scenes shot in Osaka, Yokohama, or Tokyo.

Is It Gifts and Wrappings?

Japanese are famous gift-givers. Japanese life is filled with occasions when people give each other gifts. When newcomers enter a neighborhood, they visit neighbors to the left and right, across the way, or, in apartment complexes, upstairs and downstairs, and as part of introducing themselves offer small gifts, typically soap or towels. Business people bring back souvenir gifts to their workmates when they go on business trips. Gifts are always an appropriate response to special favors, to a taxi driver who returns a dropped wallet, a doctor who fits an operation into his busy schedule, a customer, client, or boss who provides your livelihood. Weddings and funerals are occasions for gifts; the surprise for the foreign visitor is not so much having to give but receiving gifts in return. Guests leave weddings and funerals with bags of gifts given to thank them for attending and contributing through their gifts (typically cash in envelopes) to covering the expenses.

Foreigners from Europe or North America are used to exchanging gifts at Christmas, and retailers in their home countries count on one holiday season for a large fraction of their sales. Japan has two major gift-giving seasons, midsummer as well as year-end. Both are not only traditional but also the times of year when employees receive their bonuses.

Gift giving has also been stimulated by department stores' rapid adoption of Western holidays; Christmas, Halloween, and Easter are all vigorously promoted as new occasions for giving gifts. In one famous example, not only is Valentine's Day promoted as a day on which women should give chocolates to the men in their lives, but also a whole new holiday, White

Day, has been invented to allow the men to reciprocate.

Not only are gifts frequently given, they are, it seems to foreign observers, both carefully calculated and exquisitely presented. The amounts of cash given by wedding and funeral guests reflect both the relative status and the closeness or distance of giver and receiver. In department store mid-summer and year-end gift sections, gift sets are clearly priced in multiples of thousands of Japanese yen, so that both giver and receiver can understand precisely the intended weight of a gift.

Valentine chocolates are a wonderful example. They range from chocolates handmade by the giver (a sign of real affection) to imported premium chocolates (less intimate but more deferential) to *giri-choco* (obligatory chocolates), cheap mass-produced candies given by women to their bosses.

Whatever the value of the gift, however, it is beautifully wrapped and presented. One doesn't simply hand over cash when attending a wedding or funeral; special envelopes are required. Seasonal gifts may be as mundane as rice crackers or cooking oil, but the wrapping will be appropriate to both source and season. That is why serious givers go to famous department stores to purchase their gifts. The department store's wrapping communicates the giver's respect, even if the actual content could be purchased more cheaply somewhere else.[27]

The obligation to give and receive can, however, be a burden, especially in times of economic stagnation. This may be why, along with growing competition from discounters and convenience stores, Japan's famous department stores have, for several years now, faced declining sales.

Economic pressures, however, may not be the whole story. As consumerism and free competition erode traditional social structures, the obligation to give and receive may simply become less compelling. The department stores that promote new holidays and new—more individualistic—forms of giving may, in this respect, be cutting their own throats.

Is It What They Eat?

If you are invited to visit Japan, your hosts will almost certainly take you out for an "authentically Japanese" meal. Tsuji Shizuo, whose Ecole Technique Hôtelier Tsuji (the Tsuji Professional Culinary Institute) is Japan's most famous cooking school, describes such a meal as "consisting of many small courses—each a work of art on which much time and thought are spent, the receptacles, too, constituting an important part of the experience."[28]

Tsuji traces the origins of this style of cooking to the ancient imperial court in Kyoto. There, he writes, "The impoverished but cultivated court nobles learned to delight in the offerings of each changing season as it came, making the most of nature's provender when each article of food—fish, fowl or vegetable was at its prime." The food is served raw or very lightly cooked and only delicately seasoned with *dashi* (a fish stock made of dried bonito) and Japanese soy sauce. The focus of the experience is on the ingredient's original tastes, colors, and textures.

Each guest is served individual portions by kimono-clad servers moving with deliberate and studied grace. The guest of honor sits with his or her back to the rear of the room, in front of an alcove displaying a scroll painting and a flower arrangement that, like the servers' kimono, change depending on the season. The lowest ranked participant sits closest to the door. Yes, you may think to yourself, "This is the real Japan." Your hosts will agree.

You may notice, however, that if this is the real Japan, the real Japan is now only a small part of everyday Japanese lives. Imagine, for example, that our prowl around Yokohama has brought us to Yokohama Station. We are hungry and go looking for something to eat in the restaurant section of the building adjacent to the station.

We can, if we are so inclined, find a restaurant that serves the kinds of meals that Tsuji Shizuo describes. In the same section, however, there are two Italian restaurants (one of which appeals to health-conscious diners by labeling its offerings "Natural Italian"), two Chinese restaurants (one offering market stall dishes from Taiwan), a Russian tearoom, a Thai restaurant, and a beer hall whose menu features German sausages. One restaurant specializes in *omuraisu* (omelet rice), a Japanese culinary invention that consists of rice seasoned with ketchup, onions, and peppers, wrapped in an omelet, and topped with curry, stew, or simply more ketchup. All of these restaurants are filled with Japanese customers visibly enjoying their food.

Up two escalators and a short walk away is a busy street filled with young people, where the offerings include KFC, McDonald's, Starbucks, Häagen-dazs, Shakey's Pizza, Mr. Donut, and a British pub. All are doing a thriving business—as are places offering Japanese-style dishes, *soba* (buckwheat) or *udon* (wheat) noodles, *unagi* (eel), *sushi* (raw fish or other seafood) on rice flavored with sweetened vinegar, with *wasabi* (Japanese horseradish), soy sauce, and (to freshen the palate) slices of pickled ginger. One mustn't forget the *tonkatsu*, deep fried pork cutlet served with rice, a bowl of *miso* (fermented soybean paste) soup, salty Japanese pickles and a generous heap of chopped cabbage, or the *okonomiyaki*, do-it-yourself savory pancakes stuffed with all sorts of things and topped with dried bonito flakes, seaweed, and a dark brown savory sauce. Plus, of course, there are *tempura* (batter-fried seafood or vegetables) and *sukiyaki* (thin slices of beef sautéed in a heavy iron pan with *tofu*, and vegetables).

Within a half-mile radius, one can also find Indian, Mexican, and Vietnamese restaurants. At least in public places, that "authentically Japanese" meal with which we began is only one—and by no means the most popular—of the meals that Japanese now consume.

But what, we might ask, do Japanese cook and eat at home? Authoritative-sounding descriptions tell us that Japanese meals are traditionally built around a bowl of plain boiled rice, with everything else—fish, meat, or vegetable, fried, stewed, grilled, or raw—conceived as a side dish and complement to the main dish, the rice itself.

According to food critic M. F. K. Fisher, who wrote the introduction to Tsuji's Japanese Cooking, "At least half the population of more than a hundred million people like, eat, and thrive on bowl-meals from China (*ramen* in soup), and India (curry-rice), and Italy (spaghetti with tomato sauce)." Ready-to-eat, heat-and-serve, or semiprepared versions of all three dishes are now likely to appear in the meals that Japanese mothers prepare for themselves and their children, and that Japanese singles prepare for themselves if they choose to eat in instead of going out. According to market researcher Iwamura Nobuko, growing numbers of Japanese women have no interest in cooking and see little value in producing home-cooked meals for their families.[29]

Is It Japanese Religion?

Japan is often described as having two traditional and numerous new religions. The two traditional religions are Shinto, indigenous to Japan, and Buddhism, imported to Japan from China and Korea, starting in the sixth century, near the founding of the emperor-centered, legally codified state. The newer religions, those founded since then, in late Tokugawa, Meiji, or post–World War II (depending on the scholar whose thesis you prefer) have tended to have either a Shinto or Buddhist flavor.

During the Tokugawa period, Buddhism became a form of social control, as all households were required to register with temples to demonstrate that they were not Christian. Meiji saw the disestablishment of Buddhism and the creation of State Shinto, focused on the worship of the emperor portrayed as a direct descendant of Amaterasu, the Sun Goddess. Now, however, Article 20 of Japan's constitution guarantees freedom of religion, while Article 89 explicitly prohibits the use of public funds or property to support religious institutions, and the Showa Emperor explicitly denied his divinity after World War II. State Shinto has been officially disestablished.

Shinto is often described as animistic, rooted in belief in spirits who animate and control the natural world. Buddhism began as the Buddha's doctrine of the Four Noble Truths, that the world is filled with suffering, that suffering is caused by desire, that only by ending desire can suffering be eliminated, and the only way to eliminate desire is to follow the Eightfold Path of Buddhist practice.

Broadly speaking, Shinto is life affirming; Buddhism teaches detachment. Shinto is for weddings, Buddhism for funerals. These stereotypes, however, conceal a long history of interaction with Confucianism, Daoism, and later Christianity as well as between Shinto and Buddhism themselves. The results may seem paradoxical to those who cling too strongly to categorical definitions or regard exclusive practice of one religion as the norm. The keen aesthetic enjoyment of fleeting phenomena—moonlight, cherry blossoms, insect cries, or the sudden, graceful moves of martial arts, all characteristic of Zen, a form of Buddhism—seem closely akin to Shinto.

For some Japanese believers, a substantial minority, new religions have become important. A new religion was typically formed around a charismatic leader, often one who is said to have had magical healing powers. In exchange for devotion, it offers a sense of community, relief from domestic conflict and personal tragedy, and a sense of personal meaning in what may now seem an increasingly chaotic and meaningless world. Some new religions have become major institutions, some threats to public safety. Members of the largest and most famous new religion, the Buddhist-inspired Sôka Gakkai, are the core of Kômeitô, a political party that in 2003 was an important member of the ruling party coalition headed by the conservative Liberal Democratic Party (LDP). Another new religion, Aum Shinrikyô, became infamous in 1995 when its members launched a sarin gas attack on the Tokyo subways.

For most Japanese, however, religion is not a continuous focus of their lives. It is part of the landscape, like the authors' neighborhood shrine or a nearby Buddhist temple. Religion is something for special occasions, a wedding or festival at a shrine, a funeral or the annual washing of the graves in a cemetery attached to a temple.

Major shrines and temples are always packed at New Year, when crowds gather to hear the ringing of the temple bells at midnight on New Year's Eve and to make offerings to, it is said, ensure good luck in the coming months. Shrine festivals can be enormous fun, as *mikoshi*, portable shrines, are paraded through neighborhoods to mark and renew community boundaries. Some are huge tourist attractions, on the scale of Mardi Gras or the Rose Bowl parade. But the *kamidana* (Shinto god shelf) and *butsudan* (Buddhist ancestral altar) that were once common in Japanese homes have become increasingly rare.[30]

Is It The Language They Speak?

Our stroll through Yokohama will take us past signs in Japanese—in dramatic calligraphy, angular neon, or simple squarish forms—as well as people speaking that language. Speaking, reading, and writing the Japanese language is arguably one of the core aspects of Japanese identity. What, though, is that language?

Linguists generally classify Japanese as a member of the Altaic language family, which originated in Central Asia and includes such languages as Turkish, Mongolian, Manchu, Korean, Japanese, and the Ryukyuan languages spoken in Okinawa.[31] Japanese is also described as an inflected, subject-object-verb, left-branching language written in a combination of ideographs and syllabic scripts, with a majority of its vocabulary based on Chinese and European loan words (just as a majority of English vocabulary also consists of loan words).[32] What does this technical description mean?

In English, we inflect verbs to indicate singular or plural and also tense, but other information (likelihood, active or passive voice, negative forms) about verbs is communicated in other ways than by altering the verb itself. Japanese verbs are inflected to communicate all that information, but not singular or plural. Japanese adjectives, which can also function as verbs, are also inflected.

Japanese syntax is subject-object-verb: Whereas we say "I ate lunch," the Japanese equivalent would be "I lunch ate." The verb, with all the information that its highly inflected endings carry, comes last. With the verb at the end—on the right side of the sentence, as it were—it is not surprising that Japanese builds modifying phrases to the left. That is, a phrase modifying a noun or verb is placed before, not after, it.

Imagine a base sentence: Tarô collapsed (*Tarô-kun ga taoreta*). Then we might add why: Tarô collapsed [with food poisoning]. (*Tarô-kun ga [shokuchûdoku de] taoreta*: literally: Tarô because of food poisoning collapsed.) Additional information on what he had eaten and where it came from—he stole and ate a box lunch [that Emi had brought]—is attached to the left of the proper noun Tarô: *([Emi-san ga motte kita] o-bentô wo nusunde tabeta) Tarô-kun ga (shokuchûdoku de) taoreta.*

This example also illustrates the Japanese use of postpositions (compared with the prepositions of English). The *ga, wo,* and *de* all come after nouns and indicate their function: subject, object, cause. The other postpositions include *ni* (direction, place), *kara* (source), *made* (until), *e* (target), and *no* (possessive). Another is the absence of relative pronouns: No equivalent of "which" or "that" is needed for the phrases to be used to modify nouns or verbs in the sample sentence.

Note also that all the words end in vowels, except for *-san* and *-kun,* which end in n. Japanese has five vowels (*a, i, e, o, u*), which occur as single vowels and in combinations; the doubles include *aa, ii, uu, ee, oo* (usually romanized as *â, î, û, ê, ô*) as well as *ai, ae, ao, au,* and other sequences. In both examples of combinations, each of the two vowels is pronounced distinctly; both *oi* and *oo* are twice as long as *o* and are treated as two syllables. All syllables end in either vowels, syllabic "n" (an "n" sound that counts as a syllable in its own right) or the double consonants *-kk-, -pp-, -tt-, -ss-, -ssh-,* or *-tch-.* Those double consonants are unreleased—there is, for example, a slight pause in midword, but no puff of air as the first *k* of *-kk-* is pronounced, much as you might pronounce the first *k* sound in "bookcase." Those double consonants can occur only in the middle of words.

The requirement that words end in open syllables or *n* means that Japanese find loan words from consonant-heavy languages such as English difficult to pronounce. That, however, does not inhibit their adoption, with a well-assimilated term often cut down to the four-syllable form for which the Japanese language has a strong preference. Thus, for example, the graphic equalizer familiar to stereo buffs would be, in Japanese, a *gurafikku ikoraizaa,* a considerable mouthful that promptly became a *guraiko.* Similar surgery was performed on Chinese vocabulary as it was absorbed from the fourth century on.

Another feature of Japanese is the placement of honorifics after names: the general-purpose *-san* for Emi, the *-kun* used for boys, inferiors, and friends for Tarô. Those are only the start of a highly elaborated set of forms, both verb forms and separate sets of vocabulary, used to indicate the relationship (insider/outsider, inferior/superior) of the speaker to the person spoken to or about.

The use of respect language (*keigo,* in Japanese) is not in itself unusual; in English, we speak differently to our professors than to our younger brothers, for example. Respect language is, however, both more explicit in Japanese and embedded in every utterance. The relationship between the speaker and the person or topic determines, minimally, the form of the verb used and often the choice of terms. In the sample sentence, for example, the speaker or writer would be assumed to know Emi and Tarô but not be a family member of either and to be directing the utterance at someone who is also an insider and not a superior, based on the use of *-san* and *-kun* and the informal form of the final verb.

Failure to make the right choice of verb or term is not just rude, it is failure to communicate. Using a verb form suitable for addressing an "outsider/superior" when speaking to an "insider/inferior" will leave the other person wondering what you are talking about and to whom. Small children thus learn how to say "You [other kids] went home" differently from "You [teacher] went home," mastering the required verb forms and vocabulary for expressing relationships as naturally as English-speaking children learn to keep singular and plural nouns and verbs straight. Ideally, by the time those children are ready to enter the job market, they have complete control of keigo, as well as a proper appreciation of their lowly position in the organizations they are seeking to become part of.[33] (Older Japanese, however, frequently complain that younger Japanese no longer use keigo properly.)

Another feature of Japanese that overlaps with respect language is the difference between women's and men's speech, with women typically, but not necessarily, using more polite forms. What those linguistic differences, and changes in the speech of younger people, may say about gender relations in Japan has generated a large body of research of great interest to students of language change as well as sociolinguistics.[34]

The Japanese writing system was borrowed and adapted from Chinese, a process believed to have begun with the third-century contacts with the Wei dynasty and accelerated by the importation of Buddhism and the need to read Buddhist texts. Since Chinese is an uninflected language, written with ideographic characters (*kanji*, in Japanese), each of which in principle expresses a single idea, the Chinese writing system was peculiarly unsuited to writing Japanese. It had, however, all the prestige of the then-dominant East Asian culture behind it.

Initially, Japanese used kanji only to write Chinese, not their own language. The advantages of a written language were so obvious, however, that finding a way of using kanji to write Japanese quickly followed. The first stab was to use one kanji, not for its meaning but its pronunciation, to represent each syllable of Japanese. A kanji pronounced as "a" in Chinese would be used for the syllable *a*, one pronounced "sa" for *sa*, and so on. Since many kanji share the same pronunciation, it was possible to be highly playful (or confusing) in writing Japanese by selecting an array of kanji to represent the same syllables. When the *Man'yôshû*, the oldest known Japanese poetry collection, was compiled in the eighth century, Japanese had 87 possible syllables; the compilers used over 970 Chinese characters to write them.[35]

Subsequent efforts to simplify and standardize have produced two sets of syllabic writing systems, *kana*, derived from Chinese characters but used to represent the sounds of Japanese, not meanings. *Hiragana* is one syllabary, rather cursive in appearance, with one symbol for each of the syllables of spoken Japanese. The characters of *katakana*, the other syllabary, are more square looking. Thus, Japanese today is written not in one script but in a mixture of three.

Katakana are, according to the system taught in postwar schools, used to write *gairaigo*, loan words from languages other than Chinese. *Hiragana* can be used to write everything else—the nouns, pronouns, highly inflected verbs and adjectives, adverbs, postpositions, and particles that make up the Japanese language. In educated usage, however, kanji are used to write loan words (typically two-kanji combinations) from Chinese as well as new kanji combinations invented in Japan.

Another important use of kanji is to write the root forms of native Japanese terms. Thus, the first kanji in the three-character phrase *gairaigo*, "loan words," means "outside" and is also used to write the native term *soto*, "outside, external." The third kanji in gairaigo means "word, speech" and is also used to write the stem of the native Japanese verb *kataru*, "to speak, narrate." Since Japanese verbs and adjectives are inflected, the kanji assigned to a verb, for instance, is taken to apply only to the uninflected stem, with hiragana used to render the inflections.[36]

With the influx of new loan words from English and other European languages, use of roman script has also become an occasional feature of the Japanese written language. Some writers will prefer to give a term in roman letters rather than render it into katakana. Others may use roman script playfully. For example, the word "double" has been turned into a Japanese verb, *daburu*, "to double," which is sometimes written with a W followed by *ru* in *hiragana*.

The features of spoken and written Japanese described above have been used as evidence that Japanese society is organized in ways peculiar to itself. They could also be interpreted as indicating how much Japanese have in common with speakers of English—another language highly receptive to loan words and with a huge vocabulary—or with speakers of Korean, another subject-object-verb language heavily influenced by Chinese in vocabulary and writing system. How big and important a part these similarities and differences play is the critical question that faces every attempt to explain how Japanese think, feel, and behave.

EXPLAINING JAPAN

What we need now are some basic ideas to help us sort out what we've learned so far. Don't forget, however, that even the most basic ideas begin as notions in someone's mind. They emerge in a context and address specific problems. To understand their relevance to what we have learned so far, we have to keep asking ourselves, who, what, when, where, and why.

Here we begin with Ruth Benedict, the American anthropologist whose book *The Chrysanthemum and the Sword*, first published in 1946, remains perhaps the single most famous attempt to answer this question, at least among works by non-Japanese authors. (Today, it is more widely read in Japan than in the United States: If you travel to Japan, you will find it in hotel bookstores, and the Japanese you meet may remember reading parts of the Japanese translation, *Kiku to Katana*, in high school.)

The Most Alien Enemy

When Benedict did her research, America was at war with Japan. World War II was still under way. She begins *The Chrysanthemum and the Sword* with the sentence "The Japanese were most alien enemy that the United States had ever fought in an all-out struggle."[37]

Critics writing long after the war see Benedict's conclusions as stereotypes—and they are not wrong to do so. But Benedict's job was not to produce propaganda. Her job was to offer insights to soldiers fighting a new kind of war. She and her colleagues in the Office of Strategic Planning had to discover not only the aims and motives of Japanese leaders, but also "what their government could count on from the people . . . habits of thought and emotion and the patterns into which these habits fell."[38] To achieve this aim, Benedict argued, they had "to put aside for the moment the premises on which we act as Americans and to keep ourselves as far as possible from leaping to the easy conclusion that what we would do in a given situation was what they would do."[39]

When Benedict called the Japanese "the most alien enemy," the difference to which she pointed was no mere prejudice. In the Japanese, the Allies found an enemy for whom "conventions of war, which Western nations had come to accept as facts of human nature, obviously did not exist."[40] European and American generals, for example, were used to assuming that an army could be forced to surrender by killing one-fourth to one-third of its troops. The ratio of soldiers surrendering to those who died would be about 4:1. But even late in the war, when the first substantial number of Japanese surrendered, that ratio was 1:5, five times as many troops dying as surrendering, and that was seen as a huge improvement. In earlier battles the ratio had been as low as 1:250.

Why was it that Japanese soldiers would go on fighting to the death, even in situations where they could not win? And then, when captured, why did these fight-to-the-death warriors become model prisoners, meekly doing whatever they were told and not trying to escape as POWs from Europe or America would? And why was the emperor never included in criticisms of their government, their officers, and their comrades?

Unfortunately, Benedict writes, a fieldtrip was out of the question. She "could not go to Japan and live in their homes and watch the strains and stresses of daily life." She wasn't able "to watch them in the complicated business of arriving at a decision" or to observe how they brought up their children. She would have to make do with what she could learn at a distance, by reading books, watching movies, and interviewing Japanese Americans interned during the war.[41]

Not surprisingly, the Japan that Benedict describes is very much the one that the Meiji oligarchs were aiming to create, a people united by and fiercely devoted to values they saw as uniquely Japanese, united by reverence for their emperor.

Taking One's Proper Station

According to Benedict, the Japanese revered hierarchy. They believed that each person and group had a proper place in society. During the Edo period, "Every family head had to post on his doorway his class position and the required facts about his hereditary status. The clothes he could wear, the foods he could buy, and the kind of house he could legally live in were regulated according to this inherited rank."[42] Benedict states:

> The Meiji Restoration eliminated these caste distinctions but left Japanese reverence for hierarchy intact. Hierarchy is implicit in the Japanese language.
>
> Every time a man says to another "Eat" or "Sit down" he uses different words if he is addressing someone familiarly or is speaking to an inferior or to a superior. There is a different "you" that must be used in each case and the verbs have different stems.[43]

Every greeting, she noted, is also accompanied by a bow, precisely calibrated to the status of the person receiving the greeting.

To Americans who claim to prize equality and freedom, these customs may seem oppressive. Why, then, did Japanese accept the burdens they seemed to impose? To Benedict the answer was a value the Japanese call *on*, a word for which the closest English translation is "debt."

From a Japanese perspective, any favor imposed a debt. The debt was a burden because it must be repaid. Depending on the nature of the debt, moreover, repayment might be impossible. Repayment took one of two forms: *gimu* or *giri*. Gimu was owed to the emperor and to parents. In both these cases the debt was infinite. No repayment could ever be more than partial. Giri was a debt with limits, but one that must be repaid, measure for measure, in precisely the right form.

Consider, for example, a man caught between his mother and his wife. To his wife, he had giri, obligations that must be fulfilled. But the gimu he owed his mother could never be repaid. Thus, if mother and wife quarreled, he must always side with his mother, even if she behaved in ways that seemed irrational, oppressive, or vicious. A result more at odds with Western notions of romantic love and a couple supporting each other in fights with their in-laws is hard to imagination.

Here, then, was the answer to why Japanese soldiers would fight to the death, regard themselves as dead to Japanese society if captured, and criticize their colleagues but not the emperor. The gimu owed to the emperor meant that nothing short of death could repay the debt owed. Criticism could be leveled at officers and comrades who failed in the giri owed to each other. The emperor, to whom gimu was owed, was forever beyond criticism.

Giri "within the circle of *on*" was giri owed to others. But Japanese also owed giri to themselves. "Giri to one's name" involved a highly developed sense of personal honor and quick and furious anger at any sign of disrespect. Thus, otherwise passive prisoners would explode if their captors made fun of them.

We might, suggests Benedict, expect a society so preoccupied with honor and obligation to be Spartan and puritanical. But Japan was a counter-example. Japanese, she writes, are sensualists, who enjoy all the pleasures of the flesh—so long, that is, as they are kept in the right places, discreetly separated from the serious parts of life where honor and obligation rule. This compartmentalization is just another example of a highly visible Japanese habit: keeping not just people and groups but everything in its proper place.

Problems occurred only when people or things were out of place or behaved inappropriately. Thus, in traditional Japanese literature a common plot is the love affair that ends in tragedy because passion intrudes on obligation. The only way out is suicide.

The Japanese Are Not Chinese

During World War II, the Japanese were the enemy. The Chinese were allies. Throughout *The Chrysanthemum and the Sword*, Benedict draws our attention to ways in which Japanese and Chinese differ. Readers who wish to situate Japan in a broader Asian context should pay careful attention to these differences.

The Confucian ideal of filial piety is, for example, an idea transmitted from China via Korea to Japan. But in China, writes Benedict, filial piety includes the worship of distant ancestors. Ancestor halls may be shared by hundreds or thousands of people who belong to the same lineage. A shared surname implies a connection through a common ancestor, enabling strangers to cooperate. In contrast, Japanese worship of individual ancestors goes back no further than those within the memories of living household members. Sharing a surname has no particular significance, especially since most Japanese acquired surnames en masse after the Meiji Restoration. It is certainly no reason to go into business together or found a surname association to promote common interests, as Chinese do.

Gimu to the emperor was never part of Chinese thought. Loyalty was prized but rebellion justified when rulers became corrupt and unworthy. Thus, where Japan's imperial family is seen as having been part of Japan since time immemorial, Chinese history records the rise and fall of dynasties.

Giri to one's name, says Benedict, is something that Chinese find alien. "The Chinese regard all such sensitivity to insults and aspersions as a trait of 'small' people—morally small." Nobility it is not.[44]

In both societies, men display their success by taking mistresses. Chinese men, however, bring their mistresses home and make them concubines in households their wives control. In Japan, writes Benedict, polygamy is not permitted. "Only in highly exceptional cases when the girl has a child whom the man wishes to bring up with his own children does he bring her into his home, and then she is designated as one of the servants, not as a concubine. The child calls the legal wife 'mother,' and ties between the real mother and her child are not acknowledged."[45]

In all of these examples, we see fundamental differences. China is a society in which real or fictive kinship supports far-flung social networks, loyalties are conditional, households rise and fall. Japan is precisely the reverse, a society in which household counts for more than kinship. Households are expected to last forever. External relations that threaten household unity are suppressed.

These themes are also central to the work of the next anthropologist whose work we examine. They illustrate the difference between *attribute* and *frame*, the key theoretical concepts in the work of Nakane Chie.

The Vertical Society

Nakane Chie is Japanese. To her the Japanese were not an alien enemy. They were family, friends, colleagues, or neighbors. She was, moreover, writing two decades after Benedict. Nearly a generation had passed since World War II. Still, when Nakane described the lives of men who worked for large Japanese corporations in the 1950s and 1960s, she was talking about institutions created and still run by executives educated before or during the war, adapted to modern realities but clinging to prewar ideals. Their successors would grow up in a very different Japan.

In 1967, when Nakane published *Tate Shakai no Ningen Kankei (Human Relations in the Vertical Society*, later published in English as *Japanese Society*), she was involved in a debate whose roots went back to the Meiji Restoration. Should Japan become more like the West to become more modern? Or should Japan become modern but remain true to itself, asserting a unique Japanese identity? Nakane offered her own perspective, which, in retrospect, looks very much like the choice that the Meiji oligarchs made: adopting what they saw as the best Western ideas but reshaping them to fit their belief that Japan was and is unique.

On one side of what was called the modernization debate were Japanese as well as foreign scholars who, says Nakane, embraced Western theories wholesale. They argued that Japan would inevitably come to resemble other modern societies. It too, would become a democratic society that prizes individualism and embraces free-market capitalism. Distinctively Japanese customs, habits, and institutions would have to be discarded. These were merely "feudal remnants," old-fashioned and obsolete.

To the Japanese scholars who opposed this view, these same distinctively Japanese customs, habits, and institutions embodied the essential Japan. They could not be explained in terms of theories borrowed from the West. Only Japanese terms would do. (Their arguments remain alive today, in the form of *Nihonjinron*, "discourses on Japaneseness," a continuing stream of books and articles that attempt to teach the Japanese what it is to be Japanese.)

In *Tate Shakai*, Nakane situates herself between these extremes. She frames her argument in terms of social structure, a concept borrowed from the British-style anthropology she learned at the University of London. At the end of the day, however, she leans toward Japanese uniqueness.

Frames versus Attributes: Japan versus India

From her teacher, the British anthropologist Raymond Firth, Nakane learned to distinguish social structure, an abstraction that refers to the basic principles that govern relationships—between individuals, between groups, and between individuals and groups—from social organization, the way in which groups are organized as social structure interacts with other factors that affect people's lives. Her argument can be summed up in one basic claim: All social structures involve two key elements: the properties of individuals that Nakane labels "attributes" and the "frames" that define the boundaries and relationships of groups whose members work and live together, sharing the same space. In many societies around the world attributes are more important than frames. In Japan, she says, it is just the reverse. Frames trump attributes.

To illustrate the difference, Nakane turns first to her observations while doing fieldwork in India. Nakane, a Japanese woman, was startled by what happened when Indian daughters-in-law fought with their mothers-in-law.

She wasn't surprised that these quarrels occurred. Battles between mothers-in-law and their daughters-in-law are common wherever women who marry must leave the families in which they grow up and go to live with their husband's families, a pattern that anthropologists call virilocal (moving-in-with-the-husband) marriage. In this type of marriage, daughters-in-law are typically expected to obey their mothers-in-law and to learn their new families' habits. But both sides are only human. Stresses and strains are inevitable.

Filial piety, respect for the elders, tends to be strong, reinforced by close emotional ties between mother and son. So, when quarrels occur, the husband is likely to side with his mother instead of his wife. (Recall, for instance, Benedict's description of what happens when gimu to the mother conflicts with giri to the spouse.)

That is not, however, the only factor affecting the outcome when quarrels occur. In Japan's frame-oriented society, the daughter-in-law moves from one frame to another. Since the kinship attribute is weak, her ties with the members of the household she leaves are severed; she cannot look to its members for allies. If she fights with her mother-in-law, she loses. She is, thus, forced to conform.

In contrast, the Indian daughter-in-law retains strong ties to her parents, to her siblings, and to other members of her caste. Since the kinship attribute outweighs the household frame, she has allies in her fights. She wins at least some of her battles and is able to be more independent.

Nakane was also surprised by the way in which Indian fathers exercised their authority. The Indian father, she writes, disciplines his children's behavior, but he doesn't try to teach his children how they ought to think or feel, as a Japanese father would. Where, moreover, the Indian father asserted his authority by pointing to an attribute ("I am your father, do what I say"), the Japanese father spoke for the frame ("This is how WE think/feel/behave").

Nakane found these same patterns at work in the schools, corporations, and government bureaucracies of Japan in the 1960s. Here, too, she found discipline aimed at controlling not only behavior but thoughts and feelings as well. She also found total authority vested in the heads of particular groups, and customs and habits that strengthened the primacy of the group and of social relations inside it while weakening those which cut across group boundaries. Wherever she looked, she found that frames were stronger than attributes.

The Household as Model

To Nakane, the prototype for all other frames is the *ie*, the "traditional" type of Japanese household enshrined in the Meiji Civil Code.[46] Ideally the ie's core was a patriarchal stem family. The eldest son would succeed to its headship. He and his bride, who married into the family, would eventually take over from the current head and his wife. Rank within the family would reflect seniority, with the younger members obedient and respectful to the older and the older expected to provide firm discipline as well as nurturing care.

In these respects the ie resembled households in other parts of Asia, where patrilineal (father-to-son) descent and virilocal marriage result in formation of patriarchal families and rank within the family is determined by seniority. But the ie is above all a group of people who live and work together, a group whose primary objective is to ensure its own survival in competition with rival groups.

This difference shows up most clearly in rules that govern inheritance and succession to headship. In traditional Chinese families, every son has a right to inherit an equal share of his family's property. In parts of South and Southeast Asia, daughters also have rights to their own share. The inevitable result is that households rarely last more than two or three generations. The property accumulated in one generation is divided among its children and grandchildren. In contrast, in the ie there was only one heir, the successor to the headship. While normally the eldest son inherited, younger sons as well as daughters had to seek their own fortunes. The household property remained undivided. A successful household endured forever (the prototype being, of course, the imperial household).

If there were no ideal heir, no properly qualified eldest son, a replacement could be adopted—even if there were other sons. The survival and success of the household took precedence over claims based on mere kinship. The property remained undivided; the household endured.

The only exceptions to this rule were cases in which household heads voluntarily provided the assets required for junior members to set up new households, an act of generosity. These new households would, however, remain forever subordinate to the "roots" from which the "branches" had sprung. Their relation would be that of child to parent (thus, from Benedict's perspective, a matter of gimu, a debt that can never be repaid).

Even in Modern Japan

As described by Nakane, the ie recalls the total institutions described by Erving Goffman, in which every idea, emotion, and action is controlled by the institutional setting. A familiar example is a military unit whose members are bound together by the ethic of mission, unit, self: The mission is paramount, and the unit may have to be sacrificed to achieve it. The unit is second in importance, and to keep it intact individual soldiers will sacrifice themselves. Units compete with similar units, cooperating with those in the same chain of command but determined to defeat those that belong to other armies. Relations within the unit are governed by rank, which is largely determined by seniority, with latecomers junior to those who have more seniority. Relationships that cut across units may, at times, be useful but are always secondary to those inside the unit.

But what, one might ask, does all this have to do with today's Japan? Following Japan's defeat in World War II, the Meiji Civil Code was abolished. The traditional household, the ie, no longer existed as a legal entity. The absolute authority that made the father, as household head, his family's emperor, was no more.

Nakane argued that the social structure once embodied in the ie continued to shape Japanese lives—in particular, the lives of those Japanese men who followed an ideal career track, from school to lifetime employment in a large corporation or government bureaucracy. In junior high and high school, they wore uniforms modeled on Prussian originals. Their new, postwar textbooks might preach democracy, but their school days still mimicked military life, starting with morning formation and rising to bow when a teacher entered the classroom. In school clubs they learned the importance of total dedication to the group and to accept the rigid hierarchy of *sempai* (senior) and *kôhai* (junior), subservience enforced by hazing.

Those who survived the "examination hell" of nationwide entrance exams would go on to college and enjoy a brief moratorium, a moment of freedom to explore personal options. Then they would enter organizations that reinforced the habits learned in school.

For men who entered the workforce by joining large corporations just after high school or college, lifetime employment meant that the organizations they joined became the frames for the rest of their lives. Like the daughter-in-law in the ie, they were cut off from other relationships. Long days filled with work and work-related socializing made it hard to form enduring ties outside the company. Leaving one company to join another was not normally an option. Seniority-based pay, a large fraction of which was withheld for semiannual bonuses, rewarded company loyalty. Those who moved from one company to another were seen as traitors to their previous colleagues. (To this day, they are penalized in the higher taxes they are forced to pay on their retirement funds.)

Like the traditional Japanese father, the Japanese corporation did more than try to control its employees' behavior. It prescribed how they should think and feel. Company presidents' speeches were filled with calls for company solidarity. "A spirit of love for the company" and "the new familism" were typical of phrases heard everywhere. Official company philosophies echoed these themes, calling for everyone to work and feel together, to share joys and sorrows, triumphs and defeats. As mission statements, their purpose was clear: Through hard work and solidarity, the company could overcome business rivals to become an industry leader.

Like the world of the traditional family, the world of the corporation was one in which vertical relationships (leader–follower, senior–junior, parent company–child company) were stronger and more important than the horizontal ties based on shared attributes that spilled across the frames (team, section, division, company) to which individuals belonged. New employees were the lowest of the low, and those with the greatest seniority were those with the highest rank.

In the world of the corporation, the successors would, at the end of their careers, serve on the board of directors or, if they made it all the way to the top, become CEO and then chair of the board. Failure to rise to this level meant having to retire or, having risen high enough, being moved to a new job with one of the company's subsidiaries or suppliers—more junior members of the corporate family. But the rule was up or out, just as it was in succession to the ie headship.

It being unthinkable that a junior could take a senior's position until the senior moved up the ladder, vertical ties were, in principle, free of rivalry. In vertical relationships, the senior would care for his juniors, providing opportunities and training up potential successors. His care would, moreover, go far beyond an arm's length business relationship. It included concern for emotional health, playing the role of go-between at the junior's wedding, and keeping a watchful eye out for family, drinking, or gambling problems that might interfere with loyalty to the firm.

Competition was concentrated in relations between the unranked vis-à-vis each other. To ambitious individuals, dôki ("same-timers," those who joined the company en masse at the end of the same school year) were both potential allies and potential enemies. Would-be leaders found followers among new cohorts of juniors. Factionalism was endemic as followers sorted themselves into cliques (informal frames) defined by the leaders to whom they pledged their allegiance.

Legally speaking, the ie was dead. But the ie lived on in the social structures at the heart of post–World War II, modernizing Japan.

Two Very Similar Japans

Benedict and Nakane start from different perspectives. One was an American writing about her country's "most alien enemy." The other was a Japanese writing about a Japan whose rapid economic growth, already hailed as an economic miracle, was outstripping European rivals. Both attempted what many would now say is a simply impossible task, to sum up the essential Japan in one short book.[47] But the two Japans they describe at the end of the day turn out to closely resemble each other. Both reflect the thinking of the Meiji oligarchs who reworked Japanese tradition and forged a Japan that would, they believed, be a thoroughly modern and powerful nation while remaining true to its own, uniquely Japanese, self.

This is, however, a Japan with very peculiar features. It is very much a man's world, a world of men who belong to large organizations. These men lead highly structured lives, dedicated to ensuring that the groups to which they belong remain intact and succeed in competition with other similar groups. Their women stay home and raise the kids or, if they work in "the water trades" (a euphemism for the sex industry), provide men with entertainment. Is this all that there is to Japan? The answer is clearly, "No."

In his *Introduction to Japanese Society*, sociologist Sugimoto Yoshio invites us to imagine what a being from another planet would find if its purpose were to speak to a typical Japanese. If the alien began by reading the social science literature on Japan written in the sixties, seventies, and eighties, it might start out believing that a typical Japanese was a "salaryman," a male, university-educated, white-collar employee of a large corporation. He would be a member of the company union and work for the firm continuously from the time he joined it fresh out of school to the time he retired.

The salaryman was the idol of his age. His customs, habits, and motivations and the social structures that shaped his life were constantly being analyzed in an effort to understand how Japan, utterly defeated in World War II, had swiftly risen to become an economic superpower. However, writes Sugimoto, a "typical Japanese" he was not.

> To begin, the person chosen should be a female, because women outnumber men in Japan; the 2000 census shows that sixty-five million women and sixty-one million men live in the Japanese archipelago. With regard to occupation, she would definitely not be employed in a large corporation but would work in a small enterprise, since fewer than one in eight workers is employed in a company with three hundred or more employees. Nor would she be guaranteed lifetime employment, since those who work under this arrangement amount at most to only a quarter of Japan's workforce. She would not belong to a labor union, because only one out of five Japanese workers is unionized. She would not be university-educated. Fewer than one in six Japanese have a university degree, and even today only about 40 percent of the younger generation graduate from a university with a four-year degree.[48]

What, then, might her life be like? For one, partial answer, we turn to the work of our third anthropologist, Dorinne Kondo, a scholar to whom the Japanese were neither an alien enemy nor friends and neighbors like herself. They represented a heritage that Kondo, a Japanese American woman with professional aspirations, was struggling to come to grips with.

From Stories to Selves

As Kondo listened to the stories of the people whose lives she shared during her fieldwork, she was constantly asking herself, "Who am I? What do I want to be?" and writing her own story in an effort to find the answers.

In Kondo's book *Crafting Selves: Power, Gender, and Discourses of Identity in a Japanese Workplace*, one of the most dramatic moments is that in which Kondo sees herself reflected in the shiny metal surface of a butcher's display case. What she sees is a typical young Japanese housewife; she is overcome by the fear that she will never be able to escape the Japanese world in which she has immersed herself.[49]

What Kondo learned in the course of her research is that Japanese accounts of what it is to be a Japanese self vary in form as well as substance. Three cases illustrate this point.

The first is the ethics center to which her employer, the owner of a commercial confectionary plant that produces both Western and traditional Japanese sweets, sends his employees, hoping that they will emerge with renewed dedication to Japanese values. The ethics center's program is based on a clearly stated ideology. At first glance, it seems reinforce the values and social structures that Benedict and Nakane describe. Then we begin to notice some differences.

One key term is *ki,* the breath, spirit, vital force that human beings are said to share with all living things—the same ki of which martial arts instructors make so much in teaching their students to achieve the stillness and latent force needed to overcome their opponents. Ki is controlled by *kokoro,* the heart. But the ethic center's kokoro is not the warrior's stilled but implicitly aggressive heart. It is, instead, a naïve, receptive *sunao na kokoro*: "a heart accepting of things as they are, without resistance or questioning . . . a heart sensitive not to its own desires, but to the needs of others."[50]

As if lifted straight from Benedict, the ethics center's teaching continues: The sunao na kokoro is a heart deeply conscious of *on,* the inescapable burden of debt owed to others—first and foremost the parents from whom life itself is received. That debt is owed, however—not, we notice, to the emperor—but instead to employers who stand in loco parentis, providing a livelihood in exchange for loyal service. The sunao na kokoro finds its expression in behavior that is cheerful and bright, caring and cooperative, and, above all in, "working joyfully, throwing our full energy into work."[51]

Not only have the Meiji oligarchs' ideals been skewed in new directions, but their appeal has become problematic. While participating in the ethics center's training program, Kondo observes that her fellow employees oscillate between moments of deep emotion and grumbling refusal to go along. Ultimately the center is not all that successful in imposing its ideals. Her employer complains, "Most of the young guys just want to be outdoors and get some exercise. They haven't really understood."[52] He can point to only a single employee on whom the center has had a definite effect.

Then Kondo turns to a second case, the life and career of an elderly craftsworker. Instead of ideals articulated in abstract, philosophical language, she hears a picaresque narrative, the story of a life on the road. Here there is no lifetime commitment to the group. There is, instead, a passionate devotion to craft that leads repeatedly from one group and position to another.

The elderly craftsworker Ohara was born in the 1930s in Japan's cold and impoverished northeast. Orphaned shortly after his graduation from junior high school, he was apprenticed to an uncle from whom he began to learn how to make traditional Japanese sweets. Then, quitting his uncle's shop, he began a journey that led from one employer to another, adding new skills to his repertoire at each stop along the way.

During his apprenticeship and then his journey worker travels, Ohara exchanged long, grueling hours of labor for the chance to learn, room and board, and a minimal wage. But through his years of suffering, he acquired a craft from which he derives aesthetic and emotional satisfaction. Now he works at the factory where Kondo met him.

In some respects, Ohara's life story is a close parallel to the ethics center's program. Persevering through hardship and imitating established patterns were the heart of the training he endured. He acquired his skills through physical effort, learning by doing; verbal instruction was minimal. (Those who have read about life in Zen temples may now feel themselves going "Ah-hah.")

But instead of the bright, cheerful, cooperative self that the ethics center holds up as ideal, Ohara embodies a different stereotype: is a "stern, silent, severe artisan. . . . In the factory, he would work for hours without a word, occasionally stalking about to glower at his subordinates as he inspected their creations. Above all, he appeared unapproachable."[53] The self his story constructed was highly individual, with the risks as well as the rewards that being individual entails.

Ohara feared loss of physical vigor, the strength required to work long hours. He was wary of younger men, whose talents might challenge his own. His was not a lifetime position secured by its place in a corporate hierarchy. Instead the self he cultivated was rooted in personal expertise and a mastery of craft that others would find hard to duplicate.

It was, however, her third case that was most problematic for Kondo. When she interviewed the women who worked only part time, what she heard was neither philosophy nor a coherent, if rambling, narrative. She was looking for stories, but all she found were bits and pieces, fragments that didn't hang together. When women talked about their work, they described haphazard movements from one dead-end job to another, with no prospect of advancement and no chance to learn new skills. If their lives had meaning at all, it was meaning centered in their families. They felt that they had to work, to contribute to family income. But their jobs were not part of belonging to something larger than themselves. Neither were they paths to self-cultivation. To Kondo, whose own self-definition included American professional woman who finds meaning in her work, to be trapped in one of these women's lives was a frightening prospect, indeed.

Situated Listening

Kondo's work brings us straight to the heart of the problem that every anthropologist who does fieldwork in modern Japan now faces. We listen to the stories that people tell us. Our problem is how to situate them in the context in which we hear them. Is what we are told the truth—the whole truth and nothing but the truth? The answer has to be rarely. The people whose stories we hear edit what they say. The acceptable commonplace prefaced with "We Japanese" may be what they want non-Japanese (or other Japanese) to hear. This particular problem frequently arises in discussions with those in official positions. But even good friends may be reluctant to reveal what they think of as private matters.

There is evidence that concern for privacy is growing stronger in Japan. An older Japanese, a member of the "burning generation" who rebuilt Japan after World War II, remarks to me that "In our generation we were so eager to get to the *honne*, what people were really thinking and feeling, that we trampled into each other's hearts with our shoes on. The new generation is too polite." Those who know that Japanese custom requires removing your shoes before entering a Japanese home will see the force of his image. They may also know that *shinshiteki* ("gentlemanly," the word translated here as "polite") implies self-effacement and avoidance of direct confrontation. Marketing research suggests that young Japanese are increasingly averse to being preached at.[54] They prefer a "silent appeal" that attracts the attention of others without being pushy or overbearing. A young man asked if the flamboyant costume he wears when he goes to Harajuku—the teen fashion center of Tokyo where he and many others dress up in ways that seem bizarre to their parents—reflects his real self, replies: "Nobody gets to see the real me."

Tada Taku, who has won several Grand Prix in the annual Tokyo Copywriters Club advertising contest and is said by his colleagues to display penetrating insights in his work, asks, "How many of us can understand what others are thinking, even when the others are friends, lovers, parents or siblings?"[55]

Perhaps the best we can do then is, first, to crosscheck what we hear by listening to as many stories as possible told by different people. Second, we can situate what we learn by locating what we hear in relation to basic material facts that affect all Japanese lives, and noting how our storytellers position themselves in relation to critical issues that affect all modern societies: gender, generation, social class, and geography. We can look at political and economic history and ask how changing labor markets have affected life chances. We can study how demographics—later marriage, a growing number of singles, a low birthrate and aging population—have transformed families and households. We can note how urbanization, suburban sprawl, and consumerism have influenced the lives we study.

CHANGING JAPAN

To anyone reading this chapter it should be clear by now that any attempt to discover the unchanging essence of Japan—in distinctive values or social structures or everyday habits—is doomed from the start. The Japan we encounter today is only a moment in a history of change. In this, the third part of our chapter, we turn to some of the basic factors shaping that change.

The Enduring Conservative Legacy

Political scientist T. J. Pempel describes the early Meiji state as a classic conservative-authoritarian regime, with a strong centralized state in alliance with rural landlords, oligopolistic businesses, and an expansionist military. This was the Japan whose culture Ruth Benedict analyzed.

For a brief period after World War II, it seemed possible that Japan might become the kind of social-democratic state found in Scandinavia. In the early days of the occupation, militant labor unions were formed and provided the core of support for both the Japan Socialist Party and the Japan Communist Party. It was fear that the socialists would become Japan's single largest party that led to the creation in 1955 of the Liberal Democratic Party through the merger of two smaller conservative parties.

The LDP, writes Pempel, was "a vote-gathering wonder."[56] For nearly 40 years it consistently captured between 55 and 60 percent of the seats in both houses of the Diet and dominated local and prefectural governments by even larger margins. What is very interesting is that at the same time the LDP's popularity, as measured by public opinions polls, was never much higher than 40 percent. How could a party so unpopular remain so firmly in control?

The answer, says Pempel, was a new coalition in which bureaucrats and big business joined hands with farmers and small business to shut out the labor movement and the parties it supported. Bureaucrats had long played a central role in Japanese government. From the Tokugawa shogunate to the Meiji state to postwar democracy, the bureaucrats who staffed the central government ministries quietly went about running the country. As Japan mobilized for World War II, their control of banking and other key institutions was strengthened. During the postwar period, their ties with big business were renewed by what became a familiar cycle. The best and the brightest graduates of Japan's universities were recruited for bureaucratic careers. Then, at the end of those careers they retired into new jobs with the firms that their ministries regulated. Big business provided the funding required by politicians to win seats in the Diet. The bureaucrats wrote the laws that the Diet members reviewed and passed. So long as care was taken to protect the interests of the farmers and small business owners on whose votes conservative politicians depended, the system ran smoothly, despite occasional scandals when corruption became too flagrant. Following the collapse of the economic bubble in 1991, however, the stresses and strains began to show.

From a geographical perspective, the system described above unifies the interests of bureaucrats and business leaders concentrated in Tokyo with those of politicians elected from conservative districts in other parts of Japan. Politicians in rural areas mobilize support by providing a continuous stream of pork barrel spending, whose importance is only increased by the fact that construction is Japan's largest industry.

That observation may surprise foreigners, who, when they look at Japan, see not construction companies but firms like Toyota, Sony, and Canon, enormously successful in international markets, companies rightly praised for their high productivity. What they often neglect to note is (1) that these famous firms are dependent on networks of small suppliers and (2) that in other sectors of Japan's economy, productivity is half or less than that in North America or Europe.

It is not surprising, then, that as Japan's successful firms become increasingly multinational, they are doing what other multinationals do, cutting off their networks of small Japanese suppliers and shifting production overseas to places with lower labor costs. Young Japanese find it harder to find good jobs. Tax revenues fall, and funding the projects on which the current political system depends becomes increasingly difficult. The chorus of complaints about boondoggles funded to shore up rural economies that seem to do nothing but ruin rural landscapes and the basic unfairness of elections in which rural votes count for far more than those of voters who live in cities swells with every passing year.

Economic Ups and Downs

Older Japanese remember the decade from the end of the war to 1955 as a time of desperate poverty. Nearly three million Japanese had died in the war. Material losses totaled 64.3 billion yen. National wealth had shrunk to 188.9 billion yen, about what it had been in 1935. Food and energy resources were both in short supply. In a study of several generations of Japanese salarymen,[57] a man who was still a child during this period recalls an often-told story of that period: his mother selling her kimono to buy a bit of rice to feed the family.

In Japan's war-devastated cities, the housing shortage was acute, exacerbated by the influx of the approximately 6.5 million Japanese repatriated from Japan's dismantled empire in East and Southeast Asia.[58] Millions more had fled to the countryside to escape the bombing and were eager to return. This housing shortage would eventually ignite a construction boom that sent Japanese cities, especially Tokyo, sprawling into suburbs filled with ferroconcrete apartment complexes and vast expanses of stand-alone, suburban tract houses, most smaller and more shoddily constructed than the American suburban homes that inspired their construction. It would also prompt birth-control and family planning campaigns that would end Japan's short baby boom (1947–1949 vs. 1946–1964 in America) and lead, except for a minor surge when the Baby Boomers came of age, to the steadily falling birthrates that Japan has experienced ever since.

From 1955 to 1970, Japan's economy took off and grew at a pace that startled the world. Economists and historians still debate the reasons why, but four key factors seem to have played critical roles. First, the wartime destruction of Japan's industrial infrastructure had left largely intact Japan's most vital asset: a highly educated, skilled, and disciplined workforce. Wartime concentration on defense-related heavy, chemical, and precision machinery industries had, moreover, prepared this workforce to take full advantage of factor number two, a window of opportunity in a world hungry for the kinds of product—ships, steel, chemicals, optical and other precision machinery—that these industries supply.

What was still missing was factor three, capital. But following the outbreak of the Korean War in 1950, funds for "special procurements" to support the U.N. military effort poured in. Japanese economist Tsuru Shigeo notes that these extra funds doubled Japan's foreign exchange reserves and provided precisely the kick-start that Japan's economic recovery required. The take-off was then sustained by a yen artificially pegged at 360 yen to the

U.S. dollar, which made Japanese goods cheap in global markets. It was, says Tsuru, like extending special treatment to a convalescent golfer until long after he has recovered.[59]

Japanese who grew up in this period do not remember poverty. If they belonged to Japan's then burgeoning middle class, they remember the excitement of moving into new apartments or buying new homes and filling them with new appliances: first radios, sewing machines, and fans, then TV sets, refrigerators, and air conditioners. They recall the heady optimism of a world in which the dream of progress through technology seemed well within everyone's grasp. They remember when "new families" composed of hard-working dad, stay-at-home mom and a couple of delightful kids, living in material abundance in a new suburban house and driving a new automobile, were a fresh and exciting ideal.

The year 1970 was pivotal. If the 1964 Olympics announced Japan's full return to the global community of nations, the 1970 Osaka Expo proclaimed its economic triumph. The "burning generation" that had risen from defeat determined to overtake their rivals in Europe and North America could say to themselves, "Job well done." But there were other signs of change. Not all was well.

Japan was choking. The pell-mell rush to grow heavy and chemical industries had generated a rising tide of pollution, stimulating a growing wave of popular opposition. Younger Japanese were frustrated by a system into which they felt squeezed against their will. From 1965 to 1973, Japanese students were active participants in the global peace movement that opposed the Vietnam War. In 1968, Japanese universities erupted. Students seized control of buildings. Helmeted and masked demonstrators battled police.

Besides being the year of the Osaka Expo, 1970 was the year that the words "women's liberation" were introduced into the Japanese language. It was also the year when author Mishima Yukio committed ritual suicide. Mishima's final words, "Is there none among you who will join me? Not even one? So be it . . . I have seen the end!" reproach the members of the Japan Self Defense Forces for having abandoned the romantic, masculine warrior ideal that Mishima sought to embody and revive. Salarymen were called "corporate warriors." At the end of the day, however, they were only organization men.

Then, in 1971, Japan experienced the Nixon Shock; no longer would the yen be pegged at 360 to the dollar. Allowed to float in global currency markets, the yen sharply appreciated, making Japanese goods more expensive in overseas markets. That was followed, in 1973, by the first Oil Shock, when OPEC suddenly raised crude oil prices.

Japan's economy would recover and begin to grow again; but those years in the wake of the dual shocks were precisely when Japan's baby boomers, born between 1947 and 1949, entered the labor market. A weak job market dampened their once fiery spirits and forced them to learn that to get ahead they would have to remember the proverb, "The nail that sticks up gets hammered down." The peace and environmental movements lost steam. Rules and regulations multiplied as government and corporate regulators sought to regain control of what many feared had become a Japan falling into chaos. The new families created as the boomers married and began to have children became a new mass market that sustained Japan's economic growth throughout the seventies and eighties.

The authors were lucky to arrive in Japan in 1980, just one year after sociologist Ezra Vogel published *Japan as Number One,* trumpeting the message that Japan's economy was rising beyond world-class heights.[60] The *shinjinrui* or "New Breed" who came of age in the eighties were a smaller age cohort than the Boomers. They looked for jobs in a seller's market and were free to consider job options. They were able to demand more time for themselves and for socializing with friends outside their companies. Their lifestyles were captured in a novel titled *Nantonaku Kuristaru* [Somewhat Crystal],[61] the first Japanese novel to come with its own glossary of famous brands. Market researcher George Fields celebrated their consumption habits in books with titles like *Gucci on the Ginza*.[62] These were giddy times, indeed.

The collapse of the economic bubble in 1991 put an end to the optimism of the eighties, which now seemed more like hubris, the fatal pride that drives classic Greek tragedy. Once again a larger generation, the Boomer Juniors, the children of the Boomers, were coming of age just as Japan's economy slumped. Many had parents who had purchased apartments or houses while real estate prices were high and were now saddled with debt. Many saw fathers, who had devoted themselves to their companies in exchange for what they believed would be secure lifetime employment and a comfortable retirement, sacked as their employers restructured. Facing an uncertain future, a growing number delayed marriage and stayed home as what came to be called "parasite singles."

Younger Japanese are growing up in a very affluent country, but one now confronting in acute forms the issues facing all the world's economically advanced nations: new generations whose members either delay marriage or do not marry at all, falling birthrates, an aging population. Their lives are shaped by technologies unimagined when their parents were young—video games, personal computers, cell phones, and the Internet—and the need to compete in global markets where new rivals, many in Asia, now challenge Japan's dominance.

The Most Inescapable Fact

Management guru Peter Drucker says flatly that trying to predict the future is foolish, but it is, however, "possible—and fruitful—to identify major events that have already happened, irrevocably, and that will have predictable effects in the next decade or two."[63] The events he has in mind can be summed up in a single word, "demographics," changes in the structure of human populations. In the case of Japan, these changes have resembled those in other advanced industrial societies but have been, if anything, more dramatic.

In 1950, Japan's population pyramid (a graph of the population broken down by gender and age) looked like—a pyramid. It was broad at the bottom and converged to a peak at the top, the characteristic shape of a population in which there are lots of young people and the generations shrink as people grow older and die. In 2002, the graph no longer looked like a pyramid:

- At the top, where people are aged 65 and older, it was lopsided. A large dent in the side where the male population is graphed reflects men killed in World War II.
- A notch on both sides at age 63 reflects a sharp decline in births as Japan went to war with China in 1938–1939.
- A deeper notch on both sides at ages 56 and 57 reflects another sharp decline just after Japan's defeat, 1945–1946.
- Next we see, however, a sudden increase among those aged 53–55, Japan's Baby Boomers, born 1947–1949.
- Finally, however, both sides of the graph shrink inward, except for those aged 28–31, the Baby Boomer Juniors.

As of 2003, the number of Japanese aged 60 or older was already larger than the number aged 15 or younger. Japan is an aging society. The implications for Japan's pension and healthcare systems are grim. But how, after all, did this happen?

The broad outlines of the story are the same as those in other advanced industrial societies. As dependence on inherited assets (farms, shops, other real estate) declines and dependence on salaried jobs increases, the economic rationale for building and preserving a household declines. With the shift from durable skills handed down from one generation to the next to unprecedented new skills required by new technology, formal education replaces traditional wisdom. The rising costs of raising and educating children make it difficult to afford the other, more immediate gratifications that advertisers and marketers promise. With children less likely to inherit either wealth or useful knowledge from their parents and parents less able to count on their children's care in old age, the imperative to reproduce weakens.

As pundits and politicians bemoan the loss of traditional values, men and women, parents and children find themselves groping for new ways to relate to each other. As the value of marriage and child rearing becomes more uncertain, people marry later or not at all. The birthrate falls. Then, given the longer life spans made possible by modern medicine, populations age.

In the case of Japan, two factors deserve special attention: (1) the ie-based social structure described by Benedict and Nakane—a starting point for modernization very different from that of other Asian societies—and (2) the speed and intensity of Japan's transformation following World War II.

Modernization Taken to the Limit

In premodern cities and villages, homes and workplaces occupy the same spaces. Markets and religious centers are normally nearby, within walking distance. Family, work, and recreation blur into each other. By contrast, in modern cities these functions are spatially separated. Workers must leave their homes to go to factories or offices. Children go to school. Their mothers stop shopping in neighborhood stores and, instead, are lured away to supermarkets and shopping centers.

In all of these respects, Japan is a modern society—but with several important differences. The most important is the distance between home and work, especially for Japanese who work in Tokyo, the heart of Japan's largest metropolitan area.

The push to solve the housing crisis after World War II spread suburban tract housing and condominium complexes along the private train lines that radiate out of Tokyo. As Tokyo's population increased and Japan's economy prospered, property in central Tokyo became increasingly costly, forcing growing numbers of families to find housing in the new suburbs at an ever-increasing distance from the center. This trend was strong even before the real estate bubble of the late 1980s. Economist Tsuru Shigeo calculates that at height of the bubble in 1990, an average college graduate would earn a lifetime income of 166 million yen. That would not have been enough to buy even one *tsubo* (36 square feet) of central Tokyo real estate.[64] To fulfill the dream of a home of his own, the salaryman who worked in central Tokyo had to buy far from the center. It was the norm for people working in the city to spend three hours a day commuting (an hour and a half each way). For many, the commute was longer.

When the three-hour commute was added to a long workday and the after-work socializing that Japanese corporate life required, the salaried workers jammed onto commuter trains were almost never home. Leaving early in the morning and returning late at night, they had little, if any, time left for family or local community life.

Suppose, however, that Nakane was right, and Japanese social structure was, indeed, frame oriented. Frame orientation requires face-to-face interaction, and households with household heads who were almost never home, children who went off to school, and housewives transformed into part-time workers and ardent consumers—were frames falling apart. The impact on Japanese lives was profound.

Men Slipping into the Shadows

For Japanese men who commuted to work in large Japanese cities—and commuters were mostly men—their absence from home made it increasingly difficult to play the role of traditional household head. It was hard for a man who was never home to control the behavior, let alone the thoughts and feelings, of his wife and children.

An analysis of Japanese advertising describes what was going on from the point of view of the copywriters who were writing Japanese ads.

> The male who was once an absolute presence has become an obscure figure, a warrior fighting in the shadows. This marks a sharp departure from the early postwar years when men were still portrayed as the prime movers in their families, as awe-inspiring pillars of the household. . . . In the sixties, the grey warriors appeared—salarymen riding the wave of high growth as Japan's economy took off. Now father was never at home. . . . By the eighties, men mentioned in ads had no place to call their own, either at work or at home. They were like stray animals.[65]

Meanwhile, women's roles were also changing. This same study continues,

> During these same 45 years, women shed their roles as virtuous wives and housekeepers. They took control of the household and claimed equality with men in public. They became independent and began to go their own way . . . the image of women had evolved in three stages, from housewife to mother to woman.[66]

To see a woman as a housewife was to see her as responsible for housekeeping, childcare, and waiting up to feed her husband supper when he came home from work late at night. To see a woman as a mother was to see her from her children's perspective, the nurturing authority in charge of the household. She might defer to father in public, but she kept a firm grip on the family finances and, truth be told, might treat her husband privately as if he were only an older child. To see a woman as a woman was to see her in her own right, an independent consumer, someone who might have a job of her own, someone concerned about her looks, someone with sex appeal.

Changes were also taking place in how children were perceived. In the forties and fifties, children were rarely mentioned in advertising, except in birth-control ads. In the sixties, toddlers became the focus of ads for new forms of education. As Japan's economy took off and the salaryman became the ideal that every mother's son should strive for, mothers came under increasing pressure to ensure that their children did well in school. A new stereotype, the *kyôiku mama* (education mother), was born.

By the seventies, however, children no longer seemed to know their place. The children who appear in ads are, in older Japanese terms, impertinent and rude. They scold and stick out their tongues at their parents. By the eighties, they were also more calculating. A 1985 headline has a child saying, "News flash: I work for money."

Relations between Generations

One important result of market research conducted in Japan in the 1990s was the revelation that relations between generations had changed significantly—but not in a simple, linear way. Relations between the "burning generation," the corporate warriors who rebuilt Japan after World War II, and their children, the "New Breed," were difficult. The warriors appealed to traditional values and demanded an obedience that their children were no longer willing to give. The lifestyles of these generations were radically different. The older had grown up in poverty; the other enjoyed affluence and flaunted Japan's wealth in the 1980s. As one New Breed researcher remarked, "For us, getting along well [with our parents] was something to be embarrassed about." To the New Breed, being a new generation and having a distinctive lifestyle was of vital importance. Then, however, he continued,

> Today's kids don't have this attitude. In a very real sense they have all become consumers. They aren't people who make things. They are

people who buy things. They consume culture; they don't make it.

In contrast to the relationships of the burning generation and the New Breed, relations between the Baby Boomers and their children, the Boomer Juniors, are smoother and less complicated. These generations share similar tastes in casual clothes (think Gap) and sneakers (think Reebok and Nike), in the *manga* comic books that they read, and the artists whose music they prefer. Asked why, researchers point to the Boomer ideal, the "new family" composed of just parents and children. In this household, mother and father were separate but equal powers, with mother in firm control at home while father went off to work to earn the family income. No longer household heads and successors, one senior to the other but both united in dedication to a household that would, ideally, last forever, parents and children could now be friends. Their bonds would be reinforced by shared consumption of all the wonderful new products the modern economy made available. Miura Atsushi goes even further. He asserts that the new family was itself a mass-produced artifact, deliberately created by and for consumption.[67]

Suburban Life in Japan

Miura observes that to Japanese in the 1950s, when Japan was still recovering from defeat and devastation, the sheer material affluence of American life was stunning. Pursuit of this American way of life changed everything about Japanese households. First was the shift to nuclear families. Traditional households were built around three-generation families: the household head and his wife, the successor and his wife, and the household head's grandchildren. The nuclear family would be composed of a working father, a full-time housewife mother, and children. Between 1955 and 1975, 10 million new households headed by married couples were created; 7 million were nuclear family households. Nuclear family households increased from 45 percent to 53 percent of all Japanese households.

Most of these new nuclear families lived in the suburbs, at first in danchi or condominium apartments and, then, if father's career went smoothly, in their own stand-alone suburban houses. As father went off to work, mother became a full-time housewife.

Pursuit of this new way of life was not simply a matter of individual Japanese embracing the American Dream. To create domestic markets for electrical appliances and automobiles as well as new types of homes, corporate strategies promoted it. Government policies supported their efforts. In 1961, tax deductions for dependent wives were introduced. In 1962, junior high schools eliminated their old system of vocational and home economics courses taken by both boys and girls. Put in its place was a new system, in which home economics became girls-only and boys took vocational classes focused on technical skills.

These and similar steps reinforced a vision that was spreading throughout the non-communist world: Families that owned their own homes, families in which mother took charge of the home and became responsible for the children's education while father went off to work, families in which man the producer was paired with woman the consumer to generate the supply and demand that would drive economic growth—families like these would be bulwarks against communist ideology. They would play a vital role in fighting and winning the Cold War.

But like other utopian ideals, the new family would also have its problems. As the Japanese embraced the American Dream, it came under attack in its birthplace. In 1963 Betty Friedan published *The Feminine Mystique*, describing suburban housewives as leading lives devoid of meaning and plagued with unnamed anxieties. In that same year Martin Luther King, Jr. led the March on Washington. Just a year earlier,

Rachel Carson had published *Silent Spring*, warning of the growing danger of industrial pollution. As Japan's Baby Boomers were coming of age and starting new families in the early 1970s, the ideas and ideals of Friedan, King, and Carson had already spread to Japan.

As noted in the first section, Japanese students were deeply involved in the student movements of the late 1960s. But while most Japanese student radicals would—like their European and American counterparts—bow their heads to economic pressure and, if they were men, go along to get along in corporate careers, they would never fully embrace the "traditional Japanese," Meiji and wartime, legacy of older generations. They might be hardworking and appear to accept the frame-oriented and vertical structures of the business world as inescapable facts of life. But as long hours and long commutes made their new American Dream–style families only a dream after all, ironic self-distancing replaced their elders' zeal.

From Idol to Idiot: The Japanese Salaryman

In 1963, when Ezra Vogel published *Japan's New Middle Class: The Salary Man and His Family in a Tokyo Suburb*,[68] there was no question about it, the salaryman was the idol of the age. His white-collar job in a large corporation, with its regular salary, regular raises and promise of lifetime employment was the goal for which education mothers trained and groomed their sons. His promotions to section chief, and then, if he made it, to department head, were celebrated milestones in every successful career.

By 1982, promotion to department or section chief was becoming more difficult. There were too many Baby Boomers for all of them to be promoted. Even firms that had grown rapidly during the sixties and seventies simply didn't have enough places for so many new managers. By 1987, New Breed salarymen were shaking up corporate life in Japan. A study of their new attitudes observed that "While all companies have work rules, only twenty percent of salarymen follow them religiously. To most the rules seem superficial and not to be taken seriously." It found that 30 percent of salarymen disliked company trips, 50 percent didn't want to be forced to participate in company-sponsored sports days, and growing numbers preferred not to receive invitations to colleagues' weddings or funerals.

A 1995 repeat of the study found the trend to disengagement growing ever stronger. Now the newest generation was the "Bubbly Ones." Hired during the economic bubble, they were fun-loving and mostly still single; they seemed like idiots to members of older generations. The rebellious New Breed were now the "Angry Ones." Trapped in midcareer with Japan's economy stalled, they despised not only the Bubbly Ones but also their Boomer bosses, on whom they blamed their predicament. The Boomers were now disillusioned, faced with corporate restructuring and the realization that regular raises and lifetime employment were disappearing.

Of the Burning Generation, only those who had made it to board of director or CEO level were still employed by their companies. The rest had retired before or shortly after the economic bubble's collapse, while severance payments and pensions were still generous. They were the lucky ones.

These studies, however, all focused on Japanese men. What was happening to Japanese women?

Liberated for What?

In *Onna Daigaku* [*The Great Learning for Women*], seventeenth-century Neo-Confucianist Kaibara Ekiken wrote, "The only qualities that befit a woman are gentle obedience, chastity, mercy, and quietness."[69] In the Meiji Civil Code, promulgated in 1898, women were granted few legal rights. Article 5 in the Police Security Regulations of 1900 explicitly forbade women from joining political organizations or even attending meetings at which political speeches were given.[70] These laws would remain in force until after World War II.

In 1945, women's suffrage was approved. Article 14 of the Constitution of Japan proclaimed in 1946 bans discrimination on the basis of race, creed, sex, social status, or family origin. Article 24 explicitly requires the consent of both parties to marriage. The revised Civil Code issued in 1947 abolishes the ie system.

The next major change in Japanese women's legal status came in 1985, with the passage of the Equal Employment Opportunity Law. But legal status and social acceptance are two different things, especially when laws like that one contain no penalties for its violation.

Kaibara's Neo-Confucian vision had no place for the young women from rural villages who found employment in Japan's spinning and textile mills as Japan industrialized during the Meiji period. The Meiji Civil Code was silent on the service industry jobs filled by women during the first bloom of Japanese consumerism in Taisho (1915–1926), jobs still largely filled by women today. Neither anticipated what happened during the war years, when the often-quoted phrase *ryôsaikenbo*, "good wives and wise mothers," appeared as part of efforts to mobilize women's support for the war. That phrase may now sound reactionary, but at the time it presented an opportunity for women's groups to construct "more authoritative roles within the family for housewives and mothers and, by extension, new public roles for women within the state."[71]

The Boomer wives and mothers who moved to the suburbs during the 1970s were thus the daughters of women accustomed to being fully in charge of their homes. Their husbands who went off to work each day were like their fathers who went off to war. Some might pose as lords and masters. Others might want to see themselves as friends and equals. Neither was at home to interfere.

More women were, moreover, entering the workforce. The new family ideal might be a family in which father provided the livelihood while mother stayed home and cared for the children. But the costs of educating the children while keeping up with the neighbors were rising. Some women had always had to work, simply to make ends meet. Now more looked for work to be sure that their families could afford the new consumer goods that everyone wanted.

Still, however, women's careers outside the home tended to follow "the M curve," with employment figures for women rising, then falling, then rising again before sharply declining with age. More highly educated unmarried women might find jobs as "office ladies," performing secretarial and other clerical tasks in corporate offices. The less educated found employment on factory assembly lines or as sales clerks, food servers, or cashiers in retail outlets. Some became nurses or teachers. But young women typically took jobs that only lasted until they married. Then, returning to the labor force after their children started school, they could find only low-paid, part-time work. They could supplement their household's incomes but rarely earned enough to be financially independent.

Women were also becoming more educated. In 1955, only 5 percent of women received postsecondary education, and more than half of those went only to junior college. By 2002, 48.5 percent of Japanese women received some form of postsecondary education, compared to 48.8 percent of men.

Higher education combined with still limited opportunities is a recipe for dissatisfaction—and shop until you drop provides at best temporary relief. Like their counterparts around the world, Japanese women, too, find no simple answers to "What's it all about?"

What's Love Got to Do with It?

In all the industrialized countries, the age of marriage has risen, and growing numbers of individuals never get married at all. Far from being an exception, Japan is a leader in this trend. The result is a growing prevalence of "singles attitudes." A 1993 study describes these attitudes as follows:

- The self is a fenced-in paradise. There is pleasure in turning inward.
- Everyone has his own world; don't interfere with others.
- In relationships, keep a certain amount of distance, not too close, not too far.
- Keep a distance, too, from family and company, the groups to which you are attached. No stains, no smells; be self-deodorizing.
- Don't be caught up in old systems and customs. Break out of the standard models. Go your own way.
- Just drift along like a tumbleweed. Don't get tied down.

Not all Japanese shared these traits. But those who did were 36.5 percent of a 1,200-person sample, half single, half married, living within a 40-kilometer (25 mile) radius of Tokyo.

What's Happening to the Kids?

In a 1982 study, we find the observation that Japanese children lead busy lives. After school, the school day continues in cram schools or private lessons. A cram school teacher explains parents' fear that if children study only at home they won't study hard enough. Plus, he says, parents were no longer confident that they know what their children need to learn.

In this study we also hear two themes that recur in later research. The first is the observation that the children behave like miniature adults: "Today's boys and girls are like miniature wives and miniature salarymen." The second is the degree to which modern children's lives seem narrow compared to the researchers' own childhoods.

> These children have no dreams. They aren't latchkey children, but still their lives are constricted. Between study and private lessons, they aren't able to play. Looking back on when I was growing up, I remember the evenings I used to spend in a nearby vacant lot. Today's children are pitiful.

The editor who draws this conclusion remembers a time when children could slip away and escape the surveillance of parents and teachers to discover a wider world than that of the high-rise apartments, suburban houses, or classrooms to which the lives of Japanese children were increasingly confined.

Fifteen years later, a 1997 study of children about the same age, in the fourth, fifth, and sixth grades of elementary school, describes them as pragmatic, tolerant, able to mix, trend-sensitive, and—once again—like miniature adults. One new trend was familiarity with new technologies: 70.3 percent had used a personal computer; 81.2 percent liked video games.

"Able to mix" reflected a fact surprising to older Japanese. These children feel no resistance to associating with non-Japanese. They mix easily with all sorts of people instead of forming small, tight groups and excluding outsiders. Their frames are fluid and shifting ones. Casting about for an image to describe this new generation, researchers chose the water strider, the long-legged insect that skitters across the surface of ponds and puddles. These kids, this image implies, skitter over society's surface, never probing deeply. They like to be noticed but hate to be bothered; they want to be left alone. Singles attitudes are already strong among them.

Growing Old in an Aging Japan

Ruth Benedict described the typical Japanese life cycle as "a great shallow U-curve with maximum freedom and indulgence allowed to babies and the old . . . . After the age of sixty men and women are almost as unhampered by shame as little children are."[72] A 1986 study suggests that this pattern continued into the 1980s.

It depicts both children and the elderly as lacking the physical and financial resources to lead independent lives. Both are said to exhibit strong, naïve emotions, uninhibited by adult calculation. Both are described as uninterested in sex, thus comfortable bathing together.

A 1996 study presents a very different picture. It describes Japanese aged 60-plus as "lifestyle aristocrats," who value private space and time. They enjoy freedom from social demands but cling to social position. They hate being old and dress in styles that they themselves admit are more suitable for younger people. Those who can afford it pursue self-cultivation through art, music, and tasteful possessions.

Commenting on this research, Sekizawa Hidehiko notes another important difference: In 1986,

> Many of [our sample's] friends had died in World War II. They knew war and, in many cases, had been soldiers. Their friends had been killed but they had survived to grow old and have time on their hands. Talk about relaxing made them feel guilty. . . . By 1996, very few of those people were left. More than fifty years had passed since the end of the war. Retirees had experienced the war but only as children, as victims. That is the cohort whose support made high growth possible. They were the ones called worker bees, and they were ready to taste the honey. When we talked about how they planned to relax, there was no guilt involved.[73]

Beyond the Middle Class

The majority of the studies mentioned above were conducted by an organization called the Hakuhodo Institute of Life and Living (HILL). HILL was established in 1981 by Hakuhodo, Japan's second largest advertising agency, and its research reflects its parentage. Just as in reading and reflecting on the ideas of Benedict, Nakane, or Kondo, we need to be aware of the times in which this research was done and the questions it tries to answer.

The images of Japan found in HILL research depict a nation of middle-class people, salarymen and their families. They live, go to school, and work in metropolitan areas. They either live in Tokyo or quickly assimilate Tokyo trends. They are, above all, middle-class consumers.

No careful observer of modern Japan can imagine, however, that all Japanese belong to the same middle class. As we walk together to Yokohama Station, we pass homeless Japanese. They are mostly middle-aged or older men; homeless women are still relatively rare. Their unkempt hair and unbathed bodies, their ragged clothing and cardboard shelters are a visible inversion of the neat, clean, well-dressed image of middle-class Japanese.

Half an hour's train ride from Yokohama is Roppongi Hills, a monumental tribute to real estate billionaire Mori Minoru's enthusiasm for the work of the French modernist architect Le Corbusier. Conceived as the realization of Le Corbusier's vision of cites composed of gigantic towers surrounded by parkland, Roppongi Hills offers, says Mori Building's advertising, a redefinition of the Tokyo lifestyle. Too long has Tokyo been a dense, horizontal urban sprawl, a place in which home and work, recreation and shopping are so widely separated that exhausting commutes are the norm. Those who live in Roppongi Hills Residences can stroll to work in an office in Roppongi Hills Tower. After work they can go to the top of the Tower, where the world-class Mori Art Museum is the center of a complex that includes a private club, fitness center, and conference center, as well as an observation platform with a great view of Tokyo spread out below. Alternatively, they can shop or dine in the more than 200 shops and restaurants clustered at the Tower and Residences' feet, stroll in the parks that surround them, take in a late-night film at the Virgin Toho Cinema Complex, or walk to Suntory Hall, located in Ark Hills, another Mori project, to enjoy a classical concert or the opera.

It's a wonderful life indeed—for celebrities, successful entrepreneurs, or executives in multinational firms. It is not a lifestyle available to middle-class Japanese.

Geography Also Makes a Difference

To Japanese who live outside the Tokyo metropolitan area, the biggest problem with the sort of research discussed above is the way it ignores the places in which they live. Japan is divided into 47 prefectures, roughly equivalent to, though less independent of the central government, than the states that make up the United States or the Federal Republic of Germany.

Kanto, the region where both Tokyo and Yokohama, Japan's largest cities, are located, is the nine-hundred-pound gorilla of Japanese society. Tokyo is where the national government, the headquarters of most major corporations, and Japan's most famous public and private universities are located. Here, too, are the headquarters of the major mass media, the daily newspapers with national circulations, Japan's public broadcasting system, and the "key stations" that dominate Japan's five private television networks.

Kanto, eastern Japan, is frequently contrasted with Kansai, western Japan, where the cities of Kyoto, Osaka, and Kobe are located. Regional stereotypes claim that Kanto and Kansai people are very different: Kanto spawned the warrior-turned-bureaucrat ethos, whereas Kansai people are more pragmatic, more attuned to individual freedom than unwavering loyalty. Stereotypes aside, Kansai has been hurt more by the postbubble economy, since its manufacturing industries and subcontractors supplying large companies have been hard hit by shifts overseas. The experiences of people living in more rural parts of the country are different yet again; depopulation is devastating many of their communities. These differences remind us that our study of Japan still has far to go before we can claim deep understanding.

COMING TO THE END OF OUR JOURNEY

Imagine that we are walking with you back to Yokohama Station, to catch the Narita Express to the plane on which you will leave Japan. We certainly hope that you know more about Japan than you did when we met you at the station just after you arrived. But we hope, too, that you recognize how much more there is to learn about one of the world's most fascinating and rapidly changing societies. We know no better way to end this chapter than to borrow the words of Robert J. Smith, who began his research in Japan as a young anthropologist in his twenties and, when he wrote these words, was in his seventies.

> A twenty-something American embarking on the study of Japanese society and culture today brings to the commitment experience of an American society so different, and takes it into a country so changed, that I find it difficult to conceive of what the relationship might be like. For the United States of today is at least as different from that of my youth as the Japan of today is from the country I first encountered in 1946. That Japan was burned out, devastated, and prostrate in defeat—a different world. But it is too easily forgotten that the United States I had come from had only recently recovered from the disastrous effects of the Great Depression of the 1930s. Neither country was a stranger to economic hardship, and, as time passed, both achieved quite remarkable degrees of prosperity.[74]

Your journey of understanding of how that prosperity has affected Japan and perhaps changed Japan irrevocably—not just in the Kanto and not just the middle class—has only begun.

NOTES

1. Japanese is romanized in this chapter using the modified Hepburn system; place names and Japanese terms that have entered the English language are, however, expressed without

the macron indicating a long vowel. All Japanese names are given in Japanese order, surname followed by given name.
2. Theodore C. Bestor, Patricia G. Steinhoff, and Victoria Lyon Bestor, *Doing Fieldwork in Japan* (Honolulu: University of Hawaii Press, 2003) is a superb place to begin if you want to sample the results of ethnographic research in Japan and see how researchers from several disciplines have used ethnography in their studies of Japanese culture and society.
3. As the final draft of this chapter was being prepared in December 2003, a Google search for the words "Japan anthropology" produced 362,000 hits. Why not stop for a moment and check for yourself how many now appear?
4. George E. Marcus and Michael M. J. Fischer, *Anthropology as Cultural Critique: An Experimental Moment in the Human Sciences* (Chicago: University of Chicago Press, 1999). For advanced students, this is a good place to sample the debates anthropologists were having about what anthropology should be at the end of the twentieth century. But first read some classic ethnographies, to see what the authors are talking about.
5. Ruth Benedict, *The Chrysanthemum and the Sword* (New York: Houghton Mifflin, 1946); Nakane Chie, *Tate Shakai no Ningen Kankei* [Human Relations in the Vertical Society] (Tokyo: Kodansha, 1967). Both are classics likely to be found on anyone's list of seminal works about Japan. Translated, Nakane's book was published in English as *Japanese Society* (Berkeley: University of California Press, 1970). The third selection, Dorinne Kondo, *Crafting Selves: Power, Gender, and Identity in a Japanese Workplace* (Chicago: Chicago University Press, 1990), is a more idiosyncratic choice; we regard it as a modern classic. Other anthropologists might choose other works, to illustrate different approaches to anthropological research.
6. Like the one in which Dorinne Kondo sees her reflection and is shocked to discover herself looking just like a Japanese housewife (see note 49 below).
7. Kato Yuzo, ed., *Yokohama Past and Present* (Yokohama, Japan: Yokohama City University, 1990), 94. Commissioned by the city government, this book is designed to promote Yokohama. The information is accurate but also clearly slanted to make the city attractive to tourists and investors.
8. All figures cited here were the latest available when this chapter was being written in 2003. For current data see http://www.jinjapan.org/stat/. More detailed information can be found at the English-language Web sites of Japanese government ministries.
9. For current figures see http://www.worldbank.org/data/countrydata/countrydata.html.
10. For current figures see http://www.oecd.org/infobycountry/.
11. Like other aspects of the study of Japan, archeology is a field in ferment, not least because it has been so deeply involved in debates over national identity. For critical reviews of these debates and archeology's role in them, see Donald Denoon, Mark Hudson, Gavan McCormack, and Tessa Morris-Suzuki, *Multicultural Japan: Paleolithic to Postmodern* (Cambridge, England: Cambridge University Press, 1996 [paperback edition, 2001]). For an interesting and controversial survey of archaeological, linguistic, and ethnic—"racial"—aspects in Japan, see Jared Diamond's essay "Japanese Roots," *Discover* (June 1998): 86–94.
12. Joan Piggott, *The Emergence of Japanese Kingship* (Stanford, CA: Stanford University Press, 1997), provides an eminent historian's synthesis of archeological, anthropological, and historical materials concerning the formation of the first Japanese states. It is particularly noteworthy for its use of comparative perspective in a field, the early history of Japan, too often written about in purely local terms.
13. Denoon et al. are representative of scholars who point out that Japan, like other modern nations, is an imagined community, whose geographical boundaries have fluctuated widely over time.
14. An account of this process can be found in Eiko Ikegami, *The Taming of the Samurai: Honorific Individualism and the Making of Modern Japan* (Cambridge, MA: Harvard University Press, reprinted 1997).
15. For an excellent account of the development of Japanese nationalism and its many manifestations in culture, politics, religion, and throughout history see Brian J. McVeigh, *Nationalisms of Japan: Managing and Mystifying Identity* (Lanham, MD: Rowman and Littlefield, 2004). McVeigh's book cites a rich, deep literature for those interested in this topic. For another aspect of Japanese nationalism and "folk" concepts of race in Japan, see Kosaku Yoshino's chapter "The Discourse on Blood and Racial Identity in Contemporary Japan," in *The Construction of Racial Identities in China and Japan: Historical and Contemporary Perspectives*, ed. Frank Dikötter (Honolulu: University of Hawaii Press, 1997); and his "Culturalism, Racialism, and Internationalism in the Discourse on Japanese Identity," in *Making Majorities: Constituting the Nation in Japan, Korea, China, Malaysia, Fiji, Turkey and the United States*, ed. Dru Gladney, 13–30 (Stanford, CA: Stanford University Press, 1998). A brief discussion of this is the chapter on Asia in Raymond Scupin, ed., *Race and Ethnicity: An Anthropological Focus on the U.S. and the World* (Upper Saddle River, NJ: Prentice Hall, 2003).
16. Edwin Reischauer, *The Japanese* (Cambridge, MA: Harvard University Press, 1974), 135. Reischauer's classic history of Japan remains important, not least because of the role it has played in shaping foreign scholars' views of Japan. Remember, however, that it was written three decades before this chapter. Its conclusions should be taken with a grain of salt and carefully checked against more modern scholarship.
17. John W. Dower, *Embracing Defeat: Japan in the Wake of World War II* (New York: W.W. Norton/The New Press, 1999) won the Pulitzer Prize. It is, no question about it, one of the most impressive works on modern Japanese history and how Japan was rebuilt after World War II.
18. Books on the postbubble economy include Arthur J. Alexander, *In the Shadow of the Miracle: The Japanese Economy Since the End of High-Speed Growth* (New York: Lexington Books, 2003); Richard Katz, *Japan, The System That Soured: The Rise and Fall of the Japanese Economic Miracle* (Armonk, NY: M.E. Sharpe, 1998); *Japanese Phoenix: The Long Road to Economic Revival* (Armonk, NY: M.E. Sharpe, 2003); Edward J. Lincoln, *Arthritic Japan: The Slow Pace of Economic Reform* (Washington, DC: Brookings Institution, 2001). While this chapter was being written, all were frequent contributors to the Japan Forum email list, an excellent source for commentary on Japanese politics and economics (see http://lists.nbr.org/japanforum/).

19. Barrie Shelton, *Learning from the Japanese City: West Meets East in Urban Design* (New York: Routledge, 1999). This delightfully written book is a thoughtful exploration of the Japanese cityscape from the point of view of an architect and urban planner.
20. Jinnai Hidenobu, *Tokyo: A Spatial Anthropology* (Berkeley: University of California Press, 1995). Here you will find a fascinating demonstration of how the basic urban layout and distribution of property rights in Tokugawa-period Edo continue to shape the modern Tokyo cityscape.
21. For a detailed description of this process, see Kuniko Fujita and Richard Hill, eds., *Japanese Cities in the World Economy* (Philadelphia: Temple University Press, 1993).
22. The figures cited here are from Nishiyama Uzo, *Sumai kokingaku: Gendai Nihon jutakushi* [Housing neology: A history of current Japanese housing] (Tokyo: Shokokusha, 1993), 290; Inaba Kazuya and Nakayama Shigenobu, *Nihon no sumai: Sumai to seikatsu no rekishi* [Japanese housing: A history of housing and lifestyles] (Tokyo: Shokokusha, 1983), 290. Nishiyama offers a detailed explanation of the prehistoric, historic, and contemporary roots of Japanese housing. Much of the account presented in this chapter is taken from that work, augmented by the detailed illustrations of house types in Inaba and Nakayama.
23. Miura Atsushi, *"Kazoku" to "kôfu" no sengoshi: Kôgai no yume to genjitsu* [The postwar history of "family" and "happiness": Dream and reality in the suburbs] (Tokyo: Kodansha, 1999). Miura, whose numerous works inform much of the argument developed in this chapter, is a marketing planner whose background includes both sociology and design. To learn more about him and his work see his Web site, http://www.culturestudies.com/profile/index.html. Scrolling past the Japanese to the bottom of the page will bring you to English translations.
24. These statistics are as of the year 2000 and are taken from a Japanese government Web site, http://www.stat.go.jp/english/.
25. For good ethnographic and historical studies of the Ainu and Burakumin peoples in Japan see the early study by William Wetherhall and George DeVos, "Ethnic Minorities in Japan," in *Case Studies on Human Rights and Fundamental Freedoms*, ed. Willem A. Veenhoven (The Hague: Martinus Nijhoff, 1972). For more recent ethnographic work see Emiko Ohnuki-Tierney, *The Monkey as Mirror: Symbolic Transformations in Japanese History and Ritual* (Princeton, NJ: Princeton University Press, 1987); and her "A Conceptual Model for the Historical Relationship Between the Self and the Internal and External Others: The Agrarian Japanese, the Ainu, and the Special-Status People," in Gladney, *Making Majorities*, 31–54.
26. Denoon et al., *Multicultural Japan* (see above, endnote 11) is a good place to begin further research on these topics.
27. For detailed accounts of the roles of gifts and wrappings in Japanese culture, see Joy Hendry, *Wrapping Culture: Politeness, Presentation, and Power in Japan and Other Societies* (Oxford, England: Clarendon Press, 1993); and the recent ethnographic work by Katherine Rupp, *Gift-Giving in Japan: Cash, Connections, Cosmologies* (Stanford, CA: Stanford University Press, 2003).
28. Tsuji Shizuo, *Japanese Cooking: A Simple Art* (Tokyo: Kodansha, 1980), 19. Another interesting anthropological source on food in Japan and especially how McDonald's has been modified to suit Japanese tastes and culture is Emiko Ohnuki-Tierney's chapter "McDonald's in Japan: Changing Manners and Etiquette," in *Golden Arches East*, ed. James L. Watson (Stanford, CA: Stanford University Press, 1997, and soon to be released in a second edition in 2005). Ohnuki-Tierney has another more general essay on this topic in her chapter "We Eat Each Other's Food to Nourish Our Body: The Global and the Local as Mutually Constituent Forces," *Food in Global History*, ed. Raymond Grew (Boulder, CO: Westview Press, 1999).
29. Iwamura Yoko, *Kawaru kazoku, kawaru shokutaku* [Changing families, changing meals] (Tokyo: Keiso Shobo, 2003). Available only in Japanese, this book reports the results of ongoing research on the dietary habits of Japanese women and their families, using focus groups whose members kept detailed records of the meals they and their families consumed during a one-week period and their comments on questions based on those records. The research was conducted by the Japanese advertising agency, AsatsuDK.
30. To learn more and find pointers to additional sources concerning Japanese religion, see C. Scott Littleton, "Japanese Religions," in *Religion and Culture: An Anthropological Focus*, ed. Raymond Scupin (Upper Saddle River, NJ: Prentice Hall, 2000), 294–321.
31. For Japanese historical linguistics see Roy Andrew Miller, *The Japanese Language*, which was first published by the University of Chicago Press in 1967. The Altaic hypothesis continues to require further research, but the typological similarities between Japanese and Korean are now so well recognized that an annual Japanese/Korean Linguistics Conference is held in the United States. A fascinating early discussion that first hypothesized a link between Korean and Japanese is Samuel E. Martin, "Lexical Evidence Relating Korean to Japanese," *Language* 42, no. 2 (1966): 185–196. Roy Andrew Miller has been a strong advocate of both Korean and Japanese membership in the Altaic language family. See his book *Japanese and the Other Altaic Languages* (Chicago: University of Chicago Press, 1971). Again, a good overview of these issues can be found in Jared Diamond's essay "Japanese Roots" referred to above in endnote 11.
32. Samuel E. Martin's *A Reference Grammar of Japanese*, first published by Yale University Press in 1975 and reissued with corrections by Tuttle, Rutland and Tokyo, 1988, is a comprehensive study of modern Japanese. More accessible grammar guides for the student include Makino Seiichi and Michio Tsutsui, *A Dictionary of Basic Japanese Grammar* (Tokyo: The Japan Times, 1992). Two widely used college textbooks for Japanese language instruction are Osamu Mizutani and Nobuko Mizutani, *An Introduction to Modern Japanese* (Tokyo: The Japan Times, 1977); and Eleanor Harz Jorden and Mari Noda, *Japanese, the Spoken Language*, 3rd vol. (New Haven, CT: Yale University Press, 1987), 90.
33. The student of Japanese will begin learning aspects of respect language from the start. For the advanced learner, *Taigû Hyôgen* (Formal expressions for Japanese interaction), developed by the Inter-University Center for Japanese Language Studies and published by The Japan Times (1991), will provide thorough, practical familiarization.
34. For example, from the first of a continuing series of conferences on women and language (now gender and language), see Katsue Akiba-Reynolds, "Female Speakers of

Japanese in Transition," in *Proceedings of the First Berkeley Women and Language Conference* (Berkeley: University of California Press, 1985). A volume edited by Jane Bachnik and Charles Quinn, Jr., *Situated Meaning: Inside and Outside in Japanese Self, Society, and Language* (Princeton, NJ: Princeton University Press, 1994), presents stimulating work in this aspect of Japanese sociolinguistics. Ide Sachiko has written on politeness and women's speech in "Formal Forms and Discernment: Two Neglected Aspects of Universals of Linguistic Politeness," *Journal of Cross-cultural and Interlanguage Communication* 8, nos. 2/3 (1989): 223–248; and in Ide Sachiko and Naomi H. McGloin, "Aspects of Japanese Women's Language," *Journal of Pragmatics* 16 (1991): 596–599. Miyako Inoue has addressed the question of change in "Gender and Linguistic Modernization: Historicizing Japanese Women's Language," in *Proceedings of the Third Berkeley Women and Language Conference* (Berkeley: University of California Press, 1994), 322–333.

35. Miller has a good discussion of Japanese writing systems. An overview in more depth can be found in *A History of Writing in Japan*, by Christopher Seeley (Honolulu: University of Hawaii Press, 2000).

36. Imagine, for example, using a square box to represent the English verb *square. Box* plus *s* or *ed* or *ing* represents *squares, squared,* or *squaring.* The same symbol might also be used for the nouns *square* and *box* and combined with other symbols to produce *square dance* or *shoe box.*

37. Benedict, *The Chrysanthemum and the Sword.*

38. Ibid., 4.

39. Ibid., 4–5.

40. Ibid., 1.

41. Ibid., 5–6.

42. Ibid., 61.

43. Ibid., 47.

44. Ibid., 147.

45. Ibid., 187.

46. Modern scholarship suggests that while often described as "traditional," the *ie* model was invented during Meiji and based on samurai households that never accounted for more than a fraction of all pre-Meiji households. For details see Ueno Chizuko, "Modern Patriarchy and the Formation of the Japanese Nation State" and Nishikawa Yûko, "The Modern Japanese Family System: Unique or Universal?," in Denoon et al., *Multicultural Japan*, 213–232 (cited in endnote 11, above).

47. For a critical assessment of both Benedict and Nakane's group conformity model of Japanese society, see Harumi Befu, "A Critique of the Group Model of Japanese Society," *Social Analysis* 5, no. 6 (1980): 205–225. Befu is a Japanese anthropologist who grew up during World War II in Japan but eventually studied in the United States and became a leading anthropologist of Japanese society. He has a yet more current critical essay on this Nihonjinron aspect of Japanese group identity in Roger Goodman and Kirsten Refsing, eds., *Ideology and Practice in Modern Japan* (London: Routledge Press, 1992).

48. Sugimoto Yoshio, *An Introduction to Japanese Society*, 2nd ed. (Cambridge, England: Cambridge University Press, 2003), 1.

49. Dorinne K. Kondo, *Crafting Selves: Power, Gender, and Discourses of Identity in a Japanese Workplace* (Chicago: University of Chicago Press, 1990), 10–17.

50. Ibid., 105.

51. Ibid., 106.

52. Ibid., 114.

53. Ibid., 229.

54. Set up in 1981 by Japan's second largest advertising agency, Hakuhodo, HILL is a primary source of continuing research on changes in Japanese society and culture. Like other marketing research, its reports tend to have a strong Tokyo-centric and middle-class consumer bias. Pointers to English-language reports on current HILL research can be found at the HILL Web site, http://www.athill.com/ENGLISH/.

55. *Watashi no Koukoku Jutsu* [My advertising techniques]. (Tokyo: Madura Shuppan, 2000).

56. T. J. Pempel, *Regime Shift: Comparative Dynamics of the Japanese Political Economy* (Ithaca, NY: Cornell University Press, 1998), 65.

57. *Salariimen at the Crossroads* (Tokyo: Hakuhodo Institute of Life and Living, 1991).

58. Dower, *Embracing Defeat*, 48.

59. Tsuru Shigeo, *Japanese Capitalism: Creative Defeat and Beyond* (Cambridge, England: Cambridge University Press, 1994).

60. Ezra Vogel, *Japan as Number One: Lessons for America* (Cambridge, MA: Harvard University Press, 1979).

61. Tanaka Yasuo, *Nantonaku, Kuristaru* [Somewhat crystal] (Tokyo: Kawade Shobo, 1981).

62. George Fields, *Gucci on the Ginza: Japan's New Consumer Generation* (Tokyo: Kodansha, 1989).

63. Peter Drucker," The Future that Has Already Happened," *Harvard Business Review* (September–October 1997): 20.

64. Tsuru, Shigeo, *Japanese Capitalism*, 169.

65. John McCreery, *Japanese Consumer Behavior: From Worker Bees to Wary Shoppers* (Honolulu: University of Hawaii Press, 2000), 46. Much of the discussion in this section is taken from this book.

66. Ibid., 46.

67. Miura Atsushi, *"Kazoku" to "kôfu" no sengoshi*, 16.

68. Ezra Vogel, *Japan's New Middle Class: The Salary Man and His Family in a Tokyo Suburb* (Berkeley: University of California Press, 1963).

69. Hendry, *Wrapping Culture*, 20.

70. Kaneko Sachiko, "The Struggle for Legal Rights and Reforms: A Historical View," in *Japanese Women: New Feminist Perspectives on the Past, Present and Future*, ed. Kumiko Fujimura-Fanselow and Atsuko Kameda, 4 (New York: Feminist Press, 1995).

71. Sheldon Garon, *Molding Japanese Minds: The State in Everyday Life* (Princeton, NJ: Princeton University Press, 1997), 144.

72. Benedict, *The Chrysanthemum and the Sword*, 254.

73. McCreery, *Japanese Consumer Behavior*, 214.

74. Robert J. Smith, "Time and Ethnology: Long-term Field Research," in *Doing Fieldwork in Japan*, ed. Theodore C. Bestor, Patricia G. Steinhoff, and Victoria Lyon Bestor, 352–353 (Honolulu: University of Hawaii Press, 2003).

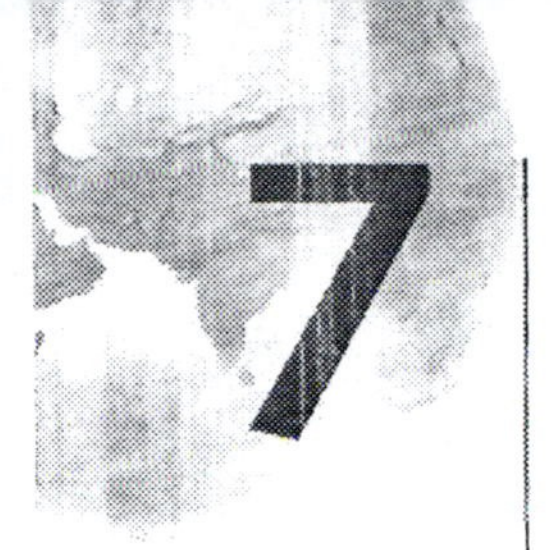

KOREA (NORTH AND SOUTH)

Clark Sorensen

GEOGRAPHY

The Republic of Korea (South Korea) and the Democratic People's Republic of Korea (DPRK, or North Korea) jointly occupy the Korean peninsula and a small part of the northeast Asian mainland. The division of Korea, when two states were set up between 1945 and 1948 as a consequence of the occupation of North Korea by the army of the then Soviet Union, and of South Korea by the United States Army, dismembered a state inhabited by a single ethnic group (the Koreans) that had been unified since AD 668. The territory of the two countries combined is about 221 square kilometers (137 square miles), making the area of the two ethnic Korean states comparable in size to Laos, but the Korean peninsula is densely populated with some 66 million people, making the population of the two states more comparable in size to that of Vietnam. South Korea, a vigorous capitalist democracy since 1987, is highly industrialized and prosperous, with a per capita income of $19,400 in 2003. North Korea, while initially successful in industrializing after 1945, has faced increasing problems of economic decline—even famine—since the collapse of its patron, the Soviet Union, in 1989. The DPRK releases few statistics, but best guesses put its per capita income around $600–$1,000 annually. Both North and South Korea claim sovereignty over the entire Korean nation. The admission of both Koreas to the United Nations in 1991, however, implies that the two states now tacitly accept the existence of each other.

Koreans celebrate their nation as extending from Mount Paektu to Mount Halla. Mount Paektu, at 2,755 meters (9,039 feet) the tallest mountain of Korea, is an extinct volcano on the North Korea–Manchuria border whose crater is filled by Lake Ch'ŏnji from which flows the headwaters of Manchuria's Sungari River. Mount Halla, whose volcanic cone rises symmetrically from the sea to 1,950 meters (6,398 feet) on Cheju Island 90 kilometers (56 miles) off the southwestern tip of the Korean peninsula, is the tallest peak in South Korea. These two volcanoes are not actually typical of the Korean peninsula, which is geologically stable and not subject to the violent volcanic eruptions and frequent earthquakes of Japan, the Philippines, and China.[1]

Korea has a temperate climate with four seasons—a cold, dry winter; a mild spring; a hot, rainy summer; and a cool, clear autumn. The southernmost parts of the Korean peninsula receive rainfall throughout the year, but most of the rest of Korea receives precipitation primarily in the spring and summer. The concentration of

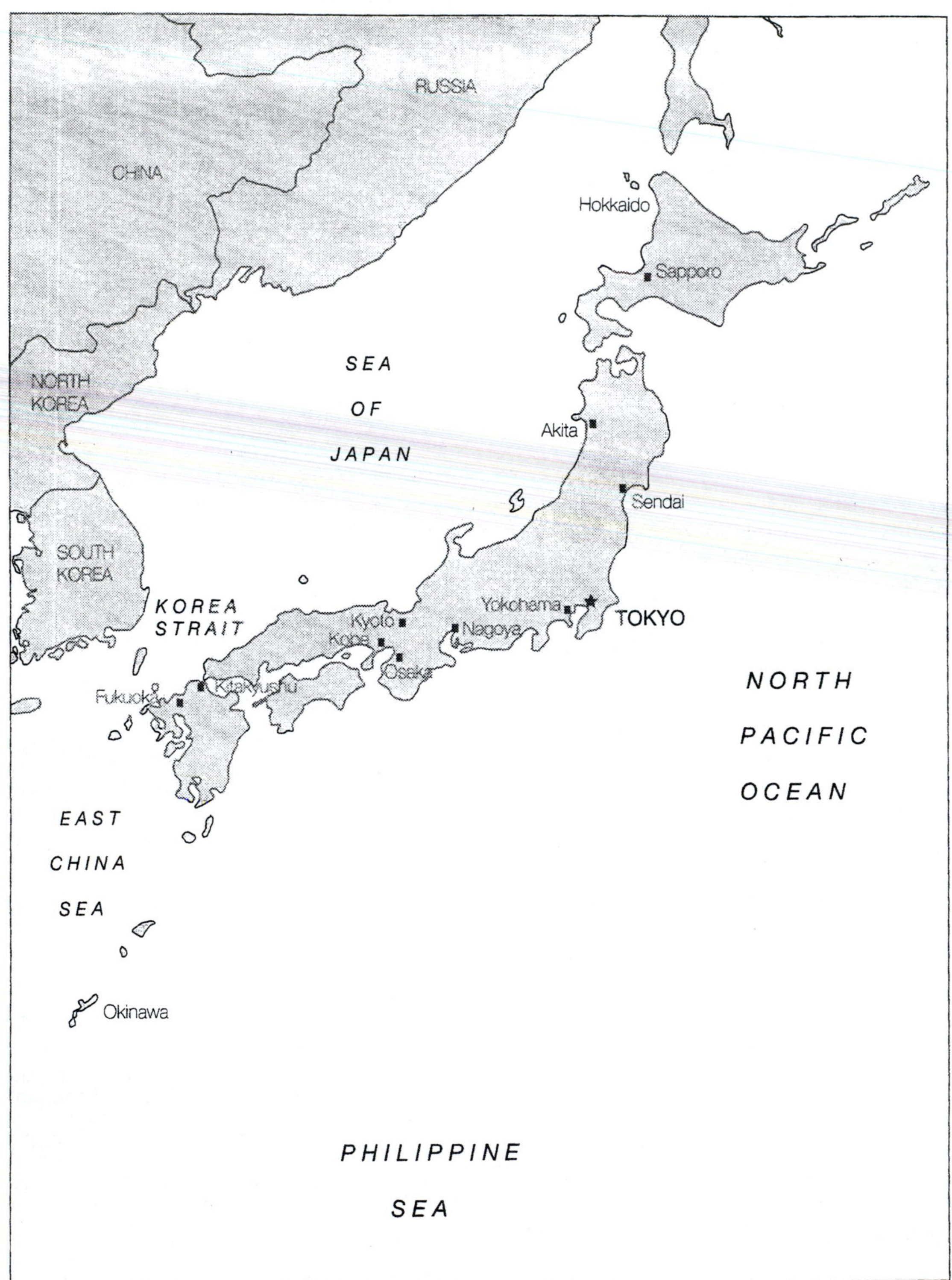
RUSSIA
CHINA
Hokkaido
Sapporo
NORTH
KOREA
SEA
OF
JAPAN
Akita
Sendai
SOUTH
KOREA
KOREA
STRAIT
Yokohama
TOKYO
Kyoto
Nagoya
Kobe
Osaka
Fukuoka
Kitakyushu
NORTH
PACIFIC
OCEAN
EAST
CHINA
SEA
Okinawa
PHILIPPINE
SEA

moisture during the growing season makes for a lush natural vegetation of great beauty and variety, as well as very productive agriculture. The main crop in the moister southern parts of Korea is irrigated rice, supplemented by dry field crops such as wheat, barley, and beans. Bamboo is grown in the very southernmost region. The main vegetable crops are cabbage, radishes, hot peppers, sesame, and medicinal crops such as ginseng. Cotton and hemp used to be grown for fabric, although these days most raw cotton and hemp is imported from China. Many farmers grow silk in the spring, and such fruits as persimmons, apples, plums, quince, jujubes, chestnuts, and peaches. Citrus fruits are cultivated on Cheju Island. As one moves from south to north on the Korean peninsula the growing season and rainy season gets shorter and less reliable. Thus, in North Korea dry field crops are a larger proportion of the fields than in South Korea, and the North Koreans have more difficulty meeting their food needs through agriculture.

Korea has few large plains, and its mountainous nature means that only 20 percent of the land can be cultivated. Although Korea's mountains are not particularly high by world standards, the slopes tend to be very steep so that people cluster in the densely populated river valleys. South Korea, with a population of almost 48 million in a country of less than 100,000 square kilometers (62,000 square miles), has a population density of about 480 persons per square kilometer—a population density surpassed only by Bangladesh (1,024) and Taiwan (622). North Korea is geographically larger than South Korea and with around 22 million people has less than half the population of South Korea. Its population density of about 186 people per square kilometer (.62 square miles) is still relatively high by world standards, however.

The two Koreas seem small and insignificant on a map compared to the massive size of China. The two Koreas combined are less than 3 percent the size of China geographically, and have less than 6 percent of China's population. Even when compared with Japan, the two Koreans reach only about half the size of their neighbor. These comparisons can be misleading, however. When compared to the major countries of Europe, for example, a united Korea would be comparable in geographical size to Great Britain and in population to Italy. Though a "minnow between whales," as the Koreans say, South Korea's economy is the 4th largest in Asia (after Japan, China, and India), and 12th largest in the world.

North Korea shares a 1,025 kilometer (636 mile) border with China along the Yalü (Amnok in Korean) and Tumen rivers. In the extreme northeast North Korea borders Russia along the last 25 kilometers (16 miles) of the Tumen River that empties into the Sea of Japan. Rail lines connect North Korea with China and Russia. South Korea's only land border is with North Korea. The border between North and South that was set up in 1945 was the 38th parallel, but this was supposed to be a temporary separation until a unified North–South government could be agreed upon by the Soviet Union and the United States. The development of the Cold War led to the creation of two separate states on the Korean peninsula in 1948. North Korea tried to unify the peninsula by force in 1950. The present boundary between North and South Korea follows the armistice line agreed upon by the United Nations forces (led by the United States), North Korea, and China on July 27, 1953. It runs considerably north of the 38th parallel in the mountainous eastern part of the peninsula, but south of the 38th parallel along the Imjin River in the western part just north of Seoul. This boundary is heavily fortified and is bordered by a 4 kilometer (2.48 miles) wide demilitarized zone (DMZ) on either side. A neutral compound where the North Korean and the United Nations Command can meet straddles the armistice line near the village of P'anmunjŏm.

The armistice line is an arbitrary point where the front lines of the Chinese and U.N. armies met in 1953. It follows no natural geographic or cultural boundary, and the people on both sides of the border are ethnically the same. Since Korea was a unified country before the division, rail lines used to radiate from Seoul (the historic capital of Korea since 1394) north across the 38th parallel to China and Russia. The Kyŏngsin line ran from Seoul through P'yŏngyang (presently the capital of the DPRK) to the Chinese border, while the Kyŏngwŏn line ran from Seoul through Wŏnsan, a North Korean port on the east coast, to Ch'ŏngjin. There it split, with one line entering China and the other Russia. All rail and road lines between North and South Korea were cut as a consequence of the Korean War, however, and from 1951 through 2003 no land travel was possible between North and South Korea except occasionally through the "bridge of no return" at P'anmunjŏm. In 2003, however, the rail line north from Seoul to Kaesŏng and a road on the east coast were reconnected, and there were plans to reconnect a rail line on the east coast as well. Russia has expressed interest in using rail lines through North Korea so that exports from South Korea to Europe can proceed by the Trans-Siberian Railway, and there has even been talk of a gas pipeline from Russia's Sakhalin Island through North Korea to South Korea.

The border area of P'anmunjŏm (Bridge of No Return) with South Korean soldiers on patrol.

Korea's position close to the North China plain—China's cultural heartland—has meant that Chinese influence has been strong throughout Korean history. Unlike many other peoples close to the Chinese heartland, however, the residents of the Korean peninsula have always had a distinctive identity, and they have been united by their own state for a good 1,500 years. Korea has also had many contacts with neighboring Japan, and the steppe peoples of Mongolia and Siberia. Although Korea was influenced very little by Japanese civilization until the late nineteenth century—being more in the position of exporting continental culture to the Japanese islands—Japanese influence has been strong since the late nineteenth century. In recent years Korean popular culture has proven popular in China and Japan, and Japanese popular culture, in turn, fascinates youth in South Korea. In general, however, Japanese influence in South Korea has been secondary to that of the United States since 1945, while Russian influence has been predominant in the North.

PREHISTORY

Early Paleolithic (ca. 1 million to 200,000 BP)

Early Paleolithic tools have been excavated in both North and South Korea. In North Korea the Hukwuri site, a limestone cave 40 kilometers (25 miles) south of P'yŏngyang, has faunal remains that date to the Middle Pleistocene, and a tool kit made of crudely chipped hand-ax-like core tools. It dates to 600,000–400,000 BP.[2]

Sokch'angni in South Korea, though dated only by stratigraphic methods, also has early Paleolithic tools. Hand axes of somewhat later age have been found in the lower layers of Chon'gongni in South Korea. Hominid remains have been found in Kumgul Cave in South Korea and been attributed to *Homo erectus.* The early Paleolithic materials in Korea—hominid, faunal, and artifactual—are broadly consistent with similar material in China that dates from 1 million to 200,000 BP, including the famous Sinanthropus finds at Zhoukoudian. During some of this time Korea was connected by land to China via the Yellow Sea, so it is plausible that *Homo erectus* lived in Korea as well as China. The Chon'gongni remains are especially important because they prove beyond a doubt the incorrectness of Movius's notion that a hand-ax tradition doesn't exist in East Asia, and that the Lower Paleolithic in East Asia is confined to a crude "chopper/chopping" tradition less advanced than the hand-ax tradition found in Africa and Europe.

Middle and Late Paleolithic (ca. 100,000 BP to 11,000 BP)

Middle Paleolithic finds are few and difficult to interpret in Korea, but tools using the Levalloisian core technique have been found at Kulp'ori dated to about 100,000 BP. This technique involves striking flakes off a prepared "core" of stone. Late Paleolithic finds from 60,000 to 30,000 BP are fairly abundant. The hominid remains dating from this period are of modern *Homo sapiens.* Obsidian blades and other sophisticated flake tools date to the late Pleistocene (66,000 to 13,000 BP). Some affinities to similar assemblages in Japan have been noted for this period. Around the Paleolithic-holocene boundary dated to around 11,000 BP, microlithic industries are found on coastal sites.

The lifestyle of the Paleolithic hominids seems to have been one of foraging in deciduous forest, with evidence of butchering of deer and wild boars. The inhabitants of Korea were probably also exploiting vegetal resources, though direct archaeological evidence for this is lacking. Evidence of a wind break in front of a hearth seems to point to small family foraging groups. Although cave sites might have had the potential for sheltering larger populations, the restricted scope of excavated sites leads archaeologists to believe that these, too, were inhabited by small family groups. The small size of the population groups in Paleolithic Korea contrasts with contemporary sites in Europe and Africa that were probably inhabited by larger hunting bands. The small size of the foraging groups is probably a consequence of Korea's forested environment at the time that precluded the development of large herds of fauna.

Neolithic (6000 to 2000 BC)

Early villages appear between 6000 and 2000 BC. These village sites contain handmade pottery and chipped stone tools found in and near semisubterranean dwellings that were heated by a central hearth. These early villages tended to contain only a few houses at any one time, and were located along rivers or seacoasts. The pottery is generally called *chŭlmun t'ogi,* or comb-pattern pottery, because it generally is decorated with designs of incised lines. These sites are found all over Korea, and scholars often group the comb-pattern pottery into geographical stylistic groups, though there is little agreement on exactly what the groups are, or where their boundaries should be. The villages seem to have been permanent settlements. Excavated hoes and grinding stones, and a famous find of stored grain at Chitamni, lead archaeologists to think these were agricultural villages that supplemented their diet with hunting, fishing, shellfish, and nut gathering. For this reason archaeologists consider these villages Neolithic in spite of the presence of chipped stone tools. Exactly when, and how, the transition to agriculture took place is not yet known. Noting the evidence for the existence of boat transportation at

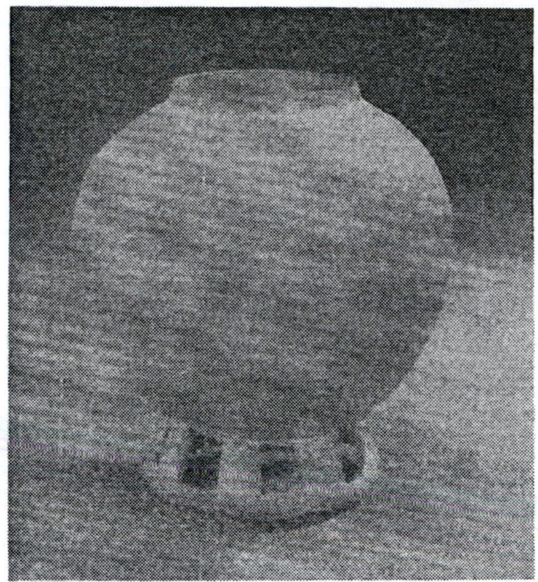

Early Korean pottery.

this time, some archaeologists suggest that the East Coast sites have affinities with contemporary Japanese Jōmon sites, the West Coast sites with China's northeastern coastal Liaoning culture, and the sites in the northeast with sites in the Soviet Maritime region.

Megalithic (2000 to 1000 BC)

A big change is found in archaeological sites between 2000 and 1000 BC. The ceramics become thick-walled, mostly undecorated *mumun t'ogi* in such shapes as jars with handles, bowls on pedestals, or steamers. Burnished red pottery that seems to have been used as a status marker is also found. Stone artifacts are generally polished, rather than chipped. The most common of these is the semilunar knife with two perforations associated with intensive rice agriculture. Indeed, finds of *sinica* strains of rice presumably introduced from North China through Manchuria date from close to the beginning of the period. Decorated pottery spindle whorls give evidence of spinning. Ritual stone daggers, and polished coma-shaped stone beads (*kogok*) made of amazonite or nephrite seem to have status-marking functions. Stone cist burials are most common, but the contemporaneous existence of smaller numbers of megalithic burial dolmens point to significant social ranking. Northern-style dolmens consist of four upright stones forming a chamber topped with a large, horizontal capstone. In southern-style dolmens the capstone is at ground level covering a stone cist. Both types are found in most of central Korea. Bronze locally made daggers are found at some sites (leading some scholars to call this period a Bronze Age), but these seem to be exclusively found in hoards or burials. Megalithic villages of hundreds of houses have been discovered.

Some Korean scholars associate the appearance of megalithic rice-cultivating villages with stone cist burials and evidence of social ranking with the earliest appearance of the ancestors of the Koreans. Relying on the traditional dating of their foundation myth, they associate Tan'gun, the legendary founder of Ancient Chosŏn in 2333 BC, with these beginnings of megalithic culture in Korea. Other scholars more plausibly point to proto-historical texts from China that mention the Eastern Bowmen (Dong-i), and in particular the Yemaek tribe. Some scholars envision the Yemaek people galloping into Korea from the north bearing Liaoning bronze daggers, semilunar knives, rice agriculture, and the custom of burying their dead in stone cists, but this seems to overinterpret the evidence. While rice and bronze were probably introduced from China and Manchuria, clear differences between Chinese and Korean pottery complexes from this period tend to cast doubt on the notion that mass migrations accompanied this technological flow. Dolmens, moreover, seem to have evolved indigenously in Korea. It seems likely that migrations of various groups from the north occurred at this time, but archaeologists have not yet been able to identify where these groups came from, and it is likely that migrants mingled with indigenous people already resident in the peninsula.

Iron Age Korea (400 BC to AD 300)

As in other countries of East Asia, it is difficult to distinguish separate Bronze and Iron Ages, since iron manufacturing comes quite shortly after the appearance of bronze. By this time, China had already developed writing, so Chinese descriptions of the inhabitants of the Korean peninsula first become available. China also had developed big states that warred with each other, and were expanding so that events there also affected developments in the Korean peninsula. Sketchy and fragmentary as they are, the Chinese texts such as the *Wei Zhi* and *Hou Han Shu* describe two broad groups of people.

The northern peoples—Puyŏ, Koguryŏ, Tong Okchŏ, and Yemaek—spoke similar languages, and lived in Manchuria and in northern and central Korea. They were in direct contact with northern Chinese states, and seem to have been ruled by horse-riding warriors who were supported by a subservient agricultural population. The upper classes were organized into exogamous clans, and marriages seem to have been accomplished through bridewealth payments of cattle and horses. The Chinese recorded that most of these people would make sacrifices to heaven in the 10th lunar month (approximately November) after the harvest. The northern peoples early on developed states—sometimes referred to as tribal leagues by Korean historians in the context of conflict and competition with China. The northern peoples also built settlements fortified by palisades.

The southern peoples—Mahan, Chinhan, and Pyŏnhan—lived in the southern third of today's Korea, and seem at this time to have a simpler level of political organization than the northern peoples. The names *Taehan* or *Han'guk* that are currently used for South Korea come from the last syllable of each of these three groups, who are also known as the *Samhan*, the "Three Hans." Agricultural peoples, the residents of the three Hans, dwelled in semisubterranean houses that were entered through the roof. Mahan in the southwest consisted of groups of villages (ranging in population from a few thousand to 10,000) scattered around the landscape that were ruled by elders. (They were probably endogamous with social ranking.) During the period before AD 300 the villages may have cooperated in loose federations, but the Mahan people were not yet building fortresses, were not horse riders, and their political organization almost certainly fell short of the state. Typically they held religious observances with singing, drinking, and dancing in the 5th lunar month (approximately June), after finishing their spring planting. The people of Chinhan in the southeast, and Pyŏnhan on the south coast, commingled and dressed similarly, but they spoke a different language from Mahan. They rode horses and built palisades. Pyŏnhan was an important center of iron production and trade within Korea, and neighboring Japan as well.

Archaeological finds from this period in Korea provide evidence of the use and production of iron, as well as the ability to make high-fired ceramic stoneware. In northern areas the typically Korean *ondol* under-the-floor heating is in evidence. Iron, sometimes cast, sometimes forged, was smelted all over Korea in small furnaces, and archaeological sites yield abundant finds of iron weapons—daggers, arrowheads, and spears—as well as items of daily use such as axes, sickles, adzes, and fishhooks. By this time bronze seems to have more symbolic than practical usefulness. Iron mirrors with increasingly fine artisanship appear, as well as horse-shaped bronze belt buckles. Typical ceramics are gray, high-fired stoneware vessels with pierced pedestals. Hoards of Chinese money sometimes are found, and jade coma-shaped ornaments are a common find.

LANGUAGE

The entire native population of Korea is Korean speaking. Korean is also spoken in the Korean Autonomous Region of China just across the border in Jilin Province, and among several million Korean émigrés elsewhere in China, Russia, Japan, North America, Europe, and Latin America. Altogether more than 70 million people speak Korean ranking it 12th in the world.[3] Korean is written with an ingenious 28-letter alphabet unique to Korea that was created by royal decree in 1443. Today 24 of the original letters, 14 consonants and 10 vowels, are still in use. Originally termed *Hunmin Chŏngŭm* (Correct Sounds for Teaching the People) the alphabet today is known as *Han'gŭl* in South Korea and as *Chosŏn'gŭl* in North Korea (both words mean "Korean writing"). Because this writing system is alphabetical, each phoneme is represented by a letter. The letters, however, are arranged so that each syllable forms a distinct graphic unit analogous to a Chinese character. The first two letters of a syllable are placed side-by-side, but the third and fourth letters of a syllable go *underneath* the first two to form a square syllabic form. Han'gŭl texts were originally written, like Chinese and Japanese, vertically from right to left without punctuation or separation of words. Modern punctuation and separation of words (known as *ttŭiŏssŭgi*) were both introduced in the late nineteenth century, and now Korean is most frequently written horizontally from left to right, though novels are often still printed vertically in South Korea.

There are six dialects (Northeast, Northwest, Central, Southeast, Southwest, and Cheju Island). For the most part these dialects are mutually intelligible, though the dialect of Cheju Island cannot be easily understood by mainlanders, and is even written with an archaic vowel not now used on the mainland. The standard language, or *pyojun-ŏ*, used in the Republic of Korea, and the standard spelling, known as *matchum-pŏp*, was devised by the Korean Language Society (Chosŏn-ŏ hakhoe) in the 1933 based on middle-class speech in Seoul. This reform introduced the current morphophonemic spelling system in which the graphic integrity of the word root is maintained even though pronunciation varies systematically according to the linguistic environment. Thus the word "chicken" is always spelled /talk/. Koreans know, however, that the /l/ is silent when the word is pronounced in isolation as /tak/, but that when it is followed by a vowel (such as the subject case marker /i/) the /l/ is pronounced and the final consonant becomes voiced, hence /talgi/. During the first half of the twentieth century fiction was written in pure Han'gŭl, but other forms of prose were written in mixed Korean and Chinese script known as *Kukhanmun*. Words of native Korean origin and all grammatical endings were written in Hangŭl, while the extensive vocabulary of Chinese origin was written with Chinese characters. (Unlike in Japanese, Koreans never write native words with Chinese characters.) The large number of Chinese loan words in Korean means that most concepts can be expressed either with homely native Korean words, or with more literary Chinese-derived vocabulary. Thus "family" can be expressed with native words as *chip*, or with Chinese loan words as *kajok* (as, say, in a sociology textbook). Since 1945 many words from English have entered the South Korean vocabulary, and since the eighties, the use of Chinese characters has gradually died out so that in South Korea today most writing is purely in Hangŭl with no admixture of Chinese characters.[4]

The DPRK initially used the Seoul-based standard language, and abolished the use of Chinese characters as early as 1949 as a "feudalistic" remnant. In 1966 the DPRK introduced an alternative to Standard Korean known as cultured language, or *munhwa-ŏ*. North Korean cultured language is based on the same principles as the South Korean standard language, but the new standard introduced a few modifications of pronunciation and vocabulary based on the speech of P'yŏngyang. The alphabetical order used in the north is also different from that of the south. Today, while North and South Koreans speaking their respective standard languages can easily understand each other, there are minor differences in pronunciation and spelling in the two parts of the peninsula. In North Korea initial *r* is both pronounced and spelled, while in South Korea initial *r* is omitted before *i* and spelled and pronounced as *n* before other letters. For example, "worker" is /rodongja/ in the north, but /nodongja/ in the south. The name Lee is /i/ in the south, and /ri/ in the north. The North Korean authorities also feel that the language in the south has become impure by accepting too many loan words from Chinese, English, and Japanese, so they have systematically encouraged the use of native vocabulary and have coined new words with native roots to replace some foreign words. Thus instead of using a Chinese loan word *ch'usu* for "harvest," North Korea promotes the use of the native phrase "autumn gathering" /*kaŭl kŏji*/. The English loan word *p'ama* (short for "permanent wave") has been replaced by the native phrase "fried hairdo" /*pokkŭm mŏri*/, and so forth.

Structurally Korean is an agglutinative language with a complex grammar and a basic word order of subject-object-verb (SOV). Unlike Chinese—to which it is unrelated—Korean is not a tone language. Though dialects in the eastern half of the peninsula north and south have pitch accent that is sometimes termed tone,[5] standard Korean lacks this feature. An interesting feature of the consonantal system of Korean is that each stop has three manners of articulation: slightly aspirated, heavily aspirated, and glottalized. Voiced consonants are found only between vowels, and are in complementary distribution with the slightly aspirated initials (e.g., initial /p/ becomes /b/ between vowels, but both sounds are spelled with the same letter). Cases (subject, object, instrumental, etc.) are marked by suffixes. What we express with prepositions in English is expressed with a small number of postpositions (suffixes) used in conjunction with a great variety of compound verbs that express direction and manner. Verb endings must be modified to express the formality of the situation and the degree of deference the speaker wishes to give to the hearer. For example, in a public situation, one might express formality and honor to one's hearer by using the verb ending *-sŭmnida*, whereas with friends and family one can express informal intimacy by using the verb ending *-ŏŏ*. Nonintimate equals can use such intermediate verb endings as *-yo* and *-ne*. Pronouns, too, must be carefully chosen with an eye to expressing the humbleness of the speaker and the honor of he who is spoken about. Whereas one might refer to a younger brother as "you" /nŏ/, the younger brother cannot use that pronoun with his older brother. In fact, selecting a pronoun can be so fraught in Korean that people often avoid the issue by addressing each other by their titles followed by the honorific suffix *nim*. A younger brother thus addresses his older brother not as "you," but as *hyŏng* (older brother), and a stranger enquiring about the older brother would asked about *hyŏngnim* (honorable older brother). Interestingly, terms for siblings vary by gender of the speaker: A boy calls his older sister /*nuna*/ while a girl calls her older sister /*ŏnni*/; on the other hand, while a girl calls her older brother /*oppa*/, a boy can call his older brother /*ŏnni*/, if he doesn't use /*hyŏng*/. All of these sibling terms are frequently extended to same-gender friends and colleagues. At work, for example, similar-aged female coworkers usually address each other as *ŏnni* (older sister), while men commonly use *hyŏng* for those older and *tongsaeng* (younger sibling) for those younger.

Finally, when speaking about persons of high status, one must use honorific case markers and vocabulary. If one is asked about a child's nap, "*Agi ka chal chassŏ?*" (Did the baby sleep well?) would do, but if one asked the same question of a person's father it would have to be "*Abŏji kkesŏ chal chumusyŏssŭmnikka?*" The honorific subject market *kkesŏ* rather than the ordinary subject marker *ka* must follow the word "father" (*abŏji*), the honorific past-tense verb for sleep *chumusyŏss-* must be used instead of the ordinary past-tense word *chass-*, and the speaker must use the honorific interrogative verb ending *-sŭmnikka.* Choice of vocabulary, pronouns, and level of grammatical formality is affected by gender and personality. Men often use blunt pronouns with their wives, while their wives use more formal terms of address. Women also seem to have a tendency to use more respectful language than men in similar situations. Many of the former status distinctions, however, have become flattened in recent years as younger people in South Korea opt for more "modern" and equal relations between genders and husband and wife, and reject excessive deference to status. This tendency to flatten status distinctions in language seems less marked in North Korea, however.

Most linguists classify Korean as a member of the Altaic language family.[6] This family includes the Turkic languages in the west, and Mongolian, Manchu-Tungus, Korean, and Japanese in the east. All of these languages are characterized by SOV word order and vowel harmony (though this feature has been lost to a great extent in modern Korean and Japanese). Japanese and Korean share certain other characteristics such as the way they make passives, and the elaboration of honorific verb endings. However, since the number of cognate words in Japanese and Korean that have been identified is limited, a modicum of doubt about the Altaic affinity of Korean and Japanese lingers among a few linguists. Archaeological evidence of movement of people down into the Korean peninsula from Manchuria and Siberia, and the distribution of the Altaic languages leads most people to assume that the ancestral Koreans must have come from this region and brought Altaic languages with them. Since Japanese is also probably an Altaic language, some of the Altaic speakers probably proceeded to Japan from the Korean peninsula, though when and how is not known. Among historians, some think the appearance of megalithic villages between 2000 and 1000 BC records the arrival of Altaic speakers, but since language leaves no material remains, this interpretation remains speculative.

Uncertainty about the genetic affinity of Korean comes from the lack of Old Korean records. Extensive and accurate texts in Hangŭl date only from the fifteenth century, and these record Late Middle Korean. (Modern Korean language dates from the seventeenth century following the Japanese and Manchu invasions.) A small number of texts in the language of Silla are written with Chinese characters (used sometimes for meaning, and sometimes for sound), and these show that language to be Old Korean Proper, the direct ancestor of Middle Korean. The languages of Paekche and Koguryŏ are known only from a few words deciphered from place names written with Chinese characters. The words in the language of Paekche show clear affinity with the language of Silla, but those of Koguryrŏ, though clearly related to Silla, seem more distant. The Koguryŏ numbers, in fact, show a striking similarity to the numbers of Japanese rather than Korean, and this is one line of evidence that has led a few scholars to speculate that the Puyŏ people who probably came down to conquer Paekche in the third century AD may have continued on to Japan (see the history section). These issues, because they are intimately linked to postcolonial Korean identity, can have a strong emotional resonance in Korea today—particularly if Korea's neighbors use issues of language affinity to challenge the antiquity, independence, or authenticity of Korean culture.

HISTORY

Earliest States

Legend places the origin of the Korean people in 2333 BC when Tan'gun, a hero descended from the union of a god and a she bear, founded *Old Chosŏn.* There was indeed an Old Chosŏn state in Korea, but it cannot be historically or archaeologically verified at such an early date. From the third century BC, however, we know from Chinese histories of an Old Chosŏn state whose capital was Wanggŏm Sŏng (near today's P'yŏngyang). The word *wanggŏm* is probably a rendering with Chinese characters of a native word that meant "king" ("king" is *imgŭm* in contemporary Korean). *Sŏng* means "fortress." Chinese sources say that King Chun of Old Chosŏn was deposed by Wiman—a refugee from the Chinese state of Yen, but a person who was probably not himself ethnic Chinese—between 194 and 180 BC. Wiman's descendents in turn were conquered by Han China in 108 BC.

After conquering Old Chosŏn, the Han dynasty in China set up a military commandary known as *Lèlàng* (*Nangnang* in Korean) in northern Korea. Japanese archaeologists in the early 1930s identified the earthen fortress of T'osŏng-ni, eight kilometers (5 miles) southwest of P'yŏngyang, as the site of Lèlàng because the seal of the governor of Lèlàng was excavated there along with other Han Chinese artifacts. Lèlàng prospered as a Chinese outpost from this time until AD 313 (North Korean historiography does not recognize Lèlàng as being part of Korean history). Many residents of the city of Lèlàng were probably Chinese, and rich Chinese-style artifacts were excavated at T'osŏng-ni, but in outlying areas the Chinese governor just gave indigenous chieftains titles, so that the commandary of Lèlàng was never completely sinified.

The Founding of the Indigenous Three Kingdoms

By the third century AD *Koguryŏ*, a branch of the Puyŏ people of Manchuria who probably spoke Altaic languages, had developed what seems like a state with its capital on the upper reaches of the Yalü River. Many anthropologists and archaeologists consider these early tribal polities in Korea to be chiefdoms that centralized authority under specific families, rather than full-fledged states with systematic bureaucracies. Early Koguryŏ consisted of five tribes (or chiefdoms), one of which supplied the kings, while lower classes supported the warrior upper classes. Koguryŏ was defeated by the Chinese in AD 245 but it was able to reorganize and conquer the last Chinese commandaries in Korea by AD 313. Koguryŏ, now a large and formidable state ruling most of northern Korea and large chunks of Manchuria, moved its capital to near today's P'yŏngyang in AD 437. Until its defeat by the combined forces of Tang China and the rival Korean state of Silla in AD 668 Koguryŏ was the most formidable state in northeastern Asia.

The time and manner of the founding of second of the three kingdoms of fourth century AD Korea, *Paekche* in the southwestern territory of Mahan, is controversial. Some historians and archaeologists think that the Paekche state gradually developed out of one of the villages with social ranking in Mahan in the second and third centuries AD. Others, noting the tradition that the royal house of Paekche claimed to be descended from the royal house of Puyŏ, regard Paekche as a conquest state established when Altaic-speaking migrants from Puyŏ in Manchuria established control in the former Mahan in the third and fourth centuries AD. The original Paekche capital was in the Seoul region. The earliest walled site found in that area that shows evidence of extensive social stratification is the fourth-century Mongch'on site in Seoul's Olympic Park. Thus the conquest theory seems most plausible at this time. Due to continued pressure from Koguryŏ and Silla, Paekche had to move its capital further south, first to Ungjin (modern Kongju) in AD 475, and then Sabi (modern Puyŏ) in AD 538.

Paekche maintained an alliance with the state of Yamato in the Japanese islands. An intriguing hypothesis regarding Korean and Japanese historical connections is that one of the reasons for this alliance is that some of the migrants from Puyŏ didn't stop migrating when they reached Paekche, but moved on into Japan contributing to the founding of the Yamato

State. Paekche crown princes sometimes lived in Japan before taking the throne of Paekche. There is evidence of borrowed Paekche words in Old Japanese poetry, and much of the early Japanese art is of Paekche origin.[7] Yamato even sent troops to try to save the doomed Paekche when it was attacked by Tang China and the rival Korean state of Silla in AD 660.

The area of Pyŏnhan on the south coast was rich in resources—particularly iron—and developed a rich commercial culture in the third and fourth centuries AD. Japanese (known in those days as *Wa*) seem to have had trading settlements there. Various polities developed—some with mounded tombs with armor and horse equipment—but *Kaya*, as this area was known, seems not to have developed a unified state and so was absorbed by Silla in the sixth century.

Silla, the last of the powerful early Korean states, developed out of the Chinhan polity of Saro in the Kyŏngju Basin in the middle of the fourth century. Silla developed at this time an elite mounded tomb culture similar to that of Kaya. The royal clan of Kim took its wives from the Pak clan, but later from among other Kims. Unlike the northern clan-based states, in Silla close marriage among cousins seems to have been common among the elite, and Silla developed a unique status system of bone ranks (*kolp'umje*) in which children of royal Kim-Pak marriages were the highest "sacred bone" (*sŏnggol*), children of royal Kim marriages with other clans were "true bone" (*chin'gol*). Only these were eligible for the throne and the highest offices in the land. Other people were classified into 6 head ranks (*tup'um*), of which the top three ranks (6, 5, and 4) were allowed to occupy the middle ranks of the bureaucracy.

Three Kingdoms Period (fourth century AD to AD 668)

The earliest histories of Korea push back the founding dates of Koguryŏ, Paekche, and Silla to the first century BC. Correlating the Korean historical sources with archaeological data, and with Chinese historical sources, however, leads most objective historians to date the emergence of a series of full-fledged kingdoms on the Korean peninsula to about the fourth century AD after the fall of the Chinese commandary of Lèlàng to Koguryŏ. By this time, relatively reliable Korean historical sources are available, and we have a good idea of the government and culture of the three kingdoms. Chinese statecraft and writing had been introduced and each of the kingdoms had a regularized and ranked bureaucratic system.

Buddhism contributed greatly to consolidation of the early states on the Korean peninsula when it was introduced from the mixed Chinese and steppe-nomad states such as Wei to Koguryŏ and Paekche in the fifth century AD, and Silla in the sixth century AD. The original religion of the residents of the Korean peninsula was a type of animism in which nature and ancestral spirits were controlled and contacted by shamans. In fact, some historians interpret Tan'gun as a kind of shaman, and see the early Silla kings as developing out of shaman-priests. Buddhism became a state religion with strong connections to the monarchs, who used the universal ethic of Buddhism to legitimize and centralize their power. Paekche Buddhist art became very refined, and exerted a strong influence on early Buddhist art in Japan. Though Silla was the last Korean kingdom to embrace Buddhism, Buddhism became an especially important prop of the monarchy there. The ruler was considered a *chakravarti-raja*, a "wheel turning king," the Indian concept of universal ruler whose chariot wheels turn over the entire world. The king was head of the "three jewels" of Buddhism (Buddha, dharma, sangha), and was considered by the faithful to be a reincarnation of Vairochana, the "Sun Buddha" of the Flower Garland Sutra. Assemblies of 100 monks to recite the "Sutra of Benevolent Kings" were used to preserve the country and grant it peace.

The Mound Tomb of Kyŏngju.

We know the most about the history and culture of the southeastern kingdom of Silla, because this is the kingdom that gradually expanded from its capital in Kyŏngju to defeat the other states and unify the Korean peninsula in AD 668. From the great mounded tombs of Kyŏngju have been excavated elaborate gold crowns like stylized antlers with dozens of coma-shaped jade pendants and gold spangles hanging from them. Silla was ruled by a king in conjunction with an aristocratic assembly known as the *hwabaek*. Constant warfare, however, gradually allowed the king to centralize authority. Silla organized its armies into "Oath Banners" with distinctive colors and uniforms. Making use of the cult of Maitreya (Buddha of the Future) as a support, aristocratic *hwarang* knights became leading Silla military figures as the three kingdoms battled for supremacy. Silla absorbed culturally similar Kaya in the sixth century. Silla allied with Paekche to wrest the Han River basin (location of present-day Seoul) from Koguryŏ, and then occupied it. Silla kept nibbling at Paekche's territory throughout the sixth century. Koguryŏ, however, was too formidable a foe for Silla at this time. In fact, Koguryŏ's general Ulji Mundŏk fought off an invasion by Sui China, a defeat that contributed greatly to the Sui dynasty's collapse, and Koguryŏ also defeated invasions by the succeeding Tang dynasty. Silla eventually allied with Tang China to conquer Paekche in AD 660. (This disaster led a large number of Paekche subjects to move to Japan where many became important personages.) Silla and Tang then united to defeat Koguryŏ in AD 668.[8]

United Silla (AD 668 to AD 918)

When Tang had allied with Silla to defeat Paekche and Koguryŏ, Tang assumed that it would rule the defeated lands as Chinese colonies. Five Chinese governorships were created in Paekche, and nine in Koguryŏ. Even the Silla king was appointed a "governor" of his own kingdom. This system didn't last for long, however. Silla allied with remnant Koguryŏ loyalists who had been settled in Paekche, and was able to drive the Chinese occupiers from Paekche by 671, and absorb Koguryŏ up to the Taedong River (approximately the P'yŏngyang area) by 676. China was not able to keep hold over the rest of Koguryŏ either, where a successor kingdom called Parhae was established.

Although the tribes, chiefdoms, and peoples who had formed the three kingdoms were linguistically and culturally related, the languages of Koguryŏ and Paekche had been distinct from each other and from that of Silla. A system for writing the language of Silla called *hyangch'al* was devised using Chinese characters sometimes for their meaning, and sometimes for their sound value, and a few poems in the Silla language written in this script have been preserved.[9] With unification, however, the Silla language became dominant throughout the peninsula, and it is this language that is Old Korean Proper—the direct ancestor of Middle and Modern Korean.

With unification, moreover, the position of the monarch was further strengthened. Silla sent off true bone aristocrats accompanied by military forces to set up five regional capitals. King Kyŏngdŏk in the mid-eighth century tried to establish a centralized bureaucratic administration, but entrenched local bone-rank aristocrats were able to maintain control of local government and prevent the central government from dispatching its own administrators to the countries. Nevertheless, the imposition of a uniform government began to forge the residents of the Korean peninsula into a unified people. It is thus from the time of Silla unification in 668 that we can begin to speak of a "Korean language" rather than of the Silla, Paekche, or Koguryŏ languages, or of "Korea" as a political and cultural entity rather than a mere geographical expression.

Unification brought a flowering of trade, learning, and culture in Korea. Hundreds, perhaps thousands, of people from Silla traveled to China—itself in the golden age of Tang—to study Buddhism and Confucianism, and even to serve in the Chinese bureaucracy. Koreans established settlements along the coast of China and dominated the trade in the Yellow Sea between China, Japan, and Korea. Arab traders in the South China Sea brought knowledge of *al Sila* to the Arab world. Kŭmsŏng, the capital located at present Kyŏngju, grew to house almost a million people in palaces, temples, and ordinary houses. Silla gold- and silversmiths reached a high degree of skill, and the Buddhist temples throughout the country exhibited a high degree of refinement in their sculpture and decoration.

Astronomy was highly developed (the seventh-century Ch'ŏmsŏngdae observatory established by Queen Sŏndŏk, and still standing in Kyŏngju, is East Asia's earliest). The arts flourished, but perhaps it was in Buddhist thought that Silla's contribution to East Asian civilization was most significant. Prominent Korean monks corresponded with their famous counterparts in China, and wrote commentaries in Chinese of wide influence. Wŏnch'uk, for example, was a disciple of the prominent Chinese translator Hsüan-tsang and wrote a commentary influential in the evolution of Tibetan Buddhism. Wŏnhyo, perhaps the most important Silla monk, was an important synthesizer of Flower Garland Doctrine in Korea whose influence reached also into China. Ŭisang was one of the chief synthesizers of Tiantai Buddhism, which he then introduced from China. Rich temples were built throughout Silla. The nine-story Imperial Dragon Temple (Hwangnyong-sa)—burnt by the Mongols in 1238—was thought to protect the kingdom. (It was the model for Japan's oldest wooden temple, the Hōryūji of Nara.) Some Buddhist prayers enshrined in the T'abo pagoda in the Pulguk-sa date to 751 and are the oldest woodblock print documents extant in the world. The Sŏkkuram temple with delicately carved stone bas-reliefs lining an artificial cave is one of Korea's most exquisite monuments. Exceptionally fine cast bells were made, and even exported to Japan.[10]

Silla reached its peak in the mid-eighth century, but then gradually declined. Strife between rival lines of descent for the throne weakened central power. Powerful local strongmen and town lords consolidated their power and blocked—even reversed—Chinese-style bureaucratic centralization. For 150 years from the end of the eighth century a succession of kings came to the throne through violence. As central power declined in the ninth century, the merchant-prince Chang Pogo was able to assemble a private army of some 10,000 men at his redoubt on Wando Island on Korea's south coast, and suppress piracy to the extent that he had a virtual monopoly on foreign trade in the Yellow Sea. He was eventually assassinated when he tried to marry the king's daughter, but other powerful merchants were also rising, one of whose sons would found the succeeding kingdom.

Koryŏ (918–1392)

As the tenth century opened, rebels set up within the territory of Silla the kingdoms of T'aebong in the central area, and Later Paekche in the southwest. Wang Kŏn, from a Kaesŏng merchant family, was able to take over T'aebong and establish the state of Koryŏ (an abbreviation of *Koguryŏ*) at his native town in central Korea in 918. Meanwhile Later Paekche sacked Kyŏngju, the capital of Silla, and so in 935 the Silla king with his leading government officials surrendered to Wang Kŏn. The following year Wang Kŏn subdued Later Paekche, and Korea was again united under a new dynasty with its capital in the central Korean town of Kaesŏng (just north of today's DMZ).

Koryŏ started out as a loose confederation of warlords and princes, but Wang Kŏn, now known as King T'aejo, gradually was able to consolidate his power by marrying 29 daughters of important strong men and military aristocrats. Throughout the dynasty, in fact, marriages with the royal house became an important way that nonroyal clans became influential. Many Head Rank Six bureaucrats from Silla moved to the new capital to be incorporated in the new polity, but the bone-rank system itself disintegrated. Local strongmen controlled the counties with the help of localized ranked descent groups, and locally dominant kin groups began to identify themselves by locale rather than bone rank. Local descent groups of high rank could send people into the central government, while those of lower status were confined to local office. The bulk of the population consisted of free peasants under the control of local officials. Throughout the tenth century the Koryŏ kings tried to expand central government power. In 958 a Chinese-style civil examination system was introduced for officials that enshrined the principle of merit, as well as heredity, for acquiring office. At the end of the century the Tang Chinese Three Department-Six Board System was introduced with its principles of central control and functional differentiation. This was the high point of centralization, however, for subsequently lines of descent established by prominent persons recruited from the countryside led to the development of a new hereditary class of central officials in the capital that came to be known as the *yangban*—the "two ranks," the military and civil officials.

The family in Koryŏ was quite distinct from the patrilineal, corporate families of later Korea.[11] The aristocrats of Koryŏ married multiple wives *and* concubines. Marriages were held at the wives' houses, where a son-in-law's father-in-law welcomed him as a resident, and where his children grew up. This system of polygyny and matrilocal residence could only be accommodated by a "visiting husband" pattern. There was little distinction in interaction or dress or between wives and concubines. Women inherited property and slaves, and divorce was frequent. The system, by allowing the creation of multiple sets of affinal ties among influential families, seems to have been an integral part of the strategic power-seeking of the Koryŏ aristocrats.

After the defeat of Koguryŏ in 668 the area around P'yŏngyang had become a lightly populated no-man's-land on the border of Silla and the Manchurian state of Parhae. Under Koryŏ, however, the area was repopulated and P'yŏngyang was made the western capital. Koryŏ persistently tried to move the border north and absorb the Jurchen people living there, but Koryŏ also had persistent problems with invasions from the north. The Khitan had destroyed Parhae in 926, with many refugees coming down into Koryŏ. A Khitan invasion in 993 was stopped, but in a second invasion in 1010–1011 the Khitan sacked the Koryŏ capital, destroying many irreplaceable historical documents. Koryŏ was able to defeat the Khitan in a third invasion in 1018. As a result of these invasions, Koryŏ completed a wall along its northern border by 1044. Koryŏ did manage to have a stable relationship with the Chin Empire that ruled Manchuria after the defeat of the Khitan.

In 1171 the military took over Koryŏ in a coup, and this regime came to be dominated by the military Ch'oe family. From that time until the assassination of Ch'oe U in 1258 during the Mongol invasions, the military Ch'oe family controlled a compliant king. The six Mongol invasions over 40 years in the thirteenth century devastated Koryŏ. The Mongols, a steppe people, had defeated the Chin Empire in Manchuria by 1215 and entered Koryŏ pursuing fleeing Khitan and Jurchen forces. At that time Koryŏ joined with the Mongol forces to mop them up. Mongol demands for tribute become greater and greater, however, and finally the Mongols invaded in 1231–1232. The military dictator Ch'oe U moved the capital from Kaesŏng to Kanghwa Island off the west coast of Korea, leaving the people to withdraw to mountain fortresses for protection. The Mongols, who relied on mobile cavalry for their military supremacy, were not able to take all the mountain fortresses, and they were never able to cross the water to threaten the capital on Kanghwa Island. On the mainland, however, they had a scorched earth policy, slaughtering all the inhabitants when a town or fortress fell after resisting. The invasion of 1254 was especially destructive, with the Mongols taking 200,000 captives and depopulating whole regions. Many cultural treasures were lost including the nine-story pagoda of the Hwangyong Temple in Kyŏngju, and the woodblocks for printing the Buddhist Tripitaka that had been carved as an act of faith during the Khitan invasion of 1010–1011. (Another carving was begun during these invasions. Completed in 1251, these wood blocks are still extant at the Haein Temple in North Kyŏngsang Province.)

The military dictators, and the Three Elite Patrols that were the core of military society, forced resistance against the Mongols despite the suffering of the common people. The dictator Ch'oe U was assassinated in 1258, but coups and countercoups prevented a change in policy until 1270, when the the Koryŏ Court finally surrendered to the Mongols and returned to Kaesŏng, but the Three Elite Patrols held out on Cheju Island until 1273. Korea's stiff resistance to the Mongols devastated the country, but unlike China Koryŏ maintained its independence upon surrender, and was not fully incorporated into the Mongol Empire. Rather it was treated as an "in-law state." The crown prince was held hostage in Beijing and forced to marry a Mongol princess. Upon ascending the throne he and his Mongol queen would move to Kaesŏng,[12] but the Koryŏ kings during this period took Mongol names, wore Mongol-style clothes, and even used the Mongol language. Certain Mongol foods and words, in fact, continued in use in the royal court right into the twentieth century. Koryŏ paid heavy tribute to the Mongol court. The Mongols founded the Eastern Expedition Field Headquarters in Koryŏ originally to plan for the two disastrous attempts of the Mongols to conquer Japan using Korean ships in 1274 and 1281, but they later used this office to make sure Koryŏ didn't get too independent. During this period, families of interpreters and falconers (falconry was a favorite sport of the Mongols) became quite powerful.

Despite its turbulent history, Koryŏ was a period of high intellectual and artistic achievement. Writing in the Korean language using hyangch'al continued, though only a few examples are extant from this period. Much writing in Chinese from the period has survived, however, such as the first extant indigenous histories of Korea, the twelfth-century *Samguk Sagi* [*A History of the Three Kingdoms*], and the thirteenth-century *Samguk Yusa* [*Remaining Affairs of the Three Kingdoms*]. Both works were based on earlier histories and documents that have now been lost. The latter contains the earliest known text of the Tan'gun myth about the founding of Korea. Buddhist thought flourished with Koryŏ monks writing works read in China and Japan, as well as Korea. The two carvings of woodblocks for printing the Tripitaka, the Buddhist scriptures, were big achievements, and as a result of Buddhist printing activity Koreans developed moveable metal type as early as 1234—200 years before Gutenberg—and were able to send to China Buddhist texts lost there in persecutions. Koryŏ Buddhist painting became extremely refined.[13] Magnificent Koryŏ paintings of *Water and Moon Goddess of Mercy* (Kwan-ŭm) have been preserved in Korea and Japan to which they were exported. The carved and inlaid celadon stoneware pottery of this period is world famous.

Buddhism continued to be the established religion, with the state administering exams for high church office. Today's dominant Sŏn (Zen) order, the Chogye order, was founded by the twelfth-century monk Chinul. Ch'ŏnt'ae (Tiantai) Buddhism was also introduced at this time. Kings and prominent families built many temples as an act of merit. Court life was enriched by elaborate Buddhist festivals. The lantern festival (Yŏndŭnghoe) held on the full moon of the first lunar month and the P'algwanhoe held on the full moon of the 11th month both combined Buddhist rites with indigenous practices of music, dance, and masked drama that have been preserved among the people even today. Buddha's birthday (the eighth day of the 4th month) and the festival of Hungry Ghosts (Ullama) on the full moon of the 7th month were other important festivals.

As the Mongol Empire began to fall apart in the fourteenth century, the Koryŏ kings began asserting their independence. Koryŏ King Kongmin (1351–1374), who came to power during a period when the Chinese were revolting against the waning Mongol power, removed the Mongol advisors and their institutions from the kingdom, and reverted to traditional Korean dress, but he found it difficult to put through the reforms necessary to reinvigorate the kingdom. He turned to the Buddhist monk, Sin Ton, who wanted to move the capital to P'yŏngyang and institute reforms, but Sin was banished in 1371 and King Kongmin assassinated in 1374. The native Ming dynasty was established in China in 1385, and was pressing Koryŏ. The court felt military action was necessary, and put the general Yi Sŏng-gye in charge of the expedition against the Ming, but rather than attack the Chinese, General Yi turned back from the border and took over the kingdom in 1392.

Chosŏn (1392–1897)

When Yi Sŏng-gye became king, he changed the name of the Kingdom to Chosŏn—land of morning freshness—taken from the ancient Chosŏn Kingdom that Tan'gun was supposed to have ruled. Apart from putting his supporters in power, and moving the capital from Kaesŏng to Hanyang (today's Seoul), King T'aejo, as he came to be known, did not make major changes in the way the kingdom was governed. His son T'aejong (1400–1418), however, introduced very extensive reforms based on Chinese Neo-confucian statecraft. The power of royal relatives was reduced. Buddhist monks were banished from the capital, and the amount of land and the number of slaves and monks the monasteries could have were reduced. A comprehensive registration system was implemented. Polygyny was abolished—only one wife could be considered legitimate; the others would be concubines whose children could not inherit the status of their father—and Neoconfucian family ceremonies as interpreted by the Chinese philosopher Chu Hsi were made mandatory for the yangban. The eventual result of this last measure was to transform the bilateral Koryŏ family system into a patrilineal one similar to that of China.

T'aejong's son, Sejong (1418–1450), is generally considered the greatest Chosŏn king. He brought the northernmost part of today's Korea into the kingdom, and is particularly remembered for the invention of an alphabet for writing the Korean language. Up until this time, the polysyllabic and grammatically complicated Korean language had been written with a cumbersome system of using Chinese characters sometimes for their meaning, and sometimes for their sound, called *idu* (*hyangch'al* in the Silla period). King Sejong ordered his scholars to study Korean phonetics and come up with a writing system. *Hunmin Chŏngŭm* (*Correct Sounds for Instructing the People*), an alphabetic script based on the sounds of the Korean language, was invented in 1443 and promulgated in 1446. It is the world's only alphabet in use that was invented from scratch, rather than by adapting an already-existing writing system, and the letter shapes are diagrams of the placement of the tongue at the point of articulation for each sound. Although the upper classes quickly began calling the new script *ŏnmun* (Vulgar Writing), and continued to prefer to write in Chinese as a sign of status and education, the script quickly spread to women and commoners throughout the Korean peninsula, and is a symbol of Korean identity to this day.

The questions of the composition of the ruling class, and of the role of slavery during this period have been controversial.[14] Many historians have attributed the Confucianization that is so conspicuous in the early years of the Chosŏn dynasty to the rise to power of a new class of Confucian literati, the sadaebu, or yangban. As we have seen, however, the yangban as a class had already been in formation during the Koryŏ period as a capital-based elite gradually separated itself from the old regional elites whose status began to decline, and recent historical work has failed to find a sharp break in the social composition of the elite between Koryŏ and Chosŏn. The yangban, moreover, seemed to use slaves both as house servants, and as cultivators. James Palais has even argued that, since the proportion of slaves in early Chosŏn was as high as 30 to 50 percent of the population, Chosŏn must be called a "slave society" just like Ancient Greece and Rome, or the American South. While many scholars question whether the term *nobi* should really be translated as "slave," the nobi could be bought, sold, given as gifts, and inherited, and unlike European serfs they were not bound to the land. The fact that slaves and masters were members of the same ethnic group, however, makes the slavery of Korea during this period extremely unusual in comparative terms.

Following a vigorous first hundred years in the fifteenth century, the dynasty was wracked by a series of literati purges during the sixteenth century. These were followed by two sets of invasions that devastated the country, and that naturally divide the dynasty into two parts. The first set of invasions by the Japanese in 1592–1595 and 1597 were the most destructive. Hideyoshi, the Shōgun who united Japan after a period of disunity, wanted to invade China via Korea, and sent some 150,000 troops to Korea in 1592. These landed on the south coast, and while Korea's navy under Admiral Yi Sun-sin put up a valiant defense with his iron-clad "turtle boats" (*kŏbuksŏn*), Korea's land forces were no match for the experienced Japanese fighters and within three weeks Seoul was in flames. Valuable historical records were burnt so that we have much less extensive knowledge of Korean history before 1592 than after. The Chinese intervened and the Japanese were eventually defeated at P'yŏngyang. The Koreans, for their part, resorted to guerilla warfare with "righteous armies" (*ŭibyŏng*) led by local literati and Buddhist monks. Japanese forces returned to Korea in 1597, but in 1598 Hideyoshi died and a settlement was reached. Thousands of potter families from the south of Korea were kidnapped to Japan, where they founded Japan's porcelain industry in the Arita area of Kyūshū.

The Japanese invasions were followed by Manchu invasions in 1627 and 1637. As a result of these four invasions Korea was devastated and depopulated, and didn't recover until the end of the century. Moreover, bitter experience with the Japanese and the Manchus made the Koreas extremely wary of foreign relations. The Koreans sent diplomats on tribute missions to China four times a year, but only one annual mission from China was allowed to visit Seoul. The Koreans dealt with the Japanese in an office at Tongnae near Pusan. Korean diplomatic missions occasionally visited Edo, the Japanese capital, but the Koreans never allowed Japanese to visit Seoul. Apart from a few contacts with the Manchus and Okinawans, other foreigners were shunned completely. Koreans, except for the few diplomatic expeditions, were not allowed out of the country, and Korea came to be known as the "Hermit Kingdom."

Nevertheless, as Chosŏn recovered from the Japanese and Manchu invasions, important economic and social changes began to appear. Despite attempts of the Confucian bureaucrats to suppress them, five-day periodic markets supplied by itinerant peddlers appeared and spread rapidly, finally being made legal in 1674. Specialized markets, like the wholesale herb market of Taegu that supplied even Japan, developed. Although private slaves continued to exist until slavery was abolished in 1894, the economic importance of slavery dropped rapidly after 1690, and all government slaves were made commoners in 1801. Agricultural production now was accomplished with small-scale owner-cultivators or tenant farmers, the latter renting their land often from large landlords. Regional cities with resident landlords, merchants, and craftworkers began to grow.

Prose and poetic writing in Modern Korean began flourishing from the seventeenth century.[15] The popular *kasa* and *sijo* forms of poetry were widely cultivated, and the first vernacular novels began to appear alongside Chinese works at this time. Early novels written by literati soon were joined by more popular works, such as *Imjin Records*, a nationalistic collection of stories set during the period of the Japanese invasions, *The Story of Spring Fragrance*, Korea's most popular folk romance, and others. These works published in the vernacular often contained criticism of the social system. The most popular of them also began to be performed in public marketplaces as *p'ansori*, a performance art in which a singer tells a story alternating narrative and song, accompanied by a drummer.

The eighteenth century was a time of peace and prosperity, but a series of weak kings in the early nineteenth century appeared just as Korea was facing pressure from the Western powers to open up. Toward the middle of the century the prince regent, or Taewŏn'gun, who ruled in 1864–1874 while his son, King Kojong, was a minor, managed to prevent foreign contacts through a program of self-strengthening based on tradition, but this ultimately proved futile. Modernizing Japan forced a treaty on Korea in 1876 that was modeled on Britain's unequal treaties with China. Inch'ŏn, Pusan, Wŏnsan, and other ports were opened to foreigners, and treaties with other major powers followed. Protestant missionaries arrived for the first time, and Catholicism—which had a presence in Korea from the late eighteenth century—was legalized. The missionaries founded modern schools and hospitals that remain important in South Korea to this day.

During this period China, Japan, and Russia vied for paramount control over Korea, while the United States tried to play a neutral role. Korean modernizers enlisted Japanese help for an 1884 coup attempt that failed for lack of sufficient indigenous support. In 1894 the Japanese jumped in when Koreans asked for help from China during the Tonghak Rebellion. This precipitated the Sino-Japanese War in which Japan defeated China and acquired Taiwan. The Japanese put advisors in place in Korean ministries to push through modernizing reforms in 1894, and even went to the point of assassinating pro-Chinese Queen Min in 1895 to neutralize her opposition. In 1896 King Kojong fled to the Russian legation, and the Koreans were able to get out from under the grip of Japan for a time.

The Great Han Empire (1897–1910)

The Koreans continued their reform efforts even after they extricated themselves from under the Japanese advisors. They elevated the status of the Kingdom of Chosŏn to Great Han Empire (Taehan Cheguk) to give Korea ritual and diplomatic equality with the Chinese and Japanese empires. New, more accurate land tax registers were made. A comprehensive, modern education system was begun. The first Korean banks were founded. By the turn of the century Seoul had electricity and telephones, electric trams, and several competing daily newspapers.

The Koreans did not have enough time to build an effective fiscal and military administration, however. When, after cementing an anti-Russian alliance with Britain, Japan attacked the Russians in Manchuria, and started the Russo-Japanese War in 1904, Japan occupied Korea despite Korea's declaration of neutrality. A series of quick naval victories gave Japan the advantage, but land fighting with the Russians in Manchuria almost exhausted Japan. Peace negotiations were begun under the auspices of Theodore Roosevelt. In the Treaty of Portsmouth, Russia conceded Japanese paramount political, military and economic interests in Korea, gave over all its leases in Manchuria to Japan, and ceded half of Sakhalin Island as well. In a later protocol American Secretary of War Howard Taft and Japanese Prime Minister Katsura agreed that the United States would recognize Japan's paramount interest in Korea, if Japan promised not to interfere or raise objections to the U.S. occupation of the Philippines. With all possibility of foreign interference neutralized, the Japanese forced Korea to accept a Japanese protectorate in November 1905.[16]

Japanese Protectorate (1905–1910)

Many Koreans initially did not think the Japanese were intent on taking full control of Korea, and hoped for modernizing reforms. As large numbers of Japanese moved to Korea, and the Japanese step-by-step took over the entire Korean government, however, people soon became aware of Japan's intentions. In 1907 King Kojong sent a secret letter to the Second Hague Peace Conference saying the Protectorate was against his will. Although the Korean delegation was not admitted to the conference, the Koreans received sympathetic publicity. The enraged Japanese then forced King Kojong to abdicate in favor of his son, Sunjong, and disbanded the Korean army. Guerilla "Righteous Armies" (*ŭibyŏng*) sprang up that took the Japanese several years to suppress. In P'yŏngyang, a major center of Protestant activity, the despair that many Koreans felt at this time found expression in a great religious revival.

Japanese Colony (1910–1945)

By 1910 the Japanese were fully enough in control to annex Korea outright as a colony. From that time, until Japan's defeat in World War II, Korea was ruled by an all-powerful governor-general appointed from among Japanese military officers. The governor-general ruled by decree, and Japanese administrators and police ran the entire country through a system of military rule. The colonial administration forced all education to be in the Japanese language, and except for one government newspaper, all Korean language newspapers were at first suppressed. Massive, peaceful demonstrations against Japanese rule, however, startled the Japanese on March 1, 1919. These demonstrations were partially inspired by President Wilson's Fourteen Points which envisioned self-rule for (Europe's) small nations, and marked the beginning of Korean mass political activity. Although the March 1 movement did not force the Japanese to grant Koreans independence, or even autonomy, the Japanese did respond to the movement by replacing Military Rule with what they called Cultural Rule.

Under Cultural Rule, a certain number of censored Korean publications were allowed, a civilian police force was created, and consultative assemblies (dominated by Japanese settlers in many areas) were created. Freedom of speech and political activity was still limited, but at least Koreans were able to discuss and write about a fair variety of subjects, and to reflect on how to achieve modernity and independence. In urban areas a modern lifestyle began to appear, as people encountered manufactured goods, magazines, radio broadcasting, and other aspects of modern life. An often suppressed, but still vigorous movement for independence continued, but after 1931 the left and right wings split. A less and less influential government-in-exile (Provisional Government) continued in Shanghai and communist insurgencies continued among Koreans in Manchuria, but the Japanese never allowed enough freedom within Korea itself for effective mass political movements to develop.

Japan moved to take over Manchuria in 1931, and then attacked China in 1937. As a result Korea experienced a modicum of industrialization—especially in the north—as it became a forward base for Japanese military activities on the mainland. At the same time, Japan's war footing made the space for cultural and political activity in Korea narrower and narrower. By 1939 publications in Korean had stopped, and Koreans were forced to take Japanese surnames. In 1944 even the public use of the Korean language was banned—a most impractical move since the majority of Koreans spoke no other tongue. During most of the Second World War, Japan and the Soviet Union had a nonaggression pact, so Korea at least was spared fighting.

Liberation, Division, and Occupation (1945–1948)

The Allied powers decided at the Cairo Conference of December 1943 that "in due course Korea shall be free and independent." In 1945 at Yalta and Potsdam the principle was established that the Soviet Union should enter the war against Japan 90 days after the defeat of Germany, but no concrete plans had been made for Korea's status after Japan's defeat. The Soviet Union declared war against Japan on August 8, but atomic bombings of Hiroshima and Nagasaki on August 6 and 9 were bringing Japan to a quick surrender. As Russian troops were nearing the border of North Korea, the United States proposed a division of responsibility with the Soviet Union at the 38th parallel just north of Seoul: The Soviet Union would take the Japanese surrender in the north, and the United States would take the Japanese surrender in the south, and a joint administration for all of Korea would be arranged afterward.[17]

The joint administration never came about. The Soviet Union occupied the area north of the 38th parallel by the end of August. They never set up a military administration, but worked through People's Committees that had been hastily organized in August and September which they reformed, when necessary, to make them sympathetic to leftist power. The Soviet Civil Administration provided advisors behind the scenes that, while they didn't rule directly, had substantial influence over policy. The U.S. forces arrived in September 1945, suppressed the People's Committees, and set up a U.S. military government (USAMGIK) that worked through the existing Japanese administration—a highly unpopular move at the time—until Japanese administrators could be replaced by Korean and American military personnel. The United States and the Soviet Union negotiated for a trusteeship over a united Korea, but distrust between the two powers and domestic opposition to trusteeship meant that these plans never succeeded. In February 1946 the North Korean Provisional People's Committee began a series of steps: uncompensated land reform, rationing of labor and materials, price controls, and nationalization of key industries that made the socioeconomic organization of the northern sector substantially different from the southern sector. Large numbers of disgruntled former landlords and business people, as well as a large proportion of North Korea's Christian population, began fleeing south while a smaller number of leftist intellectuals fled north.

In the south the U.S. military government appointed a consultative council from South

Korean political parties in February 1946. In October an Interim Legislative Assembly was created. Conditions in the south were chaotic, however, with random violence, assassinations, uprisings in 1946 and 1947, and guerillas coming down from the north. Political opinion began polarizing between left and right, squeezing out the middle. With the breakdown of negotiations with the Soviet Union in 1947, the United States turned to the United Nations, where a resolution was passed that a national assembly be created through nationwide elections to draft a constitution. This was carried out in the south, but not the north, leading to the establishment of the Republic of Korea (Taehan minguk) with its capital in Seoul on August 15, 1948, as a representative democracy in the south. The first president was Syngman Rhee. In the north the Democratic Peoples Republic of Korea (Chosŏn minjujuŭi inmin konghwaguk) with its capital in P'yŏngyang was established on September 9, 1948, as a communist state. Its premier was the head of the Korean Workers Party, Kim Il Sung. Since the regimes north and south still compete for legitimacy as the "true" government of the Korean nation, the history of the two regimes also continues to be hotly contested.

The Korean War (1950–1953)

In the late forties guerilla warfare was gradually suppressed in the south, but there were recurrent clashes between northern and southern troops along the 38th parallel. In the wake of the success of the Chinese revolution in 1949, Kim Il Sung, in consultation with Stalin and Mao Zedong, decided to attempt unification by force. The DPRK, with logistical help from the Soviet Union, invaded South Korea on June 25, 1950. The well-trained and armed North Koreans quickly took Seoul, and began moving south. The United States and its allies persuaded the United Nations to declare this civil war a war of aggression, and the United States led a United Nations force charged with defending South Korea. The initial troops the United States sent, however, were not well trained or equipped for warfare, and the North Koreans were able by mid-September to occupy all of South Korea except for a small area around Pusan. McArthur's amphibious landing at Inch'ŏn in September reversed the tide, however. McArthur's troops retook Seoul, and then without further U.N. authorization McArthur crossed the 38th parallel, and had the U.N. forces pursue the disorganized North Koreans almost to the Chinese border. Chinese entry into the war in December 1950 changed everything, and the U.N. troops were pushed south of Seoul by January 1951. Seoul, by this time largely destroyed, was retaken by U.N. forces in March of that year. The U.N. and Chinese troops fought a stalemate north of Seoul for two more years. Finally the United States, China, and North Korea forged an armistice to end the fighting. (President Rhee of South Korea refused to participate.) A ceasefire was signed, but no peace treaty ending the war has been achieved up until today. A 4-kilometer-wide (2.5 mile) demilitarized zone (DMZ) was created on each side of the demarcation line between the two sides. A place for the two sides to meet exists in the truce village of P'anmunjŏm not far from Seoul. The war had been extremely destructive. Some 500,000 North Korean soldiers, 47,000 South Korean soldiers, 1 million Chinese soldiers, 54,000 American soldiers, and 3,000 U.N. allied soldiers died. Even more Korean civilians are estimated to have died, probably at least 2 million North Koreans, and 1 million South Koreans. Bombing had reduced the major North Korean cities to rubble. Nearly half the industry and a third of the housing of South Korea was destroyed.

Politics and Development in South Korea (1948–1987)

Although South Korea's constitutions have all been more-or-less republican in form, up until the democratization process that began in 1987

South Korea's leaders were mostly authoritarian. Under South Korea's first president Syngman Rhee (Yi Sŭng-man, 1948–1960), progress was made after the Korean War in administration and education, but economic development was neglected, and South Korea was heavily dependent on the United States' economic and military aid. Rhee was overthrown by the April 19 Student Revolution in 1960 after a rigged election for vice president. This was followed an eight-month democratic interregnum, but a military coup ended this on May 16, 1961. From that time until his assassination in 1979, General Park Chung Hee (Pak Chŏng-hŭi) ran the country. He began his rule as head of a military junta, but stepped down to be elected president in 1963 when the United States pressed for a return to democracy. Under Park, South Korea experienced rapid export-led economic growth based on light industry. In 1972 as the United States was withdrawing from Vietnam, however, Park tightened his control through the so-called *Yusin* constitution that called for indirect election of the president and a partially appointed legislature. Park moved aggressively forward with his Heavy and Chemical Industrialization program. Through this program many defense-related heavy industries were concentrated in southeastern ports.[18]

The imbalances of Park's industrialization, combined with the oil shocks of the seventies, led to an economic crisis in late 1979. Amidst riots in southeastern cities, Park was assassinated by the head of the KCIA (Korean Central Intelligence Agency). At first it seemed that there would be a constitutional succession by the vice president, Ch'oe Kyu-ha. However, another general, Chun Doo Hwan (Chŏn Tu-hwan), took control on December 16, 1979. Amidst rising student demonstrations for democracy in the spring of 1980, Chun declared martial law on May 17. Subsequent prodemocracy demonstrations in the southwestern city of Kwangju were put down with such brutality that the citizens of Kwangju joined with the students in an uprising that took over the city for four days. Although Kwangju was peaceful after the troops left, the uprising was put down by force leading to the deaths of hundreds, possibly thousands, of mostly youthful citizens. Because the troops used to put down the uprising had been withdrawn from the DMZ with U.S. permission, many Koreans believe the United States was complicit in Chun's takeover of the government and suppression of the Kwangju uprising. The Kwangju Uprising, thus, is often regarded as a watershed in South Korean's attitudes toward the United States.[19]

Chun's administration (1980–1987) successfully revived the economy, but it lacked legitimacy. Suppression of labor and those advocating democracy was a continuous issue. Chun wanted his fellow general, Roh Tae Woo (No T'ae-u), to succeed him, but massive demonstrations in 1987—in which the middle classes joined students and workers—threatened to derail the 1988 Seoul Olympics, something the regime considered its crowning achievement. Roh instead acquiesced, in his June 29 Declaration, to freedom of the press, and the call for direct election of the president for a single five-year term, two of the chief demands of the protestors. While Roh, a general who had participated in the suppression of the Kwangju uprising, was unpopular with large segments of the population, the two main opposition candidates, Kim Young Sam (Kim Yŏng-sam) and Kim Dae Jung (Kim Tae-jung), could not agree on who should run against Roh, so both did. Roh, though he won only 35.9 percent of the vote, got a plurality and became president. The elections for the National Assembly had similar results: Roh's Democratic Justice Party got 42 percent of the seats for a plurality but not a majority. Even so, a process of democratization that continues to this day was begun.

That the ruling party was in the minority—a status called *yŏso yadae* in Korean—proved cumbersome. Roh was able to achieve a conservative realignment in 1990, however, by engineering the merger of his Democratic Justice Party with the conservative New Democratic Republic Party, and with Kim Young Sam's moderate Reunification Democratic Party. The merged party was called the Democratic Liberal Party, an obvious reference to the long-ruling Liberal Democratic Party of Japan. This made Kim Young Sam the obvious front-runner in the election of 1992.

Kim Young Sam's victory in the 1992 with 42 percent of the popular vote gave Korea its first civilian president since 1961. The Kim Young Sam administration consolidated democracy by purging the generals and colonels who had been major players in the military regimes, and banning anonymous bank accounts. In 1995 his administration acquiesced to popular demand by passing a law allowing former presidents Chun and Roh to be prosecuted for the December 12, 1979, coup, and the killing of hundreds of protesters during the Kwangju demonstrations in May 1980. The two former presidents were also convicted of bribery and corruption amounting to hundreds of millions of dollars. They were both sentenced to life in prison, but they were pardoned and freed by President Kim Young Sam two years later. Kim Young Sam's administration that had begun so promisingly, moreover, ended in a wave of corruption scandals and a related currency crisis that forced South Korea to seek a bailout from the IMF (International Monetary Fund) in 1997.

As the currency crisis raged in December, 1997, Kim Dae Jung finally obtained the presidency in his fourth attempt with 41 percent of the vote. It was the first time that a candidate from the discriminated southwestern province of Chŏlla obtained the presidency. It was also the first time South Korea had managed a peaceful transfer of power from a ruling party to an opposition party, thus proving the growing maturity of South Korean democracy. Somewhat similarly to Kim Young Sam, however, Kim Dae Jung's administration, which introduced financial and other reforms that over a couple of years revived the seriously damaged South Korean economy, ended in disgrace in a series of corruption scandals. Kim Dae Jung withdrew from his Millennium Democratic Party, allowing nomination of the new candidate by democratic means. The labor lawyer, Roh Moo Hyun (No Mu-hyŏn), became the surprising victor when the other strong candidate Chŏng Mong-ju, son of the founder of the Hyundai conglomerate, withdrew following Roh's besting him in a television debate. Amid rising anti-Americanism due to the acquittal of two American soldiers of negligence in the death of two middle school girls run over by American military vehicles, and concerns about possible U.S. military action against North Korea, Roh won the 2002 election against a more conservative candidate by promising to demand more equable treatment from the United States. The first year of President Roh's administration was rocky, however, with uncertainty about Korea's relationship to the United States (which still maintains 37,000 troops in Korea), and the beginning of the war in Iraq. The government decision to send 600 noncombatant soldiers to Iraq was met with massive demonstrations. Later the government decided to send 3,000 combatants as well. A realignment of the parties was begun in which President Roh expressed support for the Uri Party, something that was technically illegal. The opposition Grand National Party (Han Nara Tang), amid fisticuffs in the National Assembly, pushed through a midnight impeachment vote in March 2003, but most South Koreans reacted negatively to this move. In April legislative elections, 70 percent of the seats in the National Assembly changed hands. The Grand National Party lost 16 seats, and the Uri Party added 103 seats to their previous 49 to become a majority, the first time a left-of-center party has controlled the National Assembly since democratic interregnum of 1960–1961. The election seems to have been a generational watershed, too: One-third of the new legislature were in their forties, and 13 percent were female. The Constitutional

Court subsequently invalidated the impeachment vote.

North Korea (1948–1994)

Kim Il Sung (Kim Il-sŏng) ruled North Korea from its founding until his death in 1994, when his son Kim Jong Il (Kim Chŏng-il) became de facto ruler, though the deceased elder Kim has remained "Eternal President" to this day. Kim Il Sung had in the thirties been a guerilla fighting along the Korea–Manchuria border, but had been forced to flee with his band of guerillas to the Soviet Union during WWII. He returned to P'yŏngyang, his birthplace, in September 1945 and by December had, with his guerilla supporters, become the leader of the Korean Communist Party, North Korea Branch.[20] He worked under Soviet tutelage until 1948, and then became leader of the communist Democratic People's Republic of Korea (Chosŏn minjujuŭi inmin konghwaguk).

Already by the spring and summer of 1946—barely six months from the beginning of the Soviet occupation—the North Korean regime had confiscated and distributed tenanted land, and nationalized big industry, transport and communications, and banks. Under Kim Il-Sung the Korean Workers Party (Chosŏn rodong tang) was expanded from an elite "vanguard party" into a mass party that incorporated up to a quarter of the North Korean population. Because the North Koreans were still looking forward to unification with the south prior to the Korean War, however, they did not establish a fully socialist economy at that time. With the end of the Korean War, though, North Korea moved to collectivize agriculture and force the remaining private businesses and crafts into cooperatives to complete the transition to socialism. With substantial aid from the socialist block, North Korea began to rebuild, but Kim Il Sung was unhappy with Soviet meddling, and between 1956 and 1960 introduced the concept of *juche* (*chuch'e*), or self-reliance, into his speeches and writings.[21] This concept became the basis for justifying North Korea's autarkic approach to foreign policy and economics in which the country has tried to be as self-sufficient as possible. North Korea, for example, refused to join the Council for Mutual Economic Assistance (Comecon—a group founded in 1949 to foster a "socialist division of labor" among communist countries). During the sixties, North Korea was economically successful generally following Soviet and eastern European models of central planning, mass mobilization of people and resources, and investment in heavy industry. North Korea early on mechanized agriculture, and moved redundant labor from the cooperative farms into the cities for industrial work. Mass campaigns, such as the "thousand li horse" movement (*Ch'ŏllima undong*), the Ch'ŏngsalli Method (for cooperative farms), and the Taean Work Method (for factories) were used to create enthusiasm. After an initial spurt of industrialization in the sixties, however, upgrading technology became a problem for isolated North Korea. In the seventies Kim Jong Il, the son of Kim Il Sung, introduced the Three Revolutions Team Movement to promote the "ideological, technical, and cultural

South Korean president Kim Dae Jung (right) hugs North Korean president Kim Jong Il.

revolutions." At the same time North Korea turned to trade with the West to gain access to better technology. The DPRK's rigid central planning and its inability to export led to default on foreign debt in 1975 that made further borrowing in the West impossible. Throughout the seventies and eighties North Korea tried marginal adjustments—such as firm autonomy, money accounting, and allowing foreign investment—to revitalize its centrally planned economy, but little seemed to work. By the nineties when the DPRK was forced to trade even with Russia and China with hard currencies, chronic food shortages appeared that led to serious famine from 1994 to 1998 in which up to a million people died. Tens of thousands of North Koreans also fled across the border to become refugees in China. After nine years of shrinkage, the North Korean economy began growing again in 1999. Food shortages, however, have become chronic. The breakdown of the state provisioning system thus led the north in July 2002 to put through reforms that seemed to move them more toward a money-based economy, and there have been reports of a revival of small-scale marketing even in the cities since then. Although the degree to which the North Koreans are willing to continue with fundamental economic reform is still open to doubt, North Korea has additionally negotiated with South Korea to have an industrial park built near Kaesŏng just across the DMZ from Seoul. All of this continues in spite of serious tension with the United States over the DPRK's nuclear program, and its withdrawal from the Nuclear Non-Proliferation Treaty in 2003.

CONTEMPORARY CULTURE

Demography

At the time of liberation in 1945, the population of all of Korea was about 26 million. Only about 13 percent of Koreans lived in cities, and agriculture was the predominant occupation. Women married in their late teens and men in their early twenties. Family size averaged six persons, and at least a third of all families were stem families of parents and eldest married son.[22] The area around Seoul and the provinces to the south were densely populated wet-rice cultivating areas. In the provinces northwest of Seoul (in present-day North Korea) agriculture was predominantly in dry fields, and the population density was about half that of the wet-rice growing southern provinces. To the east and northeast of Seoul are mountainous areas in which mining and forestry were important. While the southern part of Korea was agriculturally rich, industry was predominantly in the north. P'yŏngyang was the second largest city in the country. Population movements following the breakup of the Japanese Empire, the division of the country, and the Korean War exacerbated the difference in population density between the north and south that had originally had an ecological basis. It is estimated that about 1.5 million North Koreans moved south between 1945 and 1953 settling mainly around Seoul, and secondarily Pusan. Perhaps a half-million migrated north. Almost two million Koreans returned to South Korea from Japan and Manchuria after liberation. Since that time the differing sociopolitical systems in the north and south have led to the development of two distinct demographic profiles.

South Korea

Already densely populated in 1945, South Korea received more than two million refugees from North Korea, Japan, and Manchuria in the late forties and early fifties when there was little industry. This exacerbated problems of underemployment, and led to the creation of squatter settlements in and around major cities known as *tal tongne*, or "moon villages" (because they were often located on mountainsides "close to the moon"). After the Korean War (1950–1953) a baby boom from 1954 to 1961 led to extremely rapid population growth—up to 2.6 percent a year—until the birth rate was brought down in the seventies through urbanization, later age of marriage, and government family-planning programs. Because the population growth rate during the baby boom was higher than the economic growth rate at the time, per capita standards of living fell during the fifties. The rapid industrialization of the sixties was designed partly to bring the existing underemployed urban population into the regular labor force. This was so successful that toward the end of the sixties young rural people began moving to the cities. What began as a trickle in the sixties became a torrent in the seventies and eighties. Young unmarried women could find jobs in large textile, garment, shoe, and electronics factories, as well as in the service sector. Young men found jobs as drivers and mechanics, and later on found well-paying jobs in the heavy industrial parks near Seoul and in the southeast.

The result of this process has been the concentration of most of the South Korean population in large cities. Rural areas have experienced an absolute decline in population every year since 1970, and by the year 2000 79.5 percent of South Koreans lived in urban areas over 50,000, and of those 60 percent lived in the seven cities of more than 1 million inhabitants. Seoul alone has a population of 10 million, and is also surrounded by satellite cities. The migration of so many young people off the land has led not only to a rapid decline in the rural population (in 2000 only 7.8 percent of South Korea's households were farm households), but also to the rapid aging of the agricultural workforce. Rapid urbanization and the pressure for expensive education of children have brought the birth rate to below replacement levels since 1985. Nuclear families now predominate, and stem families number only about 13 percent of the total. Single-person households, rare in the past, have become commonplace, and divorce rates at all age levels have have quadrupled since 1970, reaching 33 per thousand among those in the 15–24 age group (second highest in the world after the United States). With the very low fertility that South Korea has had since 1985, selective abortion of female fetuses led to a very high male–female ratio of 115 for first children and 204.3 for fourth or higher children by 1995. This tendency to abort undesired female fetuses in the nineties was much less marked in Seoul than in both rural and urban areas in the conservative and Confucian southeastern provinces (especially North Kyŏngsang and the city of Taegu). Identification of the sex of fetuses is now illegal and the male–female ratio at first birth now runs a less drastic 110 in all parts of the country.

North Korea

The lower initial population density of North Korea combined with the losses of population due to refugee movements and deaths during the Korean War led to a quite different demographic situation than in the south. North Korea is physically slightly larger than South Korea, but its population is less than half its southern counterpart, so North Korea had a labor shortage after the Korean War, unusual for Asia. The early mechanization of the collective farms in the sixties was designed partly to free surplus labor to enable it to migrate to urban areas for employment in the rapidly expanding industrial sector. The government also promoted high fertility until the mid-seventies, so that the North Korean population grew at an annual rate of more than 3 percent from 1964 to 1971.[23] The rapid growth in population combined with a government policy of self-sufficiency, and the inefficiency of cooperative farms in a country with limited agricultural resources has led to chronic food shortages, even famine in the late nineties, however. The government now strongly "suggests" women have no more than two children, and discourages marriage of women before 26 or 27 so the population growth rate in recent years has been around

1 percent. North Korea industrialized and urbanized rapidly up until 1980, but the distribution of population has changed little since then.

About 61 percent of North Korea's population lives in cities. North Korea's economic planners have tried to distribute industry fairly evenly around the country. P'yŏngyang, with a population of 2.7 million, is North Korea's only city over a million. Most North Korean urbanites live in cities of between 200,000 and 800,000. Household size is falling in North Korea, but not nearly so precipitously as in the south, for North Korea's secluded society seems to have made for more conservative family practices than in the south.

Economy

The post–World War II growth of the economy on the Korean peninsula is one of the world's most remarkable success stories. In 1944 Korea under Japanese rule had a per capita income of only about $80 (in current prices). Most modern, large-scale industry in Korea was owned and run by Japanese, with only menial jobs reserved for Koreans. When the Japanese suddenly left in 1945 there was a shortage of Koreans with experience in running large-scale, modern industries and ministries. Spare parts and other necessary products the Koreans used to get from Japan became difficult to acquire. The division of Korea, moreover, created additional economic problems. Most of the heavy industry that existed in Korea—metal, ceramics, chemicals, gas and electric products—was in the north. Most of the light industry—textiles, printing, food processing—was in the south. The severing of economic ties between north and south, something that was well underway by 1946, created problems for both the north and south.

South Korea

The initial problems created by the division of Korea, including the cutoff of electric power deliveries from the north where there had been extensive hydroelectric development during the colonial period, made the initial economic situation in liberated South Korea chaotic. Trained Japanese managers and engineers had to be hastily replaced by Koreans. Former Japanese-owned assets were taken over by the U.S. military government, and then had to be run or privatized by the new Republic of Korea. To this was added the immense destructiveness of the Korean War, and a rapidly expanding population. Thus, by 1960 the standard of living in South Korea had only barely climbed back to where it had been in 1945.

A thorough land reform in the late forties and early fifties in which tenanted lands were purchased from landlords and sold to tenants at reasonable prices, however, made for a high level of equality. South Korea during the fifties pursued a policy of import substitution: protecting infant industries in South Korea with high tariffs, control of foreign exchange, and licensing. Economic growth was moderate, and only possible at all because of massive foreign aid, largely from the United States. Great progress was made in expanding education, however, and competent economic planning elites were assembled.

In the early sixties the Park regime renationalized the banks, and made a number of important reforms in currency and foreign exchange controls. The government combined the former Ministry of Reconstruction, the Bureau of the Budget, and the Bureau of Statistics into the Economic Planning Board (EPB) headed by the deputy prime minister, and the EPB introduced South Korea's First Five Year Plan in 1962. As the United States began scaling down its economic aid to South Korea, the government moved toward an export-oriented economic development strategy in the Second Five Year Plan beginning in 1967. As a result of these policy changes, South Korea's growth rate shot up from an average of 4.1 percent during the 1953–1955 period to 9.6 percent in the 1962–1976 period. This initial success was made primarily on the basis of light industry, such as textiles, clothing, footwear, and human-hair wigs. In 1973, the government under Park Chung Hee introduced a Heavy and Chemical Industrialization Plan. This was an attempt to move South Korea into more capital intensive industries, but it was also influenced by the desire of South Korea to be more self-sufficient in defense industries as the United States began withdrawing from Vietnam. The government promoted investment in iron and steel, shipbuilding, electronics, nonferrous metals, and machine tools by borrowing cheap money abroad with government guarantees, and then distributing funds through the government-owned banks to entrepreneurs willing to invest in government-favored industries. During this period the government sought to raise rural standards of living through highly subsidized crop prices, but rural living standards continued to lag those of the cities. Until brought to a halt in 1979 by the Second Oil Shock, and the high levels of international debt, South Korea's growth rate in the seventies averaged 11 percent a year. In 1977 per capita GNP passed the $1,000 mark.

Following a sharp recession in 1979–1980, the Chun regime was able to revive the economy through liberalization measures, moving toward the privatization of the banking industry, and promoting the growth of nonbank financial institutions such as insurance and investment companies. The 1985 Plaza Accords, by which the United States forced Japan to raise the value of its currency, helped South Korean exports by making them more price-competitive with Japan. South Korea was also helped by low oil prices and low interest rates during this period, so that it was able to generate large trade surpluses and pay down much of its international debt during the eighties, and continue growing at more than 8 percent a year. However, the government still controlled the economy, and kept wages low by repressing labor.

This situation changed with the democratization that began in 1987. For the next three years large-scale strikes, which had been banned before, wracked the country and real wages doubled over just a couple of years. Although rapid growth continued, South Korea was no longer able to compete in the labor-intensive light industries. Light manufacturing jobs began to migrate to countries with cheaper labor such as China, Thailand, and Indonesia. The athletic shoe industry, for example, once the mainstay of the economy of the port of Pusan, moved almost entirely offshore.

By the nineties, the South Korea economy was large enough and complex enough to no longer need the Five Year Plans. The government abolished the EPB in 1993 to facilitate a move to market allocation of capital, free foreign exchange, and less centralized economic planning. By 1997, South Korea had joined the World Trade Organization (WTO) and the Organization for Economic Cooperation and Development (OECD), an organization designed to promote economic cooperation between the developed countries. Per capita income in South Korea was over $10,000 a year, making South Korea a new member of the high-income group of countries (as defined by the World Bank). These successes masked serious problems, however. Entry into the WTO had forced South Korea to open its agricultural markets, and the subsequent fall in agricultural commodity prices created widespread misery in the countryside. Although the banks were no longer government controlled, they failed to develop independent methods for assessing debt risk, and continued to making loans to companies based on their size rather than their quality, reasoning that the government would never let big companies fail. And the government failed to create effective prudential oversight of capital and foreign exchange markets. The spectacular failure of Hanbo Steel in 1997 exposed the precarious nature of South Korea's finances, and a currency crisis followed that required South Korea to request a bailout from the International Monetary Fund. The bailout was followed by a credit squeeze, bankruptcies, and high unemployment (demonstrators held up signs saying "IMF = I am fired"). The year 1998 was one of substantial negative economic growth. The South Koreans under President Kim Dae Jung, elected in the midst of the crisis, eked through a series of economic reforms making labor more flexible, and reducing the debt load of the highly leveraged large conglomerates known as *chaebŏl.* Up until the 1997 currency crisis, the South Koreans had been able to avoid downsizing layoffs and large-scale foreign direct investment in Korea, preferring to use loans to invest in (and prop up) domestically owned companies. As a result of the currency crisis, however, many chaebŏl were forced to downsize, and South Korea was forced to open itself to much more foreign direct investment. A number of Korean firms passed into foreign ownership.

South Korea today (2003) has a per capita income of $10,940, and the South Koreans are avid consumers of fashion, cell phones, electronics, and have the highest level of broadband internet access in the world in addition to high levels of credit card debt. Industry is concentrated in the Seoul-Inch'ŏn area, and in the cities of the southeast such as Pusan, Taegu, Ulsan, and Ch'angwŏn.[24] Leading industries include iron and steel, shipbuilding, automobiles, semiconductors, and telecommunications equipment. South Korean products are exported throughout the world. China, the United States, Japan, and the European Union are South Korea's most important trade partners.

North Korea

The communists who took over North Korea in 1945 believed that Korea's underdevelopment was the result of imperialist exploitation and backward social relations of production. They thus put through a program from early 1946 of land reform—uncompensated expropriation from landlords, and free distribution to farmers—and nationalized Japanese-owned and "traitor-owned" industry. This program was termed "eliminating feudal remnants." Because they still hoped for unification with the south at this time, however, they refrained from further socialization of the economy. Small businesses were allowed to continue, but rationing of labor, wage and price controls, and raw material allocation policies made it difficult for private industry to make a go of it. By the end of 1946 as much as 95 percent of agriculture was in the hands of small-scale owner-cultivators, and 97 percent of distribution was through private enterprises, but 77 percent of industry was state owned.

Following the Korean War, the DPRK implemented a full transition to socialism. Agriculture was collectivized between 1954 and 1958. Peasants were organized into work teams on cooperative farms and were compensated according to the number of labor days they earned. During this same period all other private businesses were also collectivized, with three-quarters of the businesses being reorganized as cooperatives, and the other quarter becoming state enterprises. Autarkic *chuch'e* ideology that emphasized self-sufficiency was introduced, and workers were encouraged to produce more through mass-mobilization movements, such as the Thousand League Horse movement (Ch'ŏllima undong).

The First Seven Year Plan with an emphasis on heavy industry was introduced in 1961. Collective farm organization was rationalized at this time so that each collective farm, similar in organization to a Soviet kolkhoz, corresponded to an administrative village, or *ri.* Unlike in China the economic and civil administration of the villages were not combined to form communes. The Village People's Committee continued to take care of civil affairs, while the Collective Farm Management Committee worked with the farm manager, whom they tried to make sure had at least a two-year college education, to run the collective farm. During these years there was a heavy emphasis on the "four modernizations"—mechanization, electrification, irrigation, and chemicalization (use of fertilizer and pesticides)—and the release of rural labor for employment in industry. By 1970 some 70 percent of the fields were being plowed by tractors. Kim Il Sung had introduced the Ch'ŏngsalli Method at the cooperative of the same name in 1960. This was a form of intensive guidance by party leaders in which they were supposed to visit communes, listen to the people, and then come up with solutions for their problems through "on the spot guidance" (*hyŏnji chido*). Agricultural markets where peasants could peddle crafts and home-grown produce were allowed.

The Taean Work System was the factory equivalent of the Ch'ŏngsalli Method. It, too, was introduced in 1960 when Kim Il Sung visited the Taean Electrin Plant in P'yŏngyang. Both the Ch'ŏngsalli and Taean methods put the plant or cooperative Party Committee collective leadership in charge of basic decisions, and both emphasized ideological incentives to rouse worker productivity. Unlike in their mentor, the Soviet Union, where plant managers had full authority, North Korean plant managers had to report to their corresponding party committees. Although the big push of the First Seven Year Plan led to rapid economic growth, bottlenecks in energy, labor, and transportation forced the authorities to extend the plan for three extra years making it de facto a 10-year plan.

During the seventies agriculture was further centralized to the extent that the level of fertilizer usage by individual agricultural work teams was specified. The Six Year Plan of 1971 called for increased trade with the West to help North Korea overcome the backwardness of Socialist bloc technology. The DPRK's autarkic production policy that emphasized domestic production, and the rigidity of the DPRK's central planning, however, made North Korea unable to export enough to pay for imports. When North Korea faced the first oil shock, it defaulted on its foreign debts in 1975 and added a one-year adjustment to its Seven-Year Plan. North Korea continued barter trade with countries of the socialist bloc, but since that time North Korea has found it almost impossible to acquire credit abroad, and must now pay cash for most imports from the West.

In 1973 Kim Chŏng Il, the son of the DPRK's supreme leader Kim Il-sŏng who was being groomed for succession, had launched the Three Revolutions Team movement. Work teams were sent out to factories and farms to implement the "three revolutions" (ideological, technical, and cultural). At the same time agricultural fields were extensively remade in a regular checkerboard pattern when possible. As the DPRK entered the eighties—a time when China and Vietnam began decollectivizing agriculture, making market-centered reforms, and entering a period of rapid economic growth—the DPRK authorities avoided wholesale reform (even the word became taboo), but introduced marginal adjustments to save the system. The August 3 (1984) People's Consumer Goods Production movement advocated the localization of consumer products production. Other reforms included firm autonomy, accounting in monetary units, permitting foreign direct investment (little ensued), and permitting factories and cooperative farms to operate direct sales outlets.

The collapse of the Socialist bloc in the early nineties created a severe economic crisis in North Korea as it was forced to use hard currency in economic relations with the Soviet Union from 1991, and with China from 1992. Lack of petroleum and replacement parts from the Soviet Union created transportation problems, and made manufacture or importation of the fertilizer necessary for farming extremely difficult. Trade with the Soviet Union and eastern Europe—heretofore the DPRK's most important trade partners—plunged, and North Korea had to turn more and more to trade with China, the only country willing and able to prevent North Korean economic collapse. Chronic food shortages were caused by lack of fertilizer and bad weather, but also serious deterioration of soil quality due to overuse of fertilizer, consequent lack of humus in the soil, and erosion caused by deforestation of steep slopes for crop growing that had been encouraged by central decree. By 1994 the DPRK admitted a serious hunger problem. Catastrophic floods devastated many areas in 1995 and 1996. The serious grain shortages that followed taxed the ability of the Public Distribution System to supply adequate food to North Korean households. Famine ensued, and it is estimated that North Korea had between 600,000 and 1 million excess deaths—3 to 5 percent of the population—between 1994 and 1999, the worst famine years.

The economy of the DPRK stabilized around the turn of the millennium, but at a level about 25 percent smaller than in the peak year of 1989. Current estimates of the Korea (South) National Statistical office put per capita income at around $750. As the Public Distribution System has deteriorated, the DPRK authorities have reduced the size of agricultural work teams to squads of 8–10 members, and began to tolerate more activity in farmers' markets. They substantially raised salaries and purchase prices for agricultural commodities in July of 2002. Although they still administer price controls, the authorities adjust prices periodically to reflect what they observe on the market. They have set up special economic zones in border areas, but perhaps only the one located near Kaesŏng just north of the South Korean border that is being developed by South Korea's Hyundae-Asan Corporation for opening in 2004 has much potential. Hyundae-Asan is also developing tourism in the Kŭmgang Mountain region, and North and South Korea are in the process of relinking road and rail routes for the first time since the Korean War.[25]

Social Life

Social life in both South and North Korea has gone through dramatic changes over the past 50 years.[26] Although modern city life began to appear in Korea during the colonial period, until the rapid industrialization of the seventies, most Koreans still lived traditional lives in the countryside that revolved around the corporate family, or *chip*, the lineage, the village neighborhood, and the local market town. Religion consisted primarily of male-centered ancestor worship, and a less respectable, but vigorous, tradition of spirit worship mixed with Buddhism patronized primarily by women and elaborated by shamans. Buddhist temples with celibate monks were located in the mountains, but had limited contact with the lay population. Christianity, especially Protestantism, had put down strong roots particularly in North Korea, but Christians were only about 5 percent of the population at the time of liberation in 1945.

A strong tradition of social stratification separated the yangban, the properly Confucian and educated notability descended from former high government officials, from commoners and others who traditionally had performed various services for the yangban in many villages. Although they maintained social prestige, however, many yangban families that had no recent government experience were no more affluent than their poor neighbors. Post–World War II land reform combined with democracy led many of the commoners to refuse to continue services to yangban anymore. Modern elementary education in the vernacular became widely available after World War II, but the mastery of traditional Chinese characters learned from elders at home and in small private schools known as *sŏdang* continued to carry high levels of prestige. Since that time rapid urbanization and industrialization has completely transformed both South and North Korea, but it is still important to understand the traditional lifestyle of the period before 1970 to fully understand contemporary Korea.

The Corporate Family

The traditional family, or chip, was organized corporately. Each family had clearly defined boundaries: Each person in South Korea, in fact, is still registered on a family register, or *hojŏk*, as a member of one and only one corporate family. Each family has a formal male house head, or *hoju*, who is responsible for family support, and who used to control family property, decide who could be entered on the family register (through marriage or adoption, for example), and could designate the place of residence of family members. (Most legal authority of the house head was removed from the legal code in 1989.) When a house head died, his role was continued through succession by the eldest son, so that, in principle so long as house heads continued in succession the family could never die out.

Marriages were patrilocal: A woman would be crossed off the register of her birth family and entered on the register of her marital family, and she would move from her birth family into her husband's house. Women tended to marry between the ages of 18 and 20, and these marriages were normally arranged by the family. (In poor families the marriage age of women tended to be lower, and the marriage age of men higher, than for others. For rich families the opposite was the case, so that in upper-class families it was not unusual for the wife to be several years older than her husband.) Originally the children being married were barely consulted in the process, and met for the first time at the time of their wedding. After World War II, however, the custom of *massŏn*, a premarriage meeting in which the couple involved could decide whether or not they wanted a match, began spreading from urban areas (where it had already become customary) to rural areas as well.

Eldest sons, known as *changnam* or *maji*, were expected to remain with their birth family all their lives, and continue the family through succeeding to the house headship. A daughter-in-law would be brought in for these eldest sons, creating a stem family of married parents and married eldest son. The daughter-in-law would start out under the authority of her mother-in-law, but gradually take over household affairs as she bore children. The eldest son would remain under his father's formal authority until his father's death, but the age of sixty that was marked by an elaborate celebration called *hoegap* or *hwan'gap* often marked the retirement of the parents from active management of the farm and household.

Younger sons might bring a bride into the house for a year or so, but this was always temporary. Younger sons would be given some resources to set up their own households and would over a period of time become independent. In such cases the house of the eldest son is known as the *k'ŭn chip*, or Big House, and the houses of the younger sons are known as *chagŭn chip*, or Little House. This distinction is also reflected in the kinship terminology for aunts and uncles: the children of the younger brothers called their fathers' eldest brother *k'ŭn abŏji*, Big Father, and his wife *k'ŭn ŏmŏmi*, or Big Mother. The children called all the younger brothers *chagŭn abŏji*, Little Father, and their wives *chagŭn ŏmŏni*, Little Mother. They called their own parents, of course, simply father and mother.

Within the family, a strict male–female division of labor was observed by this author in the seventies in a rural village in South Korea: Men did "outside labor" (*pakkannil*) consisting of field labor, marketing of crops and animals, and representing the family to outside forces, while women did "inside labor" (*annil*) consisting of house work, child care, vegetable gardening, primary food processing (such as husking rice and making tofu), and clothes manufacturing. (Home-based spinning and weaving of cotton, hemp, and silk continued in poor or remote rural areas up until even the sixties, though it died out in richer, more accessible areas by the twenties.) Respectable women were supposed to stay in or near the house and courtyard as much as possible, and it wasn't until the late sixties that women took over visiting the periodic markets from the men.

The corporate family has survived rapid industrialization and urbanization, but contemporary urban life naturally has required adaptation of rural patterns. Many young men and women who moved to town to take factory and other jobs in the sixties and seventies arranged their own marriages. College students today date and have an elaborate culture of many kinds of *'tings* (taken from the ending of the English word "meeting," the name for the group blind dates that were a way college boys and girls first began to meet each other in the sixties and seventies). Love matches have become most common since the eighties, but middle-class men and women may also have massŏn with possible mates who have been suggested by their parents, or others. Factory girls who marry working-class men often use their earnings to help amass their own dowry to furnish a household, but daughters also rely on their families for dowries. While dowry isn't a big issue in socialist North Korea where housing is provided by one's employer, in South Korea inflation of marriage expenses is a big problem for middle- and upper-class families: The groom's family is supposed to provide an apartment (which in Seoul can easily run to several hundred thousand dollars), while the bride's family is supposed to provide the furnishings and appliances. Many urban parents encourage first sons and daughters-in-law to coreside with them for a couple of years, but young urban wives are frequently reluctant to do this, so that neolocal residence is more common than patrilocal residence in urban Korea today. Aged parents may be taken in by their children, but often only when they become widows or widowers. When a parent coresides with children, the eldest son is still the most popular choice, but other sons may be chosen if they have been more economically successful. Mothers even sometimes prefer living with their daughter (if their son-in-law is amenable) than with a daughter-in-law whom they never got to know through coresidence in the early years of her marriage, but when this happens people tend to say things like "Moving in with your son is a right, but if you move in with your daughter your son-in-law is doing you a favor."

Rites of Passage

Rites of passage were important occasions in rural Korea.[27] Births were private affairs at home done with the aid of relatives, or, occasionally, midwives. Many women went home for their first child to allow their own mother to help with the birth. A rope known as a *kŭmtchul* would be strung in front of the entrance to the house for a number of days to prevent unwanted visitors. Many women, at this time, made offerings to the birth spirit (often called *samsin halmŏni*, or "birth spirit grandmother"), and ate special foods such as seaweed soup (*miyŏk kuk*). Capping, a coming-of-age ceremony in which boys' hair was tied into the adult man's topknot (*sangt'u*), traditionally proceeded marriage by a day or two—though by World War II most men had cut their hair short. Women had an equivalent ceremony in which their hair was done up in the adult woman's chignon (*tchok*).

Marriages and funerals were the most important rites of passage, however. Once a marriage was agreed upon, the groom's family would send a gift box of red and green silk and a marriage letter to the bride's family. In old-style weddings the groom traveled the day before with kinsmen (but not his parents) to the village of the bride, where the wedding was held. On the day of the wedding, which was held at the bride's house, the groom would first bow to his parents-in-law and present them with carved wooden "geese" (they often looked like ducks) as a symbol of fidelity. Then the bride would be brought out in her finery. She bowed twice to the groom, who returned one bow. This was repeated three times, after which a cup of liquor would be exchanged three times. The groom usually stayed at his bride's house one to three days after the wedding. Then he would bring his bride back to his family's house in a procession—the groom on a horse and the bride in a sedan chair among the upper class, on foot for the lower class. The day after reaching the groom's house they would hold a *p'yebaek* ceremony in which the bride bowed to the groom's family and all his clan relatives. Since most villages were clan villages, the bride often spent hours bowing.

Nowadays old-style village weddings are quite rare. Most marriages are love matches, or half-love half-arranged (marriages in which the parents have either introduced the couple, or been brought in to approve the match). Urban and rural couples alike usually prefer to be married in commercial wedding halls (*yesikchang*) or hotels. Christians, of course, marry in church. Brides wear white, and grooms wear Western-style suits. After walking through an arch and down the aisle together, the bride and groom stand before an "altar" and are married by a master of ceremonies (*chuhonja*) who is usually a prominent male acquaintance of the family such as a college professor, politician, or government official. The master of ceremonies often reads the educational and professional qualifications of the bride and groom before giving a wedding address full of good advice for the new couple. The wedding is completed with a cake cutting, and then a banquet for the guests. Some couples hold a *p'yebaek* after the wedding. In this case family members of both the bride and groom meet in a different room while the guests are banqueting. The couple usually changes into traditional Korean wedding outfits (court robes for the male, and a skirt and vest for the female). The bride and groom then together bow to the family members from both sides who usually present them with envelopes of money. The couple often uses this money for their honeymoon.

Old-style three-day funerals for adults with descendants incorporated practically the entire village. (Children and others without descendents were buried with a minimum of ceremony.) Children were supposed to be with their parents when they approached death, and fathers often divided their property verbally on their deathbeds. Once the death took place loud ritual keening began. Three bowls of rice were set out for the Three Messengers from Hell (who come to fetch the soul of the deceased), and relatives might go into the courtyard to call for the soul of the deceased, waving an item of their clothing. The chief mourners removed jewelry and loosened their hair. The body of the deceased was put behind a screen, where the family would wash and dress it, with the chief mourner required to hold the hand of the corpse while this was being done. On the second day the corpse was wrapped in linen, an ancestor tablet made, and the funeral bier (usually owned by the village) brought into the courtyard of the house. The burial was on the third day, with each step of the progress of the body from house, to bier, to grave marked by an ancestor worship ceremony. Once the tomb, and banquet for visitors, was completed, the ancestral tablet was brought back to the house and put in a mourning shrine where another ancestor worship ceremony would be held. The mourning shrine would be kept up for several months, and memorial ceremonies held in the house and at the grave for two years, after which the official mourning period would be over.

Although three-day funerals can still be found in rural villages, urban Koreans today use professional services to take care of the corpse. Hospitals often have a "soul repose room" (*yŏngansil*) that can be used for preparation of the body and funeral services, after which the body is transported to a cemetery for burial, or, occasionally these days, cremation.

In rural Korea the 60th birthday, the *hwan'gap* or *hoegap*, was an elaborate celebration marking the arrival of old age, and the time when men and women should retire from active farming and housework. It was celebrated like "living ancestor worship" in which descendants of the couple would bow and offer liquor to the celebrants. This was followed by an elaborate banquet. This custom is retained in urban Korea, as well, though retirement nowadays is later than 60 for most people. Rather than hold the ceremonies at home urbanites often move these ceremonies to restaurants and hotels where they become elaborate displays of conspicuous consumption. Since people are longer lived than in the past, moreover, 70th and 80th birthday celebrations have also been elaborated.

Lineage

Lineage, along with the family, has been a dominant force in Korea since about the sixteenth century. National lineage, or *munjung*, consists of all the patrilineal descendants of the founding ancestor who normally has a tomb or temple located at an ancient county seat that is considered the origin of the lineage. This site is call the *pon'gwan*. Each lineage is identified by the surname of the founder, and its pon'gwan. For each surname there are normally numerous lineages with different pon'gwan. For the common Korean surname *Kim*, for example, the Andong Kim, Kimhae Kim, Kangnŭng Kim, and so forth are all well known, but different, lineages. Although lineages seem to have become organized only as genealogies began to be published in the sixteenth century, the founding ancestor of many lineages goes back 25 or more generations to Koryŏ, or even Silla times. Hundreds of thousands of Koreans spread all over the Korean peninsula belong to the larger lineages. Nobody with the same surname and clan origin should marry. In North Korea this prohibition is maintained informally, but in South Korea it is written into the law, though there have been periodic amnesties for those who have chosen to ignore this tradition.

The national lineages, or munjung, are divided into major segments, or *p'a*, descended usually from various brothers or cousins several generations removed from the original ancestor. It is these that maintain the lineage genealogies. Although modern lineages have often created clan organizations (*chongch'inhoe*) in Seoul that try to organize the lineage on a national basis, for most people the national lineages and major segments are abstractions that have little to do with their everyday life. In rural areas, however, most villages were dominated by a single clan that, if it had claims to upper-class origin (and most organized lineages do), was consolidated by ancestor worship ceremonies called *sije* celebrated in the lunar 11th month. These ceremonies begin at the tomb of the first lineage ancestor to enter the village, and proceed to the tombs of all his patrilineal descendents until all ancestors five generations or more removed from the living have been memorialized this way. Local lineages like this often own mountain land used for burials, and may own farmland called *wit'o* whose rental income is used to finance the autumn tombside ancestor worship ceremonies. Before the Korean War elite lineages often used families of lower status, known as *myojigi*, to prepare the ceremonies and carry the paraphernalia up to the mountain tombs.

The minimal lineage of all those descended patrilineally from the same great, great grandfather, known as the *tangnae*, was the group most important for daily life. This group of uncles and cousins would meet periodically for household ancestor worship ceremonies on the death days of ancestors, and on major holidays such as lunar New Year, and the Harvest Moon Festival (*ch'usŏk*). As only the eldest son in the senior male line performed household ancestor worship ceremonies, the males of the tangnae often gathered at one or another of the Big Houses (*k'ŭn chip*) of the lineage. Often the houses of a tangnae were located near each other in villages, and first, second, third, and even fourth cousins knew and played with each other as they grew up, becoming fast friends.

In urban Korea these lineage customs have become less elaborated, and since people are scattered in urban neighborhoods, cousins meet each other less frequently and become less well acquainted. While the descendants of a living grandfather may continue to enjoy solidarity through ancestor worship, larger lineage associations have been more like voluntary associations than kin groups.

Neighborhoods

Village neighborhoods were made up both of kin and non-kin. In principle they were supposed to be socially uniform.[28] Yangban lived among other yangban, commoners among other commoners, and the small number of outcasts (*ch'ŏnmin*) were segregated among their own kind. Many of the nobility were landlords, but commoners could also become wealthy landlords. A poor yangban family could farm without losing status, but such occupations as fishing and commerce were forbidden to them, so commercial and fishing villages were always inhabited only by commoners. With the exception of Seoul, the capital, moreover, urban life was considered incompatible with yangban status. The hereditary clerks who lived within the old walled county seats, thus, were deprived of yangban status regardless of wealth or education. Within the village neighborhood, however, there was often a high degree of solidarity. Villagers exchanged labor with their neighbors (*p'umasi*), maintained revolving funds, or *kye*, to help each other finance weddings and funerals, and often held villagewide ceremonies to worship local gods.

This kind of solidarity can sometimes still be found in poorer urban neighborhoods, but in urban areas it is more common that churches, temples, schools, apartment complexes, and personal networks of kin, school, and work mates form the framework of social life.

Markets

Periodic markets linked local villages together in a network of commerce. There were a few cities before the twentieth century, so most villagers did their marketing at periodic markets known as *o-iljang* that were convened every five days at traditional locations. Usually there would be a market for each 60, or so, village neighborhoods. Most villagers were within about an hour's walk of these markets where itinerant traders would set up shop on market day to buy agricultural produce and sell simple manufactured products. Until the sixties these markets were patronized mostly by males as part of their outside labor but since then, as the economy has become more commercialized and even agricultural households are buying many household items, women have become the main shoppers. Naturally people take advance of market day to socialize: visit restaurants to catch up on the local news, or perhaps visit a shaman or fortune teller. As transportation has improved and rural population has declined, however, the periodic markets are also declining. Villagers are more and more able to take buses or drive to local cities where there is more variety and better pricing, and the rural population is no longer sufficient to support the lively markets of the past.

Issues of Ethnicity

Koreans, north and south, consider themselves a uniform ethnic group, or nation—*t'ongil-han minjok.*[29] The term *minjok* (nation or ethnic group) is used in a way that assumes that all Koreans are fundamentally related. This is represented in myth as Koreans being descended from Tan'gun, the son of a sky god who married a she bear, and who founded Ancient Chosŏn in 2333 BC (see the historical section earlier). In South Korea this myth was taught as historical fact during the fifties, and the official calendar, or *Tan'gi*, began in 2333 BC (the Western calendar was made official in the early sixties).

Although most people today think of the Tan'gun story as legend, Koreans still think of themselves as ethnically uniform descendants of common ancestors. Thus, even though North and South Korea are not politically unified (*t'ongilhan*), the Korean minjok still should be uniform (*t'ongilhan*): It is important to most

Koreans that all the Korean people share an essential homogeneity, and that all Koreans should speak the Korean language. Émigrés of Korean descent who have lost the ability to speak Korean, thus sometimes find themselves chastised when they visit Korea. Some people in Korea consider it offensive for two persons of Korean descent to use English or Japanese among themselves.

Eventual unification of North and South Korea is considered an important national project by both the northern and southern regimes. While many people in the south feel ambivalent about unification, wondering about the costs and the possible political chaos that might follow an unplanned, or sudden unification such as that of East and West Germany, they still find the notion that the North and South Korean *people* are losing their homogeneity a threat to the Korean nation. People who suggest this is so may find themselves in a hot argument.

Officially both the northern and southern regimes consider themselves the legitimate rulers of the entire Korean people. The southerners trace their legitimacy to the Great Han Empire annexed by the Japanese in 1910, but preserved through the March 1, 1919, independence movement, and a provisional government maintained in China during the years of Japanese rule. When sovereignty was returned to South Korea in 1948 under United Nations auspices, the Republic of Korea made its capital in the historic capital city of Seoul, and adopted the flag of the Great Han Empire, the *T'aegŭkki*—that has a yin-yang circle in the center, surrounded by four trigrams from the Chinese divination classic, the *Yi Ching*. During the colonial period nationalist scholars such as Sin Ch'ae-ho had decried the effete yangban class and their subservience to China. He looked to ancient Korean military heroes such as Ulji Mundŏk and Yi Sun-sin as a source of a new, strong identity. The South Korean military governments of the seventies and eighties often emphasized the importance to the nation of continuing the military tradition of Silla, whose capital was in the south. North Korea, on the other hand, traces its legitimacy to the anti-Japanese guerilla movement that Kim Il Sung, its first leader, led in Manchuria in the early thirties before fleeing to Russia in the face of a Japanese extermination campaign. The glorious legend of Kim Il Sung's anti-imperialist guerillas is emphasized in the DPRK, and Kim Il Sung is given credit for North Korea's liberation.[30] North Korea sees itself as the heir of the military legacy of the northern kingdom of Koguryŏ whose capital was in P'yŏngyang. In the north they consider South Korea to be a semicolonial appendage of the United States, and say that Korean liberation will not be complete until the north "liberates" the south. Since the Sunshine Diplomacy of South Korean President Kim Dae Jung, and his visit to P'yŏngyang in 2000, however, tensions between the ROK and DPRK have been greatly reduced, though not eliminated.

Paradoxically, although Koreans consider themselves a uniform ethnic group, there are strong regional loyalties that remain in both the north and the south. In the south, leaders of southeast origin (North and South Kyŏngsang Provinces) were heavily represented in the military regimes of the seventies and eighties. (They were referred to as the T-K faction, meaning that many of them became friends in Kyŏngbuk High School, the old elite high school in the southeastern city of Taegu, and then later moved to Seoul). The state-led industrialization of that time tended to be located in Seoul and in the southeast (Ulsan, P'ohang, Ch'angwŏn). While the southeast became heavily industrialized, people who originated in the southwest (North and South Chŏlla Provinces) tended to be discriminated against both in employment and in the location of industry. Working-class areas of Seoul are heavy with migrants from the southwest who could find no work closer to home as their native area became a poor backwater. After democratic regimes emerged in the nineties the southeast has tended to support the more conservative, authoritarian parties, while the southwest has supported its native son, Kim Dae Jung. The election of Kim Dae Jung to the presidency in 1997 allowed him to redress some of this inequality, but the southwest and the southeast continue to have strong regional identities.

Regional loyalties are also important in the DPRK. The core group of guerillas who formed the government came from the northeast (North and South Hamgyŏng Provinces). Because of this, and because the northeast was never occupied by the U.N. forces in the winter of 1950, the residents of this province are considered more loyal than those who live close to the DMZ and speak dialects close to those of Seoul. In fact, because of travel restrictions that keep most residents of the DPRK living in the area of their birth, regional dialects and identity continue to flourish there.

Apart from ethnic Koreans, the only significant minority in North or South Korea is the Chinese (mostly from Shandong Province), who at their peak in the 1930s numbered a little more than 80,000 people. Constant emigration since then has reduced their number to fewer than 25,000 in South Korea, and fewer still in North Korea. Although there are a few prosperous merchants of Chinese descent in South Korea, most of the Chinese in South Korea run small restaurants, ethnic food stores, or herb shops and have modest means. There is a degree of discrimination against them. As Korea has been more affluent in recent years, immigrants from poorer countries have moved into South Korea to take "3-D" (dirty, dangerous, and difficult) jobs. A large proportion of these are ethnic Koreans from China (the so-called *Chosŏnjok*), but in industrial areas one can also find workers from places like the Philippines, Vietnam, and Bangladesh. Rural farmers have even taken to seeking wives in China, Vietnam, or Indonesia since Korean women are have become reluctant to take on the hard work of being a farm wife. Immigrant wives have frequently had a hard time. Many of their marriages are arranged through agencies, and few foreign wives speak any Korean when they arrive. If their marriages don't work out, they often find themselves in perilous financial conditions. If they leave their marriages, moreover, they easily can lose their immigration status and custody of any children they have.

Political Issues

All political issues in North and South Korea are colored by the division of the country. Because of the competition of the two regimes for legitimacy, and the legacy of the Korean War, tensions have remained high on the Korean peninsula.

The DPRK regime indoctrinates its population with *chuch'e* ideology that apotheosizes Kim Il Sung as the founder of liberation, autonomous independence, and the Korean nation, and his son Kim Jong Il as the only one capable of continuing his father's legacy.[31] The organization of the North Korean state is Leninist—the Korean Workers Party led by Kim Jong Il sets policy, which is implemented by People's Committees (*inmin wiwŏnhoe*) at the national, provincial, county, and lower levels. The government endeavors to mobilize large portions of the population for political study and activity, but decision making is very centralized, so at the lower levels cadres, managers, and workers tend to be preoccupied mostly with carrying out orders. Fear of subversion from South Korea leads the government to impose draconian controls over mobility and the mass media. Radios and televisions are fixed to receive only government stations, and are regularly inspected to prevent alterations. Although some information about the outside world filters across the relatively porous Chinese border, only politically reliable elites are regularly allowed access to outside information. Ordinary North Koreans, thus, have little choice but to believe most of what they are told. The North Korean authorities are reported to maintain a Gulag of prison camps for those who fail to toe the line. Thus, although reports of antigovernment graffiti, or small meetings of friends and kin in which criticism of the government takes place, sometimes emerge, there seems to be little basis for independent political activity in the north, and the regime seems firmly in place.

Unlike North Korea, which has been ruled by a single, stable father–son dynasty since 1945, South Korea has had a tumultuous political history. Following the three years of U.S. military government (1945–1948), South Korea is in its Sixth Republic (or constitution) since 1948. The main political issues have revolved around authoritarianism versus democracy, support of big business, suppression of the labor and democracy movements, uneven regional development, the brutal suppression of the Kwangju Uprising in 1980, north–south relations, and the degree of deference the South Korean government should give to the United States, which still stations some 37,000 troops in South Korea to protect it from North Korea. A lively feminist movement has had important changes written into family law, as well.

North Korea has been a constant issue. Fears of North Korean subversion or invasion (borne out in some cases by infiltrations and assassination attempts) have led to curtailment of some freedoms, particularly during the Park and Chun regimes. Praise of the North Korean regime is still, technically, against the law, and selected North Korea publications have become available only in the south in the past decade. During the First Republic (1948–1960) the leader of the Socialist Party was executed for communism. The military dictatorships of Park Chung Hee (1961–1963, 1971–1979) and of Chun Doo Hwan (1980–1987) were justified, partly by the need to counter the North Koreans. These tensions have eased in recent years, however, as the overwhelming economic superiority of the south over the north has become apparent, and led the southern regime to be more self-confident.

Much of the political and economic structure of South Korea was laid during the Park Chung Hee era. The state-led industrial development of that era was achieved through government control of banks that borrowed money abroad and loaned it at cheap rates to selected large-scale conglomerates (or *chaebŏl*) who were willing, for a price, to abide by state economic

South Korea Constitutions Since 1948

First Republic (1948–1960)
- *Directly elected legislature, indirectly elected president (Syngman Rhee)*

Second Republic (1960–1961)
- *Cabinet system (Chang Myŏn)*

Supreme Council for National Reconstruction (1961–1963)
- *Military junta (Park Chung Hee)*

Third Republic (1963–1971)
- *Directly elected legislature, directly elected president (Park Chung Hee)*

Yusin Republic (1972–1979)
- *Partially appointed legislature, indirectly elected president (Park Chung Hee)*

Military Coup—December 12, 1980

Fifth Republic (1980–1987)
- *Indirectly elected president (Chun Doo Hwan), partially appointed legislature, systematic curtailment of freedom of speech and press*

Sixth Republic (1987–present)
- *Directly elected legislature (single member constituency), directly elected president, respect for civil rights*
  - Roh Tae Woo (1987–1992)
  - Kim Young Sam (1992–1987)
  - Kim Dae Jung (1997–2002)
  - Roh Mu Hyun (2002–present)

plans. The Park regime deemed democracy as dispensable (particularly during the 1972–1979 Yusin period when the Heavy and Chemical Industrialization Program was being promoted), using multiseat constituencies and a partially appointed legislature to keep control of the National Assembly, and indirect election of the president by the National Council for Unification. Students and certain Christian groups kept the movement for democracy alive through constant propaganda and demonstrations—the writings of the Catholic poet Kim Chi-ha are especially famous from this period—but during the seventies the democracy movement was relatively isolated. Because cheap labor was considered a necessary corollary of the policy of rapid export-led industrialization, the government suppressed independent, or democratic, labor unions in favor of government controlled unions (called pejoratively *ŏyong* unions) that blindly followed government policy on wages and safety.

With the bloody suppression of the Kwangju Uprising, the arrest and near execution of the popular opposition politician Kim Dae Jung, a native of Kwangju, and the establishment of the repressive and corrupt Fifth Republic under General Chun Doo Hwan, the movements for democracy and labor rights began to grow more urgent and sophisticated, and began cooperating. The government instituted in-house censorship of television and newspapers, dictating which stories should be given prominence, and what interpretive line should be followed. (Television broadcasts during this period invariably began with an uncritical report on the activities of the president.) Students in response organized secret circles to study radical ideologies and participate in demonstrations in which they marched arm-in-arm, rank-by-rank, toward helmeted and shielded police officers and military conscripts (often of the same age) wielding truncheons and tear gas. Thousands of student activists went to work in factories (illegal for college educated persons at that time) to aid in labor organizing. The Catholic Workers Movement (known under its French initials of JOC, for Jeunesse Ouvrière Chrétiènne), and the Urban Industrial Mission (Protestant) provided places for workers to meet, learn about labor law, and discuss their problems. (As third parties they could not, by law, aid in labor organizing.) Strikes were usually met by police repression and squads of hired, violent strike-breakers (known as *kusadae*, or "Save the Company Corps"). Culturally the opposition-associated populist, or *minjung*, movement, led to the creation of art, music, and literature suffused with folk forms and images. In the nineties the popular television mini-series *The Hourglass* (*Morae sigye*) nostalgically dramatized this period.

Things came to a head in 1987 as Seoul finalized its preparations for the 1988 Olympics. In May and June of that year, the democratic movement, counting on the international spotlight the Olympics brought to South Korea to prevent the government from violently suppressing them, began organizing large demonstrations demanding direct election of the president, and other reforms. Unlike in the past, the middle class seemed to support this movement (one indelible photo published at the time showed a couple of middle-aged women in high heels swinging their purses at the police). A massive demonstration took place in the port city of Inch'ŏn in June 1987. This, combined with the fear of losing the Olympics, led Chun Doo Hwan's hand-picked successor, Roh Tae Woo, to declare in a televised news conference on June 29 that he was willing to release political prisoners, restore Kim Dae Jung's political rights, remove restrictions on the press, and have free and open direct presidential elections. Roh carried out his promise, and South Korea began gradually moving toward democracy.

During Roh's presidency, a policy of *Nordpolitik* (modeled after West Germany's *Ostpolitik*)—seeking diplomatic relations with the communist countries regardless of whether they also recognized the DPRK—paid off well with most communist countries participating in the 1988 Olympics. Hungary first, and finally the Soviet Union and China, all recognized South Korea, and both North and South Korea were admitted to the United Nations in 1992. The immediate effect of democratization, however, was three years of protracted labor strife as the suppressed workers became free to demand their share of South Korea's burgeoning prosperity. Wages rose an average of 20 percent a year during this period, and began (belatedly in the eyes of some South Koreans) moving South Korea from the ranks of a cheap labor country toward one focusing on higher valued-added industry, but at the cost of the migration of some low-wage factory jobs (the shoe industry in particular) to cheaper labor countries like China, Indonesia, and Thailand.

Though democratization has introduced a certain amount of disorder into Korean politics, it seems to provide a framework through which South Korea can address its political problems. With the advent of the administration of Kim Young Sam in 1992—the first civilian president since 1961—further reforms were introduced. In 1996 some of the feeling of injustice about the Fifth Republic and the violent suppression of the Kwangju Uprising was assuaged by the trial of former president Chun for mutiny and sedition (for his December 12, 1979, coup), and Roh for corruption. Chun was sentenced to death, and Roh to more than 22 years in prison. (These sentences were eventually commuted and the two former presidents spent about two years in prison.) Social welfare legislation addressed a number of pressing problems, such as old-age pensions, and the opening of the political system allowed feminist groups to get many of the more patriarchal elements of the Civil Code revised to gender-neutral language in 1989.

The election of Kim Dae Jung, the opposition politician from the southwest, in 1997 was evidence of the maturation of Korean democracy. It was the first time South Korea experienced a peaceful change of the party in power—something that is still rare in Asia. President Kim moved to address discrimination against people from the southwest and underdevelopment there, ameliorating regional tensions, and also reduced tensions with North Korea. As South Korea moves into a more consolidated democracy fears of an authoritarian resurgence have faded into the background. While hypereconomic growth seems to be a feature of the past, democracy seems to have provided a framework within which Koreans have been able to address many of their social problems in a peaceful way. Since 1987 South Koreans have managed a steady series of reforms. Tensions over aggressive U.S. policy on North Korea—which leads many South Koreans to fear another war on the Korean peninsula—and friction over troops stationed in Korea have recently led to demonstrations. Because issues of unification and relations with North Korea will require international cooperation, however, they cannot be solved solely through domestic South Korean political activity.

Religion

The most ancient records about the inhabitants of the Korean peninsula note that they worshipped nature spirits and the souls of ancestors. Powerful male shamans contacted the heavens at important ceremonies, and dealt with troublesome spirits. The kingship of Silla, in fact, likely developed out of the role of a powerful shaman. Mahayana Buddhism arrived in the kingdoms of Koguryŏ and Paekche in the fourth century AD, and Silla in the sixth century. Eventually Buddhism was accepted by the Silla kings as an important prop for the throne. The king of Silla became associated with Vairochana, the Celestial Buddha, monks became important state advisors, and rituals such as the chanting of *dharani* (magic formulae) and of the Sutra of

Benevolent Kings (*Inwang Kyŏng*) were state occasions promoting the safety of the nation. Famous monks corresponded with their counterparts in China and contributed to the overall development of Buddhism in East Asia. During the succeeding Koryŏ dynasty (918–1392), Buddhism continued as the established religion with Sŏn (the Korean form of Zen) and Flower Garland (*Hwaŏm*) the most important sects. The royal court supported many Buddhist festivals such as the Lantern Festival, Buddha's Birthday, the Hungry Ghost Festival, and the P'algwanhoe, a festival with music and dance. The monk Chinul founded the Chogye Order, the dominant order today, which combines Zen meditation with study of scriptures.[32]

During the Chosŏn period, Buddhism was suppressed in favor of Confucianism. Buddhist court rituals were abolished, monks were banished from the capital, visits to temples were discouraged, and Confucian family ritual was imposed on the upper classes. At this time the Buddhist cremations common during Koryŏ gave way to Confucian-style burial with three-year mourning. Although Buddhism was often the personal faith of kings and queens, institutional Buddhism eventually became moribund. Monks maintained the faith in a limited number of mountain temples, but ordinary people, though they maintained many Buddhist beliefs and practices mixed in with the spirit worship of their folk religion, had little contact with the Buddhist great tradition, with scriptures, or with monks. At the time of first contact with the West in the eighteenth century, then, religion in Korea consisted primarily of Confucian ceremonialism—both family-centered ancestor worship, and state-sponsored cults such as of the grain god (*sajik*) and local earth gods—and lower status spirit and ancestral worship undertaken primarily by housewives aided by shamans. Blind persons were often trained as Sutra-chanting exorcists, or *p'ansu*.

In the late eighteenth century, when Korea was still closed to outsiders, a few Korean members of the four-times yearly diplomatic missions to Beijing visited the Jesuits there, were baptized, and brought Catholicism back to Korea. The faith spread fairly widely, despite persecutions in 1801, 1839, 1846, and 1866 in which some 10,000 believers were killed. French and indigenous priests were smuggled into Korea in the nineteenth century, but almost all of them were eventually caught and executed. Toward the middle of the nineteenth century Protestant missionaries in China and Japan were contacted by small numbers of Koreans who acquired Chinese language Bibles and, after conversion, established a number of small congregations in Korea. Because of this history South Korean Christians emphasize that Christianity—both Catholic and Protestant—was established in Korea by Koreans before the arrival of foreign missionaries. Christian missionary activity was not legalized, however, until after the first treaties with Western powers were signed (United States, Britain, and Germany, 1883; Russia, 1884; France, 1886). Full religious freedom came in 1899, and since that time a vigorous indigenous Korean Christianity has continued to develop.

Despite a strong sense of ethnic homogeneity, Koreans today are religiously pluralistic. In South Korea all religions are freely practiced. In 1995 about 23 percent of the population reported themselves as Buddhist, 20 percent as Protestant, 7 percent as Catholic, and a bit less than 1 percent as members of indigenous organized faiths such as Ch'ŏndogyo and Taejonggyo. There are about 40,000 Korean Muslims, recent converts because of contacts with the Middle East. Christmas and Buddha's Birthday are both national holidays. Forty-nine percent of the population reported no religion. Most South Koreans today consider Confucianism a philosophical system rather than a religion, but Confucian ethics underlie much of their religious culture regardless of denomination. Buddhists and the formally nonreligious often participate in folk religious practices only as needed, rather than on a regular basis.

In North Korea, though P'yŏngyang was a big prewar center of Korean Protestantism and the Catholic Church was well established there, too, the North Korean authorities began suppressing Christianity and Buddhism in 1946 and 1947 by confiscating the lands that were the economic foundation of both churches and temples, disrupting services, and laicizing monks. Religious believers, while generally not jailed, were discriminated against, so many Christians fled south at this time. Whereas all religions are considered superstitious by the North Korean authorities, folk religious activity has been suppressed primarily for being "backward" while Christianity has been suppressed because it is an "agent of imperialism." The indigenous Ch'ŏndogyo religion popular among the peasants at the time of liberation has been tolerated. Today there is one Protestant and one Catholic church in P'yŏngyang, and small house churches have survived elsewhere. Some Buddhist temples are maintained as cultural monuments, and a few monks are allowed to attend international Buddhist events.

Folk Religion

The indigenous Korean folk religion consists of high-status, male-centered ancestor worship, and lower status, female-centered cults of a variety of gods, spirits, and ancestors that require propitiation because they are active in the world.[33] The style of ancestor worship, or memorialism, known as *chesa* practiced by Koreans follows the Confucian rites advocated by the Chinese philosopher Chu Hsi and imposed by the government on the elite during the fifteenth century. There are three types of rites: household rites (*kije*), tombside rites (*sije*), and holiday rites (*chŏlsa*). In Korea only males traditionally participate in these rites, and the eldest son in the senior male line is the chief celebrant. Younger sons do not hold ancestor worship celebrations, but have to attend the rites of their oldest brother. The household rites are held in the house of the eldest son for house heads and their wives up to the great, great-grandparents, and are celebrated on the night before their death anniversary; the tombside rites are held once a year in the 11th lunar month at the tombs of ancestors five or more generations removed from the living. (These are generally high-status rites held primarily by descendants of the old yangban notability.) Holiday rites are held in the house of the senior-most male representative of the minimal lineage (*tangnae*) on lunar New Year, the Harvest Moon Festival, and other family-centered holidays. Although the timing, participation, and location of rites vary, the form of all of them is the same. A table is set up with an ancestral tablet (normally written for the occasion in Chinese on white paper and burned after the ceremony), and such food offerings as a living elder would appreciate. An incense burner is placed before the table and lit to invite the ancestors down. The celebrant makes a offering of liquor after which the other male participants kowtow twice. This sequence is repeated twice. A prayer is read in classical Chinese. The celebrants wait in silence while the ancestors "eat." After the ceremony that ends with the burning of the written prayer and the paper tablet, the male and female family members "imbibe the fortune" (*ŭmbok*) by sharing a banquet of the remaining food. Neighbors and friends are invited to the banquet that night, or the next morning.

In urban Korea today ancestor worship ceremonies continue, but they tend to be held only for near ancestors (two or three generations) earlier in the evening, and celebrants often are both male and female. Belief in the actuality of souls is not necessary to justify chesa, as this kind of ancestor worship is considered an ethical obligation in Confucianism that should make one a moral person, regardless of whether one believes in souls or not. Many urban Koreans continue the tradition, thus, for the moral training of their children. Ancestor worship used to be regarded by Catholics as idolatry, but today the ceremonies are considered memorialism rather than worship, and thus may be continued by Catholics. Though these agnostic interpretations of ancestor worship are common in Korea in the folk religion, souls not only are believed to exist, but are thought to be active in this world. Recently dead ancestors are viewed as similar to living elders with personalities, likes, and dislikes, and the capacity to visit affliction on families who botch the ceremonies. Such cases, if serious, might require the intervention of a shaman. For this reason, Korean Protestants generally regard even Confucian-style ancestor worship as idolatry. They avoid setting up tablets, offerings, and kowtowing, but they may invite their pastor over for a memorial prayer service and dinner (*ch'umo*) on the death day of someone recently dead.

Gods, souls, and ancestors can all be called *kwisin*, and are not sharply distinguished in the folk religion. Many gods are just the souls of especially powerful individuals. Other gods are genii loci, gods of particular places. Housewives used to worship many house gods with simple offerings of water and bean cake (*siruttŏk*), though these cults are much neglected in recent years. Most important in central Korea are the Lot Lord (*t'ŏju*) worshipped on the food storage terrace, and associated with the welfare of the family as an economic unit, and the Roof Lord (*sŏngju*). In years past when a new house was erected, the main roof beam would be lifted at an auspicious hour, and a shaman would hold a Peaceful House Ceremony (*ant'aek kut*) to settle the Roof Lord in the main beam. Many old houses have an inscription on their main beams recording this event. The Roof Lord is worshipped on the verandah next to the main roof beam pillar.

Local gods often protected the village. Many villages have a small shrine built on a nearby mountain slope where the village gods, often mountain gods (*Sansillyŏng*) or the Big Dipper God (*Ch'ilsŏng*), are worshipped. Other villages have a large Zelkovia tree (*nŭt'inamu*) in a strategic location in the village that is thought to be the residence of a local god (*Sŏnangsin*), and an appropriate place for offerings and prayers. While bean cake (*siruttŏk*) is appropriate for house gods, village gods require pure white rice cake (*hŭinttŏk*). In the past, some villages set up "devil posts" (*changsŭng*) at the entrance of the village to prevent the entrance of baleful supernatural influences. These consisted of logs set so the tree roots are exposed at the top, with an inscription in Chinese characters saying "Great General Under the Earth." Sometimes these were set up in pairs with the second one labeled "Female General Under the Earth," with the couple thought of as man and wife. Devil posts are rarely found anymore, however. Fishing villages frequently worshipped the Dragon King (*Yongwang*), a water deity. Ceremonies for village gods could be done in Confucian style—in which case men without pollution (i.e., no recent births or deaths in the family) make offerings to the gods in a formal style similar to that of ancestor worship ceremonies. In other cases, shamans are invited to preside over colorful ceremonies with singing, dancing, drinking, elaborate costuming, fortune telling, and spirit possession called *kut*. Most elaborate of these are the *pyŏlsin kut* of the southeastern coast that may last several days, and may include masked dance dramas and elaborate folk tales sung late into the night by the shamans. As these ceremonies are expensive villages may hold one only every few years.

The manner of a person's death, and whether they are properly buried and worshipped, determined whether their souls would be dangerous to others. Those who have had a bad death—suicide, drowning (especially if the body cannot be found for burial), death as an adult but before marriage—may die filled with *han*, a term difficult to translate, but that expresses the frustration of suffering and denial. Such souls may require special shaman ceremonies encouraging them to depart for the "other world." These ceremonies, among the most elaborate of the shaman ceremonies, consist of several "acts," or *kŏri*, in which the household gods, shaman's spirit familiars, and household ancestors are invited down to partake in a feast. The ancestors will speak through the shaman to living relatives, and the ceremony usually ends with a symbolic journey transporting the soul to the next world—often symbolized by the shaman walking along a long white cloth that she rips to symbolize the progress of the soul. *Chapkwi*, wandering souls who are not worshipped by anybody, are thought to rove from ceremony to ceremony begging food, so shamans will always throw a little millet out the front door for them.

On the Korean mainland female shamans known as *mudang*, or more respectually, as *mansin*, are the majority, but the male shamans known as *paksu* are about 20 percent of the shamans. Some female shamans who have a Buddhist orientation call themselves "bodhisattvas" (*posal*). (This term can also refer simply to a devout female Buddhist believer, as well as, of course, to a bodhisattva proper.) Shamans can make good money, but the profession is looked down upon. In the past a large proportion of shamans were hereditary, but so-called god-descended shamans (*sin naerin mudang*) have always also existed, and are most common today. These shamans experience the "shaman sickness" (*mubyŏng*), usually in early youth. When this sickness is diagnosed it is believed that a god is calling the person to become its mouthpiece, and refusal of this task will result in death. Such persons apprentice themselves to established shamans to learn the ceremonies, and when they have earned enough money as an apprentice, they have a "descent ceremony" (*naerim kut*) in which the god who has chosen them is settled.

Shamans urge their clients to keep their spirit defenses in order by having shaman ceremonies, or *kut*, for their family every three or four years. While many women visit shamans each New Year to find out about the coming year, few even among believers are this diligent. When unexplained bad luck, or other misfortune strikes, however, many women visit shamans to seek an explanation, and possibly will sponsor a ceremony to solve the problem. Because shaman ceremonies are extremely noisy and last late into the night, they are illegal in urban areas. Rather than have ceremonies at home, as is done in the villages, urbanites go to the shaman's house, or have the ceremony in a rural temple.

Indigenous Religions

The folk religion is not organized into a church. Each house head and each house mistress deals directly as priest with his or her respective ritual responsibilities. The house mistress may call in a shaman if she suspects supernatural trouble that requires a specialist, but shamans are self-selected (or god-selected) and are not organized into a systematic hierarchy with an ordered theology. There are number of syncretistic organized religions in Korea, however, that have grown out of folk belief. The oldest of these is the Religion of the Heavenly Way, or *Ch'ŏndogyo*. Its scriptures are the revelatory writings of Ch'oe Su-un that were gathered into the *Tonggyŏng Taejŏn* [*The Great Book of Eastern Scripture*] by his disciple, Ch'oe Si-hyŏng, after Ch'oe Su-un's execution for heterodoxy in 1864. Combining elements of Christianity with Daoism and Korean folk belief, Ch'oe Su-un saw heaven (*hanŭl*) as the original source of all things and the way, and rejected Christian dualism in favor of the doctrine of *innaech'ŏn* "man is heaven." Some ritual practices, such as the use of newly drawn well water, stem from Korean folk religion, while the emphasis on serving God and regular religious services reminds one of Christianity. The Ch'ŏndogyo religion, then known as Tonghak (Eastern Learning), was an important element behind the 1894 rebellion in southern Korea that precipitated the Sino-Japanese War. During the colonial period the religion came to be strongly represented in the P'yŏngyang area of North Korea, and was an important institutional force in the Korean national enlightenment movement proving popular among peasants. For this reason the Ch'ŏndogyo Youth Party was the only religious organization allowed to continue in North Korea after 1945. The religion's central church was built in Seoul in 1921, and still stands. In 1960 5 percent of the South Korean population were Ch'ŏndogyo adherents, but the faith has declined since then so that today about 0.6 percent of the population continue to be adherents.

Taejonggyo, organized in 1909 by Hongam, focuses on Tan'gun, the founder of Ancient Chosŏn in the founding myths of the Korean nation as recorded in thirteenth-century historical texts. Like Ch'ŏndogyo, Taejonggyo focuses on heaven (*hanŭl*), but in Taejonggyo this connotes three gods: God the father and creator of the universe, God the teacher, and God the King as ruler of creation. Taejonggyo considers itself the Korean religion that has indigenized Buddhism, Confucianism, and Daoism. It does not consider itself a "new religion." Since its central story consists of ancient Korean myths, the 1909 organization date is considered a renewal rather than a founding. Like Ch'ŏndogyo, its membership has declined in recent years, numbering about 7,000 in 1995.

Buddhism

As related above, Buddhism has ancient roots in Korea and is closely associated with Korean tradition. Buddhism declined as an institutional force during the Chosŏn period, but began a revival in the early twentieth century in response to the challenge of Christianity. During the colonial period the Buddhist Japanese made an energetic attempt to assimilate Korean Buddhism, introducing, in particular, married monks, a practice new to Korea. After liberation in 1945, great strife developed in South Korea between the Taech'o order of married monks, and the traditional, gray-robed, celibate Chogye order. In most cases, however, it was the Chogye monks who were put in charge of maintaining Korea's great traditional monasteries, such as the Haein-sa, location of the world's oldest wood blocks for printing the Chinese-language Buddhist scriptures, or Tripiteka, and the Songgwang-sa, one of Korea's leading teaching monasteries. The predominant Chogye order had been founded by the twelfth-century Korean monk, Chinul, who synthesized Flower Garland (Hwaŏm) thought with Zen meditation. Chinul's "sudden enlightenment and gradual cultivation" doctrine sees enlightenment as awakening to the fact that the human mind is an expression of Buddha nature (*pulsŏng*). Enlightenment is followed by cultivating quiescence and knowing. Priority is given to meditation, but reading of sutras is also important, and the order tends toward syncretism rather than sectarianism. The Chogye order maintains its head temple near Kyŏngbok Palace in central Seoul, has 25 other head temples, and more than a thousand branch temples throughout Korea. The order has responded to the challenge of Christianity by developing new institutions: Sunday schools, lay societies, meditation retreats, and even Buddhist hymns. South Korea today has Buddhist universities and many Buddhist hospitals and other charitable institutions.

Although most of Korea's Buddhists belong to Chogye temples, other forms of Buddhism have grown since 1945. Taech'o Buddhism with its married monks has already been mentioned. Wŏn Buddhism, organized in 1918 based on the teachings of Sotaesan, also emphasizes the universal inner Buddha nature, which they call *wŏn* or "perfect roundness." While accepting meditation and other Buddhist practices, Wŏn Buddhism rejects the iconography of traditional Korean Buddhism for the symbolism of the pure circle. Both male and female clergy are encouraged in Wŏn Buddhism, but only the males may marry and remain clergy. Wŏn Buddhism maintains a world headquarters and a university near the southwestern town of Iri.

Ch'ŏnt'ae (Tiantai), a sect that was introduced into Korea during the Koryŏ period but died out as a separately organized sect, has in the postwar period been reestablished. Ch'ŏnt'ae emphasizes the Lotus Sutra, rather than the Flower Garland Sutra as in Chogye Buddhism. Korea's Ch'ŏnt'ae order now has an elaborate main temple, Kuin-sa, in North Ch'ungch'ŏng Province, and numerous urban temples. The sect claims to have more than 1.5 million adherents.

Protestantism

From small beginnings in the late nineteenth century, Protestantism has flourished in Korea.[34] During the colonial period, Protestant churches were one of the few independent institutions within which Koreans could exercise leadership. P'yŏngyang became a big center where the first school of theology was established. A large number of Protestants fled to South Korea after 1945. Those that remain in the north tend to worship quietly in house churches, and have experienced a degree of discrimination. In the south Protestants now comprise about a quarter of the population. Although missionaries were important for the early church, Koreans generally believe, as mentioned above, that it is they who made the initial effort to establish the church, rather than waiting for missionaries. During the colonial period many Korean Christians identified with the story of Moses and the captivity of the Israelites in Egypt, having faith that God had a plan for Korea. The early missionaries put great effort into training indigenous leadership, so the church today is fully indigenized and Korean Protestants today have little sense of Christianity being a foreign faith.

The main denominations are Presbyterian, Methodist, and Evangelical, but each of these splintered after 1945, so there are several rival churches in each of the denominations. Some of the older, well-established congregations worship in beautiful 100-year-old stone sanctuaries with sober, dignified services. Others worship in huge mega-churches of 50,000 to 60,000 members that bus congregants into multiple services boasting closed-circuit television, a seating capacity of 10,000, and sometimes even simultaneous translation for foreigners. The Central Full Gospel Church near the National Assembly building on Yŏido Island is a well-known example of this kind of church. Small churches also abound in Korea, however, and many of the humbler congregations rent only a few rooms in a multistory building. Outside observers sometimes note the infiltration of indigenous attitudes into Christian churches. Some think the emphasis on ritual punctilio and the role of the male elders in some Presbyterian churches is reminiscent of Confucianism. The noisy enthusiasm of Born Again Christians and the descent of the Holy Spirit (*sŏngnyŏng*) into congregants at other churches reminds others of shamanism. In general, however, Korean churches tend to be orthodox and theologically conservative. Many prohibit smoking and drinking among their members. Among middle-class Christian housewives, Bible study classes are a common social activity. Many of Korea's oldest and most illustrious private universities and hospitals are of Protestant origin.

Catholicism

As mentioned, the history of Catholicism in Korea is long and illustrious. More than 100 martyrs of the nineteenth century persecutions have been canonized, the largest number for any Asian church. Compared to Protestantism, however, Catholicism was slower to indigenize its hierarchy, elevating the apostolic vicariates in Korea to dioceses only in 1962. The first Korean cardinal was appointed in 1969. Korean Catholics tend to be attracted to the solemn dignity of Catholic liturgy, and to appreciate the fact that they can continue traditional ancestral commemoration. During the seventies and eighties, the Catholic Worker Movement and the Catholic Farmers Movement were quite active. Political activists sought sanctuary in Myŏngdong Cathedral in Seoul on more than one occasion. Numerous universities and hospitals are Catholic affiliated.

Current Trends

The rapid transformation of Korea from a nation of poor but self-sufficient peasants in 1945 into two competing urban industrial nations over a 30-year period poses many questions, problems, and opportunities for Korean society. The difficulties of north–south relations have been a central issue ever since 1945, leading both Korean states to focus on security and infiltration concerns. In recent years, South Korea has forged ahead economically and developed democratic legitimacy and respect for civil rights and freedom of the press, though concerns about subversion lead them to maintain the National Security Law that makes praise of North Korea or its system illegal.

Even today neither North Koreans nor South Koreans read each other's newspapers or listen to each other's radio or television broadcasts (though some North Korean books, newspapers, and movies are now available in the south). Travel and personal contacts even among relatives are extremely limited. For this reason some Koreans express concern that the division of the country is causing the homogeneous Korean people to diverge culturally. North Korea no longer seems capable of taking over the south, but, noting the expense of German reunification, the south has also given up dreams of German-style absorption of the north. Most in the south would like to see a gradual rapprochement between north and south rather than a sudden collapse of the north that might threaten South Korea's economic and political stability. For this reason South Koreans are willing to consider aid for North Korea, have tried to arrange north–south family meetings, and have allowed a certain amount of tourism to the north. South Korea's desire for rapprochement, however, may conflict with the United States' more confrontational approach with North Korea on the nuclear issue.[35] Fears in South Korea that the United States' approach may lead to conflict on the Korea peninsula has combined with South Korea's more confident sense of their place in the world to create anti-Americanism (something that began appearing only in the 1980s in South Korea, which traditionally has considered anticommunism and pro-Americanism as the twin foundations of its foreign policy).

Since the collapse of the DPRK's most important benefactor, the Soviet Union, in 1989, North Korea has gone through a wrenching transition whose outcome is still not clear. Forced to pay world prices for imports of fuel and fertilizer, yet without the ability to export, North Korea's industries have been running at less than half their capacity, while the collective farms cannot produce enough food to feed the entire nation. Aid from China, and to an extent from the rest of the world, has kept North Korea afloat, but only barely. Some 600,000 to a million people have died as a result of famine (estimates of up to 2 million deaths have been published, but these seem exaggerated), with an equal number fleeing over the border to China. As the provisioning system of subsidized and rationed food has broken down, the North Korean authorities have been forced to turn more and more to a money economy, and the revival of small-scale markets in rural and urban areas—even P'yŏngyang—has recently been reported. The decision to reconnect rail lines with South Korea and allow an export-oriented industrial zone to be built by South Korea near Kaesŏng, not far from the demilitarized zone, may be a move toward Chinese-style market reforms.

On family, South Koreans' initial impulse after liberation, reflected in the New Civil Code of 1960, was to restore Korean family traditions that had been changed during the Japanese colonial period. This restoration, however, was opposed by feminists and modernizers because it entrenched the family head system that gave house heads patriarchal control over all women, and over younger brothers and sons (eldest sons, for example, were prohibited from partitioning, and all sons had to get parents' permission to marry up to the age of 27). It also perpetuated the disinheritance of married women, unequal inheritance among sons, male custody of children at divorce, and prohibited intermarriage between all persons with the same surname and clan origin (*tongsŏng tongbon*) no matter how distant the relationship. Wanting to abolish the house head system, and to move to an equalitarian nuclear family system, feminists and modernizers launched a coalition over several decades to revise family law. Their efforts were opposed by the traditionalists of the Confucian Association (Yudohoe) and other social conservatives who argue that Korean cultural identity is at stake. A few revisions were put through in the name of modernity in 1962 and 1977 that reduced parental and fraternal authority over younger brothers, and somewhat equalized inheritance and female rights, but more fundamental change in family law had to wait until democratization began in 1987. The most recent 1989 revisions to family law disappointed feminists because they did not abolish the house head system or the prohibition of marriage among clan members, but they did eliminate the patriarchal authority of house heads, equalize inheritance among sons and between sons and daughters, recognize female rights to custody during divorce, and instituted visiting rights for noncustodial parents. The prohibition on intraclan marriage was found unconstitutional by the Constitutional Court in 1998, so this provision is no longer enforced.

These changes in family law are closely related to current social issues under discussion in South Korea such as care for parents in their old age, son preference, abortion of female fetuses, and high rates of divorce. As eldest sons no longer routinely bring in a daughter-in-law to care for parents, middle- and upper-class parents more and more depend upon their own assets in their old age. So-called silver towns—retirement facilities—are idealized by many. In practice, however, few have the resources to take advantage of the few facilities that exist, and the majority still rely on children for care in their old age: most often on eldest sons, but frequently on younger sons, or even daughters. Although equality of sons and daughters has been written into the legal code, moreover, male preferential attitudes have not disappeared. Using ultrasound to identity the sex of the fetus is illegal, but high male birth ratios seem to indicate that abortion of female fetuses has increased as family size has fallen. The divorce rate has rising exponentially in recent years among all age groups. The reasons for this are obscure. Some of it may be related to changes in family law, but it is also possible that desires of females for the freedom and autonomy of modern marriages is colliding with the attitudes of males with more traditional attitudes.

The rapid industrialization and urbanization of Korea has, of course, greatly changed South Korea's class structure. A huge working class has developed around Korea's large industrial parks with their big industrial concerns, and an equally large New Middle Class of educated professionals working in large firms has developed. While these groups can be described statistically, important questions as to class consciousness have yet to be answered. Some researchers have reported a sharp status distinction between educated white-collar families who tend to live in high-rise apartments, and factory workers, small-scale shopkeepers, and craftworkers who live a less affluent, cultured lifestyle in low-rise housing. The evidence on the development of working-class consciousness is less certain. While some observers have claimed that workers in South Korea have developed class consciousness, it is striking that

South Korea has of yet not developed a viable working-class party.

Since the democratization process began in 1987, South Koreans have taken a keen interest in the degree to which their initial democratization has been consolidated, and civil society developed. Milestones include the election in 1992 of Kim Young Sam, the first civilian president since 1961, and the election in 1997 of Kim Dae Jung, the first president from an opposition party. Although some commentators have argued that South Korea's authoritarian political culture has hindered the development of a genuinely desired democracy, others have pointed to the broad notion that Koreans have of democracy. South Koreans tend to define democracy not simply in terms of electoral procedural norms, but also in terms of responsiveness, and accountability: the degree to which "the people" have political influence, the degree to which policy and legislation reflects the preferences and demands of the citizens, and the degree to which the politics and administration are fair and transparent.[36] While citizens' movements have sprung up to influence the political process to the extent that some believe the development of civil society has been a fundamental cause of democratization in Korea, polls indicate that most people do not think that leaders' policies reflect popular desires as of yet.

The currency crisis of 1997 in which South Korea had to accept a humiliating bailout from the International Monetary Fund forced South Korea to make far-reaching changes in its economic development policies. A country that prevented large-scale direct foreign investment, and had used state-controlled banks to channel capital into planned areas of development, and that prevented large chaebŏl from going broke by directing banks to continue loaning to them has had to change course. Since 1997 the state has had to make what opponents are calling "neoliberal" reforms: allowing large-scale direct foreign investment, layoffs, and downsizing, loosening import regulations, and forcing the chaebŏl to reduce their indebtedness. Government planners have been trying to promote South Korea as a trade, business, and finance hub for Northeast Asia. This strategy—an attempt to position South Korea between a quickly growing China and a technologically sophisticated Japan in the context of globalization—will require South Korea, a society that has long thought of itself as largely the victim of foreign forces, to accept a much greater presence of non-Koreans in their presence. Whether this policy will succeed remains up in the air.

As Korea has become modern and prosperous, a popular youth culture has blossomed. Groups singing in styles ranging from folk to punk and rap abound. Comic books (*manhwach'aek*) with superheros and elaborate science-fiction plots are popular. The movie director Im Kwŏn-t'aek has won an international following, and Korean movies, soap operas, and singers have proved popular enough in Japan, China, and Southeast Asia to be termed the "Korean Wave" (*Hallyu*). Young people have developed a culture of fashion, text messaging on cell phones while riding the subway, and playing games on the internet and in computer parlors (*P. C.-bang*).[37] Traditional sexual mores have been challenged in recent years: Several television stars have "come out" as homosexual in public, and the transgendered model Ha Ri-su has become the rage in fashion magazines, television shows, and movies.

Security and the Nuclear Issue

In addition to creating serious economic difficulties, the collapse of the Soviet Union exacerbated North Korea's security problems. Beginning with the Korean War, the United States has periodically threatened to use nuclear weapons against the DPRK.[38]

In the context of the Cold War system in which the United States protected Japan and South Korea, and the Soviet Union and China protected North Korea, this was a manageable problem for North Korea. The Soviet Union, however, recognized South Korea diplomatically in 1990, followed by China in 1992. Following the collapse of the Soviet Union, moreover, Russia's President Yeltsin in 1991 allowed Russia's mutual security treaty with North Korea to lapse. It was about this time that United States and South Korean concerns about North Korea's accelerating nuclear program became acute. The Soviet Union, which had initially aided North Korea's nuclear program, had also insisted that North Korea sign the Nuclear Non-Proliferation Treaty (NPT) that called for inspections of North Korea's facilities by the Vienna-based International Atomic Energy Agency (IAEA). Initial attempts to deal with this problem involved persuading North Korea to accept these inspections. North Korean threats to withdraw from the NPT in March 1994 led to a serious confrontation with nuclear and non-nuclear mobilizations on the part of the United States and South Korea, but negotiations were subsequently resumed. After former President Carter's visit to P'yŏngyang in 1994 the Agreed Framework was negotiated: the DPRK agreed to freeze its existing facilities and have IAEA inspections in exchange for fuel aid and the construction of light water reactors resistant to proliferation by the Korea Energy Development Corporation (KEDO), a company based in New York, but financed largely by South Korea and Japan.

Although the IAEA thought the North Koreans had diverted enough plutonium from their nuclear reactor before the Agreed Framework was in place to manufacture one or two bombs, the Agreed Framework prevented North Korea from diverting any more plutonium and creating a nuclear arsenal of significant size. However, President George W. Bush who came to office in the United States in 2000 expressed antipathy towards North Korea's leader, Kim Jong Il, and the Bush administration avoided high-level contacts with North Korea. President Bush in his state of the Union Address of 2002 frightened and angered North Korea by including it (along with Iraq and Iran) in his "Axis of Evil," and the National Security Strategy published in September explicitly mentioned North Korea as possibly subject to preemptive nuclear strike. In the first high level contact between the Bush Administration and North Korea in October of that year Undersecretary of State for East Asia James Kelly accused North Korea of running a highly enriched uranium program in contravention of the Agreed Framework. It is possible that closure of such an undeclared nuclear program could have been negotiated within the Agreed Framework. However, both the United States and North Korea at this point declared the Agreed Framework dead. North Korea subsequently expelled IAEA inspectors, withdrew from the NPT, restarted its nuclear reactors, and declared it was reprocessing plutonium—a step necessary to make it weapons-grade. Although hawks have long advocated sanctions and other pressure to force North Korea into compliance, the consequences of war on the Korean Peninsula would be horrific.[39] The United States and China, thus, are sponsoring Six Party Talks involving North and South Korea, China, the United States, Japan, and Russia. As of May, 2004, however, these talks have been inconclusive, and it is becoming more and more likely that North Korea either has, or soon will have, nuclear weapons.

These kinds of questions are usually dealt with by experts in security, but there are anthropological issues involved in addition to security issues. The anthropologist always wants to try to understand the cultural framework within which people understand the world. Shocked by the experience of being taken over by Japan, many Korean intellectuals during the colonial period and after have tried to pinpoint of causes of Korean weakness in the late nineteenth and early twentieth century. The founders of the North Korean state were among those Koreans who felt that military weakness and excessive dependence on China were the most fundamental causes for the Japanese takeover. Kim Il Sung, the father of Kim Jong Il, the present ruler of North Korea, in fact, had been a communist guerilla fighter against the Japanese in Manchuria in the 1930s. With the help of the Soviet Union he became leader of the DPRK. After the Korean War he was able to systematically put his former guerilla comrades in positions of power, and eliminate all other powerful factions—including those sympathetic to China or the Soviet Union. Those close to the leader built a personality cult around Kim Il Sung. Soon he was being mythologized as having almost single-handedly liberated Korea. At the same time the new ideology of *chuch'e*—or self-reliance—was promoted. The combination of these factors has tended to entrench a mindset in which leaders think that only a strong, autonomous military organized around the supreme leader can preserve North Korean independence. The 1998 Constitution, for example, enshrines the principle of "making the entire nation into a fortress." As the United States is a very powerful adversary, it is likely that North Korean leaders think that only the possession of a nuclear deterrent can prevent the United States from seeking "regime change" in North Korea. Thus, the decision of the North Koreans to seek nuclear weapons comes from their interpretation of the failures of Korean history, and the experience of the guerilla leaders who came to almost exclusively control the North Korean state after 1956.

This discussion of the geography, prehistory, language, history, politics, religion, and various current trends in Korea demonstrates that this region of Asia has both a long enduring tradition and disruptive, rapid, and traumatic transformations resulting from various global political trends. As we have seen, the division of Korea was primarily due to the consequences of geo-political tendencies that were prevalent during the Cold War era. The challenge that faces this region in the post-Cold War era is the capacity and the ability to these two Koreas to have mutually satisfying dialogue with one another outside of external geopolitical economic and political networks. Historically, linguistically, ethnically, and culturally the two Koreas have much in common with one another. Whether these commonalities will be sufficient to sustain mutually beneficial dialogue and peaceful cooperation is something that many people in both Koreas have hopes for in the near future.

NOTES

1. A convenient geographical sketch of Korea is in Clark Sorensen, "The Land, Climate, and People of Korea," in *An Introduction to Korean Culture,* ed. John Koo and Andrew Nahm (Elizabeth, NJ: Hollym International, 1997), 15–37. A detailed regional geography of South Korea, now somewhat dated, is Patricia M. Bartz, *South Korea* (Oxford, England: Oxford University Press, 1972).

2. A major English-language source on the prehistory of Korea is Sarah M. Nelson, *The Archaeology of Korea* (Cambridge, England: Cambridge University Press, 1993). Gina L. Barnes, *China, Korea, and Japan: The Rise of Civilization in East Asia* (London: Thames and Hudson, 1993) treats East Asian prehistory as a whole. An interesting source on the Bronze Age in Korea is Mong-lyong Choi, "Bronze Age in Korea," *Korea Journal* 24 (1984): 23–33.

3. An excellent comprehensive source on the structure and history of the Korean language is Iksop Lee and S. Robert Ramsey, *The Korean Language* (Albany: State University of New York Press, 2000).

4. Koreans sometimes say that it is difficult to understand people from another dialect area speaking quickly among themselves, but that it is no problem to communicate one-on-one with speakers of other dialects. Words of Chinese origin are still in use, but they now are almost invariably spelled alphabetically rather than written with their original characters.

5. "Pitch accent" refers to an alternating pattern of high and low pitches. Unlike Chinese tones, which are inherent inflections of each syllable that can be heard even when a word is pronounced in isolation, pitch accent refers to the relationship between pitches in a sentence. For example, in northeastern dialect, the term *pae* pronounced in isolation can mean either "pear" or "belly," but when used as the topic of a sentence followed by the affix /*nŭn*/ the tone pattern low-high (*pae-NŬN*) identifies *pae* as "pear" while the pattern high-low (*PAE-nŭn*) identifies *pae* as "belly." A similar system of pitch accent is found in Japanese.

6. An early fascinating discussion that hypothesizes a link between Korean and Japanese is Samuel E. Martin, "Lexical Evidence Relating Korean to Japanese," *Language* 42, no. 2 (1966): 185–196. Roy Andrew Miller has been a strong advocate of both Korean and Japanese membership in the Altaic

language family. See Roy Andrew Miller, *Japanese and the Other Altaic Languages* (Chicago: University of Chicago Press, 1971). A general account of language issues that also discusses the unique alphabet developed in Korea is Bill Gryson, *The Mother Tongue: English and How It Got That Way* (New York: Avon, 1990). Steven Pinker's classic work on language, *The Language Instinct: How the Mind Creates Language* (New York: HarperPerennial, 1995) deals with the history of Korean language and writing.

7. Paekche is known as Kudara in Japanese.

8. The best source for early Korean history is still Kenneth H. J. Gardiner, *The Early History of Korea* (Canberra: Australian National University Press, 1969). A number of one-volume histories of Korea treat the early period well including Han Woo-keun, *The History of Korea,* trans. Lee Kyung-shik, ed. Grarton Mintz (Seoul: Eul-Yoo Publishing, 1970); Lee Ki-baek, *A New History of Korea,* trans. Edward W. Wagner with Edward Schultz (Cambridge, MA: Harvard University Press, 1988). William E. Henthorn, *A History of Korea* (New York: Free Press 1971) emphasizes cultural elements in addition to social and political developments. A fascinating work on Japanese and Korean interconnections by Gari Ledyard is his "Galloping along with the Horseriders: Looking for the Founders of Japan," *Journal of Japanese Studies* 1, no. 2 (1974): 217–254.

9. The most extensive extant Old Korean materials are in the language of Silla, including poems. For Paekche and Koguryŏ only a few dozen words have been reconstructed from their phonetic rendering in Chinese language texts. See Lee and Ramsey, *The Korean Language* for current information on the status of research in Old Korean.

10. The major sources on Korean Buddhism during Silla and Koryŏ are Robert Buswell's two books dealing with the Korean monks Chinul and Wŏnhyo, respectively: *The Collected Works of Chinul: The Korean Approach to Zen* (Honolulu: University of Hawaii Press, 1983); and *The Formation of Ch'an Ideology in China and Korea* (Princeton, NJ: Princeton University Press, 1989).

11. The best discussions of changes in family organization from Koryŏ to Chosŏn is Martina Deuchler, *The Confucian Transformation of Korea: A Study of Society and Ideology* (Cambridge, MA: Harvard University Press, 1992).

12. Some Koryŏ kings spent considerable amounts of time in Beijing even after they ascended the throne, leaving governing to subordinates.

13. An excellent discussion of Buddhist art in Korea is Ide Seinosuke, "The World of Goryeo Buddhist Painting," in *Goryeo Dynasty: Age of Enlightenment 918–1392,* ed. Kumja Paik Kim (San Francisco: Asian Art Museum of San Francisco, 2003).

14. A good source on the rise of the yangban during the Koryŏ, and their continuation during the Chosŏn Dynasty, is John Duncan, *The Origins of the Chosŏn Dynasty* (Seattle: University of Washington Press, 2000). The major sources on slavery in Korea are James B. Palais, "Slavery and Slave Society in the Koryŏ Period," *The Journal of Korean Studies* (1984): 173–190; and *Confucian Statecraft and Korean Institutions: Yu Hyŏngwŏn and the Late Chosŏn Dynasty* (Seattle: University of Washington Press, 1996). A classic comparative study of different forms of slavery including that of Korea is Orlando Patterson, *Slavery and Social Death: A Comparative Study* (Cambridge, MA: Harvard University Press, 1982). Another major source on a comparison between Asian and African slavery is James L.Watson, ed., *Asian and African Systems of Slavery* (Berkeley: University of California Press, 1980).

15. According to Lee and Ramsey in *The Korean Language,* modern Korean appears at the beginning of the sixteenth century immediately after the Japanese invasions. Texts written before the invasions are uniformly in Middle Korean similar to that of the original texts. During the invasions the aristocratic literary tradition that this represents seems to have been broken, so that when new texts begin to appear they also reflect the changed language as it was actually spoken among these people at that time.

16. Good sources for the late nineteenth and early twentieth century Korean history include James Palais, *Politics and Polity in Traditional Korea* (Cambridge, MA: Harvard University Press, 1975); Vipin Chandra, *Imperialism, Resistance, and Reform in Late Nineteenth Century Korea: Englightenment and the Independence Club,* Korea Research Monograph 13, Institute of East Asian Studies, University of California, Berkeley, 1988; Andre Schmid, *Korea Between Empires, 1895–1919* (NY: Columbia University Press, 2002); Michael Robinson, *Cultural Nationalism in Korea* (Seattle: University of Washington Press, 1988); Carter Eckert, *Offspring of Empire: The Koch'ang Kims and the Colonial Origins of Korean Capitalism, 1876–1945* (Seattle: University of Washington Press, 1991); Gi-wook Shin and Michael Robinson, eds., *Colonial Modernity in Korea* (Cambridge, MA: Harvard University Press, 1999). One-volume histories that emphasize the modern period include Carter J. Eckert et al., *Korea Old and New: A History* (Cambridge, MA: Korea Institute, Harvard of University and Seoul: Ilchokak, 1990); and Bruce Cumings, *Korea's Place in the Sun: A Modern History* (New York: W.W. Norton, 1997).

17. The best source on the origins of the Korean War is Bruce Cumings's two volumes, *The Origins of the Korean War: Volume 1. Liberation and the Emergence of Separate Regimes 1945–1947* (Princeton, NJ: Princeton University Press, 1981); and *Volume 2. The Roaring of the Cataract, 1947–1950* (Princeton, NJ: Princeton University Press, 1991). The major sources dealing with the Korean War itself include Sergei N. Goncharov, John W. Lewis, and Xue Litai, *Uncertain Partners: Stalin, Mao, and the Korean War* (Stanford, CA: Stanford University Press, 1993); Jon Halliday and Bruce Cumings, *Korea: The Unknown War* (New York: Pantheon, 1988). The most current and fascinating account of the communist transformation of North Korea from 1945 is Charles K. Armstrong, *The North Korean Revolution 1945–50* (Ithaca, NY: Cornell University Press, 2003).

18. Good sources on South Korean politics include Gregory Henderson, *Korea, the Politics of the Vortex* (Cambridge, MA: Harvard University Press, 1968); Don Oberdorfer, *The Two Koreas: A Contemporary History* (Boston, MA: Addison-Wesley, 1997); Ilpyong Kim and Young Whan Kihl, eds., *Political Change in South Korea* (St. Paul, MN: Paragon House, 1988); and Robert Bedeski, *The Transformation of South Korea: Reform and Reconstruction in the Sixth Republic under Roh Tae Woo, 1987–1992* (New York, NY: Routledge, 1994).

19. Because of its political importance, there has been much writing in English on the Kwangju uprising. Representative

examples are Donald N. Clark, ed., *The Kwangju Uprising: Shadows Over the Regime in South Korea* (Boulder, CO, and London: Westview Press, 1988); Linda S. Lewis, *Laying Claim to the Memory of May: A Look Back at the 1980 Kwangju Uprising* (Honolulu: University of Hawaii Press, 2002); and the most current work on this topic by Gi-Wook Shin, and Kyung Moon Hwang, *Contentious Kwangju: The May 18 Uprising in Korea's Past and Present* (Lanham, MD: Rowman and Littlefield, 2003).

20. Good sources on North Korea in addition to the aforementioned work by Armstrong include the two volumes by Robert Scalapino and Chong-sik Lee, *Communism in Korea* (Berkeley: University of California Press, 1972); Helen-Louise Hunter, *Kim Il-song's North Korea* (Westport, CT: Praeger, 1999); Kongdan Oh and Ralph Hassig, *North Korea through the Looking Glass* (Washington, DC: Brookings Institution Press, 2000).

21. The formal definition of *chuch'e*, a term used in both South and North Korea, is "subject" (e.g., subject of a sentence or thought). Etymologically it means "main substance," and from these basic roots the term has been elaborated in North Korea into an ideology of "emphasizing what is important," "self-reliance," and "autarky." Similarly *chuch'esŏng* translates as "subjectivity" (antonym of "objectivity"), but also "self-consciousness" and "self-reliance."

22. The major sources on demography, family size, and population are In-hŭi Ham, "Sanŏphwa ŭi ttarŭn hanguk kajok ŭi pigyojŏk ŭimi" [The comparative significance of the Korean family following industrialization], in *Hanguk kajoksangŭi pyŏnhwa* [Changes in the Korean Family], ed. Ha Yong-ch'ul (Seoul: Seoul National University Press, 2001). Fertility rates are summarized in Kwang-Hee Jun, "Fertility," in *The Population of Korea*, ed. Doo-Sub Kim and Cheong-Seok Kim (Seoul: Korea National Statistical Office, 2004). The population of Seoul almost doubled between 1944 and 1949. In Kwang-Hee Jun's book he indicates that the total fertility rate of Korean women peaked in the 1955–1960 period at 6.3 per family. It has declined steadily since then to fall below the replacement level after 1985 and the 1995–2000 TFR was 1.55 percent. The Korea National Statistical Office 2000–2003 is a good source for precise population statistics. An earlier work on population in Korea appears in Tai Hwan Kwon et al., *The Population of Korea* (Seoul: Seoul National University, The Population and Development Center, 1975).

23. The most authoritative source on the demography of North Korea is Nicholas Eberstadt and Judith Banister, *The Population of North Korea* (Berkeley: Institute of East Asian Studies, University of California, 1992). It is based on figures released by the Central Statistics Bureau of North Korea to the United Nations Population Fund in 1989.

24. For a good overview of South Korean economic growth from the point of view of one of Korea's economic planners see Byung-Nak Song, *The Rise of the Korean Economy* (Hong Kong: Oxford University Press, 1990). An earlier good source is Edward S. Mason et al., *The Economic and Social Modernization of the Republic of Korea* (Cambridge, MA: Harvard University Press, 1980). For discussion of the major economic developments in South Korea under Park see Alice Amsden, *Asia's Next Giant: South Korea and Late Industrialization* (New York: Oxford University Press, 1989); and Jung-en Woo, *Race to the Swift: State and Finance in Korean Industrialization* (New York: Columbia University Press, 1991). For a discussion of more recent developments see Donald Kirk, *Korean Crisis: Unraveling of the Miracle in the IMF Era* (New York, NY: Palgrave, 1999); and Marcus Noland, *Avoiding the Apocalypse: The Future of the Two Koreas* (Washington, DC: Institute for International Economics, June 2000).

25. A good older source on the North Korean economy is Joseph Sang-hoon Chung, *The North Korean Economy: Structure and Development* (Palo Alto, CA: Hoover Institution Press, 1974). More recent developments are noted in Kongdan Oh and Ralph Hassig, *North Korea through the Looking Glass* (Washington, DC: Brookings Institution Press, 2000); and Marcus Noland's books, *Avoiding the Apocalypse* (Washington, DC: Institute for International Economics, 2000), and *Korea after Kim Jong Il* (Washington, DC: Institute for International Economics, 2004). On the famine see Marcus Noland, "Famine and Reform in North Korea," Working Paper WP 03-5, Institute for International Economics, Washington, DC, 2003. According to Noland's estimates, excess deaths during the famines (from 1995–1998) range from 600,000 to 1,000,000 people out of a population of about 22 million.

26. A detailed discussion of rural Korean family structure and its relationship to agricultural activity is Clark Sorensen, *Over the Mountains Are Mountains: Korean Peasant Households and Their Adaptations to Rapid Industrialization* (Seattle: University of Washington Press, 1988). For recent statistical information on gender, kinship, marriage, and social life in South Korea see Wha-Soon Byun, "Marital Status," in *The Population of Korea*, ed. Doo-Sub Kim and Cheong-Seok Kim (Seoul: Korea National Statistical Office, 2004). This study indicates that provisions for the division of property and joint custody of children (before 1989 the male's family usually retained custody) introduced at this time have been important factors pushing up the divorce rate. Another good source on family and marriage and modern change is Laurel Kendall, *Getting Married in Korea: Of Gender, Morality, and Modernity* (Berkeley and Los Angeles: University of California Press, 1996). Very good sources on class, family, and gender are Seung-kyung Kim, *Class Struggle or Family Struggle? The Lives of Women Factory Workers in South Korea* (New York: Cambridge University Press, 1997); and Denise Lett, *In Pursuit of Status: The Making of South Korea's "New" Urban Middle Class* (Cambridge, MA: Harvard University Press, 1998). On rural markets see Clark W. Sorensen, "Market and Social Structure among the Peasantry in the Yŏngsŏ Region of South Korea (1981)," *Journal of Korean Studies* 3 (1981): 82–112. An excellent recent discussion on the ethnography of class and mobility is Nancy Abelmann, *The Melodrama of Mobility: Women, Talk, and Class in Contemporary South Korea* (Honolulu: University of Hawaii Press, 2003). Current adaptations of traditional values in urban life are discussed in Clark W. Sorensen, "Filial Piety in Contemporary Urban Southeast Korea: Practices and Discourses," in *Filial Piety: Practice and Discourse in Contemporary East Asia*, ed. Charlotte Ikels (Stanford, CA: Stanford University Press, 2004). The best source on contemporary social life in North Korea is Hunter, *Kim Il-song's North Korea*.

27. Good sources on rites of passage including births and funerary rituals in Korea are Roger L. Janelli and Dawnhee Yim

Janelli, *Ancestor Worship and Korean Society* (Stanford, CA: Stanford University Press, 1982); and the works by Laurel Kendall, *Shamans, Housewives, and Other Restless Spirits: Women in Korean Ritual Life* (Honolulu: University of Hawaii Press, 1986) and *The Life and Hard Times of a Korean Shaman: Of Tales and the Telling of Tales* (Honolulu: University of Hawaii Press, 1988).

28. A classic village study in South Korea just before industrialization took hold is Vincent S. R. Brandt, *A Korean Village Between Farm and Sea* (Cambridge, MA: Harvard University Press, 1971). An older village study is Part 1 of Cornelius Osgood's *The Koreans and Their Culture* (New York: Ronald Press, 1951). Mun Woon Lee, *Rural North Korea under Communism* (Houston, TX: Rice University, 1976) is a study of rural North Korea based on interviews with refugees and defectors.

29. A good work on ethnicity and nationalism and its relationship to unification between South and North Korea is Roy Richard Grinker, *Korea and Its Futures: Unification and the Unfinished War* (New York: St. Martin's Press, 1998). Sheila Jager, *Narratives of Nation Building in Korea* (Armonk, NY: M. E. Sharpe, 2003) links ethnicity and gender.

30. North Korea was actually liberated, of course, as a result of the Allied defeat of Japan in 1945, and completed when troops from the Soviet Union entered North Korea in August 1945 to take the Japanese surrender there. Kim Il Sung did not arrive in North Korea on a Soviet transport ship until almost a month after the initial arrival of Soviet forces. This is discussed in Charles K. Armstrong, *The North Korean Revolution 1945–50* (Ithaca, NY: Cornell University Press, 2003).

31. Current politics and class relationships are discussed by Nancy Abelmann, *Echoes of the Past, Epics of Dissent* (Berkeley: University of California Press, 1996); and Hagen Koo, *Korean Workers: The Culture and Politics of Class Formation* (Ithaca, NY: Cornell University Press, 2001). A good source on North Korean politics is Oh and Hassig, *North Korea through the Looking-Glass.* A good discussion of the politics of North and South Korea is Don Oberdorfer, *The Two Koreas: A Contemporary History* (Reading, MA: Addison-Wesley, 1997).

32. A good summary of the history of Buddhism in Korea can be found in Robert E. Buswell, *The Collected Works of Chinul: The Korean Approach to Zen* (Honolulu: University of Hawaii Press, 1983). Buswell's *The Zen Monastic Experience: Buddhist Practice in Contemporary Korea* (Princeton, NJ: Princeton University Press, 1992) is an ethnography of a Buddhist temple.

33. Good sources on traditional folklore and religion including shamanism are by Roger L. Janelli and Dawnhee Yim Janelli, *Ancestor Worship and Korean Society* (Stanford, CA: Stanford University Press, 1992); and the earlier mentioned works by Kendall, *Shamans, Housewives, and Other Restless Spirits* and *The Life and Hard Times of a Korean Shaman.* For a description of shamanistic ceremonies for the dead see Clark Sorensen, "The Myth of Princess Pari and the Self-Image of Korean Women," *Anthropos* 83 (1988): 403–419. Current modifications of ancestor worship practices are treated in Kwang-Kyu, "The Practice of Traditional Family Rituals in Contemporary Urban Korea," *Journal of Ritual Studies* 3, no. 2 (1989): 167–83; and in Sorensen, "Filial Piety in Contemporary Urban Southeast Korea."

34. Good sources on Christianity in Korea include Donald N. Clark, *Christianity in Modern Korea* (Lanham, MD: University Press of America, 1986); and Chung-shin Park, *Protestantism and Politics in Korea* (Seattle: University of Washington Press, 2003).

35. A good discussion of the origins of the nuclear proliferation issue in Korea is Michael J. Mazarr, *North Korea and the Bomb: A Case Study in Nonproliferation* (New York: St. Martin's Press, 1995). A more recent treatment of the subject is Leon Sigal, *Disarming Strangers: Nuclear Diplomacy with North Korea* (Princeton, NJ: Princeton University Press, 1998). The 1994 estimates of a 90-day war with North Korea, according to Don Oberdorfer, *The Two Koreas: A Contemporary History* (Reading, MA: Addison-Wesley, 1997) are 54,000 U.S. soldiers killed or wounded and 490,000 South Korea military casualties and South Korean civilian casualties possibly in the millions. He did not give an estimate of North Korean casualties.

36. The best discussion of democratization in Korea is Doh C. Shin, *Mass Politics and Culture in Democratizing Korea* (Cambridge, England: Cambridge University Press, 1999). Other approaches include Geir Helgessen, *Democracy and Authority in Korea: The Cultural Dimension in Korean Politics* (New York: St. Martin's Press, 1988); and Sunhyuk Kim, *The Politics of Democratization in Korea: The Role of Civil Society* (Pittsburgh: University of Pittsburgh Press, 2000).

37. *Point Topic Operator Source,* a leading Web service reporting broadband research of Point Topic, Inc., reported on May 6, 2004, that South Korea has the highest broadband penetration in the world at 23.17 per 100 population in December 2003. This is due to aggressive government promotion. See http://www.point-topic.com.

38. President Truman publicly acknowledged the possibility of the use of nuclear weapons in Korea in 1950, and explicit references were made again in 1953 during the Eisenhower presidency. Nuclear capable weapons systems were maintained by the U.S. in South Korea from 1958 until their withdrawal by President George H. W. Bush in 1991.

39. Estimates of a 90-day war with North Korea are 54,000 U.S. soldiers killed or wounded, 490,000 South Korean military casualties, and South Korean casualties possibly into the millions. There is no estimate of North Korean casualties.

8 MAINLAND SOUTHEAST ASIA

Raymond Scupin

Usually, the region of Southeast Asia is divided into two geographical zones—mainland and island Southeast Asia—that include countries with different environments and histories that have contributed to cultural, ethnic, and religious complexity. The countries of mainland Southeast Asia include Myanmar (Burma), Thailand, Cambodia, Laos, and Vietnam. The countries of island Southeast Asia are Malaysia, Singapore, Brunei, Indonesia, Timor Leste, and the Philippines. This chapter will focus on mainland Southeast Asia, whereas Chapter 9 will concentrate on island Southeast Asia. Because of the cultural, ethnic, religious, and geographical diversity in Southeast Asia there have been historical problems in conceptualizing the area as a discrete region. Prior to Western colonialism in the region, there did not appear to be a distinctive indigenous conception of a "Southeast Asia." Western colonial officials, missionaries, and travelers produced early cultural configurations of the region—configurations based on somewhat naïve, simplistic, stereotypical characterizations of "race," tribes, religions, and agricultural civilizations. Although there was some pioneering research conducted by French, British, Scandinavian, and other European scholars it was not until after World War II and especially after the emergence of the Cold War and subsequent developments that resulted in the Vietnam War that both Western and Asian specialists began to conceive of a distinct cultural and political region for Southeast Asia.[1]

All the mainland Southeast Asian countries have a dominant ethnic majority with various ethnic minorities. For example, Myanmar (Burma) consists of ethnic Burmese who make up 65 percent of the population of 47 million with a variety of other ethnic groups including Shans, Karens, Mons, Indians, and Chinese. In Thailand ethnic Thais make up 75 percent of the population of 62 million with a number of other ethnic minorities such as Chinese, Malay, Indian, and smaller numbers of "Hill tribes" residing in the mountain areas bordering southern China. The countries of Vietnam, Cambodia, and Laos have ethnic majorities with smaller populations of ethnic minorities residing in different regions.

GEOGRAPHY AND ECOLOGY

A classical anthropological work on mainland Southeast Asia is titled *Hill Farms and Padi Fields*.[2] This title evokes the fundamental

Note: The author would like to thank Donald E. Brown, Richard O'Connor, Kathryn Howard and one of the brightest anthropology students that I have had in many years, Michael Tidwell, for reviewing and suggesting useful comments based on their considerable expertise and interest.

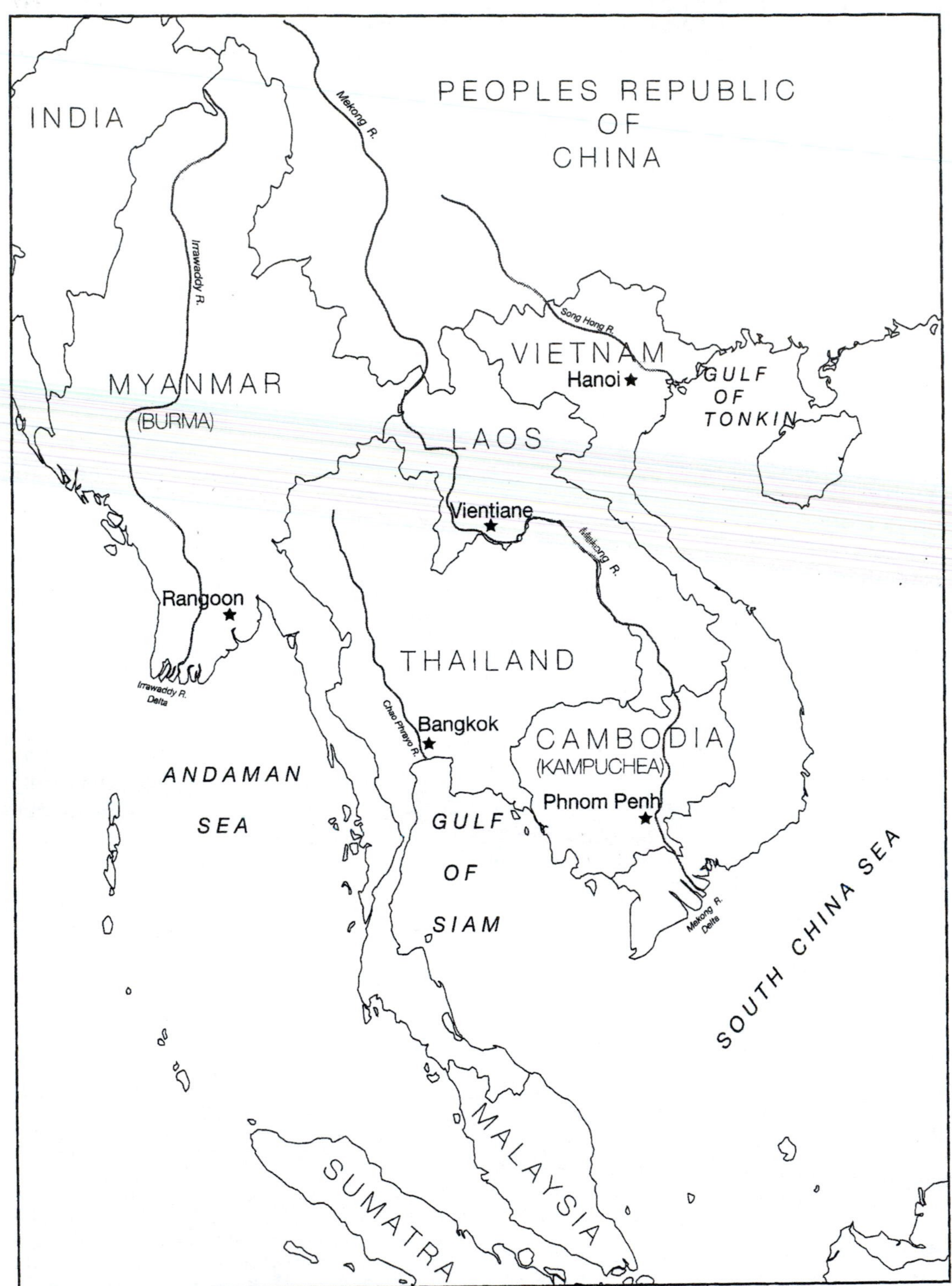
PEOPLES REPUBLIC OF CHINA
INDIA
Mekong R.
Irrawaddy R.
MYANMAR
(BURMA)
Song Hong R.
VIETNAM
Hanoi
GULF OF TONKIN
LAOS
Vientiane
Mekong R.
Rangoon
THAILAND
Irrawaddy R. Delta
Chao Phraya R.
Bangkok
CAMBODIA
(KAMPUCHEA)
ANDAMAN SEA
Phnom Penh
GULF OF SIAM
Mekong R. Delta
SOUTH CHINA SEA
MALAYSIA
SUMATRA

geographical features that have influenced the major cultures within the region. Four major river systems flow from Tibet and China into mainland Southeast Asia and were the principal routes for migrants from the north. The longest river is the Mekong, which runs near the Burmese border through the border areas of Laos and Thailand, slashes through Cambodia, and ends up at the great Mekong Delta in southern Vietnam. The Irrawaddy also flows from the Tibetan Himalayan plateau and moves directly southward through Burma ending up in the Indian Ocean. The third major river is the Red River in Vietnam and the fourth is the Chao Phraya in Thailand, which like the other two major rivers created rich alluvial soils and plains that would be available for the development of wet-rice (*padi*) agricultural cultivation. This wet-rice cultivation would provide the basis for the establishment of large-scale agricultural kingdoms that were the forerunners of the modern Burmese, Thai, Cambodian, Laotian, and Vietnamese civilizations. Other migrants from the north of mainland Southeast in what is today China settled in the hill or mountain areas. These hill peoples, such as the Hmong, Chin, Kachin, and many others, practiced shifting (*swidden*) or slash and burn horticulture (simple agriculture), which involved clearing, burning, and planting their fields and moving from place to place. These hill peoples did not develop the same cultural practices and beliefs as the wet-rice cultivators in the large-scale kingdoms.

Geographically, mainland Southeast Asia falls within the monsoon belt and most of the region is tropical. This monsoon belt affects the climate and has three distinct seasons: a hot season for three months in which the temperature can reach as high as 120 degrees Fahrenheit; a rainy season for three to four months, which is a relief from the hot dry weather; and a cooler season, which has an average temperature of 80 degrees. Historically most of mainland Southeast Asia was forested by a variety of deciduous trees including the well-known teak trees. Although the region is usually divided into the valley and hill areas, in actuality, there were three distinctive ecological zones within this region. One is where the majority of the population began to settle near the major rivers and to engage in cultivating wet rice (rice padi agriculture), or where much of the forests areas were cleared. A second zone in the foothills was more suitable for fruit orchards. The third ecological zone is *doi* (mountain areas) for the swidden agriculture or slash and burn cultivation among the hill people, as these areas were deforested with continuing population growth. Bamboo forests were also an important indigenous source for housing, baskets, cooking pots, kindling, and many other products. Moving toward the coastal regions of mainland Southeast Asia one finds mangrove and sweet water swamps that grow bushes and woods used for traditional roofing on houses.

LANGUAGE

Hundreds of languages are spoken throughout mainland Southeast Asia. Most of the linguistic diversity is evident within the hill peoples in the region. In contrast, the valley peoples who reside in the agricultural plains have been influenced by language policies that produced linguistic uniformity. Though linguists disagree on the grouping of some of the major languages, the general consensus suggests that there are four major families of languages spoken within mainland Southeast Asia. The Sino-Tibetan language family includes Chinese, Burmese, Karen, Miao (Hmong), Yao, and a number of other lesser known languages. The Austro-Asiatic family includes Mon, Khmer (Cambodian), and Vietnamese. Another major family grouping is Austronesian or Malayo-Polynesian. Only one major historical population of mainland Southeast Asia, the Chams, and some hill peoples of southern Vietnam speak Austronesian languages. Finally, the Tai-Kadai family grouping includes Thai, Lao, and Shan. Some linguists believe that the Tai-Kadai family is a derivative of the Sino-Tibetan language, while others view them as more closely related to the Austronesian. Most historical linguists maintain that the Austronesian language family was the earliest linguistic grouping in mainland Southeast Asia, but with the migration of people from China to the south, the Sino-Tibetan, Tai-Kadai, and Austro-Asiatic families came to predominate.

Language Family	Examples of the Major Languages of Mainland Southeast Asia
Sino-Tibetan	Burmese, Karen, Chin, Miao (Hmong)
Austro-Asiatic	Mon, Khmer (Cambodian), Vietnamese
Austronesian (Malayo-Polynesian)	Cham, Rhade, Jarai, Sedang, Raglai
Tai-Kadai	Thai, Lao, Shan

As mentioned above, linguistic uniformity prevailed in the plains or valley areas of mainland Southeast Asia. The spoken language of the valley people of Burma (Myanmar) has become Burmese. Siamese Thai has become the dominant spoken language of Thailand, although earlier languages such as Mon and Khmer appeared in the Chao Phraya basin. Thai is very similar to the Lao spoken by the majority population in Laos. As we will see in our discussion of the history of mainland Southeast Asia, Khmer was the prevailing language of the valley peoples for many centuries. Presently, however, Khmer is confined to Cambodia and has become the national language. Vietnamese is the dominant language of the valley peoples of Vietnam. All of these major spoken languages are what linguists refer to as "tonal languages" in that the meaning of words is determined by differences in lower and higher tones. For example, the Thai language has five basic tones: high, mid, low, rising, and falling. Burmese, Lao, Cambodian, and Vietnamese are also tonal languages, though each of these languages has a different tone system. In addition to being tonal languages, all of these languages include "honorifics," which consist of changes in vocabulary or grammar that reflects the relative status differences among speakers. For example, in Thai there are 13 terms for the pronouns *I* and *you*. The correct pronoun to be used depends on whether one is addressing his or her parents, teachers, peers, government officials, or the royal family. Status and hierarchical differences may also influence the choice of verbs. In Thai one chooses different verbs to say "to eat," depending on status differences. There is an elegant form (*raprathaan*) used with the royal family, to be used in polite company (*thaan*), to be used informally with peers (*kin*), and to be used with children (*daek*). Politeness, etiquette, and status differences play a significant role in speaking mainland Southeast Asian languages.[3]

The written languages of mainland Southeast Asia were influenced by the adoption of scripts from India and China as they had increasing contact with this region. Burmese, Thai, Lao, and Cambodian peoples adopted and modified the Sanskrit-Pali, a polysyllabic script that came with the religious texts of Hinduism and Buddhism. The most significant change was to use special marks to show where syllables were to be spoken within high tones, rising, falling, or mid tones. Other changes of the Indic-derived scripts included the modification of the shape of the letters and the deletion of unnecessary characters. Along with the adoption of the Indic script, many words from Sanskrit and Pali were imported into the languages of the Burmese, Thai, Lao, and Cambodian peoples to refer to religious, philosophical, and political–legal concepts. As we will see, Vietnamese culture and language was strongly influenced by China. The initial Vietnamese written language was derived from the Chinese-style script. For many centuries the educated

Vietnamese had to master the Chinese system of writing to become literate. Later, French missionaries worked out a system of Roman transcription for the Vietnamese spoken language called *quoc ngu*. This system of quoc ngu employs diacritical marks to indicate tonal differences and other matters of pronunciation. Eventually quoc ngu was adopted by the Vietnamese to replace the Chinese script and is used today.

PALEOANTHROPOLOGY AND PREHISTORY

As we will see in the next chapter on island Southeast Asia, nineteenth-century paleoanthropological discoveries of the fossilized remains of *Homo erectus*, an early hominid, were found in Indonesia and dated between 800,000 and 300,000 years ago. These findings coincide with the *Homo erectus* remains found in China during the same period. The earliest remains of *Homo sapiens* are also found in island Southeast Asia dating from as early as 40,000 years ago. Most paleoanthropologists believe that following the end of the Pleistocene (10,000 years ago) there was a continuous migration of modern *Homo sapiens* populations from China in the north through mainland Southeast Asia to island Southeast Asia for many centuries. Along with this migration of modern *Homo sapiens*, the cultural inheritance of mainland Southeast Asia becomes clear with the artifacts associated with skeletal remains, including stratified cave deposits subject to reliable radiocarbon dating, various Paleolithic (Old Stone Age) tools, weapons, and fossilized plants. These archaeological sites, known as the Hoabinhian culture, first discovered in Hoa Son Binh province in Vietnam, represent the hunting-gathering-fishing peoples who utilized a pebble and flake tool industry to exploit diverse forest, riverine, and marine resources. These Hoabinhian sites indicate that these people ate a wide variety of fish, snake, reptiles, turtles, mollusk, elephant, rhinos, wild cattle, pigs, and deer, as well as a multitude of plants. Their social organization consisted of small bands that inhabited seasonal shelters in caves and limestone rock crevices. In contrast to most other nomadic hunting-gathering societies, these people were producing pottery for cooking, carrying water, and other usages.[4]

For many years archaeologists and historians of Southeast Asia assumed that these original hunting-gathering peoples remained extremely primitive and backward. However, archaeological data of the past several decades have led to a radical revision of this view. It is now clear that the aboriginal people of Southeast Asia developed vigorous civilizations with organized large-scale irrigation, long-distance maritime exchange routes, specialized bronze and iron metallurgical techniques, and rich burials that included enormous amounts of gold, silver, and bronze ornamentation. All of these developments were achieved through a long prehistoric period known as the Neolithic (New Stone Age), the period in which these people began to cultivate rice. According to most archaeologists today, the wild ancestor of rice (*Oryza nivara*) was first cultivated in about 5,000 BC in southern China before radiating to all parts of monsoon Asia.

As Neolithic farmers migrated from southern China into Southeast Asia they began to replace the Hoabinhian cultures. The full-scale technology and irrigation for wet-rice agriculture was established in the plains areas of Southeast Asia by 3,000 BC. Archaeological sites in Thailand such as Non Nok Tha and Ban Chiang have yielded the evidence for rice cultivation, domesticated animals such as dogs, chickens, pigs, and cattle by this time period. A specific Neolithic technology referred to as the Don-S'on culture that emerged first in northern Vietnam had an impact throughout mainland Southeast Asia. The most remarkable artifacts

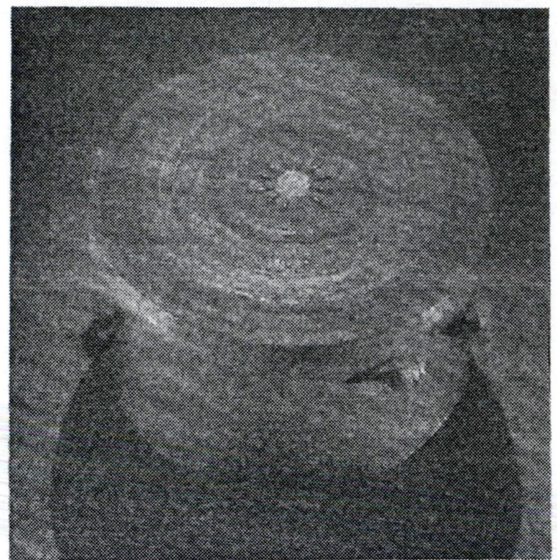

A bronze Don-S'on drum.

associated with the Don-S'on culture are the large bronze drums decorated with intricate motifs such as birds, other animals, houses, and people, along with beautiful geometric designs. The Don-S'on drums attest to a very advanced culture with sophisticated metallurgical techniques derived from China.

Gradually, the Don-S'on peoples became more sedentary farmers and employed domesticated oxen or water buffalo to prepare their irrigated wet-rice padi fields. Wet-rice cultivation fostered clusters of small populations residing in rural villages throughout mainland Southeast Asia. Their villages consisted of bamboo-with-thatch houses situated with built-in kitchens and garden areas. Leaders within the villages had larger bamboo-with-thatch structures. Of course, bamboo is a very perishable material and consequently these houses and other structures are not well preserved in the archaeological record. Yet, the archaeological data do indicate that these Don-S'on peoples were the basis of more advanced cultural developments throughout mainland Southeast Asia. Archaeologists have found that many of these Don-S'on societies evolved into what anthropologists sometimes refer to as complex *chiefdoms.* Chiefdoms are societies with a centralized political economy with ruling chiefs who manage the defense, trade and exchange, land ownership, and kinship and marriage alliances over many villages within a particular region. The development of these supravillage Don-S'on chiefdoms depended on the whether a particular chief could legitimize his status and extend his political domain. Most likely, based on the understanding of chiefdoms in other regions of the world, religious and spiritual traditions were utilized to legitimize particular families who were then recognized as the ruling chiefs. This type of political–religious legitimacy was probably precarious, ephemeral, and transistory. However, by the time of AD 100, there were many supravillage Don-S'on chiefdoms scattered throughout the whole of mainland Southeast Asia, though as we will see many other tribal horticulturalists resided in other areas, especially in the highland regions.

THE HISTORICAL PERIOD

As is evident from our discussion of the languages of mainland Southeast Asia, the cultural traditions of these areas were substantially influenced primarily by the civilizations of India and China. The written languages of India and China were adopted and modified by the peoples of Southeast Asia. These written languages also provided the source documents for understanding the history of this region of the world. Many scholars refer to Burma, Thailand, Laos, and Cambodia as the Indianized cultural region of mainland Southeast Asia, whereas Vietnam is known as the sinicized cultural region. We will begin this section with an overview of the Indian influence on Southeast Asia.

Many Indian merchants and travelers began to come across the Bay of Bengal to Southeast Asia by 200 BC or earlier. These early Indian merchants brought material goods such as weapons, clothing, jewelry, and tools that had not been seen in Southeast Asia. Some of these merchants may have been high caste *Ksatriya* (warrior caste) merchants who had considerable knowledge of the political systems, military organization, royal court rituals, and Hindu beliefs and practices of India.[5] As indicated in our discussion on prehistory, many of the indigenous agricultural settlements of mainland Southeast Asia had developed chiefdom societies. These societies were dominated by chiefs or "men of prowess," who tried to establish their legitimacy through religious or spiritual sources. Many of these supravillage chiefdoms in the region were competing with one another for territory and control of populations.

As these Southeast Asian chiefs became familiar with the model of royal governance and were inspired by tales of Hindu and Buddhist kingdoms of India, they recognized that some aspects of these Indic traditions could be utilized to buttress their own political regimes. In particular, the conception of the *deva-raja* (god-king) was borrowed to legitimize the religious cults defining Southeast Asian kingships and reinforce the traditional chiefdom's spiritual notions of descent and prowess. The courtly ideals of the deva-raja were instituted to circumvent customary norms, control rival claims to royal rank, and legitimize the acquisition of new territories. These adept Southeast Asian rulers initiated these forms of royal control by having the Hindu and Brahman priests consecrate their claims of theocratic rule through royal rites of legitimation. The royal ceremonies enacted by the Hindu and Brahman priests drew on the sacred language of Sanskrit and were used to validate the divine lineage of aspiring chiefs. Throughout mainland Southeast Asia inscriptions and monuments indicate a widespread adoption of Hindu gods and goddesses, of Sanskrit vocabulary, political forms, and Indian art, dance, and musical traditions by AD 400.

One by one, sacred capitals based on the royal conceptions of the deva-raja began to mushroom throughout mainland Southeast Asia. These kingdoms or states, known as *negara* (Sanskrit for "holy city"), were modeled on Hindu concepts of the universe. The Hindu texts describe the universe as centered on Mount Meru, the home of the Hindu gods, ringed by concentric circles known as *mandalas* that create sacred space and religious–political alliances and prohibit the entrance of evil spirits or enemies. The cosmos was populated by many kinds of spiritual beings and the deva-raja was the divine intermediary between the world of the gods and the people. These sacred capitals served as ceremonial centers, military strongholds, and a marketing and administrative nucleus for these agricultural kingdoms. The deva-rajas and their royal advisors supervised the civil and military apparatus while also protecting the religious institutions that provided for the foundations of these early states. Local spiritual beliefs and political practices were integrated with the Indic religious and legal conceptions. Thus, various animistic and shamanistic spiritual traditions were merged and incorporated into the culture of these state kingdoms. In addition, prominent local rulers in rural villages were educated to become part of the literati and political clientage. Rural manpower was recruited for conscripted labor and the military so that these regimes could grow territorially and build enormous monuments that reflected state power.

A number of major Southeast Asian states characterized by the *devarajika* style of monarchy began to flourish after the first or second centuries AD. Funan, the first of the Indianized states, developed along what is now the Cambodian and southern Vietnam coastline. Funan was a large-scale maritime state that maintained a trade linkage between China and India. Its sacred capital was comprised of ceremonial centers that ruled over regional centers and administrative towns that eventually incorporated various chiefdoms. However, another early maritime state, Champa, emerged as a polyethnic successor state to Funan and was based in southern and central Vietnam. The kingdom of Champa lasted from the second to the seventeenth century AD and extended over the central and southern coastal region of Vietnam. Yet, this kingdom was not based on Indic forms, but rather on the Islamic tradition. Islam began to diffuse into the Champa region during the eighth or ninth century AD as a result of Arab, Persian, and other Muslim traders who were trading and establishing port centers in China, and elsewhere in Asia. These Muslims had a widespread influence in both mainland and island Southeast Asia (see Chapter 9). As the Champa maritime kingdom developed many of the Cham population converted to Islam, and were ruled by Muslim religious and political officials. Following its defeat by Vietnam in 1471, Champa was gradually absorbed into the Vietnam state. As mentioned earlier, the people of Champa were the only major group who spoke a Malayo-Polynesian language (or Austronesian) in mainland Southeast Asia. This indicates that Champa had strong cultural affinities with the Malaysian cultures to the south. The kingdom of Champa had been sustained by a diverse economy of wet-rice agriculture, fishing, and maritime and overland trade.[6]

Eventually large-scale, land-based Indianized states emerged throughout mainland Southeast Asia. These land-based states were based on wet-rice cultivation and vast irrigation projects in the valley or plains area. In the seventh and eighth centuries the Mon kingdom developed in what is now lower Thailand and Burma. North of the Mon kingdom was the early Burmese Pyu kingdom. Like Funan and Champa these states had ceremonial and administrative centers and maintained long-distance trade networks with China and India. The Mon and Pyu kingdoms were important as the earliest centers of Theravada Buddhism, the religious tradition that monks brought from Sri Lanka, which eventually combined other spiritual traditions in the Indianized areas of mainland Southeast Asia. In the ninth century, Pagan, an agricultural state emerged in present-day Burma. The king of Pagan developed a more thorough-going Buddhist conception of state rule than other kings of the era.[7] A rival state developed in the ninth century, the largest land-based agrarian civilization, the well-known Khmer kingdom of Angkor. The Khmer kingdom of Angkor predominated as the major state kingdom in mainland Southeast Asia. Angkor developed in a large freshwater lake reservoir area known as Tonle Sap basin, which was linked to the Mekong River. This lake reservoir area created a natural system of irrigation that was expanded by various kings through massive engineering projects that resulted in an extensive hydraulic system producing enormous quantities of rice and other produce to support a dense population.

Between the ninth and fifteenth centuries a series of deva-raja rulers in Angkor used peasant and slave labor to construct irrigation networks and to build large-scale temple palaces of stone and brick decorated with beautiful artwork based on the Hindu and Buddhist sacred scriptures. The tales of the *Ramayana* and images of Siva, Vishnu, and other gods and goddesses are reproduced as sculptures throughout the many temples, palaces, monasteries, and walkways. Later, as Theravada Buddhism diffused into this region, images of the Buddha—surrounded by bas reliefs of various spiritual beings of Hinduism—were sculpted. The center of Khmer civilization was the great Angkor Wat, a vast temple and mausoleum symbolizing the authority of the divine king. Angkor Wat represented Mount Meru, the center of the cosmos surrounded by a large moat symbolizing the oceans of the world. The Khmer civilization consisted of some 20,000 temples with perhaps as many as 300,000 Hindu–Brahman priests and Buddhist monks. This enormous agricultural complex was supported by expanding the amount of land and labor by conquest, the taking of slaves and the use of corvee labor. Aside from labor, taxes were paid by farmers and others in the form of rice and other items such as honey, sugar, spices, wax, salt, medicine, feathers, rhino horns, ivory, sandalwood, and cloth. The epigraphy and architectural developments and other cultural evidence demonstrate that Angkor Wat and the Khmer Empire was a vast state that emphasized the rulers as maintaining connections and communication with the divine world. These deva-rajas developed these aesthetically pleasing temples and palaces to reinforce their political and spiritual legitimacy in the eyes of their populations.[8]

As is evident, these large-scale devarajika-style state civilizations were influenced powerfully by the cultural traditions of India; however, as emphasized earlier, the indigenous Southeast Asians selectively adopted certain elements of Indic culture and rejected or modified other elements. For example, the Southeast Asians did not wholly appropriate the caste system that had developed in India. The rulers and bureaucrats of these states created their own unique forms of social stratification modeled partly on Indic conceptions, but tailored to suit evolving social, spiritual, and political beliefs in Southeast Asia. Siam, or Thailand, as it developed as a major state civilization illustrates how these unique forms of social stratification varied from that of the caste system of India and will be discussed below.

The kingdom of Thailand developed slowly as a result of the gradual migration of peoples known as the Tai from southern China into the fertile rice-growing areas of the Chao Phraya River valley. *Tai* is the term referring to the speakers of the Tai language, who live in both Thailand and Laos, whereas *Thai* refers to the citizens of the country of Thailand. During this migration the Tai rulers had extensive cultural contact with the Mon and Khmer kingdoms. Through these cultural contacts, the Tai people were influenced by the Theravada Buddhist spiritual tradition. The first major historical records of a kingdom of the Thai was Sukhothai, ruled by King Ramkhamhaeng or "Rama the Bold" (1279–1299). Ramkhamhaeng identified his new kingdom closely with Theravada Buddhism and the kingdom expanded its control of populations through the support of this religious tradition, which gave moral and spiritual prestige and legitimacy to the regime. The epigraphy from that period demonstrates the first use of a written language by the Tai people. Following Ramakhamhaeng's death, Sukhothai declined but this state civilization had provided the foundations of the monarchy and religious traditions for subsequent kingdoms in Thailand.[9]

The next major Thai kingdom, Ayudhya, was established on the Chao Phraya River in central Thailand and endured from 1350 to 1767. The Ayudhyan kingdom was poised between its rival the Khmer civilization in the east and the Burmese civilization in the west. Ayudhya drew heavily from the cosmological and organization models that the Khmer and Burmese empires had developed. Through the Hindu and Buddhist concepts the monarch was perceived as the first among mortals and the promoter and protector of the religious tradition. Many Hindu and Buddhist rituals were performed by priests and monks to affirm the divine status of the king. A formal structure of government was adopted from the Khmer and Burmese that provided an administrative system with different ministeries for collecting taxes, organizing the military, recruiting labor for constructing public works, and providing a justice system throughout the region. The entire Ayudhyan society was organized into a hierarchical pattern with various departments, or *krom*, which were subdivided into more specialized units that were responsible for carrying out different functions on behalf of the royalty. In contrast to China or other regions of Asia, one of the major problems faced in mainland Southeast Asia was the shortage of manpower rather than a shortage of available land for agriculture.

Fertile land was available, but rulers had to recruit labor and manpower to the land. To control the manpower of the kingdom, every male was assigned a position in which they were to perform labor or military service for the king. Eventually, this hierarchical organizational model evolved into what was termed the *sakdina* system. *Sakdi* (Sanskrit, "energy or power") and *na* (rice fields) indicated a link between how much rank or power an individual had with respect to land ownership.

The sakdina system designated a particular number for ranking of every male and female within the Ayudhyan kingdom into a hierarchical pattern of patron–client relationships. The number was tattooed on the arm of each male and was known a "dignity mark." The king's rank was so much above everyone else's that no number was attached to it. But just below the king, the *Upparat,* or second king was given a number of 100,000. Princes and other nobles, *nai,* were given numbers ranging from 50,000 to 500 depending on their genealogical connections with the royal family. Government officials were assigned numbers 10,000 to 1,400, while government workers were given ranks of 350 to 50. The ranks of 2,400 to 200 were allotted to Buddhist monks depending on their seniority and status within the *sangha,* the monastic order. The *phrai* (commoners) numbers ranged from 25 to 10, and slaves had a number 5 assigned to them. This *sakdina* ranking system had importance for not only economic, but also political–legal circumstances within the Ayudhyan kingdom. For example, if a lower ranking male committed an offense against someone of higher rank, the penalty would be much more severe than if a higher ranking male did the same to a lower ranking male. This stratification system was rooted within the religious cosmology of reincarnation in Hinduism and Theravada Buddhism. One's social and political status or rank was influenced by *kamma* (a Pali word derived from the Sanskrit *karma*), that one inherited based on the accumulated merit and deeds from previous lives.[10]

This pattern of stratification became embedded within the Thai kingdom as it continued to develop. Following the destruction of Ayudhya by the Burmese military in 1767, the Thai monarchy reestablished itself southward and west of the Chao Phraya River in Thonburi. Finally, in 1782, a new dynasty led by the Chakri family initiated a large-scale campaign of building of temples and palaces in the sacred capital of Bangkok, east of the Chao Phraya. The form of government instituted by the Ayudhyan rulers and the sakdina system continued to structure Thai social and political life into the twentieth century. Though the sakdina system is not completely synonymous with the caste stratification found in India, it has some parallels in its effects on economic, social, and political relationships. The Khmer and Burmese civilizations had similar forms of hierarchical social and political stratification. As one can imagine, these patterns of social and political stratification have had lingering effects on hierarchy and status within these Indianized cultures of mainland Southeast Asia.

Vietnam: The Sinicized Cultural Region

As we have seen, the major mainland Southeast Asian states of what was to become Burma, Thailand, Laos, and Cambodia drew their cultural inspiration from India. Vietnam, however, had a much different historical and cultural development as it was influenced primarily by China. A millennium-long period of direct Chinese rule accounts for the sinification of Vietnam. Yet, it must be emphasized that Vietnamese people continued to have definite cultural connections with other Southeast Asian polities such as the Khmer, Champa, and various Tai societies. Thus, Vietnam was not wholly China-like, and its people developed their own distinctive form of Southeast Asian culture. The prehistory of Vietnam, as seen above, was associated with the expansion of the neolithic Don-S'on wet-rice-based regional chiefdoms. In 214 BC the Han dynasty of China established a military outpost known as Nam Viet (people of the south). By 111 BC the Chinese government had colonized most of the northern Vietnamese region. As these areas of northern Vietnam were incorporated into the Chinese empire, the people were directly influenced by cultural traditions of China. The Chinese elite were committed to "civilizing" these "backward peoples" of Vietnam. They began to nurture the Vietnamese chiefly rulers as their appointed educated elite. As the Vietnamese elite were introduced to Chinese classical education and learned to read the Chinese language, they also absorbed the political model of a Confucian-based, civil service bureaucracy with the conception of the emperor who ruled with a "mandate from heaven."

Faced by rising population pressures, the Vietnamese rulers were engaged in a policy of imperial expansion into central and southern regions. From their military and political capital city of Hue, the Vietnamese conquered the Chams, the Austronesian people who had organized the Indianized Champa civilization. By the seventeenth century, the Champa civilization was decimated. In addition, the Vietnamese also confronted the Khmer civilization as it had controlled areas in what is now southern Vietnam. The Khmers were easily dispersed by the Vietnamese. Following the defeat of the Cham and the Khmers, the Vietnamese controlled the entire coastal area including the alluvial plains of the Mekong Delta. As a result of the confrontation and contact with these Indianized civilizations, the Vietnamese often intermarried with Cham and Khmer peoples and became familiar with their beliefs and practices. However, political instability, factionalism, and a series of peasant rebellions were constant obstacles in the attempts to bring about political unity between the north and south. Major cultural and political differences between the sinified northern and Indianized southern areas of Vietnam continued to play a significant role in the region for many years. Overall, Vietnam developed a distinctive society incorporating both indigenous and external elements into its cultural fabric.

As in China, the Vietnamese emperor and members of the royal family maintained control of the local village and regional areas through the mandarins, scholarly officials who had close ties with the local gentry (property owners). The village communities in Vietnam were structured by both patrilineal kinship groups and non-kinship principles. The traditional village varied somewhat among the peasantry in northern, central, and southern areas of Vietnam. The peasants in the north adopted the Chinese method of agriculture and dike construction which proved more effective than other modes of rice production in Southeast Asia. Most of the villages were fenced by bamboo and were governed by a council of village notables who collected taxes on behalf of the state. The council determined how agricultural processes were managed, distributed the rice and other crops among the families, and administered justice. The council of notables was comprised of retired mandarins, scholars who had not passed their civil service examinations, or individuals who had more extensive land holdings than others. They kept registries of land holdings and recruited labor from among the peasantry to serve in the military or to provide corvee labor to the state. The notables were also responsible for maintaining the spiritual traditions of the villages.[11]

In addition to Confucianism, from the 10 centuries of Chinese rule, the Vietnamese elite absorbed the religious traditions of Mahayana Buddhism and Daoism that flowed from China. By the seventh century the city of Hanoi became the center of Mahayana Buddhism in the region. Yet, these religious traditions never became the exclusive religions of Vietnam. Earlier Southeast Asian forms of animism, ancestor worship, spirit guardians, and other types of spiritualism persisted in conjunction with these new forms of Chinese religions among the nonelite population. In rural villages a traditional folk culture survived the impact of Chinese foreign beliefs and practices. Despite the efforts of the Chinese government to assimilate the peoples of Vietnam into their empire, most of the indigenous people of Vietnam viewed themselves as separate from their colonizers. This tenacious commitment to their own indigenous cultural traditions resulted in numerous rebellions and resistance movements against the Chinese rulers during the thousand years of control, and the Vietnamese eventually won their independence in AD 939. Though the Chinese rulers continued to invade the Vietnamese territories, the indigenous cultural nationalism enabled the Vietnamese to retain their own unique traditions. Some scholars have referred to the "love–hate" relationship that developed between Vietnam and China.[12]

WESTERN IMPACT AND COLONIALISM

As we will see in the next chapter, the Portuguese, the Spanish, and eventually the Dutch had a considerable impact on island Southeast Asia beginning in the sixteenth century. However, it was not until the nineteenth century that Europeans began to colonize the region of mainland Southeast Asia. There were a number of Europeans who came to Thailand or Vietnam as independent traders or missionaries in the seventeenth and eighteenth centuries to establish commercial relationships. But these commercial and economic involvements did not result in immediate colonization of these countries. For example, in the 1600s a small number of French missionaries and traders tried to take advantage of political opportunities in the Ayudhyan empire of Thailand to control the area, but the local peoples reacted strongly by killing the leader and expelling the other conspirators. The full impact of Western colonialism, which marked the early stages of full-scale globalization in mainland Southeast Asia, did not begin until the nineteenth century. Of course, globalization in the region began long before the European period as India, China, and the Middle East had much earlier transformed the region.

The British were the first Europeans to control regions in mainland Southeast Asia. They perceived Burma as a political, economic, and cultural extension of their empire in India. The Burmese had very little knowledge of Europeans and badly miscalculated their military and political relationships with the British. To secure their border areas with India and to expand their colonial holdings the British confronted the Burmese in the northwestern regions of Burma. This resulted in the first of three major wars between the Burmese and the British. In the First Anglo-Burmese War (1824–1825) the Burmese underestimated the strength of the British military and were forced to cede peripheral territories at the border. A second war in 1852 (motivated by the British attempt to punish a Burmese king's arrogance) secured British control of lower Burma. Burmese monarch Mindon Min (1814–1878) and many followers were forced to move to the capital in Upper Burma at Mandalay. Mindon Min tried to embrace Western technologies and reform the Burmese economy and political system. Following his death in 1878, a political vacuum developed. Finally, a third war in 1885 was initiated by the British who were aggravated by their colonial rival, the French, who were expanding their empire in the East. In this third war the Burmese monarchy was overthrown and abolished and the whole of Burma was incorporated into the British empire centered in India.[13]

The French colonial intrusion into mainland Southeast Asia was an outgrowth of missionary outposts that had developed in the region since the seventeenth and eighteenth centuries. Small corps of French Catholic priests had entered Vietnam. Some of these French missionaries became involved in Vietnamese politics supporting indigenous rebellions against perceived corrupt rulers. A French bishop enlisted French military support for a member of the elite Nguyen family known as Gia Long, who was able to unify most of Vietnam after capturing Saigon, Hue, and Hanoi. Gia Long became the new emperor of Vietnam. With the assistance of advisors from France he modernized the military and navy, and developed roadways between various urban centers enabling them to become thriving commercial communities. Gia Long is still celebrated as the first unifier of Vietnam. However, neither Gia Long nor the Vietnamese people fully trusted the French and their apprehension proved to be justified. Under the pretext of religious persecution and harassment of Catholic missionaries, Napoleon III of France instigated the invasion of Vietnam to acquire the territory as a colony.[14] In reality, this French invasion was directed at obtaining the political and economic benefits of an imperial mission.

Initially the French conquered the lower part of Vietnam, which they referred to as "Cochin China." This included the area of the Mekong Delta that offered possibilities for plantations and other commercial interests. To defray the costs of their colonial project, the French sold millions of hectares of land to French settlers and the Vietnamese upper class to develop the Mekong Delta. Subsequently, the French extended their rule over the central part of the country around Hue, and used the name "Annam" for this region. Finally, after battles in 1883, the French took the northern territory near Hanoi calling this region "Tonkin." Under French control the name Vietnam disappeared. These three colonies were combined with Cambodia, which had been declared a "protectorate" in 1863, and with Laos which had been conquered by 1893. The French colonization of Cambodia and Laos was motivated by French–Anglo rivalries within mainland Southeast Asia. Cambodia and Laos were used as a buffer between their colonial investments in Vietnam and the British presence to the west in Burma. All of these regions were administered by the French in what was termed "French Indochina." By 1890, the French officials had "pacified" all of the political domains in French Indochina and administered these territories through direct and indirect colonial rule.

Only Thailand, or as it was known then "Siam," was able to escape Western colonialism in mainland Southeast Asia. The Chakri kings based in Bangkok, beginning with King Mongkut (Rama IV, 1851–1868) and his son Chulalongkorn (Rama V, 1868–1910), perceived that no country other than Japan was able to maintain independence from the Europeans. These kings knew that they would have to develop strategies to gain leverage with the European powers. The strategies of these monarchs in conjunction with British and French colonial rival interests enabled Siam to maintain its political independence. King Mongkut, who had lived for 30 years as a Buddhist monk before becoming king, was highly educated in both Eastern and Western traditions.[15] He and his advisors recognized both the dangers of European colonialism and the benefits of Western technology. The Siamese elite resolved to develop a rapid program of reform to develop its economic, social, political, and religious institutions to withstand Western colonial interests. With the help of Western advisors and their own diplomatic skills in playing off British against French interests, the monarchs of Siam were able to retain their political independence. King Mongkut and his son King Chulalongkorn persuaded the British and French that remaining independent would enable Siam to become a buffer state between their competing interests. In retrospect, despite losing some of its territory in Cambodia, Laos, and Malaysia through concessions to British and French interests Siam fared well during that time period in its ability to remain an independent country.

Western contact and colonialism had major consequences for mainland Southeast Asia. Western colonialism had been a byproduct of the industrial revolution that had made the Europeans pioneers in modern science and industrial technology. These new developments were introduced by Western powers into Southeast Asia, drawing this region into an increasingly global economy. Western colonialism resulted in economic, demographic, social, religious, and ultimately political transformations throughout the region. The colonists in British Burma and French Indochina mobilized the indigenous labor to produce rice and rubber on the plantations and work in the industries engaged in extracting teak wood from the forests, or mining tin, coal, or other minerals. The British and French reorganized the traditional peasant villages. Many peasants who formerly were involved in subsistence agriculture, producing for their families and providing taxes for their kingdoms, began to produce crops for the world market. As they were drawn into the global economy, they became dependent on wages and money lenders to finance the new forms of agriculture. Crops and lands were mortgaged by the peasants to pay often exorbitant interest rates. In Burma the British imported Indian money lenders to restructure and finance their colonial projects among the peasantry. These Indians were perceived by the indigenous Burmese as an alien group associated with British colonialism. In Vietnam many small farmers lost their property to large landholders, especially when prices fell for rice or other commodities on the world market. Communal property and other forms of sharing and redistribution that had been a form of insurance for traditional peasants were disrupted as people became dependent on the wage economy. The traditional peasant village economy was rapidly transformed by the colonial projects and the global economy introduced by the British in Burma and the French in Indochina.[16]

Throughout mainland Southeast Asia as populations increased in rural areas, more land was cultivated, reducing the size of forests. Population growth also caused landholdings to be subdivided into ever smaller parcels, which led many peasants to the crowded urban areas such as Rangoon in British Burma or Saigon in French Indochina. These cities were developing as "primate cities" that played a significant role in the international economy stimulated by colonial projects. They grew up around the major ports, railways, and other communication and political centers of the British and French. These cities were linked to the colonial agricultural and industrial economies and to the international systems of exchange. The urban centers contained factories that processed materials for export, handicraft production sites such as weaving, metal working, basketry, and furniture making, and service industries involved in clerical work, retail, administration, petty trade, rickshaw transportation, and so on. These primate cities were also much more pluralistic than the traditional city-states in mainland Southeast Asia. There were not only indigenous Burmese, Vietnamese, Thais, Cambodians, or Laotians, but also the Europeans and significant numbers of overseas Indians and Chinese migrants who found economic opportunities in these colonial cities. While the Europeans ruled over the civil service and military branches within the cities, many of the overseas Indians and Chinese were concentrated in occupations that were not filled by the native populations.

These primate cities became centers of Western education and culture that provided the training for the indigenous elites for clerical, administrative, and technical developments for the colonial projects. As part of their colonial projects, both the British and French developed educational institutions to enhance their administrative staff and technical services, as well as to serve as their "civilizing mission." By the twentieth century Western schools, often run by Christian missionaries, were using the same curriculum as used in the homeland. The missionaries and educators were confident that their students would adopt the same mores and values as promoted within the European curriculum. In Vietnam many of the wealthy elite families sent their sons to France to absorb Western education. However, in the rural areas of mainland Southeast Asia, education remained in the hands of Buddhist monks whose curriculum was primarily religious and in the language of the native peoples. This created a two-tier system of education that resulted in a gap between cultural orientations among the urban elite versus the rural peoples. These differences would remain an endurable cultural gap between the urban and rural populations in contemporary mainland Southeast Asia.

Since Siam was not directly colonized, the Thais responded to European colonialism much differently than Burma, Cambodia, Laos, or Vietnam. They did not develop a strong sense of anti-Western nationalism. As mentioned, Siam's monarchs took it upon themselves to modernize their nation. Four decades of a modernization campaign sponsored by the Siamese monarchs resulted in the abolition of slavery, massive reforms that affected the political bureaucracy, education, and the development of technology, the economy, and cultural traditions. This reform from above as a response to Western contact transformed the kingdom into a modern nation-state. The Siamese elite sponsored Western education both within Siam and abroad in the West for their sons to acquire scientific and technological knowledge to provide the kingdom with skills and techniques to move into the twentieth century. As the Siamese kingdom was drawn into an increasingly international and globally based economy, Bangkok became a primate city and commercial link with international trade. As development occurred, a growing overseas Chinese population came to Thailand to take advantage of new economic opportunities; they would play a significant role in the development of the modern economy in Siam.

All of the transformations resulting from Western contact created conditions for redistributing new sources of economic and political power in Siam. By the early twentieth century newly educated populations were clamoring for more representative political institutions. Eventually, as a result of economic hardship resulting from the global economic depression of the 1930s and the stresses of new cultural changes introduced from the West, the traditional monarchy had become too rigid to provide effective leadership. A middle-class group comprised of civil servants, military officers, and business people supported a bloodless coup in 1932 against the monarchy. The coup leaders argued that the absolute monarchy was no longer able to lead and promote the changes necessary for a globally based nation-state. Following the successful coup, the kings became constitutional monarchs and the government was led by various civil and military factions. Though nationalism took a different form than that of the colonized regions of mainland Southeast Asia, Thai nationalism was developed as a means to unify the country (this will be discussed in the next section).

THE RISE OF NATIONALISM, INDEPENDENCE, AND REVOLUTION

As the Western powers developed roads and railways, and the technologies for shipbuilding, printing presses, the telegraph, and educational systems to exploit the resources and labor for their own purposes, these same technologies and institutions resulted in the growth of nationalistic and independence movements that ultimately led to decolonization. Improved means of communication coupled with Western education that emphasized political freedom and democratic institutions created a milieu that promoted dissatisfaction among the elite as they recognized themselves as second-class citizens under their colonial masters. These elites began to resent, question, and reject the assumptions of Western superiority. Nationalism, a strong sense of identification with and feeling toward the nation, began to emerge within the elite-educated populations of mainland Southeast Asia.[17] Southeast Asians developed a sense of identity that went beyond their families, local communities, and local religious traditions. This nationalist identity became the trigger for stimulating anticolonial, anti-Western, and independence movements.

One of the earliest nationalist movements in mainland Southeast Asia developed within a religious context in Burma. The British made many wrong assumptions regarding their colonial project in Burma based on their experience in India. One of their problems was how they managed the role of the Buddhist monks and the *sangha* (monastic order) and its influence on the population. The British instituted their Western forms of education that were in competition with the religious traditions of Theravada Buddhism. The British tried to undermine the influence of the monks and the sangha. In reaction, the Buddhist monasteries became the centers of opposition to Western influence in Burma. An organization known as the Young Men's Buddhist Association (YMBA) was founded in 1906 by young educated intellectuals. Originally, the YMBA was modeled after the YMCA, but it gave lessons in Theravada Buddhism to counter Christian missionary efforts. This organization became the center of social and cultural life throughout Burma and promoted nationalistic anti-Western attitudes. Economic problems resulting from the worldwide Great Depression of the 1930s accelerated the nationalist critiques of the Burmese. A peasant rebellion broke out, led by a Buddhist monk Saya San, who wanted to restore a Buddhist-based monarchy. The British crushed this rebellion and executed Saya San in 1937, which served to further antagonize the Burmese. The Buddhist-based nationalist movement grew among university students and marshaled support for independence throughout the peasantry in Burma.

Vietnamese nationalism had been nurtured in the context of resistance and rebellions against Chinese political domination for centuries. However, French colonial rule had a much more devastating effect on traditional economic, social, and cultural life than that of the Chinese. The dramatic influence of globalization induced by French colonialism had radically transformed Vietnam. The harsh labor conditions and political control imposed by the French had stimulated anticolonial resistance movements beginning in the nineteenth century. The Vietnamese became concerned with not only their loss of independence, but also their loss of ethnic cultural identity.[18] The French military brutally repressed these movements through public executions, imprisonment, and murder.

In the twentieth century an educated member of the mandarin class, Phan Boi Chau, organized a nationalist movement designed to promote independence from the French. He secretly met with leaders in China and Japan to try to gain support for the overthrow of the French colonial regime. Many young sons of the elite who had benefited from higher education in France joined the nationalist independence movement. Some of these young people had returned from France only to find that there were no employment opportunities for them in the colonial structure. These young educated sons of the elite, frustrated by their prospects to serve their country, were to become important nationalist leaders.

The most important nationalist leader was Ho Chi Minh, who was born into a traditional scholar's household in 1890. At the age of 15 he was sent to a French school in Hue. Thus, Ho had both a traditional Confucian and Western style of education. He left Vietnam when he was 21 to serve as a crew member of a French merchant ship. After odd jobs in England and France he became a well-known nationalist activist in socialist circles in Paris. In 1919 Ho appeared at the Versailles Conference (the post–World War I treaty meetings) with a petition demanding the right of self-determination and independence for his country. He joined the French Communist Party and became familiar with Marxist–Leninist ideology. Ho traveled to both Moscow and China to aid the organization of the communist movement in Vietnam. He organized programs for the study of Marxist–Leninist ideals in Moscow and China. Eventually, Ho was able to bring together disparate groups of communists in Vietnam, Cambodia, and Laos to establish the Indochinese Communist Party. The form of communist ideology promoted by Ho Chi Minh was thoroughly nationalistic. Ho, like Mao Zedong in China, adapted Marxist–Leninist ideology with traditional ideas from indigenous cultural traditions. Traditional Vietnamese and Confucian ideals and images were merged with communist notions. The idea of organizing the peasants (rather than an industrial proletariat) to carry out a revolution to restore communal land and traditional property rights within the villages resonated with many of the nationalist ideals. The first stage in bringing about this revolution was to rid Vietnam of French control.

Cambodian and Laotian anti-Western nationalist movements were also fomented by French colonialism. In contrast to the French colonial projects in Vietnam that ushered in major economic and education changes, both Cambodia and Laos were viewed as "backwater" areas that served to contain British interests. The French focused on Vietnam as the center of capitalist development and their "civilizing mission" (*mission civilisatrice*). The Khmer and Laotian populations were perceived to be childlike and lazy by the French. Vietnamese civil administrators were appointed as officials throughout these regions of French Indochina. In Cambodia a peasant resistance movement stimulated by high taxes, the killing of a French tax collector, and eventually a widespread monk's rebellion marked the first phases of a nationalist movement. There were some early nationalist movements led by ethnic minorities in Laos against the French. However, the nationalist movements in Cambodia and Laos did not gain momentum until after the Japanese occupation and World War II.

In both Burma and French Indochina nationalist movements developed as a result of grass-roots movements against European colonial interests. Siamese or Thai nationalism, however, emerged as a top-down movement aimed at unification of the country. Gradually, as the Siamese state developed from its centers in Sukothai, Ayudhaya, and finally Bangkok, it incorporated bordering regions in the north, northeast, and south. Within these different geographic regions were people who were different ethnically, linguistically, and culturally from the ethnic "Tai." For example, in the south there were a large number of Malay-speaking people. Even within the capital city of Bangkok ethnic minorities such as Indians and Chinese resided among the majority Tai. Despite the ethnic diversity within the country Siamese nationalist leaders and state officials promoted a uniform ethnic nationalist identity based on notions of race, culture, and traditional conceptions of the Indianized state. The Siamese monarch, King Vajiravudh, son of Chulalongkorn, promoted what has been referred to as the Three Pillars of national and ethnic identity for the country.[19]

The Three Pillars of this Siamese collective identity consisted of the "Nation" (*chat*), "Religion" (*sasana*), and "Monarchy" (*phramahaksat*). This Siamese political and cultural code represented a symbol of a unified ethnic identity that was formulated to mediate the actual ethnic ambiguities and contradictions within the country. The first pillar, *chat*, derived from the Sanskrit–Hindi term *jati*, which translates roughly as "caste," is used by the Siamese majority to refer to birth, race, lineage, and origin. Historically, the second pillar, *sasana*, religion, was synonymous with Theravada Buddhism. The third pillar, *phramahakasat*, is an honorific term for "king" or "monarch" and embodies the vertical or hierarchical symbolic relationship between the ruler and the people in Siamese society. The Three Pillars were cultivated as the basis of ethnic and national identity within Siamese society.

Later developments in Thai history provoked extreme nationalistic policies that were based on notions of race drawn from European and Japanese sources. During the years 1932–1941, government officials drew on racist and fascist ideas from Nazi Germany and Japan to promote nationalism in Thailand. The Thai race was conceptualized to be different from that of the Chinese, Indian, European, or American. There were specific behaviors and cultural conventions that were assumed to be associated with the Thai race. Thai culture and race (*Thai Rathaniyom*) and a cultural policy based upon Cultural Rules (*Kot Wattanatham*) were publicized and propagated through the education system and media. At this time, the name of the country was changed from *Siam* to *Thailand.* Part of the reason for this name change was to distinguish the "Thai race" from the Chinese and other ethnic minorities and to encourage a more unified basis for this nationalist movement. The promotion of "Thainess" emphasizing various behaviors and etiquette was used along with other national symbols such as the Three Pillars to emphasize an ethnically homogeneous society. Official legislation was passed to expand the use of the Thai language and reduce the use of other languages such as Chinese, Lao, Shan, and Malay within Thailand. All of these policies have had consequences for ethnic minorities in Thailand up to the present.

POST–WORLD WAR II NATIONALISM, INDEPENDENCE, AND REVOLUTIONARY MOVEMENTS

World War II accelerated the nationalist movements that were growing throughout mainland Southeast Asia. The rise of Japan as a military power in the region influenced many aspects of the indigenous nationalist movements. Prior to the outbreak of war, the Japanese campaigned to gain political support in Southeast Asia through their slogan "Asia for the Asiatics." This slogan resonated within many of the nationalist sentiments being expressed in French Indochina, British Burma, and in Thailand. However, as World War II progressed, many Burmese, Vietnamese, Cambodians, Laotians, and Thais were disillusioned by the Japanese occupation of these areas. When the Japanese drove out the British from Burma, the Burmese had expected immediate independence. However, the Japanese military forces mistreated the Burmese people with forced labor projects and an explicit disrespect for their religious and cultural traditions.

In French Indochina, the Vichy government in France (sponsored by the Nazi regime) enabled the Japanese to utilize the military, economic resources, and labor during the war. Ho Chi Minh's nationalist and communist campaign grew in response to the Japanese and French Vichy occupation. He founded a new organization, the Viet Minh, to drive out both the Japanese and French from Vietnam. Ho received financial and military support from the Allies, including the United States, to further his campaign. The extreme nationalistic Thai military rulers offered to cooperate with the Japanese during the war; however, many democratically oriented Thais opposed this policy of collaboration. A Free Thai movement was formed by these democrats that sponsored political activity aimed at driving the Japanese occupiers from Thailand.

Following World War II and the surrender of the Japanese, the people of mainland Southeast Asia hoped that their aspirations for decolonization and independence could be fulfilled. In Burma, the British insisted on a need for transition until an ordered system of government could be developed. Finally in 1948, Burma was granted independence paralleling the withdrawal of the British from its empire in India. Thailand's Free Thai democratic movement supported by the Allies was able to establish an independent democratic government in 1944. However, the nationalist aspirations of the people of French Indochina were frustrated. In 1945 Ho Chi Minh led his Viet Minh to the center of Vietnamese politics and proclaimed the Democratic Republic of Vietnam (DRV) drawing on language from the U.S. Declaration of Independence at a mass rally of a half-million people. The Western Allied powers meeting at Potsdam were to frustrate the aspirations of Ho and the DRV. They divided Vietnam at the 16th parallel between the north and the south. The north was to be occupied by Nationalist China and the south by the British. With British support the French were able to restore their colonial authority south of the 16th parallel. The French also reasserted its colonial authority in Cambodia and Laos. This turn of affairs would result in a disastrous war that would have wide-ranging consequences for all of mainland Southeast Asia.

Ho Chi Minh.

The Indochina War

With the return of the French as the colonial ruler of Indochina including Vietnam, Cambodia, and Laos, the Viet Minh led by Ho Chi Minh initiated guerilla warfare against their colonial rulers.[20] A developing split in the Vietnamese populace between communist and noncommunist supporters influenced political decision making. Ho and the Viet Minh tried to heal this split by announcing the dissolution of the Indochinese Communist Party. He signed an agreement with the French allowing them to displace the Chinese troops in North Vietnam. He made a famous statement at this time in an earthy fashion: "It is better to sniff the French dung for a while than to eat China's all our lives." Following the failure of negotiations with the French the guerilla campaign directed by Ho, General Giap, and the Viet Minh continued against the French. The French responded by brutally bombarding the Vietnamese quarter of Haiphong, killing over 6,000 people. The Viet Minh began to wage very effective guerilla warfare throughout all of Vietnam. This first Indochina war lasted from 1946 to 1954 and was ended with General Giap's triumph against the French forces at Dien Bien Phu. Following this defeat the beleaguered French troops were pulled out and the warring parties reached an accord in Geneva that Vietnam would be divided between the north and south at the 17th parallel. The Viet Minh would be established in the north, whereas the south would be ruled by a noncommunist government.

The Geneva settlement was a reflection of the intensification of the Cold War, the communist victory in China, and the outbreak of the Korean War in 1950. The United States viewed the fate of Indochina as central to the "containment" of an expansionist communist China and the Soviet Union. It was feared that a Viet Minh victory would threaten U.S. security by endangering Cambodia, Laos, Thailand, and the rest of Southeast Asia and that these countries would fall like a row of dominoes. This domino policy led the United States to support the French in their military efforts against the Viet Minh. Dissatisfied with the Geneva accords of 1954, the United States began to support the anticommunist Ngo Dinh Diem as the leader in South Vietnam. Diem, a Catholic, with U.S. support began to assert full authority over South Vietnam and declared it as the Republic of Vietnam in 1955 with its capital in Saigon. In North Vietnam, the Viet Minh and Ho implemented the collectivization of agriculture and intensified its campaign to reunify the country. There were elements of the Viet Minh (who were categorized as the Viet Cong by the U.S. military) in South Vietnam comprised of peasants, workers, intellectuals, and Buddhists along with other religious-based dissident groups who began to work against the Diem government. Diem, his wife Madame Nhu, and his family developed repressive policies against the dissident elements. The Catholic family's government was perceived to be corrupt and out of touch with the majority Buddhist Vietnamese populace. Some Buddhist monks doused themselves with gasoline in acts of self-immolation to protest against the Diem regime. Madame Nhu demonstrated her arrogance and crude understandings of these protests by publicly ridiculing these monks as "barbeque bonzes." By 1960, the Diem regime had alienated all of the major sections of the South Vietnamese population.

A protesting Buddhist monk on fire during the Vietnam war.

American military and political support had flowed to the Diem regime as an aspect of Cold War politics. In 1963, the Kennedy administration recognized that Diem did not have the wide support of the Vietnamese populace. Consequently, Kennedy and the CIA aided a coup that resulted in Diem's assassination and ushered in a series of military junta regimes propped up by American military support. Meanwhile, units of the North Vietnamese People's Army went to the south to maintain their effective guerilla tactics with the Viet Cong. The next year Lyndon Johnson exaggerated a minor skirmish between the North Vietnamese and the naval spy ship the U.S.S. *Maddox* as a pretext to get the U.S. Congress to pass the Gulf of Tonkin resolution, which gave the authority to the president to take all necessary measures to deal with North Vietnamese aggression. From 1964 to 1969, over 500,000 U.S. troops were gradually introduced into Vietnam and it had become an American war. By 1965, a series of U.S. bombing missions known as Operation Rolling Thunder were aimed at destroying the Ho Chi Minh Trail that linked the North Vietnamese military to the south. This aerial bombardment had the effect of driving hundreds of thousands of refugees into the cities and defoliating major areas of the forests. "Search and destroy" methods were used by U.S. ground troops in South Vietnamese villages to identify Viet Cong. These methods frequently backfired and alienated many of the indigenous population from the U.S. military. In February 1968, at the time of the Vietnamese New Year known as *Tet*, the North Vietnamese and Viet Cong launched a massive military offensive at the royal city of Hue. This Tet offensive, which involved the occupation of the U.S. embassy, demonstrated the ineffectiveness of the American bombing and military efforts on the North Vietnamese. From the time of the Tet offensive, the United States tried to extricate itself from the Vietnam War. Finally, after many battles, U.S. bombing missions, and years of negotiations between the United States and North Vietnam, a cease-fire agreement was signed in Paris in 1973.

The Vietnam War resulted in the death of 59,000 Americans and millions of killed, wounded, and displaced Vietnamese. The militarization of South Vietnam had created a society where graft, corruption, black markets, prostitution, and other problems flourished. The North Vietnamese took over the south in 1975, renamed the city of Saigon *Ho Chi Minh City*, and formed a government called the Socialist Republic of Vietnam. But the war had spilled over into areas of mainland Southeast Asia. The country of Laos was caught up in the hostilities. The Viet Minh had sponsored the development of a nationalist and revolutionary group known as the Pathet Lao to help maintain the Ho Chi Minh Trail that ran partly through Laos. South Vietnam and the U.S. CIA tried to stifle the Pathet Lao through military incursions, secret bombings, and the development of a secret army recruited from among the hill peoples known as the Hmong. The Hmong of Laos and Thailand were drawn into the international opium drug trade. The Hmong people who were growing opium for their cash crop were recruited and trained by the CIA as clandestine guerrilla warriors against the North Vietnamese military and paramilitary forces operating in Laos. The Hmong financed their guerrilla campaign against the North Vietnamese through the cash-cropping and trade of opium, which was acknowledged by the CIA. By the time of the Vietnamese–American cease-fire agreement, Laos was the most heavily bombed country, per capita, in the history of warfare.[21] This resulted in more internal political support from the peasantry for the Pathet Lao in their efforts against the U.S. and South Vietnamese military. In addition, the Pathet Lao received massive amounts of volunteers from North Vietnam. In 1975, the Laotian government fell entirely to the Pathet Lao and established a communist regime, the Lao People's Democratic Government.

The Killing Fields

Cambodia also became a battleground during the Vietnam War. The nationalist leader Prince Norodom Sihanouk had declared independence from France during the Japanese occupation in 1945. Formerly known as an international playboy, Sihanouk became a serious nationalist who desperately tried to retain Cambodian independence from the French and to keep his country neutral and out of the wider conflagration of the Indochinese war. During the 1960s some of the Viet Minh had infilitrated procommunist groups in Cambodia. To suppress communist activity that supported supply routes on the Ho Chi Minh Trail, the U.S. military began a secret bombing campaign in Cambodian territory, in a clear violation of its sovereignty and neutrality. This bombing campaign along with South Vietnamese and American military activities drove many Cambodian peasants into a communist group known as the Khmer Rouge (Red Khmer). A political split developed in Cambodia between the anticommunist factions and the Khmer Rouge who conducted guerilla operations against Sihanouk and the anticommunists. In 1970, while Sihanouk was away at a diplomatic meeting aimed at reducing support for the Khmer Rouge, Lon Nol, an anticommunist leader, led a coup deposing him. Predictably the United States gave immediate military aid and political assistance to Lon Nol's anticommunist government. However, this U.S. political support and increased bombing and military incursions into Cambodia resulted in a wide-scale civil war between the anticommunist and Khmer Rouge forces.

The Khmer Rouge continued to recruit refugees and other peasants into their fold to maintain their effective guerilla campaign against the politically corrupt and inept military of Lon Nol's anticommunist regime. At the same time as the fall of Saigon in 1975, the Khmer Rouge marched into the capital of Phnom Penh, bringing down the Lon Nol regime and changing the country's name to *Kampuchea,* calling itself the Democratic Republic of Kampuchea (DRK). Between 1975 and 1978, the Khmer Rouge under the leadership of Pol Pot implemented a social revolution that resulted in the death of nearly two million people in Kampuchea. Pol Pot (a pseudonym for Saloth Sar, 1928–1998) had studied in Paris and had become a Marxist and then a Maoist. He was determined to carry out a radical project that entailed the abolition of the royal monarchy, the closing of schools and monasteries, and the evacuation of two million residents from the cities and their relocation into large-scale agricultural collectives in the rural areas. Intellectuals were tortured, imprisoned, and murdered along with suspected dissidents or ethnic minorities such as Chinese, Vietnamese, Cham, or others in a campaign that came to be called "the Killing Fields."[22]

POSTCOLONIAL CONTEMPORARY DEVELOPMENTS

The global context of the Cold War has had dramatic consequences for the nationalist, independence, and revolutionary movements in mainland Southeast Asia. Although the country of Burma was more distant from the center of the Vietnam War, the consequences of Cold War politics had an impact on its postcolonial developments. After independence from England in 1948, Burma faced ethnic succession movements from the minorities on its borders. These ethnic minorities such as the Chin, Kachin, Karen, and the Shan were not willing to be politically dominated by the majority Burmese populations. They were well organized and supported by either the communist insurgents or anticommunist groups. This continuing ethnic problem coupled with bureaucratic corruption and economic decline resulted in the emergence of a military government led by General Ne Win. In 1962, Ne Win led a military coup and ushered in military rule that continues until the present. This military government renamed the country *Myanmar* and rejected a Western model of economic and political development; instead it pursued an isolationist policy that separated the country from the global economy. This military government now known as State Law and Order Restoration (SLORC) has suffocated the Burmese economy and disabled any efforts toward democratic reforms. Aung San Suu Kyi (pronounced "ahng sahn suu chee"), a daughter of an important nationalist leader, has attempted to shame SLORC and the military government by leading a strong democratic movement. She has been imprisoned a number of times in Myanmar and received the Noble Peace Prize in 1991 for her heroic efforts. Many Burmese see her as the only hope for democratic processes to be implemented in the future.[23]

The Killing Fields resulting in millions of deaths in Kampuchea, created indirectly through Cold War and nationalist politics, had stunned the international community. Provoked by this holocaust and the attempts of genocide against the Vietnamese by the Khmer Rouge, Vietnamese troops invaded Kampuchea in 1978. During this period some 600,000 refugees fled to the Thai border to escape conflict and terror.

The Vietnamese installed Hun Sen as prime minister of the People's Republic of Kampuchea (PRK). The Khmer Rouge, a royalist party organized by Sihanouk, and the Hun Sen military competed for power throughout the 1980s. U.N. intervention in 1991 brought together these competing factions into a coalitional government, but it only lasted a number of years before Hun Sen launched a coup against the royalist faction then led by Prince Ranariddh (a son of Sihanouk). Hun Sen allowed democratic elections in 1998, but some democratic opposition groups contested the victory of his government. Eventually, the country's name was restored as *Cambodia* (pronounced by the Khmer as "Kampuchea") and was admitted to the Association of Southeast Asian Nations (ASEAN) in 1999, which has restored some of the confidence in the political stability of a troubled nation. In October 2004 the son of the former king Norodom Sihanouk, Norodom Sihamoni, was sworn in as king of Cambodia with an elaborate Buddhist ceremony. This event signals a return to a more traditional connection with royalty and religious authority as a means of reestablishing a sense of social and political order to a country wracked by tragedy and factional violence for many years.

Laos was spared the tragic bloodbath of Cambodia after the victory of its communist government led by the Pathet Lao in 1975. The Pathet Lao government launched a series of ambitious programs to reorganize the economy and education system according to socialist policies. To develop its socialist economic and educational projects, it relied heavily on the Vietnamese and Soviet Union patrons and planners. These socialist plans that included the collectivization of agriculture were rejected by many of the peasants. Although literacy increased in the countryside with educational developments, the overall economic plans were ineffective in increasing the standard of living in Laos. Also, as did other communist governments in Vietnam and Kampuchea, the Laos government restricted Buddhism and traditional ceremonies, viewing these as wasteful relics of an ancient past. These harsh economic, political, and religious policies led hundreds of thousands of peasant farmers, teachers, government officials, skilled technocrats, and others to flee as refugees crossing the Thai border. Eventually, in the late 1970s and 1980s, the Laotian government recognized the ineffectiveness of its socialist programs. It instituted a New Economic Policy (NEP) that returned land to the peasantry and allowed for small-scale capitalism and private investment. In an attempt to break away from their dependence on Soviet and Vietnamese aid and planning, Laos has opened up the country to international trade and tourism. Yet, so far Laos still remains a small isolated country that is struggling with procommunist conservative bureaucratic leaders and anticommunist political factions and an impoverished citizenry.

Ruled by Ho Chi Minh and the communist government, Vietnam faced tremendous difficulties as the legacies of a long war and destruction exacted its toll. The government based in Hanoi acted quickly to implement socialism into the southern economy of Vietnam. Private enterprise was abolished, land was collectivized, and small- and large-scale businesses were nationalized and controlled by the government. The ethnic Chinese, a population of close to a million people, who had dominated the South Vietnamese commercial sector were persecuted and driven out of the country. The Vietnamese invasion of Kampuchea in 1978 to reduce the Khmer Rouge genocidal policies was a costly military venture. Receiving approximately $1 billion in Soviet economic aid annually during the 1980s, many Vietnamese soon recognized that it was held hostage by another foreign imperial influence. By the time of the mid-1980s, the Vietnamese economy was a basketcase with increasing food shortages, triple-digit inflation, and economic underdevelopment. In 1986 the Sixth Party Congress of the Vietnam Worker's Party adopted an economic policy known as *doi moi*, which involved the decollectivization of agriculture, the development of an export-oriented rice and coffee production tied to the global market, international tourism, and the recruitment of multinational corporations to offshore manufacturing projects. However, this economic liberalization was not accompanied by political liberalization. Vietnamese conservative communists who had fought alongside Ho Chi Minh since the 1940s were unwilling to relinquish their bureaucratic control of the political system. Political corruption and bureaucratic control of economic investment and the effects of the Asian economic crisis of 1997 continue to plague economic and political development in Vietnam.

Cold War politics and the Vietnam War had major consequences for the country of Thailand. Beginning in 1947, a succession of military governments ruled until 1973. During the Cold War the United States gave generous military and financial support to these military governments to shore up resistance to both internal and external communist elements. During the Vietnam War Thailand was used as a base for U.S. military to launch their bombing missions and other military operations. The military governments provided some stability and allowed for capitalist economic developments in Thailand, but they abrogated any type of democratic rights for the population. Thailand was also an area for rest and recreation (R & R) for the U.S. military during the Vietnam War. Prostitution, gambling, crime, sexual slavery, and rampant political corruption developed within this time period. Because of these problems, in 1973 near the end of the Vietnam War, massive political demonstrations led by students resulted in a democratic election of a civilian government. However, this civilian government faced increasing economic and labor problems, factional splits among politicians, and armed communist insurgency movements sponsored by Laos, Kampuchea, and Vietnam. The civilian government lasted only three years and was followed by another succession of military governments. Again, in 1994, an enormous number of workers, peasants, and middle-class students and intellectuals mounted political demonstrations against the military regime. This reflected the reality that many Thais were rejecting the authoritarian-style politics of the military regime. After these mass demonstrations in 1994, a new democratically-based constitution was legislated in Thailand. Most recently, dissatisfied with the military, the corrupt civilian politicians in the government bureaucracy, and the decline in the economy since 1997, the Thai people elected a communications business leader and multimillionaire, Thaksin Shinawatra, for their prime minister.

DEMOGRAPHY AND THE ECONOMY

The last few decades have witnessed unprecedented demographic, technological, and economic transformations in mainland Southeast Asia. Some of these changes have been hinted at within the historical materials presented. Myanmar (Burma), Laos, Cambodia, and Vietnam have had traumatic historical experiences engendered by warfare, rigid governmental policies, and globalization processes. These countries can be classified as low-income countries based on per capita income, increasing populations, and meager economic development. The per capita income for Vietnam is $2,100 per year and the economic growth rate measured in gross domestic product (GDP) is 4.7 percent. The respective figures for Cambodia are $1,500 and GDP growth at 5.3 percent per year; for Laos they are $1,630 and GDP growth at 5 percent per year; and for Myanmar (Burma) they are $1,500 and GDP growth at 2.3 percent per year. Thailand, a country that has been open to the global economy, market capitalism, and has contained population growth, has a per capita income of $6,600 per year and a GDP growth rate at 1.4 percent, which makes it a middle-level-income country. (These figures compare with a per capita income in the United States of $40,100 and GDP growth rate at 2.9 percent as of 2004.) However, within all of these mainland Southeast Asian countries there are considerable inequalities among groups and regions with respect to income. Poverty in both urban and rural areas is a fundamental problem for all of these countries, although Thailand has experienced substantial declines in the proportion of their populations living in poverty compared to the other countries.

According to the most recent statistics as of 2003, Vietnam has the largest population in mainland Southeast Asia at approximately 81 million. Thailand has about 62 million, Myanmar (Burma) about 42 million, Cambodia about 12.8 million, and Laos has about 5.7 million. Cambodia and Laos have the highest annual growth rates in their populations well over 2 percent, whereas Myanmar (Burma) is growing slowly at 0.56 percent, and Vietnam at about 1.4 percent. Thailand has slowed its annual growth rate from 3 percent in 1970, and presently the population growth is close to zero population growth (ZPG). The Thai government reduced its population growth through intensive efforts at providing education and supplying birth control methods in both urban and rural areas. In no other country in Southeast Asia (or the world) has the population growth rate (negative 67 percent) dropped so precipitously as in Thailand. The Thai government is concerned presently that its population control methods have been too effective because there are not enough children to keep the population from shrinking.[24]

Life expectancy, mortality, and fertility statistics indicate substantial demographic differences among these mainland Southeast Asian countries. At the low end the life expectancy in Laos is 54 years with an infant mortality rate of 91 deaths per 1,000 live births per year. In Cambodia the respective figures for the same indexes are 57 and 64 per 1,000; Myanmar (Burma) is 61 and 49 per 1,000; Vietnam is 67 and 38 per 1,000; and Thailand is at the high end with 69 and 30 per 1,000. The legacy of war, genocide, conflict, and dislocation is evident within Cambodia in its very high levels of mortality. However, as expected within primarily rural agricultural countries such as Cambodia and Laos, fertility rates remain very high, resulting in high annual growth rates. The same pattern is also evident in Vietnam as it recovers from its wartime experience when there was a shortage of males; however, more recently, since the 1980s the population has been growing rapidly. Presently, all of the governments in these countries have developed active family-planning policies to reduce their recent growth. For many of these countries, Thailand represents a model for containing population growth.

Country	Population (2003)	Population Growth (% per year)	Life Expectancy	Infant Mortality Rate (deaths per 1,000 live births per year)	GDP (%)	Per Capita Income
Myanmar (Burma)	42 million	0.56%	61 years	49	2.3%	$1,500
Thailand	62 million	0.88	69 years	30	1.4	6,600
Laos	5.7 million	2.5	54 years	91	5	1,630
Cambodia	12.8 million	2.24	57 years	64	5.3	1,500
Vietnam	81 million	1.4	67 years	38	4.7	2,100

The distribution of population in mainland Southeast Asia is somewhat dependent upon the sophistication of the agricultural technology and capacities for economic growth. Although the highest population densities are within the large primate cities such as Bangkok, Hanoi, or Yangon (Rangoon in Myanmar), there are wide discrepancies in population densities in rural regions. The population of Bangkok is close to 10 million, Hanoi is close to 4 million, and Yangon has 4.5 million. As expected, the highest population densities in the rural areas are within the agricultural plains that adjoin the major river systems. The Chao Phraya River in Thailand, the Mekong River in Vietnam, and the Irrawaddy River in Myanmar (Burma) have the densest populations in the rural areas. These alluvial river areas contain fertile soil conditions and an ideal climate for highly productive wet-rice agriculture. Therefore, these areas allowed high concentrations of rural agricultural populations to grow over time. However, within the past few decades higher fertility levels and rural population growth in these areas has outpaced the amount of land available for agricultural production. Consequently, high rates of rural-to-urban migration have occurred throughout mainland Southeast Asia based on both push and pull factors. Push factors include war, political instability, and shortages of land for young people. Pull factors have included promises of better economic opportunities and political freedom in certain cities such as Bangkok. Thailand has the highest percentage of its population (one-third) residing in central Thailand and near its capital Bangkok. Bangkok has become the most sprawling primate city in mainland Southeast Asia.

Despite the growth of major cities in mainland Southeast Asia, agriculture continues to employ the bulk of the population in most of the countries. The exception is Thailand, where agricultural employment has decreased from 40 percent in 1960 to only 13 percent in recent years. On the other hand, agricultural land actually increased by almost one-third in Thailand, primarily as a result of forest clearance and the Green Revolution. The Green Revolution involves the adoption of hybrid genetically modified strains of crops, the use of chemical fertilizers and pesticides, the utilization of large areas of land for massive irrigation projects, and expensive farm equipment to cultivate and harvest crops. This has resulted in increased yields of crops and multiple cropping for export cash crops produced for the world market. Obviously only very wealthy farmers can adopt Green Revolution technologies, which reduces the need for large numbers of people to cultivate the land. Wealthy farmers who sometimes merge to become corporate agricultural entities purchase land from peasants and small farmers who can no longer be competitive in the global economy.

This commercialization of agriculture from a low-tech peasant system to a high-tech Green Revolution system has often led to economic and social differentiation of the rural communities, polarizing them between wealthy elite farmers and tenant farmers, or in many cases landless agricultural laborers. Less endowed farmers often go into debt to afford the expensive new equipment and the reliance on chemicals. This has increased rural unemployment and landlessness. As a result of these changes the Thai government has been actively engaged in more equity-based rural development strategies to help alleviate rural poverty and landlessness by attempting to stimulate rural industrialization projects to create jobs to absorb the surplus labor. Otherwise, many of the landless laborers will migrate to the crowded conditions of Bangkok. Some economists view Thailand as a leader compared with some other mainland Southeast Asian countries with respect to the adoption of the Green Revolution and its incorporation into the global capitalist global economy; however, the consequences of this rapid development is sometimes painful for the rural farmers.

Just as some economists perceive Thailand as advanced compared to any other mainland Southeast Asian country in the commercialization of agriculture, it is also viewed as being advanced in the integration of its industrial base with the global economy. In the early 1990s, the Thai economy was fueled by surging export commodities and internal domestic demand for its consumer products. Textiles and clothing were the top exports, but computers and other electronic goods were also important. Industrialization was spurred by many multinationals relocating in Bangkok and surrounding communities. Japanese multinationals were among the first to set up manufacturing in Thailand in the 1970s and 1980s. Other multinationals from Western countries followed. In 1996, General Motors opened a $750 million assembly plant south of Bangkok. Ford and Mazda and other multinationals developed their own plants. The Thai government offered strong financial incentive programs, low taxes, a strong domestic market, low labor costs, a government-financed automotive training institute, a reorganized port facility, a mass rapid transit system, and a new international airport to draw in General Motors, Ford, Mazda, and other multinationals.

The less developed economies of Vietnam, Cambodia, and Laos have also been trying to attract foreign investment and multinational corporations to spark industrial growth. These countries have embarked upon programs to reform their former socialist-based economies to stimulate industrial growth, especially for low-labor-cost manufacturing in textile, clothing, and shoe industries. In the 1980s Nike set up a factory in Ho Chi Minh City paying workers $10 a week. All of these former socialist countries have been involved in reprivatizing their state-run enterprises. However, these countries need major developments in their infrastructure such as roads, bridges, railways, and other transportation, which were neglected by the French colonial regime and devastated by the Indochina War. Even Myanmar, which tried to abstain from integrating itself within the global capitalist economy, has been trying to increase its foreign investments. However, due to international sanctions against the repressive government of SLORC, Myanmar has fallen behind its Southeast Asian neighbors in industrial growth. As of October 2004, a new Prime Minister, Lieutenant Soe Win, was elected. The international community awaits the development of a more open, democratic, and less oppressive government.

The neoliberal economic policies and integration into the global market economy by all of these mainland Southeast Asian countries have resulted in both stable and unstable consequences with their development. The Green Revolution and the focus on labor-intensive export-oriented production contributed to economic growth, but also resulted in negative consequences such as increasing internal economic and social stratification between the wealthy and poor. In addition, the global market economy began to disrupt local and national economies in these mainland Southeast Asian countries as of 1997.

In 1997, a major fiscal crisis began to influence all of these countries, including others in Asia. Since Thailand was the most integrated into the global economy, it began to feel the pains of the Asian fiscal crisis before the other countries. As discussed, Thailand's economy was booming in the early 1990s. Along with this booming economy, the wealthy Thai elite made deals to obtain loans from foreign banks to invest in real estate development projects, golf courses, and tourist industries. This economic development has been referred to as "golf-course capitalism." When the Asian fiscal crisis hit, the value of the Thai currency or *baht* dropped from 25 to $1 (U.S.) to 55 to $1 (U.S.). Elite investors were unable to pay back loans to foreign banks. This rippled throughout the Thai economy causing major inflation, massive unemployment, and a rapid decline in both agricultural and industrial sectors.

The 1997 Asian fiscal crisis influenced all of the economies of mainland Southeast Asia. Vietnam was forced to devalue its currency in 1998, resulting in slow economic growth. Farmers began to riot in the countryside and a widespread dissatisfaction toward government officials developed. The International Monetary Fund (IMF) and the World Bank intervened in Southeast Asian countries to develop solutions for the economies of the region. These international organizations representing the interests of global international capitalism dictated policies that involved reorganizing banks, privatizing government-controlled facilities, reducing government-funded social programs, and restructuring loans to pay back the investments in real estate, agricultural, and other industrial projects. In the socialist countries such as Vietnam the conservative bureaucrats began to blame the global capitalist system for their internal economic problems. Many leaders and other grass-roots organizations and NGOs (nongovernmental organizations) perceived the IMF and World Bank as aiding the wealthy elites at the expense of the farmers, working class, and poor. The IMF and World Bank defended themselves by saying their policies focused on reforming the financial system and the closing of inefficient and corrupt practices of the wealthy elites. As seen in other chapters in this text, the results of the Asian fiscal crisis have created economic stagnation and underdevelopment throughout East and Southeast Asia.

SOCIAL STRUCTURE, THE FAMILY, AND GENDER

Social structure and family patterns and practices differ widely among many of the people of mainland Southeast Asia. The major difference is between the hill peoples of mainland Southeast Asia who exhibit a tremendous diversity in social structure, kinship, and family relations, and the lowland or valley peoples such as the Burmese, the Khmer of Cambodia, and the Tai of Thailand and Laos. A second major difference is found between the Indianized valley peoples mentioned earlier and the sinicized valley peoples of Vietnam. We will discuss the hill peoples in the section on ethnic relations below. In this section we will focus on the differences in social structure, kinship, and family between the Indianized and sinicized valley peoples. The family, kinship, and social structural characteristics of the valley peoples of Myanmar, Cambodia, Laos, and Thailand has been referred to as "cognatic" or "bilateral." This means that both the male and female lines are relevant in determining descent and that each individual regards relatives on both his or her mother's and father's side as belonging to the same family group. The most common type of family associated with bilateral descent in this area is the nuclear family consisting of husband, wife, and unmarried children residing within a household. Beyond the nuclear family are relatives that are recognized by people on both sides of the family and are usually referred to as *kindreds.* These bilateral kindreds often provide cooperative labor-exchange groupings in wet-rice cultivation and other reciprocal economic activities in the rural areas of mainland Southeast Asia.[25] Although patrilineal rules play a role in determining the line of descent within the royal families of these peoples (matrilineal descent and matrilocal residence also has been described for some regions), the pattern of bilateral kinship tends to be the predominant pattern among the people of Myanmar, Kampuchea, Laos, and Thailand.

Among the sinicized lowland peoples of Vietnam, a strong patrilineal descent system developed along with other Confucian-based characteristics of Chinese culture. This Confucian model was adopted as the ideal type of family structure by the Vietnamese elite and was imposed on what was originally a bilateral system of family and descent. The ideal kin group in Vietnam became the patriarchal extended family that may include three or four generations.

However, in Vietnam most of the families were actually stem families that included two or more married couples of different generations. In some rural areas, neighboring households in a village are made up of closely related patrilineal kinship groups. In addition to the patriarchal stem families and lineages, some of the Vietnamese also had a strong allegiance to the clan unit based on historical and genealogical ties of blood and ancestry. These clans, as in some areas of China, would be associated with specific surnames and would be headed by a senior male.

Traditionally, the Vietnamese household would have an honored place reserved for the ancestor's altar and ancestral tablets. In some villages, there were separate ancestral shrines maintained by wealthier clans. Just as in China, during the New Year's holiday, Vietnamese family members would make memorial offerings to their clan ancestor and have a communal feast. In South Vietnam, succession of the family estate would go to the youngest son (ultimogeniture), rather than to the eldest son (primogeniture) as in China and in North Vietnam. However, in both North and South Vietnam, the eldest son inherited the rights and responsibilities of caring for the ancestral shrine.

Marriage practices also differed between the lowland peoples of the Indianized cultural regions and the lowland Vietnamese peoples. In Myanmar, Thailand, and Laos individuals usually chose their own spouses after a period of elaborate courtship. (In traditional Cambodia, marriages were typically arranged by the parents.) Courtship is usually initiated by the boy or at times a go-between is used to set up meeting for the couple. Some individuals consult astrological horoscopes to assist them in choosing their spouses. Parental approval is usually sought by the couple and parents of both families often get together to negotiate the cost of the wedding and the amount of wealth to be given to the married couple. Typically, the parents agree to an amount of bridewealth to be transferred from the groom's family to the bride's family. In Burma, a customary dowry was given to the groom's family from the bride's family. In all of these regions, the parents preferred their children to choose a partner of similar or superior socioeconomic status. Though the marriage practices were based on voluntary choice, the parents were always concerned that their children make a "good marriage." However, if the parents did not approve of the wedding, elopement was found to be quite common in these countries. Traditionally, some of the wealthy males in Burma practiced polygyny, marriage with several women. Also, although a 1935 law in Thailand outlawed polygyny, presently wealthy Thai males will sometimes take a "minor wife" (*mia noi*), a practice that usually leads to distress for the first wife. Although the rate of divorce is relatively low, divorce is in principle a relatively simple affair for couples in these bilateral Southeast Asian families.

As would be expected, in contrast to the marriage practices of Burma, Thailand, Laos, and Kampuchea, the sinicized Vietnamese marriage norms and rules are much different. The Confucian-based model of the patriarchal extended family, patrilineages, and clans influenced the marriage practices of the Vietnamese. Marriage was rigidly controlled and arranged by the members of the patriarchal extended family, patrilineage, and clan. Marriages were arranged, and for the woman, marriage represented an official transfer of loyalty from her father's family to that of her husband. Patrilocal residence was enforced and the new daughter-in-law would be under the control of her husband's paternal kin, especially her new mother-in-law. As in China, a dowry was expected to be given to the groom's family by the bride's family. In practice, however, in Vietnam the dowry customs were more loosely structured than in China and the dowry wealth was never completely merged with the husband's wealth. In the case of a husband's death or divorce, the wife and her family would retain rights of access to the dowry. Another difference between the Vietnamese and strictly Confucian model is that in some cases there were intraclan marriages. Marriage between couples with the same surname often took place in Vietnam. Overall, the Vietnamese never followed the Confucian mode of patrilineal descent rules and norms rigidly. For example, in northern and central Vietnam women retained rights to property and land and sometimes participated in clan decision making. Some households included sons-in-law, which meant that in some cases there was matrilocal residence after marriage. Undoubtedly, this reflected the earlier forms of bilateral descent that were in effect prior to the sinification of Vietnam.

Globalization, rapid urbanization, and other social and economic changes that have occurred throughout mainland Southeast Asia have influenced the form of the family and marriage practices. As methods of birth control and family planning have been encouraged by governments to reduce population, the typical family has become smaller. There has been a shift from the stem or extended families toward the predominance of the nuclear family, especially evident within the urban areas. This shift is associated not only with increased urbanization, but also the spread of universal education, the reduction of child labor, increases in geographical mobility in which children are no longer living in the same region as their parents, and a transformation of the family as a unit of production to a family of consumption. Of course, this change is more fundamental in countries such as Thailand which is more integrated with the global economy. In Thailand, modern government welfare agencies perform many of the functions formerly provided by the family. Also, with new economic opportunities available for women outside the home, Thai women can find economic security outside marriage. This has accelerated the downsizing of the family unit and has led many young educated women in Thailand to remain single for longer periods. Although globalization, industrialization, and the rural to urban migration associated with them have affected the social structure and family, the family unit remains resilient in all of the areas of mainland Southeast Asia.

In traditional societies in mainland Southeast Asia men and women were assigned specific roles, and the status of women tended to be associated with reproduction and their domestic duties within the household. However, as we will see, especially with respect to the Indianized region of mainland Southeast Asia, the status of women was not as low or as oppressive as it was in East or South Asia. Anthropologist Robert Winzeler has offered a tantalizing explanation as to why there was relative equality between men and women in these areas of Southeast Asia based on the shortage of labor and the large areas of wet-rice cultivatable land, bilateral descent, and the lack of strong centralized states.[26] Winzeler notes that traditionally in Southeast Asia, men and women complemented one another and appear to be mutually supportive in the production of wet-rice agriculture, compared to other regions of Asia. Although men prepare the fields for wet rice, women often do the actual planting of rice and are symbolically associated with fertility. Bilateral descent and the predominance of independent nuclear families that owned and worked their own land created conditions that allowed women to participate more directly in wet-rice agriculture. The bilateral descent system emphasized the equal importance of relatives on both the mother's side and the father's side, in comparison to the patrilineal descent patterns of China or India. The bilateral system of inheritance provided for children with equal shares going to both males and females. And, the states or governments of mainland Southeast Asia did not interfere directly with the rules and norms of the family and social structure. Thus, in contrast to the Western stereotype of Asian women being unequal to men, at least in the Indianized areas of mainland Southeast

Asia women are not generally considered the "weaker sex."

Even in the Indianized countries of mainland Southeast Asia, religious and other cultural factors influenced the status of women. The countries of Myanmar, Thailand, Kampuchea, and Laos are where the Theravada Buddhist religious tradition took root. Though male and female children are treated equally in most circumstances, within the Theravada Buddhist tradition, women are defined as lower status creatures because they cannot become monks, which is a high-status category. Women can become nuns (*mae chii*) in the Theravada Buddhist tradition, but cannot achieve the higher status of a monk. Anthropologist Thomas Kirsch has argued that Buddhist culture motivated males to participate in high-status roles such as the monastic organization or government service, whereas females were allowed to adapt to other nongovernmental economic roles such as market sellers or other business activities.[27] Presently in Thailand many females are employed in many nonagricultural economic activities including working in multinational factories, or as clerks, teachers, nurses, and in professional and managerial roles. In fact, following the economic boom of the 1980s and 1990s a high percentage of CEOs in Thai corporations are women. Also, female participation in the workforce is 70 percent in Thailand, higher than that of many industrial countries. Women have had the right to vote in Thailand since 1932, and women from the urban elite have often been active politically. In addition, some Thai women have been able to increase their religious status by becoming meditation teachers in which they are not viewed simply as female but as people who are transcending the categorical distinctions of "male" and "female."[28]

Despite the success of women in Thailand there been some negative trends in gender equity and development. Many Thai female workers have to work in the low-wage, labor-intensive industries such as textiles, clothing, and electronic assembly. Employers hire young females to retain loyal, submissive, and compliant workers in these low-wage industries. Working for $4 or $5 per day, these women find it difficult to achieve any economic security and stability. In addition, a number of Thai women have become involved in prostitution, which has resulted in a high rate of HIV/AIDs infection in the country.[29] The Thai government passed a Prostitution Prohibition Act in 1960, but it created many legislative loopholes that encouraged the development of a sex tourism industry. Prostitution has always been an indigenous feature of Thai life; many Thai males were and are expected to visit prostitutes as an informal rite of passage.[30] Thai males continue to be the largest clientele for the prostitutes in Thailand. However, the sex tourist–oriented prostitution first developed in the 1960s when it became popularized by the R & R activities of some 70,000 U.S. GIs serving in the Vietnam War. As the demand increased for prostitution during this period, many Thai women migrated from rural areas to Bangkok and other cities to enhance their families' incomes. Following the Vietnam War, various international sex tourist industries emerged to attract males from Europe, Japan, and other areas to Thailand; many of these men became involved in the illegal trafficking of Thai women for the sex industry in other countries. Since the 1980s, this sex tourism has led directly to the HIV/AIDs epidemic that has devastated many lives within Thailand. However, in the 1990s after recognizing an HIV/AIDs crisis, the Thai government and NGO activists launched an effective campaign that has become an international model of prevention and control of HIV/AIDs.

In contrast to the relative equality of the males and females in the Indianized countries of mainland Southeast Asia, the Confucian-based culture created conditions of inequality for many Vietnamese women. As the Vietnamese elite absorbed the Confucian patterns for establishing the household and family life, women began to be perceived as inferior in status to men. The Confucian ideal emphasized that when the husband of the patriarchal family died, the eldest son assumed authority and the mother was supposed to obey her son. Women had very few rights outside their relationship with their fathers, husbands, or sons. The postresidence marital rule of patrilocality meant that the wife would be under the control of her husband's family and patrilineage. Political leadership within the capital cities and in traditional rural villages was invested in men. Women were supposed to be confined to domestic roles and child care within the home. However, as mentioned, in actuality the gender practices in Vietnam differed from the Confucian ideal. In Vietnam some women did retain rights to land and property from their father's family. It appears that only within the Vietnamese elite groups was the Confucian patriarchal ideal adhered to rigidly. After the Vietnam War and the establishment of Communist Party rule there was an attempt to reform the traditional Confucian attitudes toward women. Women were praised and rewarded for their efforts during the nationalist struggle and revolutionary war. To celebrate the achievements of women, Hanoi has established a museum for women that highlights the importance of their role in society. Rights to divorce for both men and women were established under the communist regime. In addition, over one hundred Vietnamese women are now serving as legislative deputies in the National Assembly. [31]

ETHNIC RELATIONS

So far in this chapter, we have been emphasizing the culture and history of the valley peoples of mainland Southeast Asia. In this section, we will examine some of the ethnographic research on the hill peoples and other minorities of mainland Southeast Asia. As mentioned earlier, the hill peoples of this region practice swidden or slash and burn agriculture as the basis of their subsistence. This cultivation method involves cutting or "slashing" the vegetation and allowing it to dry before it is to be burned. The technology used in swidden agriculture has remained simple. Knives and axes are used to slash the fields and harvest the crops. Burning the leaves results in an ash that provides a natural fertilizer for the soil. The cleared area is then planted with a diversity of crops including "dry rice" (growing rice on terraced hill areas, rather than wet padi rice in the valleys), beans, tuber and root crops, chili peppers, squash, herbs, and maize. The diversity of crops grown serves as a form of insurance against risks of pests or disease from wiping out one particular crop. The crop yields are usually high during the first several years after slashing and burning, but they decline as soil nutrients become exhausted. After the exhaustion of the soil, the hill peoples allow the fields to remain fallow for several years before returning to cultivate them again. In the past, as small fields were cultivated in any one year, the people usually were able to clear another open field and shift their crops to another location. Thus, swidden agriculture was integrated within the natural ecological diversity of the tropical forest regions. However, as populations have grown among these upland peoples, there has been concern that the environments are becoming degraded due to deforestation and soil exhaustion.

The hill regions of Myanmar are an area that has attracted the attention of many anthropological research projects. Edmund Leach, a British anthropologist, completed a major ethnographic project among the Kachin people of what was then known as Burma from 1939 to 1945. As this period overlapped with World War II and the conflict between the British and Japanese in Burma, Leach was both an anthropologist and colonial officer. Leach's book *The Political Systems of Highland Burma* is widely acknowledged as a classic text that is still read by students of anthropology. The most significant lesson that Leach taught about the Kachin was that cultures of the hill peoples need to be understood in the context of wider sets of economic and political relationships. In other words, the lowland-valley civilizations and the colonial influences have had a dramatic impact on the hill peoples. In Leach's ethnography he demonstrates how the Kachin oscillated between a more democratic, egalitarian type of tribal society (*gumlao*) to that of a more autocratic, stratified "chiefdom" society (*gumsa*) based on interactions with lowland civilizations. Prior to Leach's ethnography, many anthropologists tended to describe these hill peoples as static and isolated societies. Leach challenged these earlier models, showing how the Kachin communities shifted back and forth over time between egalitarian political systems to more stratified forms modeled on the valley peoples. The Kachin people had contact with other valley peoples, primarily the Shan, who maintained a hierarchically-based Southeast Asian form of culture. Through an instrumental manipulation of symbols, marriage practices, and political alliances, the egalitarian Kachin transformed their society to become more like that of the stratified lowland peoples. Leach demonstrated that tribal societies of the hills cannot be analyzed unless they are viewed in relationship with the larger societies surrounding them.

One of the factors that triggered the transformation between egalitarian and stratified societies among the Kachin related to their social structure and marriage practices. Kachin society was comprised of different patrilineal descent groups and clans. The ideal form of marriage for the Kachin is called matrilateral cross-cousin marriage. In this form of marriage, a male is supposed to marry one of his mother's brother's daughters. Anthropologists have described these matrilateral cross-cousin marriage systems as "generalized exchange" or as "circular connubium" systems where a male gets wives from particular clans and his daughters marry males from a different clan.[32] Thus, the marriage system is arranged into alliances among circles of wife-takers and wife-givers. Upon marriage, the groom's family makes a brideprice payment to the family of the wife. Leach described how this system of cross-cousin marriage and bridewealth could be manipulated to produce more stratified forms of society. At times this system of brideprices could make wife-giving lineages wealthier than wife-taking clans. Leach described how in the Kachin system women are given a value and are exchanged for cattle, cloth, gongs, ironware, and jewelry that became the basis of wealth. When these lineages differed in rank and wealth, more powerful males could recruit lower ranking men as subordinates through lowering the amount of brideprice. The alteration of brideprice payments and the use of genealogical and political connections could produce a highly stratified society more similar to the valley peoples in Burma.

A neighboring group of the Kachin, the Chin, was studied by F. K. Lehman in the late 1950s. This group also illustrates how the hill peoples' cultures are adaptations to the lowland civilizations of the Burmese.[33] The Chin are a Tibeto-Burmese-speaking people who live in western Myanmar. Historical records indicate that the Chin were probably driven into the hills by the ethnic Burmans centuries ago. Adapted to the rugged terrain of the hills, most of the Chin are swidden cultivators who produce very few surplus crops. However, some Chin living near the Burmese lowland regions have taken up wet-rice agriculture. Like the Kachin, the Chin have domesticated pigs, chickens, goats, dogs, and mithan (a type of cattle) that they use for food. They also hunt, fish, and collect wild vegetation and fruit from the surrounding forest areas. The Chin maintained a dependent trading relationship with the lowland peoples for salt, metal, and other prestige goods. Through this trade some of the Chin villages could attain more wealth and status resulting in more aristocratic "hierarchical" forms of social and political systems. Thus, like the Kachin, the Chin oscillated between egalitarian and stratified forms of society. However, Lehman emphasizes that the Chin are neither egalitarian nor stratified, but rather they are both.

In his descriptions Lehman distinguishes between the northern Chin who were more distant from the lowland Burman population and the southern Chin who were close to the lowland civilizations. The northern Chin had developed into supralocal chiefdoms with stratified patrilineal kin groups who used exchanges of prestige goods to serve as status displays in religious feasting activities. Like the Kachin, the northern Chin maintained a complex asymmetrical social structure in which higher status lineages gave women to lower status lineages in exchange for brideprice payments and prestige goods. The southern Chin resided in close proximity to the lowland Burman populations and conducted exchange and trade relationships with them. Unlike the northern Chin and Kachin, the southern Chin did not develop the elaborate stratified, autocratic forms of chiefdoms. Like Leach, Lehman demonstrated that the variations in Chin social and political structures are a product of indirect and direct relationships with the lowland Burman civilization.

The traditional religion of the Kachin and Chin peoples has been described extensively by Leach and Lehman. Both peoples maintain beliefs in remote spiritual ancestors of chiefs and commoners that have human characteristics, and in a variety of other spirits. The ancestral spirits are the basis of what are sometimes referred to as founders' cults that associate spirits with particular territories and regions. Ancestral spirits are called upon in various rituals to aid in the welfare of the kinship groups. There is also the belief in other spirits who are held responsible for good and bad fortune. Some of these spirits are malevolent or hostile to people and cause harmful events such as death in childbirth, fatal accidents, and bad luck for hunters or fisherman. It is believed that some of the hostile or capricious spirits may interfere with the goodwill of ancestral spirits as they are approached through rituals. Major rituals were conducted by men who aspired to achieve both political and spiritual potency. These men were usually individuals who had become chiefs and were believed to be connected with the founding ancestors. Among the Kachin, the chiefs were referred to as the "thigh-eating chiefs" because they received as tribute every hind leg of slaughtered animals within their territory. The thigh-eating chiefs would perform the most important rituals and make offerings to the ancestral deities to ensure fertility to the crops. In conducting these rituals, the chiefs would gain both political and spiritual efficacy. Among both the Kachin and Chin other ritual practitioners include shamans and priests who officiate over various ceremonies, sometimes involving animal sacrifices.

Many other hill tribal peoples have been studied by anthropologists in mainland Southeast Asia. Some of the groups include the Akha, Lisu, Lahu, and the Miao or Hmong peoples of Thailand, Laos, and Vietnam. The Hmong are found in southern China and some migrants are believed to have moved into mainland Southeast Asia many centuries ago. The Hmong language is part of the Sino-Tibetan language family and has local dialectical variation depending on the region where it is found. According to Hmong mythology, their origin as an ethnic group begins with a destruction of the world by a universal flood leaving only a brother and sister. The brother and sister marry incestuously and the Hmong and their many clans are said to result from this union. In actuality, the Hmong adhere to strict rules of incest avoidance and marry outside their own families, lineages, and clans. Similar to the other hill peoples, most of the Hmong practice swidden agriculture, although some have moved into lowland areas and practice wet-rice cultivation. The most basic social unit of the Hmong is the patriarchal extended household that provides the basic psychological support for the members of the family. Beyond the household are networks of

A Hmong family.

patrilineal groups defined by descent, which are merged with patriclans. In terms of marriage, individuals must marry outside their own patrilineage and clan. Marriages are also associated with the groom's family giving a brideprice payment to the wife's family to help establish firm alliances between patrilineages and clans. In some cases, cross-cousin marriages are also a means of integrating patrilineages and clans into alliances. These cross-cousin marriages may not involve the giving of a brideprice. When a male marries a cross-cousin, his mother's brother's daughter or his father's sister's daughter, he is marrying outside the network of his own patrilineal group. Similar to the Chinese tradition, these patriclans are associated with a specific surname and are the basis of ancestral founder cults, which involve ritual and spiritual practices similar to that of the other hill peoples of mainland Southeast Asia.[34]

The hill people minorities have been dramatically influenced by nationalism, the Vietnam War, and other aspects of globalization in mainland Southeast Asia. The various governments in this region have been trying to incorporate and assimilate these hill peoples into the national culture. In many cases this has resulted in conflict between the hill minorities and the central governments. For example, the country of Myanmar for a long period has experienced major tensions and conflicts among the various minorities and the central government. When Burma gained independence in 1948, many of the ethnic minorities perceived that they were going to be dominated by the ethnic Burmese people. These smaller ethnic minorities began to foment secessionist movements and declare independence from Burma. To resolve these tensions, in 1974 the government of Burma provided for a federalist type of constitution, setting aside states for the largest ethnic minority groups including the Chin, the Kachin, and the Shan. However, armed resistance by the various ethnic minorities such as the Chin National Front against the military government of Burma continued to occur. The ethnic minorities were able to finance this resistance through black-market trade in teak, jade, and opium. Military supplies were obtained from Thailand and China. The military government of SLORC began a repressive campaign against the ethnic minorities that resulted in the death of over a million people and millions more displaced as refugees. Weary of war, some of the ethnic groups have developed cease-fire agreements with SLORC, but there are many outlying regions in which conflict continues. Presently, the United Nations is trying to bring together representatives of the military government with the ethnic minorities to provide for a more peaceful solution to the conflict.

One of the ways in which the ethnic insurgency in Myanmar was financed was through the opium trade. For many years, opium has been grown by the hill peoples of Burma, Laos, and Thailand in a region known as the "Golden Triangle." During the 1960s and 1970s, there was a rapid expansion of opium production among these people, driven by a wealthy market in the Western countries of Europe and the United States. The raw opium is produced by the hill peoples, and convoys of mules guarded by heavily armed troops led by drug lords carried the opium to heroin refineries to be processed and to be delivered to European and U.S. port cities to be cut and sold. The U.S. Drug Enforcement Agency has tried to encourage the hill peoples to replace opium with other cash crops, but the high economic value and demand for opium provides a strong incentive to keep producing this lucrative commodity. In Myanmar, a drug lord by the name of Khun Sa financed a multimillion-dollar insurgency campaign against the government in the mid-1990s. We have already mentioned the involvement of the Hmong people and the CIA-sponsored trade of opium to fund their activities during the Vietnam War. Thus, nationalism, globalization, and the Vietnam War brought the hill peoples into an international context that was beyond their local understandings.[35]

Aside from the hill peoples in mainland Southeast Asia other significant ethnic minorities have had a major influence in the region. As briefly mentioned many Indian and Chinese peoples came as migrants to take advantage of new economic opportunities that were introduced by colonial and Western developments. Indians were brought to Burma by the British as soldiers and merchants to manage new political and commercial processes introduced by colonialism. Though many of the Indians fled Burma during the Japanese occupation, some have remained as a distinctive minority. Chinese migrants surged into Thailand and Vietnam as these countries opened up to the West and the global market economy in the nineteenth and twentieth centuries. As mentioned, when the Vietnamese communist government took control, they forced the Sino-Vietnamese out of the country. However, in Thailand the Chinese had a different experience. Though the Chinese were resented for their economic successes in Thailand for some time, the Thais began to develop mutual cooperative ties with the corporations and businesses of the Chinese communities. The Chinese corporations and businesses placed the Thai military and politicians on their boards and gave them shares of stock. The military governments and politicians in turn provided government financing, political protection, and sometimes monopoly privileges for the Chinese businesses. Additionally, many of the Chinese have intermarried with the Thai. The Chinese in Thailand have successfully assimilated and have not faced the same difficulties as the Chinese have in Indonesia and the Philippines.[36]

Myanmar, Thailand, Kampuchea, Laos, and Vietnam have Muslim minorities too. Myanmar has a Muslim minority of about 4 percent or almost 2 million people within its population of 47 million. The majority of the Muslims in Myanmar reside in the central plains area and a smaller population is located on the eastern border near the country of Bangladesh. Many of the Muslims have been in Burma since the thirteenth and fourteenth centuries. Most of the Burmese Muslims of the central plains region are well assimilated. However, the Muslims who live near Bangladesh have been resisting assimilation into Burma for generations. The military government forced many of these Muslims across the border into Bangladesh in 1978. Prodded by the United Nations, many of these Muslims were allowed to return to Myanmar.

Thailand has about four million Muslims. The Muslims in Thailand comprise two different self-defined categories. The first category consists of "Malay Muslims," who speak the Malay language and reside primarily in South Thailand in a number of provinces bordering on Malaysia. The other major Muslim groups refer to themselves as "Thai Muslims" and reside in central and northern Thailand. The majority of the Muslims (about three million) are the Malay Muslims based in southern Thailand. Prior to the nineteenth century these southern Malay Islamic regions were informal tributary states tied to Thai monarchial authorities. But after the nineteenth century the Thai state began to take direct administrative control over these southern areas. The four southern provinces of Patani, Narathiwat, Satul, and Yala, bordering on the country of Malaysia, contain majority Muslim populations. As in the other areas of the Malaysian–Indonesia region, the form of Islam was based on the Sunni–Shafii tradition; however, Islam coexisted with earlier Hindu-Buddhist-animistic spiritual beliefs and practices. In addition, both Shia and Sufi elements influenced local forms of the belief system in this area.

Various Thai military governments from the 1930s through the 1970s adopted assimilationist policies toward the Malay Muslim regions through "development" (*patanakarn*) or socioeconomic and education programs. These government-sponsored assimilationist policies were perceived by the Muslims as Buddhist attempts to subvert Islamic education, political, religious, and cultural ideals. Subsequently, a number of Islamic-based factions emerged during the 1960s and 1970s in southern Thailand and became engaged in activist irredentist activities. These insurgency movements evoked repressive military campaigns by the Thai government throughout the 1960s and 1970s. Up until recently most Muslims had turned away from the extremist separatist movements, though they still want to preserve their "Malay" and Islamic identity. However, with the recent U.S. invasion of Afghanistan and then Iraq, many Muslim militants began to mobilize against the Thai state, which developed an alliance with the United States in the War on Terrorism after 9/11. Beginning in January of 2004, some Muslim militants went on rampages killing a number of Buddhist monks and attacking police and military installations. Finally, on April 28, 2004, a number of different Muslim extremists attacked a variety of police and military targets but were surrounded by the Thai military and police and were massacred. Over 30 young Muslims were killed in a major mosque in Pattani, while they shouted prayers in Arabic to call for Allah's protection. Ultimately, over 100 young teenage Muslim militants were killed that day. Sporadic violence has emerged between the Muslim militants and the Thai security forces, which most analysts connect with the U.S.–Thai alliance in the war in Iraq and Afghanistan.[37]

Because of different historical and cultural conditions the experience of Muslims in central and northern Thailand has been much different than that of their Islamic affiliates to the south. Historically, Muslims of the central and northern corridors of Thailand have migrated, either voluntarily or by force, into these regions, bringing a variety of ethnic, social, and religious conventions. Thus, they are much more heterogeneous than the Muslims of the south. And, unlike the Islamic populace to the south, these Muslims are ethnic and religious minorities residing in the centers of a predominant Thai Buddhist cultural environment. The largest group of Muslims in central Thailand, especially in the capital city of Bangkok, is descended from peoples of the southern provinces of Thailand and parts of Malaysia. As part of the assimilationist campaigns, the Thai government used forced relocation to move Malay Muslims to central Thailand. Other communities of Muslims in central Thailand, including Chams, Indonesians, and Iranians, have a long-term history that extends back into the Ayudhyan period (1351–1767 CE). Muslims from India, present-day Pakistan, and Bangladesh and a small number of Arabs have also settled in the Bangkok area. In northern Thailand most of the Muslims came from the

Islamicized portion of China, though there are also smaller numbers of Malay and South Asian Muslim migrants.

The Muslim population and settlements in Cambodia and Vietnam are intimately related to the historical development of what was known as the Champa maritime kingdom that reigned between the ninth century and the seventeenth centuries in Vietnam. Eventually, Vietnam absorbed this maritime kingdom into its political domain. The Cham Muslims of Vietnam adopted many cultural features of the Vietnamese including housing style, clothing, lunar calendar, and the sinicized 12-animal cycle of years. Traditionally, the Chams of Vietnam were involved in cultivating crops such as sugar cane, maize, banana, coconut trees, beans, and various types of chili peppers. Unlike their patrilineal Vietnamese Buddhist neighbors, the Chams maintained matrilineal groups that were embedded within matriclans that had totemic-like symbols associated with the particular clan. The Cham Islamic tradition maintained in Vietnam was based on the Shia tradition. These Cham Shia shared the doctrine of the Imamate, which revered Ali, Hasan, and Husayn. Along with the traditional Shia traditions other indigenous elements of animism, Hindu and Buddhist beliefs and practices were apparent among the Chams.

Because of continual disruptive Vietnamese military campaigns against Champa, a considerable number of Cham refugees began to migrate into Cambodia, establishing permanent communities in about 70 villages along or near the banks of the Mekong and Sap rivers. By 1975, the population of Chams in Cambodia had grown to 250,000. Traditionally most of the Cham in Cambodia in this area practiced small-scale family fishing on the various rivers. They were well known for excellent construction of boats for use along the rivers, lakes, and canals in the region. The Cham refugees who settled in Cambodia maintained a much different form of the Islamic tradition than their Vietnamese counterparts. As the Cambodian Cham had had more contact with the main currents of Islam in Malaysia and Indonesian society, they maintained a Sunni–Shafii form of Islam, as well as Sufistic, animistic, and Hindu–Buddhist religious elements. Sufistic traditions such as saint worship and praying at the tombs of Islamic saints were imported from Malaysian Islamic precepts and practices.

As a result of French colonialism and the U.S. war in Southeast Asia the Chams of Cambodia and Vietnam began to develop their own forms of ethnonationalist movements. Chams began to view their own ethnic and religious cultural traditions as different from those of both the Europeans and Americans *and* the Vietnamese and Cambodians. These ethnonationalist movements resulted in tragic episodes for the Chams. Following the victory of the Khmer Rouge in Cambodia and Ho Chi Minh's regime in Vietnam, the Chams were relentlessly persecuted by both of these regimes. Active genocidal policies were directed at the Cham Muslims by the Khmer Rouge, and some 90,000 Chams were executed by the Pol Pot regime. In Vietnam the Cham Muslims have been subjected to intensive assimilation pressures directed by the state authorities.

Various reformist and mild forms of Islamic fundamentalism known as *dakwah* movements have influenced the Muslim populace of Thailand, Cambodia, and Vietnam. In Southeast Asia, these current Islamic trends correspond with the global impact of new forms of media, including increases in print journalism, television, and general improvements in literacy, especially within the urban centers. Some Muslims from Thailand, Cambodia, and Vietnam have traveled to the Middle East for work or to participate in the Hajj. They have become familiar with recent Islamic theology and political thought, and have introduced these ideas into Southeast Asia. In the dakwah movements in Southeast Asia, Muslims are called on to devote their lives to improving the social welfare of Muslims. They promote the revitalization of Islamic cultural and religious values and sponsor a variety of community-based social programs.[38] However, as mentioned, there is an increasing radicalization of Muslims in both mainland and island Southeast Asia as the war and conflict continues in the Middle East and Islamic countries.

BUDDHISM

As discussed earlier the Indianized regions of mainland Southeast Asia (Burma, Thailand, Cambodia, and Laos) adopted the traditions of Theravada Buddhism with roots in Sri Lanka sometime between the eleventh and thirteenth centuries AD. Historical records indicate that Southeast Asian Buddhist monks, primarily from the Mon community, traveled to Sri Lanka to study the Theravada Buddhist tradition. After the thirteenth century Theravada Buddhism assumed a preeminent position in the religious traditions of the Burmese, Cambodians, Thais, and Laotians. In contrast, because Vietnam was ruled by China for more than a millennium and China had a direct and profound influence on its culture, the Mahayana Buddhist tradition, as well as Confucianism and Daoism, became the religions in this sinicized area. In this section, we will review what anthropologists have learned about these two different forms of Buddhism in mainland Southeast Asia. In earlier chapters we learned about the origins of Buddhism and the different manifestations of it in different countries. Just as Buddhism took different forms in India, China, Japan, and Korea, anthropologists find that it is expressed in different beliefs and practices in the various countries of mainland Southeast Asia.

Theravada Buddhism (wisdom of the elders) is maintained through the texts and chronicles in both the Pali language (a Sanskrit-derived language) and vernacular languages.[39] To some degree Southeast Asian Buddhists perceive themselves as the conservers of the Theravada tradition and as the legitimate heirs of the original Buddhist teachings. Some of the major Buddhist temples such as the Shewzigon Pagoda in Yangon (Rangoon), Myanmar, are believed to contain bodily relics of the Buddha Gautama himself. In addition, various images of the Buddha, including the Emerald Buddha in Wat Phra Keo in Thailand, are believed to have an inherent spiritual power that can be drawn upon to induce security and comfort. The presence of these relics and Buddhist images contributes to the sacredness of these temples. The Pali canon contains the original teachings of the *dhamma* (in Sanskrit, *dharma*) and is divided into three divisions: the *vinaya*, or monastic codes; the *suttas* (in Sanskrit, *sutras*) or discourses of the Buddha; and the *abhidhamma* (in Sanskrit, *abdhidharma*), or philosophical treatises. The Pali canon emphasizes the basic spiritual concepts of dhamma, *kamma* (Sanskrit, *karma*), *samsara* (the cycle of birth, death, and reincarnation), and *nibbana* (Sanskrit, *Nirvana*). The unifying sources of the Theravada Buddhist religious traditions, which emphasize the four noble truths and the eightfold path as the basis of morality and religious inspiration, are based on the Pali canon.

Theravada Buddhist communities are comprised of the monastic *sangha* and the laity, which are bound together through mutual reciprocity. The monastic populations of Myanmar and Thailand are very large, though the number of monks is constantly in flux. In Thailand the number of monks is approximately 200,000 including another 100,000 novices. It is estimated that there are similar numbers of monks and novices in Myanmar; however, most accounts suggest that there are far more many novices than monks, which is just the reverse in Thailand. The majority of monks do not remain in the sangha for their entire lives. Ordination as a novice or monk has served as part of a rite of passage or life-cycle ritual for many Theravada Buddhist young men. Boys and young men usually in their late teens or early 20s undergo ordination and remain monks for a limited time as part of a transition to adult life.

The ordination rite includes the shaving of their heads and the donning of the ochre-colored robes of the monk. The monks follow the sangha rules including celibacy, sleeping on mats, and fasting after noon. They may remain monks from a few months to several years or more before they return to the lay community. There is no stigma associated with returning to the lay community after being a monk. In Thailand a monastic education was often valued as a means of social mobility for young men from poor socioeconomic backgrounds. They gain a monastic education in the sangha, and then after returning to the lay community they become the principal supporters of the local *wat* or temple and may move on to become teachers or government officials. Throughout the Theravada Buddhist countries the Pali scripture is chanted by monks and is believed to help induce spiritual power and protection (*paritta*) for the community. In addition, monks also encounter the dhamma or teachings of the Buddha through spiritual meditative practices. Traditionally, it was only the monks who practiced this spiritual discipline, but today meditation is becoming widespread among the laity. Spiritual meditation is used to train the mind and body and is seen as an efficacious means of dealing with the complexities of modern life.

The central concern of most of the Theravada Buddhist laity is to "make merit" to improve their kamma, which will affect their destiny and reduce their suffering in this life and in future lives. Making merit or *thambun* (Thai) is based on leading an ethically based form of life and participating in specific ritual activities. The laity must follow the basic precepts of Buddhism that includes living without violence, sexual misconduct, lying, stealing, and excessive drinking of alcohol; and nurturing the virtues such as friendliness, compassion, sympathy, joy, charity, and even-mindedness. The thambun ritual activities include the simple offering of food to monks or supporting the ordination of a son as a monk. Thambun may also include supporting a particular wat or temple complex that includes local schooling for young people. Individuals may help keep the wat clean and donate food or money for the care of the temple. Wealthy individuals and businesses may contribute large sums of money to build a wat as a means of thambun. Thambun can also be a social endeavor for households, kin groups, or entire communities. Thambun ceremonies for the naming of a child, ordination, weddings, funerals, the opening of a business, or a political campaign are a means of transferring or sharing merit with others within their communities.

One of the major questions that has dominated the anthropological study of Theravada Buddhism is how an abstract "world renouncing" religious tradition can satisfy the interests of individuals and communities. The answer to this question in mainland Southeast Asia is that wherever Buddhism exists, it tends to exist along with other non-Buddhist spiritual beliefs and practices that are complementary to the more orthodox traditions of Buddhism. For example, anthropologist Melford Spiro found that the Burmese have an elaborate cult of *nat* worship which is parallel to the Theravada Buddhist tradition. Nats are supernatural beings who have powers that are superior to humans and can cause harmful or beneficial affects on humans. In Thailand a similar spirit cult that involves the cult of *phii*, a belief in a multiplicity of spirits that can cause suffering or comfort to individuals. Most Thais have *phii baan* or miniature spirit houses that reflect traditional Thai architecture in front of their homes, hotels, office buildings, and other dwellings. These phii baan are believed to have spirits that protect the land, property, and households of the community. Many Thai bring offerings of food and flowers and burn incense at the spirit houses to demonstrate their beliefs in the protection of the spirits. Phii and nat cults are found to be compatible with the Theravada Buddhist tradition and offer a "total field" of religious and spiritual beliefs for individuals and communities. The Theravada Buddhist tradition alone with its emphasis on the abstract spiritual goal of achieving enlightenment (*nibanna*) through the improvement of one's karma does not appear to be completely satisfying for individuals and communities. Therefore, other non-Buddhist spiritual concepts and practices coexist with the Theravada religious tradition, which satisfy these basic needs for people in both urban and rural areas.

Historically, all of the Theravada Buddhist countries integrated their religious institutions with their political order. Anthropologist Stanley Tambiah, in *World Conqueror and World Renouncer*, demonstrates how the Thai monarchy and the elite incorporated the Buddhist sangha into the bureaucracy to reinforce the legitimacy of the state. Earlier, we discussed how the Thai elite utilized the symbols of Buddhism to help build a top-down nationalist identity in Thailand. The modern sangha in Thailand has a bureaucratic structure and hierarchy that parallels the government. This bureaucratic structure monitors and supports the diffusion of Buddhist ideals throughout Thailand as it is taught by the monks in the wats. Although as we have seen in Burma, monastic education and the status of the sangha were disrupted by British colonialism, the Theravada Buddhist monastic institutions have been supported strongly by the military government as a nationalist strategy. The generals ruling Myanmar have taken extraordinary measures to retain the loyalty of the monks. However, since 2000, a number of senior monks have been actively campaigning against the military regime of SLORC and have supported the democratic movement led by Aung San Suu Kyi. This political activism on the part of the monks is worrisome to the Myanmar government, but it offers some hope for the development of a more democratic society in the future.

Since both Laos and Cambodia have been dominated by communist rule since the 1970s the Theravada Buddhist tradition and the sangha have been transformed. In Laos, since the 1950s the Pathet Laos attempted to convert monks to the leftist cause and used the sangha to promote the communist movement. The opposition to French colonialism and the U.S. bombing campaign in Laos did contribute to the conversion of many of the monks to the communist movement and paved the way for the victory of the Pathet Lao in 1975. The Laos communist government took the position that Marxism and Buddhism were compatible because they both emphasized an egalitarian way of life and both aimed at reducing suffering. The renunciation of private property by the monks was perceived as approaching the ideal of a future communist society. The government, however, undercut the moral authority of the sangha and criticized the merit-making donations and expenditures on temples as wasteful. They also used the sangha to spread party propaganda and kept local monks from participating in local decision making. During the 1970s many of the monks left the sangha or fled to Thailand for sanctuary. Eventually, seeing that Theravada Buddhism had a strong resonance for the people, the Laos government developed a policy of liberalization for religion. Presently, the ordination of monks is increasing and officials of the Communist Party are allowed to participate in Buddhist rituals. Donations to the wat and participation in the Buddhist festivals led by the monks have increased in both rural and urban areas of Laos.

Anthropologist Judy Ledgerwood has been doing ethnographic research in Cambodia on the Theravada Buddhist tradition. She notes that during the period of Pol Pot's reign in Cambodia, the Khmer Rouge set out to destroy the Theravada Buddhist tradition. Monks were forced to disrobe and return to lay life. Wats were destroyed, sometimes blown up, or converted to warehouses, clinics, and even prisons. Buddhist images were smashed and in some cases hauled off and dumped into rivers, canals, and ponds.

The library collections of the Pali texts in the Buddhist Institute in the capital city of Phnom Penh were looted and burned. Thousands of Pali texts were burned. After the Khmer Rouge were driven from power by the Vietnamese in 1979, the new Kampuchean government permitted the partial restoration of Theravada Buddhism. New monks were ordained and the government allowed the restoration of wats. Yet, the government still restricted and controlled the Buddhist institutions. They allowed only those over 50 years of age to become monks. Younger men were called upon for agricultural work, the military, and other economic development projects. The communist government did not want to see the sangha arise as an independent institution that threatened the government. They did not provide any government funding for the restoration of the wats or other Buddhist institutions. However, in the late 1980s and 1990s, the government came to realize that the sangha and Theravada Buddhism could be utilized to legitimize its political rule. The age restrictions on ordinations and taxes on the wats were removed. Theravada Buddhism was formally declared to be the official religion of Cambodia and Buddhist chant was heard again on the national radio station. Theravada Buddhist schools were reopened and with funding from Japan and elsewhere the Pali texts began to be reprinted. The numbers of monks increased rapidly. Presently, in both rural and urban areas of Cambodia the Buddhist life cycle rituals such as weddings and funerals have been revitalized. Some of the nongovernmental organizations (NGOs) have defined themselves as Buddhist organizations and are actively addressing many of the social and environmental problems of Kampuchea. Ledgerwood indicates that although the form of Theravada Buddhism has been transformed by the warfare and destruction of the Khmer Rouge, it appears that it is reestablishing itself in Cambodia.[40]

Unlike its other mainland Southeast Asian neighbors, Vietnam embraces the Mahayana Buddhist tradition rather than the Theravada tradition.[41] The Mahayana Buddhism of Vietnam includes both the Chan Buddhism and Pure Land Buddhism traditions that were prevalent in Chinese society. Though the Buddhist traditions entered Vietnam from China, the Vietnamese have created their own unique form of Buddhist religiosity. Just as in China, the political elite in Vietnam emphasized the Confucian tradition as an aspect of its traditional authority. Buddhist monks were not involved in political affairs. Before and during French colonialism Catholic missionaries entered Vietnam to promote Christianity; however, it was usually the economic and political elite who converted to this Western tradition. The majority of the population retained its ties to the Mahayana Buddhist tradition. In fact, during the period of French rule, a Buddhist revival played a significant role in fostering the nationalist and independence movement in Vietnam.

One influential heterodox Buddhist movement known as the Hoa Hoa sect emerged as a religious and political movement in the 1930s. The Hoa Hoa movement stressed moral reform and prohibited practices such as opium smoking, alcohol drinking, gambling, and arranged marriages. It organized quasi-military units that were aimed at independence from French rule. Another sect known as the Cao Dai movement also developed in South Vietnam in the 1920s and 1930s in response to French colonialism and oppression. The Cao Dai tradition was Buddhist-based, but drew from Judaism, Christianity, Islam, Daoism, and Confucianism to universalize its religious movement. This amalgam of beliefs was used to form a Cao Dai army that formed a coalition with the Hoa Hoa movement to resist the control of the French and the U.S.-backed regime of South Vietnam. As we have seen, Buddhist monks played a very active role in their political protests and acts of self-immolation to demonstrate their opposition to the U.S.-backed South Vietnam regime and the Vietnam War.

The Mahayana Buddhist tradition remained the major religious tradition of the majority of Vietnamese people, but it was never centralized by the state in the same manner as the Theravada tradition. Therefore, Buddhism was factionalized, eclectic, and diversified and combined elements of popular Daoism and other indigenous Vietnamese spiritual conceptions and beliefs that predated the entrance of Buddhism. The characteristic ancestral cult and attendant rituals of traditional Vietnamese culture were incorporated into the Buddhist tradition. As we have learned earlier, the Mahayana tradition emphasized the use of wisdom and compassion in helping individuals liberate themselves from suffering. In contrast to the Theravada Buddhist tradition that relies on the individual alone to reach nibbana, the Mahayana tradition has many different bodhisattvas, individuals who have attained enlightenment but who out of compassion postpone full self-annihilation to extend their aid to others to move toward this goal. As in China, the major Pure Land tradition is combined with the Mahayana beliefs with a particular reverence toward the Buddha Amitabha. Most Vietnamese adhere to the Pure Land form of Buddhism and believe that their actions today can influence their fate tomorrow. Thus, they have faith in merit-making acts to ensure that their future will be easier. Most of the Buddhist temples in Vietnam include images of Amitabha as well as numerous other bodhisattva statues. These images are at the center of religious practices by visitations of the laypeople who offer flowers, incense, and candles to induce spiritual power and protection. Other spirits such as *ma* who can become harmful, or *tinh* soul stealing ghosts, and a variety of popular Daoist spirits and deities also play a role in Vietnamese spiritual life.

Unlike their neighbors in the Theravada Buddhist countries, fewer males in Vietnam become monks. Yet, when they do join the monastic order they tend to make a lifelong commitment. Most of the monks practice a more rigorous form of Mahayana Buddhism, known as Thien (Zen, Chan)—a discipline that teaches that liberation—can be attained through meditation on seemingly paradoxical or incongruous statements or puzzles (in Japanese, koans). The Buddhist clergy tends to constitute the most highly educated, disciplined, sometimes politically active intelligentsia in Vietnam. Many of the Vietnamese monks have become sophisticated scholars and they established Buddhist centers for education. The monks do not depend on donations of food from the people as do the Theravada monks, but they do officiate at the various ceremonies of life-cycle events such as weddings and funerals. As in Cambodia and Laos during the period of French colonialism, leftist groups tried to convert the Buddhist clergy to a Marxist

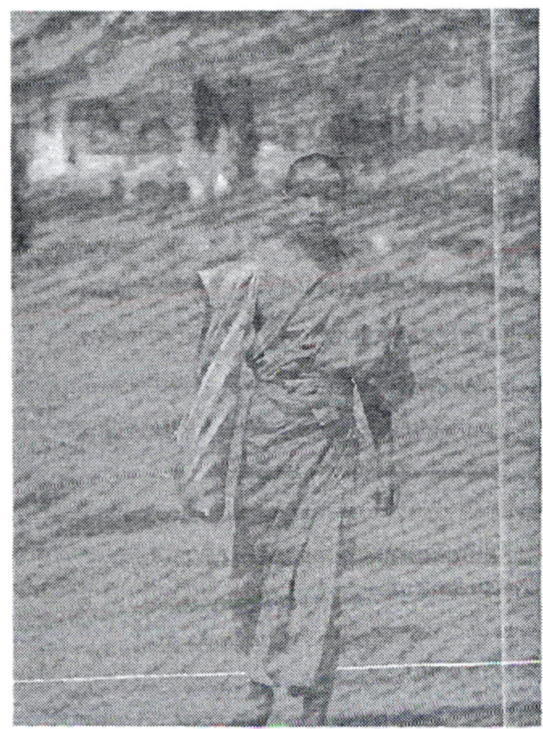

A Thai Buddhist monk.

interpretation of Buddhism. During the Vietnam War, many of the monks were accused of collaborating with communists. To defend themselves the monks tried to unite all of the factions of Buddhism, including the Hoa Hoa sect into the Unified Buddhist Church (UBC) to demonstrate their active opposition to the war.

Following the end of the Vietnam War and the communist takeover the government sought to control the Buddhist institutions. The communist government attacked the UBC and other religious organizations. Security forces raided the temples, closed down orphanages, disbanded religious organizations, and arrested prominent Buddhist leaders. The government established its own Buddhist church, which became the only recognized Buddhist religious association. This resulted in a serious rift in the Buddhist clerical hierarchy. Some of the monks acquiesced to government control while others have tried to defy the communist government. The UBC took a leading role in opposing the communist control of Buddhism. An influential monk, Thich Quang Do, wrote an open letter to the communist government detailing the long history of religious and political repression in Vietnam and called for religious freedom. He was arrested and sentenced to five years in prison for his actions. Although he was released from prison early, Thich Quang Do is constantly harassed by government and police authorities for his actions. Other monks have been working with the communist government to help preserve Buddhism. They have opened new government-funded Buddhist schools and recruit young people to improve social justice and support economic development throughout the country. Despite the difficulties encountered by the Vietnamese Buddhists, it is likely that the religion will continue to be significant for the population for a long while.

In this broad survey of the prehistory, history, and contemporary demographic, economic, social, ethnic, and religious conditions of the societies of mainland Southeast Asia, we have seen how these people have encountered many difficult challenges. Through recent globalization processes, which have brought both positive and negative consequences, the rural and urban peoples of the countries of Myanmar, Thailand, Cambodia, Laos, and Vietnam have refined, modified, adapted, and sometimes revolutionized their beliefs and practices. Of course, not all of the rural and urban people are similar. As we have seen, mainland Southeast Asia consists of people who are tribal horticulturalists of the hills, lowland agricultural peasants, and economically diversified urban peoples who are all divided among different ethnic groups. In addition, globalization and industrialization have increasingly stratified these communities into wealthy elites and middle and lower socioeconomic classes. Politically, these countries differ in respect to the degree of democratic participation and local citizen participation. In particular Myanmar has an extremely oppressive regime, but Vietnam, Cambodia, and Laos can also be singled out for excessive governmental control of their populations. In addition, all of the mainland Southeast Asian countries face serious environmental problems. Undoubtedly, the peoples of these countries will continue to struggle to develop and improve their environments, economies, social life, and political systems. As they have done throughout many generations, these people will continue to refine, modify, and adapt their cultural beliefs and practices.

NOTES

1. Political scientist Donald K. Emmerson wrote a classic essay titled "Southeast Asia: What's in a Name" published in the *Journal of Southeast Asian Studies* 15 (March 1984) on the historical problems of conceptualizing the region of Southeast Asia. Craig Reynolds addresses the same issue in his "A New Look at Old Southeast Asia," *Journal of Asian Studies* 54, no. 2 (1995): 419–446. For a more current brief essay on the origins of the concept of Southeast Asia see Robert Cribb, "The Poverty of Regionalism: Limits in the Study of Southeast Asia," *IIAS Newsletter* (November 2003): 8.

2. Robbins Burling wrote the book *Hill Farms and Padi Fields: Life in Mainland Southeast Asia* which was first published in 1965 by Prentice Hall. This classic book was recently reprinted by the Southeast Asian center at Arizona State University in 1992. Another anthropology classic on mainland Southeast Asia was written by Edmund Leach called "The Frontiers of Burma," published in *Comparative Studies in History and Society* 3, no. 1 (1960): 49–68, drew upon the same geographical and ecological conditions of the hills and plains to explicate how the various cultures of the region developed. Leach demonstrated that the hill and valley peoples not only had different modes of subsistence agriculture, but also were influenced differently by the surrounding civilizations of China and India. China, through its trade and migration, had definitive cultural impacts on the hill peoples whereas India, through its trade and influence with the valley peoples, had a major impact on the civilizations and kingdoms in that region.

3. A recent PhD thesis on language in northern Thailand by Kathyrn Howard titled "Language Socialization in a Northern Thai Bilingual Community" (University of California–Los Angeles, 2003) is extremely informative regarding the Thai language with a broad anthropological understanding of Thai society. It involves an in-depth study of how Thai children learn their linguistic concepts and vocabulary in the context of social, cultural, political, and religious beliefs and practices.

4. A recent source on the paleoanthropology and prehistory of Southeast Asia is Peter Bellwood, "Southeast Asia Before History," in *Cambridge History of Southeast Asia: Volume 1. From Early Times to c. 1800,* ed. Nicholas Tarling (Cambridge, England: Cambridge University Press, 1994), 55–136. Also, Charles Higham, *The Archaeology of Mainland Southeast Asia: From 10,000 B.C. to the Fall of Angkor* (Cambridge, England: Cambridge University Press, 1989) and his *The Bronze Age of Southeast Asia* (Cambridge, England: Cambridge University Press, 1996) and the *Early Cultures of Mainland Southeast Asia:* (Bangkok, Thailand: Amarin Publishing, 2002) are outstanding sources. Aside from the Hoabinian Paleolithic societies, a Bacsonian cultural tradition developed that had unique styles of artifacts found mostly in the Vietnam region. For an excellent overview based on archaeological and historical evidence for early ethnic groups that developed throughout mainland Southeast Asia see Richard O'Connor, "Agricultural Change and Ethnic Succession in Southeast Asian States: A Case for Regional Anthropology," *Journal of Asian Studies* 54, no. 4 (1995): 968–996.

5. Some South Asian historians such as R. C. Majumdar in his book *Hindu Colonies in the Far East* (Calcutta: N. K. Gossain, 1963) have argued that Indianization in Southeast Asia was accompanied by the founding of colonies. The French scholar George Coedes also espoused this view. In his *The Indianized States of Southeast Asia* (Honolulu: East-West Center Press, 1968), Coedes puts forth his account of the process of Indianization. However, most historians of Southeast Asia dispute this colonization model. The colonization model tended to assume that Southeast Asia peoples were backward and passive receivers of Indian culture. Contemporary scholars reject this monolithic model of colonization and the passive receipt of Indian culture. They admit that the Indian merchants may been very proactive in their cultural exchange and contacts with Southeast Asia, but that the indigenous peoples were also very proactive in selectively borrowing certain elements of Indian culture and rejecting and modifying others. For a more modern treatment of Indianization in Southeast Asia see O. W. Wolters, *History, Culture, and Region in Southeast Asian Perspectives* (Singapore: Institute of Southeast Asian Studies, 1982); and Paul Wheatley, *Nagara and Commandery: Origins of the Southeast Asian Urban Traditions,* Research Paper Nos. 207–208, Chicago: University of Chicago, Department of Geography, 1983.

6. There are a number of good sources on the Champa kingdom including early work by the French colonial anthropologist Anton Cabaton. A summary of a description of the Cham is in his "Indochina" in *Encyclopaedia of Islam* (Amsterdam: Brill Academic Publishing) Vol. 3: 1208–1212, 1971. A good historical source on the Champa kingdom is R. C. Majumdar, *Champa: History and Culture of an Indian Colonial Kingdom in the Far East,* 2nd ed. (Delhi, India: Gian Publishing House, 1985). On the origins of Islam into Champa see the French scholar Pierre-Yves Manguin, "The Introduction of Islam to Champa," *Journal of the Malaysian Branch of the Royal Asiatic Society* 58, no. 1 (1985): 1–28. More good recent sources on the Cham including the American anthropologist Gerald Hickey, *Free in the Forest: Ethnohistory of the Vietnamese Central Highlands, 1954–1976* (New Haven, CT: Yale University Press, 1982), and *Shattered World: Adaptation and Survival among Vietnam's Highland People during the Vietnam War* (Philadelphia: University of Pennsylvania Press, 1993). For a discussion of what happened to the Cham people in Cambodia during a recent period see Ben Kiernan's important essay "The Cham Muslims of Kampuchea Under Pol Pot," *Bulletin of Concerned Asian Scholars* 20, no. 4 (1988). For a brief recent discussion on the Chams in Southeast Asia see Raymond Scupin, "Muslims-Mainland Southeast Asia," *Encyclopedia of Modern Asia* (New York, NY: Charles Scribner's, 2003). A good discussion of the Chams in Vietnam was written by Japanese anthropologist Rie Nakamura, *Cham in Vietnam: Dynamics of Ethnicity* (PhD Thesis, University of Washington, 1999).

7. The most comprehensive historical account of the Pagan state is Michael Aung-Thwin, *Pagan: The Origins of Modern Burma* (Honolulu: University of Hawaii Press, 1985). His earlier chapter "Divinity, Spirit, and Human: Conceptions of Classical Burmese Kingship," in *Centers, Symbols, and Hierarchies: Essays on the Classical States of Southeast Asia,* ed. Lorraine Gessick, Monograph Series no. 26, New Haven, CT: Yale University Southeast Asia Press, 1983, is very anthropologically informed. A good discussion of the type of Buddhist state that developed in Pagan is F. K. Lehman, "The Relevance of the Founder's Cults for Understanding the Political Systems of the Peoples of Northern Southeast Asia and its Chinese Borderlands," in *Founder's Cults in Southeast Asia: Ancestors, Polity, and Identity,* ed. Nicola Tannenbaum and Cornelia Ann Kammerer, Monograph 52, Yale Southeast Asia Studies, 2003.

8. The most recent archaeological and historical survey of the civilization of the Khmer is Charles Higham, *The Civilization of Angkor* (Berkeley and Los Angeles: University of California Press, 2001). Another solid source is Ian Mabbett and David Chandler, eds., *Southeast Asia in the 9th to 14th Centuries* (Singapore: Institute of Southeast Asian Studies and

Canberra: Research School of Pacific Studies, Australian National University, 1986). A new recent source by University of Hawaii's archaeologist Miriam Stark on Angkor Wat is titled "Power, Practice and Pageantry in Ancient Southeast Asia and the Case of the Khmer Empire" (unpublished essay, available at her Web site at the University of Hawaii, 2004), which explores how global dynamics and regional power and religious authority buttressed the kingdom's development.

9. Classic interpretations of the mainland Southeast Asian kingdoms were written by the German scholar Robert Heine-Geldern in "Conceptions of State and Kingship in Southeast Asia," *Far Eastern Quarterly* 2 (1942): 15–30, and the British scholar H. G. Quaritch-Wales in *Ancient Siamese Government and Administration* (London: Bernard Quaritch, 1952). An overview of the unique forms of states in Southeast Asia is found in Carter Bentley, "Indigenous States of Southeast Asia," *Annual Review of Anthropology* 15 (1986): 275–305. The most comprehensive anthropological and historical accounts of the Thai kingdom are Stanley Tambiah, *World Conqueror and World Renouncer: A Study of Buddhism and Polity in Thailand against a Historical Background* (Cambridge, England: Cambridge University Press, 1976); and Charles F. Keyes, *Thailand: Buddhist Kingdom as Modern Nation-State* (Boulder, CO: Westview Press, 1987). A comprehensive survey of mainland Southeast Asian states and cultures is Charles F. Keyes, *The Golden Peninsula: Culture and Adaptation in Mainland Southeast Asia* (New York: Macmillan, 1977, reprinted by the University of Hawaii in 1995). A detailed history of Thailand was written by B. J. Terweil, *A History of Modern Thailand 1767–1942* (St. Lucia, West Indies: University of Queensland Press, 1983). A brief overview of Thai society, history, and culture can be found in Robert Slagter and Harold R. Kerbo, *Modern Thailand* (Boston: McGraw-Hill, 2000).

10. The classic account of the *sakdina* system of Thailand was written by Akin Rabibhadana, *The Organization of Thai Society in the Early Bangkok Period. 1782–1873* (Bangkok, Thailand: Amarin, 1996). For a discussion of a similar system of hierarchy in traditional Burma see Michael Aung Thwin, "Hiearchy and Order in Precolonial Burma," *Journal of Southeast Asian Studies* 15, no. 2 (1984): 224–232.

11. The classic work on the village in Vietnam was written by anthropologist Gerald Hickey in *Village in Vietnam* (New Haven, CT: Yale University Press, 1964).

12. A comprehensive account of the relationship between Vietnam and China is Alexander B. Woodside, *Vietnam and the Chinese Model* (Cambridge, MA: Harvard University Press, 1971).

13. For details on Burmese history see Victor B. Lieberman, "Reinterpreting Burmese History," *Comparative Studies in Society and History* 29 (1987): 162–194; and Michael Adas, *The Burma Delta: Economic Development and Social Change on an Asian Frontier, 1852–1941* (Madison: University of Wisconsin Press, 1974).

14. There were campaigns of persecution against Catholic converts and missionaries under various rulers of Vietnam. In the 1820s and 1830s the Vietnam emperor Minh Mang forbade the entrance of missionaries into Vietnam, ordered Catholic churches to be destroyed, and made profession of the faith an offense punishable by death. However, more historians of the period agree that the figures of Catholic casualties and persecution were grossly exaggerated by the French. For details on these events see Piero Gheddo, *The Cross and the Bo-Tree: Catholics and Buddhists in Vietnam* (New York: Sheed and Ward, 1970). Also see general discussions of this issue by D. R. Sardesai, *Southeast Asia: Past and Present* (Boulder, CO: Westview Press, 1989); and Milton Osborne, *The French Presence in Cochin China and Cambodia: Rule and Response 1859–1905* (Ithaca, NY: Cornell University Press, 1969) for details of French colonialism in Vietnam.

15. King Mongkut encouraged Western education for members of his palace. This resulted in the hiring of Anna Leonownens who wrote books based on her experience. Another book by Margaret Landon and later the musical and the two film versions of Anna's relationship with Mongkut, *The King and I* and the more recent *Anna and the King*, tend to portray the king in an unflattering manner. Consequently, the Thai government has banned these films from being shown in Thailand. For a historically accurate account of Anna and Mongkut see Susan Kepner's essay "Anna (and Margaret) and the King of Siam," in *Crossroads* 10, no. 2 (1996): 1–32.

16. For a good discussion of the traditional political economy see James C. Scott, *The Moral Economy of the Peasant: Rebellion and Subsistence in Southeast Asia* (New Haven, CT: Yale University Press, 1976). For a broad anthropological analysis of peasant movements including discussions of Vietnam see Eric Wolf, *Peasant Wars of the Twentieth Century* (New York: Harper and Row, 1969).

17. See Benedict Anderson, *Imagined Communities: Reflections on the Origin and Spread of Nationalism* (London: Verso, 1983) for an overview of the development of nationalism in Southeast Asia and elsewhere.

18. For a good source on nationalism in Vietnam see David Marr, *Vietnamese Anticolonialism* (1971) and his *Vietnam 1945: The Quest for Power* (1995), both published by the University of California Press, Berkeley. Two classic accounts of the origins of nationalism resulting in the Vietnam War are by John T. McAlister and Paul Mus, *The Vietnamese and Their Revolution* (New York: Harper Torchbooks, 1970); and Frances Fitzgerald, *Fire in the Lake,* (New York: Random House, 1977).

19. For sources on the emergence of top-down Thai nationalism see Walter F. Vella, *Chaiyo! King Vajiravudh and the Development of Thai Nationalism* (Honolulu: Hawaii University Press, 1978); Scott Barmé, *Luang Wichit Wathakan and the Creation of a Thai Identity* (Singapore: Institute of Southeast Asian Studies, 1993); Thongchai Winichakul, *Siam Mapped: A History of the Geo-Body of a Nation* (Honolulu: Hawaii University Press, 1994).

20. For good sources on the Vietnam War see Douglas Pike, *History of Vietnamese Communism, 1925–76* (Palo Alto, CA: Hoover Institution Press, 1978); and William Duiker, *The Communist Road to Power in Vietnam* (1996) and *Vietnam: Nation in Revolution* (1983), both published by Westview Press in Boulder, Colorado; Stanley Karnow, *Vietnam: A History* (New York: Penguin, 1983), republished with a new introduction in 1997.

21. For a good source on modern developments in Laos see Martin Stuart Fox, *Buddhist Kingdom, Marxist State: The Making of Modern Laos* (Bangkok, Thailand: White Lotus Press, 1996) and his *A History of Laos* (Cambridge, England: Cambridge University Press, 1997). An anthropological account of Laos is

Grant Evans, *The Politics of Ritual and Remembrance: Laos since 1975* (Chiang Mai, Thailand: Silkworm Press, 1998).

22. For the most comprehensive accounts of the "Killing Fields" in Kampuchea see Ben Kiernan, *The Pol Pot Regime: Race, Power, and Genocide in Cambodia under the Khmer Rouge 1975–1979* (New Haven, CT: Yale University Press, 1996); and David Chandler, *Brother Number One: A Political Biography of Pol Pot*, 2nd ed. (Boulder, CO: Westview Press, 1999). Other good sources on the tragic genocide in Cambodia include Dith Pran and Kim DePaul, eds., *Children of Cambodia's Killing Fields: Memoirs by Survivors* (New Haven, CT: Yale University Press, 1997). For more anthropological accounts of this episode and its consequences see Alexander Laban Hinton, "Genocidal Bricolage: A Reading of Human Liver Eating in Cambodia," Yale Center for International and Area Studies, Genocide Studies Program, Working Paper GS O6; and his "Why Did You Kill? The Cambodian Genocide and the Dark Side of Face and Honor," *Journal of Asian Studies* 57, no. 1 (1998): 93–122. A comparative study of genocide with a chapter on Cambodia is Eric D. Weitz, *A Century of Genocide: Utopias of Race and Nation* (Princeton, NJ: Princeton University Press, 2003).

23. Classic works on the anthropology of Burma (Myanmar) include Melford Spiro, *Buddhism and Society: A Great Tradition and Its Burmese Vicissitudes* (Berkeley: University of California Press, 1971) and his earlier work *Burmese Supernaturalism: A Study in the Explanation and Reduction of Suffering* (Upper Saddle River, NJ: Prentice Hall, 1967). Spiro utilizes a neo-Freudian perspective in comprehending Buddhism and Supernaturalism in Burma.

24. Demographic and economic data from mainland Southeast Asia are drawn from several different sources. One recent source for contemporary statistics is Dean Collingwood, *Japan and the Pacific Rim* (Guilford, CT: McGraw-Hill/Dushkin, 2003). Other sources include *The World Almanac* (2003) and the U.N. population and Vital Statistics Reports (2002/2003). For a superb introduction to geographical, ecological, demographic, and economic development issues see Thomas Leinbach and Richard Ulack, eds., *Southeast Asia: Diversity and Development* (Upper Saddle River, NJ: Prentice Hall, 2000). This text has separate chapters introducing broad themes for the entire region and also chapters focusing on individual countries.

25. On the social structure of Southeast Asia see Sulamith Heins Potter, *Family Life in a Northern Thai Village* (Berkeley: University of California Press, 1977); Keyes, *The Golden Peninsula*; and Melford Spiro, *Kinship and Burma: A Cultural and Psychodynamic Analysis* (Berkeley: University of California Press, 1977).

26. Winzeler's two essays that develop this explanation are "Sex Role Equality, Wet Rice Cultivation and the State in Southeast Asia," *American Anthropologist* 76 (1974): 563–567; and "Sexual Status in Southeast Asia: Comparative Perspectives on Women, Agriculture and Political Organization" in *Women of Southeast Asia*, ed. Penny Van Esterik (DeKalb: Northern Illinois University, 1996). Esterik's volume has other essays dealing with gender issues in Southeast Asia. Also, see Penny Van Esterik and John Van Esterik, eds., *Gender and Development in Southeast Asia*, CCSAS Proceedings no. 20, Vol. 2, Ottawa, Canada: Canadian Council for Southeast Asian Studies.

27. Kirsch's thesis was first elaborated in "Economy, Polity, and Religion in Thailand" in *Change and Persistence in Thai Society: Essays in Honor of Lauriston Sharp*, ed. G. William Skinner and Thomas Kirsch (Ithaca, NY: Cornell University Press, 1975). Kirsch developed his thesis further in "Buddhism, Sex-roles and the Thai economy," in Penny Van Esterik, *Women of Southeast Asia.*

28. On the status of women and Theravada Buddhism see Charles Keyes, "Mother or Mistress but Never a Monk: Buddhist Notions of Female Gender in Rural Thailand," *American Ethnologist* 11, no. 2 (1984): 223–241; and John Van Esterik, "Women Meditation Teachers in Thailand," in Penny Van Esterik, *Women of Southeast Asia.*

29. There is considerable literature on prostitution and the HIV/AIDS crisis in Thailand. An excellent overview is anthropologist Penny Van Esterik, *Materializing Thailand* (Oxford, England: Berg, 2000) that focuses on the general questions involving the cultural representations of women based on classical and Buddhist traditions, governmental constructions of gender, and media portrayals. Van Esterik has a chapter on prostitution and the outbreak of HIV/AIDS in Thailand. Another good essay is Marjorie Muecke, "Mother Sold Food, Daughter Sells Her Body: The Cultural Continuity of Prostitution," *Social Science and Medicine* 35, no. 7 (1997): 891–901. A number of good Thai scholars have written extensively on prostitution. See Pasuk Phongpaichit, *From Peasant Girls to Bangkok Masseuses* (Geneva, Switzerland: International Labor Office, 1982); and S. Skrobanke, Nattaya Boonpakdi, and Chutma Janthakeero, *The Traffic in Women: Human Realities of the International Sex Trade* (London: Zed Books, 1997). Another new source on sex, gender, prostitution, and sexuality and its intersection with nationalism in Thailand is Scott Barmé, *Woman, Man, Bangkok: Love, Sex and Popular Culture in Thailand* (Lanham, MD: Rowman and Littlefield, 2002). A good book that has a section on the problem of sexual slavery among young girls in Thailand is by Kevin Bales called *Disposable People* (Berkeley: University of California Press, 1999).

30. A series of essays in the journal *Crossroads: An Interdisciplinary Journal of Southeast Asian Studies* discusses the differences among indigenous Thai prostitution versus foreign-based Thai prostitution. Two essays on the indigenous Thai prostitution in North Thailand are Pamela S. DaGrossa, "*Kamphaeng Din*: A Study of Prostitution in the All-Thai Brothels of Chiang Mai City," *Crossroads* 4, no. 1 (1989) and Graham Fordham's more recent piece "Northern Thai Male Culture and the Assessment of HIV risk: Toward a New Approach," *Crossroads* 12, no. 1 (1998). One essay on the international sex tourism and its impact on Thai prostitutes is Marc Askew, "Labor, Love, and Entanglement: Bangkok Bar Workers and the Negotiation of Selfhood," *Crossroads* 13, no. 2 (1998). In this essay, Askew critiques the notion that these prostitutes are simply victims of the global political economy and sees them as actively engaged in efforts at transforming their identity.

31. A new book by Nathalie Huynh Chau Nguyen titled *Vietnamese Voices: Gender and Cultural Identity in the Vietnamese Francophone Novel*, Northern Illinois University Monograph

Series on Southeast Asia, no. 6, DeKalb: Southeast Asia Publications, 2004, helps illuminate the different ways in which male and female writers explain the context of Vietnamese culture and history.

32. The marriage practices of the hill tribes of Southeast Asia were at the center of a theoretical dispute within anthropology. The French anthropologist Claude Levi-Strauss wrote about the circular connumbiums of the hill tribes of Southeast Asia in his *The Elementary Structures of Kinship* (London: Eyre and Spottiswoode, 1949). Edmund Leach criticized Levi-Strauss's interpretation in "The Structural Implications of Matrilateral Cross-Cousin Marriage," *Journal of the Royal Anthropological Institute* 81 (1952): 23–55. For a more contemporary global analysis of the Kachin see Jonathan Friedman, *System, Structure, and Contradiction: The Evolution of "Asiatic" Social Formations*, 2nd ed. (Walnut Creek, CA: Altamira Press, 1998). A recent intellectual biography of Edmund Leach was written by his student and colleague Stanley Tambiah called *Edmund Leach: An Anthropological Life* (Cambridge, England: Cambridge University Press, 2002). It contains a superb discussion of economic, social, political, and religious conceptions that have influenced Southeast Asian studies.

33. F. K. Lehman, *The Structure of Chin Society: A Tribal People of Burma Adapted to a Non-Western Civilization* (Urbana: University of Illinois Press, 1973). For basic ethnographic descriptions of the various hill peoples of mainland Southeast Asia see Frank Lebar, Gerald Hickey, and J. K. Musgrave, eds., *Ethnic Groups of Mainland Southeast Asia* (New Haven, CT: Human Relations Area Files Press, 1964); and Peter Kundstadter, ed., *Southeast Asian Tribes, Minorities and Nations* (Princeton, NJ: Princeton University Press, 1967). For other recent materials on the hill tribes of mainland Southeast Asia see Jane Richardson Hanks and Lucien Mason Hanks, *Tribes of the North Thailand Frontier*, Monograph no. 51, Yale Southeast Asia Studies, 2001; and the collection of excellent essays in Nicola Tannenbaum and Cornelia Ann Kammerer, eds., *Founder's Cults in Southeast Asia: Ancestors, Polity, and Identity*, Monograph no. 52, Yale Southeast Asia Studies, 2003.

34. For a good ethnography of the Hmong see W. R. Geddes, *Migrants of the Mountains: The Cultural Ecology of the Blue Miao (Hmong Njua) of Thailand* (Oxford, England: Clarendon Press, 1976).

35. For an analysis of the effects of opium production on the hill tribes of Southeast Asia see Jonathan Friedman, "Generalized Change, Theocracy, and the Opium Trade," *Critique of Anthropology* 7 (1987): 15–31. For an authenticated account of the CIA's involvement in the opium trade and the Hmong see Alfred McCoy, *The Politics of Heroin in Southeast Asia* (New York: Harper and Row, 1972).

36. There is extensive literature on the Chinese community in Thailand. The classical sources are William Skinner, *Chinese Society in Thailand: An Analytical History* (Ithaca, NY: Cornell University Press, 1957) and his *Leadership and Power in the Chinese Community of Thailand* (Ithaca, NY: Cornell University Press, 1958). More recent sources include Cristina Blanc Szanton, "Thai and Sino-Thai in Small Town Thailand: Changing Patterns of Interethnic Relations," in *The Chinese in Southeast Asia: Vol. 2. Identity, Culture, and Politics*, ed. L.A.P. Gosling and L.Y.C. Lim (Singapore: Maruzen Asia, 1983). A recent book on the Chinese of North Thailand is Ann Maxwell Hill, *Merchants and Migrants: Ethnicity and Trade among Yunnanese Chinese in Southeast Asia*, Monograph no. 47, Yale Southeast Asia Studies, 1998. One interesting book that deals with the problems that the Chinese face in Southeast Asia, as well as those encountered by other ethnic minorities in other areas of the world as globalization occurs, is Amy Chua, *World on Fire: How Exporting Free Market Democracy Breeds Ethnic Hatred and Global Instability* (New York: Doubleday, 2003).

37. A recent essay by Raymond Scupin summarizes the events leading up to this Muslim violence in South Thailand in April and May of 2004. The essay is titled "Muslim Intellectuals in Thailand: Exercises in Reform and Moderation," which will be published in Omar Farouk's edited volume *Dynamics and Dimensions of Inter-Religious Contacts in Southeast Asia: Examining Buddhist–Muslim Relations in Thailand* (Singapore: Marshall Cavendish Press, 2006).

38. For a good source on the Muslims of Myanmar see Moshe Yegar, *The Muslims of Burma: A Study of a Minority Group* (Weisbaden, Germany: Harrowitz Press, 1972). For an overview of the religious culture of Muslims in Thailand see Raymond Scupin, "Popular Islam in Thailand," in *The Muslims of Thailand: Historical and Cultural Studies*, vol. 1, ed. A Forbes (Bihar, India: Center for Southeast Asian Studies, 1986); his "Thailand as a Plural Society: Ethnic Interaction in a Buddhist Kingdom," *Crossroads: An Interdisciplinary Journal of Southeast Asian Studies* 2, no. 3 (1986): 115–140; and "Interpreting Islamic Movements in Thailand," *Crossroads: An Interdisciplinary Journal of Southeast Asian Studies* 3, nos. 2–3 (1987): 78–93. See also a more recent essay on Muslims in Thailand by Scupin titled "Muslim Accommodation in Thailand," *Journal of Islamic Studies* 9, no. 2 (2001): 229–258. A classic historical and cultural source on Muslims in South Thailand is Surin Pitsuwan, *Islam and Malay Nationalism: A Case Study of the Malay Muslims of Southern Thailand* (Bangkok, Thailand: Thammasat University, Thai Kadai Research Institute, 1985).

39. For a good source on Buddhism in Southeast Asia see Donald K. Swearer, *The Buddhist World of Southeast Asia* (New York: State University of New York Press, 1995). Stanley Tambiah, *Buddhism and the Spirit Cults in North-East Thailand* (Cambridge, England: Cambridge University Press, 1970) and *Buddhist Saints of the Forest and the Cult of Amulets* (Cambridge, England: Cambridge University Press, 1984) offer in-depth ethnographic analyses of Theravada Buddhism in Thailand. Peter Jackson, *Buddhism, Legitimation, and Conflict: The Political Functions of Urban Thai Buddhism* (Singapore: Institute of Southeast Asian Studies, 1989) provides illustrative materials on the relationship between the sangha and the Thai state. For an overview of state–religious affairs in Thailand, Laos, and Burma see Bardwell L. Smith, ed., *Religion and Legitimation of Power in Thailand, Laos, and Burma* (Chambersburg, PA: Anima Books, 1978). For a fascinating discussion of Theravada Buddhism and its implications for the anthropology of religion and concepts and the politics of the divine, God, and "religion" itself see Erick D. White, "The Cultural Politics of the Supernatural in Theravada Buddhist Thailand," *Anthropological Forum* 13, no. 2 (2003): 205–212.

40. For discussions of the fate of Theravada Buddhism in Laos see Martin Stuart Fox, *Buddhist Kingdom, Marxist State: The*

Making of Modern Laos (Bangkok, Thailand: White Lotus Press, 1996). For Buddhism in Cambodia see anthropologist Charles Keyes, "Communist Revolution and the Buddhist Past in Cambodia," in Charles F. Keyes, Laurel Kendall, and Helen Hardacres, eds., *Visions of Authority: Religion and the Modern States of East and Southeast Asia* (Honolulu: University of Hawaii Press, 1994). For some of the research done by Judy Ledgerwood on recent Cambodian society see May Ebihara, Carol A. Mortland, and Judy Ledgerwood, eds., *Cambodian Culture Since 1975: Homeland and Exile* (Ithaca, NY: Cornell University Press). Ledgerwood is the leading anthropological authority on Buddhism in Cambodia and a recent essay "Global Concepts and Local Meaning: Human Rights and Buddhism in Cambodia," *Journal of Human Rights 2,* no. 4 (2003): 531–549 is indicative of her work. An excellent new source on Burmese politics, culture, and religion is by Gustaaf Houtman, *Mental Culture in Burmese Crisis Politics: Aung San Suu Kyi and the National League for Democracy,* Study of Languages and Cultures of Asia and Africa Monograph Series No. 33, Tokyo University of Foreign Studies, Institute for the Study of Languages and Cultures of Asia and Africa, 1999. Some interesting research has been carried out by ethnographer Merle Wallace on the influence of Buddhism on critical thinking in Thailand and also multiculturalism. Two recent essays by Wallace include "Today's Cultural Dilemma for the Thai Teacher: Moral Parent *and* Critical Thinker," and "The Thai Community Curriculum as a Model for Multicultural Education," *International Education Journal* 5, no. 1 (2004): 50–64.

41. For an excellent discussion of Vietnamese religious traditions see Charles Keyes's chapter "Tradition and Revolution in Vietnam" in his book *The Golden Peninsula.* For a recent report on the conditions of Buddhism in Vietnam see Robert Topmiller, "Vietnamese Buddhism in the 1990s," *Cross Currents* 50, nos. 1–2 (2000): 232–240.

9 ISLAND SOUTHEAST ASIA

Ronald Lukens-Bull

Island Southeast Asia is comprised of six countries: Singapore, Malaysia, Brunei, Indonesia, the Philippines, and Timor Leste. Malaysia, Indonesia, and the Philippines are large nations that encompass multiple geographic areas. Singapore, Brunei, and Timor Leste are small nations that have established themselves as sovereign nations for a variety of reasons. Malaysia, Brunei, and Indonesia are dominated by Malay ethnic groups. Some argue that the Philippines is as well, although many Filipinos reject that classification. The former three share the same basic language, which the Philippines does not. Singapore distinguishes itself by having a predominantly Chinese population, whereas Timor's claim to fame and independence was that it was the only lasting colony of the Portuguese in the region, and is now Southeast Asia's newest country.

This chapter offers a general introduction to the region. Like the rest of the chapters in this volume, it takes an anthropological approach. The chapter will start with a discussion of how the geography and the climate of the region shape the basic conditions in which people must live. It then turns to a discussion of the prehistory of the region, which is important not only for understanding the region but also for understanding human evolution in general. A large portion of the chapter reviews the history of region and looks at three historical processes that have shaped the societies and cultures of the region. These are Indianization, Islamization, and colonialism. The rest of the chapter concerns the region today and reviews a number of social institutions including economics, family life, gender, religion, and politics.

GEOGRAPHY

There is a great deal of diversity in the region and so it is hard to pin down defining characteristics. However, the geography of islands and ocean are important. Many of the islands are volcanic, thus the landscape transitions from coastal to mountain regions. Maritime activity is important. Specifically, fishing is such an important source of food that in some languages, Indonesian for one, the general term for all sorts of meat including beef and chicken is "fish." Vegetarians traveling in Indonesia need to ask for "no fish" rather than "no meat," which will only help them avoid beef.

No fewer than four tectonic plates meet in island Southeast Asia, which gives it one of the highest rates of seismic and volcanic activity in the world.[1] Both the Philippines and Indonesia are part of the Rim of Fire, which is a zone surrounding the Pacific Ocean in which about 90 percent of the world's earthquakes occur.

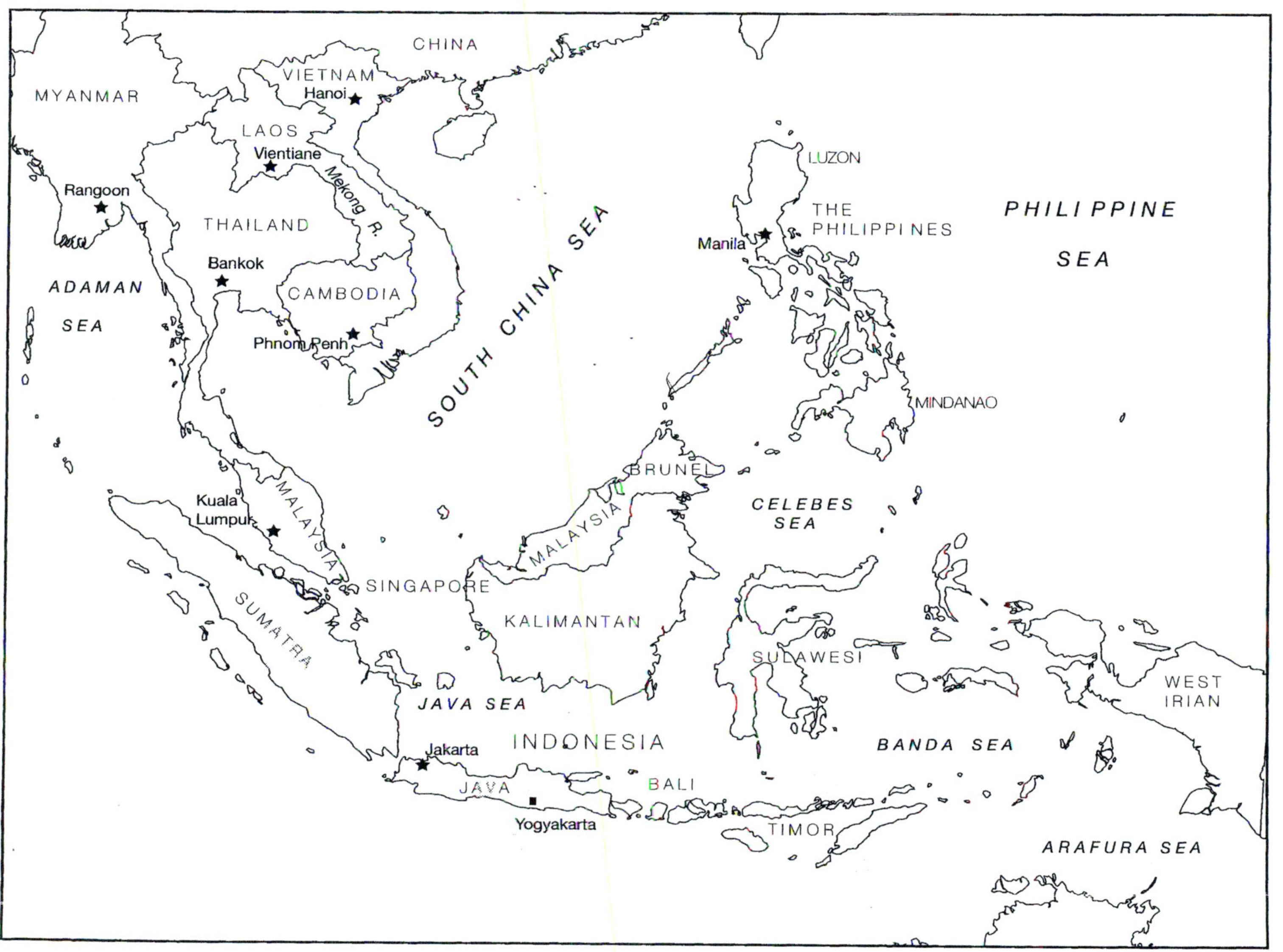

CHINA
MYANMAR
VIETNAM
Hanoi
LAOS
Vientiane
Mekong R.
Rangoon
THAILAND
Bankok
CAMBODIA
Phnom Penh
ADAMAN
SEA
SOUTH CHINA SEA
LUZON
THE PHILIPPINES
Manila
PHILIPPINE
SEA
MINDANAO
BRUNEI
CELEBES SEA
Kuala Lumpur
MALAYSIA
MALAYSIA
SINGAPORE
KALIMANTAN
SUMATRA
SULAWESI
WEST IRIAN
JAVA SEA
INDONESIA
Jakarta
BANDA SEA
JAVA
BALI
Yogyakarta
TIMOR
ARAFURA SEA

The volcanic activity of the Philippines and Indonesia gives them a higher level of soil fertility than other tropical locations.

Historically, the region has experienced a number of large eruptions. For example, the eruption of the famed Krakatau Island in 1883 sent out enough ash to affect sunsets around the world for two years. This eruption was interpreted as a sign of God's displeasure by the peasant societies of West Java, who later rebelled against the Dutch. Other volcanic eruptions, like that of Gunung Agung in Bali in 1963, have also been interpreted as signs of divine displeasure. In this case, the Hindu priests of Bali had begun early the preparations for a centenary ritual designed to restore order in the universe. They were doing this under the insistence of the embattled president, Sukarno. However, the eruption of Agung, and the fact that the lava completely skirted the Mother Temple, convinced them to postpone the ritual to its proper time.

The region is tropical, which means that the words *wet* and *hot* are frequently used to describe the climate. There are two basic seasons: rainy and dry. However, keep in mind that these are relative terms. The dry season is cooler than the wet season, but still involves temperatures up in the 30-degree centigrade (80°F) range. Annual rainfall is hard to pin down because of the variation. In many areas, it exceeds 110 inches annually.

Islands dominate the region. Indonesia has 13,000 islands, of which over 900 are inhabited. The Philippines is comprised of 7,000 islands. Singapore is a city-state on one major island. The Strait of Malacca, which is 600 miles long, about 23 meters (75 feet) deep and at its narrowest part only 1,200 meters (3,397 feet) wide, has long been important for trade in the region and today 10 percent of the world's cargo passes through it. Historically, control of this trade route connecting India, China, and Indonesia gave rise to many kingdoms including Srivijaya, Majapahit, and Malacca. Also, today Singapore, located at the southern end of the strait, is the busiest seaport in the world. The strait also gave rise to piracy, which remains a problem today given the high volume of ships, the narrow passage, and the thousands of hideaway islands.

Wet-rice cultivation is the major cropping pattern in much of island Southeast Asia. In the cooler mountainous regions other crops are favored, including cabbage, corn, and the cash crops cloves and coffee. Indonesia's coffee-growing regions produce some of the most widely sought after coffees in the world.

Island Southeast Asia is home to much of the world's remaining rainforest. Many tribal groups have lived in these forests for thousands of years. Today, deforestation has become a widespread problem. It can be attributed to three causes: changes in traditional shifting cultivation, the expansion of settled agriculture, and logging. Swidden, or slash and burn, agriculture is a sustainable technology when practiced in the traditional manner. Traditionally swiddeners will burn a small tract of forest to plant a garden, tend it for 1 year, and then abandon it for 10–100 years, during which the forest reclaims the garden. However, to be sustainable, swiddening requires a low population density and large tracts of land. Traditional swiddeners have found their territories encroached upon by two sets of interests: sedentary agriculturalists, who want to permanently convert the forest into agricultural areas, and the lumber industry, which seeks to harvest high-quality commercial lumber. The majority of the world's tropical wood exports come from the region since many of the forests have a high density of commercially desirable woods such as teak and kempas.

PREHISTORY

The study of the prehistoric era in Southeast Asia is of interest not only to area specialists but also to students of human evolution, especially those interested in *Homo erectus* and the spread of modern *Homo sapiens* throughout the world. However, the fossil record found in island Southeast Asia has been the subject of many debates because it is incomplete. The fossil record is incomplete because of three factors. First, the *Homo erectus* population in the region was never very numerous. Second, environmental conditions (climate, scavengers, etc.) did not present favorable conditions for fossilization. Third, the ever-shifting continental glaciers meant repeated sea-level adjustments and so much of the *Homo erectus* habitat is currently under water.

Island Southeast Asia, the island of Java in particular, takes center stage in certain debates about human evolution. Java Man and the lesser known Wadjak Man and Solo Man are at the center of these controversies. Java Man was discovered in the late nineteenth century by a Dutch physician named Eugene Dubois. Based on a thighbone and a skull cap (known as the Trinil fossils after the place they were found), Dubois declared that he found a "missing link" between humans and apes. He gave his discovery the scientific name *Pithecanthropus erectus.* There has been considerable debate about this find. It is now generally accepted that the femur and the skullcap were not from the same individual and some argue that the femur is from a different level from the site and is probably from *Homo sapiens. Pithecanthropus erectus,* or straight-standing ape-man, was reclassified as *Homo erectus* in 1994. There have been multiple fossil finds of *Homo erectus* in Java.[2]

Creationists love to use Java Man, particularly the Trinil fossils, to dispute evolution. They focus on two major points of contention. First is the existence of the Wadjak skulls, unmistakably modern humans, which they describe as coming from nearby the Trinil site and in approximately the same layer. Further, they claim that Dubois hid these skulls because they were older than the Trinil fossils. Second is the claim that Dubois recanted his belief that the Trinil fossils were a missing link. These claims are rejected by C. Loring Brace, a leading scholar in human evolution, who points out that the Wadjak and Trinil sites are separated by 100 miles of rugged mountainous terrain and that the dates for them are 10,000 and 500,000 years, respectively, hardly "in the same layer." As for the claims that Dubois hid the existence of the Wadjak skulls, he did not. Rather, he published about them and did so even prior to the Trinil find.

New dating techniques have suggested that the Javan materials are older than previously thought and are 1.6 to 1.8 million years old. This finding helps explain the absence of Acheulian tools in association with these fossils.[3] It suggests that *Homo erectus* might have left Africa far earlier that previously thought and that the species left before developing the Acheulian tool set. There is evidence for a tool set using nonlithic materials such as bamboo, wood, and rattan.

Other fossils suggest that *Homo erectus* lived on Java as late as between 53,000 and 27,000 years ago. If this data holds, it will be the first case of *Homo sapiens* and *Homo erectus* coexisting. This data challenges the multiregional evolutionary model, which proposes that Asian *Homo erectus* were among modern human's ancestors.

It is largely agreed that hominids reached Java on a land bridge across the Sunda Shelf, although some scholars have advanced evidence for boat travel for *Homo erectus* in the region. Some of the variation between Javan *Homo erectus* and other populations is best explained by the evidence that suggests the Javan population was isolated for hundreds of thousands of years.

Starting in about 40,000 BCE Australoid populations moved into Indonesia. From about 8000 BCE until the time of the Mongoloid migration, Hoabinhian technologies and culture thrived in the northeastern Sumatra highlands. This culture uses the same tool assemblage as that first associated with Hoa Binh in North Vietnam.[4] About 4,000 years ago, southern Mongoloids moved into the region and pushed the Australoids into the fringes of the region.

The modern *Homo sapiens* remains found in Malaysia date back to 38,000 BCE. This population was Austronesian and the ancestors of today's Negritos who are characterized by dark skin, short stature, and tightly curled hair. By about 8,000 years ago, the seas receded for the last time, leaving the region much as we find today. Starting in 2000–1500 BCE, the agriculturalist ancestors of today's Malays migrated into the peninsula.

The Philippine archipelago includes some of the last areas in the region to be settled. It was settled in three waves. The first wave was about 20,000–30,000 years ago and involved the ancestors of the Negrito peoples. Since this population was never very numerous, there are very few Negritos left in the Philippines today. The second wave was of seafaring proto-Malays who arrived from southern China and Tongkin about 10,000 years ago. These people were the ancestors of the today's mountain-dwelling peoples like the Bontoc, Ifugao, Kalinga, and Apayao. The final wave started about 2,000 years ago; Deutro Malays arrived from the Indonesian archipelago and pushed earlier immigrants to the interior highlands.

LANGUAGE

Most of the languages in island Southeast Asia belong to the Malayo-Polynesian language family. There are some Mon-Khmer speakers in peninsular Malaysia, particularly among the Orang Asli (literally, original people). However, within the Malayo-Polynesian language family there is tremendous variation. In Indonesia alone, there are over 300 mutually unintelligible languages and dialects. The Philippines has 11 languages and 87 dialects. In Malaysia and Singapore, Tamil and various Chinese dialects are also spoken. Wide-ranging linguistic diversity has lead to the establishment of national languages, namely Filipino (based on Tagalog) in the Philippines and Indonesian (a form of Malay) in Indonesia. These national languages provide the necessary foundation for national education, television, and identity. In the Philippines, nearly 75 percent of the population speaks one of four languages—Tagalog, Ilocano, Cebuano, and Ilongo—while the official languages are Filipino and English. In Singapore, Mandarin, Tamil, Malay, and English are all recognized as official languages.

English is widely spoken in Singapore, Malaysia, and the Philippines. In Singapore, the effective use of English is a marker of class position and educational level. It is socially prestigious to use English well and Singaporean television broadcasts some English language shows with no subtitles. Singaporean English, or Singlish, is a creole that reflects the mapping of English words onto Asian, most prominently Chinese grammar. One noticeable feature of Singlish is the particle "lah" that is used for emphasis and probably originates from Malay; however, some scholars trace its origins to Chinese dialects. In Malaysia, non-Malays prefer to use English over Malay when dealing with other non-Malays, even when both parties are fluent in Malay. This is partly due to their desire to deemphasize the political dominance of the Malay ethnic group.

Some languages in the region, including Balinese and Javanese, use an elaborate system of honorifics. Other Asian languages, namely Japanese, Hindi, and Korean, also use elaborate systems of honorifics that may in some ways be similar. We now turn to a discussion of Javanese, in which this system is highly developed.

Javanese has two main levels, each with its own lexicon. *Ngoko* is the basic form of the Javanese language. It is the language of thought, intimacy, anger, and most forms of natural and spontaneous expression. It is the first form one learns. Ngoko is spoken with one's mother and siblings until the age of 10 or 12, then one is gradually taught to speak more formal and polite forms to these individuals. *Krama* is more polite than Ngoko and its words tend to be longer that their Ngoko equivalents. Krama is not seen as natural or comfortable, and should be spoken more smoothly, with carefully regulated pitch and stress change; this allows frequent and lengthy pauses during speech.[5]

The choice of language level is dictated by factors of status and intimacy, not unlike similar distinctions in European languages (e.g., *tu* or *vous* in French, *tu* or *usted* in Spanish, *du* or *Sie* in German). Javanese differs from European languages in that Javanese speakers need to select each word in the sentence as opposed to just a second-person pronoun. The choice of language levels has nothing to do with what is being said, but rather is determined by the relationship between the speaker and the hearer. Generally, Krama is spoken up the status hierarchy and Ngoko is spoken down. Sometimes language choices conflict, however. A Javanese shadow puppet story exemplifies such a conflict. There were two brothers who were both kings. In private, the older brother would address the younger in Ngoko and receive Krama. However, in public, when they both were acting as kings, they each spoke Krama to the other.

While the analogy of the Javanese speech level to the T/V distinction in European languages is a useful start, it is somewhat misleading. Whereas the T/V distinction involves notions of power and solidarity, the principle underlying the Javanese language levels is *tata tentrem* which is a two-part ethic that encompasses *tata* (formal order, or the idea that everything is in its proper place) and *tentrem* (peace and tranquility of the heart). Tata tentrem is both the goal of correct behavior and the end measure by which all things are judged; if something promotes tata tentrem it is good; if not, it is bad. The world is seen as part of an unchanging and balanced cosmic order.[6] Each person in a community must have a place, and the person's behavior must conform to his or her position. The Javanese determine their relative status to someone to whom they are speaking by a process of weight and comparison. The questions asked are "Who is this person? Who am I? What is he (or she) to me?" Violation of the norms of speaking can destroy relationships and create an unharmonious state for society.

HISTORICAL INFLUENCES

The history of island Southeast Asia shows a region that has gone through several cultural or civilizational changes. The end result is a "layered" culture history in which one finds influences from Hinduism, Buddhism, Islam, and other major civilizational forces.

Indianization

One important cultural historical layer in island Southeast Asia is referred to as Indianization. This refers to the transference of Indian cultural influence, primarily in the form of Hinduism and Buddhism. Today the Hindu population in the region is very small, excluding more recent immigrants from India. Likewise, the majority of Buddhists are more recent Chinese immigrants. Indianization's influence was greatest around the areas around the Strait of Malacca and the Java Sea, namely eastern Sumatra, the western Malay Peninsula, Java, and Bali. Highland Sumatra, Nias, Mentawi, and the Philippines, among other areas, were never Indianized.[7] While there is some evidence of contact with Indian traders as early as the third century BCE, it was several centuries before these contacts lead to widespread changes in Southeast Asian societies.[8] The influence was initially and perhaps primarily at the level of society's elites and was largely associated with trade. It is unlikely that the ordinary merchants and mariners were able to effect the kinds of changes that happened. This is due mostly to the fact that they would not be overly knowledgeable about the intricacies of high Indic civilization and religion. Further, such travelers might not have much contact with local elite. Noble merchants (of the Ksatriya caste) were an integral part of this process, having both the knowledge and the social position to transmit Indic culture. The earliest Sanskrit inscriptions are dated to 200 CE[9] and up until the 1400s, the region saw a long period of rise and fall of petty "Indianized" or "Hinduized" kingdoms, the most significant being Srivijaya (for which the exact location of the capital has yet been found, although some argue that is at Palembang, Sumatra) and Majapahit in Central Java.

In the seventh century CE, Srivijaya (probably on Sumatra) replaced Funan (in modern-day Cambodia) as the dominant commercial power in Southeast Asia. This was in part due to the shift in maritime traffic from coastal waters to the high seas. The major opponents to Srivijaya were are series of Javanese dynasties collectively referred to at the Mataram polities, which were ruled by different dynasties, from the seventh to the thirteenth century. Majapahit, in East Java, was the successor to the Mataram empires. It emerged in the thirteenth century and survived for nearly 200 years, when it was challenged by the Islamic kingdom of Demak. The nobility and courtiers of Majapahit fled to the Tennger highlands in East Java and to the island of Bali.

Of significant interest is what aspects of Indian culture impacted Southeast Asia and which did not. Most significantly, Southeast Asian rulers borrowed the Indian notions of a divine king as well as Indian cosmography and patterns of warfare. Indian astrology, art, and architecture were also borrowed. We see the influence of Indian architecture in Prambanan, the ninth-century Saivite temple complex and Borobodur, the eighth-century Buddhist temple.

The Prambanan temple complex, 20 kilometers (12.4 miles) east of Yogyakarta in Central Java, was completed in the mid-ninth century by the Hindu King Pikatan of the Sanjaya dynasty. It incorporates both Hindu and Buddhist elements, which legend attributes to the marriage of King Pikatan to a Buddhist woman. One indicator of Buddhist influence is the shape of the

The Indian influence is evident at Prambanan in Indonesia.

temples. Instead of the common Hindu pattern of *linga* (phallus) topped temple, these structures are topped with a diamond shape that closely resembles a *stupa*, or a reliquary for images or remains of the Buddha. At the center of the complex are three temples, or *candi*, dedicated to Shiva, Visnu, and Brahma, the holy trinity of Hinduism. The center temple is the largest and is dedicated to Shiva. However, it also houses chambers with statues of Durga, the destroyer goddess; Agastya, the protector of Rama; and Ganesha, the elephant-headed god. The central candi are decorated with bas-relief scenes from the Hindu epic, the *Ramayana*. The complex was abandoned shortly after it was built and not rediscovered until 1733. In 1885, the site was cleared of jungle vegetation. Reconstruction was started in 1918 and continues today.[10]

Borobodur, also near Yogyakarta, was built around 750 CE by the Sailendra dynasty. Originally 42 meters (138 feet) tall, the stupa now stands at 31.5 meters (108 feet) tall and is 123 meters wide (404 feet), making it one of the three largest Buddhist monuments in the world.

There are three layers to the temple, which the pilgrim circumambulates in a counterclockwise direction. These are the Sphere of Desire, the Sphere of Form, and Sphere of Formlessness. Each layer is decorated with bas-relief depictions of scenes from the prior lives of the Buddha. As the pilgrims move through the temple, they are reminded of the stages through the which one must progress on their search for nirvana. The top section comprises three circular terraces ringed by stupas containing seated Buddha images. At the top and center is the main stupa, which rises 23 feet from its base.[11] Like Prambanan, it was abandoned and later rediscovered by Europeans. Starting in 1814 the jungle growth was cleared. Easier access to the site lead to vandalism and looting. Dutch efforts to repair the temple, starting in 1907, were doomed because the foundation was too weak. In 1973, a UNESCO support project employing 700 workers for 10 years strengthened the foundation and restored and rebuilt the temple.

The Hindu epics *Ramayana* and *Mahabharata* have provided foundations for much of island Southeast Asian art, especially theater and dance. *Wayang kulit,* or shadow puppet theater, is the dominant art form based on these epics. The puppeteer, called a *dalang,* is also a spirit medium and channels the spirits of the gods, demons, and heroes that are represented by two-dimensional leather puppets. A bright light behind the dalang projects shadows on a large white screen. Wayang kulit was historically an important form of entertainment, education, and propagandizing in the region. There are other performance arts based on these epics: *wayang golek,* which uses three-dimensional wooden puppets, and *wayang wong,* which uses masked dancers. It is interesting to note that the movements of the dancers deliberately imitate the movements of the two-dimensional puppets. In some countries, people continue to self-identify with characters from these epics and consciously model their behavior and manners after their selected character. Abdurrahman Wahid, the fourth president of Indonesia and a leading Islamic scholar and cleric, associated himself and was associated by others with Semar, a short, fat joker with a huge belly, enormous buttocks, and thunderous farts, found in the Javanese version of the *Mahabarata.*[12]

It is also important to note what did *not* transfer from India. There is no evidence that the highly stratified system of castes normally associated with Hinduism accompanied it when it came to this region. Even in Bali, which has the largest, if not only significant, remaining Hindu population, the caste system is highly attenuated. People are aware of which *varna* to which they belong, but this rarely shapes careers, marriages, or other dimensions of social life. Anyone who wishes to serve as a priest may; the only remaining vestige of the caste system is that the position of high priest is restricted to Brahmans. Further, there are no untouchables in Bali. Also, the subordination of women to men found India and China (Indianized through Buddhism) is largely absent in Southeast Asia due to mostly bilateral kinship systems in island Southeast Asia. Perhaps in a related fashion, the eroticism found in Indian art is largely missing in Hindu art in the region.

Islamization

Today, island Southeast Asia is home to about 250 million Muslims, which makes it home to more Muslims than the Middle East. Islam first came to the region in the late thirteenth century and was brought by Arab merchants and traders. The spread of Islam can be explained in part as related to the expansion of Islamic kingdoms. In the late thirteenth century, the first small trading kingdoms of Pasai and Perlak on the north coast of Sumatra adopted Islam. There were a number of political and economic factors that explain the spread of Islam to the region. Local princes, such as Iskandar Syah of Malacca, turned to Islamic states for political support against Buddhist Siam and Hindu Majapahit.

Islam also provided an ideology that supported a state and while the king could not be a god, as in a Hinduized state, he became kalipatullah, or the Shadow of God on Earth.[13] Further, the conversion of Islam by the elite cemented trade relations to Islamized trading centers in India. It was Persian notions of kingship that were the first aspect of Islam to which Malay rulers responded. The second was Sufism (mystical Islam).

There were also some strictly religious factors that may explain the appeal of Islam to Southeast Asians. The first is Islam's largely egalitarian approach: All true believers are equal before God. The second is that Islam is a dynamic faith that bridges over many of the normal aspects of life. Finally, the form of Islam brought to the region was highly mystical. Sufi mystic merchants who brought Islam to the region picked up on the strong interest in mysticism and emphasized that dimension of their faith. So successfully did they contextualize Islam with the existing tantric forms that Indonesians who still practice the Hindu–Buddhist forms use the Arabic terms *lahir* (external) and *batin* (internal) to describe different states of being.[14]

In Indonesia, the missionaries responsible for the initial Islamization of the archipelago are regarded as saints and are referred to as the *Wali Songo*, or the Nine Friends of God. The Wali Songo have great mystical feats attributed to them. Sunan Kalijaga is said to have mediated without ceasing for 40 years.[15] The founder of Demak determined the direction of prayer by putting one hand on the center pillar of the new mosque and the other on the Kabah in Mecca. Another of the Wali Songo is said to have been able to fly to Mecca for Friday prayers and be back home in Java for his afternoon repast.

Several of the Wali Songo are known for making accommodations with local culture. Specifically, they are known for their use of wayang (shadow puppet theater). One way this was done was by reinterpreting the Hindu epics. For example, in the *Mahabarata*, Arjuna has a secret weapon called the *Kalimasada*, which Javanese Muslims say is short for *Kalimah Shahada*, or the Islamic Confession of Faith. Some have argued that the highly stylized human forms in the Javanese wayang puppets reflect the influence of Islam that discourages the artistic representation of the human form. The Wali Songo are also known for incorporating the *gamelan* (percussion orchestra), the slit gong, and the *beduk* (large drum) into the call for prayer. The purported logic was that by using sounds that people already associate with large gatherings, people would be more interested in attending the prayers.

An important episode out of the Wali Songo legends is the story of Syeh Siti Jenar. Although he was one of the nine friends of God, he taught the heretical notion that since God is one there was no separation between himself and God and that he was therefore God. He was summarily executed; not for being incorrect in his assertion, but for teaching something that would confuse the common believer. This tale emphasized the importance of balancing the normative and mystical dimensions of Islam.[16] It is also important to note that this a retelling of the Persian legend of Al-Hallaj.

Another key Wali Songo is Sunan Kudus, who is said to have originated the wayang golek, the three-dimensional wooden puppet show and for building the Kudus mosque. The cultural accommodation of the Wali Songo is further celebrated in a story that relates that because the residents of Kudus were predominately Hindu, Sunan Kudus built his mosque to resemble a Hindu temple and forbade his followers from eating beef. To this day, the Kudus area, now predominately Muslim, is known for the fact that the inhabitants do not eat beef but favor water buffalo.

Because several of the Wali Songo had ties to older Hindu kingdoms, they provide a symbolic link between the rulers of Majapahit or earlier kingdoms like the Hindu Mataram politics, the rulers of the later Mataram,[17] and eventually the Sultans of Yogya and Surakarta. Today, Javanese

Indonesian Muslims at prayer in a public square.

Islamic leaders called *kyai*, who combine both Islamic scholarly knowledge and Islamic mystical practice, are said to be the inheritors of the mantle of the Wali Songo. Kyai are the main religious leaders for traditionalist Muslims and are usually the headmasters of an Islamic boarding school.[18]

The history of Islamization is parallel to European colonization. In no small part, European colonization created an atmosphere in which people sought out Islam as a way to oppose the foreign rulers. Further, the spread of Islam was limited to maritime Southeast Asia by the arrival of the Europeans.

Malaysia's Islamic history begins much the same as Indonesia's: Sufi Islamic traders and missionaries brought a form of the faith that blended with Hindu practices and Malay custom. The earliest evidence of the presence of Islam in the Malay peninsula is a late-fourteenth-century stone inscription at Tengganu. Malacca was founded in the early fifteenth century under the protection of China by Paramesvara. Either Paramesvara or his son (sources disagree) converted to Islam and ruled Malacca as Iskandar Syah from 1414 to 1424. The establishment of Malacca shifts the power balance from Sumatra to Malacca. Since Malacca is an Islamic state, Islamic traders had greater access and they and Islamic missionaries spread the faith peacefully. Sufism remained an important part of Islam in Malaysia until the eighteenth century, when scholars returning from the Arabian peninsula advocated a more Syariah-oriented form of Islam and so the community became more homogeneous and orthodox.

The development of Islam in the Philippines differs from that of the rest of island Southeast Asia. It was introduced at about the same time, and spread in the southern Philippines among major tribal groups who retained much of their pre-Islamic belief. In fact, ethnolinguistic differences are more important than Islamic identity for these groups. By the early sixteenth century, Islam was talking hold in the Manila area and was established on Mindanao and in the Sulu archipelago. The first Spanish conquistadors were met with some Muslim resistance in Manila, but within a year the resistance was largely controlled in the Manila area and Islam was unable to spread further on Luzon. Neither Christianity nor Hispanic culture in general ever took hold in the south and so Mindanao and Sulu remain predominantly Muslim and un-Hispanized. Today, the majority of the Philippines' three million Muslims live in the south in the Sulu archipelago and on the island of Mindanao. They have been divided into five major ethnolinguistic groups: Hanon, Tausig, Maguindanao, Samal, and Badjao.

The Portuguese conquest of Malacca led to the relocation of its Muslim courts to Johor on the southern end of the peninsula. This brought Brunei, a kingdom in northern Borneo, into contact with Islamic kingdoms. It is uncertain exactly when the rulers of Brunei converted. By the sixteenth century the Sultan of Brunei's authority extended to northern Borneo and into the southern Philippines. In the seventeenth century, Brunei's dominance was challenged by Sulu, an Islamic state in the southern Philippines, and lost much of its territory.

Political Theory in the Precolonial Period

To better understand the impact of Islam on the political and cultural processes that unfolded during and after European colonialism it is useful to examine island Southeast Asian political theory in the precolonial era. Any discussion of political theory in island Southeast Asia must include an examination of cosmology. In many Southeast Asian cosmologies, the cosmos is understood to be divided into the world of humans, or microcosmos, and the suprahuman world, or macrocosmos.[19] A fundamental aspect of the Javanese worldview is the notion of an unchanging and balanced cosmic order in which humanity's task is determined by immutable forces that operate through humans.

The king was seen as the center of the state. All power and authority emanated from him and all activities of the state were focused around him. This order was seen as being in perfect harmony with the organizational structure of the universe. In Malay kingdoms, this centrality of the ruler is seen in a broad range of sources and has deep roots in the pre-Islamic past. Furthermore, the ruler, rather than the Malays or the Islamic community, was the primary object of loyalty and was central to every aspect of Malay life.

In Javanese thought, the king was to be the defender and regulator of Islam and that this notion was based on the Muslim theory of the caliphate. The Malay use of the medieval Islamic kingship tradition was expressed in the adoption of titles and descriptive formula used in the Persianized Muslim world. The title *kalipatullah* (Shadow of God on Earth) was used in many parts of the archipelago. Prior to the Islamization of Southeast Asia, there was an expanding galaxy of Persianized Muslim sultans. These Persianized sultans, in many ways, resembled the kings of the pre-Islamic archipelago. Again, this is an example of how pre-Islamic practices that were congruent with Islamic ones were Islamized without having to change the basic structure or logic of the older practices.

In Persian kingship theories, sovereignty was a gift conferred on eminent men by Allah and the king was the "Shadow of God on Earth."[20] The title "Caliphate Allah" marks a claim to authority directly derived from Allah; a divine right of kings. The caliph was seen as the successor of the Prophet, not in his spiritual office, but rather as the custodian of the moral and material heritage of the Prophet. The king was Allah's *waranu*, which in literary usage meant "deputy" or "representative" but could be literally translated as "screen." It was in the sense of king as a screen that people must pass through to reach Allah and vice versa, that the king linked Allah with the people. Between the king and Allah there was no intermediary.

Only by attracting divine power and force, called *wahyu*, does someone become a sultan.[21] Wahyu was understood as a flash or beam of light that conferred an appointment on someone to complete a particular task. The original Arabic term *wahy* means "revelation" from Allah and it is the means by which Allah communicates with his prophets. Some Sufi traditions argue that it is also the way Allah communicates with saints. The equation of king and saint becomes important here in that the wahyu of the king confers upon him spiritual power and in turn, because of that spiritual power, political authority.

Important in the notion of covenant is the idea of social order, and that the chief responsibilities of the king are to guard against disturbances and to restore order if they should occur. These duties are essential because of the putative mutual dependency between micro- and macrocosmos. The supernatural and social orders conjoin in folk myths and, therefore, obedience to the sacred laws of the universe is implied in service to the king. Hence, social organization and keeping established social patterns is important not only for the daily routine of society's members, but also forms the main manifestation of cosmological harmony. By magicoreligious and physical penal means, the state enforces adherence to guard against possible deviation and to compensate for what damage has been done by past deviations.

In Javanese thought, the obligations of the state include both enforcing formal order (tata) and encouraging inner psychological order, a peace and tranquility of the heart (tentrem). Both of these obligations must be met to establish a state of perfect balance and harmony. There are three main motifs of the Javanese conception of order: unity, continuity, and harmony.

An important concept in Javanese religious thinking and political theory was the *kawula–gusti* (servant–master) relationship. The relationship of servant and lord is based on the Sufi notion of mystical union. Arising out of this mystical notion was a social theory that linked the government with the people. The people were not as much subjects as they were an extension of the ruler.

A modern enactment of these theories is the *Garebeg Malud* (feast of the Prophet's birthday). Its performance does not mirror cosmic realities; rather, it defines them and thereby establishes the state as a Sufi order whose head is the king, who is linked directly to Allah by means of his mystical adeptness. Therefore, subjects should submit to the king's will in the same sense that they submit to the will of Allah. This state of affairs is seen much in the same manner as mystical union, or merging of servant and lord.[22]

The notion that tied this all together was that a properly ordered cosmic state led to prosperity for all its residents. Of course, if prosperity was not enjoyed, then the state was considered to be improperly ordered in a cosmic sense, and the king, as center of the state, was believed to have lost his legitimacy.

Non-Islamic Southeast Asia and the Dawn of Colonialism

To balance the view of the region before the arrival of the Europeans, we will now turn to a brief discussion of two non-Islamic areas, namely the bulk of the Philippines and Bali. The non-Islamic areas also contributed much to the region's responses to colonialism.

We have very little to work with in reconstructing precolonial history in the Philippines. Even with some evidence for a pre-Spanish script, we have not yet found local accounts of life before, or at the time of, Spanish contact. Spanish records at the time of contact suggest that outside the Sultanate in the south, the Philippines was dominated by chiefdom-level societies complete with nobility, freeman, sharecroppers, and war captives. Further, the religions of the pre-Spanish inhabitants was focused on rituals to placate gods and spirits. Although there were no great unified kingdoms in the Philippines before the Europeans arrived, there had already been five centuries of commercial relations with China, Indochina, the Malay Peninsula, India, and Arab lands. The inhabitants traded sea and forest products, some as raw materials, some as finished goods for porcelain, silk, cotton, gold, and jewelry.

The Hindu courts of Majapahit fled for the eastern highlands and Bali with the rise of the Islamic kingdom of Demak. In 1630, the Balinese turned back Javanese attempts to introduce Islam. In the 1850s some Balinese kingdoms formerly acknowledged Dutch sovereignty. Slowly kingdom and after kingdom accepted the status as a vassal state to the Dutch colonial empire. In this way, they maintained a degree of autonomy. This strategy of indirect rule was consistent with the Dutch strategy elsewhere in the archipelago. The remaining independent kingdoms of Badung, Tabanan, and Klungkung were defeated militarily between 1906 and 1908.[23] The massacres of the royal families of these kingdoms are commemorated to this day as a mark of the bravery and independent spirit of the Balinese people.

Western Colonialism

The last major historical force to shape Southeast Asia was colonialism. Sinc the major colonial powers (Portu England, Holland, Japan, and

States) had different approaches to ruling their vassals, it is useful to organize this history by the colonial powers.

The Portuguese

The Portuguese made first contact in island Southeast Asia in 1509 with an exploratory expedition to Malacca. Although this mission had the charge of establishing a friendly treaty and was initially received well by the ruler of Malacca, the relationship between the Portuguese and the Malaccans took a sour turn. In 1511, four months of siege felled the city. The Portuguese soon found out that military victory did not automatically confer control of Asian trade. Because Portugal failed to monopolize regional trade, other Europeans moved into the region. After failing to conquer the port of Pasai on Sumatra, the Portuguese shifted their focus to eastern Indonesia. In time, Portugal's influence in the region was eclipsed by the Dutch, the English, and the Spanish.

The Dutch

The first Dutch ships landed in Java in 1596. In 1619, the D. Vereenidge Oostindishe Compagnie, or Dutch East Indies Company (VOC) captured Jayakarta (Jakarta) and renamed it Batavia. The VOC was less interested in ruling the East Indies than it was in exploiting it for economic gain. In 1799, the VOC was dissolved and the possession of Java was transferred to the Dutch Republic, marking the beginning of
...odern colonialism in Java. The Dutch ruled
...til 1811, when they granted control of
...sions in the East Indies to the
...rned in 1815 and remained in
...ese drove them out in

...lonialism was
...adually intro-
...s in full opera-
... assumption that
...e sufficient incentives for the production of cash crops, and that the colonial government had to force the Javanese peasants to dedicate one-fifth of their land and one-fifth of their labor to the cultivation of coffee, indigo, and sugar. With the cash payments the peasants were supposed to receive, they were expected to settle their land rent debts.[24] The Cultivation System was a period that benefited the indigenous aristocratic elite throughout Java. As hereditary succession to official posts in the Dutch administrative system became the norm, the elite's position became more secure.[25] An English writer with the improbable name of J. B. Money admired this system and recommended it to the British colonial administrators in his 1861 book *Java or How to Manage a Colony.*

Many historians hail 1870 as the turning point in Dutch colonial economic history. The Sugar Law, passed on July 21, 1870, marked the end of the Cultivation System. The Agrarian Law, passed on April 9, 1870, and the Agrarian Decree, passed on July 20, 1870, allowed long-term land grants for European enterprises. The new laws also provided for a system of land tenure for the indigenous population that restored most of their pre-1800 land rights.

This period saw the slow transition from compulsory labor to a "free" labor market. The laws granted indigenous cultivators individual hereditary rights of land ownership and the lease of "wasteland" (any land not in production) to Europeans. Eventually, Europeans rented arable lands from villagers.

The English

The British did not become a major force in Southeast Asia until the nineteenth century. After establishing a secure base in India, the British were able to challenge Dutch control of Southeast Asia. The first significant territorial claim made by the British was the island of Penang, which served as significant port until it was overshadowed by Singapore. From 1811 to 1815, the English governed the East Indies (what became Indonesia) under the leadership of Stamford Raffles, who introduced policies that outlasted the British period and until the end of European colonialism. Singapore is said to have been established by Stamford Raffles in 1819. In truth, Raffles negotiated a trade agreement with local nobility which established a trading port. After a quarrel with the port governor, Raffles took over as Resident in 1823. In 1824, Singapore became an English possession under two treaties, one with the Dutch and one with the local nobility. In 1826, Singapore became part of the Straits Settlements that were administered by the British East India Company and also include Penang and Singapore. The Straits Settlements became Crown colonies in 1867.

The British control over Sarawak and Sabah started in 1839 when the sultan of Brunei asked James Brook to put down a Dayak rebellion, for which Brooke asked the governorship of Sarawak. In 1841, Brooke began to rule Sarawak as the "White Raja." By the end of the colonial period, the British controlled a large portion of the Malay peninsula and western Borneo. In 1877, British business interests leased much of Sabah from the Sultan of Sulu. In 1880, the British government took over trading interests in North Borneo.

While the Malay aristocracy maintained their social and economic positions during British colonialism, the economic life of the Malay peasant worsened considerably. Furthermore, the British brought in Chinese and Indian migrants to work in certain fields. The Chinese were traders and moneylenders and became the backbone of the entrepreneurial class. The Indians were the primary labor sources for the plantations but also occupied a large number of educated professional service occupations.

The Spanish

The Spanish colonizers were motivated by three factors: economic gain, political control, and religious conversion. In this way, the Spanish colonial efforts in Southeast Asian were similar to their efforts elsewhere and different from the primarily economic driven efforts of other powers in the region. The Spanish's influence was primarily felt in the Philippines where Catholicism, a Hispanized cultural milieu and national government dominated. Because the Spanish did not encourage intermarriage, Filipinos were granted military, civil, and religious responsibilities.

In 1521, Ferdinand Magellan was the first European to make contact with the Philippines. He was killed by a local chief (*datu*) named Lapu-Lapu and only one ship of Magellan's fleet survived to complete the first European circumnavigation of the globe. Lapu-Lapu has become a legendary hero in the Philippines, remembered as the first Filipino leader to oppose European aggression. Before the end of that century, Spanish colonization was fully under way. Early in the 1600s, Spain had gained complete control over the islands. While direct rule was the order of the day for the colony as a whole, the countryside was controlled indirectly through *principales*, an indigenous Filipino upper class.

One of the lasting and wide-ranging impacts of Spanish colonialism was the large-scale conversion of lowland Filipinos to Roman Catholicism in just over 100 years. The Catholic missionaries were successful for a combination of factors. First was the practice of mass baptism which Filipinos may have willingly participated in because they associated them with indigenous healing practices. In any event, mass baptisms established the friars' authority over the baptized's spiritual well-being. Second, to allow better religious and secular administration of the countryside, the Spanish imported th
reduccion policy that had been successful in C
tral and Latin America. Widely dispersed
lages were forcibly relocated to a central
Both the secular government and the C
friars then had easier access to th
for the collection of taxes, keeping
and teaching the Filipinos how

Catholics. Third, Catholicism was allowed to take on a distinctly Filipino flavor. Centuries prior to Vatican II and the widespread use of vernaculars in the Mass, friars in the Philippines conducted Mass and generally communicated with their flock in local languages. Also, beliefs about local spirits became fused with Catholicism, although this seems to have been less intentional than the use of local languages. Although the friars tried to stamp out many indigenous holy places and representations of indigenous spirits and divinities, many Catholic practices blended well with existing ritual practice. Fourth, the Spanish clerics had a strong social conscience and often defended and supported the local peoples against the abuses of the military and the secular government. This basic orientation continues today with the involvement of many Catholic priests in movements based on Liberation Theology, a theological faction within the Church that calls for social justice based on biblical principles. On the other hand, the Spanish priests were hesitant to allow Filipino priests positions of authority within the Church.[26]

The Americans

The United States played a brief but significant role as a colonizing power in island Southeast Asia. The United States gained control of the Philippines as part of its victory in the Spanish–American war in 1898. At first the Filipinos expected the United States to support their bid for independence, but were disap-
...inted. In 1934, the U.S. Congress passed the
...McDuffie Act which provided for a 10-
...of self-government under U.S.
...ed by full independence.
...occupation, independ-
...946. It is interest-
... Philippines
..., rather than
...ines Indepen-
...years in length,
...hilippines had a profound affect on that nation; the United States implemented public education for the masses and the general use of English. The United States also rapidly Filipinized the bureaucracy and military and set up an elective assembly in 1907.

The Japanese

The brief Japanese period proved that the West was not invincible. Following the Japanese defeat of the Allies, the Japanese established the Greater Asia Co-Prosperity plan. Initially, many Southeast Asians welcomed the Japanese occupation. However, in time many resented the Japanese presence. In some ways, the Japanese occupation was harsher than European colonialism, in part due to the Japanese' interest in exporting rice. On the other hand, the Japanese organized independence committees that formed the basis of independence movements after the return of the Europeans. The Japanese period ended after the return of the Allies at the end of World War II. Shortly afterward, the European colonizers reclaimed control of their colonies. However, Nationalist efforts started under the Japanese continued and eventually led to independent states.

Postcolonial History

Indonesia declared its independence from the Netherlands on August 17, 1945. This independence was not easily gained. The long and, at times, desperate war for independence was finally won on December 27, 1949. Following independence, Sukarno governed Indonesia. The first years of the postindependence Sukarno regime have been called the Liberal Democracy period or the Democratic Experiment. The year 1957 marked the beginning of the Guided Democracy period. In 1965, Guided Democracy ended abruptly. In the early morning of October 1, 1965, a number of generals in the Indonesian army were murdered. These murders were blamed by the military on the *Partai Komunis Indonesia*, or PKI (Indonesian Communist Party), but it is commonly accepted that the U.S. CIA was involved.[27] What followed was a bloodbath of epic proportions, in which up to a half-million people were executed. In the aftermath of these events, Suharto emerged as the president of Indonesia. Suharto stepped down in May 1998, amidst economic crisis and student protests; Suharto had long used the symbols of Javanese kingship to justify his regime and the economic crisis of 1997 showed that he was no longer able to grant prosperity to the land and so was no longer sanctioned by God to rule. In 1999, the first democratic elections since 1955 led to the election of Abdurrahman Wahid, a nearly blind Muslim cleric. He was impeached in June 2001 for failure to turn around the economy; Megawati Sukarnoputri, the daughter of Indonesia's first president, became its fifth president.

In 1957, Britain granted independence to Malaya. In 1963, Singapore, Sarawak, and Sabah were incorporated into Malaya to form the Federated States of Malaysia. The government was one in which the head of state rotated among the sultans of the nine composite states and the head of government was an elected prime minister. Since Sarawak and Sabah are on the northern end of Borneo, their inclusion in Malaysia triggered a conflict with Indonesia that controlled the rest of the large island. In 1965, following race riots, Singapore seceded from the Federation. The conflict with Indonesia ended in 1966, with a reformation in which the inhabitants of Sarawak and Sabah decided to join Malaysia.

After World War II, the Philippines gained its independence. In the years immediately following independence, the United States reduced tariffs on Philippine imports to the United States which allowed American interest to exploit the Philippines' natural resources. In this same time frame, the United States negotiated 99-year leases for military bases. In 1965, Ferdinand Marcos became president. After being reelected in 1969, Marcos invoked a state of emergency in 1971 after a serious of terrorist attacks and invoked martial law in 1972. During martial law, Marcos's most outspoken opponent was Benigno Aquino. Aquino was sentenced to death in 1977, but in 1980 was allowed to go into exile. In 1983, two years after the end of martial law, Aquino returned to the Philippines and was brutally murdered at the Manila airport. Eventually his murder was linked to the military. In 1986, Aquino's widow, Corazon, was victorious over Marcos in the presidential election. Ferdinand, along with his wife Imelda, spent the rest of his life in exile.

Timor Leste, or East Timor, consists of the eastern portion of the island of Timor which, in the colonial period, was disputed and then divided by the Dutch and the Portuguese. Political shifts in Portugal in 1974 established the independence of all its colonies including East Timor. During the process of decolonization, Indonesia entered (some would say, invaded) East Timor and administered it until 2001. At first, this action was generally accepted by the United States and neighboring Australia. In time, however, human rights groups pointed out the excesses of the Indonesian military. After the fall of Suharto, his successor B. J. Habibie started a process that gradually led to the withdrawal of Indonesian forces and administration from East Timor and the establishment of a new nation.

CONTEMPORARY CULTURE

The demographic data illustrates a couple of key points. First, the population growth rate is very high in this region. In fact, most countries are actively trying to reduce population growth and encourage their citizens to have fewer children. The notable exception is Singapore which is trying to encourage college-educated, mostly Chinese, couples to have at least one child.

Some Basic Demographic Information

	Population (millions)	Projected 2025 Population (millions)	Infant Mortality Rate	Percent Population under Age 15	Percent Population over Age 65	Urban Population (%)
Indonesia	204.3	276.4	66%	34%	4%	31%
Philippines	73.4	73.4	34	38	4	47
Malaysia	21.0	32.8	11	36	4	51
Singapore	3.5	4.5	4	23	7	100
Brunei	.3	.5	52	35	3	67

Source: Demographic information from "Demographic and Social Patterns," by Graeme Huego, in *Southeast Asia: Diversity and Development,* by T. Leinback and R. Ulack (Eds.), 2000, Upper Saddle River, NJ: Prentice Hall.

Economics

Wet-rice cultivation is the major cropping pattern in much of island Southeast Asia. Wet-rice cultivation starts by planting seeds in a nursery bed. Meanwhile the fields are prepared—soil is broken up and the fields are flooded, the water being controlled by a system of dikes and irrigation canals. The seedlings are transplanted early in the rainy season. This can involve many people to get the work done on time. After the transplanting there is little to do during the growing season except to maintain the dikes and regulate water flow. The rice field forms a complex constructed ecosystem that also includes frogs, fish, and ducks, all of which may be kept or collected as food. Harvest can involve many people from the surrounding village. In some places like Bali millennium-old terraces continue to produce rice.

The Balinese irrigation system is particularly interesting in that rather than being controlled by the state, it is regulated by series of water temples and priests. The priests, by coordinating certain rituals, coordinate when each part of the island receives water for rice cultivation. Although the Balinese system is well established it may speak to the hydraulic hypothesis of state formations forward by Karl Wittfogel. Wittfogel argued that irrigation projects necessarily require state apparatuses to ensure fair distribution of water. The Balinese cases suggest that irrigation can be regulated outside the offices of the state. Because the climate would allow growing year-round, the limiting resource is water. Modernization projects, as part of the Green Revolution, tried to move the Balinese away from the religiously organized irrigation system; people were able to crop whenever they were ready. The results were disastrous: Pest damage increased and farmers were forced to use more pesticides which in addition to being expensive put additional strain on the environment. The prior cropping patterns had the effect of limiting pests by removing all of their food in one area at the same time. In 1992, a multidisciplinary team led by anthropologist Stephen Lansing set out to model the traditional irrigation system using then cutting-edge computer technology. They returned to Bali to demonstrate their model to both the temple priests and the government irrigation officers. The end result was a renewed appreciation for the traditional irrigation system.[28]

To deal with issues arising from high population density in certain areas and the need for more agricultural land, both Malaysia and Indonesia have engaged in large-scale resettlement and land conversion projects. The Malaysian program, called the Federal Land Development Authority (FELDA), is generally recognized as the more economically successful of the two. Both have been criticized for having negative environmental impacts. The Indonesian program, called *transmigrasi*, has also been criticized for creating social hierarchies between new arrivals and long-term residents of resettled areas. In transmigrasi, entire villages may be relocated from densely populated places like Java, Madura, Bali, and Lombok to less populated areas like Sumatra, Kalimantan, Sulawesi, and Irian Jaya. Transmigrants are given capital to build houses and farms. Since they are always of a different ethnic group from those who may already live in the area, the government funding they receive sometimes creates resentments.

Oil is very important in some areas. While Indonesia is a member of OPEC, other Southeast Asian countries are not. Malaysia has reserves of 3 billion barrels. Indonesia's reserves are estimated at nearly 10 billion barrels. Brunei's largest company is Brunei Shell Petroleum, half of which is owned by the governments. The majority share of the second largest company is held by the sultan's brother. In this way, Brunei is an oligarchy with the sultan as prime minister and minister of finance and domestic affairs and most important government positions are held by his family. Since major oil fields are located near key trouble spots, namely, Timor, Aceh, and Papua (formerly Irian Jaya), it is sometimes difficult to distinguish the politics of independence from the economics of oil.

Tourism has become an important element of island Southeast Asian countries. It is the second leading source of foreign exchange in the Philippines, the third in Singapore, and the fourth in both Malaysia and Indonesia. National governments advertise widely to bring in tourists. Indonesia's "Visit Indonesia Year" (1991) became "Visit Indonesia Decade" (1991–2001). Some areas have been overrun by tourists; small fishing villages have become beach resorts. Without the tourists, the economies of many towns in the region would completely collapse. Tourism is seen by many as a mixed blessing. While it provides a source of revenue, it places the well-being of many families on the vagaries of the tourist trade. After major disruptions like riots or terrorist attacks, shopkeepers may find their income severely reduced as tourists change their destinations to locations they perceive as more safe. In Indonesia, shopkeepers report a steady downturn ever since the May 1998 student riots that brought down President Suharto. Events like the bombing of pubs and nightclubs in Kuta, Bali, in October 2002 have only made things worse.

The money to be made in the tourist trade comes from a number of sources. Of course, there are the basics of hotels, food, transportation, and souvenirs. But there is also a steady trade in personal services: hairdressing (braids, cornrows, and the like), nail care, massage, laundry, and sex.

The souvenir trade has sometimes impacted local art markets in interesting, and some would argue, detrimental ways. In Bali, for example, the needs of tourists have made changes in the art forms ranging from subtle to nearly complete. Subtle changes include making pieces small enough to fit into suitcases or making larger pieces collapsible so that they may be shipped easily. Less subtle changes have been the creation of new forms that suit Western tastes. The most detrimental impact has been a reduction in the quality of the work. Since tourists may not be well educated about the art forms and the level of quality they should expect, enterprising artisans of mediocre talent have flooded the market. On the other hand, new and interesting art forms have emerged. One found in Indonesia involves taking wooden masks similar to those traditionally used in wayang wong, or masked dance, theater and applying designs using the lost-wax technique traditionally used in creating batik cloth. The early versions of this new form were exquisite and detailed. However, a common pattern repeated itself and now one finds cheap painted imitations more often. This is not to blame the artisans; people must eat, after all.

The benefit of tourism is distributed unevenly. Sometimes the hotels are owned by large corporations or absentee landlords. They do not have to live in the communities overrun by tourism. Also, it is not unusual for the nightly cost of a room in even a moderate hotel to be more than the monthly earnings of a hotel employee.

Sometimes related to tourism is the informal economy. Legions of street peddlers ply the streets of cities engaged in small-scale commerce. In Jakarta, peddlers of chewing gum, peanuts, and water will hop onto a bus (and not pay based on an understanding of shared poverty with the driver), sell their wares to passengers, and hop off a few blocks later to run back to the starting point and repeat their efforts on the next bus. Similarly, youths with musical instruments, but sometimes little talent, will board, play a brief piece, and ask for contributions to support their art. Traffic-choked streets swarm with peddlers selling drinks to thirsty drivers, cheap toys to take home to waiting kids, newspapers and magazines, and other low-cost items. Beggars tap on windows and transvestites shimmy in front of them for small coins. The most ingenious scheme remains those who rent out their bodies to be the extra needed passengers for drivers to use the carpool lanes.

Kinship and Gender

Most of the peoples of island Southeast Asia practice bilateral descent. That is, a person's descent is traced back through both male and female lines and that both Mom's kin and Dad's kin are counted equally as family. Since Islam favors patrilineal patterns of descent and inheritance, Muslim populations have an overlay of patrilineality on top of their indigenous system. There are some groups that are matrilineal—that is, descent and inheritance is traced through women. The most famous of these are the Minangkabau who are also Muslim. An interesting cultural issue for them is how to balance the matrilineality of their traditional culture with the patrilineality of their Islamic faith. The solution has been to create two descent systems around two separate economies. The matrilineal descent system centers on farmland and an agricultural economy. The patrilineal descent system centers on trade and a mercantile economy. In part, these dual systems mean that young Minangkabau men will leave home for several years to seek their fortunes and to build and expand trade networks. After becoming well established they will return home to marry.

Javanese Muslims face a bit of an odd situation when defining close kin. Islam does not include first cousins in its definition of closest kin (*isih muhrim*) but these family members are included in the traditional Javanese concept of closest kin (*sedular cedak*). This is important since "closest kin" cannot marry. Further, the touch of an opposite-gendered member of closest kin does not require ritual purification before prayers. However, the Islamic definition of closest kin includes children, regardless of genealogy, who are suckled by the same woman.

Some pious grandmothers have devised an ingenious way of having all their grandchildren be closest kin under Islamic law: they suckle them all. Thereby, people who would have been seen as less than "family" by the Islamic system but who need to be seen as family by the Javanese system are redefined as such through nursing. By allowing each of her grandchildren to nurse a woman can make them all closest kin under the Islamic system as they are seen under the Javanese system. By making both kinship systems match, cousins then would not be left in ambiguous situations where they would not know how to behave.

There is a general sense that, in island Southeast Asia, women enjoy a greater degree of equality than in other areas of the world. In some senses, this is correct. However, recent work has looked at the ways in which women are placed in structurally inferior positions.[29] For example,

Javanese society requires women to be more polite than men in most situations, particularly within the family. However, it is men who are more likely to cultivate politeness and formality through the language levels as a way to demonstrate superior status and authority. Further, a woman must take the risk of making social gaffes to preserve the status of her husband.

In both Malaysia and much of Indonesia, on one level men are seen as being more reasonable and responsible than women; they are dominated by reason whereas women are driven by emotion. In Java, women control finances because men are seen as being incapable of doing so; if given money a man will spend it irresponsibly, most likely to obtain illicit sex. However, as some scholars argue, this fiscal responsibility does not automatically translate into authority and prestige. A women's prestige is intimately connected with her husband's. Therefore, a women controls the money to keep her husband from doing things that will muddy his prestige (argue over money, get involved in illicit affairs, etc.) to protect her own standing in society. In the end, the subtext is that men are neither reasonable nor responsible but are given the social prestige of being both.

In much of island Southeast Asia, third genders, transvestism, homosexuality, and other nonstandard genders and sexualities are somewhat tolerated and accepted. In Java, there is a third gender known as *waria,* which is a contraction of the words *wanita* (woman) and *pria* (man). A clear distinction is made between waria and homosexuals. Waria do not have sex with other waria; they only have sex with men. These women-men engage in a number of economic activities include hairdressing, *ngamen* (singing/performing on the street for handouts), and prostitution. Most waria are known as such in their community but tend to keep their attire low key in their neighborhoods. However, outside their neighborhood they dress in full drag in a quite explicit and ribald fashion.

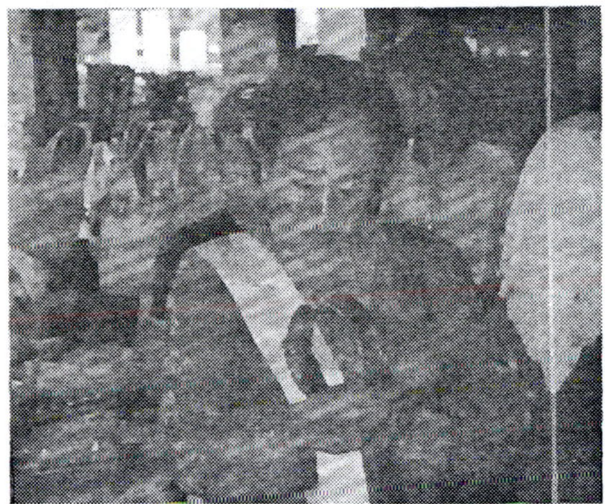

Waria: The third gender.

Sometimes, waria live with men as husband and wife and are generally considered to be married, even without the benefit of a formal wedding. Some even argue that this is morally superior to the situation of a man and woman living together without the benefit of marriage. When a waria lives with a man, the waria takes care of all the man's needs: cooking, cleaning, washing and ironing clothes, and general taking on the role of a good wife. They are considered to be married by their neighbors.

Supporting the notion of waria marriage as a legitimate form of marriage are the expectations and practices surrounding the male partner's desire to have children. Usually this means taking a woman as a wife. The man must ask the waria for permission first and sometimes even sets up a separate household. The practice of asking permission and setting up a separate household mirrors precisely the Islamic requirements for multiple wives.

Childrearing

Since childrearing practices shape the kinds of adults a society values it is useful to briefly examine the childrearing practices of a few Southeast Asian societies. In the past, childrearing has not been closely examined by anthropologists, although this is the institution in which society and culture is reproduced most effectively.[30]

On the Hindu island of Bali, young children are seen as gods, as ancestors reincarnated. Since they are divine their heads must be kept upright at all times, even when nursing. For the Balinese, reincarnation takes place on a very short cycle. Children are not allow to venerate ancestors of their great-grandparents' generation because they may be reincarnations of a people from that same generation. So, when a baby is born the Balinese seek the services of a diviner to determine whom the baby is reincarnating.

The Balinese believe that if a child is not treated with respect she may decide to leave the human world and return to the world of the gods. Deceased infants do not need to be purified by cremation because they are still considered free of sin.

The Balinese and the Javanese believe that a person's life will be influenced by four spirit siblings. The siblings are physically linked with the placenta, which must be treated with respect and properly buried. The Javanese bury the placenta of a boy just outside the house fence so that the boy will grow into a man who goes out in the world and earns his fortune, but close to the fence to ensure that the boy will return to his family with his earnings. A girl's placenta is to be buried next to the house, so that she will remain close to home and be a dedicated wife and mother. The Balinese make offerings to the spirit siblings so that they will protect the child and ensure the child's well-being.

Balinese parents are held responsible for molding their child's character. The first thing parents do in this regard is consult with trance specialists who will determine which ancestor's soul has been reincarnated and ask if there are any special requests for this lifetime. The specialists may also recommend that parents do things like make offerings to protect against an ancestor's greed or lusts. Personality traits are believed to be also influenced by day of birth, which is reckoned in terms of the intersection of a 7-day week yielding a 35-day cycle. A medium (*balian*) will be consulted to determine what a person's birthday means for personality and what prayers and offerings can be made to alter any undesirable characteristics. Renaming a child can also help counter negative personality traits that emerge.

The care of children on Bali centers on protecting the child's *bayu* or life force. A child's bayu can be weakened by loud noises and crying. Babies must be handled with extreme care and calm. Physical discomfort and rough handling will weaken an infant's bayu which is already weakened by virtue of being a newborn. Because infants and young children can become ill when emotionally taxed, mothers are encouraged to nurse their child before they start to cry. They are also expected to share their bed with the child at night until their third birthday.

Javanese society values adults who are tightly woven into an interdependent network of friends and family who at the same time are always aware of the place of both themselves and others in the intricate social hierarchy that typifies Javanese society. Various dimensions of childrearing practices seek to encourage this modal personality.

On Muslim Java, children cannot be seen as gods, but they are treated as very special and honored creatures who are at the same time not fully Javanese, not fully human. These two factors mean that children are deeply honored but since they are not fully rational, they cannot be expected to be treated as rational beings and therefore they are not punished in any way until they are five or six years old. Starting at age six, a child must start speaking to his father in the respectful form of Javanese. Degrees of familiarity on one hand and power on the other are marked in the Javanese language by selecting among three ranked choices for each word in a sentence. One uses the higher status words for people of higher status, for example one's father. A six-year-old child has been using the familiar form his entire life. Now Dad (and Mom) require that he address his father with words that he does not know. Which means that all he can say for a long time is "Yes, Sir." The once warm relationship with Dad becomes cold and distant. This is especially true for boys: Girls are allowed a slightly more familiar relationship with their fathers, but not as familiar as the one that all young children have. It must be so if the child is to be become fully Javanese and master the skill of negotiating social status through language use. In Java, whereas the relationship with Dad becomes rigid, formal, and fraught with tension, the relationship with Mom continues to be warm, attached, and loving. This has incredible implications for gender socialization, male bonding, and a number of other social psychological issues.[31]

The Semai, an Orang Asli group in Malaysia, practice a form of childrearing that is almost completely absent of punishment per se, and completely absent of corporal punishment. Children are taught the importance of *bood*, which is translated as "reluctant and shy." If a child is asked to do something, he may reply that he *bood*, which means that he refuses to do it. When asked why he does not hit a disobedient child, a Semai parent is likely to respond with a question like "What if she hits you back?" or "What if he dies?" The Semai prefer a form of discipline based on natural consequences—if a child is playing with a sharp knife, adults will intone the warning "sharp, sharp," but will otherwise not intervene. Since the child explores a new object somewhat tentatively, he is rarely, if ever, seriously hurt. And with a small nick, the child receives a clear reminder of the value of adult advice. The Semai are a nonviolent people, and because they value highly nonviolent responses to social stress, they use nonviolent childrearing to achieve this social goal.

The Semai also practice long-term breastfeeding, usually weaning around the fourth or fifth year of life—although there are reports of children as old as nine, alternately nursing and smoking a cigar. In addition, children feel comfortable leaning against any adult. This is not seen as an act of great affection but does suggest a sense of basic acceptance within the community.[32]

Filipinos cherish children; they as seen as gifts of God. Infants are seen as pure, almost sinless little angels, despite the Catholic doctrine of original sin. However, newborn babies who are unbaptized are considered not yet fully human. Before baptism, babies are constitutionally weak and particularly susceptible to illness. If they die before being baptized, they cannot enter heaven. Parents will grieve more over the loss of an unbaptized child because God will care after a baptized child.

Whenever possible, adults will cuddle and caress children. Both mothers and fathers are involved in the care of children. A father, tired from a day's work, would rather play with his child than nap. When children disrupt adult activity, such as ceremonies and rituals, they are gently moved out of the way and simply told not to do it again. Corporal punishment is not completely absent from Filipino childrearing, but it is seen as a last resort.

Children are also seen as investment in the future; as a way of ensuring care for oneself in

A Filipino family.

old age. Traditionally then, birth control has not been popular, even more so because Catholicism discourages its use. Pregnancy is seen as having both natural and supernatural causes. Repeated intercourse is seen as necessary for a woman to become pregnant; once or twice is not sufficient. Both Catholic and spirit beliefs come into play in explaining the spiritual components of conception. During the first nine days after birth the mother is not allowed to do any hard work. The husband will take over household chores in the rare event that female relatives are unavailable to help the family.

Filipinos, like the Javanese, consider colostrum to be harmful to the newborn babies and so the child is not breastfed right away. Breastfeeding starts on the third or fourth day. If the mother's milk does not come in, she eats a wide array of milk-inducing foods. If these fail, she performs a ritual to induce milk production. Because sleeping on the stomach is said to auger a difficult and short adult life, babies are made to sleep on their backs or sides.

Nursing becomes infrequent when the baby starts to teethe because of a tendency for babies to bite. If a nursling bites her mother's nipples, she is scolded angrily and spanked. Sometimes nursing is stopped and often this frustrates the child who may tear her hair out and scream. Various sweet foods are offered as replacements. If the mother resumes the nursing relationship, it is with the stern warning that further nipple biting will lead to the immediate termination of the nursing relationship. Weaning usually occurs after the first year and often well in the second or even third year of life. This transition from infancy to childhood is sometimes traumatic. One strategy for weaning is for the mother to rub her nipples with ginger, pepper, and soot. Another is to put worm excrement on them and tell the child the nipple is too dirty for nursing. At night, when the child is crying and begging for her mother's breast, she will be told that a monster will come and get her if she does not stop crying. Finally, a mother might cover her breasts with the flowers of the male papaya to dry out her milk supply.

Once children are strong enough, they go out and play with children roughly the same age, with their older siblings being responsible for their supervision. This creates strong bonds with age mates that will last throughout their lifetime. Children are taught to distrust strangers, primarily by being warned not to accept food or candy from them.[33]

Ethnicity Issues

Island Southeast Asia is ethnically diverse with several hundred ethnic groups speaking mutually unintelligible languages. Malaysia consists of the ethnically Malay population comprising 58 percent of the population of 21 million people with other ethnic minorities such as the Chinese, Indian, and other smaller groups making up the balance. The small country of Brunei with approximately 300,000 people also has an ethnic Malay majority, a Chinese minority, and smaller numbers of other ethnic groups. In contrast, 77 percent of Singapore's more than 3 million people is Chinese, although of various Chinese ethnic groups. Singapore also has significant Malay and Indian minorities. Indonesia has a total population of about 210 million people. About 60 percent of Indonesia's population lives on the island of Java and ethnic Javanese make up 45 percent of the total national population. Other ethnic minorities on different islands of Indonesia include the Sundanese, Acehnese, Madurese, Alorese, Sumatrans, Balinese, Moluccans, Iban, Dani, and many others. Ethnic Filipinos are 95 percent of the 77 million people in the Philippines.

In Malaysia, to be Malay means to speak the Malay language, have Malay customs, and to be Muslim. The link between Malay identity and Islam is so strong that the Malay phrase for converting to Islam is "*masuk Melaya*" or "entering Malayness." By the time the British arrived, this strong association had already been established.

The Tennger are a Hindu–Buddhist group living in the mountains of East Java. The Tengger do not see themselves as an ethnic enclave of non-Javanese but as heirs to a deep-rooted Javanese historical tradition. The Tengger think of themselves as Javanese, as belonging to but one among a variety of related "Javanese" religious traditions; they are often referred to by lowlanders as "real" Javanese (*Orang Jawa asli*). The example of the Tengger's adjustment to the fall of Hindu Majapahit in the fifteenth century and the ensuing Islamization of Java produces some insights that might help in understanding the general dynamics to Islamization. Islamization in East Java has tended to occur on the village level, with the village leaders deciding the nature of the village religion. Conversion has not been a personal matter, and perhaps not even a religious matter. It has often occurred in response to national-level politics. The sociopolitical nature of conversion has a long history in Java. The Islamization of East Java was associated with a steady stream of Central Javanese and Madurese immigrants brought in by the Dutch for coffee agriculture. Interestingly, the "coffee line" (1,200 meters) (3,937 feet)—the altitude above which coffee does not thrive—still provided, in 1985, an approximate line of demarcation between Tengger and Islamic settlements.

In much of island Southeast Asia, the colonizers created a plural society. Europeans, Chinese, and natives lived each in their own world as constituent elements in a plural society.[34] Dutch colonial policy and practice reified group boundaries and strengthened the plural nature of society. For instance, Dutch policies segregated the Chinese as a separate social entity with its own captains. Without Dutch intervention and protection, either the Chinese would probably have swallowed up the natives or they might themselves have been assimilated within a single homogeneous society. Certain industries and economic opportunities were preferentially given to the Chinese because they were seen by the colonizers as having keener intelligence and greater industry compared to the locals.

Throughout island Southeast Asia, overseas Chinese have moved into positions of great economic power. As a group, they have been compared to the Jews of Europe; being kept from landowning they turned to trade and moneylending and so amassed great personal wealth. In Indonesia there is considerable tension felt toward the Chinese. Until recently, Chinese inhabitants of Indonesia, even those whose families had lived there for 300 years, were considered outsiders and not full citizens. I recall the story of two Javanese youths who injured each other in a knife fight. The taxi driver who recounted the tale blamed the incident on the Chinese, because they had such control over the economy. The Javanese youths were so stressed that they were driven to violence against each other. To counter this antagonism, many Chinese have given up Chinese names and some have even converted to Islam.

Despite the fact many Chinese are citizens by birth and come from families who may have been in the region for centuries, they are treated in some ways as second-class citizens. The separation works both ways: Peranakan Chinese, or Babah of Malaysia, are descendents of Chinese traders and Malay women. Although they speak a language that is intelligible to the student of Malay, they call it *Bahasa Babah* and see it as a different language. In fact, linguists recognize Bahasa Babah as a creole with a Chinese substrate (grammar and syntax) and a largely Malay lexicon (vocabulary).

In both Indonesia and Malaysia, there is the idea of the true "sons of the soil" (Bumiputera in Malaysian, Pribumi in Indonesian); that is, those who are the true and rightful inhabitants of the land. This definition excludes Indians, Chinese, and later immigrants. Preferential treatment is given in education, finance, and other areas to Bumiputera in Malaysia. However, Bumiputera, which can be glossed as "indigenous," excludes the Orang Asli, tribal peoples whose ancestors were, undisputedly, in the region before the ancestors of the Malays. We now turn to a discussion of the experiences of tribal peoples in island Southeast Asia.

TRIBAL PEOPLES OF SOUTHEAST ASIA

In addition to the lowland agriculturalists that have been the focus of this chapter, island Southeast Asia also has large numbers of tribal peoples. They are frequently found in the hilly interior of the islands and typically engage in either foraging (hunting and gathering) or swiddening (slash and burn horticulture) as their economic base. Foragers are interesting to anthropologists because there are few left in the world today and because they give us a clue to how all humans lived prior to the development of agriculture. They are an imperfect model because they are not stone-age remnants but modern people connected to and participating in the world system. As discussed earlier, many Southeast Asian foragers belong to the Negrito ethnic stock. They are short, dark-skinned, and kinky-haired.

The Orang Asli, or Original People, of the Malay peninsula comprise over 18 ethnolinguistic groups varying in size from 100 to 20,000 individuals. In 1995 there were a total of 90,000 Orang Asli in Malaysia. The majority of the groups speak Mon Khmer languages of the Aslian subfamily related to the languages spoken in mainland Southeast Asia. A few groups speak Malay dialects and are hence considered by the Malaysian government to be "proto-Malays." We have already read an account of the lives of one Orang Asli group, the Semai, in the section on childrearing. The Orang Asli face a number of challenges that fall into three categories: government intervention, development and encroachment, and regroupment and Islamization.[35] Many Orang Asli groups have been placed on government reservations, experienced development projects in their territories that are of little benefit to them, and been pressured to convert to Islam and "masuk Melayu" which in some way then strengthens the Malays' claim of being indigenous.

The Batak are a Negrito group that live in riverine valleys on the island of Palawan in the Philippines. Traditionally the Batak lived primarily by foraging, although there is some evidence to suggest that they have been involved in the trade of forest products for centuries. With the expansion of lowland Filipinos on the island, the Batak have responded in a number of ways. The first was to move further and further into the interior. The second was to engage their new neighbors in trade for forest goods (honey, rattan, and copal). This interaction gradually led to the Batak working as wage laborers for their neighbors. The Batak still occasionally live off the land for periods of weeks to months, but in the end return to the permanent village established by the government.

The Batak are undergoing a process that has been described as being on the road to tribal extinction.[36] Being part of Philippine society has had a number of impacts on the Batak. First, their nutritional status and other indicators of physical health have declined. Second, their overall numbers have dramatically decreased. In part, this has been due to intermarriage with lowland Filipinos. Finally, there is a loss of culture. They are abandoning traditional practices because they fear being labeled primitive by their lowland neighbors. However, they are not replacing them with functional equivalents. For example, they have abandoned their traditional shamanic healing practices but do not have access to biomedical clinics.

An interesting case study of foragers concerns the Tasaday. In 1971, the Marcos government proclaimed that they had discovered a stone-age people living in the backwoods of the Philippines. Western journalists and film crews came out and documented a group living in caves, wearing leaf clothing, and collecting food with stone tools. In 1986, journalists returned to the area to find them living nearby in a village, wearing clothes, and engaged in other economic pursuits. The world was shocked; had the Marcos regime pulled an elaborate stunt on the world? Or had stone-aged people evolved in a few short years? Perhaps a third explanation more fully explains the complexity of the situation. Many forager groups in the Philippines today are engaged in a multitude of economic activities including wage labor and small-scale agriculture. They periodically make extended "camping trips" of a few weeks to a few months in which they practice their traditional foraging subsistence practices. It is possible that the "Tasaday" were exactly such a group. It is also possible that they were persuaded by a government official to go on a camping trip and to wear leaves for the duration of it.

In the headwaters of Sulawesi, a tribal group in the Bambang area practices a headhunting ritual, called *pangngae*, which uses a purchased coconut surrogate. The pangngae creates a cosmological order between the people of the headwaters and other populations on Sulawesi. Religion is not an ethnic marker for the people of the headwaters, many of whom have converted from the *mappurondo* religious order to either Christianity or Islam. Historically, the ritual cycled between using real heads and using coconut surrogates. When the Dutch colonialists and missionaries first came to the headwaters, the mappurondo communities were in the surrogate phase of the cycle. Because of the influence of the Dutch and later the Indonesians, they have remained in this phase.

The traditional victims of the mappurondo headhunters were the Mandar, a downstream Muslim population with which the people of the headwaters have had trade and work relationships for a long time. In the mappurondo cosmology, a relationship is created between lowland and upland peoples in which the upland people of the headwaters are the elder brother and the Mandar lowlanders are the younger brother, a socially inferior position. In reality, the trade and work relationship between the two communities establishes the Mandar as superior; the pangngae and the taking of "Mandar heads" reestablishes the proper relationship between the siblings. Interestingly, the Mandar have no notion of ever being the victims of mappurondo headhunting.[37]

Contemporary Islam

Islam is the majority religion in three island Southeast Asia countries: Brunei, Indonesia, and Malaysia. It also plays an important role in the Philippines where it is the majority religion in the southern part of that country. We have already discussed how, in Malaysia, Islam has become synonymous with Malay identity. The *dakwah* (prosyletization) movements of the 1970s in Malaysia, Singapore, and Brunei led to a more homogeneous and orthodox form of Islam than Indonesia. Islam in the Philippines has never been completely unifying for the Muslim groups. However, in recent years several separatist groups in the southern Philippines have espoused Islamic ideologies.

During the 1970s an Islamic revitalization movement developed in Malaysia primarily among young Malays who had moved from rural areas and were adapting to the new demands of education and modernist developments. Known as the dakwah movement, it led to an increasing emphasis on religious ritual, mosque and religious school attendance, the introduction of Arabic dress and language, and political Islamic themes in Malaysia. Despite the fact that Islam is perceived as a universal religion that is antithetical to racism, nationalism, and parochial identities, the dakwah movement in Malaysia has tended to be bound with the ethnic identity of Malayness. The dakwah movements tended to concentrate on the Malay community, and to be associated with the politics of that ethnic bloc in Malaysia. Even though some of the Chinese convert to Islam as a means of assimilating to Malay culture, they are not integrated within the Malay ethnic community. Islamic religious revitalization has exacerbated the ethnic divisions among the Malay, Indian, and Chinese population in Malaysia. The overtly pro-Malay and pro-Islamic programs of the Malaysian government have revived apprehensions among the non-Malay communities.[38]

Since Indonesia has the largest Muslim population in the world and the highest percentage of Muslims in Southeast Asia, it is useful to consider Islam in Indonesia in great depth. There are two major variants of Sunni Islam in Indonesia, which are generally referred to as Traditionalist and Reformist. Traditionalists are typified by their use of classical Islamic texts and their affiliation with pesantren and the organization Nahdatul Ulama (NU; Renaissance of Islamic Scholars). Reformists, who are affiliated with the organization Muhammadiya, seek to reform Indonesian Islam so that it draws primarily on scriptural sources.[39]

The Traditionalist variant is centered on pesantren, and their headmasters, kyai, are hence the leaders of this religious community. The theologies, considered opinions, legal theories, and findings and mystical theories of Traditionalist Islam are found in texts called *kitab kuning*. The pesantren community holds them to be of high importance in determining how to live as good Muslims in a globalizing and modernizing world. They are critical components of pesantren curricula.[40]

The Reformist branch of Indonesian Islam, which is in part affiliated with Muhammadiya, has established Islamic schools modeled after the pesantren, but none of these are recognized as true pesantren by Traditionalists. Muhammadiya takes a position that the basis of Islamic Law (*shariah*) is the Qur'an, *hadith* (the sayings and actions attributed to the Prophet), and personal interpretation. They thereby reject historical developments in Islam and classical Islamic scholarship.

Dutch Orientalist policies reified traditional customary law (*adat*) and authorized "religious Islam," while simultaneously repressing any assertion of "political Islam." This resulted in the rise of new popular forms of Islam that instilled critical attitudes toward native authorities. Muslim institutions, especially the Islamic boarding schools—the pesantren led by local scholars or kyai, which were hierarchical and authoritarian—spread throughout Indonesia and distanced themselves from state authorities. This diminished the capacity of the state or the pesantran institutions to induce and support any forms of civic engagement at the local level throughout the archipelago.

However, pesantren have historically played an important role in rural communities in Java. The kyai (headmaster at a pesantren) is often believed to possess *barakah* (blessing from Allah), which lead to reports of supernatural, or magical occurrences. Since barakah can be transmitted from its holder to others, a kyai's popularity and authority is partially derived from his value as a source of barakah. The kyai's involvement in the community has ranged from serving as consultants about the problems of everyday life and purveyors of traditional medicines to leading revolutionary cadres in times of great political and economic crises, often against Dutch colonialism and in support of the independence movement.

Prior to the twentieth century, pesantren were the only formal educational institutions found in Java and in most of what is now Indonesia. They taught an almost exclusively religious curriculum to a mix of students including future religious leaders, court poets, and members of the ruling class. First the Dutch, then the Nationalists, and later the Republic of Indonesia promoted an educational system focused on science, math, and other "secular" subjects. In response to the demand for this type of education, as early as the 1930s many pesantren added government-recognized curricula. Starting in the 1970s, these new curricula became an important part of the pesantren community's strategy for negotiating modernity. These changes have shaped both the daily round as well as a general sense of what kind of education a pesantren should provide. It is common for parents to seek schools that give their children the necessary skills and knowledge to do well in the modern job market and the moral and religious training to be good Muslims and upstanding citizens.

Pesantren exist for children and youth of all ages and at all stages of education—primary, secondary, and tertiary. While there are pesantren for both males and females, they are generally gender segregated. Today, 20 to 25 percent of Indonesia's primary and secondary school children are educated in pesantren-based schools. In some areas, such as Aceh, this number may be as high as 40 percent.

It is common for pesantren to engage modernity by opening government curricula schools at the junior high and high school levels. Contemporary pesantren at this level aspire to deliver both the pre-twentieth-century pesantren curriculum and the newer government curriculum with the hope of graduating alumni who have the religious knowledge and morality of a religious leader as well as the basic education needed to pursue further education at the college level.

An additional, even central, component of pesantren religious education is Islamic mysticism or Sufism. Key texts are studied and mystical practices, such as *dikir* (chanting religious formulae; literally, remembrance of God) are integrated into daily activities. Sufism as practiced in pesantren insists on a mysticism subject to normative Islam and distinguishes intellectual, emotional, and organizational components of Sufism.

For contemporary Islam in the region, an important question is to what extent can an Islamic-based society provide civil institutions that promote both pluralist and democratic proclivities? "Clash of Civilization" arguments perpetuate the notion that civil institutions are incompatible with and cannot be sustained within Islamic societies.[41] The Huntington hypothesis has been widely debated both among scholars and Southeast Asian Muslims.[42]

Sukarno, Indonesia's first president, argued that religion should be separate from the state and eventually promoted the ideals of *Pancasila*, a syncretic blend of nationalist, Muslim, Marxist, liberal democratic, and populist trends throughout Indonesia. Earlier Muslim intellectuals who founded the Muhammidiyah movement inspired by Islamic reformism stemming from Middle Eastern roots were divided over what role the state should play in enforcing Muslim authority. These Muslim modernists were caught between a conservative-fundamentalist and politically militant Islam and the forces of secularism. Meanwhile, independent Indonesian society under Sukarno's leadership was spiraling downward into a morass of clientage-based factionalized struggles among the communists, conservative and reformist Muslims, landowners, peasants, and merchants that undermined any form of civil society. The Suharto regime repressed Muslim activist politics while playing the Islamic card to sanction state authority against both communism and Western liberalism. However, during the New Order government new Muslim public intellectuals emerged representing a globally-based Islamic resurgence that would have a dramatic impact on Indonesian politics.

During the New Order (1965–1998), the Islamic community was politically neutered. Suharto's New Order regime consolidated all political opposition into two broad parties, the Indonesian Democratic Party (PDI) representing the Nationalist Party, Catholics, Protestants, and other nationalist groupings; and the Party of Unity and Development (PPP) that represented four different Islamic parties including the modernist Masyumi and traditionalist Nahdlatul Ulama. In addition, the government tried to deprimordialize the ethnic or religious base of Islamic politics by forbidding these political parties to operate at the subdistrict or village level. The newly formed government political party, Golkar, was the only political group allowed to be involved in local-level village politics. This undermined any sort of voluntary organizations that would be essential to civil democratic processes throughout Indonesia. Golkar itself was rigidly controlled by the state and both the state and Golkar remained subject to Suharto's authority. Muslim intellectuals, inspired by newly developing dakwah (the call to a deep profession of faith) movements throughout the Islamic world, recognized the need to either transform this dictatorial regime through constructive engagement or adopt a noncooperative stance toward Suharto's authority.

During the New Order, a new sort of Islamic scholar emerged in Indonesia. This new breed of scholars has Western education in addition to, or even instead of, traditional Islamic education. Their role in the Indonesian Islamic community is not yet clearly defined. They are learned and respected men, but they are not traditional *ulama*. Within the Indonesian Islamic discourse about development, they are trying to define three things: (1) their role within the Indonesian Islamic community, (2) their role in national politics, and (3) the role of Islam in the Republic of Indonesia. One way in which Muslim intellectuals define these things is through a careful selection of the symbols, models, and metaphors used to discuss development. Different groups select different Islamic symbols to emphasize.

An important Muslim organization founded initially by university students known as the Association of Muslim Indonesian Scholars (ICMI) was led by Dr. B. J. Habibie, a German-trained technocrat who became a close associate of Suharto who wanted to induce economic development through the development of aircraft manufacturing. Although this organization was coopted by the Suharto regime, its membership consisted of some Muslim intellectuals including Nurcholish Madjid who were committed to a civil, pluralistic, and democratic Indonesia and other Muslim activists who were factionalized over the role of the New Order regime and Islam in Indonesian politics. From within ICMI, Madjid criticized those factions who were hostile to Christian and Chinese populations in Indonesia and eventually targeted the Suharto regime itself for its undemocratic and corrupt practices. These undemocratic practices were demonstrated dramatically in 1994 with a government ban of several major Indonesian magazines that had published articles critical of both Habibie's and Suharto's involvement in corruption. This ban had the unintended consequences of stimulating democratic and Muslim forces that would inevitably bring down the Suharto regime.

Another Muslim public intellectual and politician, Abdurrahman Wahid, popularly known as Gus Dur, arose within the ranks of the Nahdlatul Ulama (NU) organization that provided the stimulus for activating a democratic movement opposed to the Suharto regime. Gus Dur was also an ally of the Indonesian Democratic Party (PDI) led by Megawati Sukarnoputri, daughter of Sukarno who had attracted wide support within both the military and as a critic of Suharto. Suharto strategists perceived the threat of an NU–PDI political alliance that would undermine its authority. They began to target Wahid and Megawati through a broad-based propaganda campaign that questioned their credentials as authentic Muslims and linked them with the reactionary mass killings of 1965–1966. Eventually, the regime sponsored a violent attack on Megawati's PDI headquarters and blamed it on a marginal communist political organization. This ploy inflamed some Muslim rightists who carried out mass demonstrations in support of Suharto. But Muslim public intellectuals such as Wahid and Madjid became allies in opposition to these devious strategies and called for the development of a pluralistic civil society in Indonesia that would counter the Suharto repressive and corrupt New Order.

There is no one-size-fits-all form of democracy satisfying universal needs, nor is there one single form of modernity, but rather a variety of configurations and reconfigurations that reflect family resemblances. The Indonesian case study illustrates the precarious nature of a democratic-civic-pluralistic form of Islam. Historically, the advance of Islam in Indonesia initiated plural and diffuse centers of powers, but these tendencies were stifled by centralizing European colonialist projects. Postcolonial Indonesian politics confronted secularist, ethnic, religious, and nationalist voices including the extremes from the ultraconservative and leftist circles of power. Yet, Muslim public intellectuals arose to militate against both an absolutist form of Islamic state and the use of Islam for reinforcing authoritarian corrupt regimes. This does not guarantee that a civil form of Islam will be sustained in Indonesia or reproduced in other historical, cultural, or political settings, but it sets the stage for an ongoing struggle for these institutions throughout the Muslim world.

Contemporary Christianity

With 60 percent of Asia's Christian population, the Philippines is the only predominantly Christian nation in Asia. As a legacy of Spanish colonialism, Catholicism remains a central part of Filipino private and public life. However, approximately 11 million out of the total 65 million Christians are non-Catholic.[43]

It is interesting to note that Filipino priests have become part of the liberation theology movement and thereby have argued that it is the responsibility of the church to address the needs of the poor. Historically, they have used this sort of religious argument to work for liberation from colonial rule by both Spain (1565–1898) and the United States (1898–1946). These teachings were also used to support the People's Power revolution that peacefully removed Ferdinand Marcos from power in 1986. In general, the clergy have worked to establish human rights, social justice, and freedom as an expression of the gospel.

In pre-Christian Philippines, certain people, objects, and places were considered sacred. These practices have been Christianized. Today, members of the clergy, both Protestant and Catholic, are highly respected. They are sought after as social and political allies because of their influence over the general population. Certain pilgrimage sites have been Christianized by being associated with saints. Other sacred sites have emerged when saints have manifested themselves in those places.

As might be expected, Easter is a central holiday. Many business and services are closed from noon on Holy Thursday until Easter Sunday morning. Good Friday is a special day; it is a taboo day for fishermen. It is seen as an omen of terrible fates, so fishermen fear for their lives if they go out fishing on that day. Statues of saints or even of Christ himself are paraded through communities. In some areas, live actors enact Passion Plays, depictions of the final hours of the life of Jesus.

At various holidays, namely All Saints' Day on November 1 and Fiesta de Mayo on May 5, Filipinos commemorate the dead. Twenty-four-hour vigils are held at gravesites which are decorated with flowers and candles. Families will also feast with the dead, sharing food and prayers with the deceased.

Protestant missionary activity started in earnest during the American colonial period. These missionaries were motivated by the desire to correct or purify what they saw as overly indigenized forms of Christianity. Since the missionaries came from different denominations, they formed a missionary alliance that gradually evolved into the National Council of Churches in 1929, which is run by local churches rather than foreign mission boards. Because neither

Spanish colonialism or Roman Catholicism penetrated remote areas, new Christian denominations, including Seventh Day Adventists and Jehovah's Witnesses, actively seek to win converts. Although once almost exclusively Roman Catholic, there are now a variety of forms of Christianity in the Phillipines.

In other areas, Christianity is less hegemonic. In many highland areas in Malaysia and Indonesia, tribal people have converted to Christianity. These conversions way be as much for political reasons as for motivations based on faith. In Indonesia, since everyone must declare a religion, tribal people sometimes select Christianity because it gives them a way of being distinct from their Muslim neighbors, connections to the worldwide Christian community for economic and political support, and the allowance to still eat their favorite food, pork. In the highlands of Central Sulawesi, the many Torajans have converted to Christianity. However, this conversion has not been easy. Traditional Torajans engage in elaborate funerary rites which last for days and include the sacrifice of buffalo and other animals to the deceased. Many Torajan Christians still want to perform these rituals because they see it as what makes them Torajan. Also, there is a certain appeal of these rites to tourists, so they have an economic benefit. The Torajan Christians attempt to define their old ways as *adat*, custom rather than religion, but the followers of the old ways are less than convinced. So are Western missionaries who wish that Torajan Christians would completely abandon the forms of their old religion and act in properly Christian ways.

Southeast Asian Hinduism: Bali

Bali is the site of the largest extant Hindu group in the region. The Balinese separate reality into three worlds: that of the gods, that of humans, and that of demons. They believe in reincarnation like Indian Hindus, but unlike Indians they believe that the time frame is very short. After a birth, the Balinese employ mediums and oracles to determine who is being reincarnated in the baby. For the Balinese, one of the most important spiritual goals is to balance good and evil. This is played out in many of their rituals. For example, the Barong-Rangda dance ritual pits Barong, a lion-headed dragon who represents order and cooperation against Rangda, a widow witch who devours children, who represents chaos and self-interest. In the long drama, the villagers come to the aid of Barong and have their *krises* (daggers) turned against themselves by the magic of Rangda. The battle ends in a tie, representing for the Balinese the notion that the goal is to find the proper balance between good and evil.

Another ritual that demonstrates the Balinese interest in finding balance is the Eka Dasa Rudra. People from all over Bali bring elaborate offerings for both gods and demons. This ritual is only performed every one hundred years and brings a balance to good and evil, returning the world to a state of complete neutrality. It was last performed in 1970. In 1963, several Balinese priests were convinced by then President Sukarno to start preparations for the ceremony early. Indonesia was in a state of crisis and Sukarno hoped that the ritual would help ease tensions and serve to legitimize his continued rule. Mount Agung erupted, destroying several villages but sparing the central temple. The priests and the people took this as a sign to stop the preparations and to wait until the proper time to hold the ceremony.

Contemporary Animist Religions

The Ngaju of Central Kalimantan are participating in local and national debates about *adat* (custom) and *agama* (religion). In Indonesia, everyone must declare one of five officially recognized religions (Hinduism, Buddhism, Catholicism, Protestantism, and Islam). Beliefs and practices not recognized by the Ministry of Religion are categorized as mere custom (adat).

The *tiwah* secondary mortuary ritual is the central ritual of *Kaharingan*, the Ngaju religion. To the Ngaju, to rebury the bones of one's relatives is an important responsibility that is part of a complex set of social and cosmological laws called *hadat*. Besides the national forces that attempt to define the tiwah as custom, there are local actors trying to enact this definition as well. Not unlike other parts of Indonesia, Christian and Muslim converts wish to define the religious practices of their ancestors as custom so that they do not have make a firm break with their heritage. Unlike the Toraja of Sulawesi, Christian Ngaju do not participate in traditional mortuary practices because Kaharingan has achieved official recognition as a religion, as a form of Hinduism. Christians do not generally tiwah their dead. However, they do participate in the less religious components of the tiwah and will erect small memorials above the graves of Christian dead during a tiwah for another villager or family member.[44]

CURRENT TRENDS

Three major factors are dramatically shaping the societies of contemporary island Southeast Asia: economic crisis, political crisis, and terrorism. In 1997, economic crisis hit Southeast Asia. No country went unaffected; however, Indonesia is the only country not to have fully recovered. Indonesia's lack of economic recovery is intimately linked to its political crisis that started in May 1998 with the fall of President Suharto. Indonesia and the Philippines have been struggling with the emergence of democracy. In this context, increased terrorist activity has emerged.

Economic Crisis

Previous economic crises in the region primarily impacted the lowest economic levels of the population; this one, however, also affected the middle and upper economic classes. Several countries in the region had dramatic increases in the number of people living below the poverty level. But this does not tell the whole story. The definition of "poverty level" may disguise how many people are facing economic hardship. For example, Indonesia defines the poverty level as having an income of 55 cents (U.S.) a day in urban areas and 40 cents a day in rural areas. Therefore, many people surviving on less than $1 per day were not defined as being poor. However, even with these measures, the percentage of Indonesia's population living in poverty jumped from 10.1 percent in 1997 to 37 percent in mid-1998. Malaysia's definition of poverty in 1999 was about 425 RM (Ringiit Malaysian) a month (or about $4 (U.S.) a day) which put the 3.7 percent of urban households below the poverty level. Some argue that urban poverty line should be set at 750 RM which would lead to 23 percent of urban households being considered poor. However, these percentages fail to put a human face on the soaring unemployment, increased school dropouts, people returning to the countryside, and increases in crime.

In Malaysia, the economy reversed itself from an average annual growth of 8 percent to contracting by 6.6 percent in 1998. It is interesting to note that as part of its response to the crisis, Malaysia cut by 10 percent the salary of government ministers and senior civil servants. Further, Malaysia refused IMF aid because it saw the IMF requirements for reform as too rigid. Malaysia welcomed aid from Japan and other sources, though.

Indonesia and Malaysia were hit harder by this crisis than Singapore or the Philippines. The general consensus among analysts is that the domestic causes of the crisis include macroeconomic imbalances, structural deficiencies in financial sectors, and shortcomings in political and corporate governance. How hard a country was struck is directly related to how serious these problems were within its borders. For example, a long history of corruption by the Suharto regime was one of the key factors in that country's economic collapse.[45]

Political Crisis

The economic crisis in Malaysia directly led to a political crisis. Finance Minister and Deputy Prime Minister Anwar Ibrahim was prepared to accept the IMF's demands for fundamentally restructuring the economy and opening it to great foreign investment and competition. These moves and his austerity package that cut ministerial salaries, deferred major investment project and generally reduced government spending by 18 percent was met by bitter opposition from Prime Minister Mahathir. Some suggest that Mahathir was protecting the business empires of himself and his circle that had been built through cheap credit, government contraction, and protections from foreign competition. A book titled *50 Reasons Why Anwar Cannot Become Prime Minister* was distributed at the annual meeting of UMNO in June. This book made explicit accusations of sexual impropriety as well as corruption against Anwar. In September 1998 Anwar was fired from the cabinet and was later dismissed from UMNO. He was convicted on corruption charges in April 1999 and on sodomy charges in August 2000. Human rights groups, Amnesty International, and Human Rights Watch have expressed concerns about whether Anwar's trials and appeals were fair. Some analysts have argued that while Mahathir's government has maintained control that is losing its hegemony, that is an almost unquestionable control. This crisis of hegemony is threefold: economic, political, and ideological. Mahathir's economic dealings are being questioned, significant opposition can now be found in organizations like Persatuan Islam se-Tanah Melayu (PAS), which is drawing some of the support from ethnic Malays from UMNO. Finally, the persecution of Anwar and his family to protect the political order went way beyond acceptable *realpolitik* and so Mahathir faces a significant loss in moral authority.[46]

During Indonesia's first 53 years of independence, a handful of traditional Javanese theories of leadership and their accompanying symbol set were important in legitimizing the regimes. Suharto had leaned heavily on Javanese theories and symbols of kingship, which holds a ruler legitimate as long as the land is prosperous. As the economic crisis deepened in Indonesia, the recently "reelected" Suharto regime was beset by scores of student protests throughout Indonesia. In short time, university students became the vanguard of a nationwide reform movement that led to Suharto stepping down in May 1998. Sticking to the Javanese theories and symbols he had long used, Suharto said that he was going to retreat from the world and spend his time in prayer and meditation so that the land might be prosperous again. Suharto's named successor, B. J. Habibie, called for elections several years ahead of schedule. In October 1999, the People's Assembly named Abdurrahman Wahid the fourth president of Indonesia despite the fact that Megawati Sukarnoputri's Indonesian Democracy Party—Struggle held the most seats in the assembly. At the time, there was concern by conservative Muslims about the suitability of a woman as president.

After the end of the Suharto regime, there was debate about the nature of the presidency and the symbols upon which it would draw. Since Suharto had drawn on Javanese kinship theories, there was an understandable desire to avoid such symbols in the post-Suharto era. At the time, there was a sense in much of the Islamic community that Indonesia might need someone who was more than simply a president, someone who could serve as the spiritual leader of the nation. In this regard, Megawati was not suitable and so her political ally Abdurrahman Wahid was elected. Abdurrahman is a kyai, a Javanese Islamic leader who combines the learning of an *'alim* (Islamic scholar) and the mysticism of a Sufi *syehk* (master). Some of his followers have gone as far as to call him a living saint. Others accept that he is kyai but argued that the trappings of kyai leadership do not belong in the office of the presidency. There are dimensions of the kyai leadership model that are incompatible with democracy—the idea that a kyai is a little king of his pesantren and his followers, for example. The process of democratization has also started to change ideas about kyai leadership including demands for fiscal accountability.

Abdurrahman Wahid's presidency ended in July of 2001. His continual shakeups of the military hierarchy were so resented that they eventually united officers against him. Unfounded corruption allegations against him, and his firing of key members of his own cabinet advisors including allies of Megawati, turned many proreform moderates against him. Some of his political allies came to view Gus Dur as imperious, acting as if he had no need of coalition partners to govern when in fact, near the end of his reign he controlled only a minuscule percentage of parliamentary votes. Eventually, Gus Dur turned to authoritarian tactics to try and stop the parliamentary moves against him. He made no secret of the fact that he wanted to declare a state of emergency and dissolve the parliament, unilaterally declaring that the impeachment moves against him were unconstitutional without acknowledging the wide power given to parliament in Indonesia's constitution. The army's decision to side with the parliament put it in the paradoxical position of defending democracy against Indonesia's great democratic hope. In his last desperate act as president, when he tried to impose a quasi-state of emergency, the army and police politely declined to go along. Gus Dur, a man who came to power through astute parliamentary politics, was judged to be an utter failure at the daily politics necessary to run the country effectively.

While Megawati Sukarnoputri was his vice president, Wahid's relationship to her became more politically distant. Gus Dur detected that she was beginning to gain more popular support from different factions especially in Indonesia. Increasingly, those who had previously argued against Megawati because she was a woman changed their argument. Essentially because she was merely a political leader and further the system of checks and balances prevent the president from having absolute control, a woman could be president. Megawati Sukarnoputri became the fifth president of Indonesia when Gus Dur was removed from office.

In 2004, Indonesia underwent its third set of democratic elections since declaring its independence in 1945. In April, the MPR or People's Consultative Assembly was elected. However, for the first time this body was not responsible for naming the president and in October 2004, the people of Indonesia elected Susilo Bambang Yudhoyono as the first directly elected president in the nation's history.

Terrorism

The aftermath of the September 11, 2001, attacks on the World Trade Center and the Pentagon has greatly affected Muslim populations in Southeast Asia. Prior to those attacks, a number of processes were developing in Muslim politics in the region, namely Islamization, globalization, democratization, and the negotiation of modernity and tradition. For Indonesia, these processes meant that expressions of Islam not previously witnessed in the country gained footing, for example, the emergence of radical groups like Laskar Jihad and Jemaah Islamiyah in the early to mid-1990s. In Malaysia, the rivalry between two Islamic parties led to Islamization becoming a state project, which led to concessions to Muslim conservatives.

The September 11 attacks horrified most Southeast Asians and many could not believe that terrorist attacks would occur within their own borders or even that terrorist cells linked to al Qaeda were operating in their own nations.[47] In May and June 2001, Malaysia made the first arrests of terrorist operatives in the region. In October 2002, Indonesia was rocked by the bombing of a pub in Kuta, Bali.

The major terrorist network in the region is *Jemaah Islamiyah* (JI). Evidence collected after the arrest of 15 members of the JI cell in Singapore suggested that JI had created alliances with the Moro Islamic Liberation Front in the Philippines and a militant group in southern Thailand. The hope was to set up a network to facilitate cooperative arms procurement and training.

JI is linked to al Qaeda but is not controlled by it. The relationship between the two organizations is multifold: overlapping membership and shared operations planning and execution, including the September 11 attacks. JI was founded by two Indonesian radical clerics, Abu Bakar Ba'syir and Abdullah Sungkar, both of whom were living in exile in Malaysia. Other major figures associated with the creation of JI are Riduan Isamadduin, also known as Hambali, and Mohammed Iqbal Rahman, also known as Abu Jibril. Hambali and Abu Jibril were alumni of the Afghanistan jihad and had been recruited into al Qaeda. In 1994, they were given the task of creating a network in Southeast Asia. Although founded in the early 1990s, JI's first terrorist acts were committed in 2000. These included the attempted assassination of the Philippine ambassador to Indonesia, and a spate of church bombings through Indonesia. By April 2001, they had also been responsible for a series of bombings in Manila, the assassination of local Malaysian politicians, and bombings in southern Thailand. They have also claimed responsibility for the bombing of a Balinese nightclub in which over 200 people were killed, and the August 2002 bombing of the J. W. Marriott Hotel in Jakarta. The switch to nonmilitary, or "soft," targets is attributed to the arrest of a large percentage of the senior leadership between December 2001 and January 2002. Today, JI has four regional commands: (1) peninsular Malaysia, southern Thailand, and Singapore; (2) Java and Sumatra (Indonesia); (3) the Philippines, Brunei, the island of Borneo, and Sulawesi (Indonesia); and (4) developing cells in Australia and the Indonesian province of Papua (formerly known as Irian Jaya).[48]

The Moro Islamic Liberation Front (MILF) and the Free Aceh Movement, Gerakan Aceh Merdeka, or (GAM) are sometimes considered terrorist groups. However, they are better understood as separatist groups because they differ in scope and aims from groups like JI. GAM seeks to secede from the Republic of Indonesia and create an Islamic state in North Sumatra. Likewise, MILF wishes to establish an Islamic state in the southern Philippines separate from that nation.

At this point, almost all the governments in the region are taking their counterterrorist efforts seriously. However, in some cases, notably Indonesia, it took major terrorist attacks before the government acknowledged the threat.

THE TSUNAMI

The high rates of seismic activity mentioned at the beginning of this chapter manifested itself on December 26, 2004, with an earthquake in the Indian Ocean that created a tsunami that killed over 250,000 people. The hardest hit area was the Aceh province in North Sumatra, Indonesia. The relief and reconstruction efforts in Aceh have been complicated by politics. Aceh

The tsunami in Aceh, Indonesia, December, 2004.

has been involved in periodic rebellion against the Indonesian government since its beginning (and against the Dutch colonial regime before that). As part of its efforts to suppress the Free Aceh Movement (GAM), the Indonesian government has not allowed any foreign travelers or observers into the region. This restriction caused some delay in getting foreign aid workers on the ground. More puzzling is the delay involved in getting Indonesian resources to Aceh. As late as February 2005, mass graves remain uncovered. Some observers conclude that the Indonesian government's indifference to Aceh has been an attempt to crush or discredit GAM. Unfortunately, some foreign journalists and policy makers have accepted the Indonesian government's depiction of GAM as a terrorist group associated with al Qaeda. The tsunami significantly reduced GAM's numbers and yet the Indonesian army has focused on pursuing the few remaining rebels.

On the other hand, the U.S. military's involvement in rescue efforts has gone a long way to repair its tarnished image after the Abu Ghraib scandal. Indonesians do not hold any animus against Americans, but oppose U.S. foreign policy in the Middle East. The United States could use this opportunity to build a strong ally especially by working with Islamic organizations who are leading the effort to help the Acehnese rebuild their lives.

Another issue the international community must pay attention to both in Aceh and in other areas affected by the tsunami is efforts to move shoreline communities up to 2 kilometers (1.2 miles) inland. This will have a strong negative impact on local fishermen. Further, as some Acehnese fear, it will lead to a land grab with the government and corporations taking control of the coastal lands for the development of hotels and resorts at high profits which will not be shared with the Achenese people.[49]

This chapter has introduced the major geographic, ecological, prehistoric, linguistic, historical, social structural, political, and religious beliefs and practices that have had an influence on island Southeast Asia. These influences have produced a tremendous cultural diversity throughout the many island areas in the region. The peoples in island Southeast Asia continue to confront significant challenges as they wrestle with the new pressures of globalization that bring into being both diversifying and unifying tendencies for their cultural traditions. The symbols of globalization associated with America, Japan, China, India, and elsewhere have invoked both resistance and emulation among the populations in the area. Undoubtedly, the people in island Southeast Asia will continue to innovate and modify their indigenous, local cultural forms and practices just as they did in the past. Southeast Asian and Western anthropologists continue to collaborate to produce significant insights into these rapidly changing cultural traditions and practices. We will continue to track both global and local tendencies to gain insights on how people of island Southeast Asia adapt and adjust to the twenty-first century and beyond.

NOTES

1. For an excellent introduction to Southeast Asia that includes physical geography, economics, history, and politics, the best source is the edited volume by Thomas Leinback and Richard Ulack, eds., *Southeast Asia: Diversity and Development* (Upper Saddle River, NJ: Prentice Hall, 2000).
2. An interesting and readable account of the study of human evolution on the island of Java is Carl Swisher, Garniss H. Curtis, and Roger Lewin, *Java Man: How Two Geologists' Dramatic Discoveries Changed Our Understanding of the Evolutionary Path to Modern Humans* (New York: Scribner's, 2000). Another useful source on the subject is C. Loring Braces's classic article "Creationists and the Pithecanthropines," *Creation/Evolution* XIX (1986–1987). Reprinted by permission on http://www. talkorigins.org/faws/homs/ brace.html, accessed September 30, 2003. For a general treatment of human evolution, look at Frank Poirier and Jeffrey McKee, *Understanding Human Evolution*, 4th ed. (Upper Saddle River, NJ: Prentice Hall, 1999).
3. Acheulean tools are a lithic (stone) tool industry normally associated with *Homo erectus*. This stone tool tradition is characterized by teardrop-shaped hand axes chipped on both sides, picks, and cleavers. For an excellent source see Kathy D. Schick and Nick Toth, *Making Silent Stones Speak: Human*

Evolution and the Dawn of Technology (New York: Simon and Schuster, 1993).

4. See the discussion of the Hoa Binh culture in Chapter 8 of this volume.

5. The relevant resources in the study of the Javanese language and its social uses are Joseph Errington, *Language and Social Change in Java: Linguistic Reflexes of Modernization in a Traditional Royal Polity* (Athen, OH: Ohio University Center of International Studies, 1985); John Wolff and Soepomo Poedjosoedarmo, *Communicative Codes in Central Java* (Ithaca, NY: Cornell University Southeast Asia Program Linguistic Series VIII, 1982); Gregory Moedjanto, *The Concept of Power in Javanese Culture* (Yogyakarta, Indonesia: Gadjah Mada University Press, 1990); and Nancy Smith-Hefner, "A Social History of Language Change in Highland East Java," *Journal of Asian Studies* 48, no. 2 (1989): 257–271.

6. The classic article of Javanese cosmology and beliefs is Justus Van Der Kroef, "Javanese Messianic Expectations: Their Origin and Cultural Context," *Comparative Study in Society and History* 1, no. 4 (1959).

7. An excellent introduction to the prehistory of this region is Peter Bellwood, *Prehistory of the Indo-Malaysian Archipelago* (Honolulu: University of Hawaii Press, 1997).

8. For students interested in reading about the history of Asia in an outline form, I recommend John Bowman, *Columbia Chronologies of Asian History and Culture* (New York: Columbia University Press, 2000). This excellent book provides historical summaries for the major countries of Asia from prehistory to modern times. A readable narrative summarizes the key points, while detailed chronologies recount significant events.

9. To describe historical dates, we will use the scholarly notations *BCE* for Before Common Era and *CE* for Common Era instead of the liturgical notations *BC* for Before Christ and *AD* for *Anno Domino* (In the Year of Our Lord). This allows us to acknowledge that among the myriad historical calendars people of the world use, there is one we use in common. However, the scholarly notation allows us to disassociate that common calendar from the understandings of a specific religion.

10. For a basic introduction to the Prambanan temples see "The Prambanan Temples" on *Travelling in Indonesia*, http://www.emp.pdx.edu/htliono/pramban.html, accessed April 22, 2004.

11. Perhaps the best review of the Borobodur site is the information compiled by the World Heritage Foundation to establish it as a World Heritage Site in "World Heritage Review: The Borobodur Complex" (2003), http://www.worldheritagereview.org/news/fullstory.php/aid/44/The_Borobodur_Compound.html, accessed February 9, 2004.

12. For a good study of the Javanese shadow play and the role it plays in the lives of people, see Ward Keeler, *Javanese Shadow Plays, Javanese Selves* (Princeton, NJ: Princeton University Press, 1987).

13. The classic studies of precolonial states in island Southeast Asia are A. C. Milner, "Islam and the Muslim State," in *Islam in Southeast Asia*, ed. M.B. Hooker (Leiden, the Netherlands: Brill, 1983); Soemarsaid Moertono, *State and Statecraft in Old Java. A Study of the Later Mataram Period, 16th to 19th Century* (Ithaca, NY: Cornell University, 1968); P. E. de Josselin De Jong, *Ruler and Realm: Political Myths in Western Indonesia* (New York: North Holland, 1980); and Theodore Pigeaud and H. J. De Graaf, *Islamic States in Java 1500–1700* (The Hague, the Netherlands: Martinus Nijhoff, 1976).

14. The classic ethnographic study of Java, the one said to have launched Java studies in the United States, is Clifford Geertz, *Religion of Java* (Chicago: University of Chicago Press, 1960). It is important to note that this work has proved controversial. Geertz divides Javanese religion into three variants: *abangan*, *santri*, and *priyayi*. The nominally Muslim peasant villagers adhere to the *abangan* tradition, which is said to be highly syncretic. *Santri* are middle-class traders, village chiefs, and well-to-do peasants whose economic lives center on the market. *Santri* are more conservative in their expression of the Islamic faith than either the *abangan* or the *priyayi* and are associated with *pesantren*. The *priyayi* are white-collar government bureaucrats descended from the traditional aristocracy and practice a form of religion derived from the court Hindu–Buddhism of the pre-Islamic era. At first it was widely accepted and its categories were used by other social scientists to explain complex social behavior. In the mid to late 1980s, it started to come under criticism from both Indonesians and Western scholars. Today, its basic analysis is held highly suspect.

15. An interesting study comparing two Muslim cultures is Clifford Geertz, *Islam Observed: Religious Development in Morocco and Indonesia* (Chicago: University of Chicago Press, 1968). Geertz compares how common Islamic concepts, like that of saints, are expressed in very different ways in two different countries.

16. An important critique of the Geertzian paradigm was Mark Woodward, *Islam in Java: Normative Piety and Mysticism in the Sultanate of Yogyakarta* (Tucson: University of Arizona, 1989.) Woodward demonstrated that the religious practices of Java are best understood as forms of Islam and not syncretic or Hindu–Buddhist traditions. A more recent treatment of the debate is found in Andrew Beatty, *Varieties of Javanese Religion: An Anthropological Account* (New York: Cambridge University Press, 1999).

17. The later kingdom of Mataram was Muslim and used the name of the earlier Mataram dynasties to enhance its legitimacy.

18. For a good introduction to the Wali Songo, see "Wali Songo: The Nine Walis" on *Sejarah Indonesia: An Online Timeline of Indonesian History*, http://www.gimonca.com/sejarah/walisongo.shtml, accessed April 21, 2004.

19. The classic study of Southeast Asian political theories is Robert Heine-Geldern, "Conceptions of State and Kingship in Southeast Asia," *Far Eastern Quarterly* 2 (1942): 15–30.

20. For the classic treatment of Persian political theories, which greatly influenced Muslim Southeast Asia, turn to Ann Lambton's two-part articles "Quis Custodiet Custodes: Some Reflections on the Persian Theory of Government," *Studia Islamica* 5 (1955): 125–148; and 6 (1956): 125–146.

21. The seminal work on Javanese theories of power, and hence politics is Benedict Anderson, "The Idea of Power in Javanese Culture," in *Culture and Politics in Indonesia*, ed. Claire Holt (Ithaca, NY: Cornell University Press, 1972). For a specific analysis of the Javanese courts, examine Aart Van Beek, *Life in the Javanese Kraton* (New York: Oxford University Press, 1991).

22. For a detailed account of this ritual see Mark Woodward, "The Garebeg Malud in Yogyakarta: Veneration of the

Prophet as Imperial Ritual," *Journal of Ritual Studies* 5, no.1 (1991): 109–132.

23. For a good introduction to modern Bali, see the volume edited by Linda Connor, *Staying Local in the Global Village: Bali in the Twentieth Century* (Honolulu: University of Hawaii Press, 1999). For this discussion, I draw upon Michel Picard's contribution "The Discourse of Kebalian: Transcultural Constructions of Balinese Identity.

24. Peter Boomgaard's *Children of the Colonial State: Population Growth and Economic Development in Java, 1795–1880* (Amsterdam: Free University Press, 1989) remains a solid treatise on colonial Java.

25. A good introduction to Indonesian history is Merle Ricklef, *A History of Modern Indonesia* (Bloomington: Indiana University Press, 1981).

26. A good introduction to the history of Catholicism in the Philippines is Susan Russell's Web article "Christianity in the Philippines," http://www.seasite.niu.edu/crossroads/russell/christianity.htm. For an introduction to the general history of the Philippines which includes a discussion of the indigenization of Catholicism, see John Larkin, "Philippines History Reconsidered: A Socioeconomic Perspective," *The American Historical Review* 87, no. 3 (June 1982): 595–628. For a deeper treatment of these issues see Fenella Cannell, *Power and Intimacy in the Christian Philippines* (Cambridge, England: Cambridge University Press, 1999).

27. A good starting place for examining CIA covert operations is Ted Gup, *The Book of Honor: Covert Lives and Classified Deaths at the CIA* (New York: Anchor Books/Doubleday, 2001).

28. This project is documented in the movie *The Goddess and the Computer*, Documentary Educational Resources, 1988.

29. A fantastic book on gender issues in Southeast Asia is a volume edited by Aihwa Ong and Michael Peletz, *Bewitching Women, Pious Men* (Berkeley: University of California Press, 1995). In addition, Peletz's *Reason and Passion: Representations of Gender in a Malay Society* (Berkeley: University of California Press, 1996) is a classic.

30. For an interesting treatment of childrearing throughout the world refer to Judy Deloache and Alma Gottlieb, eds., *World of Babies: Imagined Childcare Guides for Seven Societies* (New York: Cambridge University Press, 2000). In this innovative book, the contributors each wrote a chapter as if they were writing a childcare manual for members of the particular society about which they were writing. Marissa Diener's chapter on Bali, "Gift from the Gods: A Balinese Guide to Early Child Rearing," was an important source for this discussion.

31. The classic study of Javanese family life is Hildred Geertz, *The Javanese Family: A Study of Kinship and Socialization* (Glencoe, IL: Free Press, 1961).

32. For the classic study on the Semai see Robert Dentan, *The Semai* (New York: Holt, Rinehart and Winston, 1968).

33. A classic treatment of Filipino childrearing and education is F. Landa Jocano, *Growing Up in a Philippine Barrio* (New York: Holt, Rinehart and Winston, 1969).

34. The classic reference on plural societies is John S. Furnivall, *Netherlands India: A Study of Plural Economy* (New York: Macmillan, 1944).

35. For a detailed but unsettling account of the Orang Asli contemporary situation see Robert Knox Dentan et al., *Malaysia and the Original People: A Case Study on the Impact of Development on Indigenous Peoples* (Boston: Allyn & Bacon, 1997).

36. The definitive treatment on the Batak is James F. Eder, *On the Road to Tribal Extinction: Depopulation, Deculturation, and Adaptive Well-Being Among the Batak of the Philippines* (Berkeley: University of California Press, 1987). The reader should note that in island Southeast Asia, there are a number of unrelated groups called Batak.

37. For a compelling treatment of this community see Kenneth M. George, *Showing Signs of Violence: The Cultural Politics of a Twentieth-Century Headhunting Ritual* (Berkeley: University of California Press, 1996).

38. A seminal work on this topic is Judith Nagata, *The Reflowering of Malaysian Islam: Modern Religious Radicals and Their Roots* (Vancouver: University of British Columbia Press, 1984).

39. The seminal studies of Muhammadiya are James Peacock, *Muslim Puritans* (Berkeley: University of California Press, 1978) and *Purifying the Faith: The Muhammdijah Movement in Indonesian Islam* (Tempe: Arizona State University Program for Southeast Asian Studies, 1992).

40. The most important work in English about pesantren is Zamakhsyari Dhofier, *The Pesantren Tradition: A Study of the Role of the Kyai in the Maintenance of the Traditional Ideology of Islam in Java* (Tempe: Arizona State University Program for Southeast Asian Studies, 1999). Other interesting works include Ronald Lukens-Bull's article, "Two Sides of the Same Coin: Modernity and Tradition in Indonesian Islamic Education," *Anthropology and Education Quarterly* 32, no. 3 (2001): 350–372; and his article "Teaching Morality: Javanese Islamic Education in a Globalizing Era," *Journal of Arabic and Islamic Studies* (2000): 26–48.

41. "Clash of Civilizations" was a phrase popularized by Samuel Huntington in his article that used the phrase as the title "The Clash of Civilizations," *Foreign Affairs* 72, no. 3 (1993): 22–49.

42. An important source for this discussion is Robert Hefner, *Civil Islam* (Princeton, NJ: Prinecton University Press, 2000) and his more recent contribution of a survey of recent trends in Islamic radicalism and its impact on Indonesia titled "Indonesian Islam at the Crossroads," *Van Zorge Report on Indonesia* 4, no. 3 (2002): 12–20. Other anthropological accounts of Islam in Indonesia are by John Bowen, especially *Muslims Through Discourse: Religion and Ritual in Gayo Society* (Princeton, NJ: Princeton University Press, 1993) and his recent *Islam, Law and Equality in Indonesia: An Anthropology of Public Reasoning* (Cambridge, England: Cambridge University Press, 2003).

43. For a basic treatment of Christianity in the Philippines see Kathleen Nadeau, "Philippines," in *Worldmark Encyclopedia of Religious Practices* (Gale Publishing, 2004). For more advanced reading, I recommend Wilfredo Fabros, *The Church and Its Social Involvement in the Philippines, 1930–1972* (Quezon City, Philippines: Ateneo de Manila Press, 1988); and Kathleen Nadeau, *Liberation Theology in the Philippines: Faith in a Revolution* (Westport, CT: Praeger, 2002).

44. See Anne Schiller, *Small Sacrifices: Religious Change and Cultural Identity among the Ngaju of Indonesia* (New York: Oxford University Press, 1997).

45. For a summary and analysis of the Asian economic crisis of the late 1990s see Frank Ching, "Social Impact of the Regional Financial Crisis" and Linda Lim, "The Challenges for Government Policy and Business Practice," both in the report *The*

Asian Economic Crisis: Policy Choices, Social Consequences and the Philippine Case, published by the Asia Society at http://www.asiasociety.org/publications/update_crisis_ching.html, accessed April 9, 2004. It should be noted that Ching's essay does not address the Philippines but discusses the regional context and includes discussions of Thailand, South Korea, Malaysia, and Indonesia.

46. A useful introduction to the circumstances around Anwar Ibrahim is "Anwar Ibrahim" in *Wikipedia: The Free Encyclopedia*, http://en.wikipedia.org/wiki/Anwar_Ibrahim, accessed April 26, 2004. A fuller discussion of Malaysia politics under Mahathir is John Hilley, *Malaysia, Mahathirism, Hegemony, and the New Opposition* (New York: Zed Books, 2001).

47. For a compelling treatment of Muslim politics before and after September 11, see Suzaina Kadir, "Mapping Muslim Politics in Southeast Asia after September 11," published by the European Institute for Asian Studies at http://www.eias.org.

48. A short but excellent introduction to terrorist networks in Southeast Asia is Zachary Abuza, "Funding Terrorism in Southeast Asia: The Financial Network of Al Qaeda and Jemaah Islamiyah," *NBR Analysis* 14, no. 5 (December 2003). For a fuller treatment see his *Militant Islam in Southeast Asia: Crucible of Terror* (Boulder, CO: Lynne Reiner, 2003).

49. The academic assessment of the tsunami's impact is still being developed. However, a useful early account is John R. Bowen, "After the flood: Islamic volunteers, with help from the U.S., can rebuild Aceh," *St. Louis Post-Dispatch*, Sunday, January 16, 2005. Another interesting post-tsunami analysis is the Oakland Institute's "Aceh Abandoned: The Second Tsunami" (http://www.oaklandinstitute.org/?q=node/view/145), accessed February 20, 2005.

Chapter 1
Introduction to Asia

Dr. Raymond Scupin is professor of anthropology at Lindenwood University. He received his BA degree in history and Asian studies, with a minor in anthropology, from the University of California–Los Angeles. He completed his MA and PhD degrees in anthropology at the University of California–Santa Barbara in 1978. Dr. Scupin has continued extensive ethnographic fieldwork in Thailand with a focus on understanding the ethnic and religious movements among the Muslim minority.

Dr. Scupin has authored a number of widely used textbooks for undergraduate teaching in anthropology for Prentice Hall. These textbooks include *Religion and Culture: An Anthropological Focus* (2000); *Race and Ethnicity: An Anthropological Focus on the United States and the World* (2003); *Cultural Anthropology: A Global Perspective,* 6th edition (2006); and *Anthropology: A Global Perspective,* 5th edition (2004).

Chapter 2
Afghanistan

Dr. Homayun Sidky is an Afghan American anthropologist. Currently he is associate professor of anthropology in the Department of Anthropology at Miami University, Oxford, Ohio. Dr. Sidky received an MA in sociology from the University of Miami, Florida, and holds a PhD in cultural anthropology from Ohio State University. His areas of interest include the anthropology of religion, ecological anthropology, anthropological theory/history of anthropological thought, and political Islam with a focus on the Taliban and related movements. Dr. Sidky has conducted field research in Afghanistan, Pakistan, Nepal, Easter Island, and Australia. The author of numerous scholarly articles and books, his most recent publications include *Perspectives on Culture: A Critical Introduction to Theory in Cultural Anthropology* (Prentice Hall, 2004); *A Critique of Postmodern Anthropology: In Defense of Disciplinary Origins and Traditions* (2003); *Halfway to the Mountain: The Jirels of Eastern Nepal* (2002); and *The Greek Kingdom of Bactria [Afghanistan]: From Alexander to Eucratides the Great* (2000).

Dr. Deborah S. Akers is a cultural anthropologist at Miami University in Oxford, Ohio. Dr. Akers has lived and conducted fieldwork in Dubai, United Arab Emirates, as well as in Jeddah, Saudi Arabia, where she has maintained residence for the past 20 years. The geographical areas of her research include the Middle East (Saudi Arabia and Arabian Gulf), Central Asia, and South Asia (Afghanistan and Nepal). Her research focus is on political tribal systems and political Islam in Saudi Arabia and the Gulf. Her other areas of interest include culture conflict and resolution in the Islamic world.

Dr. Akers' essays include "Human Rights in Saudi Arabia: Voices from Within," "Cosmopolitanism as Political Engagement among Afghan Women," "An Uighyur Woman in Mekka, Saudi Arabia: The Hajj as Political Engagement," "Afghan Aborigine Muslims in the Outback," "Women's Self-Immolation in Post Taliban Afghanistan," and "Reverse Hajj: Wahhabism in Xinxiang, China."

Dr. Akers also holds a Juris Doctorate, which she has used in her position as liaison officer with the U.S. Congress Foreign Affairs Committee on Bosnia and Iran and staff attorney and then director for oversight with the Committee on House Administration for the Smithsonian and the Library of Congress.

Chapter 3
India

Dr. Anne Hardgrove holds a PhD in anthropology and history from the University of Michigan, Ann Arbor. She conducted fieldwork in Calcutta and northern India among the diasporic Marwari trading community. Her book *Community and Public Culture,* based on that ethnographic and historical research, has been published by Columbia University Press and Oxford University Press in India. This ethnographic and historical work focuses on trade, ethnicity, gender, social, political, religious, and cultural life of this community. Dr. Hardgrove's current ethnographic research focuses on gender, sexuality, transnationalism, and religion, and is tentatively titled *The Global Erotic: Translating the Kamasutra.* She is presently teaching at the University of Texas, San Antonio, in history and anthropology.

Chapter 4
Pakistan

Dr. Anita M. Weiss, professor of international studies at the University of Oregon, received her PhD in sociology from the University of California at Berkeley. She has published extensively on social development and gender issues, including *Walls within Walls: Life Histories of Working Women in the Old City of Lahore,* 2nd ed. (Oxford University Press, 2002); and *Culture, Class and Development in Pakistan: The Emergence of an Industrial Bourgeoisie in Punjab* (Westview Press, 1991). She edited *Islamic Reassertion in Pakistan: The Application of Islamic Laws in a Modern State* (Syracuse University Press, 1986); and she most recently coedited (with Zulfiqar Gilani) *Power and Civil Society in Pakistan* (Oxford University Press, 2001). She is currently completing a book manuscript titled *Interpreting Islam, Modernity and Women's Rights: Implementing CEDAW in Pakistan, Tunisia and Malaysia,* which addresses the way Muslim states are grappling with international human rights to construct a practical understanding of Islamic views on women's human rights.

Chapter 5
China

Dr. Pamela A. DeVoe is the Community Connections manager at the International Institute of St. Louis, a nonprofit organization working with refugees and immigrants. With graduate degrees from the University of Wisconsin, Milwaukee (BA in anthropology), the University of Missouri (MA in anthropology and postdoctorate in cross-cultural mental health), and the University of Arizona (PhD in Asian studies with a minor in anthropology), her areas of specialization and past publication center on a range of intra- and international migration issues. She has conducted research in a variety of cultural settings, from the Seminole Indians in Florida, and the Taiwanese in Taiwan, to diverse refugee groups (such as Sino-Vietnamese, Vietnamese, Lao, and Somali) in the midwestern United States on topics involving education, gender, religion, economics, and social change. Dr. DeVoe conducted research among Southeast Asian refugees in the St. Louis area through the International Institute of St. Louis.

Dr. DeVoe has published widely on topics ranging from Taiwanese family structure to refugees and refugee issues in the Midwest, including "Refugee Work and Health in Mid-America" featured in her edited volume *Selected Papers on Refugee Issues* (Arlington, VA: American Anthropological Association, 1992) and more recently "The Silent Majority: Women as Refugees" and "Symbolic Action: Religion's Role in the Changing Environment of Young Somali Women."

Chapter 6
Japan

Dr. John L. McCreery is an anthropologist who has lived and worked in Japan since 1980. For 13 of those years, he was a copywriter and creative director for Hakuhodo Incorporated, Japan's second largest advertising agency. His academic credentials include a BA in philosophy (Michigan State University, 1966) and a PhD in anthropology (Cornell University, 1973). His dissertation, *The Symbolism of Popular Taoist Magic,* was based on two years of fieldwork in Taiwan. When asked how an anthropologist became an adman, he replies, "In Taiwan I studied magicians. In Japan I joined the guild." Recent publications include "Traditional Chinese Religion" in Raymond Scupin, ed., *Religion and Culture: An Anthropological Focus* (Prentice Hall, 2000) and John McCreery, *Japanese Consumer Behavior: From Worker Bees to Wary Shoppers,* 2000.

Ruth S. McCreery has a BA in Sociology (Reed College, 1968) and an MA in East Asian studies (Yale, 1976). She met and married John at Cornell in 1969. The couple's honeymoon was the field research for John's PhD in anthropology. It was Ruth, then a PhD candidate in Japanese literature at Yale, who brought John and daughter Kathryn to Japan in 1980. In 1985, she founded The Word Works, Ltd., a supplier of fine translation, copywriting, editing, and desktop publishing services to both Japanese and international clients. Her publications include *A Japanese Touch for the Seasons,* numerous catalogs for the Tokyo Metropolitan Museum of Photography and other museums, and, most recently, translations of *I-mode Strategy* (2002) and *I-mode Ecology* (2003) by Natsuno Takeshi.

Chapter 7 Korea

Dr. Clark Sorensen was graduated with distinction from the University of California at Berkeley in 1970 with a degree in cultural geography. He received his MA in Korean regional studies from the University of Washington in 1974, and his PhD in anthropology from the same institution 1981 after doing fieldwork in an agricultural village in Kangwŏn Province, South Korea, for 14 months in 1976–1977. He did additional fieldwork in the same village in Kangwŏn Province in 1983, which formed the basis for his book *Over the Mountains Are Mountains: Korean Peasant Households and Their Adaptations to Rapid Industrialization.* This fieldwork was followed by additional fieldwork in 1985 and 1986 in two different provinces in South Korea (South Ch'ungch'ŏng and South Kyŏngsang Provinces) which formed the basis for a number of articles and has provided material with which he still works.

Dr. Sorensen joined the East Asian Studies Program at the Jackson School of International Studies at the University of Washington, Seattle, in 1989. Among his more recent articles are "Education and Success in Contemporary South Korea," in *Comparative Education Review* (1994); "National Identity and the Construction of the Category 'Peasant' in Colonial Korea," in Michael Robinson and Giwook Shin, eds., *Colonial Modernity in Korea* (Harvard University Press, 1999); "P'yŏngyang," in *Grolier's Encyclopedia of World Cities,* in press; and (with Song-Chul Kim) "Filial Piety in Contemporary Urban Southeast Korea: Practices and Discourses," in Charlotte Ikels, ed., *Comparative Perspectives on Filial Piety in Contemporary East Asia* (Stanford University Press, in press). He visits Korea annually to keep up with developments in that rapidly changing country.

Chapter 8 Mainland Southeast Asia

Raymond Scupin (see above)

Chapter 9 Island Southeast Asia

Dr. Ronald Lukens-Bull is an assistant professor of anthropology, within the Department of Sociology, Anthropology, and Criminal Justice, at the University of North Florida in Jacksonville, Florida. He earned a BA from Seattle Pacific

University in 1988, and an MA and PhD in social-cultural anthropology at Arizona State University in 1991 and 1997, respectively.

Lukens-Bull's research and teaching focuses on the anthropology of religion, Islam in particular; Southeast Asia, primarily Indonesia; identity politics; modernity and globalization; and the anthropology of education.

Since 1986, he has traveled 10 times to Southeast Asia, spending in excess of 25 months in the region. To date, Lukens-Bull has published three books: He edited *Sacred Places and Modern Landscapes: Sacred Geography and Social-Religious Transformations in Asia* (Arizona State University Program for Southeastern Asian Studies, 2003); and *Jihad ala Pesantren di Mata Antropolog Amerika* (*Jihad ala Indonesian Islamic Boarding Schools in the Eyes of an American Anthropologist*), Gama Media, in Press. His new book, published by Palgrave Macmillan, is titled, *A Peaceful Jihad, Negotiating Identity and Modernity in Muslim Java,* 2006.

PHOTO CREDITS

CHAPTER 1

AP Wide World Photos, 4; Lawrence Migdale/Pix, 8; Corbis/Sygma, 12.

CHAPTER 2

H. Sidky, 22, 35; WorldPictureNews, 87; Getty Images, Inc.—Agence France Presse, 88; Getty Images, 90.

CHAPTER 3

The Bridgeman Art Library International Ltd., 108; AP Wide World Photos, 121; Getty Images Inc.—Stone Allstock, 125; Corbis/Bettmann, 126; Corbis/Digital Stock, 138.

CHAPTER 4

The Stock Connection, 149; Robert Harding World Imagery, 156; AP Wide World Photos, 166; Robert Harding World Imagery, 170.

CHAPTER 5

David R. Frazier Photolibrary, Inc., 187; Corbis/Bettmann, 204; Contact Press Images Inc., 205; Getty Images Inc.—Hulton Archive Photos, 208.

CHAPTER 6

Art Resource, N.Y., 235; The Stock Connection, 239; Creative Eye/MIRA.com, 240; Corbis/SABA Press Photos, Inc., 241 (top); Rough Guides DK, 241 (bottom); EMG Education Management Group, 245.

CHAPTER 7

AP Wide World Photos, 282; Dorling Kindersley Media Library, 284; Index Stock Imagery, Inc., 291; AP Wide World Photos, 303.

CHAPTER 8

American Museum of Natural History, 340; Getty Images Inc.—Hulton Archive Photos, 353; AP Wide World Photos, 354; Peter Arnold, Inc., 369; David R. Frazier Photolibrary Inc., 377.

CHAPTER 9

Ronald Lukens-Bull, 390, 393, 403; Peter Arnold, Inc., 405; AP Wide World Photos, 418.